THE ROCHDALE HANGMAN AND HIS VICTIMS

JACK DOUGHTY has had a varied and interesting career. He played professional Rugby League with Oldham but following a serious injury he moved into amateur acting before graduating to television and a few appearances at Oldham Repertory Theatre. From this he went on to performing song and dance routines in Music Hall. This was followed by a dramatic change in direction when he became involved in professional boxing, opening a gym in Bacup, Lancashire. In 1988, Jack opened a new gym at Rochdale, before leaving there in 1993 to open a boxing gym at Shaw, Oldham. During this period he and his family have built up a successful business, which his sons, Danny and Richard, have now taken over completely.

For the past twelve years Jack has managed and trained fighters as well as staging regular Sunday afternoon promotions. Though he finds it necessary to promote in order to develop young boxers, he has always been far more interested in training techniques and spends much of his time in the gym. He has produced three British champions to date, ably assisted by Tony Ogden, his fitness conditioner, and trainer Godfrey Brown.

Apart from the theatre and sport Jack was always interested in reading and studying crime and his first venture into print reflected this with *Come at once — Annie is dying* (1987). This was followed by *The Rochdale Thunderbolt* (1991), a biography of the boxer Jock McAvoy. He has also written a radio play for the BBC, *The Shadow of Slim*, and a stage play, *The Cato Street Conspiracy*, which was performed at The Little Theatre, London. Jack has completed one more book — as yet unpublished — and is working on his autobiography.

The Rochdale Hangman and his victims

by

Jack Doughty

Jade Publishing Limited,

5, Leefields Close, Uppermill, Oldham, Lancashire, OL3 6LA.

This first impression published by Jade Publishing Limited 1998.

ISBN 1 900734 14 1 The Rochdale hangman and his victims.

© Jack Doughty 1998

All rights reserved.

Printed in Great Britain by

K. Taylor Printing, Oldham, Lancashire.

Typeset by

Jade Publishing Limited, Uppermill, Oldham, Lancashire.

British Library Cataloguing in Publication Data

Doughty, Jack,

    The Rochdale hangman and his victims.

    1. Ellis, John, d. 1932. Executions and executioners - Great Britain - Biography.

    1. Title

    364.6'7'092

    ISBN 1 - 900734 - 14 - 1

This book is sold subject to condition that it shall not, by way of trade or otherwise, be lent, re-sold, hired out, or otherwise circulated without the publisher's prior consent in any form of binding or cover other than that in which it is published and without a similar condition including this condition being imposed on the subsequent purchaser. No part of this publication may be reproduced, stored in a retrieval system, or transmitted, in any form or by any means, electronic, digital, mechanical, photocopying, recording or otherwise, without the prior written permission of the publisher.

ILLUSTRATIONS

The author and publisher have used their best endeavours to ascertain the copyright of the pictures used in this work. In most cases originals, or direct copies from originals, have been supplied from photographic libraries and other sources. Some photographs, erroneously attributed in other works to individuals or organisations which obviously did not take them in the first instance, have added to the difficulty in tracing copyright holders. Others, while correctly attributed, appear no longer to exist in the relevant archive and so have been copied from available material. However, we will readily acknowledge, in a future reprint — should one be produced — any proven copyright inadvertently infringed in this publication.

We are grateful to Martin Smith, Chief Photographer, for the useable pictures from a damaged copy of the *Oldham Chronicle* of 1920; and Anne Swadel, Picture Archivist of *The Courier*, Dundee, for her assistance with pages from *Thomson's Weekly News* of 1923–4; and to Mrs. M. Maybury, of Blackpool Central Reference Library, for supplying copies of pictures from the *Blackpool Gazette and Herald* of 1921 with the permission of that journal.

The following pictures were supplied by Topham: 1, 2, 3, 6, 26, 28, 29, 30 and front cover, 33, 34, 38; Paul Popper Limited: 37; by Hulton-Getty: 9, 10, 14, 16, 31; by Mirror Syndication International: 4, 5, 8, 12, 15, 17, 18, 19, 20, 27, 32, 35, 36; courtesy of the Metropolitan Police: 7, 13; Mail Newspapers-Solo: 11; by Hannah Haynes: the cover photograph of John Ellis; *Oldham Chronicle*: 24, 25; *The Courier, Dundee*: 39, 40, 41, 42, 43, 44; and *Blackpool Gazette and Herald*: 22, 23.

CONTENTS

	Preface	xi
1	An Adventurous Spirit	1
2	Double Event	11
3	Murder at Moat Farm	19
4	Incitement to Kill	31
5	Murder of 'The Little Yankee'	41
6	Close to Home — the Shaw Murder	49
7	The Man Who Pulls the Lever	67
8	North of the Border	79
9	The Newcastle Train Murder	87
10	Four Hangings in Ten Days	97
11	The Notorious Dr Crippen	103
12	Cowardice or Courage?	123
13	Hope to the Very End	135
14	The East End Gambling Den Murders	143
15	Seddon — a Study in Avarice	149
16	The Hooded Man	163
17	The House on Saratoga Road	173
18	Unequal Justice	185
19	The Liverpool Sack Murder	217
20	Brides in the Bath	227
21	Terror on the Gallows	245
22	Unpremeditated	255
23	The Tragedy of Roger Casement	263
24	Whimpering Bullies	281
25	The Hanging of Three Soldiers	289
26	The Wallasey Double Murder	297
27	The Gruesome Remains in Regent Square	313
28	The Body in the Sandhills	325
29	The Child in the Cellar	333
30	Kevin Barry — 'For the Cause of Liberty'	347
31	Arsenic and Major Armstrong	357
32	Ronald True and Henry Jacoby	377
33	Mrs Thompson and Bywaters	387
34	Steady Decline	417
	List of Executions	433
	Bibliography	439
	Index	441

ACKNOWLEDGMENTS

I would very much like to express my thanks for the help I received from the staff of the Local Studies Centres at Oldham and Rochdale while researching this book. Also those at the British Newspaper Library at Colindale, St Catherine's House, London, and the custodians of the Mormon records at the Church of The Latter-Day Saints, Rochdale.

I am also indebted to Hannah Haynes of Rochdale, co-author with the late David Tipper, of *De Balderston II*. With her vast and intimate knowledge of the district of Balderstone she was able to help in establishing the locations of properties occupied by the Ellis family at various times, and also gave me access to notes left by David Tipper.

My gratitude is also extended to Pamela Daniels for proof reading the typescript.

As always, I must pay tribute to the patient and painstaking work of my faithful secretary, Sheila Whitworth, without whom the job would be so much more difficult.

Jack Doughty,
November, 1998.

PREFACE

It is an interesting fact that more public executioners have come from Lancashire and Yorkshire than from any other part of the British Isles, though this is, perhaps, hardly surprising when it is taken into account that two families, the Billingtons and the Pierrepoints, provided seven executioners or assistant executioners between them. Going back as far as 1853, Thomas Askern, from Maltby in Yorkshire, carried out hangings, mainly in his own county. Bartholomew Binns, who originated from the North-East but had settled at Dewsbury, was appointed in 1883, following the death of William Marwood, a Lincolnshire man, who had held the job for eleven years. James Berry of Bradford, Thomas Scott of Huddersfield, William Warbrick of Bolton and Robert Wade of Accrington, were all hangmen in the latter part of the last century, with Berry, who reigned for over seven years, up to that time the longest serving.

James Billington, from Farnworth near Bolton, was placed on the official list of executioners in 1884, shortly after the appointment of James Berry. When Berry retired, in 1891, Billington was acknowledged as senior man and was assisted at various times by his sons William, John and Thomas.

One of William Billington's assistants was John Ellis of Rochdale. Another was Henry Pierrepoint, who served from 1901 until 1910 and was eventually joined on the official list by his brother Tom. The Pierrepoints came from the village of Clayton, near Bradford, Yorkshire, though Henry later moved to Huddersfield. John Ellis held office from 1901 and carried out his last execution at the end of December 1923. During that period a whole string of executioners and assistant executioners came and went, with Lancastrians very much the dominant faction. There was one Yorkshireman, Albert Lumb from Bradford, and five from the other side of the Pennines; William Willis, William Conduit and Robert Wilson from Manchester, George Brown from Ashton-under-Lyne and Tom Phillips from Farnworth. After Ellis's retirement two other Lancashire men, Henry Pollard of Blackburn and Lionel Mann from Rochdale, joined the official list, and in 1932 Henry Pierrepoint's son, Albert*, whose Uncle Tom had resigned in 1929, was appointed. Albert, who had settled in Lancashire, served until 1956, when yet another Lancastrian, Harry Allen, took on the job.

It obviously takes a particular kind of person willingly and deliberately to snuff out the life of a fellow human being. But what sort of person would be attracted to such a calling? In virtually every case the executioner was an ordinary sort of family man, in some instances even mild and insignificant, a description quite often given to John Ellis, the subject of this book.

* Albert was later landlord of a public house, 'Help the Poor Struggler', at Hollinwood, Oldham.

It has been claimed many times that certain hangmen were later very much affected by feelings of guilt and remorse over what they had done, particularly when women had been numbered among their victims. Whatever unknown demons haunted the mind of John Ellis in the latter part of his life will never be established with absolute certainty. Quite apart from the fact that he began to suffer with his nerves, there is no doubt that he became mentally unstable. It was widely believed at the time that the onset of his mental problems could be traced back to the hanging of a woman, Edith Thompson, following the sensational Thompson and Bywaters case of 1922.

CHAPTER 1

AN ADVENTUROUS SPIRIT

John Ellis was born on 4th October, 1874 at 18, Broad Lane, in the Balderstone district of Rochdale. This was not the present number 18, but a cottage some yards further up on the same side, at the corner of Turn Hill Road, which, as near as can be ascertained, was the one now numbered 26, the original street numbering having been altered following demolition and re-building over a period of many years. This district was part of what was originally known as Buersil Fold, and took in the area around the present Craven Heifer public house.

John Ellis's mother, Sarah Ann (née Dawson), was a typically hard-working Lancashire housewife. His father, Joseph James Ellis, a sternly religious man and a strict disciplinarian, ran a barber's shop on the Oldham Road, well down towards the town centre and close to the Swan With Two Necks pub, which stood more or less opposite to the present Wood Street.

It would appear that Joe Ellis, as well as being thrifty, had a very good business head on his shoulders, for while running his hairdresser's shop and bringing up a family, he was saving his money and steadily buying up various blocks of property in the district. He eventually finished up with a substantial number of houses, and was able to live off the rents comfortably in his old age.

Apart from John, the eldest, there were five other children in the family: Ann, Ellen, Isabella, James Preston and Emily, who died in 1883, aged two. Her death certificate states that the child died of croup and that the mother was present at the death. This would obviously have been a very sad time for the family, though infant mortality was common in those days.

John Ellis's parents usually referred to him as 'our Johnny', but as he grew up he was known among the locals as Jack. All of Joe Ellis's children attended the Red School, a Methodist Chapel and Day School, which stood on Oldham Road next to The Plough public house. The old school has long since been demolished, and at the time of writing the site is occupied by a car and van hire firm.

Not so many years before, Balderstone had been very much a country district surrounded by fields and farms. Apart from Rochdale itself, the nearest communities were at Thornham and Royton, going in the direction of Oldham, and Shaw in the valley to the east. Like each of these communities, Balderstone had its share of weavers' cottages, some of which still survive. In these three-storey stone dwellings the spinning and weaving was originally done by hand, but by the mid-nineteenth century power looms had made the old hand loom obsolete. Huge purpose-built cotton mills were springing up everywhere, providing work for many thousands in the North of England. At their peak these mills could use all the labour they could get, and large numbers of young children were employed long hours for pitifully low wages. Known as 'part-timers', they would work in the mill in the mornings and attend school in the afternoons. The following week this would be reversed, with school in the morning and work in the afternoon, and so on. By the mid-eighteen-eighties laws had been passed to ensure that no child under the age of ten was allowed to work, but for children above that age half-time working continued until 1918, when, following the passing of a new Education Act, all children were obliged to remain at school until the age of fourteen.

It is unclear at what age young Jack Ellis started work. It is possible that he went part-time, but when he left school he was put to work in his father's barber's shop, lathering the customers before his father shaved them. He did not really take to the job, even though his father assured him that hairdressing was a good, steady trade, and that if he put his mind to it and worked hard, the shop would be his some day. But the idea of spending a lifetime cutting hair and shaving people did not appeal to him at all. Yet, knowing that his father would never listen to his opinion and would force him to stick it out, he came to the conclusion that there was only one thing for it. He would run away from home.

It could well have been the case that his aversion to barbering was only part of it, for Jack Ellis had always possessed an adventurous spirit, which his father's strong personality had done little to quell. He was not at all sure that he wanted to go for good. It was more a question of getting away from the nest for a while and seeing a bit of life elsewhere.

One day, when he was about fifteen, his father went off to Manchester on business, and seizing his opportunity, Jack left the shop and met some other boys, whom he persuaded to join him on his little expedition. They would visit other towns he told them, places they had only heard about, but never seen. They would have no trouble finding work he assured them. In the meantime, they would not starve, as he had saved up his money and had a sovereign in his pocket. At first they were as keen as he was, but in the afternoon got cold feet and decided to go back home, much to young Ellis's disgust.

Left alone, he realised it was now so late that he dared not return home himself, and rather than risk his father's wrath, he settled down for the night in a nearby stable. It was midsummer and quite warm, but with the turn of the night the air grew chilly, and he woke up shivering in the early hours and set off in the direction of Bacup.

Not far along the road he came face to face with an uncle on his way to work, and held his breath as he passed by him. In the dim light of dawn he was not recognized and pressed on, arriving at Bacup later that morning. From there he tramped on over the steep, winding moorland road to Burnley.

He was tired and hungry and soon found a lodging house where he put up for the night. Some other lads were staying there and he became friendly with them, but made the mistake of admitting that he had some money. They were a lot sharper than he was and managed to relieve him of most of it by conning him, rather than actually robbing him, though it added up to the same thing. Ellis soon realised that there was no future in sticking with this bunch, whether they were friendly or not.

Next day he attempted to get work at a barber's shop, but when he told the barber that he came from Rochdale and had some experience as a latherboy, the barber said he was familiar with Rochdale and knew most of the hairdressers there. The boy became very uneasy and hurriedly left the shop.

The barber must have contacted someone in Rochdale, for when Ellis returned to the lodging house he was told that his father had informed the police that his runaway son was in Burnley and they were now on the lookout for him. It was obviously time, either to hit the road again, or go back home. Jack, however, was not ready to give up his new-found freedom so easily, and off he set, this time striking out in the direction of Nelson and Colne.

As he plodded along he fell in with a man who was also on the tramp, which was by no means unusual in those days. The first thing Jack's new companion asked him was; 'Have you got any money?'

By now, of course, he was a little wiser, and though he still had two or three shillings in his pocket, he replied that he had only a penny, whereupon his new friend said he would show him how to get some money.

'Do you know any songs?' he was asked.

'Yes, one or two', said Jack.

'Right, start singing them', said the tramp, taking off his cap. 'We'll soon have some money for a meal and lodgings'.

Somewhat hesitantly, young Ellis began to warble, and sure enough, after a while, one or two passers-by, moved, no doubt, more by pity than by appreciation of his vocal talents, began to drop coppers into the hat. Ellis was most gratified and grew in confidence. In fact, throughout the rest of his travels, which were to take him up into Yorkshire and even as far as

Sunderland and Newcastle, he tried the singing routine several more times, with varying success.

One night he had a nightmare in which he dreamt that his mother had died. This worried him so much that he wrote a letter home, informing his father of his whereabouts and enquiring after his mother's health. The reply came back by return of post, assuring him that his mother was well and very much wanted him to come home. His train fare was enclosed. So, somewhat sheepishly, the runaway returned to Rochdale.

Though he was pleased to be back, it was no more than a few weeks before the wanderlust returned. A couple of lads, who had heard all about his adventures on the road, persuaded him to lead them on a similar excursion, so off he set again, this time heading in the direction of Bury, some eight miles distant. When it began to get dark and Ellis's companions realised they would be forced to sleep out in the open they wanted to go home, but by then it was far too late. Jack was angry and tried his best to persuade them to continue, but one night of sleeping rough was enough to convince the intrepid travellers that the wayfaring life was not for them, and by daybreak they were on their way back to Rochdale.

Jack was now afraid to face his father, and in fact, never did go home, for although he eventually made his peace with his parents, he went to live with an aunt. This is obviously why he is not listed as residing at 18, Broad Lane in the 1891 census, along with the rest of the family. He was also replaced in his father's shop by his sister Ellen, who was not too keen on the job, but was given little choice. Jack lost no time in finding work, as a stripper and grinder at the Eagle Mill in Queen Victoria Street, Balderstone, off the Oldham Road. Perhaps the fact that he met a young girl there named Annie Whitworth, helped to settle him down, for he remained at the mill for the next five years, during which time he and Annie were married at the parish church, Middleton, on 20th April, 1895. He was twenty at the time, and Annie, or Annie Beaton Whitworth, to give her her full name, twenty-two. The bride came from the nearby village of Thornham. Her mother was a native of Dumbarton, Scotland, and her father, Samuel, a local man, is described on the marriage certificate as a 'fustian cutter'. The young couple first set up home at Balderstone Fold, off the Oldham Road, close to what is now Balderstone Road, but by the time their first child was born two years later, they were living just around the corner at 398, Oldham Road.

It was while working at the mill that Ellis suffered an injury to his back, which caused him to be off work for some months, and would, in fact, leave him with a weakness for the rest of his life.

Eventually, he left the mill and got a job at Tweedale and Smalley's, the textile machinery makers in nearby Castleton, and it was during an idle conversation with workmates there one dinner time that the idea of becoming a public executioner first entered his mind. Listening to the men as they discussed a forthcoming hanging, Ellis suddenly piped up;

'That's just the sort of job that would suit me'.

'You!', was the incredulous cry.

'Yes me', replied Ellis. 'I'd like to be a hangman'.

This naturally prompted roars of laughter, for a less likely candidate for such a profession could hardly be imagined, and Ellis was somewhat surprised himself that the statement had actually come from his lips. He could not think why he had said it, and at no time throughout the rest of his life could he ever give a valid reason for wanting to follow the trade of executioner. He always said, 'I just wanted to be one. That's all there was to it'.

But was it? Was he really being honest with himself? Ellis was by no means an imposing figure of a man. He was slight of build and undistinguished in looks and personality. It is obvious, however, that somewhere deep down he still retained that longing for adventure. That urge to be something more than just an ordinary millworker, and the desire to see something of life beyond the confines of a Lancashire mill town had to be satisfied, even if the only way to do it also meant seeing something of death. Perhaps this was the reason. Perhaps he was also determined to be someone special, but was clearly ill-equipped for the role. Maybe he realised this and took the only option that occurred to him. A hangman would be someone special. Notorious, if not famous. Surely, that would be far more desirable than going through life as a nobody. Though many would agree with such a sentiment, few would go to the lengths to which Jack Ellis was prepared to go to satisfy a yearning to climb out of the shadows of anonymity and into the glare of the public spotlight.

There is, possibly, one other clue as to what might have planted the idea of taking up the profession of Public Executioner in young Ellis's mind. The local cobbler, whose business happened to be next door to the Ellis home in Broad Lane, was a keen student of the hangman's art. He spent many long hours in his back room developing an idea he had formulated for a new type of scaffold. He built a full-scale model which he always intended to patent, though it came to nothing in the end. Though the cobbler would never allow visitors to view the contraption, for fear that his idea might be stolen, he was so enthusiastic that he could not resist the temptation to talk about it to customers and cronies. So it is fairly obvious that the Ellises, along with the rest of the neighbours, would have known all about it.

Whatever his reasons for that initial expression of interest in the hangman's job, Ellis found that the idea stayed with him until it became something of an obsession. One evening, he plucked up enough courage to mention it to his wife. Her reaction was one of shock and amazement. Annie was a very positive, no-nonsense type of woman, in many ways the more dominant figure in the household. The very idea of the insignificant Jack Ellis aspiring to such a calling must have stunned her. Apart from which, as a respectable, god-fearing Methodist, she viewed the suggestion with the utmost disdain and told him to forget it. Ellis knew better than to argue and immediately dropped the matter, but did not forget it. Instead, he decided to mull it over for a while, before making his next move.

In the meantime, finding the work at Tweedale and Smalley's becoming more and more taxing due to his physical disability, Ellis opened a hairdresser's shop at 451, Oldham Road. After getting the business off the ground he wrote to the office of the High Sheriff of Lancashire, asking how a person should go about getting a job as an executioner. The reply advised him to write to Wilson, Wright and Wilson of Preston, who acted as Under-Sheriffs. When the answer came from them it was, again, something of a disappointment, for they in turn suggested he write yet another letter, this time to Major R.D. Cruikshank, the Governor of Strangeways Prison, in Manchester.

This he did, and was pleasantly surprised to receive a letter shortly afterwards informing him that the Governor would see him on 14th March, 1901, and requesting that he bring some references with him. Ellis called at the houses of several gentlemen of some standing in the community, including the Reverend W.J. Bradford, the local vicar, and managed to get them to furnish the required testimonials.

At this juncture, he mentioned nothing further to his wife, but on the day in question he duly presented himself at Strangeways Prison and was admitted through the outer gate only. It was snowing and very cold, but he was made to wait outside the main building for some considerable time before being led inside and on through into the Governor's office.

Major Cruikshank cut a rather stern figure, but turned out to be a kind, considerate man, who was interested in discovering just why Ellis wished to become an executioner. He was somewhat nonplussed when Jack could only reply that he was not at all sure himself. Nevertheless, the interview went quite smoothly, mainly due to the fact that Major Cruikshank was a patient man and treated young Ellis with the greatest courtesy.

'Of course', he said, 'Billington is still doing the job you know, and doing it quite satisfactorily'.
'Yes, I know sir', replied Ellis, 'but he can't go on for ever'.
'No, but if you should be appointed you would obviously have to act as an assistant for possibly quite a long period of time'.
'Yes sir', said Ellis, 'I understand that'.

'And you would not earn a lot during that time'.

'No sir, I wouldn't expect to'.

When the Governor realised that his little talk had failed to put the young man off and that Ellis was very much in earnest, he said he would report to the Prison Commissioners and that Ellis could expect to hear from them in due course.

On returning home, he made no mention of his interview with the Prison Governor, but when a letter arrived from the Home Office instructing him to report to Newgate Prison, in London, for a week's training, he had no option but to break the news to Annie. She was rather annoyed to think that he had still gone ahead despite her objections. After much heated discussion, however, she must have realised that he was not going to change his mind, and in the end she had no alternative but to accept the situation. It is also possible that the extra money would have been taken into account, for the Ellises now had a young family to keep, a daughter, Sarah, having been born in the summer of 1897, and a son Joseph James, just over two years later, in 1899.

Telling his father and mother proved even more difficult. Joseph Ellis felt that the news would bring disgrace on the family, and his mother was very upset indeed. All she could say was,

'What will people think about us?' When he pointed out that it was the law of the land and that somebody had to do it, she replied,

'Then let it be somebody else, not you'.

Of course, their objections failed to deter him, for he was quite resolved to go through with it, and soon he was on his way to London. On arrival, he was immediately struck by the hustle and bustle, as well as the sheer vastness of the metropolis. His first sight of Newgate came as something of a shock. It was the most grim and forbidding place he had ever laid eyes on, and on entering, he found the inside to be just as dismal and gloomy, with dim gaslights burning day and night. He was led down a long, stone-flagged passage and was shown into a large room with white-washed walls. This was the hangman's room and had been used by the likes of Marwood, Calcraft and Berry, the initials of some of its previous occupants being carved on the walls.

Ellis slept fitfully that night, almost as a condemned man might. The stark, sombre setting did not help, and he was glad when morning came. After breakfast he was taken to meet Chief Warder Scott, who led him into the death chamber and indicated a large hole in the flag floor.

'That's the drop', he was informed.

A couple of planks were placed over the hole by two warders and Ellis was invited to stand on them and look down into the pit. Though in a highly nervous state, he tried not to show it, steeling himself as he stepped gingerly onto the planks. He now found himself peering down into the eerie blackness of a twelve-foot-deep pit, and a sudden feeling of panic swept over him. Fighting hard to control his nervousness, he nodded, and stepped back onto firmer ground. An assistant warder named Shepherd entered, carrying a dummy. It was fully clothed and appeared very life-like indeed.

Under instruction from the Chief Warder, Ellis proceeded to pinion the dummy, before placing the noose around its neck. The planks having been removed, the trap doors were now pulled up and the dummy placed on them. Ellis was told to pull a lever, and as he did so the trap doors fell downwards with a heavy thud and the dummy disappeared into the hole.

The entire scene was so realistic that any newcomer might have been excused for becoming unnerved by it all. But Ellis somehow managed to keep a firm grip on his emotions, a point which the warders did not fail to note. The rest of the week was spent in learning all about the pinioning straps, the placing of the noose, calculating the length of the drop, according to the build and bodyweight of the victim, and various other aspects of the hangman's job.

On the final day of his training Ellis was given a test, which was witnessed by the Governor of Newgate, Colonel Milman. This time he had to pinion the dummy in the cell, as in a real execution. It was then carried to the scaffold, where Ellis quickly completed the job by pulling the white cap over the dummy's head and lashing the legs together with leather straps just below the knees. He slipped the rope over the head, making sure that the brass ring at the base of the loop came just behind the left ear.

At a signal, Ellis pulled the lever, the trap doors banged open and the dummy plunged down into the pit. Ellis's work on the scaffold had been accomplished smoothly and competently in under a minute and the Governor appeared well pleased.

On returning to Rochdale, Ellis noted that although Annie was still unhappy about the situation she was at least interested enough to enquire how he had fared. Ellis was quietly confident, and on 8th May of that year, 1901, was delighted to learn by letter that his name had been officially added to the list of executioners and assistants. The rates of pay were £10, plus expenses, for the executioner, with the assistant receiving only two guineas (£2.10p).

His delight, however, slowly turned to disappointment as the weeks and months slipped by without any sign of an appointment to assist at an execution coming his way. He was beginning to get very disheartened indeed, when suddenly a letter arrived from the Governor of Newcastle Gaol, informing him that he would be required to act as assistant at a double execution due to take place there on 7th December. The condemned men were John Miller, proprietor of the fairground roundabouts on the seafront at Cullercoats, near Whitley Bay, and his nephew, John Robert Miller.

The victim, Joseph Ferguson, had been married to the widow of John Miller's brother. The widow had come into a considerable amount of money on the death of her first husband, and Ferguson would no doubt enjoy the benefit of it. The Millers were apparently unhappy about this state of affairs and nurtured a growing hatred for the man who had stepped into their dead relative's shoes. Threats were issued, and the whole thing blew up suddenly one night when the two Millers burst into Ferguson's house and stabbed him to death in front of his wife.

At the trial, the younger man made no attempt to hide his guilt, but alleged that, while under the influence of drink, he had been goaded into committing the crime by his uncle. It was also stated that the Defendant was somewhat simple-minded. The older man, on the other hand, claimed that he had taken no actual part in the stabbing. He also denied that his nephew had acted under his influence.

Pointing out that the victim had been murdered in the most horrifying manner, having been stabbed viciously and repeatedly until his body was a mass of gaping wounds, the judge remarked that the older man had made no attempt to restrain his nephew after the first blow was struck. Had he done so a murder might well have been prevented. Instead, he stood by and did nothing.

Both men were sentenced to death, giving John Ellis the opportunity to take part in his first execution.

CHAPTER 2

DOUBLE EVENT

On the morning of 6th December, 1901, John Ellis made his way to Rochdale Station to catch the train to Newcastle. As he went through the barrier and onto the platform, he saw that the train was already in and the engine driver was in the act of pointing out a small plump man to some of the people standing on the platform. The man had just alighted from the train and appeared to be stretching his legs while he waited for it to pull out again. Very soon he was surrounded by a small crowd. Ellis asked who the man was and was surprised to be told,

'That's the hangman, Billington. He's on his way to Newcastle to hang the Millers'.

Showing no reticence whatsoever, Ellis stepped forward and boldly addressed the hangman so that all could hear,

'Good morning, Mr Billington', he said. 'I'm going with you to Newcastle'.

The little fat man turned sharply on the young intruder and barked at him in a strong Lancashire accent that was even broader than his own,

'Tha's doin' nowt 'ut sort'.

'Well that'll be up to you. But we're both going to the same place, Newcastle Gaol. I'm John Ellis and I've been appointed to assist you'.

'Well, I'll be damned!' said Billington.

Ellis produced the Governor's letter, and after looking it over, Billington invited him to share his carriage.

During the journey the hangman explained to Ellis that he was, in fact, William Billington, son of the renowned James Billington. James it was who had actually been given the appointment at Newcastle, but having caught a chill and been laid up, he had requested that the job be undertaken by his son, William, to which the Commissioners had readily agreed. The two hangmen had been instructed to report to the prison no later than four o'clock that afternoon, and once inside, would not be allowed out again until after the executions had been carried out on the following day. As they had plenty of time in hand after arriving at Newcastle Station, Billington suggested that they go into a public house for some refreshment. Inside, they could not help noticing three well-dressed women. They were talking quietly in a corner and Ellis became quite perturbed when he realised that one of them was weeping. Soon all three were sobbing and dabbing their eyes, and it became clear from snatches of their conversation that they were relatives of the condemned men.

'Come on', said Billington. 'Let's clear out of here'.

Ellis followed as Billington slipped quietly out of the pub. He felt sorry for the women and probably realised for the first time the full significance of the job he had taken on and the mental anguish it could involve.

By the time he and Billington had entered the prison and heard the gates close behind them, he was in full control of his emotions and ready to focus his mind firmly on the job in hand.

After being shown to their quarters the executioners were taken before the Governor, who told them that the original plan to hang the two Millers together would have to be changed, as there was more than a hint of trouble between the condemned men and he feared it might blow up if they were to come face-to-face again. It was therefore decided that the younger one, John Robert Miller, should go to the scaffold at eight o'clock and his uncle at nine-thirty.

Ellis then went with Billy Billington to inspect the gallows. After the rope had been set up a sandbag was attached to the end of it and lowered into the pit to hang there overnight, the object being to test its strength and also to take out the stretch.

The hangmen were next taken to view the elder Miller through a spy-hole in the cell door. This was always done for the purpose of looking over the condemned man's physique and, in particular, his neck. These, along with his body weight, which was the most important factor in the calculation, were taken into account when determining the length of the drop.

As there was only one condemned cell the younger man was confined in a room within the prison hospital. During his incarceration he had become noisy and aggressive, and felt very bitter, blaming his uncle totally for the terrible fate which had befallen him and screaming out the direst threats against him.

On that last afternoon of his life young Miller's mind seemed to give way completely. His yells and threats now turned to crying and screaming, which he kept up throughout the night. Unfortunately, Ellis's room was on the same floor and he had very little sleep, spending most of the night listening to the young man's heart-rending cries. He was thankful when morning came, but felt very nervous and uneasy, and there is no doubt that the condemned man's mental breakdown and terror of the gallows had a lot to do with this.

Early in the morning, the two hangmen made their way to the scaffold for the purpose of inspecting the gallows and making a final check on their equipment. As he hauled up the sandbag and tested the trapdoors Billington appeared cool and totally in control. This helped to calm Ellis, though he still feared that young Miller would cause them plenty of problems when his time came.

On returning to the main building, they were told that it was time to go to Miller's cell, and Ellis was glad that the waiting was almost over.

As the cell door was opened, Ellis saw at once that a change had come over the condemned man. He was no longer screaming, but just stood there staring vacantly into space, almost oblivious to all that was going on around him.

Within seconds Billington had swiftly and efficiently whipped his hands behind his back and pinioned his wrists.

The walk to the scaffold passed without incident. So much so that, to Ellis, this first experience of an execution seemed somehow unreal and, momentarily, as he looked at the doomed man, a good looking, well-built young fellow, he found it difficult to take in the scene. It was just like a dream; something he was witnessing, rather than taking part in.

At last, young Miller was up on the scaffold and looking slowly around with a dull, dazed expression on his face. He appeared to be uncertain as to what was happening to him, and asked, indicating the Governor, the Chaplain and other officials,

'Why are all these people here?'

He turned and began to walk away from the gallows, as if to go back to his cell. Billington quickly caught him by the sleeve and the two executioners led him gently back and placed him on the trapdoors.

Miller made no effort to resist as Ellis fastened the straps on his lower legs and Billington placed the noose around his neck and tightened it. Slipping on the white cap, he immediately instructed his assistant to stand clear. As Ellis stepped back Billington pulled the lever and the trapdoors shot open to send Miller plummetting down into the pit.

Ellis stood there gritting his teeth as he took in the expressions on the faces of those present. The Governor, for one, appeared very shaken and suggested that the two hangmen join him in his office for a glass of brandy. It was only then that they discovered that this had also been *his* first experience of an execution.

After the young man's body had been left hanging there for one hour, as required by law, it was taken down and removed to the mortuary. The hangmen now made ready to carry out the second execution, and on arriving at John Miller's cell, found the prisoner reasonably calm, though obviously feeling the strain. There were no incidents, however, Miller's nerve holding out to the end.

It was all over, and Ellis felt very relieved indeed. That morning he had experienced a feeling almost of blind terror. Now he felt calm and elated. He knew he had acquitted himself well and was relieved to note that the experience had not left him shaken.

Already he had learned something, and also found a justification for what he was doing. For after working with Billington he realised that while feeling pity, he could make the ordeal less harrowing for the condemned person by carrying out his work as quickly and efficiently as possible. At least, that was the way he rationalised it.

On a spring day in 1902, a group of boys were booting a football around on Tottenham Marshes in North London. The ball was kicked off the pitch and bounced into a ditch, and on going to retrieve it one of the footballers discovered the body of a young woman. She had been brutally murdered. The corpse, which was badly mutilated, was estimated by the pathologist to have lain there since the previous night, a Saturday. Though there was nothing on it to assist with identification, the body was, in fact, that of Charlotte Cheeseman, a twenty-one-year-old cigar factory worker, who had lived locally with her married sister.

That morning, her boyfriend, a young man named George Woolfe, called at the house and asked for her. He was told by the sister that she had not been home all night. Woolfe appeared surprised at this and remarked,

'I missed her last night'.

He left, returning in the afternoon and also in the evening. Still there was no news. They were not to know it, of course, but by that time the body had been removed to the mortuary and was lying there unidentified.

Once the identification had been made the police began their inquiries and soon discovered that the dead girl had been keeping company with Woolfe, and had gone out to meet him on the afternoon of her death. They also learned that the lovers had quarrelled some time previously because of Woolfe's having taken exception to the fact that another man had been paying Charlotte a little too much attention. This had apparently, blown over, and the two had become close again, seeing each other almost every evening and going for long walks together.

Woolfe was not considered a suspect at this stage, particularly in view of the fact that he had made every effort to contact Charlotte following her disappearance and had appeared very worried indeed.

However, when the police made efforts to get in touch with him at his Hoxton home he was nowhere to be found, and further inquiries over the next few days, failed to unearth any clue as to his whereabouts.

About a week or so after the discovery of Charlotte's body, two soldiers were sitting in the barracks of the Surrey Militia, when one of them, who was idly scanning the pages of a Sunday newspaper, remarked to his friend, a man named Slater,

'Look at this, a murder in Tottenham'.

'Yes?'

'You come from somewhere round there, don't you?'

'What about it?' asked Slater.

'Just listen to this', said his pal, and read out the article.

After listening intently, Slater said, very seriously, 'You don't think I did it, do you?'

'Well of course not', replied the other soldier. 'Why should I think that?'

There the conversation ended, but though Slater's friend was slightly puzzled, as far as is known, he did not relate this odd episode to anyone else, until detectives paid a visit to the camp several days later. He was then astonished to learn that the man he knew as 'Slater' was none other than George Woolfe, the murder victim's missing boyfriend.

Woolfe was immediately arrested and charged with the crime. The evidence against him was largely circumstantial, yet appeared extremely damning.

The couple had been seen together in a public house around nine-thirty on the Saturday evening, the night of the murder. A tram conductor also remembered the couple travelling on his tramcar that evening around nine o'clock. Two other witnesses gave evidence of seeing a couple strolling in the direction of the Marshes that night, and although neither could make a positive identification, one possibly significant detail, which both witnesses had noticed and commented on, was the fact that the young man was slightly shorter than the girl. This had also been the case with Woolfe and Charlotte Cheeseman.

It had been noticed on the Sunday that Woolfe's face bore scratch marks, which he claimed had been caused during a fight with another man in Hoxton around midnight on the Saturday. A number of witnesses were put up by the Defence, including the man Woolfe had fought with, who admitted that the altercation had taken place but could not remember scratching Woolfe's face.

In the witness box, Woolfe admitted that he had been with Charlotte on the evening in question, but told the court that she had left him before seven-thirty. He was very convincing, as were his Counsel, but in the end, the fact that he had run away and joined the army told very much against him and the jury brought in a verdict of guilty.

John Ellis duly received a letter from the Governor of Newgate, requesting him to stand ready to come to London for the execution, when he would again be required to act as assistant to William Billington.

On arrival, Ellis left his belongings in the executioner's room and went with Billington to take a look at the condemned man, who was not much more than a boy. He was on the small side, being no more than 5ft. 5½ ins. and around 9st. 6lbs. in weight.

As the two hangmen peered at him through the spy-hole in the cell door, he appeared not to have a care in the world. There he sat, chatting away quite happily to the two warders who attended him, clearly making their job a lot easier, for normally it could be quite a harrowing experience, having to remain with a condemned man hour after hour, day after day, in some cases growing to like him and to feel pity for him. No doubt Woolfe's gaolers did feel sorry for him, but the fact that he did not appear to feel sorry for himself certainly helped to lift much of the gloom that would have been expected to pervade the death cell.

When he did mention the case during his confinement, Woolfe persisted in protesting his innocence. In those days there was no such thing as a Court of Appeal, but a sentence could, of course, be commuted to life imprisonment on the intervention of the Home Secretary, and Woolfe was, without doubt, hoping against hope that such would be the case. Unfortunately for him it was not to be, yet once he was made aware of his fate he did not crack up, but showed the same degree of courage he had exhibited throughout his time in prison.

When Billington and Ellis entered the condemned man's cell shortly before eight o'clock on the morning of 6th May, 1902, Woolfe appeared quite calm and in control of himself. He remained silent as his arms were pinioned. On being taken from the cell he heard the Chaplain begin to intone the prayer as the little procession began to move slowly along the passage. Then, as if intent on speeding up the proceedings, Woolfe quickened his stride, and completely oblivious to the restraining hand of the warder on his shoulder, moved forward with short, hurried steps.

Ellis later remarked that he gave the impression of a man late for an appointment. The two hangmen and the rest of the procession, in fact, were hard-pressed to keep up. It was a very odd sight to see a man literally hurrying to his doom.

Woolfe was clearly anxious to get it over with, and on reaching the scaffold stepped quickly on to the trapdoors. Within seconds his legs were strapped, the noose fixed in place and the white cap adjusted. A signal, then Billington pulled the lever and Woolfe's body disappeared into the pit. Ellis later claimed that the entire operation had been carried out in no more than 25 seconds.

George Woolfe was the last person to be executed at Newgate, and Ellis was always very proud of the fact that he had helped dispatch him in double-quick time.

When the old prison was demolished, not long afterwards, Ellis managed to acquire a piece of one of the wooden beams, from which he had a walking stick made. It was a souvenir he treasured for many years.

This stick eventually came into the possession of Irene Noble, a niece of Jack Ellis. Just below the handle is a silver band, inscribed with the words: *Relic of Newgate Prison Hangman's Room 1770—1902. J. Ellis, Rochdale.**

Ellis also assisted Henry Pierrepoint at three executions during the course of 1902. Pierrepoint himself was fairly new to the job, but struck Ellis as being very sure of himself. He was certainly far more outgoing than the Rochdale man, and set about the job as though he had been doing it for years.

Richard Wigley, who was hanged at Shrewsbury in March 1902, was Pierrepoint's first assignment as Chief Executioner, but the authorities must have had every confidence in Pierrepoint, although he had assisted at only two previous hangings. Wigley, a slaughterman, had cut the throat of a ladyfriend, Mary Bowen, in a pub at Westbury, Shropshire.

Ellis's two other jobs as assistant to Pierrepoint in that year, were the hangings of William Brown at Wandsworth for the murder of his wife at Mortlake, and of George Place at Warwick for the slaying of Eliza Chetwynd, her baby and her mother at Baddesley Ensor in Warwickshire.

All three executions went smoothly and without incident.

---

* In 1996, with the help of Hannah Haynes, co-author of *De Balderston II*, the walking stick was passed on to Mr John Gwilliam, a grandson of Jack Ellis.

CHAPTER 3

MURDER AT MOAT FARM

John Ellis was now an established executioner, though still acting as assistant to the main man. Over the next twenty years the insignificant little barber from Rochdale, whom you would never notice in a group of people, would not only become the Crown's senior hangman, but would put to death some of the most notorious murderers in British criminal history. These included Crippen, Seddon, George Smith, the Brides in the Bath killer, and Edith Thompson, the female half of the sensational Thompson and Bywaters case. He would also be called upon to dispatch the Irish patriot, Sir Roger Casement, following one of the most melodramatic and controversial cases of the century.

The execution of Mrs Thompson was said to have affected Ellis very badly, and would later be linked with the serious personality problems with which he became afflicted following his retirement from the job. Edith Thompson was one of three woman he would hang during his career, and each one of these executions is believed to have had a profound effect on him. Ellis himself always denied this, though he admitted that they worried him to some extent at the time.

Frederick Seddon and George Joseph Smith were both vicious killers who preyed on women, employing a deadly mixture of charm and cunning to relieve their victims of money and property before doing away with them.

The year 1903 would see Ellis come face-to-face with his first female victim, Mrs Emily Swann, and also Lothario, seducer, thief and killer, Samuel Dougal — his first encounter with a murderer in the Seddon-Smith mould.

In January 1897, Samuel Dougal came out of prison, where he had served twelve months for passing worthless cheques. He was fifty-one years old, and though it was not known at the time, had left behind him a trail of crime and shattered lives.

A former soldier, Dougal, a well-built man of above average height, with a neat grey beard and upright military bearing, still cut an impressive figure, despite the fact that he had seen better days and was, at this point in his life, at a very low ebb.

A Londoner, born and brought up in Bow, he had been fortunate enough to receive a good education, and in 1866, at the age of twenty, joined the Royal Engineers, being posted to Chatham in Kent, where he later married a local girl. Though the couple stayed together and eventually had four children, Dougal certainly ruined the marriage, for he was constantly on the prowl for other women. His wife had little option but to put up with the situation. She was probably still under her husband's spell, and in any case, was tied because of the children.

In 1873, Dougal was posted to Halifax, Nova Scotia, and took the whole family to Canada with him. Within a couple of years he had been promoted to the rank of sergeant. He must certainly have neglected his family, for almost all his off-duty time was spent in the company of females. Not surprisingly, he was usually short of money, and quite apart from the fact that he possessed a voracious sexual appetite, he was always on the lookout for women of some means, whom he could fleece of their savings. This obviously necessitated deeper involvement, which placed an even greater strain on the marriage, leading to constant rows and bitter recriminations.

One day, in 1885, Dougal's wife was suddenly taken ill with violent attacks of vomiting. In less than a week she was dead. There is no record of what happened to the children, but within a very short time the sergeant had married an English girl from a reasonably well-off family. How much he managed to wheedle out of her is not known, but although she also died after a short illness, no questions appear to have been asked, or suspicions aroused.

There was yet another affair in Canada, with a farmer's daughter, from which Dougal no doubt expected to benefit financially. Though they never married, a child was born, after which he callously abandoned her.

Soon after this, Dougal left the army with a small pension and, for some reason, turned up next in Dublin, where he obtained work at the Royal Military Hospital. Within a matter of months he had met and married Sarah White, a local girl, who was many years his junior and of quite striking appearance. None of this, however, resulted in Dougal settling down to a happy married life. At every opportunity he would pursue any woman he fancied, especially when he could smell money. The young Irish girl was not prepared to put up with such treatment and eventually left him. It was a new experience for Dougal to have someone walk out on *him*, but one which did not appear to worry him unduly, for he simply carried on as before, chasing women and swindling those gullible enough to fall for his persuasive charms. In 1896, he was sentenced to twelve month's imprisonment for forging cheques and was released the following year, a sadder, if not much wiser, man.

For many months after his release from prison Dougal drifted aimlessly around London, scratching a living as best he could, but always keeping up appearances in case the right opportunity should present itself, which it did eventually.

In the autumn of 1898, he took a room at 37, Elgin Crescent, off Ladbroke Grove, and it was while residing there that he had the good fortune to encounter Miss Camille Holland, a fifty-six-year-old spinster of excellent background and breeding. It was mentioned in the newspapers later that the two had met through a matrimonial agency, while other reports claimed that they had simply been introduced by a mutual acquaintance.

Whatever the truth of this, it is a fact that Miss Holland was immediately captivated by the smartly turned out ex-military man, who lost no time in ingratiating himself with the spinster, whom he identified at once as the ideal prey.

Camille Holland had been engaged to a naval officer, who had unfortunately died. Since then her parents had also passed away, leaving her a fortune of between six and seven thousand pounds, a considerable sum in those days, the interest from which produced a comfortable income. Miss Holland was quite a pretty lady. Petite, and always neatly dressed, she could certainly have made a good marriage had it not been for the fact that her natural shyness and reserve tended to inhibit would-be suitors.

Dougal, of course, had no such inhibitions, and there can be no doubt that he made it his business to extract from Miss Holland the details of her wealth. He then began to formulate his plan to relieve her of it.

Posing as a retired army officer with a pension, but temporarily short of funds, Dougal soon persuaded Miss Holland to co-habit with him. The fact that this was very much in conflict with her upbringing and all her principles only goes to show the hold Dougal already had over her. In all probability, he either claimed to be single, or spun her a yarn to the effect that he had a wife and was in the process of getting a divorce, the latter scenario being the most likely, for this would conveniently forestall any question of marriage. He was, of course, still married to Sarah White, who had borne him two children, only one of whom survived.

The couple lived in rented property in various parts of the South while looking around for their ideal home, which they eventually found near Saffron Walden in Essex. It was an ancient farm in a very unusual setting. There were two connected moats, the smaller of which encircled rough scrubland. Within the larger moat stood the farm buildings, the only access to the house being by way of a wooden bridge, which faced the front porch.

It was known at the time as Coldham Farm, but the couple soon changed the name to Moat Farm. Miss Holland's furniture, which had been kept in storage in London, was sent for, while in the meantime, the place was painted and decorated.

In this idyllic setting, the couple, who had passed themselves off as Mr and Mrs Dougal, were very happy for the first few weeks. Then a young servant girl was engaged through an agency. From the day she arrived Miss Holland's life was in danger, though of course, she was not to know it. One look at the young servant girl's pretty face and shapely body was enough for Dougal. He simply could not resist making approaches to her. The girl, however, complained to her mistress, who was so shocked and angry that she ordered Dougal to pack his bags and leave.

Over the following two days, Dougal tried his best to get round Miss Holland, while contemplating his next move, and she relented at least enough to allow him to take her out one day in the pony and trap.

As they left Moat Farm and set off along the lonely country lane, Dougal must have been carefully turning over in that fertile brain his plan for the murder and disposal of his mistress, no doubt having come to the conclusion that Moat Farm was the perfect setting for what he had in mind.

Though the farm looked pretty in the summertime, it was an isolated and lonely spot. In the late autumn and in winter, even the moat could look drab and gloomy. With the flowers gone and only the thick, coarse reeds swaying forlornly in the wind around the dark, stagnant water, it could be a very eerie place indeed, especially at night. The main road and the nearest house were both over a mile distant, and few people ever came by. It was the last place on earth for a genteel lady like Camille Holland to be — with a man as desperate and as evil as Samuel Dougal.

Later that day the servant girl saw the pony and trap return, and was surprised to note that Dougal was alone. He explained that his wife had decided to go to London to do some shopping and would return by train later that evening, when he would pick her up at the station. He did, in fact, go out several times during the course of the evening, but by bedtime there was still no sign of 'Mrs Dougal'. Next morning, Dougal told the girl that he had just received a letter from his wife telling him that she had decided to take a holiday.

Fearing to be left alone in the house with him, the servant girl promptly packed her bags and left. That same morning, Dougal lost no time in contacting the agency for a replacement, and there followed a succession of young girls, some of whom were apparently quite willing or were persuaded to cater for Dougal's sexual requirements. None stayed very long, but several certainly indulged the master, for reports of scandalous goings on at the farm were not long in reaching the ears of the locals. On one occasion, a young woman was seen riding a bicycle around the farmyard with not a stitch of clothing on her.

Surprisingly perhaps, no one appears to have questioned the fact that the mistress of Moat Farm was never seen. Dougal went into town regularly and from time-to-time cashed cheques purportedly signed by 'Camille C.

Holland'. At the same time he was systematically obtaining possession of the dead woman's stocks and shares by craftily forging her signature on various letters and documents. Over a period he also rifled her account at the National and Provincial Bank, transferring all the funds into an account he had opened in his own name at the Birkbeck Bank.

Dougal seemed quite happy to remain at the farm. He was living the life of a country squire and even went so far as to purchase one of the new-fangled motor cars. It was the first one ever owned by anyone in the distict and caused quite a stir whenever he drove it into town.

At some time between the disappearance of Camille Holland in 1899, and 1902, a very pretty young woman with dark hair and an Irish accent arrived at the farm. She was Sarah White, Dougal's third wife, to whom he had written, asking her to join him. Instead, she came seeking a divorce. There is no record of how long she stayed and she could not have realised the danger she was in, or she would never have gone to the lonely farmhouse at all. Apparently though, she was one female who was strong-willed enough not to fall for Dougal's smooth talk. He could see that her mind was made up, and though she was an exceptionally good-looking woman, she had no money to speak of, so he saw little point in arguing. He agreed to the divorce and proceedings were instituted, with Dougal as the petitioner. A decree was eventually granted, but before it could become absolute, the King's Proctor, after looking into Dougal's background, intervened, and the decree was declared null and void. The failure of the petition made little difference to Dougal, but must have been a bitter blow to the young Irish girl, who was anxious to rid herself of him.

It had been nearly four years since the lady whom the locals understood to be Mrs Dougal had been seen in the district, yet no one apparently felt it necessary to go to the law, though there was much whispering and gossip. But when weird stories of bodies concealed in cupboards and in cellars began to circulate they soon reached the ears of the police, who were eventually prevailed upon to investigate.

Superintendent John Pryke, of the Essex County Constabulary, an extremely able and experienced detective, visited Moat Farm early in 1903. He was greeted cordially by the confident, smiling occupant, who made him welcome, remarking that it was not often that he received visitors. After being invited to view the new motor car, which he did with interest, the Superintendent informed Dougal of the purpose of his visit. Could he account for the apparent disappearance of his wife?

'No', was the reply. 'Unfortunately, I can't. I drove her to Stanstead Station with her two trunks. That was over three years ago, and I haven't seen her since'.

In view of the rumours going around, the Superintendent asked if Dougal had any objection to his looking around the farm, and was assured that he was quite welcome to do so.

However, not having a search warrant, Pryke could hardly go probing around in drawers and cupboards, and had to be satisfied with a brief tour of the living room, kitchen and bedrooms, with Dougal in attendance. He then looked around outside, checking the outbuildings and adjacent land. Finding nothing that might furnish a clue as to the missing woman's whereabouts, he thanked Dougal and left.

Though he had discovered nothing of any significance, Pryke was far from satisfied. For a man whose wife had been missing for such a period of time Dougal had seemed surprisingly complacent. True, he had conveyed the impression that she had simply left him, yet he had not appeared in the least put out when Pryke had asked if he might look around the farm.

After further investigation Pryke made the inevitable discovery that Dougal had been cashing cheques signed by a 'Camille C. Holland'. Inquiries at the bank, where the money had originally been deposited, convinced the Superintendent that Camille C. Holland and the woman known as Mrs Dougal were one and the same. As Dougal had been cashing cheques bearing her signature since her disappearance, there was certainly something very much amiss.

On asking to see the cancelled cheques, Pryke was disappointed to learn that they had all been returned to Dougal in accordance with the normal procedure. Then, just as Pryke was about to leave the bank, a single cancelled cheque, which was about to be posted off to the farm, was located on a desk.

Close examination indicated that the signature thereon was probably a forgery, and soon after this, Miss Holland's signatures on a number of letters to her stockbroker were also deemed to be fraudulent.

Following the visit of the police, Dougal, who must have realised that it was only a matter of time before the forgeries were discovered, packed a bag and left the farm. His first stop was the Birkbeck Bank, from which he drew out all the funds in his account. He then promptly disappeared.

Once it was discovered that Dougal had left the farm the police acted quickly. From the Birkbeck Bank they were able to obtain the serial numbers of the banknotes he now had in his possession. Several days later a teller at a bank in central London drew the attention of a superior to a five pound note he had been asked to change by a customer who was still at the counter. The police were summoned and arrived within minutes. The fugitive was arrested and escorted to the police station in Old Jewry.

When only yards away from the entrance Dougal decided to make a dash for it. Unfortunately for him, he ran into Frederick's Place, a *cul-de-sac*, and was quickly recaptured.

The next day, he was handed over to the Essex County authorities, who had already made a number of visits to the farm following Dougal's disappearance. Several items of women's clothing, later identified as belonging to the missing woman, along with other personal possessions, including a couple of large boxes or trunks, which could very well have been the ones that Dougal claimed she had taken away with her, were discovered.

At this stage, with no clear evidence to show that Dougal had done away with the missing woman, the only charge that could be brought against him was one of forgery, but the police were not prepared to let it rest there, and within days of Dougal's arrest Detective Inspector Bower of Scotland Yard had been brought in to work with the local constabulary.

After a briefing from Superintendent Pryke on the details of the case, Bower was taken to Moat Farm. He took his time looking over the place, and though nothing suspicious came to light he was left with the strong feeling that somewhere on the farm lay the key to the mystery.

As an experienced detective, Bower knew that much hard work was now required. A minute search of the house and outbuildings revealed nothing. Teams of policemen painstakingly combed the undergrowth and shrubbery surrounding the property. Again nothing was discovered. It was clear that the moat would have to be dragged, and a gang of labourers was drafted in to carry out this highly unpleasant task. Soon they were up to their thighs in foul-smelling water, mud and slime, and after a few days of this, several of the men fell ill and had to give up. The rest toiled doggedly on. Then, just as Bower was beginning to give up hope of ever finding anything, one of the searchers called out excitedly that he had located what appeared to be a human bone. At once the policemen converged on the spot, while other workmen went to the assistance of their colleague. The excitement grew as further bones were brought to the surface. Bower was confident that a find of real importance had been made, but his hopes were soon dashed, for on closer examination it was ascertained that the remains were those of some farm animal, possibly a calf.

The police operation at Moat Farm had been going on for several weeks with no breakthrough whatsoever, and Bower was under considerable pressure from his superiors to wind things up. On learning, through his solicitor, of the disruption at what he considered to be his property, Dougal threatened to sue the police. To make things worse, Bower was told that if nothing was discovered soon the digging would be stopped and the authorities would proceed with the prosecution of Dougal on the forgery charge only.

Bower was becoming desperate. He still believed that Moat Farm held some terrible secret and he was determined to discover it. Then came a very fortunate break in the case. While talking to some of the locals one day he pricked up his ears when mention was made of a ditch, which one of them recalled had been filled in two or three years before. Though no trace of it was to be seen, its position was eventually ascertained as running down one side of the smaller moat. Digging began at once, but after excavating the earth to a depth of several feet, there was still nothing to show for almost a week's hard, back-breaking work.

Bower was not a man to give up easily, but he knew he was almost beaten. He now played his final card. Sending for the man who had filled in the ditch, he asked him to look over the excavation very carefully, just to be absolutely certain that they had reached the bottom of the original ditch. He was assured that they had not, that there was still some way to go. So the diggers set to again.

On 27th April, 1903, a woman's shoe was discovered. It proved to be the breakthrough. The earth around it was carefully scraped away to reveal the fully-clothed body of a woman.

The mud-encrusted corpse was removed to a greenhouse and placed across three chairs, where Dr George Pepper, the Home Office pathologist, began his grisly task. Though the features were unrecognisable, the garments on the body were proved to be those which Camille Holland had worn on the day of her disappearance. The identity of the body was clearly determined at the trial, which took place at Chelmsford Assizes two months later, through the evidence of a dentist whose patient the wretched victim had once been. A gaping hole in the skull led to the discovery of a bullet lodged in the brain. This was matched with others found at the farm. The victim's undergarments were still quite clean and in good condition, as were her lace-up boots. These were identified in court by the man who had made them, his name and a reference number being plainly readable.

Almost everything Dougal had told the servant girl following Miss Holland's disappearance was proved to be false. It was proved that the dead woman had not travelled to London that evening as he had stated. It was shown in addition that it would have been impossible for her to have gone to London and returned by train the same day, as no trains ran so late.

Dougal had told the servant girl, at around 7a.m. on the following day, that he had received a letter from his wife that same morning stating that she intended to stay in London. However, it was proved conclusively that no postal delivery could have reached the farm by that time. If Miss Holland had gone to London on the evening train she could not possibly have posted a letter in time for it to have reached the sorting office at Clavering in any case.

So, the inevitable verdict was one of guilty and Dougal was sentenced to be hanged. The job was given to Billy Billington, while John Ellis received a letter informing him that he was to act as assistant.

About one week prior to the execution of Samuel Dougal the two Lancashire hangmen travelled to Chelmsford Gaol to execute a young soldier named Charles Howell, for a murder committed at Colchester.

While passing along a corridor, the warder in attendance pointed out to them the cell of the Moat Farm murderer, and they stopped for a moment to peer at Dougal through the grille. The killer of Camille Holland lay on his bunk, apparently asleep.

'He seems to be in very good spirits', the warder told them. 'He gives us no trouble and doesn't seem at all worried about his position'.

The reason for Dougal's confident demeanour soon became clear. He had written to the Home Secretary, explaining that the killing had been accidental. He had been showing Miss Holland his revolver when it had suddenly gone off. In a panic he had buried the body.

Dougal was apparently quite certain that his explanation would be accepted and that he would be reprieved. However, three days before the sentence was due to be carried out, word came through from the Home Office that no reprieve would be forthcoming. On being given this news, the murderer broke down and wept, professing to be worried about what might become of his daughter, aged twelve, whose mother had been his third wife.

Later, he sat in silence, staring ahead and refusing to talk to anyone. He ate very little, and as Tuesday 14th July approached, paced up and down his cell almost the whole time.

Dougal appeared most anxious to receive the ministrations of the Chaplain, the Reverend Blakemore, who pressed him to make a full confession, but this he refused to do, still insisting that he was innocent of murder. The only confession he was prepared to make was that he had killed Camille Holland accidentally. The Reverend Blakemore, however, did not intend to leave it at that and persisted in his efforts to get the wretched prisoner to admit his crime. More than once he agreed to do so, but always drew back when it came to admitting the truth.

Billington and Ellis arrived at the prison on the afternoon of 13th July, and were taken to see the Governor. After being informed that the condemned man weighed 11st. 7lbs. and stood a little over 5ft. 9ins. tall they again viewed Dougal through the peephole and decided that a drop of 6ft. 8ins. would be about right. The scaffold was then given the usual test and all was ready.

Ellis slept quite soundly that night, though it is doubtful if the same could be said of the prisoner. The Rochdale hangman was awakened by a warder around 6a.m. and given a cup of tea, after which, he proceeded to the scaffold to make sure that everything was in order. He and Billington then learned that the prisoner was in a very bad state, and it was decided to place two planks across the drop so that a warder could stand on either side of the condemned man, ready to support him in case his nerve should crack.

On going into Dougal's cell, just before 8a.m., the hangmen were surprised at the number of people present. These included Inspector Fox, the man who had arrested the murderer. He had been granted special permission to attend the execution.

Though Dougal looked haggard and totally drained, he was quite smartly turned out in the dark blue coat and striped trousers he had worn at his trial. His patent leather buttoned boots were well polished and his shirt white and starched.

It was obvious, though, that the prisoner was in a highly agitated state mentally, and a measure of brandy in a tin mug, handed to him by a warder, appeared to calm him somewhat.

As his wrists were pinioned behind his back Dougal made no attempt to resist, and he seemed to have his emotions reasonably under control as he stepped out of the cell to walk to the scaffold. Even so, as he stood on the trapdoor, the two warders took their places beside him.

Billy Billington was, as usual, intent on getting the job done as quickly as possible. With the white cap over the condemned man's head and the rope adjusted, the Bolton hangman was about to pull the lever when the Chaplain suddenly called out 'Stop!'

Billington and Ellis were quite taken aback at the Chaplain's sudden intervention, and both said later that their first thought was that a last minute reprieve had come through.

Then the Reverend Blakemore asked in a loud voice

'Dougal, are you guilty or innocent?'

There was no reply from the prisoner, and the two executioners, standing there in shocked silence, exchanged bewildered looks as the Chaplain asked again.

'Dougal, are you guilty or not?'

It was most irregular for a clergyman to interfere in this way and Billington was less than pleased about it.

Still the condemned man remained silent. Billington, by this time somewhat exasperated, took the lever and applied downward pressure, then Dougal was heard to cry out, 'Guilty, sir!', just an instant before the trapdoor banged open and he plummeted into oblivion.

Billington was very upset at the Chaplain's method of eliciting Dougal's dramatic last-second confession, while the Reverend Blakemore appeared quite elated. His high-handed action, however, was the subject of a number of newspaper reports at the time and also resulted in questions being asked in the House of Commons.

The Reverend was, in fact, heavily criticised for his interference, and received a letter from the Home Secretary demanding an explanation for his behaviour. No doubt he explained that his intentions had been to save the prisoner's soul. Whether such an explanation was acceptable or not we shall never know, but soon after the incident he was transferred from Chelmsford Prison to Winson Green in Birmingham.

Thirteen years later Ellis travelled to Birmingham to hang William Allan Butler, who, in a fit of jealousy, had stabbed a woman to death. The prison Chaplain, who could make no impression at all on the unrepentant Butler, was none other than the Reverend Blakemore, who confided to Ellis that his intervention on the scaffold at Chelmsford Gaol that day had done his career no good at all.

CHAPTER 4

INCITEMENT TO KILL

William Swann, a glassblower, lived with his wife Emily in a modest cottage in Wombwell, near Barnsley, Yorkshire. Their lodger, John Gallagher, was a thirty-year-old miner, to whom Mrs Swann had taken rather a fancy. An affair soon developed between the pair, and before long the two men had words, with the result that Gallagher was asked to leave the house, which he did, finding lodgings nearby.

The Swanns, however, seemed to be constantly at each others' throats, with the glassblower quite frequently losing his temper and beating his wife. As a consequence of this Gallagher went to the house on a number of occasions and threatened him.

Eventually, no doubt realising that there was very little future in pursuing the relationship with Mrs Swann, Gallagher decided to leave the district and move to Bradford. Fate, however, was destined to play a deadly role before he was due to depart.

On the afternoon of 6th June, 1903 Mrs Swann knocked on the door of a neighbour's house and entered with a shawl around her head. She appeared to be very agitated, and once inside threw the shawl back and blurted out, 'Just look what Bill's done!'

Her features were in a shocking state, all swollen and black and blue. As luck would have it Gallagher was in the house, and leaping from his chair, the miner yelled,

'I'll go and give him something for doing that!'

He dashed out of the house, followed by Mrs Swann, and was seen by a neighbour to enter William Swann's house shouting,

'I'll put him in his coffin before morning!'

Neighbours later told the police that the sounds of a struggle then came from the Swanns' house, and Mrs Swann was heard to shout,

'Give it to him, Johnny!'

After a while, Gallagher emerged and returned to the house he had left. He was heard to say,

'I've broken four of his ribs and I'll break four more!'

After sitting down for a short time he rose and again left the house, saying,

'I'll finish him off before I go to Bradford!',

He re-entered the Swann's house with the words,

'I'll murder the pig before morning. If he can't kick a man, he'll not kick a woman!'

Neighbours claimed that there were sounds of a further disturbance coming from within the Swann's house, and Emily was again heard encouraging Gallagher as he attacked her husband. After ten minutes or so Gallagher and Mrs Swann appeared at the door. Holding hands, they returned to the house of their friends and announced that William Swann was dead. Within a very short time the police were on the scene. Mrs Swann was placed under arrest, but Gallagher was nowhere to be found.

Soon it became clear that he had left Wombwell altogether, but extensive inquiries in Bradford, his original intended destination, failed to produce any clue as to his whereabouts. He had, in fact, fled in a panic once the enormity of the crime had dawned on him. He had no idea where he was going and tramped to various towns up and down Yorkshire before arriving at Middlesbrough, where he had relatives. It was there that the police finally apprehended him. By this time, Gallagher was in a very sorry state. Having been on the road a number of weeks, often living rough and getting very little to eat, he seemed relieved to have been caught.

Gallagher and Mrs Swann were placed on trial together. The Defence attempted to show that Gallagher had gone to the Swann home to chastise a brutish husband, and that neither he nor Mrs Swann had connived at William Swann's death. However, the fact that he had been heard to say, 'I'll finish him off before I go to Bradford', did not help his case.

The judge pointed out to the jury that in law it is possible to be found guilty of murder without laying one's hands on the victim.

'If one person incites another to commit murder and murder is committed, then the instigator is equally guilty in the eyes of the law'.

After only half-an-hour's deliberation the jury found both prisoners guilty. The judge then revealed to the court a piece of evidence which the Prosecution had obviously found it unnecessary to put forward before.

When Gallagher had been arrested he told the police that Emily Swan had hit her husband with a poker a number of times and that he himself had not touched William Swann, although he had been present. Whether there was any truth at all in this statement, it was not used against Emily Swann, and certainly had no bearing on the outcome of the trial.

When asked if she had anything to say before sentence was passed, Mrs Swann said, quite calmly,

'I am innocent and I'm not afraid of death. Because I'm innocent I know I will go to God'.

No recommendation for mercy was made and an attempt to set up a petition fell on deaf ears. At this point, Mrs Swann still retained her equanimity and Ellis, for one, would have been very relieved had he been aware of this, for he certainly did not relish the idea of hanging a woman, an experience he had yet to face, and one which had many times entered his thoughts. During Ellis's period in office quite a number of women were to be found guilty of murder and sentenced to hang. In most cases they were ultimately reprieved, much to the relief of the public generally, among whom there appeared to be the feeling that to hang a woman was a monstrous act, whereas a male murderer received no such sympathy.

Emily Swann, at forty-two years of age, was her lover's senior by some twelve years, and was the mother of eleven children, all grown up. Members of the family, which was said to be a very respectable one, were shocked and devastated, especially her eighty-year-old mother. When news of the Home Secretary's decision to let the law take its course was received, a letter was forwarded to the King, appealing for an exercise of the Royal clemency, but His Majesty declined to interfere.

Both condemned prisoners spent many hours with the prison Chaplain. Gallagher and Mrs Swann met for the first time following the trial, when they were taken to a special service in the prison chapel on Christmas Day. They were not allowed to communicate, but looked across at each other while in the pews. After the service they were each taken to their respective cells, where they sat down to a hearty Christmas dinner, which both were reported to have enjoyed.

Mrs Swann, a short, dumpy woman, talked to the wardresses quite openly, and seemed more worried about the disgrace she had brought on her family than about her own fate.

Before deciding on the length of rope required to hang their victims the two hangmen gathered together all the necessary statistics.

Gallagher, at 5ft. 5¾ins. weighed under ten stone, while Mrs Swann, who weighed just under nine stone, stood only 4ft. 10½ins. tall.

On the night before the hanging, Ellis was particularly edgy. So far the condemned woman had stood up to her ordeal remarkably well, and he was hoping fervently that she would not crack at the last moment.

Just before nine o'clock on Tuesday morning, 29th December, Billington and Ellis entered Gallagher's cell and proceeded to pinion him. The miner appeared reasonably calm.

As they moved on to Emily Swann's cell Ellis asked one of the warders accompanying them,

'How is she holding up?' The warder shook his head.

'If you look through the inspection hole you'll see that she's in a heap on the floor'.

Although he did not show it at the time, Ellis admitted later that he was horrified to hear this. On reaching the cell the hangmen in turn peered through the grille, and were met by a sight which was enough to make their blood run cold. It was quite true. There she lay on the stone floor, moaning and groaning pitifully. It was a most distressing spectacle, which had clearly affected the two wardresses attending her. As the execution party entered the two women were trying vainly to pacify the prisoner, while at the same time attempting to get her back on her feet. She appeared to have fainted and now seemed dazed and somewhat confused.

Apparently, she had held up reasonably well until an hour or two before she was due to die, then the full realisation of her fate had hit her.

Billington turned to one of the wardresses and said,

'Get some brandy as quickly as possible'.

When the brandy arrived, Mrs Swann was prevailed upon to take a good long drink. The effect was quite miraculous. Immediately she appeared much steadier. A few minutes later her courage seemed to have returned. The hangmen were then able to pinion Mrs Swann's arms behind her back. As the party left the cell and moved towards the scaffold one of the wardresses broke down and wept. On seeing this her colleague also burst into tears. The ordeal had been just too much for them, for though no doubt thorough professionals, they were only human and had become attached to the diminutive Mrs Swann during her time in custody.

The weeping wardresses were not allowed to go near the scaffold, for the condemned woman was taken from their custody before the party reached its destination. It was at this point that Emily Swann saw her lover again, though he did not see her, for he was standing with his back to her as she reached the scaffold. The two nooses hung there side by side. Almost before Mrs Swann could take in the scene the white caps had been slipped over the heads of both prisoners. As Billington placed the rope in position around Gallagher's neck Mrs Swann suddenly called out,

'Good morning, John'.

Gallagher immediately stiffened. He had had no idea that Emily Swann was standing close to him until that very moment. There was a pause, then he replied,

'Good morning, love'.

The final words were uttered by Mrs Swann.

'Goodbye, John. God bless you'.

Seconds later the trapdoors clanged open and the tragic lovers plunged to their deaths. The doctor certified that both had died instantly, a clear indication that the Lancashire hangmen had carried out their work satisfactorily.

The ordeal was over, but did the memory of Emily Swann's heart-rending cries, just prior to the taking of her life, remain buried deeply in the dark recesses of John Ellis's mind? This could well have been so, as later events would appear to indicate.

That same year, 1903, a murder occurred at Thames Ditton, Surrey, which Ellis would in later years refer to as 'the murder Crippen might have copied'.

It would be another seven years before the sensational Crippen case broke in the newspapers. Dr Crippen, an American, was living in this country at the time the Thames Ditton murder was committed, and might well have followed it in the newspapers. However, there is absolutely no evidence that he was in any way influenced or inspired by the way William Tuffin murdered his wife in 1903, though certain elements of the two cases might possibly be considered similar.

Tuffin, a twenty-three-year-old carman, or tram driver, with a wife two years his junior and a baby of 15 months, had been married only a short time when he made the acquaintance of Mary Stone. Mary, who was just twenty and worked as a housemaid, soon had Tuffin so besotted that he began to think of a way to rid himself of his wife Caroline. He became totally obsessed with the idea, and hardly a day passed without him racking his brains to find a way to do it.

In April 1903, Caroline Tuffin simply vanished, or so it appeared. One day she was seen as usual by friends and neighbours, the next she was gone. Not only that, but Mary Stone lost no time in stepping into her shoes, and soon afterwards Tuffin let it be known that his wife had died. Oddly enough the neighbours had witnessed no funeral, but Tuffin did not bother to explain this to anyone. In fact, he claimed to be so grief-stricken that he would not discuss the matter of his wife's alleged demise at all.

One of the neighbours, however, mentioned it to the local insurance agent, whose company held a policy on the missing woman's life. The agent decided to drop in on Mr Tuffin about two weeks after Caroline's disappearance. He said he was very sorry to hear of Mrs Tuffin's death and assured the bereaved husband that there would be no delay in his company's paying out on the policy. Tuffin was taken aback at the insurance man's sudden appearance. Insurance money had not even entered his mind, and he knew instinctively that he would have to tread very carefully. There can be little doubt that the insurance man shared the scepticism of the neighbours, and his suspicions were strengthened considerably when Tuffin at first refused to sign a claim form. He must have known he was on very shaky ground, but after further insistence by the agent, he at length agreed to sign. That done, he was asked to produce a death certificate. Tuffin now panicked and began to mumble and stammer in a confused way. Yes, he said, he would obtain the certificate and let the agent have it, obviously knowing full well that he had no chance whatsoever of producing it.

The agent had not long left the house when Tuffin received another shock. His wife's brother arrived and demanded to know where his sister was. After failing to convince his brother-in-law that Caroline had gone away, Tuffin appeared to break down and said that his wife had died during childbirth. The brother was far from satisfied, particularly as he had not been informed of any death or funeral and could not even elicit a straight answer from Tuffin when he asked where she was buried. He left the house determined to get to the bottom of the mystery, and Tuffin now realised that the game was up. Next day it was discovered that both he and Mary Stone had vanished. There is no record of what they did with the baby. Possibly it was left with relatives.

It is easy to see why Ellis drew a parallel between this and the Crippen case. For apart from the eternal-triangle aspect, it concerned a man who had done away with his wife, concealed her body and was unable, under questioning, to explain her disappearance convincingly. Then, with the law closing in, the murderer and his mistress went on the run.

The body of Caroline Tuffin was not dismembered, nor was it even hidden, for when the police came looking for Tuffin and eventually broke into the house they found the remains of Caroline in a locked room. She had been badly battered about the head and lay on her bed, an axe and a hammer, both heavily bloodstained, beside her.

The runaways were soon tracked down and brought to trial. There was such strong feeling in the district where the Tuffins had lived that the prisoners' guard was doubled on their journey to and from the court on the day of the trial.

Tuffin's Counsel attempted to prove insanity, but without success. The extent of Mary Stone's involvement in the crime therefore became the main issue. The girl herself claimed that on the night of the crime she had been staying at the house and had gone up to bed, leaving Tuffin and his wife downstairs. She had heard nothing unusual during the night and on the following morning was told by Tuffin that his wife had gone away. She said she had not known of the presence of the body in the house until the police told her about it. The testimony of one of the medical witnesses, however, cast doubt on this latter statement, for the doctor told the court that in his opinion it would have been impossible for anyone living in the house to remain unaware of the presence of a decomposing body.

The jury took only half-an-hour to decide that Tuffin was guilty of wilful murder, and that Mary Stone was guilty of being an 'accessory before the fact.' On hearing this, the judge, referring to the latter part of the verdict, asked the jury members,

'Gentlemen, do you realise what that means? It means guilty of wilful murder'.

He was assured by the foreman of the jury that he and his colleagues were well aware of precisely what their verdict implied.

'Very well', replied the judge. He then donned the black cap and sentenced both prisoners to death.

However, as far as the Home Office was concerned, this verdict was indeed a dubious one. For although the background to the case may have indicated that the crime was premeditated, the evidence did not clearly substantiate this. Therefore, if this issue could not be settled beyond doubt, how could the jury safely arrive at the conclusion that Mary Stone was an accessory before the fact?

It was proposed by the Sheriff that Mary Stone be removed from her cell at Holloway Prison to Wandsworth, where Tuffin was held, the intention being to carry out a double execution on the morning of 11th August.

The Home Secretary opposed this, possibly because he was still considering the case against Mary Stone. In the meantime, however, arrangements were made for her to be hanged at Holloway on 12th August. Henry Pierrepoint was engaged to carry out both executions, with Ellis as his assistant.

Mary Stone, though, was reprieved one week before she was due to die, her sentence being commuted to penal servitude for life.

It is extremely unlikely that the two Northern hangmen ever travelled together on the same train. For one thing, Henry Pierrepoint had taken a dislike to Jack Ellis, for some reason or other. It is by no means clear what that reason was, though the two men were certainly miles apart in terms of personality. Jack Ellis was no prude. He liked a bet on the horses, a game of cards and a glass or two of ale, but beside Pierrepoint, he must have appeared very insipid indeed. The powerfully built Yorkshireman, who worked at the Huddersfield Gasworks when he was not out on a 'hanging-job,' was a volatile man to say the least, and extremely eloquent and outgoing. He could tell a good tale, and when off duty and drinking he always liked to be the centre of attention, seldom leaving the pub until he was either drunk or 'skint.' He loved a sing-song, and would still be warbling long after he had arrived home to be greeted by the long-suffering, but always forgiving Mrs Pierrepoint.

Jack Ellis, on the other hand, was by no means an imposing figure of a man, being rather pale, slender and developing a slight stoop. In his neat, dark suit, stiff collar and bowler hat, he could quite easily have been taken for a bank clerk. He was certainly not the type of fellow Henry Pierrepoint would normally have made a friend of. But the real reason for Pierrepoint's apparent aversion to the Rochdale man is far more likely to have been professional jealousy. This seems surprising on the face of it, for although coming into the business at around the same time as Ellis, Pierrepoint had clearly made the more rapid progress. If he feared that Ellis might eventually overtake him to become acknowledged as chief executioner, his fears were not unfounded, for this is exactly what happened. After that, Pierrepoint became very bitter indeed, and his intense dislike of the Rochdale man was ultimately communicated to his elder brother Thomas, who later joined Henry on the official list. Tom Pierrepoint would become one of the longest serving hangmen in history. He worked with Ellis on quite a number of occasions, and never had much time for him.

Ellis always travelled by train, and rather than go down to Rochdale Station he often preferred to make his way across the fields to nearby Castleton, where he would call at the Bridge Inn to have a drink and a chat with the landlord, Henry Wood, an old friend. After spending a leisurely half hour at The Bridge, he would board the train for Manchester and pick up his connection to London, or wherever he was bound.

When Ellis arrived at Wandsworth, Henry Pierrepoint was already there. Very little conversation passed between the two of them. Just what was necessary and not much more. When they went along to view their victim that evening they found Tuffin to be a small, weak-looking individual of only 5ft. $3^{1}/_{4}$ins. and 9st. 2lbs. A drop of 7ft. 7ins. was decided upon by Pierrepoint, whose calculations proved to be absolutely correct, for the little man is said to have died instantaneously. He had made a full confession and seemed to be quite resigned to his fate and reasonably calm when he went to his death. Either that or he simply froze, for he stood quite still as the white cap was placed over his head and the rope adjusted. Then Pierrepoint drew the lever and Tuffin plunged into oblivion.

During the latter part of 1903 Ellis was involved in two further executions. On 2nd December, he assisted John Billington, brother of William, at the hanging of Charles Wood Whittaker in Manchester, found guilty of the murder of a woman friend, Ellen Range, at Collyhurst. It was John Billington's first time as number one, though he had already assisted at well over a dozen executions.

On 15th December, Ellis assisted Henry Pierrepoint at Hereford. The victim was 61-year-old William Haywood, who, after battering his wife to death, had later been seen conveying her body along the street in a wheelbarrow. Though Haywood had previously spent time in an asylum, his plea of insanity was rejected by the court, which found him guilty and sentenced him to the gallows.

Three months later Ellis again assisted John Billington, at the execution of Henry Jones at Stafford, Jones having been found guilty of the murder of Mary Gilbert, the woman with whom he was living. In a fit of jealousy he had cut her throat and then his own. However, after doing a thorough job on his victim, he had gone much easier when turning the knife on himself, and sustained only superficial injuries. He gave the hangmen no problems, and went to his death showing genuine remorse for what he had done.

CHAPTER 5

MURDER OF 'THE LITTLE YANKEE'

The year 1904 saw Ellis still acting as assistant to both John and Billy Billington, and on other occasions to Henry Pierrepoint. In that year, Ellis was called upon to assist John in the execution of one George Breeze, whom he subsequently referred to as 'the bravest man I ever hanged'.

On the morning of 6th July, 1904, Breeze strangled to death Margaret Jane Chisholm at her home at Seaham Harbour on the North-East coast. Breeze, a twenty-one-year-old footballer, had lodged with Mrs Chisholm and her husband, who was a close friend and a member of the same club.

After the murder Breeze gave himself up to the police in Sunderland, telling them that he had killed the woman because he loved her and could not have her.

At the Police Court he said,

'If I am sentenced to die I hope there will be no question of a reprieve, or I will curse anyone who signs his hand to it'.

The judge at the Assizes was so taken aback at the prisoner's insistence on his own guilt that he remarked to Counsel,

'I think you had better show some evidence that this man is fit to plead'.

Dr Gilbert, the prison medical officer, was then called, and assured the court that the prisoner was indeed in a fit condition, mentally, to plead.

Having pleaded guilty, Breeze was asked by the judge if he wished to say anything, to which he immediately replied;

'No sir. I just wish to die. And I'm not sorry for what I've done'.

'And you still say you're guilty?'

'Yes sir', was the reply, 'quite guilty'.

'And you don't wish to be defended?'

'No'.

After sentence of death had been passed, the prisoner called out to the judge as he was being led away,

'Thank you very much, my lord. I hope there will be no talk of a reprieve'.

Then off he went to the cells with a broad grin on his face.

Before sentence of death could be carried out a petition for reprieve was circulated, probably by relatives and friends, based on the grounds of possible insanity, but the Home Secretary could find no cause to intervene.

When Ellis entered Durham Gaol on the afternoon prior to the execution he was told that Breeze appeared to be just about the happiest man in the prison, and on entering the passage leading to the condemned man's cell, Ellis was amazed to hear hearty laughter coming from within. Peering through the aperture in the door, he saw Breeze sharing a joke with two warders, both of whom were smiling, while the prisoner himself was leaning back on the wall, roaring with laughter. It was an amazing scene and one which Ellis never expected to witness in the condemned cell.

Though Breeze was not laughing when he mounted the scaffold he was very calm and totally devoid of fear. He even called out, 'So long', to reporters standing in the corridor through which the execution party passed, and as the white cap was slipped over his head the condemned man still had a smile on his face.

In August, William Billington and John Ellis hanged Samuel Holden at Birmingham for the murder of Susan Humphries, Holden being allowed to smoke a cigar as he walked to the gallows.

Before the year 1904 ended Ellis again acted as assistant to Billy Billington, the two Lancastrians travelling by train to Cardiff, where they hanged Eric Lange, convicted of the murder of John Jones, landlord of a public house, during the course of a robbery.

In the early part of 1905, a murder was to occur as a consequence of which John Ellis would be called upon to travel to Ireland for the first time. Again the senior executioner was William Billington. The setting for the crime was Cork in Southern Ireland, and the principals in the affair were two friends who lodged together in the house of Mrs O'Connor. The two men were totally different types. John Foster, an ex-policeman, was a huge man of 6ft. 2ins. and hefty build, while his mate, William Regan, was a tiny fellow who stood no more than 5 feet tall. Regan, an old US Army pensioner, was known as 'The Little Yankee'. A more sharply contrasting pair would have been very hard to find.

Regan was the proud possessor of a gold watch and chain of a rather unusual design. Attached to it was a large gold horseshoe locket. It was without doubt Regan's prize possession and one of which he was very proud. He would never consider selling the piece, but liked to show it to friends and acquaintances in beer houses which the two men frequented.

On the afternoon of 3rd December, 1904, he was seen in the town with his friend Foster, but when Foster returned to the lodging house around six that evening he was alone. Regan, in fact, seemed to have disappeared completely. His prized watch and locket, however, had not disappeared with him, for Foster was known to have them in his possession.

The police decided to keep a eye on Foster rather than move in and arrest him, but some ten days after Regan's disappearance the body of 'The Little Yankee' was fished out of the River Lee at the Exhibition Grounds.

It was clear that he had been murdered. Within hours of the discovery of the body John Foster was in custody, charged with the crime. It was ultimately proven in court that he had robbed his friend, before beating him about the head with a blunt instrument and dumping his body in the Lee. The ex-policeman was found guilty and sentenced to hang.

The crossing to Ireland was only the second time that Ellis had been to sea, the first occasion having been a short trip down the coast to Brighton, during which he was seasick. So the prospect of braving the notoriously rough Irish Sea was one that filled him with the greatest dread. As it turned out, the apprehensive hangman came through it very well, for though the sea was quite rough, he had conditioned his mind to expect such a nightmare crossing that the reality was nowhere near as bad as he had anticipated.

The execution was due to take place at Cork on the Tuesday following the weekend of the arrival of Billington and Ellis at the prison. As chief executioner, Billington secured permission to leave the gaol and stay in the town until the Monday, but when his assistant applied for the same privilege he was told that having been fixed up with accommodation within the prison he must not leave it until after the execution. They were not to know it at the time, but the Irish authorities would attempt to detain them even after the hanging had been carried out.

Billington did not return until the Monday afternoon, and delighted in relating to Ellis, the marvellous time he had had over the previous two days.

When the two hangmen were taken to 'view' their victim, both were at once struck by his outstanding physique, which several months in gaol had done nothing to diminish. On learning that Foster weighed 16st., and taking other factors into account, they decided that the length of the drop should be 5ft. 9ins. After testing the scaffold and its equipment, they left a sandbag hanging from the rope in the usual way and retired for the night. Ellis, however, slept very little. He was kept awake by the sound of rain, which poured down heavily all night long and did not let up until early morning. By 8a.m. a crowd of several hundred people had gathered outside the prison gates to wait for news of the carrying out of the execution.

On approaching the condemned cell, the hangmen were informed that they were not allowed to enter it.

'But we have to pinion the prisoner's hands', said Billington.

'Then you will have to do it by hiding yourselves somewhere and then approaching the prisoner from behind before he reaches the scaffold', they were told by the Chief Warder.

It was no use arguing. So the executioners concealed themselves in a room off the passage along which the party would pass on the way to the scaffold. After the retinue had passed by, the hangmen left their hiding place and followed quickly, coming up behind the prisoner just prior to his mounting the scaffold.

They were naturally very worried that he would put up a fight, but to their extreme relief he allowed them to place his hands behind his back and pinion them without offering the slightest resistance, which was just as well, for a man of such size and strength could without doubt have put up a tremendous struggle had he chosen to.

The execution itself went without a hitch and was over very quickly. The two hangmen were then left with the problem of getting away from the scene, for they had been told that they must remain in Cork until after the Coroner had held an inquest on the body of the executed man. To make sure that they did not leave, a warrant was issued for their arrests, but taking great exception to this, they decided to ignore it and leave at once.

Fortunately for them, one of the prison officers laid on a car to drive them to Dublin immediately after the execution, and when the Coroner opened the proceedings and called for Billington and Ellis to give evidence there was no response.

The Coroner was very angry and pointed out to the court that,

'We have come here in the interests of the community for the purpose of ascertaining whether the prisoner Foster was executed in accordance with the law. The executioners are not present and should be. I intend to adjourn until this day next week. In the meantime we must make sure that the warrants have been served on them'.

But by the time the inquest was resumed the following week they were safely back in England.

A month after his little adventure in Ireland Ellis and Henry Pierrepoint acted as assistants to John Billington in a double execution at Wandsworth. The condemned men, Albert and Alfred Stratton, aged 20 and 23, two brothers from Deptford, had been found guilty of the slaying of Thomas Farrow and his wife, whose bodies were discovered in a room above their shop. They had been battered to death. Two men were seen leaving the shop, and the Stratton brothers, both of whom had appalling criminal records, were arrested and subjected to an innovation in the detection of crime, fingerprinting.

With things looking bad for them the brothers soon showed their true colours, each attempting to place the blame on the other. Both were found guilty and sentenced to death. They were the first to be convicted on fingerprint evidence.

In August, 1905, Ellis assisted Henry Pierrepoint at Maidstone in Kent, at the execution of Ferat Mohamed Benali, one of a group of five Algerian pedlars, who had murdered the leader of their band for the money he had on him. On peering at the prisoner through the aperture, the hangmen were rather taken aback at the slight build of the man. His body was as small and light as a child's, and it was eventually decided that a drop of 7ft. 6ins. would be necessary to hang him. In loose-fitting, Arab clothing with a red waist-band, the condemned man, who was, in fact, little more than a boy, showed no fear as he was pinioned.

On the scaffold, he began to pray in his own language and the name 'Allah' was muttered a number of times. A moment later he had plunged to his death through the trapdoors and all was silent.

The hanging of Thomas Tattersall at Leeds for the murder of his wife Rebecca, turned out to be John Billington's last. While preparing the drop he fell into the pit, injuring himself. Though he was still able to carry out the execution, he later became ill, and died not long afterwards. On the day of Billington's accident at Leeds, 15th August, 1905, Ellis was assisting Henry Pierrepoint to hang Arthur Deveraux, at Pentonville, for the murder of his wife Beatrice and their twin sons.

In November, Ellis assisted Pierrepoint in the hanging of William George Butler at Pentonville for the murder of his sweetheart, Mary Allen. December proved to be a very busy month indeed for the lethal Northern pair. On the fifth, at Worcester, they hanged William Yarnold, an army veteran found guilty of the murder of his unfaithful wife. From Worcester they took the train north, where at Newcastle-upon-Tyne, they executed Henry Parkins on the following day. Parkins's crime had been committed in one of the city's lodging houses, when, during a drunken brawl, he had stabbed to death a fellow lodger, Patrick Durkin.

On 20th December, Pierrepoint made the long train journey to Maidstone, in Kent, for the execution of Samuel Curtis, who had murdered Alice Clover, the mother of his three children, by cutting her throat, then leaving her to bleed to death in the street. Pierrepoint 'broke in' a new assistant, William

Fry, from Weymouth, who obviously did not take to the job, as he was never heard of again following the execution of Curtis.

Pierrepoint and Ellis ended the year with three executions in three days: at Stafford on the 27th and at Leeds and Derby on the following two days.

The Stafford hanging was the result of a particularly cruel and brutal murder committed by one Frederick William Edge, who lost his job and consequently got into arrears with his rent at the house where he lodged in Neilson Street, Newcastle-under-Lyme.

Eventually, his landlady, Mrs Evans, was told by her husband to inform Edge that he would have to move out, as they could not continue to keep him rent free.

Edge became very angry at this, but agreed to leave. Later that same day he was nursing the Evans's five-month-old baby, which he was in the habit of doing. Once the baby had gone off to sleep he gently placed it on the couch, at which point Mrs Evans went upstairs, leaving Edge sitting in the kitchen with the sleeping child.

Not very long afterwards she heard the front door open, then bang shut, and assumed, quite correctly, that it was Edge leaving the house. A few minutes later she came downstairs and heard a gurgling noise coming from the kitchen. Rushing in, she was met by a most horrifying scene, for the baby's throat had been cut in such a manner as to leave the infant almost decapitated.

The lodger, who had taken his revenge on the Evans family in the most cowardly way imaginable, surrendered himself immediately at the local police station, the bloodstained murder weapon, a razor, still in his hand.

On arriving at Stafford Gaol, Pierrepoint and Ellis were rather surprised to note that the perpetrator of this vicious, most callous crime was a weedy-looking young man of twenty-three, wearing gold-rimmed spectacles.

The executioners decided that a drop of 6ft. 10ins. was called for and carried out their work quickly and efficiently. Tears streaked the cheeks of Edge as the white cap was slipped over his head. A few seconds later he had disappeared into the pit.

Victim number two, that Christmas, was George Smith, who had murdered his wife Martha, at Ilkley, the previous September.

The couple were the parents of two small children, and not only was Smith a poor provider, but his wife was eventually forced to go out to work to keep him, as well as the children.

Despite the reliance on the wife's wages, Smith seemed intent on making Martha's life as difficult as possible, and frequently beat her. Once he went to the house were she was employed in domestic service and assaulted her there. He then insisted that she leave her employment, which she did, going to her mother's house at Wakefield with the children.

Knowing he would soon find her there, she looked around for further employment and managed to obtain a position at a large house in Ilkley. It took Smith no more that a few days to track her down.

On the particular day that Smith arrived at Ilkley the family had gone out, leaving Martha Smith alone in the house. At around two-thirty that afternoon Smith was seen to enter by the back door. Three hours or so later the daughter of the house returned and was stunned to find the new servant lying in a pool of blood on the kitchen floor. She had been stabbed no fewer than forty-nine times. Within a couple of days Smith was arrested, still wearing bloodstained clothing and carrying a silk handkerchief which had belonged to his murdered wife's employer. He also had in his possession a butcher's knife, which had gone missing from his lodgings in Leeds on the day he had travelled to Ilkley.

In court, he claimed that he had been provoked by his wife, who told him that she was seeing another man, which was quite untrue. The inevitable verdict of guilty was brought in by the jury, and in passing sentence of death, Mr Justice Jelf described the murder as one of the most brutal crimes it had ever been his lot to try.

Smith seemed quite unmoved on hearing of his fate, but on being lodged in Armley Gaol, Leeds, he became very aggressive, threatening the warders and swearing that he would attack the hangmen if they dared come near him. Smith, an out-of-work bricklayer, was fifty years of age and at 5ft. 4ins. was a stocky, strong-looking individual.

When Pierrepoint and Ellis went to the condemned man's cell to take a look at him on the day prior to his execution he was having his tea. Observing him through the inspection hole, they saw nothing untoward about his behaviour until the meal was finished, when he suddenly jumped to his feet, and snatching two pillows from the bed, began to swing them wildly around his head. Eventually becoming bored with this, Smith threw down the pillows and began to pace his cell, a strange, angry look on his face.

'He's going to be a difficult one', observed Pierrepoint to his assistant.

'Yes, I'm afraid so', was the reply.

A drop of 6ft. 9ins. was decided upon and the hangmen entered the cell prepared for problems. However, to their surprise the condemned man made no fuss at all. When Pierrepoint approached him, fully expecting trouble, Smith very obligingly placed his hands behind his back, while the hangman pinioned him from the rear.

After that he went to his death without a murmer. It turned out, in fact, to be one of the smoothest and least trying hangings at which Ellis ever officiated.

Later that day the two hangmen travelled to Derby to execute John Silk, a Chesterfield man, who had been sentenced to death for the murder of his mother. Silk, a former soldier, had served in the army for over eight years, and on being discharged, had gone to live in Spa Lane, Chesterfield, with his crippled mother.

Though he supported her, he was a man who frequently got out of control when under the influence of alcohol. On these occasions he had been known to attack his mother. On the day of the murder, a Saturday, while drinking heavily, he told two friends,

'A murder will be done in Spa Lane tonight. It'll be our old girl'.

He was not taken seriously, and staggered off, still muttering threats.

On arriving home, he immediately began to quarrel with his mother. A lodger who was present became very apprehensive as Silk became more threatening and violent. Grabbing a lamp, the drunken man smashed it to the floor, plunging the room into darkness.

At this point the terrified lodger fled from the house, and it was not until the following morning, when a newspaper boy called, that the old lady's dead body was discovered on the floor of the living room. A broken crutch lying beside the old woman bore grim testimony to the terrible violence she had been subjected to by her son.

Silk, fast asleep, was found in an adjoining room. He was arrested at once, but told the police that he remembered nothing of the previous night.

When Pierrepoint and Ellis arrived at Derby to hang him they found Silk to be a cowardly, cringing specimen, who filled them with revulsion.

At 5ft. 9ins. and 11st. 3lbs. he was given a drop of 6ft. 3ins. Silk's legs were like jelly as he was led to the scaffold. He was so terrified that as he stood on the trapdoors he began to sway, as if about to faint. With the bag already over his head, Pierrepoint quickly slipped the noose around his neck and adjusted the knot. Then, just as the condemned man's knees gave way and his body sagged, the lever was pulled and the murderer plunged down into the hole.

CHAPTER 6

CLOSE TO HOME — THE SHAW MURDER

John Ellis was never called upon to hang a person from his native town, but in 1906 he came within a few miles of it, for the closing month of the year 1905 saw a sensational murder case hit the headlines. It would lead, not only to his officiating at the execution a few months later, but also attending the trial at Manchester Assizes.

The murder in question occurred in the nearby mill town of Shaw *, which stands between Rochdale and Oldham and is very close to both. Though little more than a village at that time, Shaw was already growing into a booming centre for cotton spinning, and probably contained more mills per square mile than any other town in Britain.

On the last day of the year 1905, a Saturday, a young man of nineteen was brought before the magistrates at nearby Royton, charged with having feloniously murdered his sweetheart, a girl of seventeen named Katherine Geraghty.

John Griffiths, known as Jack, lived at 7 Moss Hey Street, Shaw, and worked in the blowing room at the nearby Lyon Mill. The dead girl had lived close by at 12, Middle Street, and also worked at the Lyon, in the cardroom.

It was stated in court that the girl had been sent by her mother with a two shilling piece, at 8-30 in the evening, to the Blue Bell Inn, to fetch a pint of beer and three pennyworth of whisky.

When Katherine failed to return with the beer, her father, John Geraghty, went to look for her. Seeing no sign of her on the street, he went to the Blue Bell Inn and enquired of the manager, John Lord, if his daughter had been in. But the publican, who knew the girl well, as she came for the supper beer every night, said he had not seen her.

Early the following morning the girl's dead body was discovered by Robert Griffiths, father of the prisoner, at his place of work, a stable just off Greenfield Lane, which was close by his home.

Griffiths, who was employed by William Brierley, a fishmonger, to look after his pony, had locked up the stable at 6-30 on the previous evening. At that time there were two sacks hanging up on nails on the wall by the stable door.

Samuel Holden, who lived in Cowlishaw Lane, Shaw, and worked for the Sanitary Department, entered the yard where Brierley's stable stood, at

* Shaw being part of the district of Crompton.

around 10-30 that night to empty the ashpit, and noticed what he took to be a pile of sacks thrown over something on the ground. He did not bother to investigate, but completed his work, then left.

On returning to the stable at five minutes to six on the following morning, Robert Griffiths also saw the sacks lying on the flags near the stable door, then noticed a pair of clogs protruding from beneath them. Thinking it was a sleeping man, Griffiths kicked the clogs, and on getting no response, lifted the sacks. There was the girl, lying on her back, her hands crossed on her breast. Griffiths lifted her head, but realising at once that she was dead, he ran to fetch a policeman. At that time, because it was still dark, he was unaware that the dead girl was Katherine Geraghty.

A local bobby, PC David Moffat, reached the yard within ten minutes or so, and was soon joined by a colleague, PC Davenport, who stood guard over the body, keeping people going to the mills, on the footpath, well away from the stable, while Moffat hurried off to report the grim discovery to his superiors. He was soon back at the scene, to be joined later by Dr Forbes Kinnear, the Police Surgeon, who quickly ascertained that the girl had been strangled. The face was blue and swollen, and the eyes protruding. Bloodstained froth was coming from the mouth and nostrils.

By 8 a.m. it was daylight, and Davenport began to examine the ground around the body. The first thing he noticed was a pot jug on the flags in front of the stable. As it was unbroken, it had obviously been placed there and not dropped. More important, perhaps, were traces of footprints leading from where the body lay, across a passage by the end of the Greenfield Mill. One set branched off to the left towards Stott's Yard, on the other side of which was the yard of the Dawn Mill.

PC Moffat knew Katherine Geraghty quite well. In fact, she had been involved in an ugly scene one Sunday evening three weeks or so previously while out walking with her mother in Market Street, Shaw, when John Griffiths, the boy with whom she had been keeping company, approached and made a grab at her. Moffat had separated them and asked Griffiths,

'Have you been ill-using this girl?'

'Yes', replied Griffiths, defiantly, 'and I'll do it again'.

He then claimed that the girl's mother had hit him with a poker, and indicated a mark on his face.

All this was witnessed by a large crowd of people, and PC Moffat reported the matter that same night, with the result that Griffiths was bound over to keep the peace at Royton Police Court some ten days later. Prior to this incident, Griffiths had been seen on other occasions to strike the girl.

It was hardly surprising, therefore, that among the first persons questioned following the discovery of Katherine Geraghty's body was John Griffiths. Around 9 o'clock that morning three police officers arrived at the Lyon Mill and asked to see Griffiths. At the time the suspect was with Will Turner, a carder, under whom he worked. On being called into the office, Griffiths was questioned by Inspector Hinds of the Oldham Police as to his movements on the previous evening. Though he was able to give a clear account of all he had done that night, the police seemed far from satisfied. After they had left the mill, Turner asked him,

'Jack, did you see Katie last night?'
'No', was the reply.
'You're sure?' asked Turner.
'Yes', said Griffiths. 'I didn't see her'.
'Where were you last night?'
'I went to the Duke of York corner and stood talking there with some of the lads. Then I went over to the Temperance Club'.
'What time did you get there?'
'Oh, about ten minutes to nine, or it might have been ten-past'.
'Who were you with at the Duke corner?'
'O'Connor and Garside and one or two others', he replied.
'Well you should think on who you were with and what time you left them'.
'I'm not sure of the time'.
'Who did you see at nine o'clock?' Griffiths replied that he had not seen anybody.
'Well somebody saw you', said Turner.

Griffiths then turned away, sobbing, and said he was going home. Turner, however, advised him not to, saying that he would be better off staying at work.

'If you go home', he told him, 'people will be staring at you and following you about. There's nothing to be frightened of as long as you tell the truth'.

Was Griffiths overcome with grief at the terrible fate that had befallen the girl he was in love with, or because he was implicated in her murder? And what exactly had been his movements on the previous evening?

According to seventeen-year-old factory hand, John O'Connor, he had been standing outside the Duke of York pub at the junction of Greenfield Lane and Market Street, talking with another lad named Thomas White, when Griffiths walked up and joined in the conversation. This was at around ten minutes to eight, and Griffiths mentioned that he had just come from the house of Mrs Winterburn, a neighbour.

Over the next half-hour, several other locals, Joe Garside, Arthur Sutcliffe and Griffiths' brother Charlie, arrived on the scene and stood there talking. It was a mild night for the time of the year.

As near as could be ascertained from them John Griffiths had left the group at around 8-20, saying he was hungry. He had gone off down Greenfield Lane in the direction of his home in Moss Hey Street.

At around 8-30 that night two local women, Maria Morris and Clementina Leach, saw a man and a woman standing on the footpath on a corner near the bottom of Greenfield Lane. The man's face was towards them and they were later able to identify him as John Griffiths. As the girl's back was to them they could not be sure as to her identity, but noted that both the man and the woman were about the same height.

Soon after this, a man named Mark Sanderson was walking up Greenfield Lane when he saw a man and a woman standing on the footpath, deep in conversation. After passing them he heard a slight scuffle and looked round. The man appeared to have his hands on the woman's shoulders, but as it was quite dark Sanderson could not be sure just what was going on. When he was further up the street he looked back again and heard a girl's voice cry out 'Oh, don't!' and 'No, I shan't'. The man appeared to be pulling her towards the Greenfield Mill, near the spot where the body was later discovered. Sanderson thought little of the incident at the time and carried on up the street.

James Taylor, a carter, who lived at 2, Leach Street, was standing outside his front door that night between half-past-eight and nine o'clock, and also saw a man and woman standing talking on the pavement at the corner of Greenfield Lane and Moss Hey Street, which connects with the top of Leach Street. He could not identify them, but was able to tell the police later that he had seen the man grab hold of the woman by her shawl and drag her towards the Greenfield Mill.

William Ward and Fred Sutcliffe, both members of the Shaw Temperance Club, saw Griffiths in the club at about twenty-past-nine that evening. He walked through the gymnasium and went upstairs to the billiards room. They had the impression that he had just come into the club, but could not be certain.

At about 9-20 that same night, Thomas Kay Stott was sitting alone in his house in Thomas Street, Shaw, when he heard a noise, 'as if someone had kicked a bucket over'. Stott's house was close to the yard of the Dawn Mill, and he remembered that when walking along the street that day he had looked through the railings and noticed an old bucket lying around in the mill yard. On hearing the noise that night he assumed that someone was in the yard and had either accidentally kicked the bucket in the darkness, or perhaps had used it to stand on, to climb over the railings and into the street. Anyone doing so would at that point have been quite close to the Temperance Club.

On the following morning, James Bailey, a moulder, who lived in Horton Street, Shaw, found a two shilling piece on the pavement near the Temperance Club. He put it in his pocket, but later, on reading the report of the murder in the newspapers, he handed it over to the police.

Though things did not look too good for young Griffiths there was no clear evidence to show that he had been in the girl's company on the night in question. As to the murder itself, no one had witnessed it or heard any cries coming from the direction of the stables, though quite a number of people had been in the vicinity during most of that evening.

Had it not been for PC Harry Davenport it is possible that no clue linking Griffiths to the killing would ever have been discovered. Davenport it was, who had had the presence of mind to keep all passers-by well clear of the area around the body until daylight broke. Had this precaution been overlooked it is more than likely that the footprints left in the soft ground nearby would have been obliterated. Davenport's discovery of these resulted in Inspector Hinds and Superintendent McQueen returning to the scene later in the day with a pair of clogs belonging to Griffiths. When a comparison was made by placing the clogs beside the footprints they were found to match perfectly, right down to the irregular impression left by a broken iron on the right clog.

Back at the police station traces of what appeared to be blue powder were noticed on the clogs and a further inspection was made of the area around the Dawn Mill. Close to a wall in Stott's Yard a blue substance known as ultramarine, a sodium aluminium silicate containing sulphur, had been spilt and lay scattered around. On the other side of the wall was the yard of the Dawn Mill, and directly in line with the blue substance a set of footprints was clearly visible pointing inwards, towards the wall, as if someone had climbed over and dropped down into the Dawn Mill yard. Nearby, an old bucket lay on its side. There was now enough evidence for the police to place Griffiths under arrest.

At the magisterial hearing, which was packed to the doors, it was clearly shown that he had left his friends at the Duke corner around 8-20 on the night of the murder and had not arrived at the Temperance Club until some time between nine and nine-thirty. Though most of the evidence against him was circumstantial, the clog prints were to prove quite damning, and it came as no surprise when he was committed to stand trial at the Manchester Assizes. Mr J.H. Butterworth, Griffiths' solicitor, then applied for permission to brief Counsel under the Privileges of the Poor Defendants Act, and this was granted.

That Griffiths came from a poor family there can be little doubt. In fact, the entire neighbourhood was poor, as were all such working class areas in the country in 1905, especially in the North. The *Oldham Chronicle*, however, put it a bit stronger than that, referring to both victim and accused as 'belonging to the lower working class, whose home surroundings are not such as would be likely to cultivate much refinement of feeling or conduct'.

On the day following the prisoner's committal at the Magistrates' Court, Superintendent McQueen received an anonymous letter dated 25th December, 1905, and postmarked Ashford, Kent.

Dear Katie,

She was the pride of my heart, but now she has gone and I can't help her. We had a few words together when she went to fetch the supper beer, and I soon done it for her. She didn't utter a sound, just said "Don't do it Jack". God help what I have done. I am an innocent man. I didn't know what to do with her body, so I got some old bricks from a wall and laid them over it. God bless her, I said when I left her. She's gone. I waited to see if I could see anything in the papers and I saw in the People on Sunday that they had accused my old pal John Griffiths over it. By the time you get this I may be miles away. I am spending Christmas at my mother's house in the best of spirits. I suppose I shall have to swing for it when I'm caught. Cheer up John G --------. God bless you for the crime you are accused of. They always get the wrong man for anything of that sort. Wishing you all a Happy New Year. As for Kate she is gone.

Yours truly ------ S.H.B.

When the letter was posted Griffiths had been in custody for over four days. Despite the evidence against him, there were quite a number of people in Shaw who appeared to have doubts, and the fact that a band of gypsies had camped in the neighbourhood led to much gossip and speculation among the locals, especially when it was revealed that Kate had been seen talking with a young man from the camp. Also, the fact that the gypsies had not been seen in Shaw after 20th December was considered significant.

The trial of John Griffiths commenced on Monday, 3rd February 1906, with the Prosecution parading no fewer than 35 witnesses.

John Ellis, quite apart from his chosen profession of executioner, was what might be termed a student of criminology. He followed every case reported in the newspapers with avid interest, whether professionally involved or not, and the fact that the Shaw murder was so close to home made it even more intriguing. So much so, in fact, that the Rochdale hangman resolved to go to the Manchester Assizes and for the first time in his life witness a murder trial.

On the day of the trial Ellis locked up his hairdresser's shop and set off for Manchester alone, his wife Annie having declined an invitation to go along, as she felt only revulsion for such events as murder trials.

On arriving at the courthouse, Ellis was somewhat taken aback at the size of the crowd packed around the entrance. Some people were so anxious to gain admission that the police had no option but to push them back down the steps.

Ellis hung around outside for nearly two hours. By that time most of those who had been unable to get in were now moving off, and as the crowd began to thin out Ellis went up the steps. On being told by a constable that the court was full the hangman made known his identity and was admitted.

Mr Langdon, K.C. and Mr Rhodes conducted the Prosecution's case, while Mr Shawcross, instructed by Mr J.H. Butterworth, represented the prisoner.

The judge, Mr Justice Grantham, took his seat at 11a.m., and Griffiths, on being charged, spoke up clearly and confidently,

'Not guilty'.

Before the case commenced, Mr Shawcross requested that all the witnesses who were present in court, be removed. This was done, only the medical witnesses being allowed to remain.

Apart from those previously mentioned, a number of other witnesses recalled seeing a couple standing talking at the lower end of Greenfield Lane between eight-thirty and nine on the night of 19th December, while several others testified to the fact that Griffiths had arrived at the Temperance Club around twenty-past nine.

A factory worker named Miles Needham, told the court that he saw Griffiths enter the billiard room by the back entrance, which was not the usual way in. He had not appeared ruffled or upset in any way, but seemed quieter than usual.

Several witnesses were produced to show that the prisoner was a violent person with a vicious temper and an insanely jealous streak.

One of these, John Newall, a collier living in Newhey, said he was talking to Katherine Geraghty one evening a couple of months previously when the prisoner came up to them and began acting aggressively towards him.

Questioned by Mr Shawcross, Newall admitted that Griffiths had been standing on the other side of the road and that he, Newall, had gone across to speak to him.

'And you started to quarrel with him, didn't you?'

'No', replied Newall. 'I told him I didn't want any bother'.

'Didn't you say "wait till I get my pit clogs on tomorrow"?'

'No, I didn't say that. He threatened me and began punching me in the body and in the face. He knocked me down in a door-hole'.

Bridget Smith, known to her friends as 'Delia', of 1, Moss Hey Street, said she had known the murdered girl well, and also the prisoner, and that on a Sunday night in early December she saw them standing together in Greenfield Lane. Katie had called to her,

'Delia, come here'.

'I went across and asked what was to do. She told me that Jack Griffiths would not let her go either up the street or down. He hit her in the face and when I told him to stop it he said he would "knock my bloody head off".'

John Bardsley, of Heyside, a little piecer, said that on 6th December he was working with the prisoner and asked him about the bother on the previous Sunday. Griffiths told him he had wanted Katie to go for a walk with him and she wouldn't go, so he gave her a 'love tap'.

A few days later he sent Bardsley with a message for Katie, asking her to meet him down by the Dawn Mill. She sent word back that if he didn't stop bothering her he'd 'get three months'. When Griffiths heard this he told Bardsley to tell her that he'd 'do for her before Christmas'.

Asked to explain the expression 'love tap', the witness said it was only a playful bit of a slap.

After PC Davenport had given evidence, a plaster cast of the clog print and the right clog belonging to the accused were examined minutely by Mr Justice Grantham, who then ordered the clog to be passed around for the jury to examine, the judge instructing the jury members to handle it very carefully by holding it by the rear end. One of the jurymen received a sharp reprimand when Mr Justice Grantham remarked irritably,

'Look here, you're holding it just as I told you not to!'

The similarity of the right clog, which had one of the irons broken, and the cast, which had an identical break, was pointed out to the jury.

Mr Shawcross attempted to show that, as the prisoner was frequently in the area around the Dawn Mill and Stott's Yard, the clog impressions in the soft ground could have been made sometime prior to the night of the murder, but this possibility was refuted by PC Davenport, who pointed out that there had been a number of showers over that period of time and the many people going to and from the mills would surely have obliterated them had this been so.

Dr Forbes Kinnear told the court that he saw the body of the girl lying near the stable at 7-50a.m. on 20th December. It was obvious that the victim had been strangled. There was a mark encircling the neck, which appeared to have been caused by a thin cord, and it was clear that a considerable amount of force had been used.

In reply to Mr Shawcross, Dr Forbes Kinnear said that in his opinion the girl had been dead for at least three hours and not more than twelve.

'Was the body still warm when you first arrived on the scene at 7-30a.m. doctor?' asked Shawcross.

'Yes'.

'But if a body had been dead for a number of hours would it not cool much more quickly on a December night, and out in the open air?'

'Not if it were covered up, as this was'.

'Are you prepared to swear that death did not take place after ten o'clock?'

'I am prepared to swear', replied the doctor, 'that death had not taken place longer than twelve hours before I saw the body or shorter than three hours before'.

Dr Forbes Kinnear's evidence was backed up by that of Dr Ashton of Edinburgh, a Police Surgeon practising at nearby Chadderton, who pointed out that as it was a mild night with no wind a body covered by sacks would cool much more slowly.

After Mr Rhodes had announced that the case for the Crown was complete, Mr Shawcross said that he did not intend to offer any evidence.

The truth was that he had little or nothing to offer, and had had to be content with his cross-examination of the Prosecution's witnesses, a task he had performed very ably in view of the overwhelming evidence.

In summing up, Mr Rhodes told the jury,

'As my learned leader stated in his opening, this is one of those cases in which you, the jury, have to decide whether the prisoner is guilty or not, purely on circumstantial evidence. From the evidence one thing is clear. That the poor girl met her death at some time between 8-10p.m., when she left her house, and 10-50p.m. when the nightsoil man noticed a pile of sacks near the stable door. Now the prisoner could not satisfactorily account for his movements between around 8-15p.m., when he left his friends at the Duke of York corner, and 9-20p.m., when he was seen entering the Temperance Club.

'There were a number of witnesses who swore to having seen a couple standing arguing at the bottom of Greenfield Lane, which is close to the spot where the body was later found. One was identified as the murdered girl, while the man with her was about the same height as Katherine, as also is Griffiths. As to the footprints, whoever murdered the girl was probably the person who wore these clogs, the impressions of which led to the wall of the Dawn Mill, which was climbed. Those impressions have been proved to be identical to the soles of the clogs worn by the prisoner. It seems as if some providence has brought home the guilt to this man. The guilt of this crime against the girl he had professed to love'.

Mr Shawcross, in summing up for the Defence, said he felt that the police had begun their investigations with a preconceived idea as to the identity of the guilty party.

'When police enter upon an investigation with a preconceived suspicion dominating their minds, they see signs of guilt where otherwise they would not see them, and the most trivial events assume great importance. The Prosecution has left no stone unturned to bring home the guilt to this poor lad. They have taken a number of unrelated incidents and made a chain out of them.

'They said he had a motive for the crime, that on the 19th December last he was seen in the company of the deceased not far from where the body was found. That after he had committed this crime he went through Stott's Yard, climbed over the wall into the Dawn Mill yard and made his way to the Temperance Hall. Then they say that a two shilling piece was missing from the girl's purse, and a two shilling piece was found next morning on the footpath near the Temperance Hall — Mr Langdon seemed almost ashamed to mention this in his opening speech. They say that a piece of string was found in the prisoner's pocket, and they wound up by saying that when charged with the offence he showed signs of agitation and fainted.

'Much has been made of Griffiths' assault on the girl in Market Street, Shaw, when a number of other people were present. It was said that he threatened her, but I suggest that it was merely the idle threat of a man in a fit of anger. If he had harboured any serious intentions towards the girl, do you, the jury, think he would have been such a fool as to tell the police officer?'

Mr Justice Grantham began his summing-up by pointing out that circumstantial evidence can be more important and trustworthy than direct evidence. That in dealing with circumstantial evidence the jury was dealing with evidence dependent on actual facts, which could not lie.

'Such as in this very case. The clog with the broken iron, the blue on the clog and on the ground. Although these do not prove that the prisoner murdered the girl, they prove that the person who wore the clogs was at the place where the crime was committed. If there is sufficient circumstantial evidence to connect the links together to make a complete chain, that evidence is more valuable than direct evidence'.

The judge also pointed out that the jury was entitled to look at the antecedents of the prisoner and his connection with the deceased to see whether or not they could find a motive for the crime.

The prisoner's previous assaults on the girl showed that he was a man with no control over his emotions. It seemed incredible, said the judge, that he had actually threatened to do something very serious to her before Christmas.

'As to the anonymous letter', Mr Justice Grantham told the jury. 'You might be safe in saying that it is rubbish. The man who wrote that letter did not, of course, commit the murder'.

The jury then retired to consider their verdict and were out no more than thirty-five minutes. Amid a very profound silence, each juryman solemnly answered to his name, then, in response to the Clerk of Assizes, the foreman announced that they had found the prisoner 'Guilty, with a strong recommendation to mercy on account of his youth'.

The customary question was then put to the prisoner, who stood very erect and replied,

'Yes sir, I have not done it. I'm innocent'.

His Lordship then donned the black cap, and in passing sentence of death on the prisoner, remarked that he had tried a good many cases in his time, but had never had to try one in which such brutality had been used for so little reason.

Just before being escorted from the dock Griffiths surprised everyone in court by remarking quite audibly,

'Well, I've nobbut once to dee'.

The judge seemed rather taken aback, and the expression on his face clearly showed his disapproval of the prisoner's remark and his general attitude.

Griffiths, under sentence of death in Strangeways Prison, Manchester, continued to maintain his innocence. The execution was fixed for 27th February, and on the 14th the condemned man wrote the following letter to John Wright, an employee of the Jubilee Colliery, Shaw, under whom he had worked before leaving the pit and going into the cotton mill. The letter ran;

Dear Johnny,

I write these few lines hoping to find you in good health as it leaves me at present. I believe you had a visit from our Charley on Friday and that you are doing your best for me, and I'm very glad to hear it. I wish I was working with you now instead of being in here. I'd be much happier than I am now. Dear Johnny, you said that the

Vicar of Shaw was at our house and he has decided to move in the matter, and I'm glad to hear it, for I have not done it ------

From your faithful friend. J.Griffiths.

According to Wright, Griffiths worked under him for three or four years, and during that time had been a competent and conscientious worker.

On reading Griffiths' letter there is little doubt that John Wright would have been very much impressed by the earnestness of his former workmate's plea of innocence. Yet within the space of twenty-four hours the condemned man was to effect an amazing about-face.

Possibly the prison chaplain's ministrations had something to do with it, but it is more likely that Griffiths' Counsel had convinced him that if he *was* guilty a confession and sincere expression of remorse might well influence the Home Office when the question of reprieve was considered.

Whatever the precise reason, Griffiths sat down and wrote the following letter to his parents, dated 15th February, the day after he had written to John Wright proclaiming his innocence:

Dear Mother and Father,

I write these few lines hoping to find you in good health as it leaves me at present. Dear Mother, I'm sorry to tell you that it was me that murdered my dear Katie, and it is no use, I cannot keep it in any longer, and dear mother, I hope that you are not vexed with me for not telling you what I did when you came to see me, and I hope you will keep that photo of Katie for my sake. Dear mother, you might go and see Mrs Geraghty and tell her from me how sorry I am for what I've done. You told me some friends were coming to see me, but I'd rather they didn't come. Please tell Johnny Wright to burn that letter I sent him, for what I told him in it was not right. Dear Mother, I should have told you yesterday when you asked me, but after you had gone I was very sorry I did not tell you the truth, but I know you will forgive me. I hope you will all try and bear and try and forget, as it is none of your faults and none of you to blame for what I've done. Please give my love to brothers and sisters and tell them I hope none of you will be bad friends with the Geraghtys for my sake. Don't forget to remember me to the Winterburns family, and I hope you will have that medal of mine made into a brooch. I'm glad to say I feel a lot better since I admitted what I have done. So I think I will conclude. Don't forget to put that photo of Katies in with mine for my sake.

Your unfortunate son. JOHN GRIFFITHS.

Once Griffiths had admitted his guilt numerous prominent people in the area were either asked to support petitions for reprieve or initiate them.

The condemned man's solicitor, Mr J.H. Butterworth, informed local newspapers that he was prepared to forward sheets to anyone who could gather signatures for the purpose of obtaining a review of the death sentence, which should be sent either to his Manchester office or to Old Market Chambers, his Rochdale office.

A memorial headed 'To The Secretary of State For Home Affairs' was drawn up by The Vicar of Shaw, the Reverend James W. Pinniger, which read:

> *We, the undersigned inhabitants of Crompton desire strongly to support the recommendation for mercy made by the jury on behalf of John Griffiths, now under sentence of death for the murder of Katie Geraghty, in view of the fact that he has confessed to the crime. Our grounds for doing so are (1) The youth of the prisoner, he being only 19. (2) Our belief that owing to bad home influences and degrading surroundings he has not had so good a chance as most of ourselves.*

The letter was also signed by another prominent local man, Mr John Morris, Secretary of the Shaw Temperance Society.

In a letter to a local newspaper, the Reverend Pinniger stated that, after being in correspondence with the prison chaplain at Strangeways, he was absolutely convinced that the prisoner's hitherto callous attitude had now given way to one of remorse and repentance.

The Reverend then made a further attack on the boy's family by stating that in his opinion Griffiths' 'criminal instincts' had been fostered, if not developed, by the evil influences he had been subject to, just where he ought to have found protection and guidance.

'I mean his own home and surroundings'. He then went on to state:

> *'No one can more deeply deplore the crime than I do. It was of a most revolting nature, and justifies the severe censure passed upon it. But if the sentence could be mitigated to penal servitude there would be at least a prospect of liberty to a lad so young, and a chance of his being able to make a better start amidst better surroundings'.*

The pleas of those determined to press for a reprieve of the death sentence did not fall on deaf ears. Within a few days of the publication of the Reverend Pinniger's letter Mr J.H. Butterworth was claiming that over 2,500 people had already signed, with more sheets pouring in.

Few people apparently spared a thought for the family of the deceased. Not only had the Geraghtys lost a daughter in the most horrific circumstances imaginable, but their feelings were now ignored, as the local vicar pleaded on behalf of her killer.

It is perhaps not surprising therefore, that the girl's father, John Geraghty, passed away during this period, and her mother moved with the rest of the family to another part of the town. Sympathy appeared to incline very much towards the condemned man, and it was pointed out in the newspapers that he was clean living and teetotal, played football for the Shaw Temperance Club, used the gymnasium and was also a militiaman, who had once won a sum of money and a medal for marksmanship.

The number of signatures on the petition was increasing rapidly, and to add insult to injury as far as the Geraghtys were concerned, all the members of the jury involved in the trial had signed an appeal and forwarded it to the Home Secretary, pleading for mercy on the grounds of the condemned man's youth.

Even the Bishop of Manchester sent a telegram to the Home Secretary pleading for mercy on the grounds that there had been no premeditation involved.

Although he had confessed to the crime, Griffiths insisted that he had never intended to commit murder. His version of the events of the night in question were that he had met Katie by chance when she was on her way to the Blue Bell Inn, and had pulled her in the direction of the stables 'In a playful way'. She had said 'Leave me alone, I'll come', and had gone with him.

As they stood talking by the stable an argument developed, in which the incident of Katie's mother striking him with the poker was mentioned. Griffiths was very bitter about this, while Katie took her mother's side.

Griffiths claimed that as the argument became more heated he had grabbed hold of her by the neck with both hands in a fit of temper.

'Then she suddenly fell. I was alarmed. I listened to hear if she was breathing, and she wasn't. I got frightened and threw some sacks over her body. Then I left the place quick. I had no intention of killing her'.

Probably there had not been premeditation. Perhaps Griffiths' account was true in essence, though he had made no mention of any cord or string being used, yet the marks on her neck clearly pointed to the fact that something of that sort rather than bare hands had caused strangulation.

Leaving aside, for a moment, the problem of the cord, it seems a great pity that Griffiths did not make his confession earlier. Had he done so, it is possible that the charge might well have been reduced to one of manslaughter. As things now stood it was basically a question of the Defence desperately trying to save his neck by persuading the Home Secretary to commute the sentence to one of life imprisonment.

In the meantime, John Ellis, who had taken a more than usual interest in the case, received a communication from the authorities to the effect that he would be required to assist Henry Pierrepoint in carrying out the execution of Griffiths on Shrove Tuesday, 27th February, 1906.

On Sunday 18th February, just over a week prior to the date set for the hanging, crowds of people turned up in Shaw to view the scene of the crime. As the day wore on literally hundreds trooped down Greenfield Lane and converged on the stable. It became so bad that those living in the cottages nearby began to throw buckets of water on the unwelcome sight-seers. Eventually, most of them went away, but it would be many months before the Moss Hey corner of the village would return to its former peaceful existence.

The Defence solicitor and the family and friends of Griffiths were still working desperately to save the young man's life. By the end of that week, it was claimed that over 11,000 signatures had been collected and sent off to the Home Office in London.

On the Sunday morning, it became known that the Home Secretary had declined to intervene and a notice was posted on the door of the prison announcing that the sentence of the law would be carried out.

That day, Griffiths received a visit from his father's employer, William Brierley, who ran a Shaw fish and poultry business, and later his father and his brother Robert turned up at the prison. When the two saw the notice pinned up on the gates announcing that Griffiths would be executed at 8a.m. on the Tuesday morning, both broke down and wept.

When they were shown into the Governor's office they were still very upset, and were asked by the Governor,

'Whatever have you come for? You will only make things worse for the boy. You will upset him. He was as happy as a lark when I left him a few moments ago. You will make him downhearted'.

The Governor eventually agreed to let Griffiths' father see him, but not the brother. Robert Griffiths senior, did, in fact, find his son in good spirits.

'I've done the murder', he said, 'and it's only right that I should suffer for it. I'm all right and I'm prepared for the worst'.

'Well, as long as you are prepared, keep up your spirits and die like a man'.

'I will do', replied Griffiths.

Griffiths made it clear to his father that he did not want a reprieve, as he would not wish to live with the thought of what he had done. It would be true to say, that when they said their final farewell, the son was the more composed of the two.

On leaving the prison, Robert Griffiths and Robert, the son, were both in a very emotional state, and to make matters worse, hundreds of people were waiting outside to gaze at them and pester them with questions. After pushing their way through the crowd, they were followed through the streets, and only escaped from the mob by going into the Woolpack Hotel. They were led out through a back exit, and by a roundabout route, to the railway station. Mr Griffiths stated later that he had never had a more unpleasant experience in his life.

Jack Ellis arrived at the prison on Monday afternoon, the day prior to execution day. Though he had now been a hangman for four years he continued to be cast in the role of assistant, and wondered if he would ever be upgraded.

Along with Henry Pierrepoint he was taken to the condemned cell and was surprised to find the prisoner in quite good spirits, laughing and joking with the warders on duty in his cell. He appeared, in fact, far more cheerful than the warders, who were doing their best to humour him, though they appeared somewhat strained in doing so.

The hangmen were informed that Griffiths had been weighed and measured, and that his weight was 11st. 2lbs. and his height 5ft. 7ins. He looked to be of sturdy build and a drop of 6ft. 9ins. was decided upon.

Rain was falling heavily the next morning as the two hangmen arose very early to prepare for the execution. But the weather did not stop hundreds of people gathering outside the prison gates, as they always did, to stand vigil and await the announcement that the sentence had been carried out.

On entering the death cell, the executioners were surprised to find Griffiths still bright and smiling. His bravery aroused in Ellis a feeling of admiration, for he stood, as Ellis put it, 'as straight as a soldier on parade, and the smile never left his lips as we pinioned him'.

Then an even more amazing thing happened. As the procession of officials left the cell to make their way to the scaffold, with the Chaplain just ahead of the prisoner intoning the prayers, Griffiths hurried forward, breaking almost into a run. The warders were also forced to hurry in order to keep up with him, as onto the scaffold he rushed. Henry Pierrepoint was quickly beside him. The noose was slipped around his neck, adjusted, and the white bag placed over his head, all within a matter of seconds. Then, at a signal, the lever was pulled and it was all over. Jack Ellis always claimed that although he felt only revulsion at what the Shaw lad had done, he could not help admiring the amazing courage and fortitude shown by Griffiths as he went to his death.

Just over a month later Henry Pierrepoint was assisted by his elder brother, Thomas, when he hanged Harry Walters at Wakefield, for the murder of Sarah Ann McConnell, a widow with whom Walters had co-habited in Sheffield. Thomas, who had only recently been placed on the list, was taking part in his first execution.

Not long after this, Henry broke in another new man, William Willis from Manchester. Like Ellis, the newcomer wore a large, heavy moustache, but there the similarity ended, Willis being a thick set, strong-looking individual. The venue was Nottingham and the victim Edward Glynn, a sailor found guilty of murdering his lady friend by repeatedly stabbing her.

Before the year was out Ellis carried out two further jobs with Henry Pierrepoint, dispatching Frederick Reynolds, at Wandsworth, and an ex-soldier, Walter Marsh, at Derby.

CHAPTER 7

THE MAN WHO PULLS THE LEVER

Before the end of the year 1906, John Ellis received a letter informing him that he would be required to carry out a hanging at Strangeways, Manchester. For the first time since his appointment, five years earlier, he would act as senior executioner. This did not mean that Pierrepoint had retired or been sacked. It was simply that Ellis had been promoted to the senior list.

Ellis was delighted. He was well aware that a man could spend his entire career as an assistant and never progress beyond that station. Apart from the money, a huge difference existed between the duties of the assistant and the senior executioner. Though the assistant was always present and helped with all the arrangements, such as the testing of the scaffold and the checking of the equipment, it was the senior man who bore full responsibility for ensuring that the job was done in a thoroughly professional manner, and as swiftly and smoothly as possible.

The assistant, in fact, actually carried out only one task on his own: the strapping together of the condemned man's legs on the scaffold. The senior man calculated the length of the drop, which had to be pretty accurate to avoid any horrific consequences, such as decapitation or slow strangulation. He was always the one who pinioned the man in the cell, covered his head with the white cap, or bag, and slipped the noose over his head, making sure that the knot was in position behind the left ear. Finally, he would pull the lever, which released the trapdoors.

Ellis knew he would now carry a tremendous responsibility on his shoulders, but after five years in the job, during which he had assisted at no fewer than twenty-eight executions, including three doubles, he was confident that he was quite capable of justifying the trust now placed in him by his superiors, and realised that they had obviously been impressed with his work.

We cannot, of course, be sure of exactly how he felt about being the one who would personally kill the condemned man or woman. Ellis professed to having no qualms about executing a murderer, and at that stage in his career, this was probably quite true, but in later years his mind would become troubled by doubts and uncertainties.

Now though, at the beginning of what he confidently believed would be a long and fruitful term of office, he was savouring the situation and looking forward very much to his first engagement as senior hangman. He was rather deflated, therefore, to read in a newspaper that the condemned man, who had been sentenced to death for the murder of a warehouseman at Preston, had had his sentence commuted to life imprisonment.

The new senior executioner had not long to wait, however, for his next appointment, for only a week or so later, he was informed that he would be required to officiate at the execution of John Davies, at Warwick. Ellis was not to know it then, but his first job as the man in charge was to prove very trying, in more ways than one.

John Davies was fifty-three years old and lived at Aston, in Birmingham. He had been married for many years, but after a torrid affair with a married woman named Jane Harrison, had left his wife and gone to live at Garston, Liverpool. Being religiously inclined, Davies became well known around the docks for his missionary work, but frequently travelled back to Birmingham to visit Mrs Harrison, whose husband was suffering from a mental illness.

The woman had two grown-up sons, who tried their hardest to break up the affair, but to no avail. Eventually, however, it was Davies himself who was to cause a rift in the liaison. Perhaps because of the fact that the lovers lived some distance from each other, relations became a little strained, and Davies began to display a jealous streak, which only made things worse. On his visits he would question her closely, which she naturally resented, and bit by bit, the relationship began to deteriorate. Inevitably, the day came, when, after a bitter quarrel, Mrs Harrison told Davies that she wanted no more to do with him. He left the house swearing that she had not seen the last of him.

Early one October morning, soon after her sons had left for work, neighbours heard the sound of angry voices coming from the Harrisons' house. Davies had been lurking about and had gained entry after seeing the sons leave. The lovers' quarrel became so loud and fierce that a next-door neighbour opened her door to try and hear what was going on. At that moment Jane Harrison appeared at the door of her house crying,

'What shall I do? What shall I do?'

Blood was pouring from her neck and her head hung grotesquely to one side. As she staggered out into the garden Davies came out of the house and the neighbour began to scream,

'Murder! Murder! He's cut her throat!'

Other neighbours, who had obviously heard the commotion and were already standing at their doors, now rushed to help, with the result that Davies was apprehended even before the police arrived on the scene. He was then handed over to the law and placed in handcuffs. Mrs Harrison, meanwhile, was removed to the hospital, were she died shortly afterwards.

At his trial, Davies claimed that the wound had been self-inflicted, but he was not believed. In sentencing him to death, the judge, Mr Justice Ridley, pointed out that it was very significant that when arrested, Davies had said,

'It was all through jealousy'.

When Ellis received the letter informing him that he was to proceed to Warwick to hang John Davies he showed it proudly to his wife. Annie had never liked the idea of his doing the job, but she must have realised that it was one which probably few men could handle.

'Well', she remarked. 'I hope you give satisfaction'.

Ellis was quite pleased with Annie's reaction. Coming from her it almost amounted to enthusiasm. As he journeyed to Warwick the full realisation of the great responsibility on his shoulders now dawned on him, and though he knew he would get by, he could not quite shake off a feeling of apprehension as the train chugged along steadily towards the Midlands.

The condemned man had never recovered from the shock of hearing the judge solemnly pronounce sentence of death, and was in a very low state when Ellis observed him for the first time through the door grille in his cell. His mood alternated between stony silence, when he just sat staring ahead, as if in shock, and wild demonic outbursts. He simply could not come to terms with his situation.

On Christmas Day, the prisoner had received a surprise visitor. It was Mrs Davies, the wife he had abandoned for Jane Harrison. She was accompanied by their son, and the visit proved to be extremely painful and harrowing for all three.

When Ellis had completed his calculations with regard to length of drop, he encountered his first problem, for the Under-Sheriff demanded to know what figure he had arrived at. When Ellis told him that 7ft. 9ins. would be about right, the Under-Sheriff, well aware of the fact that Ellis was making his debut as senior man, promptly informed him that he had got it wrong.

'That's too much', he said. 'I've seen more executions than you have, and I consider that a most unsuitable drop'.

'Very possibly you have', replied Ellis. 'But seeing an execution and performing one are two distinctly different things'.

Rather annoyed, the Under-Sheriff gave it as his opinion that a drop of four to five feet would be quite sufficent.

Ellis was shocked. He knew full well that so short a drop would hardly be enough to hang even an exceptionally heavy man. As Davies was only 5ft. 3ins. and nine stone-odd, it was obvious that it would take a very long drop to hang him.

'Very well', said Ellis. 'If you'll take full responsibility, I'll do it'.

Backing down, the Under-Sheriff replied that he had better please himself.

'Then I'm giving him 7ft. 9ins.', said Ellis firmly.

William Willis, who was to assist, found himself acting out the role of condemned man in the hangman's quarters on the night before the execution, when Ellis used him to practise his pinioning technique.

On the following morning, the two hangmen entered the cell to find Davies in a pathetic state. He looked so terrified that Ellis could not help feeling sorry for him, and after pinioning him and opening up his shirt collar, the hangman whispered a few quiet words of comfort to him. Unfortunately, the death cell was situated quite a distance from the scaffold, which was not at all usual, and for the whole of that painful journey along stone corridors and down a flight of steps, Davies looked around him at each face, as if desperately trying to find a sympathetic one.

Once on the scaffold, Ellis was determined to end the man's agony as swiftly as possible and slipped the noose quickly over the prisoner's head and tightened it around his throat. Then on went the white cap. Meanwhile, the assistant had strapped together Davies's legs and all was set.

As the assistant stepped clear of the trapdoors Ellis was aware that the Chaplain was still chanting the prayers. He grasped the lever and pulled.

Davies disappeared into the pit and Ellis's gaze was transfixed by the rope. It did not kick back or even swing. In fact, there was barely a quiver. He knew then that the job had been successfully carried out, and this was soon confirmed. Davies had died instantly.

On his return to Rochdale later that day, Annie questioned him closely about the execution and how it had gone. When he related the details she just nodded, almost approvingly. It was the first and only time she ever asked him about his work.

Ellis was back at Warwick Gaol again within a matter of weeks. This time to hang one Edwin Moore for the murder of his mother. Again Willis was to assist.

An ex-soldier, who had served in India with the Royal Warwickshire Regiment, Moore, like many other servicemen, had got into the drinking habit while in the army, and continued in similar vein after his demob.

One night he quarrelled with his mother while in a drunken state, and deliberately set fire to her blouse. On seeing it blaze up, and his mother rush screaming into the kitchen, Moore was shocked enough to recover his senses somewhat, and attempted to save her by smothering the flames.

Meanwhile, the police had been called and arrived to find the woman dead. When Moore showed them his hands, which were in a bad state, they at first assumed that an accident had occurred. It was only after questioning Moore's eleven-year old brother that they realised a crime had been committed.

At his trial, the Defence barrister attempted to show that his client's behaviour had been due to the fact that he was subject to fits of violence because of sunstroke suffered in India. This line, however, failed to convince the jury, which found him guilty of murder.

Moore received no sympathy from any quarter and no efforts were made on his behalf to obtain a reprieve. Yet despite the enormity of his crime, he made a very strong impression on the warders and all who came into contact with him in the prison, for he was courteous to everyone and showed sincere repentance.

The manner in which he conducted himself, from the time the hangmen went into the cell to prepare him, to his last moments on the scaffold, induced feelings of profound admiration in all those present, to such an extent that one of the warders actually wept, and was not ashamed to admit it afterwards.

On his next two assignments Ellis found himself acting as assistant to Henry Pierrepoint, which would be the case on a number of occasions before the Yorkshireman finally retired in 1910.

When William Edward Slack, a forty-seven-year-old painter from Chesterfield, appeared in court at Derby charged in June 1907 with murder, he created such havoc by his repeated outbursts and continual interruption of witnesses' testimony, that the judge, Lord Colcridge, who was experiencing his first murder trial, was at times in grave danger of losing control of the proceedings.

At some time previously, Slack had begun a clandestine relationship with a married woman named Lucy Wilson, but like most men in such situations, still expected loyalty from his wife. When Mrs Slack left him he made strenuous efforts to find her, travelling to nearby towns, often on foot, enquiring at police stations and even placing advertisements in local newspapers in an effort to trace her. When a woman's body was recovered from the River Trent, Slack was frantic with worry. He was certain it must be his wife, but on checking, was greatly relieved to discover that this was not the case.

The shock of it, however, seemed to bring Slack to his senses, and when he did eventually track down his wife to Nottingham, there was an emotional reunion. A tearful, but very happy Mrs Slack returned with her husband to Chesterfield to start all over again.

The couple's newly-found happiness was to be short-lived, however, for not long after the reconciliation, Slack was in Derby Gaol, charged with murder.

Around noon on the day the crime was committed, Slack was seen talking to Lucy Wilson outside the theatre where she and her husband were employed, and was overheard by a passer-by to make threatening remarks to the woman.

Soon afterwards he was back at the house in Avondale Road, where he was working at that time, and told a workmate that a woman might call by to see him. Later that afternoon Lucy Wilson turned up, pushing a pram, and asked to see Slack, who left his work to talk to her. They were engaged in conversation for at least twenty minutes. The woman was clearly in an agitated state, while Slack appeared calm and very much in control of his feelings.

Eventually, Lucy Wilson disappeared down the street with her pram, while Slack returned to his work. A few minutes later, however, he left the job and set off after her.

By this time it was around 5p.m. A postman on his round was walking along Highfield Road when he noticed a couple standing on the pavement, talking, a pram beside them. After passing them he heard a sound which he later described as 'a noise like someone chopping wood'. Turning around, he was shocked to see the woman lying on the ground and the man striking her repeatedly about the head with a hatchet.

The postman ran back to the scene, but there was little he could do, the woman was obviously dead. Slack told him,

'I've killed her. I'm going to give myself up'.

The postman set off at once towards the town centre to summon help, and on glancing back over his shoulder saw Slack kneel down beside the victim. Curious, he stopped for a moment to watch what the murderer was doing, and was amazed to see him tenderly kiss the dead woman on the lips. He then rose, took charge of the perambulator and surrendered to the police.

Though Slack may have been full of remorse immediately following the murder, his attitude had undergone a great change by the time the trial began some three months later. Amazingly, he attempted to throw all the blame for the murder onto the victim, explaining that Lucy Wilson had tried as hard as she possibly could to persuade him not to take up again with his wife. He pleaded that he had never meant to harm her and had only finally lost control when she had made insulting remarks about Mrs Slack.

In one of his outbursts in court, Slack, addressing the judge, said,

'She made remarks about my wife and I told her to be good and go home. My wife is a good person, sir, and there was this woman standing there calling her names. She rushed at me. I'd had the hatchet out of my pocket scraping the top of the paint brushes, and when she called my wife I struck her with it. Then I threw it over a garden wall. It was done in a second. When I saw what I'd done I said to myself, "Slack, what have you done"?' It seemed to go dark, as if there was going to be a great storm, and I don't know where I struck her. It seemed to be about the head. I don't know how often I struck her. I think it was about three times, but the doctor says about six, and he ought to know'.

Slack then turned to the jury, and, waving his arms about, told them,

'It seemed to light up then, like a flash of God's beautiful light, and I said "look what you've done Slack ". When the postman came up, and then another man, I had already thrown the axe over a garden wall, and I told them, "It's not my wife, but it is my child". She was not dead when I went to kiss her and I'm sure she said "Oh Will". I'm sure I never struck her while she was down. God above knows, that when I put the axe in my pocket that morning, I had no intention of murdering the woman'.

During the judge's summing up, Slack became extremely agitated and shouted,

'I will have the truth. You are suggesting things that are not true'.

He held up his jacket in front of the judge before slinging it down on the floor. Then, dressed in his painter's overalls, he sat down on the floor himself and began to pull nervously on his moustache. After a moment or two he began to weep.

When the judge referred to what the murdered woman was supposed to have called Slack's wife, the accused painter pointed in the direction of the jury,

'What would one of those gentlemen — what would that man with the white hair say if I called his wife a — ?'

He was cut short by one of the warders, who advised him that he was not helping his case by continually interrupting the proceedings. Still he persisted,

'What would the judge do if I called his wife an evil name? I don't care if it does me harm. The worst is the worst, isn't it?'

The judge, commendably keeping his own feelings under control, attempted to calm the prisoner. He told Slack,

'Your best friend would ask you to be silent'.

He then addressed the jury:

'Gentlemen, you must discharge your duty, uninfluenced by all of this'.

It took the jury members only a few minutes to find a verdict of 'Guilty'.

When asked, in accordance with the usual procedure, if he had anything to say, Slack launched into another monologue, which became a torrent of words as he grew more and more distraught.

After he had been calmed down yet again, the judge donned the black cap and prepared to pronounce sentence. Several warders now closed in around the prisoner in case he became violent.

'Prisoner at the bar', the judge began, 'the law regards human life as sacred, so sacred that the taking of it is—'

'Oh, I'm not listening to this', broke in Slack.

He then pushed a couple of warders out of the way and deliberately turned his back on the judge.

At this, Chief Warder Morrell grabbed the prisoner round the neck and forced him to turn around and face the judge again.

'I will not add to your distress by any unnecessary words', Lord Coleridge told him gently. 'I am not really your judge. I am only the temporary minister of human justice'.

'No', sneered Slack, 'but I've been judged by a lot of old farmers and that. Anyway, what do I care?'

As sentence of death was pronounced, Slack again interrupted by stamping his feet loudly on the floor of the dock. He then pulled out a few strands of hair from the side of his head and threw them into the air.

'See! That's what I care. That's the man I am!'

As the judge droned finally,

'…and may the Lord have mercy on your soul', his words were all but drowned by Slack's shouting.

Struggling and cursing, the condemned man was hustled down the steps of the dock to the cells below, from where his bellowing was clearly audible in the courtroom.

As Slack waited in gaol for sentence to be carried out he somehow convinced himself that if a petition for reprieve was begun he would get off. Though he acknowledged that he was guilty of killing Lucy Wilson, he never believed for one moment that the blame lay with him. He told the warders guarding him,

'If there is a God, and most people believe there is, he will yet show that I am innocent of wilful murder. There was no malice aforethought. It was done in a spilt second almost, after I'd tried to persuade her to go home. But no, she had come out with the express purpose of either drowning herself or that beautiful, sweet little child'.

He said that after his wife went missing he had feared she might be drowned, and vowed to himself that, if he found her alive, he would go back to her and never leave her, but that, after the reconciliation, Lucy Wilson would not leave him alone.

A few days before the execution Mrs Slack visited her husband, who seemed totally convinced that he would be reprieved. So much so, that when they said goodbye that day, he told her that he would soon be back with her.

In an interview with the Prison Chaplain and the Governor, she was assured that this was not so. There was no hope, whatsoever, of a reprieve, the Governor told her, while the Chaplain said that he was very disappointed that he had failed in his efforts to get her husband to accept the seriousness of his position.

When the hangmen arrived at Derby Gaol on 15th July, they were told that the prisoner's mood was never the same from one hour to the next. In one sentence he would call on the Almighty for his help, and in the next, totally deny the existence of a God.

Ellis was just a little apprehensive on hearing of Slack's tendency to violent outbursts and wondered if there would be any problems when it came to going into the cell to pinion the prisoner.

'I don't think you'll have much trouble with him', said one of the warders, 'but, of course, you can never tell. He's a funny one alright'.

They were more than normally anxious that all should go smoothly, and paid particular attention to all the prisoner's physical proportions, spending a good deal of time observing him through the cell's grille.

After noting the thickness of his neck and logging his height and weight at 5ft. $4\frac{1}{2}$ ins. and 10st. 9lbs., Pierrepoint finally decided to give the condemned man a drop of 7ft. 7ins.

Next morning, one of the warders told Pierrepoint that Slack was in a fairly quiet mood, but had refused to listen to the chaplain's exhortations.

When the hangmen entered the condemned cell and came face to face with their victim they were met with what appeared to be a show of arrogance. For though Slack must by this time have accepted that there would be no reprieve, he still did not crack. In fact, if anything, he seemed determined to play the role of aggressor, rather than that of lamb to the slaughter.

As Pierrepoint went to pinion his arms, he snapped, 'What are you trembling at? I'm not going to run away'.

The hangman was quite taken aback, and maintained afterwards that he was not trembling. Pierrepoint was an executioner of considerable experience, it is therefore more likely that Slack's words were uttered out of sheer bravado. He must have been in a highly nervous state and was trying desperately to hide the fact.

As the hanging party approached the scaffold Slack uttered his final words:

'My last thoughts are of my wife'.

The Chaplain then began to intone the prayers and was immediately interrupted by the prisoner,

'Stop it! I want none of that!'

The Chaplain, taking no notice, droned on. They now had Slack on the trapdoors and were determined to get the job done as quickly as possible. It was all over within a matter of seconds. Once the lever had been pulled and the victim disappeared into the pit, Pierrepoint breathed a sigh of relief. The man who had caused so much trouble in court had given them no real problems. All executioners experienced feelings of tension before a hanging. They knew that they were always open to criticism if anything went wrong. So having come through what could well have proved to be a difficult assignment, given the condemned man's erratic personality, Pierrepoint and Ellis were more than pleased to have completed their work without a hitch, and journeyed North in good spirits.

Though Ellis had the feeling that the Yorkshireman was none too pleased at the idea of his having been promoted, the two of them had worked quite well together, yet Ellis could hardly wait to work as number one again. His elevation to the position of senior executioner brought with it, of course, increased earning power, which was very welcome indeed, for the size of his family was steadily increasing. A second son, Austin, had been born in 1902, and another daughter, christened Annie Beaton Ellis, early in 1904.

Ellis and Pierrepoint found themselves paired once again only a month later, when they travelled to Wandsworth to hang Richard Brinkley, a Fulham man, who had been found guilty of a double murder in a quite amazing case, which could well have been given the title 'Murder by Mistake'.

In attempting to swindle an elderly widow, by tricking her into signing a paper which, unknown to her, was actually a will leaving her money and property to him, Brinkley ran up against the problem of witnesses. The following night, while drinking in a public house, he somehow managed to persuade two acquaintances, named Parker and Heard, to sign the will.

Not long after this, the widow died suddenly and Brinkley soon produced the will, which was contested by relatives of the deceased. With solicitors becoming involved, Brinkley started to panic, and decided that as Parker and Heard were in a position to testify against him, they must be done away with. His first stop was Parker's home in Croydon, which he visited on the pretext of buying a dog that Parker had for sale. On arriving at the house he produced a bottle of beer, which was left on a table in the kitchen while the two men went to another part of the house to look at the dog.

Soon afterwards, Parker's landlord, Richard Beck, and his wife Elizabeth, went into the kitchen, spotted the bottle and decided to help themselves. A glass was also poured out for their daughter. Within a matter of minutes all three were writhing in agony, and though the daughter eventually recovered, her father and mother were found to be dead on arrival at the hospital. Analysis of the bottle's remaining contents revealed a large quantity of prussic acid. The victims must have died in unbelievable agony, their insides, literally, being burned away.

Brinkley was found guilty of murder at Guildford Assizes and sentenced to be hanged, Pierrepoint and Ellis carrying out the assignment on 13th August, 1907.

CHAPTER 8

NORTH OF THE BORDER

Ellis's first assignment of 1908 came as the result of a completely motiveless murder. It was committed by one John Ramsbottom, who was living at the time with his wife and baby at the Prince of Wales public house, Gorton, Manchester, which was kept by his mother-in-law, Mrs Mc'Graw.

One day the landlady was startled to hear what sounded like a gun going off in an upstairs room. She and her son James ran to investigate. As she entered the room Mrs Mc'Graw saw her daughter lying injured on the bed, while Ramsbottom stood there holding a revolver. On seeing his mother-in-law enter, he immediately fired at her, but missed, the bullet bursting a water pipe. As James Mc'Graw entered the room Ramsbottom fired again. This time the bullet found its mark and Mc'Graw slumped to the floor. As Mrs Mc'Graw screamed in horror the killer fled out into the street, still holding the gun, and ran straight to his mother's house in nearby Openshaw.

At the Prince of Wales all was weeping and chaos. The young wife was badly wounded, but eventually recovered. The baby, only three months old, had lain asleep on the bed throughout all the commotion and shooting, completely unharmed, and had not even woke up. Unfortunately, James Mc'Graw was dead, the victim of a totally unnecessary, and senseless killing. Quite obviously, there had been some sort of family squabble, which had got out of hand, with Ramsbottom losing his head and going berserk with the gun.

The case excited tremendous interest in Manchester, but Ramsbottom appeared completely indifferent to it all. He refused to engage a solicitor and would not co-operate with the members of his family, who urged him to plead temporary insanity. He simply kept on repeating that he wanted to die.

Neither judge nor jury gave him an argument, and he was duly sentenced to death, Ellis being engaged to assist Henry Pierrepoint in carrying out the execution at Strangeways on the morning of 12th May, 1908.

On entering the condemned man's cell the hangmen were met with a smile and a friendly nod. The spring morning was warm and sunny, and outside the prison the usual large crowd had gathered to wait for the fatal hour to strike. As they stood around in the street, conversing among themselves in quiet tones, they were no doubt discussing the scene being enacted within as the hour drew near. Most of them would have been amazed had they been able to witness the prisoner's demeanour at that moment, for

Ramsbottom appeared to be in total control of his emotions, almost relaxed in fact, and still smiling.

With the prisoner standing on the trapdoors, legs strapped together, head covered and the rope in position, Pierrepoint was about to pull the lever when he saw the white cap moving and realised that the condemned man was trying to say something. Leaning a little closer, the hangman could just make out the words,

'God bless my wife and child'.

Pierrepoint then stepped clear and pulled the lever.

Soon after this Ellis accompanied Henry Pierrepoint to Hull, where they hanged Thomas Siddle of York, who had cut his wife's throat with a razor. The condemned man was in a state of almost total collapse on the day of the execution, and practically had to be carried to the scaffold.

It was also in the year 1908 that Ellis received his first commission to carry out a hanging in Scotland. The condemned man was Edward Johnstone, an Irishman from Londonderry, who had been found guilty of a particularly horrendous murder committed in the village of Saline, near Dumfermline, in Fifeshire.

The victim was a pretty twenty-five-year-old Glaswegian girl named Jane Wallace Withers, whose throat had been slashed one Sunday morning at a cottage in the village where the couple had found overnight lodgings. Johnstone, a miner, aged thirty-two, was an insanely jealous person, who would take offence if the girl even glanced in another man's direction.

Though he had no cause to doubt his girl friend's fidelity he nevertheless became obsessed with the notion that she might have kissed another man. For some reason he made up his mind to kill her, perhaps because he surmised that once she was dead he would no longer be tortured by feelings of jealousy and possessiveness.

After almost decapitating her with a razor, he ran from the cottage as the owner, Mrs Christie, raised the alarm. Johnstone was at once pursued by two young local men, James Smith and Hugh Watson, who caught up with him after he had fallen while crossing a stream. When he got to his feet it was seen that he still gripped the razor.

'Drop that razor', Watson demanded.

'Is she dead?' asked the murderer.

On being assured that she was, Johnstone smiled,

'Good... now I'm a happy man. For some time I've been planning to kill her. This morning I decided to do it'.

Johnstone offered no resistance, and allowed the two men to escort him back to the village, where he was placed under arrest.

After the post mortem, arrangements were made for the burial, which sadly, not a single mourner attended, possibly because the victim had broken all ties with her family to take up with Johnstone.

The gaol at Perth was an ancient building even then, having been erected at the beginning of the nineteenth century to house French prisoners of war. Not one prisoner had been executed there, however, until John Ellis arrived to dispatch Edward Johnstone. Though it was the Rochdale hangman's first visit to the gaol, it would not be the last, for twelve months later he would be back again to execute a killer named Edmunstone, who had been found guilty of the murder of a young boy.

There was a strong feeling among the public that Johnstone's words and actions pointed to a clear case of insanity, and a petition for reprieve, bearing 639 signatures, was forwarded to the Home Office. Then, as the weight of public opinion shifted even further in that direction, a second petition produced a total of nearly 1,600 more signatures.

These proved of no avail, however, and a couple of weeks prior to the date set for the execution Ellis received a letter from the Deputy Town Clerk of Perth, which stated that he had been instructed by the magistrates to inquire if he would be willing to undertake the duty of executioner on 19th August. Ellis, of course, wrote back accepting the appointment and arrived in Perth on the previous day.

It being his first trip North of the Border, the hangman was very much taken with the great natural beauty of the countryside. In those days travel was not something readily available to a humble local barber, and Ellis considered himself fortunate to be in such a position. Very few of his neighbours back home had ever been much further than Manchester, and they were always keen to listen to Ellis as he talked of the many places of interest he had visited during the course of his 'other' work.

The Rochdale hangman liked to talk while cutting hair in his shop, or in the taproom of his local pub, for he was fond of a glass of ale, but he was always careful not to reveal too much when it came to discussing a particular execution. He had no intention of jeopardising his job. It was a position he had worked long and hard to attain, and at that point in his career it was one he valued very highly.

On reaching Perth at nine o'clock in the morning, Ellis was met by Chief Constable Garrow, who took him to the prison, where an excellent lunch was laid on, after which he was invited by the Chief Constable to take a trip in the country. It was the first time that Ellis had ever had the pleasure of riding in a motor car and he enjoyed it immensely. The scenery he later described as 'magnificent'. He was very sorry when the thirty mile round trip came to an end and he was obliged to focus his mind once more on the grim reality of the job in hand.

As he peered through the grille in the door of Johnstone's cell that evening, the prisoner, unaware that he was under scrutiny, sat quietly in his chair, apparently deep in thought. Two warders were seated there with him, and not a word passed between the three of them as Ellis observed the scene.

Johnstone, fair-haired and quite handsome, was a wiry 5ft. 6ins. and weighed around 11 st. After some deliberation, Ellis decided on a drop of 7ft. 4ins.

Johnstone had been visited in his cell that day by his son, aged seven, and his mother, his wife having died some three years previously. The mother could not hold back her tears, while the prisoner himself was also deeply affected.

The mother told one of the warders that her son had always had a warm and lovable disposition, and it was only after growing up and being no longer under her influence that he had changed for the worse, which was probably something that any mother would say.

Later in the evening the hangman received a visit from two doctors connected with the prison. Though friendly and helpful, they both professed to be very knowledgeable when it came to discussing the forthcoming event and hangings in general. One said that, in his opinion, an executed man died from stangulation rather than a broken neck. When Ellis asked him if he had ever witnessed an execution he was forced to admit that he had not, but had talked to a number of doctors who had, and after reading a great deal on the subject had arrived at his conclusions.

The second doctor gave it as his opinion that though hangmen always claimed that death was instantaneous, a man usually kicked for a minute or two on the end of the rope, and that a man could not be dead when the rope jerked.

'That may have been the case in years gone by', Ellis replied, 'but not anymore'.

'I'll believe it when I see it', one of them replied.

'Very well', said Ellis, 'in the morning you *will* see it'.

That same evening, the Rochdale hangman inspected the gallows even more thoroughly than usual. Perth prison, having never previously hosted an execution, had no gallows of its own. The lever and trapdoor had been borrowed from Glasgow, while the gallows itself had been constructed by a local joiner, who appeared to have made a sound job of it. Before leaving the scene Ellis suspended a heavy sandbag on the end of the rope and left it hanging to take the stretch out.

Back in his quarters, Ellis was visited by the Governor of the prison, who informed him that he had arranged to have the condemned man removed from his cell on the ground floor to one close to the scaffold.

Ellis was not happy about this and explained to the Governor that it was his usual practice to test out the trapdoors for the last time at around six-thirty on the day of execution. As the prisoner's new cell was close by he would be bound to hear it and this might cause him unnecessary distress.

But the Governor intended to move Johnstone at around six o'clock next morning and would not be budged. So Ellis offered to get up at five to carry out the test. This plan was agreed to and Johnstone spent a reasonably restful night, after which he ate a good breakfast. He was then attended by the Reverend Walter E. Lee, and listened intently to his ministrations.

In those days an unusual custom prevailed in Scotland, whereby a magistrate would enter the condemned cell, immediately prior to the execution, to ask the prisoner if he wished to make a statement. When the question was put to Johnstone he replied that he had no public statement to make, that he had no complaints and was resigned to his fate, adding that he had been treated with the utmost kindness by the warders and officials.

When Ellis and his assistant entered to pinion the prisoner they were somewhat taken aback by the man's calm and composed manner. Never flinching as the executioners went about their business, and with no hint of nervousness or false bravado, Johnstone smiled and said,

'Do your work well now boys'.

There was a short stairway to be negotiated, just before the scaffold was reached, and Ellis took hold of the prisoner's arm in case he should falter at the last moment. But Johnstone climbed those steps as firmly as any in the group. As he stood on the trapdoors he was still fully in control of his emotions, and even inclined his head so that Ellis could slip the rope around his neck. It was quite unnerving. Then, as Ellis was about to place the white cap over his head Johnstone looked the hangman straight in the eye and said quietly,

'Goodbye'.

As Ellis replied 'Goodbye', he was aware that, while the condemned man's voice was firm and controlled, his own betrayed just a hint of emotion.

When the execution was over the doctors present confirmed that death had indeed been instantaneous, and a few days later the Rochdale barber received a copy of a document which had been forwarded to the Home Office. It read:

> Mr John Ellis carried out the sentence of death passed on Edward Johnstone within the General Prison, Perth, on August 19th 1908, and performed his duties to the entire satisfaction of the Magistrates of the Burgh of Perth.

Ellis was always very proud of this commendation, and regarded it as a sort of certificate, or proof of his ability as an executioner.

Ellis's next three assignments were all with Henry Pierrepoint: at Warwick, where they hanged Henry Parker for the murder of Thomas Tomkins at Coventry; at Cardiff, where they executed Noah Collins for the murder of his fiancée at Abertridwr; and at Leeds, where they dispatched Thomas Meade for the killing of his wife Clara.

Ellis then travelled to Exeter, where he hanged nineteen-year-old Edmund Elliot for the murder of his sweetheart, Clara Hannaford, William Willis acting as assistant.

In May, 1909, Ellis accompanied Henry Pierrepoint to Swansea to execute William Joseph Foy for the murder of his common-law wife, Mary. Though the killer was only twenty-five-years-old and the victim just a few years his senior, the pair had sunk to the lowest level of society and were living rough, often finding shelter in the huge caverns outside Swansea, where previously, great smelting furnaces had blazed.

One night Foy walked up to a policeman in the street and asked to be locked up.

'What for?' he was asked.

'For murder', was the reply. 'I've thrown Sloppy Mary down a hole in the old works'.

Foy explained that the two had had a fierce argument, which ended when he grabbed her, swung her round and flung her into the pit. When they found the victim she was indeed dead. Foy was tried for murder and found guilty.

The condemned man came from quite a good family and had no excuse for having sunk so low in life. Even so, his father and other relatives made great efforts to save him by petitioning the Home Secretary, but to no avail.

A highly emotional meeting with members of his family, during which Foy expressed his regret for the pain he had caused and admitted that his sentence was justified, took place just a few days before the execution.

After this final meeting the condemned man steeled himself for what he knew was now inevitable. He decided he would have to accept things as they stood and make the best of them. Asked what he would like for his last breakfast, Foy ordered steak and onions, bread, butter and tea, and appeared to relish the meal.

When Pierrepoint and Ellis were shown into his cell on the last morning he appeared bright and cheerful. A tall, well-built fellow with sandy hair, Foy maintained his calm to the very end. He had been given a cigarette and asked for a light before his hands were pinioned. As he took a long drag, then slowly expelled the smoke from his mouth, it was obvious that he was really enjoying that last cigarette.

On the scaffold the stub of the cigarette still hung from the corner of his mouth, and was not removed even when the white cap was slipped over his head and the rope adjusted. Just before his head was covered he seemed to have a smile on his face. This was noted by both hangmen and others present, and an hour later, when the body was examined, the smile was still there with the dead cigarette end still between his lips.

Foy's bravery certainly moved the Under Sheriff, Mr George Isaacs, who remarked to the executioners,

'What hard hearts you must have. If it were up to me none of them would hang. I wouldn't have your job for a pension'.

In July, 1909, Ellis was involved in the execution of two men with very similar names, in the space of three days. They were John Edmunds, who had raped and murdered Cecilia Harris at her isolated Welsh farmhouse, and Alexander Edmunstone, found guilty of the murder of a sixteen-year-old clerk named Michael Brown in Fife, Scotland. In the first instance, at Usk, Ellis assisted Henry Pierrepoint, while at Perth on 6th July, he did the job himself.

There followed another run of executions with Pierrepoint. First, that of Madar Dal Dhingra, an Indian student studying at London University. His victim was Sir William Curzon Wyllie, treasurer of the National Indian Association. The murder, really an assassination, occurred in the foyer of the Imperial Institute in London. The killer also shot another man, who attempted to detain him. Dhingra was a lightly-built young man in his mid-twenties, who weighed well under eight stone, necessitating a very long drop of 8ft. 3ins. He was terrified when led to the scaffold, and it was a great relief to the hangmen when it was all over.

Next came John Freeman, hanged at Hull for the murder of his sister-in-law, Florence, having cut her throat after a bout of heavy drinking.

Early in 1910, Pierrepoint and Ellis hanged an ex-seaman named Joseph Wren for a particularly gruesome murder at Burnley, Lancashire. Out of work and down on his luck, Wren spent most of his time wandering the streets. He told an acquaintance that he intended getting sent to prison 'even if it meant committing murder.' Unfortunately, he was not taken seriously. Later the same day Wren was seen near the railway sidings at Bank Hall Pit. He was accompanied by a three-year-old boy named John Collins. An hour or so after this sighting, Wren approached a policeman and informed him that he had just committed a murder. It was quite true, for the little boy was soon discovered with his throat cut. Wren, who must certainly have been very disturbed mentally, was executed at Manchester on 23rd February, 1910.

A week after this Ellis again assisted Pierrepoint at the execution of George Henry Perry at Pentonville, Perry having stabbed to death his lady friend, Anne Correll, at Ealing. Three weeks later he worked with Henry Pierrepoint for the last time, when they hanged William Butler at Usk for the murder of an elderly couple, Charles and Mary Thomas, at Bassely, near Newport, during the course of a robbery.

After carrying out a few more executions, Henry Pierrepoint decided he had had enough and resigned. There can be no doubt that John Ellis was very pleased to hear the news. From this point on he would be top dog, acknowledged as Chief Executioner and first choice for all the most important assignments.

CHAPTER 9

THE NEWCASTLE TRAIN MURDER

The year 1910 would prove to be one of the most memorable in the career of John Ellis, for in that year he would number among his victims, Dr Crippen, one of the most notorious murderers in the annals of crime. This event occurred near the end of November, a month which turned out to be unusually busy for the Rochdale hangman.

Before that, however, in August, Ellis was engaged to carry out the sentence of death on John Alexander Dickman, one of the leading characters in an extremely interesting and controversial case which became known as the Newcastle Train Murder.

On a miserable, wet Friday afternoon in March, William Charlton, a porter at Alnmouth Station in Northumberland, opened one of the carriage doors of the train which had just pulled in from Newcastle-upon-Tyne. Though at first the carriage appeared empty, Charlton immediately spotted a large amount of blood on the floor. On closer investigation he ascertained that it was seeping out from under one of the carriage seats, beneath which a body had been stuffed. The victim lay face downwards, his smashed spectacles close by on the floor, along with his felt trilby hat. He had been shot a total of five times in the head and face. Two of the bullets were larger and of a different type and calibre than the others. It appeared obvious, therefore, that two guns had been used in the killing.

The dead man turned out to be John Innes Nisbet, a forty-four-year-old wages clerk employed at Stobswood Colliery. Nisbet had been in the habit of travelling from the colliery every other Friday to the bank at Newcastle to collect the wages. He would then take the 10-27 slow train, which ran to Alnmouth, thirty-five miles north of the city, getting off at Widdrington, the nearest station to the colliery. On these mornings Nisbet's wife would be at Heaton Station, which was close to his home, and would wave to him as the train passed through.

On that particular Friday, Nisbet, who normally collected as much as a thousand pounds at the bank, was carrying no more than £370, as there had been a strike at the mine and the men were owed considerably less in wages than usual. The money had been placed in canvas bags, which were then locked in a leather bag. There was no sign of the bag or the money.

On questioning other travellers, the police learned from two men, Percy Hall and John Spink, who were employed as cashiers at other pits, that they had been on the same train as the murdered man that morning and had both seen Nisbet walking along the platform with another man, who was wearing a light-coloured overcoat or raincoat.

That morning, Mrs Nisbet was on the platform at Heaton Station as usual, but as her husband normally travelled in a rear compartment she failed to locate him at first, and only spotted him when he leaned out of a window further up the train and waved to her. Mrs Nisbet hurried up the platform, and on reaching her husband's carriage, which was close to a tunnel, noticed that it contained another passenger. As he was side-on to her and had his coat collar turned up, she could not make out his features very clearly.

When Hall and Spink got off the train at Stannington Station they nodded to Nisbet as they passed the window of his compartment and also noted that there was another man occupying the same carriage, which was near the front of the train, close to the engine.

At Morpeth, a couple of miles further on, a man in a light-coloured overcoat got off the train. Ticket collector John Ather remembered him because his ticket had been valid only as far as Stannington, and he had paid the 2½d excess fare. Another passenger later recalled that the compartment in which Nisbet was known to have travelled, appeared to be unoccupied when the train left Morpeth Station to continue on its journey to Alnmouth.

The clue to the murderer's identity came from a local artist named Wilson Hepple, who told the police that he had been on the platform at Newcastle's Central Station on 18th March when he saw John Dickman, a man he knew quite well, in the company of another man whom he did not know, but whom he now believed was John Nisbet. Though he had not actually seen the two men get into the train together, he had seen them standing talking near the open door of a carriage, and on glancing back a few moments later, noted that they were no longer on the platform.

It was quickly established that Dickman answered the description of the man who had paid the excess fare at Morpeth, and Detective-Inspector Tait of the local police force was sent to Jesmond, where John Dickman lived, to interview him.

Dickman, a forty-three-year-old bookmaker, who dabbled in various other enterprises and always appeared to be scratching for money, was a former colliery worker himself, having previously been employed as a secretary at one of the local pits.

The detective did not have a warrant for Dickman's arrest, as at this stage, he was not even a suspect, merely someone who might be able to help the police with their inquiries. Dickman at once assured Tait that he was quite willing to give any information he could.

Yes, it was true that he had seen John Nisbet at Newcastle Central on the morning of the murder, as the two were in the booking hall at the same time. Dickman had then bought a sporting newspaper at the bookstall and gone into the refreshment room until it was time to catch his train. He had travelled on the same train as Nisbet, but had not shared a compartment with the murdered man.

Detective-Inspector Tait was not altogether happy with Dickman's story, but thanked him for his co-operation and suggested he go with him to the County Police Head-quarters at Gosforth to make a statement. Again Dickman was only too happy to oblige.

'This shouldn't take very long', he told his wife. 'I'll be back to my tea'.

At Police Headquarters Dickman was interviewed by Superintendent Weddell and made a statement to the effect that he had bought a third class train ticket to Stannington, as he had intended to call on a Mr Hogg at Dovecot Colliery. Unfortunately, the train had passed through Stannington Station before he realised he had missed his stop. He had got off at the next station, which was Morpeth, and started to walk back towards Stannington, but was taken ill and decided to return to Morpeth. From there he had taken the 1-40p.m. train back to Newcastle.

Asked to account in greater detail for the time spent between leaving the train at Morpeth and returning there later, he said he had been sitting down resting in a field, and in any case, had only just missed the 1-12 train.

The police now harboured doubts about his story, particularly in the light of Wilson Hepple's certainty that he had seen Dickman talking to the murder victim by the door of one of the train's forward compartments. For Dickman insisted that he had spoken to no one at Newcastle Central and had not shared a compartment. By this time, Mr Hogg had been contacted at Dovecot Colliery and questioned as to Dickman's alleged appointment with him. Hogg denied any knowledge of this and stated emphatically that no such appointment had ever been made, that Dickman had no business to transact at the colliery and that he was not expecting him, although he did admit that Dickman had recently got into the habit of dropping in on him.

Dickman was now placed under arrest while further inquiries were made. In his possession was found the sum of £17-9-11d, which was surprising, as he was known to be very short of money. The cash was in a canvas bag similar to one given to the murdered man at the bank on the morning he had collected the wages.

Following a thorough search of the area, the leather bag which Nisbet had been carrying was discovered at the bottom of a disused pit shaft between Stannington and Morpeth. The lock on it was secure, but a large hole had been cut in the side of it. The colliery manager at the Isabella Pit, where the shaft was situated, told the police that Dickman had worked there some nine years previously and was well aware of the existence of the disused shaft and the fact that the bottom of it was under water.

A pair of blood-stained gloves, found amongst Dickman's belongings, was shown to the prisoner, who could not satisfactorily explain them, apart from replying rather vaguely that he thought he had cut himself sometime previously and touched the spot while wearing them.

Minor items such as the gloves were not, however, enough to convict him of murder, but when an identification parade was set up, the witness Percy Hall had little hesitation in picking out Dickman as the man in the light-coloured overcoat he had seen on the platform with Nisbet at Newcastle Station.

During a preliminary hearing at the Magistrates' Court the dead man's widow gave evidence. As she started to leave the witness box Mrs Nisbet glanced over at the dock, caught a side-on view of the prisoner and sank to the floor in a faint. Later she explained that the profile of Dickman and that of the man she had seen in the train compartment, which her husband had also occupied, were one and the same. The shock of seeing it again had been too much for her.

Dickman, who continued to proclaim his innocence, was ably defended by Edward Mitchell-Innes, who brought out in court that the identification parade in which Percy Hall had picked out Dickman was badly handled and something of a farce. Apparently, the witness was allowed to see the prisoner even before the parade was assembled. Altogether, there were nine men in the line-up and on being led into the room Hall had clouded and confused the issue by saying:

'If I was assured that the murderer was amongst the nine men in this room I would have no hesitation in picking him out'.

But despite the fact that the identification parade had been little better than a shambles, still a massive weight of circumstantial evidence pointed the finger at Dickman.

William Hogg for example, claimed that Dickman had called on him at Dovecot Colliery on a number of occasions in the weeks leading up to the murder. There had been no apparent reason for these visits. They had been absolutely pointless as far as Hogg was concerned, and in the opinion of the Prosecution were an indication that Dickman had been in the process of planning and rehearsing the crime and needed an excuse to explain his frequent journeys on the 10-27 from Newcastle.

John Ather, the ticket collector at Morpeth Station, told the court that Dickman had had his ticket, along with the excess fare of $2\frac{1}{2}$d, ready in his left hand as he passed through the barrier, the implication being that he was concealing the leather bag containing the colliery wages under his overcoat and clutching it with the other hand.

Thomas Simpson, a Newcastle gunsmith, explained to the court that two of the bullets taken from the dead man's head were of a larger calibre than the others, and it followed, therefore, that two different guns must have been used to kill Nisbet.

Mitchell-Innes naturally seized on this piece of evidence to suggest that if two different guns had been used, then presumably the murder was committed by two men. If this was in fact so, then there was little substance in the Prosecution's case against his client.

Despite this, and the fact that the evidence was, to a great extent, purely circumstantial, the jury decided that the prisoner was guilty as charged and Dickman was duly sentenced to death by the presiding judge, Lord Coleridge.

Asked if he had anything to say, Dickman replied,

'I can only repeat that I am entirely innocent of this crime'.

Though it was not discovered until after the trial was over, the answer to the riddle of the different calibre bullets had been there on the floor of the railway carriage in which the dead body was found. A tiny wad of rolled-up paper, which appeared to be nothing more than litter, was picked up by one of the investigating police officers and fortunately retained, although its significance was not realised at the time.

The killer had used only one gun. Two of the bullets in his possession had obviously been of a smaller calibre, and he had wrapped them in paper to make them fit into the larger-bore revolver.

Dickman's appeal against his conviction failed, and shortly afterwards the Under-Sheriff of Northumberland, Mr E.G. Harvey, wrote to John Ellis offering him the choice of two dates to carry out the execution. There had been quite a number of death sentences passed in various parts of the country around that time, and Ellis had to refuse an engagement at Warwick after agreeing to carry out the execution of John Dickman on 9th August.

No sooner had this been arranged, than a letter arrived at the barber's shop from the Under-Sheriff of Yorkshire, Mr Gray, asking if Ellis was available to officiate at a double execution at Leeds. As this had also been set for 9th August he had no option but to refuse. Thomas Pierrepoint, brother of Henry, was given the Leeds job, but at the last moment one of the condemned men was reprieved.

While Dickman languished in his cell awaiting death, his legal representatives continued to fight hard on his behalf. Pressure was brought to bear on the Northumberland Police, with the result that the Chief Constable was eventually forced to admit that the identification parade had been handled in a very slipshod manner indeed, which was, without any doubt, grossly unfair to the prisoner.

The publication of such facts as this in the newspapers led to a public outcry, many people being of the opinion that while Dickman was an apparently guilty man, the evidence had not been sufficently conclusive to prove it beyond a reasonable doubt. Though Dickman had been seen on the platform with the murder victim, apparently in conversation with him, he had denied speaking to anyone at the station that morning, after buying his ticket.

On the other hand, neither the gun nor the money had been found, and indeed never were. The leather satchel discovered at the bottom of the disused pit shaft could not be directly linked to Dickman, but the fact that he had known of the shaft and had been in the vicinity of the mine that day told heavily against him.

Nevertheless, perhaps because of the botched indentity parade, a doubt had been created in the public mind, and many letters of protest were received at the Home Office, along with demands for a reprieve. In various parts of the country people walked around with placards demanding a stay of the execution and an immediate re-opening of the case.

Ellis arrived in Newcastle Gaol on 8th August to find hundreds of protesters outside the gates. As he approached the entrance, accompanied by Willis, his assistant, a cab drove up and a woman, who was immediately recognised by some in the crowd as the condemned man's wife, stepped out. Had the attention of the crowd not been diverted by Mrs Dickman's arrival, Ellis, who was carrying the leather bag containing the tools of his trade, would no doubt have been spotted and pestered. As it was, the two hangmen were able to follow the woman, and were immediately admitted on producing proof of indentity.

John and Annie Dickman talked together for the last time that day. At the end of a tearful and obviously very painful meeting the condemned man asked the warders present if he might be allowed to kiss his wife goodbye. As this was contrary to prison regulations his request was refused and Mrs Dickman was led away, sobbing bitterly.

Had the public been aware of this little episode there is no doubt that even greater condemnation would have been heaped on the authorities. The public, however, were totally ignorant of certain facts pertaining to the prisoner which had not, and could not, be released to the press.

In the course of the investigation of the train murder, a number of incriminating items were found in Dickman's house linking him to the murder of a money-lender named Herman Cohen at Sunderland the previous year. The money-lender had been battered to death, his safe robbed, and his finger callously hacked off in order to remove a gold ring.

It was ascertained that Dickman, who was heavily in debt to Cohen, had been in his office a short time before. Had he been acquitted of Nisbet's murder, he would have been charged immediately with the killing of the money-lender.

On taking a surreptitious look at the prisoner, Ellis was immediately struck by the thickness of his neck. He also noted that Dickman, a smart-looking man with a neat moustache and well-groomed hair, was well built, with strong, square shoulders. Only 5ft. 5ins. in height, he weighed around 11st. 6lbs., and Ellis decided that, taking everything into account, particularly the thickness of the neck, an extra long drop would be necessary. After giving it some thought, he worked out a drop of 7ft. 1in.

In the condemned cell Dickman continued to proclaim his innocence. He was very difficult to deal with and complained all the time, with the result that the warders, who could have made his last days a little easier to bear, lost all patience with him. This gives some idea of their exasperation with the prisoner, for as a rule a condemned man was treated with the utmost kindness and consideration by the warders.

Even the Chaplain found it extremely difficult to warm to him. Whenever the question of religion was brought up Dickman would immediately change the subject. All he wanted to discuss was his case and the prospects of a reprieve.

At six-thirty on the morning of 9th August Ellis and his assistant, Willis, tested the rope and the trapdoors. All was working smoothly. As they left the execution shed and were crossing the prison yard Ellis noticed a lone figure perched on the roof of a nearby house. Immediately the Governor was called and the man pointed out.

'We must get him down from there', ordered the Governor.

An officer was sent to the house, but the man on the roof, who turned out to be an enterprising journalist, simply refused to budge, his argument being that as he was on the roof of a private house, over which the prison authorities had no jurisdiction, they could not force him to come down. After much arguing the prison officers, having failed to persuade him to vacate his precarious perch, had no alternative but to return to the gaol, leaving the journalist to enjoy his grandstand view of the proceedings. At that time no reporters were allowed to attend an execution, so this particular pressman, while unable to witness the execution close up, had certainly stolen a march on his colleagues, at least so he thought. The Governor, however, was quite determined that the man on the roof should see as little as possible. A large sheet of canvas was hung across the open front of the shed, which had the effect of blocking out the view from the roof.

Inside the prison the Chaplain was talking earnestly to the condemned man, exhorting him to confess rather than die with a lie on his lips. Dickman, however, was adamant.

'No, I will admit nothing of the sort', he insisted. 'I am an innocent man'.

As soon as Dickman saw the two executioners enter his cell he glared at Ellis and began to button up his coat in an irritated, angry manner, causing the hangman to suppose that the prisoner was about to offer some sort of resistance.

Ellis approached him gently.

'Right, we're ready', said the hangman.

Dickman simply stared at him, but made no attempt to resist as Ellis swiftly and expertly strapped his wrists behind his back. But just as Ellis thought that everything was going smoothly, Dickman suddenly turned to him and said,

'I'm not going to die with my coat on. I want to take it off'.

Ellis, rather taken aback, said nothing, but thought rapidly. Once he had a condemned man's wrists strapped, the last thing he wanted to do was to release him, in case he took further advantage and caused a scene. On the other hand it was probably best not to antagonise him at this point, and so Ellis reluctantly decided to accede to his request. There was what Ellis later described as 'a nasty gleam' in Dickman's eye, and he interpreted this as spelling trouble unless the prisoner got his own way.

After removing the straps Ellis stood by quietly as Dickman removed his coat. Just why he did not wish to die in it was not made clear, and Ellis had no intention of tempting providence by entering into a discussion on the matter. Once the coat was off Ellis again pinioned the prisoner, then led him out. Dickman did not say another word as he was led to the scaffold, and within a minute or two it was all over.

His execution, based on the evidence made public, was considered by many to be a miscarriage of justice, and led to a further outcry from those who supported the call for the abolition of the death penalty. Very few people knew the full facts behind the conviction and execution of John Alexander Dickman.

On the very morning that Ellis hanged Dickman, Thomas Pierrepoint was officiating at his first execution as number one. He had been operating as an assistant for the previous four years or so, having taken part in over twenty executions, all with his brother. Now, Henry having retired a month previously, Tom Pierrepoint found himself promoted to Chief Executioner, though still junior to Ellis, who was now acknowledged as senior man.

Pierrepoint's first time in charge saw him execute John Roper Coulson at Leeds, for the murder of his wife and five-year-old son. He was assisted by William Warbrick from Bolton, who had first taken up the hangman's trade as far back as 1893, working the next twelve years exclusively as assistant. Having retired in 1905, Warbrick was called back in August 1910 to work with Tom Pierrepoint, due to the fact that there was a shortage of trained men at that particular time. It was the last time he would work on the scaffold.

CHAPTER 10

FOUR HANGINGS IN TEN DAYS

For some unknown reason the year 1910 produced an almost unprecedented number of murder convictions throughout the country, and though several of those condemned were ultimately reprieved, Britain's executioners were kept very busy.

To the Ellis family, it seemed that the head of the household was on the road more often than he was home. The peak month was November, when Ellis was engaged to carry out four hangings within the space of ten days, with three of these on consecutive days.

Victim number one, on the 15th November, was Thomas Rawcliffe, who strangled his wife before attempting to kill himself by taking rat poison.

A petition for reprieve having failed, the condemned man simply went to pieces, and as Ellis slipped the rope around his neck and covered his head with the white cap Rawcliffe sagged at the knees. Ellis realised at once that he had fainted and only managed to keep him upright with the help of the rope. The hangman then let go, stepped smartly to one side and pulled the lever, sending his victim plunging down into the pit. It was the first execution carried out at Lancaster Castle for over twenty-five years.

On the 22nd of that month Ellis travelled to Liverpool to hang Henry Thompson, sentenced to death for the murder of his wife.

The couple lived in York Street and frequented the local beerhouses. When drunk they often quarrelled, and Thompson regularly assaulted his wife. At times the attacks were so violent that she feared for her life. One Saturday night a woman who lodged at the house was suddenly startled by a loud banging on her door and screams of 'Let me in for God's sake! Please let me in!'

On being let in, Mrs Thompson, who appeared terror-stricken, pleaded with the lodger to hide her. Knowing what a brute the husband was, the woman told Mrs Thompson to get down between the bed and the wall, but Thompson was soon on the scene. Barging his way into the room, he shoved the lodger roughly out of the way and soon located his wife's hiding place. In a raging temper, he dragged her off to their own room by the throat. As the door banged shut the neighbour could hear Mrs Thompson pleading with her husband to let her go, as he was choking her. Later on that night the neighbour heard further banging, then a sort of bumping noise, as if someone or something was being dragged along the bedroom floor.

Over the weekend all appeared quiet. No further sounds of violence came from the Thompsons' room, nor was either of them seen. On the Monday morning the neighbour crept upstairs and tried the door. It was unlocked. Stepping quietly inside, she discovered Thompson fast asleep on the bed. Beside him lay his wife, a red handkerchief covering her face. Soon a second neighbour was on the scene, and though very frightened, the first neighbour plucked up the courage to remove the handkerchief.

Henry Thompson awoke sometime later to find a policeman looking down at him. Asked to explain his wife's death, he said he thought she had had a fit, then collapsed. After examining the body, however, the doctors had no hesitation in attributing the cause of death to strangulation. Thompson was immediately arrested and placed on trial.

An attempt was made by the Defence to prove that the accused was not responsible for his actions, and his manner and remarks in court were certainly rather odd, and not what one would normally expect from a reasonably sane person. However, neither judge nor jury was impressed by this argument and Thompson was found guilty and sentenced to be hanged.

Asked if he had anything to say to the court before sentence was passed, the prisoner replied,

'No, let 'em get on with it. I don't care. I'm not frightened of death'.

The judge then donned the black cap and proceeded to pass sentence.

'Henry Thompson, he began —

'Yes my lord', broke in Thompson. 'I'm not guilty'.

'Silence!' one of the police officers cried.

'No I won't be silent', replied the prisoner, defiantly. 'Anyway', he continued, turning in the judge's direction, 'I'm not guilty, so you can sentence away!'

The judge did precisely that, condemning Thompson to death and ending with the usual 'and may the Lord have mercy on your soul', to which the prisoner replied insolently,

'Amen'.

Then, as the prison officers moved in to escort him back to the cells, Thompson impudently called out to friends and acquaintances in court,

'So long, Jack' and 'I'll be seeing you, George', then strutted brazenly off down the steps to the cells below.

In the condemned cell at Walton Gaol, Thompson proved to be something of a handful for the warders. He continued to display a cocky attitude throughout his confinement, and claimed to be a Buddhist, saying that this gave him extraordinary powers and made him unafraid of death. He said, though his body might die, his spirit would not, and he threatened to come back to haunt them. When Ellis observed him through the grille on the evening prior to execution he saw a man of 5ft. 10½ ins., weighing over 12 stone. A big man for those days. The prisoner, who appeared to be of the rough and ready type, still maintained his brash, unconcerned manner, and insisted on cracking grim jokes concerned with hangings in general and his own fate in particular. Knowing that the infamous Dr Crippen was due to be executed at Pentonville the day after he himself would face the hangman, Thompson remarked with a broad grin,

'I shall be ahead of Crippen at the other shop. So I'll be senior to him'.

When the prison doctor asked Thompson if the thought of suicide had entered his mind after he had killed his wife, he replied,

'Not me. Why should I do somebody out of a job when he's getting paid to hang me?'

During that last evening, Thompson continued to unsettle the warders with his outlandish remarks and strange behaviour. At one point, he decided he would hold a rehearsal of the hanging, and placing a chair in the centre of the cell he suddenly climbed up onto it and said,

'Look, I think it'll be as simple and as quick as this'.

He then jumped down onto the floor.

'There you are. It'll be over just like that'.

The warders, who had never before witnessed such outrageous behaviour in a condemned prisoner, were absolutely staggered and felt extremely uncomfortable indeed.

All this bravado seemed, to Ellis, so extreme that he could only conclude that the man must, in reality, be absolutely terror-stricken, and would probably go completely to pieces when the time came for him to face the hangman.

He could not have been more wrong, for on the following morning Thompson allowed himself to be pinioned and escorted to the scaffold as though he had not a care in the world. After that very unusual experience Ellis always said,

'I never hanged a cooler man'.

Ellis left Liverpool that day by train for London, where he had a date with a certain Dr Crippen, whose crime, apprehension and subsequent trial had made headlines throughout the world. This fascinating case will be dealt with in the next chapter.

After carrying out the execution of Crippen at Pentonville on the morning of 23rd November, 1910, Ellis moved on to Reading Gaol, where he was scheduled to execute William Broome, a twenty-five-year-old ex-soldier, who had served in South Africa and India.

Broome had been sentenced to death for the murder of seventy-year old Isabella Wilson, who had run a second-hand shop on the Bath Road, at Slough, Berkshire. The old lady's dead body was discovered by a visiting relative in a room at the rear of the shop. She had been bound, suffocated and robbed.

When local police could make no headway in the case, Scotland Yard detectives were called in, and within a very short time, had arrested William Broome, who had drawn attention to himself by visiting a chemist's shop and requesting treatment for two ugly scratches which marked the side of his face, and which he was most anxious to cover up.

Worse still, he remarked later to his landlady,

'It's very awkward having these scratches on my face. People might think I've been out robbing somebody'.

When asked how he had got the injuries Broome gave different stories to various people. After telling the chemist that he had brushed against the wing of a car near Paddington Station, he told his girlfriend the injury had been caused by a boxing glove. To Chief Inspector Bower of Scotland Yard, the detective who placed him under arrest, Broome said that it had been inflicted on him by a man with whom he had quarrelled outside a public house in Camden Town. Broome also claimed to have been in London when it could easily be proved that he never left Slough all that day.

It was Mrs Wilson's normal practice to go for a lie down in the back room of the shop each day around 1p.m. It was believed by the police that the intruder had been a person well aware of her habits. That person had got into the shop and slipped into the back room, then smothered the old woman with a silk shawl and a cushion before ransacking the place.

Though the victim was known to keep a large sum of money in gold sovereigns on the premises, only a few coppers were found after her murder. A piece of paper was also discovered, in which some of the sovereigns had been wrapped.

Dr Willcox, of the Home Office, after carefully examining the discarded paper, gave it as his opinion that it had contained a total of nineteen sovereigns plus two half sovereigns.

When Broome's lodgings were searched exactly that number of coins was discovered. This was naturally claimed by the Defence at the trial to be mere coincidence, but the Defendant's case was not helped by the fact that his Counsel failed to challenge the Prosecution's allegation that he had been very hard up immediately prior to the murder. A later attempt to remedy this on appeal by calling his mother as a witness was disallowed by the Lord Chief Justice, as she had not been produced as a witness at the trial.

A bicycle, seen by a passer-by leaning against the wall of the shop that afternoon, was referred to a number of times by Counsel for the Defence. Possibly its owner, who was never identified, had something to do with the murder. As neither he nor the bike was ever traced, such conjecture in the end proved to be of little help to the Defendant.

Though Broome had changed his story a number of times and told various untruths, it was pointed out that he had done so because he had flown into a panic on being arrested. The testimony of Dr Willcox regarding the number of coins which the paper might have held appears somewhat flimsy, and it is a fact that the evidence produced was largely circumstantial. But it was very compelling nevertheless, and overwhelming.

To the very end, the Defence clung to the theory that the mysterious bicycle, which had disappeared shortly after its sighting, had without doubt belonged to the killer.

But the jury was unconvinced and brought in a verdict of wilful murder, and within a few hours of hanging Crippen, Ellis was peering through the grille at his next victim. He saw before him a young man of stocky build, standing 5ft. 5ins. tall. Broome weighed 11 stone and had a thick, powerful-looking neck. While measuring out a drop of 7ft. 9ins., Ellis was approached by one of the warders, who told him of a conversation he had had with the condemned man on the previous evening.

'You have heard of men walking firmly to the scaffold', Broome had said. 'Well I won't. You'll have to carry me'.

From what he had gathered from the warder Ellis did not feel that Broome was out to cause trouble by putting up a fight. He probably doubted his own ability to keep his nerve when the time came for him to walk to the scaffold.

Ellis, by now an experienced executioner, turned again to the old faithful brandy bottle.

'Give him a stiff drink just before I come in to pinion him'.

This was done, and on entering the cell, it was quite clear to Ellis that Broome was in control of his emotions, though only just. When the time came to leave the cell the prisoner summoned up all the nerve he possessed and stepped forward quite briskly. Then, with everything apparently under control, the condemned man shocked all those in attendance by suddenly crying out, just as the rope was placed around his neck,

'I'm innocent!'

The Chaplain stopped praying and all were silent. Ellis, however, hesitated only a split second before pulling the lever.

Broome died instantly, but his last utterance left a strong impression on the hangman. In this particular case, he could not bring himself to believe that Broome was the sort of person to lie when about to die.

The Rochdale hangman, a keen student of criminology in his own way, always felt that justice would have been better served if Broome had been reprieved until some more concrete evidence could be found to back up all the circumstantial evidence produced at the trial.

One thing he was very sure of. Men convicted in cases where there was far less doubt had had their sentences commuted to life imprisonment and so escaped the death penalty. The whole business, in fact, left Ellis with a very uneasy feeling.

CHAPTER 11

THE NOTORIOUS DR CRIPPEN

Hawley Harvey Crippen was born at Coldwater, Michigan, in 1862, the son of Myron and Andresse Crippen. The father, who ran a dry goods business, was one of the most prosperous men in the town. Hawley's uncle, who was the local family doctor, had a great influence on him, and the boy grew up determined to follow him into the medical profession.

After finishing his studies at the University of Michigan, Hawley took his MD and qualified as a homoeopathic physician. Homoeopathy was the creation of Dr Hahnemann of Leipzig in the 1790s. It is the treatment of disease by drugs in minute dosage, and aims to effect a cure by producing symptoms similar to those they are designed to remove. So, though Crippen was never a qualified medical practitioner in the accepted sense, he was determined to make good, and while in his early twenties, made his first visit to England, where he gained experience by assisting in a London hospital for very little remuneration.

In 1887 he married an Irish girl, Charlotte Bell, who unfortunately died some five years later. A child of the marriage, christened Otto Hawley, was sent to live with his grandparents in California, while Hawley Harvey Crippen moved on to New York, where he managed to obtain a position as assistant to a doctor in Brooklyn.

At some time in 1892 Crippen made the acquaintance of Cora Turner, whose original surname, Mackamotzki, betrayed her Polish ancestry. Cora was very keen to succeed as an opera singer, though from all accounts her voice was hardly good enough to warrant such lofty aspirations, and certainly did not match her enthusiasm. But a singing career was something on which she had set her heart, and at only nineteen she considered herself still young enough to study and eventually make the grade. But coming from a very poor background, this was proving to be extremely difficult. Cora, however, was resourceful and not short of male admirers, several of whom, apparently, helped to pay for her lessons.

Cora's buxom figure and sensual charms immediately attracted the doctor, and though they were complete opposites in almost every way it is not difficult to understand what drew them to each other. To Cora, Crippen, a man more than ten years her senior, represented security, something she had never known, plus a possible source of finance for her singing lessons. The fact that he was a small, insignificant-looking man did not worry her in the least. It is doubtful, in any case, if she even considered remaining faithful to the little doctor, whom she married in Jersey City in the autumn of 1892, only six months or so after the death of his first wife.

Cora's hopes of a better life, however, were somewhat slow to materialise. The so-called 'gay nineties' in America were gay and glamourous for some, no doubt, but for the majority times were very hard indeed.

Homoeopathy was considered an alternative medicine. There was no such thing as a goverment health plan, and the majority of the population was so poor that even the conventional family practitioner found it increasingly difficult to collect the money his patients owed him, so alternative physicians were far from prosperous, and the Crippens, like many others, struggled to survive. Even the fact that Hawley had previously gained a diploma as an eye and ear specialist proved to be of little extra financial help.

It was tempting for men in Crippen's position to become pedlars of quack medicine. While people could not afford the services of a proper doctor they somehow managed to find the money to buy all sorts of concoctions, mostly of dubious content, with which to dose themselves. Enormous sums of money were being spent on newpaper advertising by the purveyors of these cure-alls, and whether they worked or not, many became household names, such as Trench's Remedy, 'the world-famous cure for epilepsy and fits', Poplets, said to cure 'all ladies ailments', and Clarke's Blood Mixture 'take it for Eczema, Boils, Pimples, Sores and Eruptions'.

Usually, the advertisers attempted to inject a suggestion of medical authenticity into their copy by referring to a doctor by name, such as 'Dr Blosser', who was prepared to send a free trial pack of herbal cigarettes, said to be pleasant to smoke and very beneficial to those suffering from catarrh, asthma, catarrhal deafness or frequent colds.

Perhaps most horrifying of all were those which claimed to cure such killer diseases as tuberculosis, and included a letter from a person swearing that he, or she, had been a victim and was now completely healthy again, thanks to the benefits of a certain treatment said to be cheap and effective.

One of these was signed by a 'Norah M. Jones of Pembrokeshire in Wales' and witnessed by a G. Meyrick Price, 'Commissioner for Oaths'.

To go to such lengths to get money out of sick people was indeed shameful and scandalous.

Soon Crippen had abandoned all the lofty principles of his chosen profession and joined a company by the name of Munyon's Homoeopathic Remedies in New York City. Working under the dynamic Professor Munyon, Crippen made such rapid progress that before long he was opening new offices for the firm in other cities. He was making enough money for Cora not only to take her singing lessons with the best teachers available, but also to go out and buy expensive pieces of jewellery with which to adorn her ample figure. She flirted with all sorts of mostly small-time theatrical characters, for she had now begun to conceive the idea that a career in Vaudeville might be just as rewarding as one in opera. The fact was, however, that her voice was nowhere near good enough to carry an aria, and never would be. This decision did not please Crippen at all, since Vaudevillians were at that time perceived by many as brash, unrefined vagabonds.

In his travels around America, Crippen left his wife alone for weeks on end. She had no children to occupy her and never could have, so it is not surprising that, being the type of woman she was, Cora should seek the company of other men.

At some time in the late eighteen-nineties Crippen's firm sent him to London to open up a new branch office in Shaftesbury Avenue. It is possible that it was not intended that he should remain permanently in England, or Cora would no doubt have accompanied him. However, after a separation running into several months, during which time Crippen must have wondered what his wife might be up to, and with whom, Cora joined him in London.

There is no doubt that she arrived in this country determined to take the London stage by storm. American artists were always popular and Cora had, after all, received a certain amount of classical training. She was also bright, vivacious and overflowing with enthusiasm. On the debit side was the fact that she was by no means the ideal build for the role she intended to play on the Music Hall stage. Buxom women in those days were considered, if not beautiful exactly, most certainly bonny, for slenderness was considered skinny and unattractive. Cora, unfortunately, as well as being 'well-built' was also short, and has been rather unkindly described as 'dumpy'.

This, coupled with the fact that her talent was apparently limited, was by no means a formula for success in London, where audiences were very demanding and competition extremely fierce. Nevertheless, Cora, who if nothing else was never short of confidence, was soon making the rounds of agents' offices. Now that her husband was relatively successful she spared no expense when it came to flashy clothes and jewellery with which to impress, and eventually managed to get a few engagements at some of the smaller venues such as the Bedford Music Hall in Camden Town, where she was once booed off the stage. It may have been a far cry from the London Pavilion, but at least she could now claim to be a member of the theatrical profession.

By this time it had occurred to her that talent or no talent, the name Cora Crippen would be unlikely to take her very far, and after a spell as 'Cora Motzki' she was now appearing on the halls as 'Belle Elmore'. Though always a long way down the bill, she occasionally found herself rubbing shoulders with such 'topliners' as Florrie Ford, Ella Shields, famous for her rendition of 'Burlington Bertie', and George Lashwood, who was always impeccably turned out and who made his name by singing great favourites of the day such as 'Riding On Top Of A Car', and 'In The Twi Twi Twilight'.

The big problem was, that once having given the heavy-set American warbler a spot on the bill, few managements were keen to re-book her, with the result that engagements were few and far between.

Cora blamed her husband for her lack of progress on the halls. He had been against it from the start and had never given her his full backing she said. This was totally untrue, of course, for despite any misgivings he might have had, Hawley had been forced to go along with Cora, who always got her own way in everything. In addition to financing her extravagances in regard to clothes and jewellery, he had never denied her anything and had always been prepared to go along to the theatre to watch her perform and also accompany her to various theatrical functions, even though he usually felt ill-at-ease among Cora's friends.

To make life still more unbearable, Crippen was dealt a shattering blow when the head of the company, Professor Munyon, suddenly fired him from his highly-paid position. Apparently, it had come to Munyon's ears that Crippen's wife was on the Music Hall stage, and that Crippen himself had theatrical connections. As far as Munyon was concerned this was not acceptable. Crippen had to go.

Now Hawley really 'got it in the neck' from Cora, for when Crippen attempted to explain that they would have to economise, she flew into a rage and carried on spending as usual. When the bills started to come in there was more trouble, but with the bank balance at a very low ebb, even Cora had to face facts. There was nothing for it but to give up their comfortable rooms in Guildford Street and move to cheaper accommodation near the British Museum. Cora was very unhappy and continued to take out her anger and frustration on her long-suffering husband.

Following a short spell with a rival patent medicines firm and an unsuccessful attempt to run his own company, Crippen managed to get himself taken on as consultant at the Drouet Institute for the Deaf, a firm dealing in all sorts of patent remedies, including an alleged cure for deafness, which was by all accounts of very little help to the sufferer.

The bulk of Drouet's business was transacted on a mail order basis, with clients sending in cheques and postal orders, along with a letter describing their symptoms. Crippen's job was to read the letters and make a diagnosis, which would be sent to the patient in the form of a standard letter couched in medical terms, along with the remedy.

Of course, no self-respecting doctor would ever have taken such a position. John Ellis, who followed the case avidly when it had broken in the newspapers, later remarked, that according to one report Crippen had received his degree from an American College and was, therefore, 'hardly on the same high footing as our own doctors'.

Drouet's business, in fact, involved far more paperwork than doctoring, which is where Ethel Le Neve comes into the picture. Ethel, a seventeen-year-old shorthand typist and bookkeeper, had been with Drouet's only a short time when Crippen joined the firm in 1901. She was pretty in a quiet sort of way and very efficient. Crippen took a liking to her from the day they met, and she to him. Unlike Cora, Ethel was kind and considerate and obviously looked up to him, which made him feel very good, for it was an unusual experience for the little doctor. There was clearly a strong attraction between them from the start, which did not develop into anything physical for a long time.

Ethel was so good at her work that within a couple of years she had risen to become head of the ladies' department. Much more of her time was now spent liaising with Dr Crippen, which drew them even closer. It was clear that he was unhappy at home, and eventually he began to confide in her as to the reasons why. Soon they became lovers, and took to spending a few hours together in back-street hotel rooms, which was far from satisfactory, but the only way at that time. Although there was a difference in age of more than twenty years between them, this did not seem to them to matter at all. They liked the same things and enjoyed each other's company, quite apart from the physical attraction, which had now developed into something very passionate.

Despite this, and the fact that both yearned to spend their lives together, they did nothing about it. Ethel once met Mrs Crippen when she dropped into the office one day, and did not like her at all, which was to be expected, and though she certainly did not badger Crippen, Ethel did begin to feel just a little resentful, knowing that he and his wife still socialised with Cora's theatrical friends. It was, however, something that Crippen could hardly avoid, and though Ethel understood this she still found it painful.

Mainly because of bad publicity in regard to several of its products, Drouet's had gone out of business, and Ethel was working with Crippen in a dental practice, located in Albion House on the same floor as his old employers, Munyon's. Crippen had gone into partnership with a fellow American, Dr Gilbert Rylance, in a company calling itself The Yale Tooth Specialists, and was passing himself off as a dentist.

In 1905, the Crippens, their circumstances now somewhat improved, were able to move into a three-storey, semi-detached house, 39, Hilldrop

Crescent, in Camden Town, North London. It was Cora's idea, of course, and cost Crippen over £50 per annum in rent. Cora was in her element, spending lavishly on decorations and furniture and sparing no expense, for she always had to have the best. Whenever Crippen was at home he was never allowed to relax, Cora would be constantly finding jobs for him around the house and garden. He never complained and became quite handy, particularly when it came to planting rose bushes and various other chores in the garden. But Cora never seemed satisfied, and the neighbours would often hear her giving him orders as if he were a paid servant.

The visits of the theatricals had now become more frequent, as Cora was eager to entertain and show off her new house. It had been quite a while since Cora had had a theatrical engagement, but she was still popular among the Music Hall fraternity and always threw herself wholeheartedly into their numerous social gatherings and fund-raising activities. Soon she was installed as Treasurer of the Music Hall Ladies' Guild, a group set up to raise money and organise benefit concerts for performers who had fallen on hard times.

Crippen had never felt very comfortable among Cora's friends, who now visited the house on a regular basis, coming to tea and holding meetings there. At these times he had to be very careful not to show his displeasure or Cora would be likely to lose her temper and castigate him verbally, whether other people were present or not. In such situations he never argued with her, but always went out of his way to calm the situation.

Though Hawley, generally speaking, was out of tune with Cora's friends, the exceptions were Mr and Mrs Paul Martinetti, with whom they often had supper, then played whist. Paul Martinetti was a mime artist of some renown, and he and his wife Clara had become very friendly with the Crippens. Once he got to know them well Crippen looked upon the Martinettis as being just as much his friends as Cora's. Though she understood, Ethel felt left out of another part of his life as well as the obvious part, that of living with him as his wife. Crippen always assured her that he considered her his wife in every way other than legally, and even took to calling her 'wifey', an Americanism no doubt, which may or may not have helped pacify her. In all probability he also led her to believe that he and Cora slept in separate rooms, but this, in the main, was untrue. Cora had a voracious sexual appetite, and when none of her gentlemen friends was at hand she always knew that she could call on her husband.

When Cora decided to take in boarders, including a number of foreign students, to help finance her extravagances, her husband was the one who bore the brunt of the extra chores involved. Cora liked to stay up late at night and was by no means an early riser, the result being that Hawley was expected to get up at the crack of dawn to light the fires, cook breakfast for the guests and even polish their shoes, after which he would take his wife a cup of tea and prepare his own breakfast, before leaving for the office, where he could enjoy his day in the company of the devoted Ethel.

This very unsatisfactory state of affairs continued for many months, running into years. During this time Cora had a whole series of boy friends, which included lodgers and, of course, theatricals. One in particular, an American Music Hall artist named Bruce Miller, a former pugilist, would often call at the house and take Cora out for the evening, or come when Crippen was out and spend time with her. The two grew very close, and Crippen once found a love letter which Miller had written to Cora.

The Doctor, however, said nothing to his wife, but told Ethel about it. At this stage there can be little doubt that both were hoping that Cora and Miller would decide to go off together, leaving the way clear for Crippen to obtain a divorce.

After an affair lasting several months, however, the Yankee Vaudevillian decided to return home to his wife and children. This did not please Cora, who took out her frustration on her hapless husband, frequently finding fault with him and comparing him, unfavourably, with the other men in her life, most of whom were just casual lovers. There were times when Cora would take a particular fancy to some young man, and this would last for a while before he either moved on or she tired of him. The tragic players in this unholy triangle continued to drift along year after year on a course that was clearly taking them nowhere.

Though all three were obviously unhappy, the one most to be pitied, perhaps, was Cora herself. At least the lovers had each other. As far as we know, no one at all really cared for her.

But though Hawley and Ethel never lost hope, both knew deep down that Cora would never divorce him. It was 1910. Crippen was nearly forty-eight and Ethel twenty-seven. He was getting older and it showed. His hair, which was sandyish, was thinning, with a pronounced bald patch on top. His moustache tended to be rather straggly, and the eyes, which peered out from behind wire-rimmed spectacles, had an odd bulging look about them.

Perhaps Crippen looked at himself in the mirror one morning and decided that one way or another he had to change things. Something had to be done. That same day he called at Lewis and Burrows, chemists, in New Oxford Street, where he bought five grains of hyoscine, a crystalline substance used in minute dosage as a sedative, but which is, in fact, a deadly poison. Crippen regularly ordered drugs from the shop, so his visit would excite very little interest among the staff, even though hyoscine was probably not one of his usual purchases. He would, of course, have been required to sign the Poison's Book.

Apart from her husband, the last people to see Cora Crippen alive were Paul and Clara Martinetti. On 31st January, 1910 the Martinettis came to supper. They did not notice anything different that night in the behaviour of either Crippen or his wife. As usual, they played whist afterwards, not leaving until well past midnight. It was bitterly cold outside and Cora sent her husband to look for a cab. When it arrived the Martinettis buttoned up tight against the icy wind, said goodbye to their friends and climbed into it. Their final recollection of that last evening was of the Crippens standing in the doorway of 39 Hilldrop Crescent waving them off.

A couple of days after the visit of the Martinettis, the Secretary of the Music Hall Ladies' Guild received an envelope from Crippen containing bank books and other documents connected with Cora's work as Treasurer, and also a letter of resignation, in which Cora explained that she had been called away urgently to be with a close relative in America who was dangerously ill. Cora's friends were very surprised that she had left without even saying goodbye, but when questioned, Crippen assured them that she had been called away unexpectedly and had had no time to contact anyone.

That same day Crippen told Ethel that his wife had gone away. He offered her several items of jewellery, which she accepted, mainly to please him. Later he visited a pawnbrokers in Oxford Street, where he pawned other pieces of jewellery. Over the next few days Crippen sold off most of his wife's clothes, including her theatrical costumes. Shortly after this it was noted by the neighbours that a young lady had moved into 39, Hilldrop Crescent, whom Crippen was passing off as his housekeeper.

As the weeks went by a number of Cora's friends enquired about her and were all given the same story: she was still in America and he had no idea when he could expect her to return. The Martinettis, in particular, were rather puzzled and disappointed at their friend's failure to send even a postcard.

In the middle of February, Crippen was asked by Clara Martinetti if he would like to buy tickets for a charity ball to be held at the Criterion restaurant on the twentieth of that month. He was not expected to refuse and bought two, though he did not have to use them. Foolishly, however, he turned up at the ball with Ethel. Worse still, she was wearing his wife's jewellery. One piece in particular, which Cora's friends could not fail to recognise, was a very distinctive brooch in the shape of a rising sun.

Not surprisingly, the Martinettis and other friends of Cora began to harbour doubts, especially when Crippen told them that he had received news that his wife was very ill with pneumonia in California.

'I'm very upset', he told Clara Martinetti, 'and I'm thinking of going over there at once'.

However, he did not go, and in late March Mrs Martinetti received a telegram from Crippen, informing her that his wife had passed away.

'She died yesterday at six o'clock'.

A shocked Clara Martinetti informed the Music Hall Ladies' Guild, and a couple of days later the theatrical paper *Era* published an obituary notice.

It was Easter, and Crippen, far from mourning his wife's passing, took Ethel on a weekend jaunt to France, sailing for Dieppe in late March. Meanwhile, several of the ladies of the Music Hall Guild were communicating their suspicions to the police, who showed very little interest at first.

Then John and Lil Nash, a couple of performers, who were good friends of Cora, called at the house and began asking questions. Crippen seemed evasive and tripped himself up on a number of points, which caused the Nashes to feel very dubious indeed. After leaving the house they contacted the police and made it clear that, in their opinion, Crippen's explanation of the sudden disappearance of his wife was far from convincing. At last, it was decided to send someone to 39, Hilldrop Crescent, to make enquiries, and the following day Chief Inspector Dew and Detective-Sergeant Mitchell were knocking on Crippen's door. On finding no one at home, they went on to his office. He did not appear particularly surprised to see them and answered their questions in a direct, forthright manner.

> 'I'll tell you quite frankly', he said, 'the story I put out regarding my wife's death is untrue. She is still alive. She left me for an entertainer named Bruce Miller, and as far as I know has gone off to America to join him. I told people she had gone to visit a sick relative because I was ashamed. When I realised she was never coming back I told them she was dead'.

The police had no reason to disbelieve him at this point, but to be on the safe side they asked if he had any objection to a search being made of his house. As he could not very well refuse, the Doctor said he had no objection at all.

Dew and his colleague returned to Hilldrop Crescent with Crippen and went through every part of the house, but found nothing.

> 'Well, there appears to be nothing here that might help us. Still, we must try to find your wife, Doctor. I suggest you put an advertisement in the newspapers asking for information as to her whereabouts'.

'Yes', said Crippen, 'that's a good idea. I'll do that'.

Accordingly, Crippen wrote out the following advertisement,

Will Belle Elmore communicate with H.H.C. or the authorities at once. Serious trouble through your absence.

It was never delivered to the newpaper office and was later discovered in the house by detectives.

After the police had left that day, Crippen panicked. He was sure they were on to him and made immediate plans to leave the country. What he did not know was that the Chief Inspector and his colleague, having found nothing suspicious at 39, Hilldrop Crescent, had come to the conclusion that Crippen was probably telling the truth. Apart from taking down further details regarding relatives with whom she might have communicated and any other information that might help to establish the missing woman's whereabouts, they had no further plans to call at the house again.

The day following their visit, however, Crippen and his mistress were on their way to the continent, and when Dew turned up at the Doctor's office on 11th July to ask a few more questions he was told that Crippen had not been seen for several days. Dew went at once to 39, Hilldrop Crescent, to find the house locked up, with no sign of any occupants. It was now clear that something was very wrong. The house was opened up and this time a thorough search of the place was made from top to bottom. Apart from a revolver and a quantity of ball cartridges, found in an upstairs drawer, nothing of interest to the police was discovered. The gun, however, was not considered to have any real significance, and the police continued their search. Even the garden was dug up, ruining the flower beds which Crippen had planted at his wife's behest.

After three days nothing had come to light which might help the investigation. Only the fact that Crippen had bolted told Dew that something was obviously amiss. When he had almost come to the conclusion that no clue to Cora's disappearance lay in the house, he suddenly thought again of the cellar, which was actually part of a basement containing the breakfast room and kitchen. Dew decided to take one more look down there. Entering the basement area, he walked down a dark passage which ran from the kitchen to the back door. In the coal cellar he glanced around thoughtfully. Just coal, firewood and various other items of old rubbish. As he paced up and down he noted that the floor was of brick. Scraping the coaldust away with the edge of his boot, Dew peered more closely at the bricks. Then taking a poker, he began to probe between the joints. He now found that some of the bricks were so loose that he could prise them up. He called out to Mitchell, who brought in a spade from the garden and set to work. After several more bricks had been removed the spade sank into the earth beneath and suddenly the two policemen were aware of an overpoweringly nauseous stench which drove them up the steps and into the garden.

Gulping in some welcome fresh air, they steeled themselves, rolled up their sleeves and returned to their grim task.

After removing more bricks and digging deeper, the toiling policemen made a gruesome discovery. Wrapped up in a man's pyjama top was what could only be described as a horrible mess of human remains. The head was missing and there were no bones, as the body had been filleted, leaving only internal organs, flesh, skin and muscle.

On the floor of the cellar was found a metal hair curler. Still adhering to this were several strands of human hair about six inches long, which were bleached blonde and dark at the roots.

Dew reported his find to his superiors, and the Assistant Commissioner, Sir Melville Macnaughten, was soon on the scene.

The pyjama top bore the label of *JONES BROTHERS LTD, SHIRTMAKERS, HOLLOWAY*, and after wrapping it around the grisly remains, the murderer had buried the bundle in lime, in the mistaken belief that this would destroy what little was left of the victim. If he had used quicklime*, this would, in fact, have been the case. However, plain lime was used, which had the effect of preserving the remains that for all those weeks past had lain buried no more than a few feet from where Crippen took his meals in the breakfast room.

On 16th July a warrant for the arrest of Dr Crippen was issued and the hunt began. Newspaper headlines screamed out details of the 'London Cellar Murder' and gave descriptions of the Doctor and his young mistress. Now the hue and cry was on, not just throughout Britain, but also on the continent and of course the United States, to where Crippen, as an American, might well have decided to flee. All railway stations and seaports in this country were being carefully watched, and the name 'Crippen' seemed to be on everyone's lips.

Dr Bernard Spilsbury, then a young pathologist at St Mary's Hospital, London, but destined for an outstanding career, was about to leave for a holiday at Minehead, with his wife and young child, when word came through that his presence was requested to work on the Crippen case, although at that time the suspected murderer was still at large.

Spilsbury, who had been following the case in the newspapers, did not hesitate. His wife and the baby went to Minehead without him. He would try to join them later.

At that time, Spilsbury was a junior member of a very experienced team, and working on the case with such eminent men as Drs Willcox, Luff and Pepper was a great privilege. Spilsbury himself, of course, would later become far more prominent than any of them, a man not only acknowledged

* Burnt lime, not yet slaked with water.

as one of the finest in his field, but a much sought-after medical witness at most of the major murder trials.

The organs of the chest and abdomen were examined, along with four pieces of skin and muscle. One of these pieces of skin was from the lower part of the abdomen and showed traces of an operation scar about four inches long, which was broader at the lower end. As the sexual organs were missing it was impossible to determine the sex of the victim. 2.7 grains of the poison hyoscine were found in the remains.

Further investigation soon revealed the fact that Cora Crippen had undergone an operation for the removal of an ovary sometime previously, and her body carried a scar very similar to the one described in the pathologist's report.

On Wednesday, 20th July the cargo ship *Montrose* sailed out of Antwerp bound for Quebec. Among the two hundred or so passengers on board were a middle-aged man, Mr John P. Robinson, and his son, whom he claimed was sixteen. The majority of those on board were emigrants to the New World, travelling steerage class, packed into the holds and sleeping on bunks. There were, however, a limited number of cabins for those who could afford to pay the extra, and the two Robinsons occupied one of these.

The Master of the *Montrose* was Captain Henry Kendall, who noted on first meeting them that the Robinsons were a rather odd pair. The boy's hips appeared unnaturally wide in his ill-fitting suit, while his hands and feet were small and dainty. Moreover, he moved in a mincing sort of way. Also, Robinson would often hold his companion's hand when they were on deck and probably believed that no one was watching.

The Captain, however, was suspicious from the start, and being something of an amateur sleuth, decided to keep a close watch on the strange couple.

The older man, in a grey frock coat and trousers, seemed somewhat over-dressed for a passenger on an emigrant ship, while the boy's clothes, though of good quality, were a very poor fit indeed and totally unsuitable for his shape, which was decidedly feminine, as were his features. Even the hat he wore looked out of place on his head. It appeared to be several sizes too large, and Kendall suspected that it was padded inside the band to stop it falling over his eyes.

Kendall knew all about the London Cellar Murder and the hunt for Crippen. Could it be that the world's most wanted man was actually here, aboard the *Montrose*, along with his mistress?

It did not take a detective to realise that the pair did not behave as would have been expected in a normal father and son relationship, for as well as holding the boy's hand the older man would occasionally kiss him on the cheek in a way that seemed more passionate than affectionate.

Captain Kendall, on close observation of 'Mr Robinson' at dinner, was quite sure the man had false teeth, a point mentioned in some newspapers giving the fugitive's description. Kendall still had, in his cabin, a copy of *The Daily Mail* of 14th July, 1910, which he had bought in Antwerp. In it were reported full details of the murder of Belle Elmore and the hunt for the missing husband. There was also a picture of the wanted man, with a heavy drooping moustache and eyes that seemed almost to be popping out of their sockets behind a pair of wire-framed spectacles. Mr Robinson was clean shaven, and though he wore no spectacles the Captain had not failed to notice the tell-tale marks on either side of his nose which indicated that he normally used them. But there was no mistaking those bulging eyes. No disguise on earth could have hidden them. Kendall knew that he had to do something, and very quickly, for the *Montrose* was by now over a hundred miles out of port, and though the old ship was fitted with the new-fangled Marconi wireless system, its range was somewhat limited. Another day or so at sea and there would be no chance of getting a wire to England. So the Captain sat down and wrote out his message which was passed on to the wireless operator, who was told to send it immediately and was sworn to secrecy. As near as can be ascertained the wire read as follows:

> *Have reason to believe that Dr Crippen and Miss Le Neve are among the passengers on this ship, she dressed as a boy, but undoubtedly feminine— Travelling as Mr Robinson and son. We are due in Quebec on July 31st. Now await instructions. Capt. Kendall.*

On reaching Scotland Yard the message was quickly relayed to Chief Inspector Dew, who, on the authority of Sir Melville Macnaughten, at once booked a passage for four people, himself, his colleague, Detective-Sergeant Mitchell and prison wardresses Foster and Stone, on the liner *Laurentic*, due to leave Liverpool for Canada on the following day. The *Laurentic*, being a much faster vessel than the *Montrose*, was expected to reach Quebec well ahead of the smaller ship.

The press quickly got wind of what was going on and the newspapers were soon full of the great drama and exciting chase being enacted on the high seas. Diagrams appeared on the front pages showing the respective positions of the two ships, and the question was asked; 'Will the pursuing *Laurentic*, carrying the two Scotland Yard detectives, overtake the *Montrose*, on which suspected murderer Dr Crippen and his mistress are believed to be travelling?'

It would appear that the source of these newspaper reports had been Kendall himself, for the Captain, not content with his role as amateur sleuth, was eager to tell the world of his part in the apprehension of the notorious Dr Crippen and had sent off a second wireless message, this time to the *Montreal Star*. The *Star* had, in turn, relayed the details to a London newspaper, and within twenty-four hours, talk of the great sea chase was on everyone's lips.

Although scarcely able to contain himself, Captain Kendall tried to behave as normally as possible, while still maintaining a close watch on the Robinsons, who, while keeping themselves very much to themselves, seemed to be enjoying the voyage. They spent a lot of time on deck, in a quiet corner, just sitting there talking and obviously very happy in each other's company.

The first indication Kendall had that his wire had been received was when a wireless message reached the ship from the *Daily Mail*, asking for full details. This was quickly followed by messages from several other London newspapers.

On 27th July, when they were just one week out of Antwerp, a message was received from Chief Inspector Dew on board the *Laurentic* , confirming the fact that the *Montrose* had been overtaken and that the *Laurentic* was now well ahead of her and steaming towards Quebec. The message ended;

'*—Will board you at Father Point'*.

Four days later, on the morning of Sunday 31st July, Inspector Dew, accompanied by Detective-Sergeant Mitchell and several officers of the Canadian Police Force, stepped aboard the *Montrose* and shook hands with Captain Kendall. After a brief discussion the visitors were taken below to the Captain's cabin and Mr Robinson sent for. On being confronted by the Chief Inspector, the little man, still dressed in his grey frock coat, stood there in silence until Dew at last spoke up.

'Good morning Doctor. I believe we've met before. Chief Inspector Dew of Scotland Yard'.

Crippen stared back at him for a moment, then replied, 'Yes, good morning Inspector'.

'I'm arresting you for the murder of your wife Cora Crippen in London last February', the Inspector informed him.

As the arrest was made on Canadian territory a local police officer then produced the warrant, along with one for Ethel Le Neve, who was arrested in her cabin, where she had been reading. Ethel was so shocked that she fainted.

The *Montrose* sailed on up the St Lawrence river to Quebec, where the two runaways were taken ashore, as hundreds of people thronging the quay gaped at them. They were duly returned to England on the *Megantic*, knowing that they now both faced the ordeal of a murder trial at The Old Bailey.

When the *Megantic* reached Liverpool on 28th August the dock was packed with people, all waiting to catch a glimpse of the, by now, notorious pair. When Crippen came down the gangplank with his police escort, his face almost hidden behind the collar of a heavy overcoat, he was roundly booed and jeered at, the public apparently having decided he was guilty, even before he was placed on trial.

The same thing happened at London's Euston Station, where they were met by several police officers and taken by cab to Bow Street Police Station. Both were charged, Crippen with wilful murder and Ethel with being an accessory after the fact.

Though Crippen and his mistress had caused him no problems during the time they had been in his custody, Dew was glad, nevertheless, to get them off his hands. When the officers from Bow Street had taken charge of the prisoners, the Chief Inspector felt as though a great responsibility had been lifted from his shoulders.

Of the three ships involved in the drama, one, the *Laurentic*, ended her days in tragic circumstances during the First World War, when she struck a mine off the north coast of Ireland in January, 1917 and sank within a matter of minutes, taking 350 crew down with her.

The trial of Hawley Harvey Crippen opened at the Old Bailey on 18th October, 1910. Lord Alverston, the Lord Chief Justice, presided, with the very capable Richard Muir leading for the Prosecution. Mr Arthur Newton, Crippen's solicitor, was keen to brief that giant among barristers, Edward (Later Sir Edward) Marshall Hall for the Defence. Unfortunately Marshall Hall was abroad on a long holiday, and though discussions took place with the famous barrister's representatives, in the end, the reins were handed over to one Alfred Tobin, a capable enough man but a 'lightweight' compared to the likes of Muir and Marshall Hall.

It is highly unlikely, in any case, that even the redoubtable Marshall Hall could have succeeded in getting Crippen acquitted, although he later let it be known that he would not have tackled the case in the way Tobin had.

The truth is that the dice were heavily loaded in favour of the Prosecution and Muir took full advantage of this fact, using his expert witnesses to the full and driving home every telling point with great effectiveness.

On the witness stand, Bernard Spilsbury told the court that the cutting up of the body had been carried out by someone with considerable anatomical knowledge, which obviously pointed to a person with Crippen's background.

The old operation scar on the strip of abdominal skin clearly connected the remains in the cellar with Cora Crippen, while a pair of men's pyjama trousers found in an upstairs drawer at 39, Hilldrop Crescent matched perfectly the pyjama top in which the rotting flesh and viscera were wrapped.

Cora had last been seen alive at her home by the Martinettis on 1st February. At that time she was in the company of her husband. She was never seen again, and Crippen had continued to live at the house. His subsequent flight and the discovery of the gruesome remains in the cellar were clearly enough to hang him.

Mr Tobin attempted to show that it was impossible to establish, with any degree of certainty, that the remains were those of the missing woman, and in the witness box Crippen insisted that he knew very little about surgery and had never carried out a post-mortem in his life.

He even went so far as to state that in his opinion his wife was still alive, probably in America, and that the remains in the cellar had been put there on one of those occasions when he had been away from home.

The jury, however, was unimpressed, and as expected, brought in a verdict of 'Guilty'. As this was announced, the Doctor, who had been leaning on the rail of the dock, turned pale and sank down into his seat. Before sentence was passed he again protested his innocence, then, looking very shaky, he was led from the dock to the cells below, where he promptly collapsed.

A few days later Ethel Le Neve was placed on trial, and after a hearing lasting only a matter of hours, was acquitted.

Assuming that Crippen was in fact guilty, it is unlikely that he would have admitted to his mistress that he had actually murdered and mutilated his wife. It is possible, therefore, that Ethel herself believed the story of Cora having run off to America with another man. Certainly, she would have been unwilling to countenance the possibility that her tender-natured lover had actually done away with his wife, and in such a callous and brutal fashion.

Ethel's acquittal was a great relief to Crippen. Since their arrests he had clearly been much more concerned with her fate than with his own. He was allowed to write to her from his prison cell, and expressed his hopes that she would make a new life for herself abroad, should his appeal fail.

Within a couple of days of Crippen's sentencing, John Ellis received a communication from the Under Sheriff, Mr Metcalfe, asking if he would be prepared to undertake the execution on 8th November at Pentonville. The Rochdale hangman accepted at once, but as Crippen had appealed against his sentence the execution was cancelled. The Appeal Court judges, however, dismissed the appeal, and the execution was re-scheduled for 23rd November.

Ellis immediately informed the Under Sheriff that he had been engaged to hang Henry Thompson in Liverpool on the 22nd and William Broome at Reading on the 24th. Metcalfe saw no problems with this, pointing out that Ellis could quite easily travel from Liverpool following the first execution and be at Pentonville later that day with plenty of time to prepare for the carrying out of Crippen's sentence on the following day. So Ellis, no doubt feeling somewhat under pressure, agreed.

Since word had filtered out that Ellis was to execute the infamous Dr Crippen, the hangman's life had been a misery, with people pestering him in his shop and stopping him on the street, all wanting to discuss the Crippen case and its grisly details and to solicit his opinions.

Ellis, therefore, attempted, as far as was possible, to leave Liverpool and make the journey quietly and inconspicuously. After settling into his quarters at Pentonville, Ellis headed for the condemned man's cell to observe the prisoner through the peephole, and was at once struck by his demeanour, for Crippen sat there looking calm and relaxed as he wrote a letter, breaking off occasionally to chat to the warders, who sat close by. He looked anything but the monster portrayed in most of the newspapers. But as later events would prove, Crippen's apparent calmness and serenity, hid from the warders all that was going on in the prisoner's mind.

Ellis had been informed by Metcalfe that Crippen's height was just 5ft. 4ins. and his weight 9st. 10lbs. The Under Sheriff suggested a drop of 7ft. 6ins., but Ellis decided that 7ft. 9ins. would be about right and measured off the rope accordingly. He then tested the scaffold, left everything in readiness for the morning, and retired to his quarters.

In the condemned cell something of a drama was about to unfold. With Crippen still seemingly relaxed and in control of his emotions, having undressed and settled down for the night in his bunk, the two warders made themselves as comfortable as possible in their chairs close by and prepared for what would be a long night's vigil.

Spending the last hours with a condemned person was always nerve-racking, and a great strain on the men who had to do it, especially when the prisoner was as pleasant and gentlemanly as Crippen. His dignified bearing and courtesy had made a profound impression on the warders, who would, nevertheless, be very relieved when it was all over, for they were entrusted with a great responsibility.

After Crippen had been in bed an hour or so he appeared to become quite restless, making awkward twisting movements beneath the blankets. The warders, at first, put it down to simple tossing and turning, but when the movements were repeated, one of them went over to investigate.

'Are you all right?' the warder asked.

'Yes', replied Crippen. 'Just a little restless'.

The warder then noticed that the prisoner's spectacles were not in their usual place on the chair beside his bed and asked him where they were.

'They're here', replied Crippen. 'I have them here'.

He was told to get up while the bed was searched. The glasses were there all right, but one of the lenses had been removed from its frame and broken, leaving a jagged edge, which Crippen had obviously intended to use in a bid to cheat the hangman.

He should never have been allowed to retain the spectacles, of course, but the mild-mannered little doctor had conducted himself in such a way while under sentence of death that he had obviously lulled his gaolers into believing that he could be trusted completely, for he had never given them the slightest trouble and had done exactly as he was told at all times.

Ellis arose around 6-30a.m. and went off to make sure that everything was in place. It was a damp, cold and foggy morning, but, as usual, the morbidly curious began to assemble outside the prison gates even before daylight. Normally a bell would ring out the death toll as the procession left the condemned cell, but on this occasion the custom was dispensed with out of consideration for three other prisoners lying under sentence of death in the prison. Of these, two would be ultimately reprieved. The third, Noah Woolf, would face the hangman a month later.

Crippen was up early and was allowed to dress in his own clothes, which included the familiar grey frock coat in which he had made his last sea voyage. He was taken to the Roman Catholic chapel, within the prison, to attend a special service. Apart from the prisoner and the priest, just three warders were present. Crippen was, in fact, a convert to Catholicism, and ironically enough, it was his victim, Cora Crippen, who had introduced him to the faith.

Whether Crippen's visit to the church had fortified him or not, he certainly appeared quite calm at this point, yet on the other hand he ate very little of the breakfast that was put before him at eight o'clock that morning.

He was due to be hanged at 9a.m. and the last hour was spent with the priest. If he confessed to the murder of his wife, his confession was never made public, though, of course, any such revelation would have remained secret in any case.

At a few minutes before nine o'clock the principals gathered outside Crippen's cell. At a signal from the Under Sheriff, Ellis and his assistant stepped inside. Crippen was seated on a chair in the far corner, a warder standing on either side of him. One of the warders, who was speaking to the prisoner in quiet tones, stopped and looked up as they entered. Crippen stood up and meekly allowed himself to be pinioned, not uttering a word as the job was swiftly and expertly executed. The prisoner was unshaven and of course wore no collar, yet he still looked quite smart, and more composed than might have been expected for a man in his position.

For this execution Ellis initiated a new procedure. Instead of walking behind the condemned man, as was the normal practice, the hangman let his assistant accompany the prisoner and the rest of the procession, while he went on ahead. When the party arrived at the scaffold Ellis was already there and ready to place the condemned man on the trapdoors without even the slightest delay, the idea being to keep things moving and get the job done, thereby causing the victim as little mental anguish as possible. Ellis used this method at all his subsequent executions.

As Ellis stood on the scaffold and watched the execution party approach, the condemned man immediately behind the praying priest, he noticed with some surprise that Crippen had just the trace of a smile on his lips. Perhaps he was having pleasant thoughts of his beloved Ethel, or more likely his strong religious faith had fortified him for the ordeal. Crippen did not even have the opportunity to take in the scene before the white cap was slipped over his head, his legs strapped together and the rope adjusted. A glance around by Ellis to see that all was in order, then the hangman's hand was on the lever. A quick pull, and bang! The trapdoors had opened and the little doctor was gone.

After one hour had passed, the prison Doctor descended into the pit to pronounce Crippen dead. Later, he came to Ellis and gave it as his opinion that the hangman had been given too long a drop. This complaint was apparently based on the fact that the post mortem had revealed that every bone in the victim's neck had been broken. Ellis, for his part, considered this a compliment. To him it was a clear indication that Crippen had died instantly.

The demise of the notorious doctor did nothing to lessen public interest in the case. Ellis himself became well known as 'the man who hanged Crippen'.

More than ever he was pestered to reveal all that had occurred in the prison and particularly on the scaffold, and was even offered £1,000 plus all expenses to undertake a lecture tour of America to speak on Crippen. Of course, he was obliged to turn it down. Otherwise, it would certainly have been the end of his career as an executioner.

It is a fact that the name of Crippen is as well known today as it was in 1910, when he was finally apprehended and brought to justice. For some reason, the case captured the imagination of the public and has held it ever since. All the right ingredients were there: the clandestine love affair; the mild-mannered little man dominated by an uncaring, unfaithful, spendthrift wife, whose Music Hall connections, tenuous though they may have been, gave just a touch more colour to the background of the case; the unexplained disappearance of the wife; the discovery of the gruesome, rotting remains in the cellar; the flight of the lovers and their dramatic capture; the trial; Ethel's acquittal; the hanging of the Doctor, whose waxen figure has for many years fascinated visitors to Madam Tussaud's Chamber of Horrors in London, were all elements which added up to a truly fascinating murder mystery.

Dr Hawley Harvey Crippen was, in life, the most insignificant of men. In death, he became one of the most infamous characters who ever lived.

CHAPTER 12

COWARDICE OR COURAGE?

The behaviour of a condemned man, when the time comes for him to face death by execution, can be interpreted a number of ways, depending on one's point of view. To John Ellis, and probably to most people in those days, if a man going to the gallows co-operated fully with those who were about to put him to death, he had died bravely. In other words, if he was prepared to be preached to, if he responded to the Chaplain, let them pinion his hands behind his back and lead him in a procession to the scaffold, strap his legs together, cover his head, then stand perfectly still while the rope was placed around his neck and the knot adjusted, that man had gone to his death with dignity and courage.

On the other hand, if a victim went to pieces under the pressure, if he wept and pleaded for his life, then he was considered a coward. Fair enough. But what about the prisoner who resisted when the execution party came for him? Should he too be considered a coward because he was fighting for his life, hopeless though that resistance might be? According to Ellis the answer was 'Yes'. Perhaps he was right, but many would disagree. A condemned man might be guilty of murder; nevertheless, when about to be murdered himself, why should he make it easy for those employed to kill him? To John Ellis, this type of man was as cowardly as the man who simply crumbled when the dreaded moment arrived.

Such was the case with William Palmer, whom Ellis hanged at Leicester Gaol in July 1911. Palmer went absolutely berserk when his time came, putting up the most fierce and terrifying resistance that it would ever be the Rochdale hangman's misfortune to face in a prison cell. A Manchester man, Palmer was fifty years old when he went to his death, and though it was not realised at the time of his arrest for the murder of an elderly widow in the Leicestershire village of Walcote, he was the possessor of an appalling criminal record stretching back over many years.

On 24th January, Ann Harris, who lived alone in her cottage, was discovered on the floor of her tiny kitchen, clad only in a nightdress. A piece of webbing, tied tightly around her neck, with the other end attached to the leg of a chair, had caused death by strangulation.

The house had been ransacked, with drawers thrown open and contents scattered around the floor, including two empty purses, while a third purse, containing two half-sovereigns, a shilling and five farthings, was found on top of a chest of drawers, having been missed by the intruder.

Though a painter by trade, Palmer did not work regularly, and had taken to hawking for a living. Finding things very hard in his home territory, he went on the tramp, eventually arriving in the Leicestershire area. He was very scruffily dressed and carried a collection of bootlaces, which he hoped to sell along the way.

One of the first people Palmer accosted was a clergyman, the Reverend C.E. Ward, Vicar of Bitteswell, who gave him a few coppers, remarking,

'What's a fine strapping fellow like you doing on the road?'

Having extracted a promise from Palmer that he would not spend the money on drink, the vicar gave him a few words of advice and sent him on his way.

That same night the itinerant turned up at a lodging house in Lutterworth, but was refused admission because he arrived too late to sign in. Despite the fact that it was a very dark and cold winter's night, the proprietor refused to stretch a point, quite possibly because he did not like the look of the stranger. Whatever the reason, Palmer was forced to tramp on. Before leaving Lutterworth he asked a policeman the way to Northampton, then set off in that direction.

Later that night, Mrs Elizabeth Gibson, a widow living in Voss Yard, Walcote, noticed a man striking matches close to the house occupied by Ann Harris. He appeared to be trying to find the keyhole. Though she thought this very odd, Mrs Gibson, unfortunately, did nothing about it. Next morning her neighbour was found dead on the floor of the kitchen.

That same morning Palmer was seen at Lutterworth Railway Station, buying a ticket for London. From there he travelled to Folkestone, where his sister lived. At the station in Folkestone he asked a porter for directions, and seemed very edgy, remarking,

'I fancied somebody was following me'.

On the way to his sister's, Palmer stopped at an inn. In contrast to his impoverished state of the previous day, he seemed to be rolling in money, and even treated a group of local fishermen to a round of drinks. The landlord later told the police that as he chatted with his new-found friends, the stranger, who was very shabbily dressed considering his obvious affluence, behaved rather oddly, glancing nervously towards the door every time a customer came in. But the landlord, naturally, did not worry, for the man spent ten or twelve shillings, which was quite a sum in those days.

The more he drank, the less apprehensive he became, and eventually, after having consumed enough to feel merry and very talkative, he left the inn and made his way to a second-hand store, where he bought an overcoat for three shillings, before setting off once again for his sister's house.

Palmer was in Folkestone for the best part of a week, most of which was spent in public houses, before the police caught up with him. His trail had not been too hard to follow, and when Detective-Inspector Taylor arrested him he was still drinking heavily. He insisted that his name was not Palmer, but William Thompson, and that he knew nothing about any murder in Leicestershire.

Asked where he had got his money from, he told the detective that he had found it near Rushden, in Northamptonshire. He was taken by the police to Rushden and asked to point out the spot, but then changed his story and took them to a field near Claybrooke Magna, in Leicestershire.

In the cistern of a public lavatory, which Palmer had been seen to enter at Rugby, a watch and chain were found, along with a purse and a reading glass. These items had all been the property of Ann Harris.

Before Mr Justice Pickford in the Assize Court, Palmer stood in the dock looking brazen and quite unconcerned, despite the seriousness of the charge, and from time to time would burst out laughing as various witnesses gave their evidence. It took the court only a short time, however, to determine Palmer's guilt, and on hearing the verdict his manner changed dramatically.

'I'm innocent. I know nothing about it. I hope you'll have mercy on me' he said, addressing the judge.

The judge then passed sentence of death on the prisoner. Some, however, apparently believed the sentence harsh, since all the evidence was circumstantial, and a petition was prepared as efforts were made to secure a reprieve. Signatures were obtained both in Manchester and in Leek, Staffordshire, where Palmer had lived for a period.

From the death cell Palmer wrote to Mr J.H. Pendlebury, Secretary of the Manchester Prisoners' Protection Society, stating,

> *I can assure you that I am as innocent of this crime as our Lord Jesus Christ, who is in Heaven, and I am going to suffer an unjust punishment, just as he did.*

Pendlebury was convinced, and made great efforts to save him from the hangman's noose, but without success.

In due course, Ellis received a letter from George Roylatt, Under Sheriff of Leicestershire, asking if he would be available to carry out the execution of Palmer at Leicester Gaol on 19th July. Ellis replied that he would, and arrived in Leicester on the afternoon of the 18th to be met by his assistant. They were housed in comfortable quarters for the night and well looked after by the prison staff. After an enjoyable tea they were taken to the shed where the scaffold stood, which was some forty or fifty yards from the main building.

During the evening, Ellis got his first glimpse of Palmer through the peephole. The hangman had been most surprised when given the prisoner's measurements by the prison medical officer. On viewing the condemned man, Ellis could well believe that he was indeed $14\frac{1}{2}$ stone. Though no more than 5ft. 6ins. he was very stocky and muscular and looked extremely powerful. On the other hand the prisoner's neck appeared rather flabby, a fact that caused Ellis to ponder long and hard before finally deciding on a drop of only 5ft. 8ins., one of the shortest he ever gave.

It was around this time that Palmer's previous record came to light. He had spent several years in South Africa, where he had been tried and sentenced to death for the murder of a Colonial. He was quite a young man at that time and because of his youth the death sentence was commuted. After several years in a South African gaol he was released and returned to England. It was also claimed that, at the time of his arrest for the murder of Ann Harris, he was wanted for questioning in the case of the murder of a man in Manchester.

Ellis and his assistant spent a quiet evening in the company of several of the warders, who told them that although Palmer had been sullen and moody during his incarceration, he had given them no real problems. The only thing he would ever talk about was his innocence and the petition for reprieve. Even though this had been denied he still harboured hopes of a last-minute intervention by the Home Office, though in reality there was no possibility of it happening.

Ellis saw nothing in the situation to worry him. Having so much experience of executions by this time, he simply expected Palmer to react in the same way as all the others. Though devastated, the condemned man would, in the end, bow to the inevitable. He had to, for there was nothing he could do about it. At this point he would have been well prepared by the Chaplain to accept his fate. The possibility of a prisoner putting up any kind of physical resistance was highly unlikely, and in ninety-nine cases out of a hundred he would go like a lamb to the slaughter. William Henry Palmer, however, was not about to oblige.

The condemned man hardly slept at all on his last night. All he wanted to do was talk. As always, the conversation centred on the Walcote murder and his insistence that he was innocent. On several occasions during the night he got very excited and cried out,

'I'm innocent, and I'm going to be murdered in the morning. I tell you I never killed that woman!'

When the Chaplain entered the cell, and attempted to communicate with the condemned man Palmer turned his back on him, and despite the minister's persistence, continued to ignore him.

When Ellis and his assistant entered the cell that morning the first thing the Rochdale hangman noticed was the prisoner's breakfast lying on the table, practically untouched. There stood Palmer in the centre of the room, glaring at them and looking very powerful and formidable indeed.

As was the normal practice, Ellis approached the prisoner, then stepped behind him and took hold of his left arm. But this prisoner did not submit in the normal way. Ellis's assistant had now taken hold of his other arm, but he still refused to have them forced behind his back.

'You warders!' he yelled. 'Are you going to stand there and let these fellows murder me?'

On hearing the shouting the Governor entered the cell and tried to calm the prisoner, but it was no use.

'I'm innocent', he cried out, 'and I'm not going to be murdered!'

He then tore his arms free, shoved the two hangmen away and lashed out with his foot at Ellis's assistant, just missing him, which was fortunate, as the prisoner was wearing heavy hob-nailed boots.

Pandemonium now broke out in the cell. The four warders in attendance all pounced on the prisoner, who fought like a tiger, kicking, punching and even biting his captors. Four other warders were rushed to the scene and piled in. In all there were now ten men engaged in a frantic struggle to subdue the prisoner, who was still laying about him, shouting, swearing and fighting like a maniac. Ellis received a couple of blows to the head before Palmer was eventually forced over until he was lying face down with several warders sitting on top of him. Only then was Ellis able to pinion his arms, while the condemned man, gasping for breath, still remained defiant as he shouted and swore at those holding him down.

'You're only making things harder for yourself', the Governor told him.

'Pull yourself together and act like a man — not like a coward'.

'I'm innocent', came the reply, 'and I'm not going to let you murder me'.

After a minute or two Palmer was hoisted to his feet and held tightly by four rather dishevelled-looking warders. The fear now was that the prisoner would fight all the way to the scaffold, and that it would prove almost impossible to get him to toe the line marked on the trapdoors.

With this in mind, Ellis decided to dispense with normal procedure. As the condemned man was hustled out of his cell, down the passage and out into the yard Ellis whispered to his assistant,

'Don't pinion his legs. As soon as we get him on the trapdoors be ready to step clear. I'll have the rope in place'.

When the execution party was about ten yards from the scaffold Ellis took the white cap from his pocket and slipped it over Palmer's head. A few more seconds and he was on the scaffold with the rope around his neck. Swiftly, Ellis adjusted the knot, stepped back and pulled the lever.

It was all over, and everyone breathed a sigh of relief. The murderer was dead, but what a tremendous struggle he had put up. In Ellis's view Palmer's behaviour amounted to nothing less than cowardice, but at least he showed spirit in fighting for his life.

Generally speaking, the Rochdale hangman's victims in that same year, 1911, reacted to their desperate plight in a way that he very much admired.

George Newton, a youth hanged at Chelmsford Gaol for the murder of his fiancée, Ada Roker, by cutting her throat with a razor on Christmas Eve, 1910, was one of them.

Newton was possessive to the point of paranoia, and killed her in a fit of jealous rage. It was certainly a most tragic case. Newton simply could not bear to see her even laugh and joke with any other man and was constantly challenging her to explain what had passed between herself and any male she had spoken to. When the whole thing finally blew up and ended in murder, the pair were only one week away from being married.

After leaving the house Newton returned to his lodgings, and handing the bloodstained razor to a relative, calmly announced,

'I've just cut Ada's throat'.

He then went to the sink and began to wash the blood off his hands. Within a very short space of time Newton was arrested and charged. Faced with an almost impossible task, his Defence decided on a plea of insanity. They blamed their client's alleged madness on his exposure to sulphurous fumes during a long period of employment at the Stratford Gasworks.

Dr Dyer, the medical officer at Brixton Prison, told the court that he had never known noxious fumes to cause mental illness, nor had he found any evidence of insanity in Newton during the time he had had him under observation. Several witnesses were called to testify that there was madness in the prisoner's family, but the jurymen were unimpressed and brought in a verdict of guilty, with a recommendation for mercy because of the fact that he was only nineteen.

The presiding judge, Mr Justice Grantham, seemed quite put out by this.

'I agree that the prisoner is guilty', he told the jury, 'but it's a strange thing to say that he should not be punished in the same way as an older person'.

Newton made it clear though, that he did not have any desire to live, and was very brave right up to the end. Ellis gave him a drop of 7ft. 6ins. and carried out the job with his usual clinical efficiency.

Hanging a young lad was not the most pleasant duty to have to perform, especially for a man with sons of his own, and Ellis did not relish it at all. Not long after the pronouncement of death Ellis was aboard the train and on his way home to Rochdale, glad to have got it over with.

Ellis's assistant on this occasion was a new man, William Conduit of Manchester, who took part in only one other execution, a double event, before packing the job in.

Tom Seymour was a sailor from Liverpool, who got married rather late in life. His wife had a little money from a legacy, so they were not too badly off. But for some reason they seemed to quarrel most of the time, though their friends did not think their frequent arguments were of a serious nature. How wrong they were.

One evening a relative called at the Seymour house and was invited inside by the husband. On entering, the visitor got the shock of her life, for in a corner of the room lay the body of Mrs Seymour. She had been battered to death, and to make the crime even more horrendous the killer had taken a shovelful of hot ashes from the grate and thrown them over the body, presumably to soak up the blood, which was running freely. Seymour told the horrified relative that he was responsible, then left the house and headed for the local police station to give himself up.

Seymour obviously felt that there was no point in covering up or making excuses, and informed the magistrate that he was guilty and had no intention of attempting to defend himself. At his trial he was not represented by Counsel, and when asked how he intended to plead he responded without hesitation by replying,

'Guilty'.

A plea of guilty to a charge of murder was very rare indeed. No matter how clear-cut the case against him may have appeared, an accused person was almost always advised to plead 'not guilty' unless, of course, the Defence was attempting to prove insanity, for example. When a man was facing the death penalty the courts were always extremely anxious to make sure that he received every consideration and a fair trial, so that there could be little margin for error.

Bearing this in mind, the judge, Mr Justice Avory, asked the prisoner,
'Do you understand what you are pleading guilty to?'
'Certainly I do', replied Seymour.
'Do you mean to tell us that you intended to take away the life of your wife?' asked the judge.
'I mean that I killed her. Although I'm not saying I murdered her'.
'Did you kill her intentionally?'
'Yes I did. I killed her intentionally'.
'And do you understand that the only sentence I can pass upon you for this crime, if you insist on pleading guilty to it, is the sentence of death?'
'Certainly I do', Seymour again replied.

Even after this frank admission of guilt Mr Justice Avory still refused to accept the prisoner's plea and ordered him to be removed to the cells. The judge then asked one of the barristers in court, Mr Kenyon, if he would be prepared to look through the depositions, then speak to the prisoner, just to make sure that he fully understood the case against him.

This was done, and later in the day Seymour was again placed in the dock. It was soon clear that neither his plea nor his off-hand attitude had changed one iota.

'Do you still wish to plea guilty?' he was asked.
'Yes', came the reply.
'Do you still say that you are guilty of the wilful murder of your wife?'
'Yes!' replied the prisoner, almost angrily.
'I understand', said the judge, showing infinite patience, 'that learned Counsel, whom I asked to look over your case, has spoken to you and explained the situation. Now do you thoroughly understand exactly what you are pleading guilty to?'
'Of course I do', replied Seymour.

The judge indicated to the Clerk of Arraigns that he should proceed. The Clerk rose and addressed the prisoner,
'Thomas Seymour, you stand convicted of murder on your own confession. Have you anything to say why the Court should not pass sentence of death on you according to law?'
Seymour shrugged his shoulders and replied,
'No, absolutely nothing'.

The judge placed the black cap on his head and pronounced sentence.

The execution was set for 9th May, 1911, and when Ellis arrived at Walton Gaol, Liverpool, on the previous day, he found the prisoner as unrepentant as he had been at the trial. As the hangman weighed him up very carefully through the peephole he wondered if Seymour would prove troublesome.

The man was 64 years old, but possessed a wiry physique for his age. The warders assured Ellis that although the condemned man had not caused any trouble, he still maintained a truculent, 'couldn't-care-less' attitude and had shown not the slightest sign of remorse for what he had done, nor did he seem to care in the least about the consequences.

When Ellis entered the cell to pinion him, Seymour was silent, but stared grimly ahead, as though determined to prove himself totally unafraid. He walked firmly, almost boldly, to the scaffold.

Because of the prisoner's wiry frame and light build Ellis had decided on a very long drop indeed, 8ft. 2ins. This proved just about right, for the little man died instantly.

Among Ellis's assignments for the year 1911 was a double execution at Pentonville. The condemned men were Francisco Carlos Godinho and Edward Hill. Their crimes were unrelated, Godinho having committed murder whilst at sea, while Hill, a man with a bad record, had been found guilty of the murder of his wife only nine days after they were married.

Godinho was a steward aboard the British owned *SS China*, and was under the direct orders of the first-class stewardess, Alice Emily Brewster, a middle-aged spinster, who, though inclined to be somewhat brusque, was good at her job and not unpopular with her staff generally. The one exception seemed to be Godinho, who harboured resentment towards her that eventually developed into a deep hatred. As the two were in constant contact, things got worse, and when the stewardess began receiving abusive notes Godinho immediately came under suspicion.

On the voyage home from Sydney to London the whole thing finally came to a head in the most tragic way. The ship had docked at Colombo, and on the third morning after leaving the port, Miss Brewster's body was discovered in one of the cabins, just below an open porthole. This was considered very significant because, since it was the monsoon season, orders had been issued by the Captain that all portholes be kept shut.

It was, therefore, suspected that the murderer had opened the porthole with the intention of disposing of the body, and had been disturbed before he could complete the job.

The ship's doctor, on examining the body, came to the conclusion that the victim had died from blows to the head, which could have been inflicted by an instrument such as a port key, of which there were several on board.

Because he was known to have quarrelled frequently with Miss Brewster, Godinho was one of the first to be questioned. He immediately denied any involvement in the murder, but when asked to produce his port key, was unable to do so. He said he had looked for it but could not find it. A search of the ship was quickly set in motion and the missing port key soon discovered, lying in a bathroom sink with water running over it to wash off bloodstains. Also hanging up in the bathroom were Godinho's trousers, which had obviously been scrubbed in a vain attempt to eliminate bloodstains.

This may have amounted to no more than circumstantial evidence, but it was nevertheless damning, and a statement made by Godinho later, at Bow Street Police Station, certainly sealed his fate, for what he told the police was tantamount to a confession.

In broken English, he said,

'If I say it is my fault will you pardon me? Is King George here? If I say it is my fault and ask pardon, will he relieve me? It is Coronation ten days ago, so maybe he will relieve me, or if he no pardon me will they put me in gaol and hang me up? It both our faults. We fighting'.

Despite the obvious inference of guilt in that statement, the Defence Counsel at Godinho's trial argued that a statement made in the hope of receiving a pardon cannot be used as evidence at a trial. This would only apply of course if the detectives interrogating a suspect actually promised him a pardon as an inducement to confess to the crime. Mr Justice Avory, presiding, admitted the statement as evidence.

Ellis, as always, followed the case closely in the newspapers. It ran for two days at the Central Criminal Court, before the jury reached a verdict of guilty. Godinho's lawyers then went to the Court of Appeal, where the sentence of death was confirmed, to be carried out on 17th October.

Three days later, Edward Hill was placed in the dock at the Central Criminal Court, where the judge was again Mr Justice Avory.

Hill and his wife Mary Jane had been married on the 16th July that year. Both were middle-aged, and while Mrs Hill was a decent, honest woman, she was unfortunately unaware of her new husband's background and record, which could not, of course, be mentioned in court until the matter of sentencing came up, should he be found guilty.

During their first week of married life, Hill, despite promises, failed to furnish his wife with any housekeeping money whatsoever, and as there was no food in the house she was reduced to borrowing twenty-two shillings from her mother-in-law. Before she could spend any of it, however, the money disappeared from her purse, and she was forced to the conclusion that her husband had taken it.

In the early hours of the morning of 25th July Hill came home drunk. He left the house again at 10a.m. Soon after this a policeman noticed smoke coming from the house and broke in to investigate. He found, in the bedroom, a paraffin lamp which had caused the mattress to smoulder and then burn. On the floor lay Mrs Hill, a linen bandage tied around her neck and two pillows nearby. She had been strangled and suffocated.

Hill was quickly found and arrested, and immediately protested his total ignorance of the matter.

'I don't even know the woman', he said. 'I'm not married. I'm a single man. This is all a mistake. It's my brother you want'.

After being found guilty, Hill's previous record was read out to the court. Over a period of more than twenty years he had indulged in dishonesty and violence, and in 1903 had been sentenced to ten year's penal servitude for setting fire to a house.

Hill's Counsel appealed against the sentence of death, the case being dealt with at the Court of Appeal on the same day as Godinho's, and with the same result, which is no doubt why the two men were scheduled to be hanged together.

On arriving at Pentonville on the day prior to execution, Ellis was taken to view the condemned men and was rather taken aback by the great difference in their respective physiques. While Godinho was just under six feet tall and very thin, Hill was a stocky individual, who stood no more than half an inch over five feet. Yet despite this, Hill, at 9st. 8lbs. was the heavier man by over a stone. After much deliberation Ellis finally decided on a huge drop of 8ft. for Godinho, while Hill was given 7ft.

All went according to plan until the condemned men reached the scaffold. Both had appeared composed when pinioned in their respective cells, and had walked calmly enough to the death-shed to the accompanying drone of the Chaplain's prayers for the dying, but when placed on the trapdoors they began to show signs of wilting under the strain. Ellis's two assistants quickly lashed their legs together, while the hangman slipped on the white caps and adjusted the two nooses. Just as these tasks were being completed Ellis noticed Godinho lurch slightly, then Hill did the same. He knew that both were feeling faint and called on his assistants to support a man each.

It was something that Ellis had seen many a time before. Though not in a dead faint, a man may not be in a complete state of consciousness. When this happened even the merest touch of a supporting hand on the condemned man's arm could be enough to steady him, which is exactly what happened in this case. On feeling the grip of the assistant hangman, both Godinho and Hill made determined efforts to pull themselves together, and in that brief moment Ellis pulled the lever.

The year 1911 also saw the birth of Ivy, the Ellis's fifth and last child. By the time Ivy was born the family had moved from 398, Oldham Road to number 400, next door, a larger house. All Jack Ellis's children attended St. Mary's day school, Balderstone, and went to Church and Sunday School. In an interview in 1977, Mrs Sarah Robinson, Jack Ellis's eldest daughter, told David Tipper, then the Vicar at St. Mary's, of going from Sunday School to her grandparents' house for tea. Old Joe Ellis and his wife Sarah Ann had by this time moved from the original family home in Broad Lane to 314, Oldham Road, just a few doors away from the Bridge Inn. Joe, who had sold his barber's shop in Oldham Road, took another one in William Henry Street, but eventually sold up and bought a house at Cleveleys.

CHAPTER 13

HOPE TO THE VERY END

In December of 1911, Ellis was the executioner in a double hanging at Strangeways, Manchester, the first such event at the prison since 1884, when Henry Hammond Swindells and Kay Howarth were put to death. Swindells, from Oldham, had been found guilty of the murder of James Wild, an in-law, during a family quarrel. Kay Howarth murdered and robbed Richard Dugdale, of Wakefield, while the victim was visiting Bolton in the course of his work as a commercial traveller.

Now, a quarter of a century later, the victims were Martyn and Tarkenter, both of whom came from towns just north of Manchester. Walter Martyn, aged twenty-three, was found guilty of strangling his girlfriend in Plumpton Wood, a secluded spot between Rochdale and Heywood, following a lovers' quarrel, while John Edward Tarkenter, who lived at Heyside, near Oldham, cut his wife's throat during one of their frequent arguments, when he flew into a rage and completely lost control.

Although Martyn was clearly guilty of having strangled Edith Griffiths, he insisted that he had never had any intention of causing her death. His plea of manslaughter, however, failed to convince the jury. He was found guilty of murder, with a recommendation for mercy. His conviction, though, was by no means a popular verdict, and great efforts were made to obtain a reprieve, a total of 2,150 signatures being forwarded to the Home Secretary, Mr McKenna, on his behalf.

Tarkenter, on the other hand, was perceived by just about everyone as a callous, vicious murderer, who evoked little sympathy from any quarter.

The Tarkenters had been married more than twenty-two years, and lived in Hilton Street, Heyside, with their son. It would be true to say that Tarkenter had never treated his wife Rosetta with much kindness or respect, and on at least four occasions the couple had split up after bitter quarrels.

A former soldier, Tarkenter, who was forty-three-years-old, worked as a cotton spinner. He liked a drink and it was usually while under the influence that he would set about his wife, who was by all accounts a decent, respectable and hard-working woman.

One morning, the Tarkenters' next door neighbour, William Cuddy, heard Rosetta screaming.

'That's Rosie', he remarked to his wife. 'They're at it again'.

The Cuddys, however, did not take too much notice. They knew that Tarkenter was a violent man who often knocked his wife about. Her screams therefore were not taken seriously by the Cuddys.

Later that day, Cuddy met John Tarkenter in the street. Tarkenter had been to the Star Inn, in Shaw, for a drink. He had bought a small bottle of brandy before leaving, telling the landlord that it was for his wife, who was not well. He told Cuddy the same story, then asked him if he would go and get a couple of bottles of ale.

When Cuddy returned with the beer, Tarkenter was just coming down the stairs.

'How is she now?' asked the neighbour.

'A bit better', was the reply.

When the two men had finished the beer, Cuddy returned to his own house. An hour or so later, Tarkenter answered a knock on his door and was rather taken aback to find a police constable standing there. Apparently a whisper had got around that Rosetta Tarkenter had been heard screaming early in the morning and had not been seen during the day. Some nosey, or perhaps concerned, neighbour had informed the police, who had simply sent a constable to check that everything was all right.

The constable, PC Kerslake, asked Tarkenter where his wife was.

'Oh she's gone down to Shaw. To the washhouse'.

'How did you get that cut on your hand?' asked the constable.

'Oh that', replied Tarkenter. 'It's nowt. I had a bit of bother'.

'Can I just go upstairs to have a look round?' asked the constable.

'What d'you want to go upstairs for?' asked Tarkenter.

'I told you, to have a look round'.

'Have you got a warrant?'

'Well, no...'

'Then you've no right to be going upstairs in my house'.

With that Tarkenter showed PC Kerslake the door. After the constable had gone Tarkenter left the house himself and went to see his brother, whom he asked to treat him to a drink, adding,

'It's the last one I'll have with thee. I've cut Rosie's throat'.

'You've what?' asked the stunned brother.

'Aye it's reet', said Tarkenter, producing a razor. 'I did it with this'.

As it was obvious that Tarkenter had been drinking, his brother did not believe his story, but when Tarkenter's son arrived home from work between five-thirty and six o'clock that evening to find the house, and in particular the kitchen, in an untidy state, he knew something was wrong. Going upstairs, he received a terrible shock. There was blood everywhere, and on the bed lay his mother, her throat cut.

Within the hour Tarkenter was tracked down, and made no attempt to deny his guilt.

'I knew you'd come for me', he told the arresting officer. 'I cut her throat and I know I'll have to swing for it. I'll tell you what I've done with the razor if you'll buy me a pint of beer'.

His offer was ignored and he was placed under arrest and conveyed to the 'lock-up'.

At Royton Magistrates' Court he did himself no favours, for his behaviour made a very bad impression on everyone present. Apparently one of his toes was hurting and he seemed far more concerned with this than with the business in hand. On one occasion he lost his temper and swore at one of the witnesses.

At the Assize Court he was better behaved, but still exhibited a callous indifference regarding what he had done. Tarkenter's line of defence was that his wife had nagged and goaded him while making allegations against his character. This had so enraged him that he had lost his head and used the razor on her, under extreme provocation. This line of defence was hardly convincing, and it was no surprise when he was found guilty of wilful murder and sentenced to death. Tarkenter received the sentence quite coolly, while standing rigidly to attention like the soldier he had once been.

John Ellis was duly engaged to carry out the double execution. As always, he had already made himself familar with both cases through the newspapers, and there was some doubt in his mind as to whether both sentences would be implemented, for Martyn's family and friends, and of course his solicitor, had been making strenuous efforts on his behalf and were very hopeful that the Home Secretary would intervene. Nevertheless, Ellis knew that full preparations must still be made.

Around the end of November the hangman received a letter from Captain Haynes, the Governor of Strangeways Prison, asking if he would require two assistants rather than the usual one. Bearing in mind that the scaffold at Strangeways was somewhat cramped, Ellis replied that he would prefer to have just one.

Ellis knew from experience that the people of Manchester always took a great interest in executions, and apart from thronging the street outside the prison on the morning of a hanging, a fair number of curiosity seekers would usually turn up on the afternoon before, in the hope of catching a glimpse of relatives visiting the condemned person or even the executioner and his assistant as they arrived to take up their quarters.

Being well aware of this, Ellis decided to arrive there early, and though a handful of idlers had already assembled he managed to slip by them without being recognised.

Tarkenter's mother had paid him a visit a few days previously. When Ellis arrived the condemned man's son, his sister and his brother were visiting him for the last time. In a letter to his relatives Tarkenter had asked them not to speak of his crime when they came to see him, yet he himself could not resist referring to it.

According to one of the warders he was in good spirits for most of the time they were there. He expressed remorse for what he had done and accepted that he deserved to die for it. Still, emotions were very much aroused when he finally addressed his son, and when the relatives took their leave after more than half-an-hour spent with the prisoner, a few tears were shed.

When Ellis took a look at the condemned man through the peephole early that evening he appeared sullen and introverted, the warders being unable to have any meaningful communication with him.

In another part of the prison, Martyn had also taken leave of his closest relatives, and had been informed that the Home Secretary had no intention of interfering with the course of the law. On receiving the news he seemed to sink into a deep depression, yet still insisted that he might yet be reprieved. When Ellis peered in at him, Martyn was leaning on the edge of a table and gazing at the cell door, as if hoping that the Governor was about to enter, bringing good news.

Ellis waited for him to move, or at least turn his head, so that he might catch a glimpse of his neck. But the prisoner did not move, although Ellis stood there observing him for nearly twenty minutes. At last Ellis decided to go away and come back later. When he did, over half-an-hour afterwards, the prisoner still had not moved. Several times the hangman went away and returned later, only to find Martyn in exactly the same position.

Around 9p.m., Ellis again took up his position outside the cell and lifted the lid of the inspection hole, to find that Martyn was about to have his supper and get ready for bed. Ellis was able to get a good look at his neck. He had already inspected the drop and now went away to make his calculations. No word had been received from the Home Office, so it was certain that the two would die at 8a.m. next morning.

Martyn, who was 5ft. $5^1/_2$ins. and almost 10st. 10lbs., was given a drop of 7ft. 6ins., while Tarkenter, who stood 5ft. $4^1/_2$ins. and weighed 11st. was given 7ft. $7^1/_2$ins.

The day dawned damp and misty, a typical December day for Manchester. Very early that morning Martyn was taken from his cell and placed in one not far away from the scaffold, close to the cell in which Tarkenter was confined.

Before 7a.m. Ellis and his assistant had completed all of their preparations. Around 7-30 the officials began to assemble: Sir George Pilkington, the High Sheriff of Lancashire, along with Captain Haynes, three aldermen, the Prison Chaplain, and another clergyman, the Reverend J.H. Hannan, Dr Edward, the Prison Surgeon, and the Under-Sheriff.

Shortly before eight, Ellis was given the signal to enter the first cell, Tarkenter's. The condemned man submitted himself readily enough to the pinioning process, as did Martyn when his turn came. Ellis later stated that there was a look on the young man's face that would have melted a heart of stone.

The procession then formed up in the passage with the two clergymen at its head. Tarkenter strode down the corridor with a firm step, as did his partner in death, though in Martyn's case a much greater effort was needed to steady the nerves.

To reach the gallows the procession had to cross another corridor, pass through one door, then through another on the left which led straight onto the scaffold.

Martyn was the first to take up his position on the drop. Ellis gave him no time to take in the scene, but immediately slipped the white cap over his head, then the rope. The same thing was swiftly repeated with Tarkenter, as the Chaplain intoned the prayers for the dying.

Within minutes the double execution was completed. According to Ellis both men died instantaneously and painlessly. They may well have died quickly, but how he could be certain that they felt no pain is something the Rochdale hangman never explained.

During the last weeks of 1911, as Ellis perused the newspapers, avidly following any interesting criminal case that caught his attention, it must have been quite obvious to him that he could look forward to a period of very brisk business in the first quarter of the New Year.

One of these cases Ellis always referred to as 'The Warder's Prophecy.' Though he made it a strict rule never to discuss the executions themselves, he was certainly not averse to chatting with his customers in the barber's shop about the latest sensational robbery or murder. Though solving crime was not his business, he was always keenly interested in criminology and never short of an opinion or two.

The warder in question was employed at Knutsford Gaol in Cheshire, a prison which Ellis had never visited, for during the eleven years he had been an executioner only three men had been hanged there, and Henry Pierrepoint had done the job on each occasion.

One day a prisoner named John Williams, who was in gaol for assaulting his wife, was whitewashing the walls of one of the cells. As he was a painter by trade he had been put to that work soon after his arrival, and on this particular day he was being supervised by one of the warders, who happened to remark,

'This is the condemned cell, you know. If you don't learn to control that temper of yours you could quite easily find yourself occupying it one of these days'.

The warder's words turned out to be amazingly prophetic, for the very next time it was used, Williams was, in fact, the occupant. The painter, who was Welsh, had been married for only a few months when he began to ill-treat his wife Hilda. After he had served a short spell behind bars, the couple were reconciled. It was not long, however, before trouble again flared up, with Williams first becoming violent, then attempting to commit suicide.

Had it not been for the intervention of a friend he might have died. As it was, he received a prison sentence for his trouble. In prison again, Williams, discussing his suicide attempt with the Governor, claimed that he had cut his throat, when it was common knowledge that he had taken poison. This odd mental aberration was later used by the Defence, at his trial for murder, as evidence that Williams was mentally abnormal.

After being released from prison, Williams discovered that his wife had gone to Birkenhead, and so he moved to that area himself. They were soon talking about what the future held for them and considering the possibility of getting back together again.

They parted on good terms, and Hilda promised to have tea with her husband at his lodgings a few days later. All went well, and at the end of quite a pleasant evening, Williams offered to walk his wife back to the house of her employers, where she had a room.

She never reached her destination. About ten-thirty that night Hilda Williams was found in an alley with her throat cut. The murderer was quickly apprehended, for John Williams was discovered no more than fifty yards from the dead body. He was mumbling incoherently, and when searched, was found to be in possession of a blood-stained razor.

In the police cells he was still mumbling away to himself and was heard to mutter,

'I've murdered Hilda ... I hope God will forgive me... I've killed her all right. I've put her in heaven and I'm going there too'.

For a while Williams was quiet, then he began singing Welsh hymns. His behaviour, in fact, was such that a defence based on the theory that the accused was of unsound mind was the obvious course. A number of witnesses were brought from Wales to support this claim, including a doctor, who testified that Williams was so weak-minded that he could not have understood the seriousness of his actions. A second doctor, however, produced by the Prosecution, declared him to be perfectly sane. Yet, despite being found guilty and sentenced to death, Williams firmly believed he would be reprieved.

Ellis arrived at Knutsford Gaol on a bitterly cold afternoon in March and called in at the office of Major Nelson, the Governor of the prison, to discuss the following day's execution. He was informed that Williams had given no trouble, but still entertained hopes that the Home Secretary would intervene. The Governor knew full well that this was not likely to happen, but did not have the heart to say this to the prisoner, who was constantly enquiring if any word had come through from the Home Office.

Ellis went down to the cells to take a look at him. Williams was sitting there, quietly conversing with one of the warders as the hangman peered at him through the aperture. He was 5ft. $8^{1}/_{2}$ ins. tall, and very thin, weighing no more than 9 stone. Ellis decided on a drop of 7ft. 9in, and went off to examine the gallows.

Next morning, when Ellis and his assistant entered the death cell, Williams appeared reasonably calm. No word having come through regarding a commutation of the sentence, he had pulled himself together, totally accepting his fate. As a former Welch Fusilier, he announced to the Governor that he would die like a soldier. When the time came to walk to the scaffold he certainly did not let himself down, striding firmly along the passageway and stepping unhesitatingly onto the drop with head held high.

The operation went so quickly and smoothly that it was all over almost before the Chaplain could get very far with his prayers. So much so that Major Nelson remarked on it at the subsequent inquest,

'It was one of the smoothest and swiftest executions I've ever seen, and took no more than thirty-five seconds from start to finish'.

CHAPTER 14

THE EAST END GAMBLING DEN MURDERS

Millstein's Jewish restaurant stood on Hanbury Street, Spitalfields, in the heart of London's East End. In the autumn of 1888, when Jack the Ripper brought terror to the streets of the neighourhood, Hanbury Street had hit the headlines when the horribly mutilated body of Annie Chapman, a drunken prostitute, was discovered in a yard at the rear of No 29, a lodging house in which seventeen people had slept on the night she was murdered.

At that time, both Mr and Mrs Millstein, later to become victims in the gambling den murders, were young teenagers. With their respective families they had arrived in England in the early 1880s, along with many hundreds of other refugees, fleeing the horror of Russia's pogroms, to find shelter and a meagre living indeed, in the mean streets of the East End.

Like many other hard-working, industrious Jews the Millsteins prospered, and by the time he had reached his early thirties, young Millstein had married and opened his own bakery shop in Hanbury Street, which he later developed into a small restaurant.

The young couple loved children, but had none of their own, which is no doubt why they took in Mrs Millstein's orphan step-sister, who was eight-years-old.

The restaurant was located at the front of the building, at ground level, with the Millstein's living quarters, including the bedroom, to the rear. On the first floor lived a family by the name of Verbloot, while the floor above this was occupied by a young woman in very poor health.

There was also a cellar below the shop, and one autumn day in 1911, Millstein, whose business was doing very well indeed, decided to utilise this area by opening a gambling club. It was to prove a fateful decision.

It was, of course, an illegal venture, and though Millstein did not actually run the gaming personally, he took a share of the profits. He also loaned money to some of the gamblers against various items such as jewellery and watches.

All went well during the first few weeks, but as the gambling den became better known and more and more men — among them some decidedly shady characters — were seen coming and going well into the early hours, the place began to gain an unsavoury reputation. Several of the neighbours complained to Mrs Millstein, who had been very unhappy about the venture from the beginning and who now tried to persuade her husband to shut it down. Millstein, though somewhat uneasy about the situation, was loath to give up such a lucrative business.

In the end, Mrs Millstein enlisted the services of her brother-in-law, a linotype operator, who lived in Hackney, and after a heated argument the two of them managed to convince the husband that if he did not shut down the gambling den, and quickly, he would only succeed in ruining his restaurant business. His brother-in-law warned him that if he did not come to his senses he would not hesitate to go to the police. Only then did Millstein capitulate.

Yet though he agreed to close it down, he could not resist keeping it going over Christmas, when he felt that takings would be high. He therefore decided that the operation would cease the following week, immediately after the Christmas Day and Boxing Day sessions.

When word got around among the gamblers that Millstein was closing down they were none too happy, but they turned up in large numbers on the last night and Millstein, as usual, received a good share of the spoils.

After all the gamblers had left the premises, Millstein locked up and joined his wife in their living quarters. Only one door was left unlocked, for it was Millstein's custom to unbolt the back entrance door to the cellar so that an Irishwoman, who worked for him, might let herself in early in the morning.

It was around half-past-two on Wednesday morning, 27th December, that Marks Verbloot, one of the occupants of the first floor flat, was awakened by what sounded like a low moan. He could not be sure, but it seemed to come from above, and he therefore concluded that the young woman who lived in the room above must be feeling ill again.

The moaning and groaning continued intermittently for over an hour and Verbloot was unable to get back to sleep. At around four o'clock he thought he could smell smoke and realised that there was some in the room. He got up at once and woke his father, telling him,

'I think there might be a fire downstairs'.

He opened the window and stuck his head out. Down below he could see a dull glow, and taking a small, heavy brush, he aimed it at the Millstein's bedroom window just below. The glass broke and smoke began to pour out.

The Verbloots now realised that everyone in the building was in grave danger. Young Verbloot immediately grabbed a whistle, which he kept in a drawer, and rushed to the front window. After blowing it frantically he dashed downstairs into the street and blew it again and again. A police constable was quickly at the scene and it was then noticed that the front door of the restaurant was open.

The constable entered the premises, followed by Verbloot and made his way to the rear of the shop where the bedroom door was located. It was locked, but as the key had been left in the lock on the outside they were able to open it. The room was filled with smoke, which was coming quite clearly from the bedcovers and the mattress. The latter had been ripped open and lay smouldering on the floor.

Two fire engines had arrived at the scene, and as the firemen entered the premises, the constable, peering through the smoke, discovered the body of Millstein, clad only in vest and trousers, lying on the floor in a pool of blood. There was a stab wound on the right side of the chest which had penetrated the lung.

On lifting the smouldering mattress, the firemen found the body of Mrs Millstein. Her nightdress was heavily stained with blood, the result of numerous stab wounds to the head and body. The tongs and poker from the grate lay on the floor, broken, and there were clear signs that the Millsteins had put up a tremendous struggle while fighting for their lives, for several chairs and other items of furniture had been knocked over. As most of the cupboards and drawers lay open it was also obvious that the place had been ransacked.

There was no shortage of clues around the place, as Chief Inspector Wensley, a famous Scotland Yard detective, soon discovered when he arrived on the scene. A large and extremely sharp carving knife, stained with blood, lay on the floor. On a shelf was a bottle containing just a drop of petrol, the rest having been poured over the bedding. There was also a box of Swan Vestas matches, on the sides of which were red smudges, which had obviously been made by blood-stained fingers.

The most significant clue of all was a coloured neckerchief, which it was soon ascertained did not belong to either of the Millsteins. This was also stained with blood, and the Chief Inspector conjectured that it might well have been torn from the killer's neck during the struggle.

On learning of the gambling den, Wensley at once set out to track down all who were known to frequent it, and particularly those who had been there on that last night. Eventually, all were traced and cleared, except one, a twenty-two-year-old Polish costermonger named Myer Abramovitch. On visiting his lodgings they learned that he had not been seen there over the previous twenty-four-hours. A watch was kept on the house overnight, but Abramovitch did not put in an appearance.

In the early hours of the morning, however, the fugitive was spotted by an acquaintance standing by a coffee stall on the corner of Leman Street and Commercial Road. Over a hot drink, the acquaintance, a Jewish tailor's cutter, prevailed upon Abramovitch to go with him to Leman Street Police Station. An hour later he was being questioned by Chief Inspector Wensley.

It was an open and shut case, for the suspect was actually wearing clothes which had belonged to the murdered man, and there was blood on them. In his coat pocket were two watches and chains, which it was later proved had been left with Millstein by gamblers against loans of money. In a trouser pocket were found gold coins to the value of £2-10s.

When asked about the murders, Abramovitch immediately replied,

'I done it. I done it because I lost all my money gambling'.

Then noticing a blue silk neckerchief on the desk he pointed to it and said,

'That's mine'.

Volunteering such information was not the wisest thing Abramovitch could have done, and as the Coroner, Mr Wynn Baxter, later remarked at the inquest on the bodies of the murdered couple,

> 'If the accused man had set out to manufacture evidence for the Prosecution he could not have done it more thoroughly. In establishing a motive the jury need look no further than the fact that Abramovitch was very hard up, having lost all his money in the gambling den. And while he undoubtedly entered the premises with the intention of robbing them, I do not believe that he went there with the idea of committing murder'.

That may very well have been so, but according to the law, if a person kills while engaging in a crime, such as robbery for example, he is still guilty of murder, even if the killing is not premeditated.

Such was clearly the case with Abramovitch, who had been discovered by the Millsteins while burgling their living quarters, and had murdered them, probably in a blind panic. On realising what he had done, he had attempted to set fire to the place in an effort to cover up his crime.

At his trial before Mr Justice Ridley at the Central Criminal Court, the Defence Counsel, Mr Elkin, attempted to prove that Abramovitch suffered from intermittent bouts of 'mania', or mental derangement, and that during one of these he had killed the Millsteins. To support this claim a witness was unearthed to swear that he was sometimes referred to as 'Mad Myer', but at the last minute the witness backed out and refused to testify.

Abramovitch was found guilty and sentenced to be hanged. As he stood in the dock the condemned man could not hold back his tears, and continued to weep bitterly while being taken down to the cells.

Mr Elkin immediately lodged an appeal, which was heard by Judges Channell, Avory and Hamilton. Elkin attempted to show that Mr Justice Ridley, in his summing-up, had not left the jury to make up their own minds, particularly on the possibility that Abramovitch had committed the murders while of unsound mind. He also pointed out that as the weapons used did not belong to the accused, but to his victims, he could not have gone to the house with murder in mind.

Returning, once more, to the question of temporary insanity, Elkin pointed out that it was clear that the murders had been committed by a man in a mad frenzy, who was not responsible for his actions. He then asked the Appeal Judges if he might introduce further witnesses to support the 'Mad Myer' theory.

This was refused, and Mr Justice Channell, in delivering the Court's final judgment, stated that there were no grounds for interfering with the verdict. The appeal was therefore dismissed and the sentence of death must stand.

Abramovitch had not helped his own case by freely confessing in the first place, and also by volunteering the information that he had 'done it' because he had lost all his money gambling. It is certainly true that it would be more difficult to bring criminals to justice if only the suspects had the sense to keep their mouths shut when arrested.

John Ellis was originally engaged to hang Abramovitch at Pentonville Prison on 27th February, 1912, but because of the appeal, the date was put back to 6th March. Ellis arrived at Pentonville on the afternoon of the fifth and was taken to the prisoner's cell to have a look at him.

The man he observed through the spyhole was short and stocky, swarthy in appearance, with dark eyes and a mop of untidy black hair. He looked very frightened. As Ellis watched, Abramovitch began to pray with the Jewish Rabbi who was with him. The heads of both were covered, the Rabbi wearing the usual black skull cap and Abramovitch his own cap. Each man also wore a *talith*, or prayer shawl, and as the words of the prayers were uttered in the Hebrew tongue their bodies swayed to and fro as they became completely absorbed in the ceremony.

It was an unusual sight to see in a prison and the warders in attendance quickly realised the value of the Rabbi's ministrations, for Abramovitch's fear seemed gradually to subside, and by morning he was relatively calm. Though he had passed a restless night and could not face breakfast, he appeared to be in control of his emotions. When Ellis entered the cell with his assistant, Rabbi Isaac was with the condemned man, who showed no sign of resistance when the hangman went to pinion him.

Once outside the cell the Rabbi led the way to the scaffold, Abramovitch following close behind with a shambling gait. Once on the drop the prayers were resumed. The prisoner now appeared very shaky, but managed to remain standing without assistance. Ellis and his assistant quickly completed their work and stepped clear. Then the lever was pulled and it was all over.

After witnessing the scene in the cell, when the Rabbi prayed with the condemned man, Ellis realised that in the whole of his career thus far, he had executed no more than a couple of men of the Jewish faith, a fact which he felt was very much to the credit of the Jewish community.

CHAPTER 15

SEDDON — A STUDY IN AVARICE

While in London for the purpose of hanging Myer Abramovitch, Ellis took the opportunity to spend some time in the spectators' gallery at the Old Bailey, where the trial of Frederick Seddon, the notorious poisoner, and his wife, Margaret, was taking place.

It was a case which had hit the headlines of every newspaper in the country, and after taking his seat Ellis listened with great interest and admiration as Sir Rufus Isaacs, later Lord Reading, began his opening speech for the Prosecution. Ellis was captivated as much by the Attorney-General's cultured, beautifully modulated voice as he was by the skill and clarity with which he outlined his case.

Seddon sat there listening intently, every now and then fingering the ends of his waxed moustache thoughtfully. He seemed very calm, as did his wife, who would from time to time whisper in his ear, causing him to nod and smile. The pair certainly did not behave like two people who were on trial for their lives.

The reason for their relaxed, almost confident demeanour in court was not too difficult to understand. First, the case against them was built entirely upon circumstantial evidence. Secondly, they had been fortunate enough to obtain the services of one of the most outstanding advocates of his day, Edward Marshall Hall, who became so fascinated by the case that he handed over a number of briefs he was working on at the time, to other members of his staff, so that he might concentrate on defending the Seddons.

How did the Seddons, a very ordinary, insignificant-looking couple, come to find themselves in the Old Bailey dock? There can be little doubt that it was Seddon's greed that had put them there.

Apart from being avaricious, Frederick Seddon was also an exceedingly mean man. An area supervisor for the London and Manchester Assurance Society, Seddon, who was forty-years-old, considered himself god-fearing and thrifty and insisted that his wife and family embrace the same virtues.

Born at Liverpool in 1871, he had gone to sea as a cabin boy. Shipwrecked off Cape Horn, he had managed to reach the Falkland Islands and remained there for some months, earning a meagre living at sheep farming. Eventually, Seddon managed to get a ship bound for Liverpool and home. He continued to travel the seas until the age of twenty, when he gave it up and found a job as an insurance canvasser.

Though starting at the very bottom, he made rapid strides. Good at figures and meticulous, if pedantic, in his dealings, Seddon was absolutely determined to succeed and make money. Through a series of promotions he was sent to Barrow-in-Furness, to Oldham, then back to Liverpool. After several years' hard work, during which he managed to accumulate a little money of his own, he was given the position of Superintendent at Islington, London, and made a very good job of it. Though he was somewhat parsimonious when it came to spending, he liked a drink, was a heavy smoker, and often visited Music Halls, where he occasionally picked up women.

As well as his insurance job, he ran a second-hand clothes shop in the Seven Sisters Road in Islington, North London, with the assistance of his wife. He also dabbled in the buying and selling of property, and drove a very hard bargain, especially if he sensed that the person he was dealing with was desperate.

In 1909 Seddon bought 63, Tollington Park, a large Victorian terraced house with a basement, and though it was not very far away from the shop, Tollington Park was quite 'up-market' by comparison.

Seddon's idea was to let the new property to tenants, but after advertising and failing to get an immediate response, he decided to rent out the shabby upstairs rooms of the second-hand shop and move his family of wife, five children and aged father, plus a servant girl, into the Tollington Park house. It was so spacious that there was still a whole floor vacant after the Seddon family had been accommodated on the ground and first floors. The basement was also made use of, partly to provide Seddon with an office, for which he charged the insurance company five shillings a week. As he also charged his two teenage sons six shillings a week each for their board and lodging, Seddon was obviously going to be well in pocket once he had rented out the top floor rooms. Within a short time after moving in, these rooms had been let, the tenant remaining for about six months before giving notice and moving on.

Seddon re-advertised the top floor rooms and soon received an enquiry from a spinster in her late forties named Eliza Barrow. This was in the summer of 1910, and Miss Barrow, who had been living not very far away in Evershot Road with some relatives by the name of Vonderahe, brought with her a boy of eight named Ernest Grant and a Mr and Mrs Hook, a rather down-at-heel couple, who were related in some way to the boy. Hook turned out to be a gossipy type and confided to a very interested Seddon that the spinster had several hundred pounds, mostly in gold, in a strongbox, which she always kept in her room.

Miss Barrow volunteered the information that young Ernest and his sister were orphans on whom she had taken pity. She had sent the girl to boarding school and taken the little boy to live with her.

It appeared to Seddon that the Hooks were just a pair of scroungers who had attached themselves through the child, to Eliza Barrow, whom they knew to be quite well-to-do. For the top floor Seddon charged twelve shillings a week, in advance, and Miss Barrow paid him in cash from the strongbox, which she dragged out from under her bed. The landlord's eyes gleamed as he caught a glimpse of its contents — several bags containing gold sovereigns plus a bundle of banknotes.

It transpired that her relationship with the Vonderahe's had ended acrimoniously, and it soon became clear that Miss Barrow was by no means an easy person with whom to get on, let alone live with. Though she was obviously devoted to the boy she could not abide the Hooks, who were living rent free and continually asking her for money, for they appeared to have no income of their own whatsoever. It was Mrs Hook's responsibility to keep the rooms clean, but Miss Barrow continually found fault with her work.

Within a couple of weeks of their moving in, a series of quarrels occurred between Miss Barrow and the Hooks, with the result that the spinster asked Seddon to get them out of the house. Seddon did not tackle the undesirable couple face to face, but pinned a notice on the door of their room, informing them that they were required to quit the premises forthwith. The unwanted couple kicked up a fuss, and even accused Seddon of being interested in the spinster's money himself, but eventually left.

Had it not been for the fact that Eliza Barrow was well off, it is highly unlikely that Seddon would have considered her a suitable tenant, for she was a slovenly, overweight woman of around forty-eight, who tended to lounge around all day. Her rooms were always untidy and soon became filthy and smelly through neglect. She also liked a drop of gin, which made her irritable and unpleasant.

Nevertheless, Seddon made it a point to stay and chat whenever he called for the rent, and on other occasions when he could find an excuse to speak to her. Miss Barrow soon realised that Seddon was very shrewd when it came to handling money, and in soliciting his advice she was quite open in discussing the amount of capital she possessed, and also details of her various investments.

She told him that she owned a public house in Camden Town, The Buck's Head, and a barber's shop in the same block. She also had £1,600 in Indian stock, some jewellery and several hundred pounds in the bank. She was worried about her investments, she said. The people to whom she leased her properties were a constant source of trouble to her, and the Indian stock had been falling in value. Could Seddon offer any advice?

Seddon, of course, was only too pleased to be of assistance. After further discussion Miss Barrow began to show an interest in her landlord's suggestion that it might be a good idea to sell the Indian stock and use the money to purchase an annuity. He would be glad to handle such a transaction for her and could get the papers drawn up at once.

Miss Barrow was very relieved to think that her affairs were in good hands, and shortly afterwards signed over the stock to Seddon in return for an annuity of £103–4s. Her new advisor was most helpful to her. She was normally very dubious about people's motives, but appeared to trust Seddon totally. Within weeks she had transferred the leases of the pub, the barber's shop and a tenement building over to him for a further annuity of £208, and being a pretty shrewd person herself, no doubt felt that she had done an excellent bit of business, for having previously made tentative inquiries, she was well aware that Seddon was paying her more than she could have obtained from an insurance company or bank. The landlord handed over the money regularly and watched as she added it to her little hoard in the strongbox.

It was not long before he had persuaded Miss Barrow that as banks were shaky at that time and one had, in fact, collapsed, she might be wise to withdraw her savings. She agreed, and he obligingly accompanied her to the London and Finsbury Savings Bank, following which a sum in excess of £200 was placed in the strongbox for safe keeping. All that Miss Barrow now possessed was, in one way or another, under Seddon's control.

Though always very security-conscious, the spinster felt safe in the house of a man like Seddon. She insisted, however, that the little boy, Ernest, share her room. In fact, they actually slept in the same bed.

Seddon could not have been more helpful. He was always knocking at her door to enquire if everything was satisfactory, or if there was anything she needed. He even arranged for his fifteen-year-old daughter, Maggie, to cook and clean for her. Of course, he charged for this service.

In January 1911, Seddon sold the Indian stock for £1,519, and used the money to buy a number of properties in Stepney.

Miss Barrow did not enjoy the best of health and her life-style certainly did not help, for she seldom left the house, she and the boy taking all their meals in her rooms. During the month of August Miss Barrow began to feel very unwell. The weather that month was hot and clammy, which made things worse, and the Seddon house was plagued with flies, especially the top floor.

Eliza Barrow took to her bed complaining of stomach pains, diarrhoea and sickness. Dr Sworn, the Seddon's family physician, was called in and arrived late at night. The smell of sickness in the darkened room was appalling. The doctor mentioned that he had recently treated a number of similarly afflicted patients. He prescribed for the illness and promised to return the following day, a Sunday. On arriving that day, he was taken upstairs by Mrs Seddon, and entering Miss Barrow's bedroom in the daylight, was at once struck by the squalid conditions in which she was living. Apart from the stench, the place was filthy and swarming with flies.

As the patient had not improved, Dr Sworn suggested that she might be better off in hospital, but Miss Barrow would not hear of it, saying that she was happier in her own bed, with Mrs Seddon looking after her.

After leaving the sickroom, Dr Sworn told the Seddons that he felt very unhappy about the boy being exposed to all the germs, and was appalled when he was told that Ernest was still sleeping in Miss Barrow's bed. Seddon promised to try to do something about this, and also about the problem of the flies.

When the subject of Ernest was broached, however, Miss Barrow would have none of it, insisting that she needed to have the boy beside her. Dr Sworn again visited on the Monday. The patient was still very ill, and Mrs Seddon told the doctor that she could not take the medicine he had prescribed, a mixture of morphia and bismuth. The doctor then prescribed citrate of potash and bicarbonate of soda.

Because of the heat, the windows had to be left open, and the flies continued to swarm in, attracted by the filth and the stench. After the doctor had left, Miss Barrow gave Margaret Seddon cash to go and buy fly papers and instructed her not to get the sticky ones, but those that had to be wetted. Mrs Seddon got them from Meacher's Chemist's shop in Stroud Green Road, and they were placed in saucers of water on the mantlepiece.

While Miss Barrow was still very poorly, Seddon's sister Emily and her daughter arrived on a visit from their home in the Midlands and stayed for several days. It was around this time that Miss Barrow again began to worry about her wealth. She sent young Ernest to get Seddon, saying she needed to talk to him urgently. Leaving his guests and climbing the stairs to the top floor, the landlord found his tenant in a somewhat agitated state.

'I want to make a new will', she told him. 'I want to do it now'.

Seddon assured her that she was not dangerously ill, and that there was, therefore, no need to do anything in haste. On her insistence, however, he agreed to draw up a will himself, although he later claimed that he had done all in his power to persuade her to wait until she was feeling better, then arrange an appointment with a solicitor.

She said she intended to leave everything to Ernest and Hilda Grant, including all personal effects, furniture and jewellery. All was to be kept in trust until the young Grants came of age, with Seddon as sole executor. Miss Barrow was propped up in bed, her spectacles produced and the will signed. It was witnessed by Seddon's wife, Margaret, and his father, William, who was in his seventies.

Later that evening, Seddon visited a Music Hall and arrived home grumbling that the box office had tried to cheat him out of sixpence. 'They picked on the wrong man', he snapped, with a self-satisfied sneer. This was true enough, for anyone who could get the better of Seddon when it came to money matters had to be very sharp indeed.

Meanwhile, Mrs Seddon continued to nurse the patient, who was very difficult to handle. That night the little boy came downstairs to say that Miss Barrow, whom he referred to as 'Chickie', was asking for Mrs Seddon. Both Seddons went upstairs, accompanied by Seddon's sister, Emily Longley, who had offered her assistance. On reaching the sickroom, however, Mrs Longley felt so nauseated by the smell that she was forced to withdraw. Seddon soon did the same, leaving his wife to cope with the situation.

Miss Barrow was retching, and appeared to be frothing at the mouth. After settling the patient down once more, Mrs Seddon left her and went to bed. In the early hours of the morning they were again called by young Ernest, who told them that Miss Barrow was out of bed. When they reached her room they found her on the floor, moaning.

'You shouldn't be out of bed', said Seddon. 'Come on, let's get you back in'.

With the help of his wife, Seddon managed to get the patient back into bed.

'I'll stay with her', said Mrs Seddon.

'Look, I can't stomach the smell in here', said Seddon. 'I'll be just outside the door'.

With that, he sent Ernest to sleep in another room, got his newspaper and pipe, and settled himself outside on the landing, while Mrs Seddon tried to get some medicine into the patient, who kept on insisting that she was dying. Eventually, she drifted off into a restless, fitful sleep, with Mrs Seddon close by in a chair by the bed.

It was around 6a.m. when Seddon looked in again to find that his wife had dozed off. He peered closely at the bulky woman in the bed, then shook his wife.

'I think she's stopped breathing'.

Mrs Seddon awoke with a start.

'What?' Seddon's wife rose slowly from her chair. 'Is she…?' Seddon took Miss Barrow's pulse, then announced,

'Yes…, she's gone'.

Later that morning Seddon went to Dr Sworn's surgery and informed him of Miss Barrow's demise. Without even viewing the body the doctor wrote out a certificate, giving 'epidemic diarrhoea' as the cause of death.

Seddon next visited a local undertaker and arranged for his former tenant what amounted to a pauper's burial, to be carried out without delay, the body to be buried in a public, or communal grave. Even though this was the cheapest possible funeral, he still haggled with the undertaker, informing him that the deceased, who was not a relative, had left very little money. In the end the price was reduced from £5 to £3-7s-6d.

While Margaret Seddon ordered a wreath, her husband visited a local jeweller's shop with a watch, which he later claimed had been given to his wife by the deceased. He had the jeweller remove the name of Miss Barrow's mother from the back of it.

That same day, two insurance collectors arrived at the house to pay in their takings. One of them later stated that he had watched Seddon counting a large amount of gold, which he took from a bag.

'He seemed to be flaunting it', said the collector.

Miss Barrow was buried two days later, on 16 September, 1911, at Islington Cemetery, where the remains of Cora Crippen, such as they were, were interred. Only the Seddons were present, young Ernest having been packed off to relatives at Southend.

It was about a week later that Miss Barrow's relations, the Vonderahes, heard about her death by chance and went at once to 63 Tollington Park, which was only a few minutes' walk away. They were very angry that they had not been informed of Miss Barrow's death, or invited to the funeral. Seddon replied that he had written a letter to them and even described the notepaper, which, he said, had a black edging. He showed them a copy of the letter. He had posted the original to their address in Evershot Road, he said.

'We're no longer living at 31 Evershot Road', Vonderahe told him. 'We moved to Corbyn Street over a month ago'.

'Oh well, that's why you didn't get my letter'.

'All our other mail has been re-directed to us, but not your letter', said Vonderahe.

'Oh, I'm sorry. But I'm sure you'll get it'.

'There's no point in getting it now, is there?' snapped Vonderahe. 'Eliza's dead and buried'.

He demanded to know what had happened to Miss Barrow's belongings, her private papers and also the money, which he knew she always kept by her.

Seddon explained about the will and claimed that he had found less than £10 in her room. He produced bills from the doctor and the undertaker and also mumbled something about young Ernest Grant's food and lodging.

'All in all', said Seddon, 'I make it that I'm about £1-10s out of pocket'.

The Vonderahes were far from satisfied and still very incensed. Before leaving they pointed out that there had been no need to have Miss Barrow buried in a public grave, as there was a family vault, which the deceased woman had often mentioned, in Kensal Green Cemetery.

Soon after this, the entire Seddon family went off to Southend for a fortnight's holiday. On their return in early October, they were again visited by Mr Frank Vonderahe, who wanted more information about Miss Barrows' affairs, particularly her will.

When asked about the ownership of the Buck's Head Public House and the barber's shop, Seddon admitted,

'I own them now, and it's all perfectly legal'.

This was, of course, quite true, but Vonderahe was still unhappy about the situation, especially when it transpired that all that appeared to remain of the spinster's wealth amounted to no more than £16 or so. Vonderahe was shocked and left the Seddon house determined to take the matter further. After talking things over again in some depth, the Vonderahes decided that the time had come to contact the police. Within days an order was obtained to have the body exhumed.

According to her death certificate the deceased's heart had given out as the result of a bad attack of epidemic diarrhoea. In carrying out the post mortem, Sir William Willcox, assisted by Bernard Spilsbury, found the internal organs in a well-preserved state, with no disease apparent. A considerable quantity of arsenic was, however, present both in the organs and tissue. Seddon was arrested early in December and committed for trial. It was over a month later that his wife was also taken into custody and charged.

Assisting Sir Rufus Isaacs, for the Crown, were Richard Muir, Sidney Rowlett and Travers Humphreys, a formidable team indeed. Surprisingly enough, when Seddon found out that the Attorney-General himself would be in court to lead for the Prosecution, far from being dismayed, he was delighted, and looked forward to doing battle with the great man, for he was expecting to be called to testify.

It turned out to be the lengthiest capital case in which Edward Marshall Hall ever engaged, lasting ten days. The Prosecution's contention was that Miss Barrow had died from arsenic poisoning, and that the only people who could have been in a position to administer the fatal dose were the Seddons. It was calculated by the Prosecution's expert witnesses that as much as five grains of arsenic could be extracted from one fly-paper if it were placed in boiling water. Two such grains constitute a fatal dose.

Mrs Seddon, who was defended by Mr Gervais Rentoul, gave evidence, and though she did not make the best of witnesses, and broke down sobbing a number of times, it appeared from her evidence that she had been used by her husband. She came across as a pathetic creature, who was prepared to do anything Seddon ordered.

When Seddon took the stand he appeared very sure of himself. Too sure, in fact, and though he acquitted himself very well, his 'cocky', self-satisfied manner did not help his cause at all. Indeed, his smug, over-confident demeanour, and the arrogant way in which he dealt with almost every question put to him, clearly antagonised most of those in court, even his own Counsel, who is said to have remarked to a colleague,

'If the evidence doesn't convict this man, his conceit will'.

While pointing out to the jury that the Prosecution relied totally on circumstantial evidence, Marshall Hall admitted that Seddon had, without any doubt, shown himself to be a man possessed of 'monstrous meanness and covetousness', even to the point of arranging the cheapest possible funeral for Miss Barrow and obtaining from the undertaker what really amounted to a commission of 12s-6d for introducing the business.

Marshall Hall's main argument though, was that no proof had been produced to show that Seddon had administered arsenic to the victim, or had even handled the fly-paper.

From the tenor of his closing speech it was evident that while the Attorney-General was quite adamant in demanding a 'Guilty' verdict in respect of Seddon, he was by no means as insistent when it came to the question of the wife.

The jury, after deliberating for over an hour, brought in a verdict of 'Guilty' in the case of Seddon, while Margaret Seddon was found 'Not Guilty'.

At this point the two Defendants embraced, and Mrs Seddon wiped away a tear. Seddon, again assuming an air of total calm and confidence, addressed the court: 'The Prosecution has not traced anything to me in the shape of money, which is the great motive suggested by the Prosecution for me to have committed this diabolical crime, which I declare, before the Grand Architect of the Universe, I am not guilty of.

As he made this short speech Seddon raised his hand and gave a Masonic sign. There were, no doubt, a number of Freemasons present in the court. The judge, Mr Justice Bucknill, was one, and he did not fail to note Seddon's sign. Judge Bucknill, who was Provincial Grand Master of Surrey, appeared very much affected on learning that the accused was a brother Mason, on whom he was about to pass sentence of death.

When the black cap had been placed upon his head the judge began to speak rather haltingly, as if the words were difficult for him to get out.

'I do not know exactly how you poisoned this woman, but I do believe that you wished to make great pecuniary profit by felonious means. I have no wish to harrow your feelings, but...

'It doesn't affect me sir', cut in Seddon. 'You see I've got a clear conscience'.

Ignoring this, the judge continued, 'In the short time you have left, try to make your peace with the Almighty...'

'I'm already at peace'. Seddon again interrupted, in a loud, clear voice.

'I appeal to you'. said the judge, his voice shaking with emotion. 'You and I are members of the same brotherhood, which makes this very painful for me, although it makes no difference as far as my duty is concerned. It may be some consolation to you to know that I agree with the verdict in regard to your wife. Whatever she did, she did it to help you. I am satisfied that the jury have decided wisely, and that they have done justice to you both'.

Judge Bucknill then passed the death sentence, which Seddon listened to without the slightest sign of emotion. He walked from the dock as though he had not a care in the world.

Despite having been found guilty, the condemned man apparently felt confident that the sentence would be overturned on appeal. In the meantime, the execution date was fixed for 18th April. John Ellis, who had returned home to Rochdale after sitting through the first day of the trial, followed the case very closely in the newspapers. A week or so after it had reached its conclusion, a letter arrived in the post assigning him the job of executing Seddon. As well as being a Freemason, Seddon was also a Buffalo, as was Jack Ellis. This, however, would make no difference as far as the Rochdale hangman was concerned.

At the Appeal Court, Marshall Hall made a tremendous effort on his client's behalf, the case taking up two full days. But in the end the appeal failed.

Still Seddon refused to give up hope. His wife Margaret was doing all in her power to save him, writing to newspapers and even publishing her husband's touching letters, written to her from the death cell. She also got up a petition to be sent to the Home Office, and enlisted the help of her children in obtaining hundreds of signatures.

In the end it was all for nothing, and by the time Ellis arrived at Pentonville, on the afternoon of 17th April, Seddon had already been informed that the Home Secretary had refused to intervene. Though he must surely have felt very low at this point, Seddon did not show it. Instead of bemoaning his fate, he simply asked to see his solicitor. In granting this request, the Governor naturally assumed that the prisoner wished to discuss his will. It turned out, however, that he merely wanted to find out what certain articles of furniture, which he had sent to auction, had realised. When given the figure he flew into a temper, banging his fist down on the table and declaring scornfully, that in view of the quality of the items, 'the sum was nothing short of derisory'.

Those present were shocked and amazed that such a matter could occupy his mind when he was about to go to the gallows.

Seddon was still agitated about the furniture when Ellis observed him at exercise. As the hangmen watched him through a window, he was allowed to stroll around a lawn, accompanied by the Chaplain and two warders. Watching with Ellis was the Governor, Ellis wearing a warder's cap in case the prisoner should catch a glimpse of him through the window and realise that it was the hangman, weighing him up. Precautions such as these were always taken in an effort to ensure that those under sentence of death were not subjected to unnecessary stress.

As he walked with Seddon, the Chaplain appeared to be trying hard to explain something to the prisoner, but Seddon kept on shaking his head, interrupting him and gesticulating in an animated fashion. Though he could not hear their conversation, Ellis got the distinct impression that while the Chaplain was trying to save his soul the condemned man was still preoccupied with discussing the auction and the disappointing sum he had received for his furniture.

While in custody, Seddon had been a prolific letter writer. He wrote to a number of people, but mainly to his wife. The letters were unusually lengthy and contained, surprisingly enough, many religious and biblical references, giving the impression that the writer was some sort of martyr about to be put to death unjustly.

Never for one moment did Seddon let anyone forget that he was standing by his claim of innocence to the very end. One day he said to the warders,

'This is clearly my destiny and I trust I will meet my fate bravely, as a Christian. No mercy in human law has been extended to me. I'm the victim of a gross miscarriage of justice. My execution will be a judicial murder. If a man on trial is deprived of the benefit of the doubt, to which he is justly entitled, then there is no excuse for the law when it makes the error of condemning and executing an innocent man'.

In letters written in his cell, Seddon mentioned that he had been a lay preacher and Sunday School teacher, also a prominent Freemason and a member of the Order of Buffaloes. He had been married for eighteen years and had five children, ranging in age from one year to seventeen.

After his close observation of the prisoner, Ellis decided on a drop of 7ft. 1in. Seddon weighed a few pounds under ten stone and stood only 5ft. 3½ins. in height. Yet, because of his bearing, he gave the appearance of being a much taller man.

Ellis's assistant on this occasion was Tom Pierrepoint, who, like his brother, did not get on too well with the Rochdale hangman. Apart from the fact that the two were complete opposites in almost every respect, there appears to have been an element of jealousy on Pierrepoint's part, perhaps because Ellis had made such rapid strides in the job and had taken over the mantle of Number One Executioner from Henry Pierrepoint. It is more than probable that Tom considered that Ellis should be *his* assistant, rather than the other way round.

When Ellis and Pierrepoint entered the condemned cell on the morning of 18th April, the prisoner, as usual, stood proudly erect. If he was downhearted he had no intention of showing it. He was again dressed in his own clothes, according to the normal practice, and looked trim and smart. His breakfast had consisted of only tea, bread and butter, and he had hardly touched it. As usual, the Chaplain was present, and though he attempted again to communicate with the prisoner, Seddon would only repeat over and over again that he was innocent.

Outside the prison the usual crowd had already assembled, and it was rumoured that Margaret Seddon had taken a room opposite the prison, where she had stayed the previous night. It was said that she was now among the crowd outside the gates, waiting there until the notice was posted up proclaiming that the death sentence had been carried out.

Once the pinioning of the prisoner had been completed and the procession began to form, ready to proceed to the scaffold, Ellis left the cell and went on ahead. At this point the Chaplain, the Reverend Swanston, began to recite the usual prayers, but Seddon refused to join in.

On leaving the death cell, the procession turned right, into a short passage, then right again into the prison yard and straight on ahead to the scaffold. From the cell to the scaffold was no more than twenty yards, and as the condemned man entered the yard he was immediately confronted by the sight of the noose, with Ellis standing beside it. Though it was barely discernible, Seddon was just slightly unnerved. Ellis noticed this and also the fact that the prisoner looked very pale. For a moment Seddon closed his eyes, as if to shut out the spectre of the gallows. Seeing this, the two warders flanking him took hold of his arms, but it was not really necessary, for Seddon was still in control of himself.

Immediately the prisoner's feet were on the trapdoors, Tom Pierrepoint strapped his legs together, while Ellis slipped on the white cap and adjusted the rope. Then both men stepped clear and Ellis pulled the lever.

According to Ellis the chief warder timed the execution on his behalf, and reported that from the condemned man's leaving the cell until he disappeared into the pit, the entire operation had taken no more than twenty-five seconds.

CHAPTER 16

THE HOODED MAN

It was in the year 1912 that the case of 'The Hooded Man' first hit the headlines. A man who gave his name as 'John Williams' was arrested and charged with the murder of a police officer at Eastbourne, Sussex. It was clear from the outset that the entire case was likely to centre on the question of the identification of the killer. For this reason, the greatest care was taken to ensure that the arrested man's head and shoulders were well covered up while he was being transported from London, where he was arrested, to Eastbourne, where the crime had been committed.

Though it is common procedure these days, it was a completely new idea in 1912, and was carried out on the advice of Scotland Yard. The prisoner cut a very odd figure as he was hurried through the railway station, head and shoulders covered by a flimsy dark blue fabric with white spots.

The story of the 'Hooded Man' was an amazing one indeed, and first came to the notice of the public as the result of the shooting of Parade-Inspector Walls of the Eastbourne Police.

The scene of the crime was 6, South Cliff Avenue, the residence of Countess Sztaray. As the Countess was leaving the house one day to go for a drive, her coachman informed her that he was sure he had seen a man on the roof above the porch just as they drove off. The Countess ordered him to drive her back to the house immediately. On reaching number 6 they could see nothing amiss, nor any sign of the man, but the Countess decided to telephone the police. Inspector Walls responded to the call and was there within minutes.

'There's a man on my porch', the Countess informed him.

As the coachman, David Potter, pointed out the spot where he had seen the intruder, the Inspector stepped back and shaded his eyes to look up at the balcony. If the man was still there he was obviously crouching down, out of sight.

'If you're up there, you'd better come down', called out Walls.

Receiving no reply, he tried again,

'Hello...' Then, trying a softer approach, the Inspector called out,

'Look here old chap, you might as well come down'.

There was a movement on the balcony, and Walls, thinking that the man was about to climb down by the side of the porch, went around to the right, pushing his way through the shrubbery. At that moment the report of a gun was heard and David Potter saw the Inspector sink down to his knees. He then managed to drag himself upright and stagger to the gates.

No doubt the coachman's attention was drawn to the plight of the shot policeman, or perhaps he even dashed back into the house for safety, but whatever happened, he certainly made no attempt to apprehend the gunman, who made good his escape, apparently without being seen by anyone who could give the police a description.

The unfortunate Inspector Walls was rushed to the hospital, but quickly expired, and the hue and cry immediately went up for his killer.

It was yet another case that Ellis followed in the newspapers, and one which interested him greatly. For though the crime itself was unremarkable, as the facts of the case unfolded the accused man proved to be a highly interesting character, whose true identity was to remain something of a mystery for quite a considerable time.

It was obvious from the outset that the man on the balcony had been there for the purpose of breaking into the house. Eastbourne had been a prime target for burglars over the preceding months, and the Countess was known to be a very wealthy woman, who was often seen at various functions dripping with jewellery.

Sent down from Scotland Yard to take charge of the investigation was Chief-Inspector Bower, the man responsible for bringing to justice Samuel Dougal, the Moat Farm murderer, some nine years before.

Along with two detectives from the C.I.D., Bower went over the front garden very thoroughly, paying particular attention to the ivy-covered balcony as they searched for fingerprints. A light fawn trilby hat was found in the bushes, while careful scrutiny of the soft ground revealed several clear shoe impressions.

Working with the local police force, the Scotland Yard men made extensive enquiries in Eastbourne and surrounding towns, but failed to come up with a positive lead. Then, working on a tip-off, Bower returned to London, headed straight for the buffet at Moorgate Railway Station and made an arrest. As the prisoner would have to be transported to Eastbourne, the Chief-Inspector gave the order to cover his head and shoulders.

The introduction of this precaution was brought about because of problems and complaints caused by methods adopted by the police, which had resulted in prisoners accused of serious crimes being exposed to public scrutiny, and even photographed by the press, soon after being picked up and before being formally identified by witnesses.

On being taken into custody, the suspect was handcuffed and conveyed to Eastbourne. Bower was well aware that his entire case might well rest on the identification evidence of Potter, the coachman, along with the testimony of a young lady named Florence Seymour, who was said to have had a romantic involvement with the prisoner.

As Potter's description of the man he had seen on the balcony was very vague indeed, the Chief-Inspector was relying rather heavily on Miss Seymour, which was hardly surprising considering that her initial statement clearly pointed the finger at the arrested man. When questioned, she told the police that Williams had been out with her on the evening of the murder, and that after taking a stroll they had sat down on a seat just at the point where South Cliff Road meets the sea front and about one hundred and fifty yards from the home of Countess Sztaray. He had left her there and was gone about half-an-hour. When he left he had been wearing a trilby, but returned bare-headed.

The two of them then set off to walk to his lodgings, and on the way he threw a package containing a rope onto the beach, where it was found the next morning. She also told the police that on the following day she had seen Williams cleaning a revolver. He had explained this by saying,

'I'm cleaning my fingerprints off this gun. I'm well known to the police and I'm getting rid of it. If they should find it I don't want my prints to be on it'.

Soon afterwards Williams went to the beach and buried the revolver in the sand. After a lengthy search the gun was dug up to be produced later in evidence.

By the time the case came to trial, however, Miss Seymour had completely changed her story, insisting that she had been confused about the times and that she and Williams had been at the pictures when the murder was committed. Despite this, the jury took only fifteen minutes to find the prisoner guilty, after a trial which had lasted three days.

Ellis duly received a letter asking if he would be available to carry out the sentence of death at Lewes Gaol on 29th January, 1913, to which he replied that he would.

Oddly enough, although no executions had taken place at Lewes for almost twenty years, there were two scheduled for that month, and on 12th January, two weeks before he was due to hang Williams, Ellis arrived there to dispatch Albert Rumens, a labourer, who had murdered a ten-year-old girl in a wood at Wadhurst, in East Sussex. The victim had been out blackberrying, and when she failed to return home after several hours, an organised search culminated in the discovery of her body. She had died from suffocation in a crime that was apparently without motive.

Rumens, an inoffensive little man, who was well known in the area, claimed he could remember nothing about the incident, but although he appeared simple-minded the jury decided that he was responsible for his actions. The hanging of Rumens proved to be a straightforward, routine job as far as Ellis was concerned, and when it was over he spent some time discussing the forthcoming execution of Williams with the Under-Sheriff.

He was told that the prisoner was feeling very low. Pending his appeal, Williams had written a letter to the Home Secretary, informing him that his fiancée, Miss Seymour, was pregnant, and requesting permission to marry her before the child was born.

Somehow the condemned man's request was made public and reported in the newspapers, prompting many people to sympathize with the tragic couple. Of course, there were two sides to the question. On the one hand, to save a child from the stigma of illegitimacy was considered important in those days, while on the other, it could be claimed that to have a father who was hanged for murder was much worse.

After due consideration the Home Secretary replied that he was unable to accede to the prisoner's request. It quickly became clear that large sections of the public felt that the refusal of William's request was callous and inhumane, and questions were asked in the House of Commons in regard to the case.

The Home Secretary replied that he had followed accepted Home Office practice in dealing with the request, and added that there were also special circumstances connected with the case. An appeal was pending, and a marriage would have prevented the woman from giving evidence had the Court of Appeal so desired. Also, an element of sentiment would have been introduced into the case, which in reality would have no bearing on the guilt or innocence of the prisoner.

While Ellis was at the prison he learned a few more facts regarding the true identity of the man who called himself John Williams, facts that would not become known to the public until after the execution.

The story was that the mother of the condemned man was old and sick. She had not seen her son for a very long time, as he had spent periods abroad, during which he regularly communicated with her by letter. The mother was well aware that her son was a shiftless adventurer, who could never settle down to a steady, productive life. Yet she had no idea that he was incarcerated in Lewes Gaol under sentence of death. He feared that the shock, should she find out how he had ended up, might very well kill her. For this reason he was quite prepared to die under an assumed name.

The condemned man's real name was George McKay. He was the son of a highly-respected clergyman and was born in Edinburgh in 1883. He had first appeared in court at the age of nine, charged with stealing, but was let off. His next court appearance, however, earned him a fine of £1, and by the time he was fourteen George was involved in more serious crime. After breaking into a shop he was caught and sentenced to seven days in prison.

Being very agile, he began to specialize in burglary, and on being arrested yet again, was sent on board a training ship for young offenders. But far from putting young McKay on the straight and narrow, life at sea only served to steer him in the wrong direction, for part of the training involved climbing rope ladders, and by the time his sentence was completed he was as nimble as a chimpanzee and even better equipped for breaking and entering than before.

On being released, however, McKay decided to try his luck in the army, and enlisted in the Royal Scots Regiment. In 1899, at the age of seventeen, he was sent to South Africa to fight in the Boer War. McKay had only been out there a matter of months before he was sentenced to three months' imprisonment for robbing the stores.

After completing his sentence he proved himself to be a man of some courage when he was shot in the face during a battle at Lydenburg in September 1900, and left for dead on the field.

When he regained consciousness, he found himself cut off from his regiment, alongside a comrade who was badly wounded. McKay would have had a much better chance of survival had he made his way back to the British lines alone, but he decided that he could not leave the wounded man. Although weak from loss of blood, he managed to half-carry, half-drag his comrade over rough terrain, eventually linking up again with his regiment, in a sorry state and on the verge of total collapse from hunger and sheer exhaustion.

After several weeks in a military hospital McKay recovered, the only disfigurement being a scar on his face, which in no way detracted from his rugged goods looks. Back with his regiment, he promptly deserted and joined up with an irregular corps known as the Canadian Scouts.

But he could never keep out of trouble for long, and in 1902 was court-martialled and sentenced to two years' hard labour, after being found guilty of one of the most despicable crimes imaginable — stealing from his fellow soldiers.

At this time he was calling himself 'John Thompson' but when his sentence was completed, he headed for Kimberley, and on making certain underworld contacts there he began to use the name 'Harry Wilson'.

In 1904, in the High Court of Kimberley, he was found guilty of theft and receiving stolen property and sentenced to terms of eighteen and nine months hard labour respectively. He served his time in gaol at Cape Town.

After his release, McKay decided to try his luck in Johannesburg, but the authorities there kept a close watch on him, and at the first opportunity, deported him as an undesirable.

By the middle of 1907 he was back in England, still looking for easy money and calling himself 'Sydney Hamilton'. Initially, he was based in London, then for some reason or other moved to Somerset, where, in October 1907, he got nine months' hard labour at Wells Quarter Sessions for housebreaking.

At liberty once again, McKay returned to London. He was becoming well-known among a certain section of the underworld, and was noted for his smartly-tailored suits, impeccable manners and smooth, confident style. It was quite obvious that he fancied himself as a Raffles-type gentleman thief, and there is no doubting the fact that he fitted the description perfectly, the only difference being, that unlike the great cracksman of fictional fame, McKay tended to get caught.

In September 1908, while working the South Coast, he was arrested at Folkestone, charged with burglary, and sentenced to twenty-one months' hard labour under the name of John Williams.

On release, he went back to London and his old haunts, and was soon in trouble again, being sentenced to twelve months' imprisonment for housebreaking, at London Quarter Sessions in November 1910.

McKay, or Williams, as he now preferred to be known, had still not learned his lesson, for after finishing his sentence he made immediate contact with other London criminals and began to formulate plans to concentrate on the South Coast, where towns such as Eastbourne and Brighton offered rich pickings.

During this period he had taken up with Florence Seymour, who was young, slim and very pretty. Though she did not approve of his way of life, Miss Seymour became very much attached to her new friend and the two spent a good deal of time together. She must have known about his criminal connections, though he made every effort to keep her out of that side of his life. He told her very little and she did not ask too many questions. Though he never had a job, he always seemed to have money in his pocket.

That fatal day, when he had left her sitting on the form near the sea front and returned later, she knew that something very serious had happened. What she did not know was that her lover had just committed murder and that both their lives were ruined. On being questioned by the police, she had simply told them the truth, but later changed her story. It had made no difference to the outcome. The man she knew as John Williams was to die, and she was carrying his child.

From the day Williams was sentenced to be hanged, to the actual day of the execution, many weeks had passed, what with the appeal, followed by the request by the prisoner to marry Miss Seymour and its subsequent rejection by the Home Secretary. The result being that the baby was born before Williams went to his doom. This led to a further request to the Home Office, that the condemned man might be allowed to see the child before he was put to death.

This time the prisoner's request was not denied, and on the day prior to the day of the execution Florence Seymour and her baby made the journey to Lewes, unaware that the hangman was travelling on the same train. Ellis and his assistant saw her board the train in London, but did not realise who she was until they had arrived in Lewes and she was pointed out to them on the platform. Most people felt very sorry for her, and she appeared frail and vulnerable as she stood there tightly clutching her baby.

As Ellis had some time to spare before going to the prison he suggested to his assistant that they might drop into a pub near the station. As the two settled down over their drinks, Ellis's attention was drawn to a bulldog pup owned by the landlord.

'That's a fine looking dog', said Ellis, patting the animal.
'Aye, he is that', replied the landlord. 'You interested in dogs sir?'
'I am that', said the hangman. 'I breed 'em'.
'Do you now?'
'Aye, whippets and bulldogs, and I wouldn't mind making you an offer for this one'.
'No, he's not for sale'.
'I'll gi' thee ten pound for him. How's that?'
'No, no, thanks just the same, but I'm not interested'.

After Ellis had left the pub a customer told the landlord that the man who had made him an offer for the pup was none other than the Rochdale hangman, John Ellis.

'Well I'll be damned!' said the landlord. 'What about that, eh?'

This incident had an amusing sequel some two years later, when Ellis was in the South of England to hang George Smith, the 'Brides in the Bath' murderer, at Maidstone Gaol, and called at the same pub with a warder friend. The warder began to discuss dogs with the same landlord, who was upset at having lost a valuable bitch the previous week.

'I've still got one of her pups though. He's a fine specimen. One of the best I've bred. As a matter of fact the hangman, Ellis, offered me twenty pounds for him when he was a young 'un''.

Realising that the landlord had not recognised him, Ellis chipped in, 'Is that a fact?'

'Aye, it's right. Ellis is very interested in bulldogs you know'.

'Yes, I think I've read something about that somewhere', said Ellis, winking at the warder.

He and his friend then left to share the joke at a safe distance, with the landlord none the wiser.

On arriving at the prison, Ellis was told that Miss Seymour and the prisoner had already had their final meeting, which had proved harrowing to those who witnessed it. Though kissing was normally not permitted, the condemned man had been allowed to kiss his child for the first and last time.

Ellis made his way to the condemned cell to take a peep at the man he would hang on the following morning, and was immediately impressed with the prisoner's fine physique. At 5ft. 8ins. he weighed just over 10-and-a-half stone, but was all muscle and looked every inch an athlete.

Ellis realised at once that the prisoner would require a longer drop than it would take to hang another man of similar proportions, and decided to allow 7ft. 6ins.

Though Williams was no coward he was naturally very tense and spent a restless night. When Ellis learned of this he suggested a drop of the 'old faithful' brandy, but Williams, not wishing to show even the slightest indication of weakness, refused it. If he felt jittery, he certainly made every effort to control his emotions and appeared quite steady when the hangmen entered his cell. There he stood, as if he had been waiting for them, looking very smart in the frock coat he had worn at the trial. He remained silent as his hands were pinioned, then stepped out into the passage to be escorted to the scaffold.

The weather that morning was damp and misty, but despite this a small crowd gathered outside the gaol, as usual, to await the signal that the deed was done.

As Williams stood there on the trapdoors he appeared completely oblivious to all that was going on around him, just staring out over the heads of all the officials who were clustered around the scaffold. With the white cap over his head 'The Hooded Man' was once again hooded, and within seconds was dead.

Following the execution, Ellis was handed an envelope, which had been delivered to the prison that morning. It was post-marked London and addressed to 'The Public Executioner, Lewes Gaol'. It was a rather vague and rambling letter in which the writer remonstrated with the hangman for taking up such a profession when there were so many other ways of making a living.

If you wish to practice hanging, the letter ran, *then practice upon yourself. Even that would be wrong, but if you are built that way and believe it good that would be the quicker way out for you. Thou shalt not kill means that neither you nor anyone else shall do so.*

Ellis kept the letter as a memento, but it clearly made no impression on him, for he continued to practise his trade. He had always believed very firmly in the principle of an eye for an eye. He had never for one moment doubted it. The doubts would come later.

It was around this time that Ellis carried out an execution, which, though it could not be said to have affected him exactly, did at least touch in him a feeling of real sympathy for the victim. If the Eastbourne murder was referred to as the 'Hooded Man' case, then the hanging of a young man at Chelmsford, in December 1912, could well have been remembered by Ellis as 'The Case of the Frightened Youth'.

On the evening of 12th September, 1912, two young girls were out walking in Abbey Lane, West Ham, London, when they passed a courting couple. When they were a few yards further on they heard a cry of 'Help!' Looking around, they saw first the girl, then the young man, fall to the ground. The two witnesses fled from the scene, one of them later claiming that she had seen a razor lying on the ground close to the couple.

Within minutes the girls were back on the spot, along with a policeman and another man, who had heard them scream. In the darkness of the lane it was difficult to take in the scene which confronted them, but with the help of the light from a nearby gaslamp it was possible to make out two figures, both writhing on the ground covered in blood. Closer examination revealed that their throats had been cut.

The young girl, whose name was Clara Carter, was close to death and soon expired, while the young man was rushed to the hospital and eventually recovered. When he was fit enough to answer questions he had a very strange tale to tell. He gave his name as Beal and said that for many months he had been unable to obtain employment. As Clara was set on marriage, Beal's lack of a job was obviously worrying her. According to him she was not altogether stable mentally. He said she had bad dreams and constantly complained that people were talking about her.

On the night she died, she had again brought up the question of marriage, and he had been forced to resist once more, reminding her of their financial circumstances. She had then begged him to marry her despite the problems, and while gently refusing, he had leaned over to kiss her. Suddenly, he felt a sharp pain on his throat and realised that she had stuck something into his neck. She had then cut her own throat. The razor, which was found lying nearby, belonged to Beal, who said that she must have removed it from his pocket as they embraced.

Beal's story could have been true, but the fact that the victim had three bad cuts across her throat, rather than a single slash, told heavily against him at his trial. Furthermore, Clara, after receiving one of the cuts, might have been able to call 'Help', but she certainly could not after receiving three, for each single cut was serious enough to have caused her death, and each was so severe that after administering the first one she would not have had the strength to administer a second, let alone a third.

It took the jury an hour to find Beal guilty. His appeal failed, and Ellis was commissioned to execute him at Chelmsford Gaol on 10th December, 1912.

After receiving the final ministrations of the Catholic priest, Father Shepherd, Beal waited for the hangmen to arrive. Ellis entered the cell along with his assistant to find the prisoner, a well-built lad of twenty, looking frightened and haggard. His hands were pinioned behind his back, then, as Ellis began to loosen his shirt collar, Beal looked appealingly into his eyes and said,

'Don't hurt me, will you?'

Ellis, who very rarely spoke to a condemned person, was at once touched, and replied,

'Don't worry lad. You need have no fear. It'll all be over very quickly. You'll not suffer, or feel anything'.

Ellis then gave the boy an encouraging pat on the shoulder and left the cell.

As he waited on the scaffold, the hangman could hear the voice of the priest and the murmured responses of the condemned man as the procession drew nearer. Ellis was determined to make this one of the quickest hangings he had ever carried out. Yet, brief as it was, it still turned out to be a terrible ordeal for young Beal. Immediately he was on the trapdoors his legs were strapped together, and as Ellis moved to slip on the white cap he could see that Beal, who at that moment looked no more than a boy, was fighting to keep back the tears. Then the noose was slipped over his head and the knot adjusted. All this, which had taken only seconds, seemed to last an eternity, so great was the strain on all those involved.

Then Ellis stepped back and jerked the lever. It was all over, and the Rochdale hangman breathed a deep and heartfelt sigh of relief.

CHAPTER 17

THE HOUSE ON SARATOGA ROAD

John Ellis now had a very full life indeed. Apart from having a wife, three daughters and two sons to keep him occupied, he had always been interested in animals, and at various times kept poultry, rabbits, bulldogs and whippets. He was a member of the Antediluvian Order of Buffaloes and a keen follower of Rochdale Hornets Rugby League Club.

Founded in 1871, Hornets was one of those clubs that split from the Rugby Football Union in 1895, over broken-time payments to players, to form the Northern Union, which eventually became the Rugby League. In their first season the Hornets had a very poor team, finishing bottom of the table. But gradually their fortunes improved, and in the 1911-12 season Ellis was a delighted spectator when they beat Oldham by 12 points to 5 at Broughton, to win the Lancashire Challenge Cup.

Apart from his family and his hobbies, Ellis still had his barber's shop to run. He also liked a drink and was a regular at several of the local alehouses, where he was constantly kidded about his 'other job'. He seemed not to mind, and probably secretly enjoyed the notoriety it brought him, though he would never have admitted this.

The executioner's job kept him steadily employed, hanging murderers whose crimes, though often horrendous, did not capture the imagination of the public in the same way as those of Crippen and Seddon. Yet beneath the surface of many of these little-known cases lay some intriguing stories.

The year 1913 produced a number of such cases and three in particular stand out, mainly because they involved the horrifying crimes of matricide and infanticide. The perpetrators were Pat Higgins, an Irishman living near Linlithgow, Scotland, Augustus John Penny, a Hampshire man, and Frederick Ernest Robertson, who, because he had a wooden leg, was known as 'Peggy'. Higgins was hanged at Calton Gaol, Edinburgh on 2nd October, and the other two on consecutive days, Penny at Winchester on 26th November, and Robertson on the 27th at Pentonville.

On a warm June day, two farmhands were out for a Sunday afternoon walk in wild country near the Scottish village of Winchburgh, which lies roughly midway between Linlithgow and Edinburgh, when their route took them past a disused quarry. It was an area through which few local people ever passed, and the two men might never have gone that way had it not been for the fact that one of them was new to the district, and was keen to explore the countryside.

The quarry had filled up with water to a good depth and the two men noticed an object floating just a few yards from the edge. With the help of a tree branch they managed to drag the bundle towards them and were horrified to discover that what they had stumbled upon were the badly decomposed bodies of two young children, tied together with a piece of cord.

Medical examination soon established that the bodies were those of two boys, aged around five and eight years respectively. No clue as to their identities could be found on the bodies and it was impossible to determine just how long they had been in the water. The one fact that was crystal clear was that they had been cruelly murdered.

The scene of the terrible tragedy was a lonely and desolate place indeed. To reach it from the village meant crossing several fields, following the railway lines for a good distance, then climbing a steep hill. Yet it occurred to the police that the murderer had, in all probability, made the journey from Winchburgh, as there was not another town or village for miles around.

Though extensive enquiries were made in the surrounding districts, it was soon established that no reports of missing children had reached the police. The discovery, of course, was the subject of much discussion among the local people, who were quite unused to having anything of a sensational nature occur in their midst.

Who were the children, and who had so callously ended their young lives? It remained a complete mystery for some weeks. Then one of the locals suddenly remembered that a man by the name of Pat Higgins, who had lived in the district previously before moving on, had had two young sons. Another person then recalled having remarked to Higgins that he had not seen the two boys around for some time, and was told by the Irishman that he had put them in a home.

Another of the locals passed this story on to the police, adding that he believed Higgins was still living somewhere in the area.

As Higgins was known to be a widower, who had found it very difficult to cope with the children while at the same time trying to make a living, he had received plenty of sympathy from the local people, none of whom believed that he could possibly have harmed his children.

Nevertheless, the police decided that they should track down the Irishman, find out where the children were living and make sure that they were all right.

Accordingly, an early morning visit was made to a lodging house in Broxburn, just a few miles beyond Winchburgh, going in the direction of Edinburgh, where the keeper told them that he did not know of a man named Pat Higgins, adding, however, that he had not been in the job very long. He offered to take them upstairs so that they might question some of his regulars.

Upstairs he knocked on the door of a cubicle, which contained two beds, one occupied by a man who had lodged there off and on for a few years. Addressing this lodger, the policeman explained that they were trying to track down a man who had previously been in trouble for neglecting his children. On hearing this the occupant of the other bed sat up and said,

'I believe I'm the one you want'.

The man was indeed Pat Higgins, and when he failed to provide a satisfactory explanation as to the whereabouts of his children, he was placed under arrest. He was taken to the mortuary, and on being shown the pathetic remains, broke down and admitted that the bodies were those of his two boys.

While Higgins was awaiting trial, details of his past life began to emerge. It was a sad story indeed, but a common one in those hard days, when many people lived in dire poverty, very often with little or no shelter from the elements, were inadequately clothed and seldom knew where the next meal was coming from.

After leaving Ireland, Higgins had joined the Scottish Rifles at the age of nineteen, and served a number of years in India before being discharged, when it was discovered that he was subject to epileptic fits. Life as a civilian, however, proved very difficult for him, for though army life was tough and regimented, at least he could be sure of food and a bed.

Higgins found it almost impossible to get work, and was forced to tramp all over the country. He managed to find a job here and there, but nothing permanent. While working in the vicinity of Winchburgh he had met and married a young local girl, and though the marriage eventually produced two sons, this did not result in Higgins settling down, for he left his family behind for long periods, sending money home whenever he could. At other times he took the family with him on his travels, and it was while the boys were still quite young that a tragedy occurred. While they were staying in Fife the mother was taken ill and died.

Higgins was now forced to bring up the boys on his own, while still faced with the prospect of having to scatch around to find work. There were times when they were placed in the care of the authorities, but as Higgins was expected to contribute to their maintenance, things were no easier for him and he was obliged to have the children with him most of the time.

In the past, he had often spoken of emigrating to Canada or America, where he believed his sons would have a better chance in life, but of course he could not find the fare. He still entertained hopes of working and saving so that one day his dream would become a reality, but even when in employment he was not very good at managing his finances and things never seemed to improve.

Once again he returned to the Winchburgh district, where he found work at the brickworks, boarding the children out with a widow in the village. By all accounts he was a good worker, but his wages were very low, and after paying for the boys' keep there was very little left. The result was that he himself often slept in the brick kiln, where his bed, though hard, was at least warm.

The last time the two boys were seen by any of the villagers was some time in November 1911, when a miner saw them walking along the quarry road with their father. Later that evening the same man met Higgins in the village. He was alone, and when asked where the boys were, Higgins related an odd story to the miner.

He told him that two ladies had taken a fancy to them while travelling on a train to Edinburgh, and that believing it to be in the children's best interests, he had parted with them. Surprisingly enough, the miner did not doubt the truth of Higgins' story, and therefore did not bother to mention it to anyone else at the time. It is almost certain though that Higgins had murdered his children that same day, for they were never seen again until their bodies were discovered some twenty months later.

At his trial the Defence were unable to produce any evidence whatsoever to substantiate Higgins' story of the two ladies on the train, nor did any such ladies come forward, despite the publicity the case received in the press. In an attempt to escape the death penalty the Defence pleaded insanity on behalf of their client, but to no avail, although in bringing in a verdict of 'Guilty' the jury added a recommendation for mercy.

The judge, Lord Johnston, in passing sentence, described the killings as, 'A heinous crime against God, man and nature'.

Surprisingly, as Higgins was led from the dock, he seemed very little affected and even paused to smile and wink at several of those in the public seats.

It had been sixteen years since an execution had taken place at Edinburgh's Calton Gaol, and those in charge were not sure how to go about the job. First they wrote to John Ellis asking if he were prepared to undertake to hang Patrick Higgins on 2nd October, of that year, 1913. Ellis replied that he was available on that date and quite willing to travel up to Scotland. Several days later he received a second letter in which it was mentioned that he would be expected to provide all the pinioning straps, rope and tackle, and even the white cap.

This was most unusual. In earlier times hangmen had indeed carried these items with them to each execution, but this practice had ceased years before, due mainly to the fact that hangmen had often indulged in the unsavoury practice of selling pieces of rope for souvenirs. All Ellis ever brought with him was a tape measure, a ruler, a pair of pliers and a spare rope.

With only a week to go Ellis wrote a letter to the Prison Commissioners in London. Three days later he received a reply from the Deputy-Governor of Pentonville, informing him that a box containing the necessary equipment was on its way to Edinburgh. Having dealt with that problem, it occurred to Ellis that he ought to check to make sure that an assistant to the hangman had been appointed. He received the following reply:

> *An assistant has not been engaged. On previous executions in Edinburgh the warders in the prison have rendered any help that was required.*

Ellis was far from happy with this arrangement, for though he could carry out an execution with the help of prison warders, he much preferred to have a trained man at his side. If the Chief Executioner happened to be taken ill, or meet with an accident, how could a prison warder be expected to assume responsibility?

Ellis replied at once by telegram, strongly advising the authorities in Edinburgh to reconsider. They did not argue the point, and an assistant was duly engaged.

On arriving in Scotland, Ellis was overwhelmed by the hospitality he received. Instead of being treated as a paid servant, as he usually was, he found that he was welcomed more as an honoured guest.

In England, the hangman, after taking up his quarters in the prison, was not allowed out until the execution was over. Here in Edinburgh Ellis was asked if he would prefer to dine in the city. Not only did the Rochdale hangman visit several local restaurants, but he was also given a conducted tour of the police headquarters, where he was shown many interesting exhibits in the criminal museum. He was also introduced to a fingerprints expert, who took his prints, saying 'I hope these are never used in evidence against you!'

On observing Pat Higgins through the peephole, later that evening, Ellis was struck by the prisoner's strong physical appearance. He was 38 years old, stood only 5ft. 4ins. and weighed no more than ten stone, but he looked very hard and in excellent condition. Though not very heavy, he was certainly wiry, and Ellis had great difficulty in making up his mind on the length of drop. In the end, he decided to allow 8 feet, which was an exceptionally long drop.

The priest in attendance found Higgins responsive to his ministrations, and later it was rumoured that the prisoner had confessed to him his guilt of the murders. The priest, of course, would not confirm this.

Two days before the day of execution a touching scene was played out in the cell when the prisoner's mother arrived to visit her son for the last time. On the following day, other relations came and Higgins put on such a brave face that several of those in the party went away with the impression that the condemned man felt little, if any, remorse. This, however, was far from the truth, for it seemed to the warders, who had got to know him well, that Higgins was acting bravely so that his relatives would go away feeling a little less down-hearted, knowing that he was holding up well.

The condemned man left a letter thanking all at the prison for the kindness and consideration shown to him. He also admitted that his sentence was just, and added that he had been brought to his present position 'through drink and neglect of religion'.

As Higgins was pinioned in the cell, the prison clock began to boom out the hour of eight. Before it was finished the prisoner was standing on the trap doors with the rope in place around his neck and his head covered by the white cap. Then, just as the priest intoned the words 'Into Thy hands, O Lord, I commend thy spirit', Ellis drew back the lever and Pat Higgins disappeared into the hole.

The length of drop proved to be just about right. Higgins' confession had cleared up any lingering doubts about the Winchburgh murders, and the deaths of the two little boys had been avenged.

Augustus John Penny returned from the Royal Navy after twelve years' service, to live with his mother and an elder brother at Copythorne in the New Forest. His mother was not particularly keen to have him there and made it quite clear to him that her love and loyalty was directed exclusively to her elder son, who had remained with her while Augustus had gone off to sea.

Soon after his return, his mother told Augustus that she had made over the land adjoining her cottage to his brother. He claimed later that she had taunted him about his brother, and driven him to such anger that he had rushed into his bedroom, grabbed a gun, which he had borrowed for the purpose of shooting pigeons, and had shot her in the head. Penny gave himself up to the police and was charged with murder.

At his trial it was claimed in Penny's defence that he had been drinking at the time and that it might, therefore, be appropriate to reduce the charge to manslaughter. It was also claimed that the Defendant had been a good son to the victim, who had been a bad mother.

After deliberating for over half-an-hour, the jury returned a verdict of 'Guilty' on the capital charge, with a recommendation for mercy on the grounds of the victim's character and probable provocation.

Great efforts were made on the prisoner's behalf by his solicitor, Mr T.E. Brown, who, in promoting a petition for reprieve, actually managed to secure the signature of the High Sheriff, Mr R.C.H. Sloane-Stanley. Many hours were spent in putting together information favourable to Penny's cause. This was then placed before the Home Secretary, along with a strongly-worded appeal for clemency, and about a week before the date fixed for the execution, word was received from the Home Office that the petition was being very carefully considered. Not only that, but the Home Secretary had even gone so far as to request a report from the police regarding Penny's previous character.

Despite all these efforts, however, no word was received from the Home Office over the following days. Then, on Sunday, 23rd November, three days prior to the date set for the execution, the Governor of the prison, Captain Clements, received a letter from the Home Office which stated that after further review and consideration of all the circumstances surrounding the case, the Home Secretary could see no reason to justify advising His Majesty to interfere with the course of the law.

When the Governor conveyed this news to the prisoner, Penny broke down and wept. He had allowed himself to believe that he would be reprieved, which made the shock of hearing the bad news even harder to bear. Several of the warders were also affected at seeing the emotional state of the prisoner.

Ellis arrived at Winchester Gaol on the afternoon of 25th November, and after an interview with Captain Clements, went to see the condemned, whom he found to be a heavy-set fellow of around 14 stone, standing 5ft. 6ins. tall.

Penny was not only devastated at the rejection of his plea for clemency, he was also deeply remorseful, as he had been during the whole of his time in prison. On his mother's death he had inherited a small part of her estate. This he had pledged to cover the cost of his defence.

On the day of the execution Ellis entered the condemned cell to find Penny dressed in the brown suit with black armband which he had worn at his trial. He had managed to pull himself together and co-operated fully as the executioner pinioned his hands behind his back.

On the table Ellis noticed a letter addressed to Captain Clements. The hanging party then proceeded to the scaffold. Ellis had allowed a drop of 7ft. exactly, which proved to be as near perfect as it was possible to be, for Penny died instantaneously.

The letter he had left behind was read out at the inquest, which was always held following an execution, and ran as follows:

> *Sir, I wish to thank all the officers for the kindness shown to me during my incarnation [sic] in this prison both before and after my conviction, including yourself, the medical officer and the chaplain — Believe me, Yours sincerely, Augustus John Penny.*

A house in Saratoga Road, Hackney, was the setting for a particularly gruesome multiple crime in that same year, 1913. Normally let as two flats, ground and first floor, the building had been standing empty for a number of weeks when new tenants moved into the upper floor. Soon they were complaining to the landlord that a noxious smell was emanating from the lower section of the house. The landlord at once called in his builder, who instructed a workman named Liddon, who happened to live next door to the flats, to investigate.

Liddon's first thought was that the smell must be coming from the drains, but on checking he found them to be clear. He then prised up a couple of floorboards in one of the rooms, but though the smell was very strong he could find nothing. Liddon next went down into the cellar and noticed that a section of one wall had apparently been taken down and re-built in a rough and ready fashion.

He set to work and soon opened up a large hole. The cavity behind was about 18 inches deep, and peering inside, Liddon saw what appeared to be a quantity of old sacking and a blanket. Taking a rake, Liddon dragged these items out of the hole. As they hit the flag floor of the cellar Liddon leapt back in horror, for out of the blanket tumbled three small bodies.

Liddon gaped at this horrifying sight for several seconds, unable to move. Then he rushed upstairs and into the back yard, gasping for air.

The police arrived on the scene very quickly, and following a thorough examination of the premises, the rapidly decomposing little bodies were removed to the mortuary.

It did not take the police very long to discover the identities of the last tenants of the lower flat. They were Mr Frederick Ernest Robertson and his wife and three children, twins Frederick junior and Nelly, aged two, and Beatrice, only ten months old.

One evening, shortly after the discovery of the bodies, Detective Inspector Haigh saw a man with a wooden leg walking past him in Shepherdess Walk, City Road. Haigh stopped the man and asked him if his name was Fred Robertson, to which he replied that it was.

'I'm arresting you on suspicion of having murdered your three children. You must come with me'.

Robertson began to sob, then agreed to accompany the officer. At the police station he was told,

'The bodies of three children, believed to be yours, have been found concealed in the cellar of your former home in Saratoga Road.

'I don't know whether they're mine or not', replied Robertson. 'I haven't seen them'.

'Then where are your children?' asked the Inspector.

'I abandoned them', was the reply. 'I left them in the street near to Howerton Workhouse'.

The prisoner's wife, however, told a different story. Mrs Robertson, who was only twenty-two years old, was questioned by detectives in the Infirmary where she lay ill.

She said that the family had moved into the house at Saratoga Road in June of that year. Three days later she was admitted to the Infirmary and had not seen her children since. Her husband, to whom she had been married for three years, had visited her a number of times. When she asked about the children he always said that they were all right.

'He told me he'd taken them to the Salvation Army. He was always a good father to them'.

In a letter to his wife, Robertson had written 'You'll be glad to know that the children are very happy'.

The letter was dated 15th July, yet the children had been dead since the end of June. Robertson had moved out of the house on the same day as the Smiths, the occupants of the upper floor.

Mrs Smith told the police,

'My husband and me first lived with the Robertson's at a house in Millfields Road. When we moved to Saratoga Road on 21st June, they went with us. Mrs Robertson was poorly and was taken to the Infirmary three days later. On the afternoon of 28th June, I had a conversation with Fred Robertson. It was just before he went out, and he asked me to put the children to bed. I told him I would and he said not to undress them because he was trying to get them into a Salvation Army home and would come to fetch them. I thought Salvation Army officers would be calling for them, but Fred came back on his own about half-past seven that night. He asked me if they were in bed and I told him they were. Then me and my husband went out shopping and left Fred in the house.

'When we got back he was sitting in the kitchen and I asked if the children had gone yet. He told us that a man had called and taken the baby and was coming back for the other two next morning.

'Next morning, Fred came up to our bedroom and brought us a cup of tea. I asked about the children and he said "It's all right. A man came for them at six o'clock this morning". I told him they must have been very quiet, for we hadn't heard them go.

'We saw Fred a few times, over the next week, and he asked us not to tell anybody where the children were, because he didn't like it to be known that they were at the Salvation Army'.

Mrs Smith told the detectives that Robertson had said he would not stay in the house because the landlord would not 'do up' the rooms. When he left, she and her husband had also left.

'While the children were there', said Mrs Smith, 'I always put them to bed and made Fred's bed. But after Saturday 28th June, I didn't go in the room again, and the door was kept locked. He told me not to go in again. Said he'd make his own bed'.

Two clues were unearthed to connect Robertson with the bricking up of the three bodies in the cellar. First, a wad of newspaper which had obviously been used to smooth over the plaster, which had been very roughly applied. The remnants of this had been left on the floor of the cellar. The date, which was barely discernible, was 28th May, 1913. At Robertson's new lodgings in Islington the police found a quantity of plaster wrapped in part of a newspaper which bore the same date.

The other clue was far more damning. A piece of blanket covering Robertson's bed, at the Islington house, matched exactly that in which the bodies had been wrapped. At the trial the two pieces of blanket were placed together, and fitted perfectly.

While it was now obvious that Robertson was clearly linked with the deaths of his three children, still the question remained as to how they had died.

In the witness box Dr W.H. Willcox, the Home Office analyst, told the court that he had found no trace of poison, nor any evidence of disease in the bodies, and offered it as his opinion that they might well have died from suffocation.

Mr Purchase, defending, said that there was absolutely no evidence to back up such a supposition, and pointed out that there was no proof that his client had been guilty of anything more than the unlawful concealment of the bodies.

'The law provides for such a case', he told the jury. 'But not for the forfeiture of a man's life based on guesswork. My submission is that in the whole of this case there is nothing that is consistent with murder, only with the offence of disposing of the bodies. The Crippen case centred on the cause of death, but that vital point is missing from the evidence against Robertson'

The jury, however, were unimpressed. They knew full well that a man who would go to the length of tearing down part of a cellar wall to conceal three bodies must certainly have a guilty secret. Not surprisingly, Robertson was convicted and sentenced to be hanged.

An appeal was lodged on his behalf, which merely had the effect of delaying the carrying out of the death sentence by a couple of weeks. There now only remained the question of whether or not Robertson would confess to the crimes. When Ellis arrived at Pentonville on the day prior to the execution he had not done so.

The Rochdale hangman had come by train from Winchester Gaol after executing Augustus John Penny that morning. Though he was tired and hungry, he immediately asked to see the Governor and the chief warder, as he always preferred to be briefed as quickly as possible, in case there were any particular problems in regard to the condemned man, and also to get his measurements. These were given as 5ft. 3ins. and 10 stone.

Ellis then asked to be taken to Robertson's cell. He wondered what manner of man he was about to see: a man who could murder three little children, his own, in fact, then so callously and calculatingly dispose of their bodies.

But on viewing the prisoner through the grille, Ellis found himself looking at a man who certainly did not appear to be the monster one might have imagined. Robertson had a mass of dark curly hair, and though normally clean shaven, he now sported the beginnings of a beard, due to the fact that prison regulations forbade a condemned man to go anywhere near a razor.

In most of the prisons that Ellis visited regularly he got on well with the warders and always made it a point to get to know their names and to talk with them. In this way, he learned as much as possible about the person he was about to hang. This could be very helpful in ensuring that the execution went smoothly. Unfortunately, Pentonville was one of the few prisons where the executioner was not encouraged to mix with the staff, so Ellis could discover very little about the prisoner, apart from the fact that he was bearing up reasonably well, and had not confessed to the crime.

Before retiring for the night, Ellis checked the scaffold and thoroughly tested the drop, then left a sandbag hanging from the rope and went to see the Under-Sheriff, Mr Metcalfe.

Metcalfe told him that he had fixed the drop at 7ft. 3ins. Ellis nodded his agreement. He and Metcalfe had worked together on so many executions, and he trusted his judgement to such an extent that he was quite happy to let the Under-Sheriff decide the length of the drop, Metcalfe being the only Under-Sheriff in the country whom he allowed to do so.

Next morning things went very much according to plan. Robertson gave no trouble as he was pinioned in the cell. No words were exchanged, and though quite often sympathy was felt by the prison staff towards the condemned man, after getting to know him in the weeks leading up to the execution day, it was not expected in Robertson's case. Who could feel anything but revulsion in the presence of a man who had murdered three helpless little children?

Surprisingly, however, a certain sympathy *was* felt. For as the procession moved solemnly along the stone passage en route to the scaffold, one sound could be clearly heard above the Chaplain's prayers. It was the tap-tap of Robertson's artificial limb, reminding Ellis and his associates that they were about to put to death a cripple.

After that thought had registered, Ellis kept firmly fixed in his mind the terrible things that this man had done.

Once Robertson was in position on the trapdoors with everything in place, Ellis waited momentarily, but it was clear that no confession would be forthcoming. He pulled the lever and Robertson plunged to his death. No one ever discovered exactly how the children had died. That secret went to the grave with him.

CHAPTER 18

UNEQUAL JUSTICE

Daniel Wright Bardsley was one of Oldham's most respected traders. His bookseller's and stationer's shop in Yorkshire Street had been established over twenty years and was highly successful. A conservative, god-fearing man, whose grey hair and beard made him appear somewhat older than his fifty-four years, Mr Bardsley was a regular attender at the Salem Moravian Church. He was also a member of the Oldham Lyceum and a keen supporter of local amateur theatre.

As a boy, he had attended Mr Buckley's school in Queen Street. In those days, such items as books, pens, pencils and so on were purchased direct from the local stationer's, and young Daniel was often sent to collect them from the High Street shop of Mr W.E. Clegg, the well-known stationer and bookseller. Mr Clegg took a liking to young Bardsley, finding him well-mannered, respectful and eager to please.

When Daniel left school, at the age of thirteen, he was offered a position at Clegg's and was delighted to accept. Mr Clegg had not been wrong about him, for the boy was intelligent and worked so hard that within a matter of months he had acquainted himself with virtually every aspect of the business and could be trusted to carry out his duties just as efficiently as any of the older, more experienced members of the staff.

Over the next twenty years, Daniel played a major part in the expansion of Clegg's business, particularly in supplying schools throughout the North of England. Around 1892 Mr Clegg moved his business to Market Place. Daniel was now in his early thirties and decided that the time had come to strike out on his own. He opened a shop at 36 Yorkshire Street, and did so well that he was soon obliged to take larger premises in the same street, at number 43, near the bottom end of the 'iron railings', a well-known local landmark.

He became so immersed in the business that his social life was extremely limited, so it was hardly surprising that he had never married. For a number of years he had lived with his brother John in nearby Egerton Street. John was not involved in the business, having a good position at Platt Brothers, the textile machinery company.

Daniel Bardsley, though he could not be described as a physically strong man, was in good health and capable of working very long hours at the shop. In fact, he was in the habit of staying quite late some nights, and it was not unusual for him still to be there in the early hours of the following morning.

Bardsley's staff was made up of two female assistants, Annie Leach and Clara Hall, and a boy of eighteen named Edward Hilton, who was employed as a packer and general errand boy. Hilton was a youth of rather low intellect. As a young lad he had attended a special school at Chaucer Street, for children with learning problems, but the teachers there could do nothing with him and he was sent to Sandalbridge, an institution at Alderley in Cheshire, where he made no improvement whatsoever. After this, having committed some minor misdemeanour, he was placed in the hands of Mr Millward, the Police Court Missioner. The boy was obviously mentally defective, and the Missioner decided that a two-year spell at a special school in Canada might well do him some good. Getting him to agree was not too difficult, but once there, young Edward found that he did not like it at all. He soon wrote home saying that he was very lonely and homesick and asking for money to get him back to England. At first his pleas were ignored by his father, who insisted that he stick it out, but later the father took pity on him and sent the money. On his return Edward found it difficult to hold on to a job and held a number of menial positions, in each of which he proved unsatisfactory.

On Saturday 26th July, 1913, Daniel Bardsley opened up the shop as usual at 8-30a.m. and at around 1p.m. went home for lunch to 89 Egerton Street, which was only a matter of minutes away. He was back at the shop just after 2p.m. and was still working in his upstairs office when the last of his staff left at around 10-30p.m. A very long day indeed, but in those days it was normal for shops, especially in the town centre, to stay open until very late on a Saturday.

Edward Hilton put up the gates in the front doorway of the shop and left the premises by the back door at around 10-20p.m. According to a later statement by Miss Annie Leach, he went upstairs and had a conversation with Mr Bardsley before leaving. After Hilton had gone home, Miss Leach went upstairs with the day's takings of £2. It was not unusual for the shop takings to be so low, as most of the business was done through schools and libraries. Miss Leach, who was aware that Hilton had fallen well short of expectations, asked her boss whether or not he had decided to let the boy go.

'Well, he doesn't want to go', was the reply. 'He's asked for another chance'. Mr Bardsley did not say what he intended to do about Hilton, but as Miss Leach was about to leave, he called her back and asked for the address of a young man who had recently been employed at the shop. The two young women then left for home, Mr Bardsley staying behind as usual, to work on his accounts.

A couple of hours later James Greaves, a night watchman employed by the Upper Yorkshire Street Private Watch, of which Mr Bardsley was a member, was making his rounds. As he passed the Town Hall he observed two police constables standing on a corner, and glancing up at the Parish Church clock, noted that it read 12-45. Greaves then continued on his rounds, trying doors as he made his way down Yorkshire Street.

James Greaves, who lived in Frankhill Street, close to the town centre, was a watchman of considerable experience. He had been in the job for over twelve years and was known to be a thoroughly reliable and conscientious man. A couple of years previously he had captured an intruder who had broken into the Coliseum Theatre for the purpose of burglary, and who was subsequently sentenced to 18 months' imprisonment.

After checking the front doors, he made his way to the rear of the block. On this narrow thoroughfare, Church Lane, a large yard served several business premises, each of which had its own gate, giving access to a smaller yard and the back door. Had he seen a light in the upstairs room of Bardsley's Book Shop, Greaves would have thought nothing of it, for he knew that Daniel Bardsley often worked late in his office. On this particular occasion, however, according to the night watchman, the premises were in darkness and the back door secure.

It was well after three o'clock in the morning before Greaves reached the same spot on his next round. Everything was quiet as he made his way down the alley, and all appeared normal until he reached the back gate of number 43, which was now standing open. Stepping inside the yard, he tried the back door of the shop. It was on the latch, but not locked, as it should have been. Greaves could not get the door open more than a few inches, as there appeared to be something wedged behind it. Putting his shoulder against it, he managed to force it open enough to get inside, and on shining his torch on what had caused the obstruction, Greaves gasped in horror. On the floor lay the dead body of Daniel Bardsley, his feet up against the door and a pool of blood on the floor beneath his head.

Greaves made sure that no one else was in the room, but did not go upstairs. He shut the back door and within a few minutes was at Oldham Police Station, which was situated in the Town Hall building at the top of Yorkshire Street. He was accompanied back to Bardsley's shop by Inspector Johnson, who made a brief examination of the body before checking the premises. On the ground floor was the shop and the back room where the body was discovered, plus a small kitchen. The upstairs consisted of three rooms, two at the rear of the premises and a larger one at the front. This had served as Mr Bardsley's office and was the room in which he had last been seen alive.

The Police Surgeon, Dr Fort, had been sent for, and while he waited for the doctor to arrive Inspector Johnson examined the scene more closely. Initially, he did not assume that Mr Bardsley had been the victim of foul play. He might well have had a fall and sustained a head injury. Close by, however, lay an Indian club and a dumb-bell, both of which seemed to the Inspector to be out of place in a booksellers' and stationers' shop. On closer examination, he found what appeared to be traces of blood on the club. On the floor close to the body lay Mr Bardsley's bunch of keys and several letters addressed and stamped, ready to post. The key to the back door was also found on the floor.

Dr Fort was soon on the scene, and after a brief examination arranged for the body to be taken to the mortuary. The same afternoon, Dr Jackson, pathologist at the Oldham Royal Infirmary, carried out a post mortem, which revealed that the head had been battered by two or more blows, delivered with such tremendous force that the skull was fractured from its base all the way up to the forehead. There was also a gaping wound in the throat, as though the chin had been forced down onto something solid.

Annie Leach and Clara Hall were contacted on the Sunday morning, and both were badly shaken when told of the tragedy. Miss Leach, who had been with Mr Bardsley for over eleven years, told the police that she had delivered the shop takings to Mr Bardsley in his upstairs office, leaving a float of twenty shillings in the shop till. She also mentioned that on the Saturday morning Mr Bardsley had sent Clara Hall to Hirst's, the jewellers, as he wished to buy a signet ring. She had returned with six rings, on approval, and placed them on Mr Bardsley's desk.

Around noon that day Detective-Inspector Pigott and Detective Jones called at 195, Manchester Street, where Edward Hilton lived. They spoke to his father, who was a barber, informing him of the tragedy and explaining that they wished to speak to the boy, as he had been one of the last people to see Mr Bardsley alive. Hilton was questioned, and as a result of the interrogation and also the state of his clothing, he was taken into custody.

As a direct result of their interview with Hilton the police made a second arrest later that day, that of Ernest Edwin Kelly, aged 20, at his home in Ward Street, off the Rochdale Road. He was told that Hilton had confessed to the killing and had said that a pal had also been involved, the pal being Kelly.

The two youths were brought before the magistrates on the following morning, charged with murder. The court was packed, but it was after 11-30 before the case was dealt with and Kelly and Hilton placed in the dock. A press photographer who attempted to take a picture of the two men was ordered out of the courtroom by a police constable. Both Hilton and Kelly were under-sized individuals and rather poorly dressed, Kelly's clothing, in particular, being rough and dirty.

The Chief Constable, Mr D.H. Turner, announced that Ernest Edwin Kelly and Edward Wild Hilton were charged with having feloniously, wilfully, and with malice aforethought, murdered Daniel Wright Bardsley at number 43, Yorkshire Street, some time between 10-30p.m. on 26th July and 3a.m. on the 27th.

It was revealed that Hilton had been given notice of the termination of his employment at the time of the killing. He was believed to have left the shop at 10-20p.m. that night and, as far as was known, Mr Bardsley was alone when the two female assistants left at 10-30p.m. The Indian club and the dumb-bell were put forward as exhibits by the Chief Constable and were examined by the magistrates. The club was an old one and was chipped and dirty-looking. It weighed between four and five pounds and there were dark stains on it which could well have been blood stains, and also a number of grey hairs still adhering to the rough edges of the wood.

When charged, Hilton replied,

'Not guilty. I never touched him with the club. I never touched him with anything. I gave him a drink of water, that's all'.

Kelly said, 'Guilty for me. I hit him on the head once with the club and threw it down. And he, (indicating Hilton), hit him twice, then ran upstairs'.

The court was told that no money had been found in the pockets of Mr Bardsley's clothing, and the till drawer was found open and empty, so it would appear that robbery was the motive. Possibly, the robbers had been surprised by Mr Bardsley and had attacked him with the Indian club. Neither it, nor the dumb-bell, had been on the premises prior to the murder.

Mentioning that a small amount of the stolen cash had been recovered, the Chief Constable went on to state that certain items of clothing had been sent to the Public Analyst, among them a pair of socks belonging to Hilton, which were saturated with what he believed to be blood. He therefore proposed to ask for a remand for one week. Mr Nicholson, of Mr F. Megson's office, appearing for Hilton, said he had no objection. Kelly was asked by Mr Hesketh Booth, the Clerk to the Magistrates, if he had any objection to this. He replied that he had not. The prisoners were then taken down to the cells.

At the inquest, evidence was given by Mr John Andrew Bardsley, brother of the deceased, by the night watchman and also by Detective Jones and

Inspector Pigott, who told the court that, on being interviewed at his home, Kelly had said,

> 'Well, come into the front room. Don't let my mother hear'. Once in the front room, he had said, 'I'll show you where I put all I got'.

Detective Jones had then accompanied the youth into the back yard, where Kelly indicated a spot near the wall of a closet, or outside toilet. The sum of 9s-6d in silver, 1s-8$\frac{1}{2}$d in copper, four rings and four keys, were found buried under a few inches of dirt. Kelly was taken to the police station and told to strip. His coat and also his socks were badly stained with what appeared to be blood.

That same evening, Detective-Inspector Pigott had accompanied Hilton to a back passage off Painter Street, where the youth had reached into a hole in one of the yard walls and pulled out a handkerchief in which were wrapped 23s-6d in silver, 4$\frac{1}{2}$d in copper and two gold rings. Hilton admitted that it was the property of Mr Bardsley.

Finally, the Coroner addressed the jury:

> 'Well, gentlemen, you have heard all the evidence. Can you please come to a verdict?'

The jury members retired to a private room. After they had left the court Hilton could no longer hide his emotions and gave way to tears. The prisoners were not kept waiting long, however, to hear their fate, for after only thirteen minutes the jurors filed back into the courtroom, looking very sombre indeed.

The foreman announced that they were in unanimous agreement. The verdict was one of 'Wilful Murder' against both prisoners. The Coroner remarked that, in his opinion, the jury could hardly have arrived at any other verdict. Though having been found guilty by the Coroner's Court, the two youths would still be required to return again and face the magistrates. In the meantime, they were locked up in Strangeways Prison.

On the Thursday following his untimely death, the body of Daniel Wright Bardsley was conveyed from his home in Egerton Street, in a coffin of the finest English oak with silver mounted handles. The blinds of every house in the street were drawn and a large crowd assembled to watch the funeral cortège depart for GreenacresCemetery, a procession of ten carriages following the horse-drawn hearse and several hundred people lining the pavements along the route. Among the many floral tributes was one sent by Mr and Mrs J. Hilton, the parents of Edward Hilton.

On Monday 12th August, Hilton and Kelly were brought up at Oldham Police Court. Among those present were Mr Pearce, representing the Public Prosecutor's Office. Mr W. Lees appeared for Kelly, while Mr R. McCleary, instructed by Mr Nicholson, appeared on behalf of Edward Hilton. After the evidence of the Public Analyst had closed the case for the Prosecution, Mr McCleary informed the court that he proposed to call his client to the witness stand, to give his account of what had occurred at the bookshop on the night in question. Mr W. Lees immediately rose and said that it had not been his intention to call his client, but he would now be obliged to do so, as it was only fair that Kelly's evidence should be put on record as well as Hilton's. This proved to be a wise move, for as it turned out, each attempted to throw most of the blame for what had happened on to the other.

Hilton told the court that he had got to know Kelly at around the time that he had gone to work at Bardsley's.

He was asked by Mr McCleary,

'At some time before ten o'clock that night had you occasion to go into the back yard of the shop?'

'Yes sir', was the reply.

'Did you see someone there?'

'Yes sir, Kelly'.

'What did he want?'

'He asked me if I wanted to go to Hollinwood Wakes* with him'. I said, '"yes", I'd go. He asked me if I had any money and I told him I would have when I'd got my wages'.

'What did he say then?'

'He asked me if Mr Bardsley had any. I told him, "yes, but it's in the safe".'

'What did Kelly say next?'

'He said, "We'll attack him".'

'What did you say to that?'

'I said, "No, we'll wait till he's gone home".'

'What happened then?'

'Kelly went off home, and I saw him again after I left the shop'.

'At what time would that be?'

'About twenty-past-ten'.

Hilton explained that it was his duty to fix the gate in the doorway at the front of the shop and lock the front door. After going upstairs to see Mr Bardsley and drawing his wages, he had left as usual by the back door, leaving it on the catch. He had then met Kelly again.

'Had he anything with him?'

'Not that I know of'.

* Annual Fair.

Hilton told the court that he had waited around the corner with Kelly until the two girls left. He had then gone back into the shop and Kelly had followed.

'Did you know that he would follow you into the shop?'
'No sir'.
'What was your reason for going back into the shop?' asked Mr McCleary. 'I'd left my apron behind'.
'When you got inside, did you see Mr Bardsley?'
'Yes sir'.
'Did he say anything to you?'
'Yes, he asked me what I wer' doing there, and I told him I'd come back for my apron. He told me to go and get it, and I went into the shop'.
'When you were in the shop did you hear anything?'
'Yes, I heard a noise like, "Oh!".'
'What happened then?'
'I came out of the shop into the back room again'.
'What did you see when you got into the back room?'
'I saw Mr Bardsley falling against the steps'.
'Did you see anyone else there?'
'Yes, Kelly. He had that club in his hands. He wer' close to Mr Bardsley, who wer' trying to get up. He had one hand on the floor and the other on a shelf'.
'What was Kelly doing?'
'He wer' going to hit him again'.
'Did you say anything'.
'Yes, I said, "Wait a bit till I get out of the shop, or I'll get catched".'
'What happened next?'
'Kelly hit him with the club on the left side of his face'.
'Did you say anything?'
'Yes, he wer' going to hit him again and I told him not to do'.
'Did you do anything?'
'I told him God would punish us if he did it again'.
'Did Kelly say anything?'
'Yes, he swore, then he hit him again. Then he dropped the club on the floor. I picked it up and put it on a box'.
'Was Mr Bardsley conscious during this time?'
'Yes, sir, he wer' trying to get up'.
'Did he touch you at all?'
'Yes, sir, when I wer' giving him some water — that wer' after'.
'Oh yes, but we'll come to that later. Did you get some blood on you?'

'Yes, after I put the club on the box I saw that my hand wer' full of blood'.
'Did Kelly remain in the room?'
'No, he went upstairs, and I went with him. While we were up there I heard Mr Bardsley moaning and I came back down'.
'What happened when you came down again?'
'I filled a cup with water and poured some down Mr Bardsley's throat'.
'Then what?'
'He got hold of my hand and tried to get up. Kelly wer' still upstairs and I called out to him that Mr Bardsley wer' trying to get up. He came running down and got hold of the club. He wer' going to hit Mr Bardsley again and I grabbed hold of his arm, but he hit him again, on the left side of his head'.
'Did you do anything?'
'Mr Bardsley wer' making a noise and I got a cloth and wiped his face with it. Kelly told me to put it in his mouth so that people outside wouldn't hear him making a noise'.
'Did you put it in his mouth?'
'No, sir, only on his face'.
'What happened next?'
'Kelly got hold of the cloth and screwed it up, then put it in Mr Bardsley's mouth. Then he went through Mr Bardsley's pockets and pulled some letters out of his coat pocket, then some keys from his trouser pocket'.
'Anything else?'
'Yes, he got a handful of money and put it in his own pocket. Then he got some silver and a small parcel. There were six rings inside. He gave two of them to me and kept the other four. Then he gave me some silver. About 5s-6d'.
'What next?'
'Well, he got the keys off the floor and we went upstairs. I tried to open the safe with a screwdriver. Kelly said "No, that's no good, I've got the keys here". He tried to open the safe with the keys, but none of them would fit. He then tried to force it with the screwdriver, but couldn't open it. I left him and went downstairs and into the shop. I got some money from a box on a shelf. Then I left and Kelly followed after'.
'Where did you next see Kelly that night?'
'It wer' later on. At the corner of Rock Street'.
'Was that the last time you saw him?'
'Yes'.
'Did you at any time hit Mr Bardsley with that club?'
'No, sir'.

'Or with the dumb-bell?'
'No, sir, that wer' not used at all'.
'Or with anything?'
'No, I only gave him a drink of water'.

Hilton may have been of low intelligence, but he had answered every question put to him clearly and quite convincingly. Mr Pearce now rose to cross-examine.

'Were you under notice to quit Mr Bardsley's shop?'
'Yes'.
'When did he give you notice?'
'About ten minutes past ten on Saturday night'.
'To leave when?'
'To leave on the week following'.
'Was that when he paid you your wages?'
'Just before he paid me my wages'.
'What money did he pay you that night?'
'Sixteen shillings'.
'Did you spend any money that night?'
'Yes, I spent 3s-2d'.
'And what did you do with the rest of the money?
'I gave it to my mother next morning'.
'How much did you give to your mother?'
'Fifteen shillings and sixpence'.
'Did you know that Mr Bardsley had those rings?'
'Yes'.
'How did you come to see them?'
'He had them in his hands at half past three that afternoon, when he wer' telling me to go and deliver some parcels to the Lyceum, in Union Street'.
'When you and Kelly went into Mr Bardsley's shop that night you intended to rob it, didn't you?'
'Yes'.
'You say the cloth was put into his mouth. Was it in his mouth when you left?'
'Yes sir'.
'I think it was on Friday the 25th that you made the arrangement to go with Kelly to Hollinwood Wakes on Saturday the 26th'.
'Yes'.
'Did you suggest to him that Mr Bardsley would be alone and you could rob him?'
'No, sir'.
'Did you say to Kelly "Have you got anything to hit him with?".'
'No, sir'.

'Did Kelly say "Yes, I've got a club in our yard"?'
'No, sir'.
'I suggest to you that after he mentioned the club he said "Lend me a penny and I'll catch a tram and go and fetch it", and you lent him sixpence'.
'No, I lent him sixpence, but not for that'.
'After Kelly came back with the club and met you again round the back, did you both get into the shop through the back door and find a hiding place?', he was asked by Mr Lees, representing Kelly.
'No, sir'.
'While you were in the hiding place did Mr Bardsley come downstairs to lock the back door?'
'He's just said that he was not in any hiding place', cut in Mr McCleary.
'I know that', replied Mr Lees. 'Did Mr Bardsley come down to fasten the back door?'
'I couldn't tell you what he came downstairs for. I saw him come down when I was going in for my apron'.
'In the shop, did you say to Kelly "Here, take this club. I might not hit him hard enough"?'
'No, sir'.
'What time elapsed between your going into the shop and leaving it?'
'It wer' twenty-five-to-eleven when we went in'.
'How do you know that?'
'On account of the girls going out. I guessed at the time because they said it wer' half-past-ten when they came out'.
'What time did you leave?'
'When I left the shop it wer' twenty-five-to-twelve'.
'What were you doing in there for an hour?'
'Trying to get into the safe'.
'How long did it take to settle Mr Bardsley?'
'He wer' struck seven times'.

Hilton's assessment of the time, 11-35p.m., could not have been accurate, for according to the nightwatchman it would have been close to 1a.m when he checked the back door of the premises. Either that, or the watchman was mistaken. If he had, in fact, tried the back door and found it secure as he claimed, then Kelly and Hilton must have been inside at the time, for when they left the scene the back door was unlocked and the gate stood open.

Quite possibly the watchman did not, in truth, carry out a check on the rear of the block on his first round as claimed.

Soon afterwards Kelly took the witness stand to be examined by Mr Lees. The youth, described as a hoist attendant employed at Platt Brothers, told the court that he had just turned twenty and had only met Hilton three weeks or so before the murder. On Friday night, the 25th, they had gone together to the pictures, and before parting, Hilton had said,

'Come up tomorrow night and meet me outside the shop and we'll go to Hollinwood Wakes'.

According to Kelly, he had met Hilton in the back yard of the shop that Saturday night before ten o'clock. Hilton told him that he thought Mr Bardsley was going to sack him, and added,

'He'll be in by himself tonight, after they've all gone'.
'What did you say to that?', Kelly was asked by Mr Lees.
'I said, "What about it?".'
'And what did he reply?'
'He said, "We'll rob him. Have you anything to hit him with?" I told him I had an old club, and he said, "Well, fetch it then".'
'And did you?'
'Yes, it didn't take me long. I got the tram there and back, and got off outside Bardsley's front door. Then I went round the back. Hilton came out and said that the two girls would be leaving in a few minutes. So we hid round a corner till they'd gone'.
'Did Hilton suggest that you both take off your boots, so as to move about quietly?'
'Yes, and we did. We left them round the corner near some ladders. Then we crept in at the back door of the shop. We waited about ten minutes, then Hilton said, "You take t'club. I might not hit him hard enough".'
'And did you?'
'Yes'.
'And shortly afterwards, did Mr Bardsley come down the stairs?'
'Yes'.
'And where did you hide?'
'I wer' in the cellar and he wer' under the stairs facing me. Only about two yards away'.
'What happened then?'
'Mr Bardsley came down and locked the back door. It wer' dim in there, and Hilton said, in a man's voice ,"Hands up".'
'What happened when he said, "Hands up"?'
'Mr Bardsley made a rush for the gas and turned it up. Then he ran to the back door and tried to get out, but he'd just locked it and the key wer' in his pocket'.
'What did he do then?'
'He wer' running away from t'back door and fell on his face'.

'At this time, was he struck with the club?'
'Yes, I struck him on the shoulder just as he wer' falling'.
'What did you do next?'
'I threw t'club down and turned him over on his back'.
'Why did you do that?'
'Because I thought he'd hurt himself very much with falling'.
'And had he?'
'No, only his nose were bleeding'.
'What made you think he was not badly hurt?'
'Because when I turned him over he tried to get up, but then Hilton hit him on't th'ed wit' club'.
'What happened then?'
'Hilton threw t'club down and started going through his pockets'.
'Did you both go through his pockets?'
'Yes'.
'After you'd been upstairs and failed to open the safe, did you both come downstairs, Hilton first, and did he tell you that he'd given Mr Bardsley a drink of water?'
'Yes, and I said, "Is there anything in here to mop his face with?" and he went and got this cloth like'.
'What was done with the cloth?'
'I took it and wiped Mr Bardsley's face with it'.
'And after that?'
'He opened his eyes and wer' feeling for something to lift himself up with'.
'What then?'
'Hilton had the key and wer' unlocking the back door. Then we went outside and put us boots on'.
'Did Hilton then go back on his own into the shop?'
'Yes, he said he'd forgot something'.
'Did he say what he had forgotten?'
'No. He said he would meet me in Rock Street. I got there and waited about five minutes, but he didn't come. So I went across Tommyfield and saw him agen't' Market Hotel'.
'What happened then?'
'We went round Cheapside and down New Radcliffe Street, then down Grosvenor Street and onto Middleton Road. We went into a closet near t'Newland Mill,* and divided up the money and the rings'.
'So as far as you know, how many blows were struck?'
'Two blows, one on t'shoulder and one ont'th'ed'.

* Oldham Technical College was later built on this site.

Mr McCleary said he did not wish to question Kelly, but the witness was asked by Mr Pearce,

'For what purpose did you take that club to the shop?'

'I took it with the intention of striking him, but not with the intention of doing him much harm'.

So ended the evidence. The two prisoners were then formally committed to take their trial at the next Manchester Assizes. Before the magistrates rose Mr Lees applied for financial aid under the Poor Prisoners' Defence Act, pointing out that the total sum would be only two guineas for the solicitor and one guinea for the barrister, and mentioning that Kelly was in a very poor way. The application was granted.

It was on 24th November, over a month later, that the two Oldham youths were brought up at the Assizes to stand trial for murder. Before the proceedings opened a considerable crowd had gathered outside the court buildings, but the general public were not allowed inside until all of the 'legal' people, including the judges, had arrived. When the doors were finally opened there was a rush to get the best seats. A large number of ladies took possession of the gallery seats, leaving standing room only at the rear of the court.

Mr McCleary said that he appeared for the prisoner, Hilton, and wished to make an application to the court.

'When the case was before the magistrates the prisoners made statements on oath, each implicating the other. That being so, the application is that his Lordship should direct that there be two separate trials'.

His Lordship had the power to do so, he said, citing a precedent at Stafford Assizes in 1857 in the case of Regina v Jackson.

Invited by the judge, Mr Justice Bramwell, to give his opinion on this point, Mr Gordon Hewart, K.C., M.P., conducting the Prosecution for the Crown, said that he could see no benefit to either of the prisoners in separate trials, while Mr Roe-Rycroft, instructed by Mr W. Lees on behalf of Kelly, opposed the application, pointing out that at the Magistrates' Court Mr McCleary had called his own client first, and the total effect of Hilton's evidence had been to throw the blame on to his co-Defendant. If the application were acceded to it would be prejudicial to Kelly.

Mr McCleary did not agree, arguing that,

'Mr Roe-Rycroft wants to make his own defence out of me'.

After further arguments were put, the judge came to his decision.

'Having regard, particularly to the fact that one of the prisoners has objected, and for a reason that I can appreciate, I must decline to grant the application'.

The prisoners were then called, and were brought up from the cells and placed in the dock. Both were respectably dressed on this occasion. In place of the mufflers they had worn at the Magistrates' Court, each sported a smart collar and tie. Both boys, however, appeared very subdued, and it was clear that they now fully realised the seriousness of their situation. When charged, both replied, 'Not Guilty'.

The entire circumstances of the case were then presented to the court by the Prosecution, from the time the shop was closed for business and the staff left the premises on that fateful Saturday night, to the arrest of the two suspects on the following day. Mr Hewart went into great and gory detail in describing the horrific scene that greeted the night watchman when he pushed open the back door and shone his torch on the dead body of Daniel Wright Bardsley in the early hours of Sunday morning, 27th July.

'The victim's head and face were covered in blood. It was all over his hair and his beard. There was blood on his clenched hands, on his shirt front and even on the goods stacked on the shelves around him. The shelves, in fact, had blood on them up to a height of two feet from the floor. There was a pool of blood under Mr Bardsley's head. There was an Indian club and a dumb-bell lying around and also keys and letters there on the floor, addressed and stamped and apparently ready to post. Everything, in short, pointed to the conclusion that the unfortunate man had been attacked with great violence just as he was about to leave the premises. He was murdered and his pockets rifled. The blows which caused the injuries were repeated blows of considerable force. The next question is then, who were the perpetrators of this repulsive and cowardly crime?'

As the case proceeded both prisoners were called to the stand to give evidence, along with a number of other witnesses, including the two young lady shop assistants and the night watchman. Their evidence, however, did not differ in any significant detail from that given before the magistrates.

Mr Ernest Arthur Wagstaff of Manchester, the analyst, stated that he had found both the Indian club and also the dumb-bell to be smeared with blood, and there were grey hairs on both exhibits. He had found some blood on Hilton's trousers, but nothing on those of Kelly.

After the examination of Hilton, which had taken an hour and a half, was completed, Mr McCleary called Dr W.N. East, resident surgeon at Strangeways Prison, who stated that the prisoner Hilton had been under his care for almost four months.

'And what do you say as to the boy's state of mind', asked McCleary.

'Just a minute', interposed the judge. 'I don't quite follow this. You have put forward a defence that he had no part in the murder, only the robbery. Are you now going to put forward a defence on the grounds of insanity?'

'No sir, not at all'.

'Then it's not relevant. So what's the good of placing it before the jury?'

'Very well, if your Lordship pleases. I won't call the evidence'.

In his summing up Mr McCleary laboured the point that while Hilton might be guilty up to the hilt of the crime of breaking-in and robbery, he would put it to the jury that this was a matter very different from the capital charge. He added that he did not think that the jury would consider Kelly's story to be accurate, and pointed out that his client had told substantially the same story from the very beginning, and had been subjected to the most severe cross-examination. He placed much emphasis on the fact that Hilton had given the victim a drink of water. It was suggested by Kelly that Hilton had been guilty of brutality. They knew that there had been extreme brutality on the part of someone, and if they were convinced that Hilton had given Mr Bardsley a drink of water while he was suffering, was that not humane and therefore inconsistent with brutality?

Speaking on behalf of Kelly, Mr Roe-Rycroft began by saying that at the Magistrates' Court Hilton had sought to throw practically the whole of the blame for the crime onto his client.

'I do not try to excuse Kelly for the part he took. If two persons act in the furtherance of a crime, both are responsible'.

Roe-Rycroft maintained that while the victim may have been attacked by both during the course of the robbery, the joint act ceased once the two had left the premises. He then went on to suggest that Hilton had returned to the scene of the crime on the pretext of having forgotten something and had completed the murder.

Mr Justice Bramwell, in summing-up, was relatively brief and very much to the point. He said that the proposition was so simple that it was hardly necessary for him to expound it to the jury.

'These two persons agreed together to commit a felony, and agreed, in order to carry out that common purpose, to use violence, which might cause the death of the victim or grievous bodily harm. If death ensues from that violence, then both are guilty of murder. Kelly admitted that he struck one blow after Mr Bardsley had fallen and injured himself. Hilton has claimed that he was never a party to any agreement that violence should be used on Mr Bardsley. He said he begged Kelly not to strike him again. Can the jury accept this?'

The judge then went on to consider Hilton's own evidence as to what took place after he had said, 'Don't hit him again or God will punish us for it!'

'He took Kelly upstairs to show him where the safe was, and when Mr Bardsley moaned he brought him down again. He said he did not put the cloth in his mouth, but wiped his face with it. Afterwards, they went through the victim's pockets and divided the spoils. Can the jury believe that a person who protested against violence would then take part in the division of the plunder? It is no answer to the proposition of law I have put to you to say that the prisoners did not intend to kill the man they proposed to rob. It is impossible to suggest that both men were not party to the violence that was used. Both admitted that they combined to rob the victim.

'The jury have more than once been reminded of the extreme youth of the prisoners. This, of course, might make your duty more painful, but it cannot alter either the law or the facts. Your duty is to render your verdict according to the evidence, and this you must do, irrespective of persons or the ages of those persons'.

The jury then filed out. Very few of the spectators left the courtroom, and there was an expectant buzz as they waited for the verdict. The jury took only twenty minutes or so to decide the fate of the two young men. In delivering the inevitable verdict of 'Guilty', the foreman added,

'We recommend mercy in the case of both of them, on the grounds of their youth'.

Both Kelly and Hilton appeared composed as they waited for the judge to pronounce sentence, neither showing the slightest emotion. When asked if they had anything to say why the court should not pass judgment according to law, each in turn replied,

'No'.

'You have been convicted of a cold-blooded murder', said the judge gravely, 'aggravated, if such a crime can be aggravated, by the callousness with which each of you has given evidence in this court, seeking to put the blame on your fellow criminal. The jury believe that you are too young to die the degrading death to which, by law, you are subject. It lies not with me to express any opinion or to hold out any hope to you as to the effect of the jury's recommendation for mercy, which will, of course, be forwarded to the proper quarter, where alone it can be considered. You hurried your victim into eternity without giving him time to make any preparation to meet his maker. The law is more merciful to you. It gives you that time.

'My duty is to pass upon you the sentence of the law; which is that each of you be taken from hence to a lawful prison, thence to a place of execution. That you there be hanged by the neck until you are dead, and your bodies be then buried within the precincts of the prison where you shall be confined before your execution. And may the Lord have mercy on your souls. Amen'.

It would be quite true to say that the people of Oldham were shaken to the core when details of the crime first appeared in the newspapers. That a hard-working, highly respected, local tradesman should be murdered, and in such a callous and brutal manner on his own premises, was almost too shocking to believe. The locals were up in arms, outraged and screaming for punishment to be meted out to the culprits, who were already in custody. Once the death sentences were pronounced, however, a surprisingly large number of people suddenly seemed very concerned about the two young men now incarcerated in Strangeways. The shock and horror of the crime itself had apparently, within a few short weeks, faded gradually from the public mind. The mental agony and the pain would now be borne only by those closest to the victim, for the death of Daniel Bardsley was yesterday's news. The public's concern was now for the murderers.

Petitions for reprieve were instigated all over the town and much further afield. Signatures were obtained in their thousands, and at a rapid rate, for great urgency was called for, as time was running out.

An uncle and aunt of Hilton, Mr and Mrs George Hibbert, of Shaw, were allowed to visit their nephew in his cell on Saturday, 13th December. They found him looking quite cheerful. He expressed regret for what had happened and said that he hoped for the best, but was prepared for the worst. He blamed his fate on going about with bad companions, and insisted that he had never done anything to Mr Bardsley except give him a drink of water.

A warder told the visitors that both prisoners were in such good spirits that he had come to the conclusion that they did not fully appreciate their position. Perhaps, having been told by their families that over 20,000 people had signed petitions on their behalf, they did not believe that they were heading for the gallows.

On Sunday morning, 14th December, a letter was delivered by special messenger to Strangeways Prison. It was addressed to the Governor, Major Nelson, and read:

> *Home Office, Whitehall, December 13th 1913.*
>
> *Sir, In reply to the petition received by this office on behalf of Edward Wild Hilton and Ernest Edwin Kelly, now lying under*

> *sentence of death at His Majesty's Prison in Manchester, I am directed to acquaint you that in the case of Edward Wild Hilton, in view of his youth and mental weakness, the Secretary of State has felt warranted, in all the circumstances, in advising His Majesty to respite the capital sentence with a view to commutation to penal servitude for life, but in the case of Ernest Edwin Kelly, he regrets that, after considering all the circumstances of the case, he has failed to discover any grounds which would justify him in advising His Majesty to interfere with the due course of the law.*

News of their son's reprieve was conveyed to Mr and Mrs Hilton by the Reverend Eaves, curate of St Andrew's. They were naturally greatly relieved, but at the same time offered their sympathy to the parents of Kelly.

Great shock and strong feelings of incredulity and indignation were expressed by the majority of Oldhamers at the difference in treatment of the two lads. As details of the evidence produced at the trial were discussed over and over again, it became increasingly clear that public opinion was very sharply divided as to which of the two had contributed most to the killing. A surprising number of people, in fact, appeared to believe that Kelly had told the truth when he claimed that the victim was not terminally injured when he and Hilton left the premises together that night. As Hilton had gone back into the shop on his own and did not immediately re-join Kelly, many people suspected that he might well have completed the job.

Very few people could fail to agree that as the two had acted in concert they were equally guilty. So if one was to be hanged, they both should hang, and if one was to be reprieved, then the same mercy should be shown to the other.

A mass meeting was held outside the premises of Platt Brothers, where Kelly had worked, on the day following the receipt of the Home Secretary's letter, a Mr Jesse Mills presiding. A stormy meeting ended with a resolution being passed, stating:

> *That this meeting, representing all classes of workers at Messrs. Platt Bros & Co., Werneth, strongly protests against the decision of the Home Secretary in respect of the petition for Hilton and demands equal treatment for both men. Copies of this resolution to be sent to the Mayor of Oldham and the Home Secretary.*

The Mayor of Oldham, Alderman Herbert Wilde, had already sent a telegram to the Home Office, which ran:

> *Oldham Murder; Great indignation that Hilton only should be reprieved. Public meeting tonight to recommend reprieve for Kelly. Will forward copy of resolution… Wilde, Mayor.*

Amidst all the furore, a certain barber in nearby Rochdale was following the case with a growing feeling of apprehension. Jack Ellis had been informed of the appointment two weeks previously and had accepted with some misgivings. As an experienced executioner he knew he had no option but to accept, even though the town of Oldham was very close to Rochdale. Mind you, only a few years before he had hanged young Jack Griffiths from Shaw, and Shaw was even closer. He knew all about the petitions for reprieve which had been flying about. If they succeeded, all well and good. If they failed he would simply do his job and that would be the end of it. What he had not reckoned on was that one lad would be reprieved and the other would have to die. Ellis was now in a very difficult position, and made it a point not to discuss the case, particularly in view of the fact that when it was mentioned in his presence, he found himself the recipient of cold and hostile looks. The news of Hilton's reprieve was made public only a couple of days before he was due to hang Kelly. At this stage, frantic efforts were being made to persuade the Home Secretary to relent and grant a second reprieve. Ellis must surely have been hoping against hope that this would happen.

In a letter to his parents, written on official prison notepaper, Kelly insisted that he was innocent of the charge of murder.

> *In the first place, if the crime had been done while I was there I would have had blood on my clothes like Hilton had... I told Hilton to get the cloth and I wiped Mr Bardsley's face with it. He opened his eyes and said... 'Oh dear, where am I?'...I said to him to lie down and he'd be all right in a minute. Hilton unlocked the back door with a key he'd got out of Mr Bardsley's pocket and we went out. When we'd got to the end of the entry Hilton said, 'Oh, I forgot something', and went back, while I went on to the end of Rock Street. I didn't see Hilton for about a quarter of an hour after, and that was up in Market Place.*
>
> *I remain your loving son, E.E. Kelly*

As well as the meeting at Platt's, a number of others were convened at various factories in the town, and a great deal of pressure was put on the Mayor to call a public meeting. With time short, Alderman Wilde immediately agreed, the meeting being arranged for that same evening, Monday 15th December, in the large room at the Town Hall. It was called for 8-15p.m., but by late afternoon it had become quite clear that the size of the crowd would far exceed the room's capacity. The Mayor lost no time in setting up an overflow meeting to be held at the Salvation Army Citadel in Union Street. Even so, the turn-out at the Town Hall was absolutely staggering.

Long before the meeting was due to commence, the area to the front of the Town Hall was packed with people, with more arriving all the time. The elevated area opposite, below the churchyard and behind the iron railings, was also crowded. As the time for the commencement of the meeting approached, those inside the Town Hall began to feel rather uneasy, for it was becoming apparent that the densely packed crowd, which by this time had swelled from hundreds into thousands, was in a very ugly mood. One of the reasons for this was believed to have been a rumour that Alderman Mrs Lees, of the well-known Lees family of Werneth Park, bore some responsibility for the difference in treatment of the two prisoners, and that she had used her influence more on Hilton's behalf than on Kelly's. Some people even went so far as to claim that she had actually been against a reprieve for Kelly. All this, of course, was totally untrue, but because of the excited state of the majority of working people in Oldham, this gossip had, unfortunately, taken a hold in the town, to such an extent that the very high level of respect that Mrs Lees had always enjoyed, and to which she was certainly entitled, considering her outstanding record of service to the community, her charitable work and wonderful generosity, appeared to have been completely forgotten.

The crowd outside the Town Hall that night was in an ugly temper, with threats being shouted against the Home Secretary and Mrs Lees, whose safety could not have been guaranteed had she stepped out into the street to face that milling, unruly mass of humanity.

Seeing the size and the mood of the crowd, a section of which could certainly have been described as a mob, the Mayor decided, after consultation with the Chief Constable and members of the Town Council who were present, not to open the Town Hall's doors, but to speak to the crowd from one of the upper windows of the building. Having opened the window, however, and attempted to make himself heard above all the racket, the Mayor withdrew and held a further heated consultation with the Chief Constable. Eventually a megaphone was produced and the Mayor and Mayoress, along with Alderman Mrs Lees, appeared at one of the middle windows of the upper floor.

The Mayor himself was cheered as soon as he was recognized, but the moment Mrs Lees stepped forward a loud hooting and booing came from the crowd. The Mayor tried vainly to get some order, but the booing continued. It seemed amazing that a lady who had done so much for the town and been held in such high esteem only a matter of days before, should have suddenly become so unpopular. Many people in the crowd were shouting for her to go away, but Mrs Lees would not be put off. She just stood there staring down at the hostile crowd, and quietly, but firmly, murmured to those standing at the window with her,

'I shall stay here if I have to stay all night'.

Then at the top of her voice she called out defiantly to the howling mob,

'Are you going to listen to me?' She was answered by further booing and yelling, which continued unabated, until eventually, the Mayor, shouting through the megaphone, told them,

'When I heard of the indignation in the town I called this meeting tonight'. At this there were cheers.

'In the meantime, I have sent a telegram to the Home Secretary, informing him that we in Oldham are very dissatisfied with what has taken place, and to say that if one boy has been reprieved then the other should be. (More cheers)

'Now just listen a moment. Let me ask you to be quiet while I explain with regard to Mrs Lees'.

This only resulted in further unfavourable reaction from the crowd, but the Mayor doggedly persisted.

'Whatever Mrs Lees has done for one...'

Again uproar, which continued for over a minute before the Mayor could continue,

'Mrs Lees signed the petition for both'. (More booing)

'She also went to see both lads in prison. She has done as much for one as she has done for the other'.

There were cries of 'No!', 'No!'

'Yes, I say, yes', persisted the Mayor. 'Mr Barton, M.P., has sent word that he will approach the Home Secretary with me to put the following resolution'. He then produced a paper and read aloud:

> *This public meeting of the inhabitants of the town of Oldham is strongly of the opinion that inasmuch as the death sentence of Edward Wild Hilton has been respited, the same clemency ought to be extended to Ernest Edwin Kelly, the other prisoner, and earnestly hopes that the Secretary of State will be able to give effect to this recommendation.*

The Mayor then told the meeting that he intended to leave for London early the following morning, to seek an interview with the Home Secretary. There were shouts of,

'Go now!'

'We shall ask him in the first instance—'

'Demand it', shouted someone in the crowd.

'We want him to put off the execution for at least a week', continued the Mayor.

'We shall ask him that and let him know what a demonstration there has been here tonight in favour of a respite. (Cheers) Mrs Lees will second the resolution'.

The mention of her name again brought forth loud booing, which noticeably increased in volume as Mrs Lees attempted to speak. It was obvious, however, that the lady possessed a great deal of courage, and clearly had no intention of being intimidated by the mob. She just stood there as the booing continued for what seemed like several minutes, then, as the noise gradually subsided, she spoke calmly and deliberately,

'I beg to second the resolution'.

At this there was more booing and heckling, and it was several more minutes before she could continue. Nevertheless, she waited patiently, and eventually, as they quietened down somewhat, she said,

'I believe that a rumour has been circulated to the effect that I have used my influence on behalf of Hilton, but not on behalf of Kelly. Any influence, I may have, has been used on behalf of both youths equally'.

There was another burst of jeering, which caused the Mayor to appeal to the noisier element to,

'Behave like Englishmen'.

'I signed the petition for both youths', went on Mrs Lees, 'and I also obtained the signatures of a number of influential men in the town. I saw both Mrs Hilton and Mrs Kelly, and I have visited both their sons in Strangeways'.

Even this did not seem to pacify the crowd, and as Mrs Lees went on to say, her voice getting louder as she attempted to speak above the noise,

'I have written to the Home Secretary and several MPs,...' the booing and shouting again increased in volume. The Mayor this time yelled through the megaphone,

'Please, please... be Englishmen... be Britishers. After hearing what Mrs Lees has had to say, and knowing her character, you should certainly be satisfied with the explanations given. Now, you have heard the resolution moved and seconded. Those who are in favour of going to the Home Secretary say 'Aye'.

At this there was a tremendous roar of assent.

'And to the contrary?' To this question there was not one single 'No' and the Mayor declared the resolution carried.

The Mayor then called upon the crowd to disperse, and although he got little response at first, the majority did eventually begin to drift away, encouraged by the police, who had handled the situation very well indeed. The street had, however, been completely blocked for almost two hours, bringing the tramcars to a halt, but they were soon on the move again. Meanwhile, Mrs Lees and the other councillors remained inside the Town Hall for quite a while before leaving for their homes.

The Deputy Mayor, Alderman Ashworth, had taken charge of the overflow meeting at the Salvation Army Citadel, when the name of Mrs Lees again came up. She was ably defended by Mr Ashworth. When he explained to them that she had visited both boys in their prison cells and had gone out of her way to console the stricken parents, they were won over and responded with a spontaneous burst of applause.

The feeling of the meeting was that, in view of the terrible crime, the capital sentence should be carried out, but as the Home Secretary had intervened in the case of Hilton, it would be a grave injustice to hang Kelly. It was the opinion of the Deputy Mayor that the Home Secretary had been strongly influenced by the medical opinion in regard to the state of Hilton's mind.

'If Kelly had been put to the same test', said Alderman Ashworth, 'and been judged in the same way, they might have found that he was also feeble-minded. I can't understand anybody with a healthy mind doing such a dastardly deed'.

His words were greeted with a great burst of applause.

On the following morning, the Mayor and Deputy Mayor, along with the Chief Constable and several others, left for London on the 9-20a.m. train, due to arrive at Euston at 1-15p.m. That same afternoon, John Ellis, attaché case in hand, boarded the train at Rochdale. His destination: Victoria Station, Manchester, close to Strangeways Prison. If Kelly was to be saved there was very little time left.

That evening a letter appeared in the *Oldham Chronicle* :

> *Sir, It is an uncomfortable sensation to feel ashamed of your fellow-townspeople, but the disgraceful scenes of last night, when Mrs Lees was abused by those who should know and appreciate her so well, makes one feel that, after all, the mob is as ignorant and unthinking in Oldham as in other places one has considered less reputable. Even allowing for the excitement and natural indignation at the discrimination (or want of it) which resulted in the reprieve of one of the wretched youths under sentence of death and left the other one (who is popularly supposed to be the less guilty) to suffer the extreme penalty, the occurrence was deplorable. If they wanted a target for abuse, why did they not select the lawyers, or those responsible for the conduct of the trial, who either suppressed or failed to elicit facts concerning Hilton's*

bad character and former life, which would have materially assisted the judge and jury to form a better opinion as to the relative guilt of the accused? As for Mrs Lees, hers is the experience of the reformer of all ages…to be reviled and misunderstood… If the Mental Deficiency Act, or a similar one, had been in force some years ago we should probably not have to deplore the loss of a worthy and respected citizen in the person of the late Mr Bardsley.

The letter was dated 16th December, 1913 and signed, 'Agnes Dornan'

The Mayor's deputation from Oldham was not exactly received with open arms on arriving at the Home Office in London. They did not, in fact, get to see the Home Secretary at all, but were instead met by Sir Edward Troup, Permanent Secretary to the Home Office, and Mr Blackwell, solicitor, and this in spite of the fact that the Mayor's party included two MPs. After going exhaustively over each point raised in the petition they were told that the matter would have to be put before Mr McKenna. They were asked if they could return at 5p.m. that evening, which they did. Then, after being kept waiting for half-an-hour or so, they were told that each point was being studied very carefully and it was suggested that if they returned to Oldham a wire would be sent off to them later that evening. They declined, and were back at the Home Office by 9p.m. After being kept waiting again, for quite some time, they were called into an inner room and handed a letter signed by Sir Edward Troup. Not being happy with the letter's contents, they demanded to see Mr Reginald McKenna, the Home Secretary. An official conveyed the message, and finally, a letter written and signed by the Home Secretary was handed to the deputation.

It read:

I am very sorry to be obliged to refuse to see you. I have given the fullest and most anxious consideration to the representations which have been made to me to mitigate the sentence passed on Kelly, and I deeply regret that I can come to no other decision than that which has been conveyed to you, and it must be regarded as final. R McKenna

Still refusing to accept this, the Mayor's deputation proceeded to 10 Downing Street and attempted to gain an audience with the Prime Minister, who refused to see them.

While the Mayor was in London, trying in vain to see the Home Secretary, the Mayoress sent a telegram to Buckingham Palace, pleading with the Queen to intervene on Kelly's behalf.

It read:

> *May I approach your Majesty to assist us in our endeavour to obtain a reprieve for Kelly, one of the Oldham murderers, who is to be executed tomorrow morning. Hilton, the other prisoner, has been reprieved, and great indignation has been aroused by the decision of the Home Secretary not to treat both prisoners alike. The public feel that the least guilty of the two is to be hanged.*
> *Wilde, Mayoress, Oldham*

At Strangeways Prison the hours and the minutes were inexorably ticking away. While Ellis was making his final preparations and examining the drop and the apparatus, the condemned man was visited by members of his family, several of whom were distraught. When they left the prison that afternoon, being aware that the Mayor's deputation was at that very moment in London pleading for young Kelly's life, they were still hopeful, but by late evening they must have realised that the reprieve was not going to come through.

That evening, a large crowd gathered outside Kelly's home in Ward Street, Oldham. Like almost everyone else in the town they were waiting for the Home Secretary's final decision. When it was made known there was a remarkable display of sympathy from the crowd, many among them weeping. Friends and relatives did their best to comfort the parents, but Mrs Kelly was very badly affected and was in a state of virtual collapse. What she had to say was largely incoherent, but she kept on moaning that her son had not been treated fairly, and that justice had not been done.

Once it was finally accepted that the Oldham deputation's last ditch attempt to sway the Home Secretary had failed, it seemed that all hell was let loose in the town. Large groups of people, mostly men, the majority of whom were young, some inflamed by drink, amassed around the steps of the Town Hall and caused a fearful row. The Home Secretary's name was constantly shouted out, as the mob, which included a number of screeching, raucous females, gave vent to its anger and frustration.

The police were given a very hard time, but managed to keep things under control. Before the evening was out, however, the force would be stretched to its limits, for an unruly-looking mob was already on its way down Manchester Street, heading for Werneth Park, the residence of Mrs Lees and her family. A number of shop windows were smashed as the wrath of the crowd increased in intensity and their ranks swelled rapidly as many more joined them along the way. By the time the gates of Werneth Park were reached the crowd had grown to enormous proportions. Fortunately, the police were on hand to deal with the problem, but when the mob attempted to enter the grounds the police forced them back, and after a struggle, managed to shut the gates and secure them. This reverse seemed to madden the crowd, and their wrath was then directed at Werneth Police Station and Fire Station, both close by. The demonstration had now become a riot.

Telephone calls were made to various other local police stations as bricks were hurled through the windows and the situation threatened to get totally out of hand. The gallant handful of beleaguered bobbies inside were subjected to an extremely harrowing time until the promised reinforcements, which comprised plain clothes as well as uniformed men and a squad of mounted police, began to arrive on the scene. The anger of the mob was then directed at the newcomers, who came under attack from a fusillade of bricks, bottles and various other missiles as they forced their way into the crowd and attempted to break it up. Gradually, the rioters were driven back, and though a few decided to give up and go home, there were many others who seemed determined to linger all night if necessary and cause as much trouble as possible. The police were hissed and booed, but stood their ground and showed commendable patience and restraint in the face of great provocation.

Meanwhile, many hundreds of people were still congregating in the vicinity of the Town Hall, and as the evening wore on their numbers were swollen by people coming out of the town-centre pubs, many of whom were only too eager to join in any kind of demonstration. There was much hooting and general disorder, shouts of 'No work tomorrow' and various references to Mrs Lees, none of which was complimentary.

There were also cries of 'Let's march to Strangeways!' which gathered such momentum that before long a group of several hundred had formed and set off on the seven-mile tramp to Manchester.

By 11p.m. the trouble at Werneth appeared to have died down somewhat, and a concerted attempt was made to clear the streets. But the crowd responded by hurling another shower of bricks, stones and bottles at the police. One officer was hit on the shoulder, while another was struck in the stomach by a half-brick which then came to rest on his saddle. One of the horses was also injured, sustaining a nasty belly-wound. Despite the enormous pressure they were under the police were handling an horrendous and frightening situation with remarkable courage and coolness.

Having done as much damage to the Police Station and Fire Station as possible, short of burning them down, the rioters now turned their attention to other Corporation property, the tramcars passing up and down the road between Oldham and Manchester making easy targets. Completely ignoring the fact that members of the public were on board, the hooligans hurled bricks indiscriminately at the windows, striking fear into the unfortunate

211

passengers and causing an appalling amount of damage. Several of the drivers had narrow escapes, one being hit full in the face by a brick.

At the top of Edward Street, a policeman who tried to prevent a man throwing a brick at one of the tramcars was surrounded and attacked. He drew his truncheon, but was pounced upon and the truncheon torn from his grasp. In defending himself he received many kicks and blows before being rescued by his fellow officers. Near the top of Featherstall Road a police-sergeant was very roughly handled and kicked about the body.

While all this was going on groups of people were still holding protest meetings, one of which took place around the house of Hilton's parents in Manchester Street, where at least three hundred people had gathered. Most of the speakers appeared to be half-drunk, while much of their audience was made up of young women and girls who seemed to be thoroughly enjoying all the excitement. The situation, however, was extremely serious, the damage having reached alarming proportions. More tramcars were attacked, with trolleys being pulled off their wires, while the windows of the Oldham Motor Company's showrooms were smashed, and an attempt was made to overturn a taxicab.

The rioters were now joined by those on their way down to Manchester, who willingly pitched in to make matters even worse. Though the situation appeared to be out of control the police stuck doggedly to their task, with the mounted men continuing to drive the mob back. Eventually, by the early hours of the morning, the situation had eased somewhat, though there were still hundreds of people who stubbornly refused to disperse, loitering around the streets.

Many of the marchers had already continued on to Manchester. Now two further groups set off after them. Windows were broken and street lamps smashed as they went on their way. Just after midnight they passed through Failsworth. Along the route they were joined by others chanting, 'Kelly will not hang', and by 1a.m. were nearing the gaol.

The departure of many of the rioters for Manchester had certainly eased matters around Werneth, but it was getting on for 3 o'clock before all was quiet, most, if not all, of the trouble-makers having gone home to their beds. An all-night guard was stationed around Werneth Park, and the police remained on the alert in case of further trouble.

The mob, many of whom had armed themselves with sticks, shovels and crowbars, had now arrived at their objective, and had congregated at the end of Southall Street, opposite the prison gates, looking very menacing indeed.

The Manchester police had been alerted, having heard all about the riots in Oldham, and were ready for trouble. Men had been drafted in from divisonal stations all around the city, and by early morning over 250 policemen were on duty outside the prison gates and on the streets around the gaol. Another gang from Oldham and other areas north of Manchester was stopped at the bottom of Cheetham Hill Road and prevented from joining those already outside the prison. When they became aggressive the police charged and they scattered, running off in all directions.

Posted up outside the gaol was a notice to the effect that Kelly was to be hanged at 8 o'clock that morning, and several of those in the crowd came closer to read it. Their numbers were increasing rapidly, and with the arrival of Deputy Chief Constable Vaughan on the scene, a line of constables was formed to make a solid wall across the gateway.

On first being sentenced, neither Kelly nor Hilton could have held out any hope of a reprieve, so terrible had been their crime and so outraged had public opinion been against them. But following the commutation of Hilton's sentence and subsequent pressure on the Home Secretary to intervene also in the case of Kelly, it is likely that the prisoner had begun to entertain hopes that he would not, after all, face the hangman. Now, with the last slim chance having disappeared, it would not have been surprising if he had simply gone to pieces. This did not happen. From first arriving at the gaol he had proved an easy prisoner to handle, giving the warders no problems and becoming quite friendly with them. He seemed to relish his meals, and his appetite remained healthy right up until the time he went to bed on the last night. Of course, he had been told that all the efforts on his behalf had come to nothing. He did not sleep well and on rising could not face his breakfast, but smoked a couple of cigarettes, which seemed to help him to relax.

At a few minutes before eight o'clock the execution party gathered outside the condemned cell. As Ellis entered, Kelly was praying earnestly with the Prison Chaplain, who stood back as the hangman approached. But before Ellis could pinion him the prisoner asked if he might speak to the Governor, who stepped forward. Kelly thanked him for his kindness and asked if he might shake hands with him. 'Of course', replied Major Nelson, and offered his hand.

When the pinioning was completed Kelly walked to the drop with a firm step. He did not speak, but looked straight ahead as the noose was slipped around his neck and his head covered. Seconds later the tolling of the prison bell told the thousands gathered around the gaol that it was all over. Kelly was dead. Though many people now began to drift away, a massive crowd still packed the area around the entrance to the prison, while the wall of constables remained in position. Shortly after the tolling of the bell an offical emerged from within and posted a notice on one of the huge doors, proclaiming that the sentence had been carried out.

After it was all over the Governor remarked to a colleague that he had witnessed many an execution, but had never known a man go more bravely to his death.

'There was no swagger, mind you. He just went pluckily and betrayed no fear. He was simply resigned to his fate. He paid the greatest attention to the Chaplain all the time he was here. The Chaplain was most kind, and Kelly repaid that kindness by the deep interest he took in his spiritual ministrations'.

Had he been present Ellis would have been pleased to hear the Governor add, 'The execution was carried out in the most perfect manner. The prisoner would not have felt any pain, as death was instantaneous'.

As he travelled back on the train to Rochdale that morning there was much talk among his fellow passengers about the hanging of Kelly and the reprieve of Hilton. Sitting there with his pipe, unrecognised by those around him, Jack Ellis pondered over the happenings during the weeks leading up to the execution. Of course, as well as following every important case in the newspapers, he had been closely involved for a number of years now in the whole business of being appointed to hang a convicted man, the uncertainty pending appeals and public petitions, the Home Secretary's final decision, often at the eleventh hour, followed either by the carrying out of the death sentence or the receipt of a letter officially informing him that a reprieve had been granted. But never, in all his experience, had he ever known of a case like the one in which he had just played a part. In Ellis's opinion, all the furore, the arguments, the riots, the deputations to London and the additional heartache endured by the Kelly family could have been avoided.

He was quite correct, for the case was, in fact, clear-cut. Kelly and Hilton made a plan to enter and rob Mr Bardsley's premises, and they went armed. The bookseller was killed — brutally murdered. Each attempted to throw the blame on his companion, but the fact that one might have contributed more to the demise of the victim than the other was totally irrelevant. In the eyes of the law, Kelly and Hilton were equally guilty, and the judge was fully justified in passing sentence of death on both.

However, faced with an avalanche of letters and petitions, the Home Secretary, Mr Reginald McKenna, decided, in his wisdom, to grant a reprieve to Hilton only, on the grounds of his youth and the fact that he was known to be feeble-minded. It was a major blunder that led, not only to public outrage and bitter arguments for many months, even years, afterwards, but also to riots on the streets of Oldham and a great deal of damage both to public and private property. It could all so easily have been avoided, had the Home Secretary either allowed Ellis to carry out his assignment and hang both Kelly and Hilton, or commuted the sentences of both to imprisonment for life.

Ellis knew that he had done no more than his duty, but in acting as the instrument of the law he was only too well aware of the anger and hatred that could be directed against a public executioner in such a controversial case.

CHAPTER 19

THE LIVERPOOL SACK MURDER

Christina Bradfield was a forty-year-old spinster who ran the Liverpool office of her brother, a well-known tarpaulin manufacturer. She had a small staff consisting of a lady typist, a twenty-two-year-old packer named George Sumner and a handcart boy, Samuel Eltoft, aged eighteen.

Miss Bradfield, who lived across the River Mersey in Birkenhead, ruled the office with a firm hand. Though she was a pleasant lady, she would not tolerate insolence or insubordination and kept a sharp eye on her two young male employees.

One evening Miss Bradfield failed to return home after work, and though a thorough search was made for her over the next few days, no clue as to her whereabouts was discovered. Her family was frantic with worry and the police totally baffled.

Then one evening a barge-man named Francis Robinson, on reaching a lock near Lightbody Street, found his progress halted when he attempted to open the lock gates. As they would open only so far he was unable to get through, and realised that some object must be trapped in the gates below the water line. Probing around with a boathook, Robinson struck something soft, and pulled. A bulky sack at once floated to the surface. On closer examination the sack turned out to contain the body of Christina Bradfield. She had been battered to death. Her eyes were badly discoloured and there were wounds on her head and face.

On seeking out the two young men employed at the tarpaulin works the police soon tracked down Eltoft, but failed to locate the whereabouts of his workmate, which immediately threw suspicion on the missing Sumner.

Young Eltoft cracked under questioning. He told the police that on the previous Wednesday evening, when Miss Bradfield had told them that they could go home, he had left the premises with Sumner, but that his companion had asked him to wait outside the building while he went back inside, saying, 'I won't be long, just wait here for me'.

According to Eltoft, Sumner was inside a long time. It seemed like half-an-hour. When he finally emerged he was pushing a handcart, on which was a bulky object, covered by a tarpaulin.

'He told me to take the handcart and follow him. We set off along Great Howard Street, with me pushing the cart behind him. We went over a field, then came to some rough ground and we couldn't go any

217

further. George then threw off the tarpaulin. There was something in a sack on the handcart and we dragged it down to the canal and threw it in'.

Eltoft may have been attempting to cover himself by throwing all the blame onto Sumner, but his story of the removal of the body from the warehouse was certainly true, for a number of witnesses now came forward, who had seen two youths pushing a handcart through the streets that night.

Over the next few days a great hue and cry went up for George Sumner, who appeared to have vanished completely. All over the country both police and public were on the lookout for the missing man, who had left his lodgings soon after the discovery of the body had been reported in the newspapers.

A reward of £50 was offered for information leading to his capture, and the captains of all ships docked in the port were asked to be on the alert in case the fugitive should be on board, amongst the passengers or crew. When this failed to produce results the police received an anonymous tip-off that Sumner had reached London, and an intensive search of the capital was undertaken.

While all this was going on he was spotted in a Liverpool street by an old acquaintance, who followed him to a lodging house, then informed the local police, who made the arrest within a matter of minutes. He was picked up on his twenty-third birthday, and his first words to the police were,

'I'm glad its over'.

The first thing he told them was that his name was not Sumner, but Ball, and that he was one of eleven children. He said he came from a very unhappy home, and after leaving it had changed his name, as he intended to begin a new life and wanted nothing further to do with his family.

His story of the murder of Miss Bradfield, however, differed considerably from that of Eltoft. According to Ball, Eltoft left the warehouse first, while he himself was sent upstairs to turn out all the lights.

'When I came down', he said, 'I saw a man come from behind a bundle of sacking. He had a marlin-spike in his hand and he hit Miss Bradfield on the head with it. Then he pointed a revolver at me and told me to stand back. I was on the stairs and could move neither up nor down'.

In court Ball explained that only after the man had snatched Miss Bradfield's handbag and rushed out of the warehouse was he able to come down the stairs and approach Miss Bradfield, who was covered in blood. Soon after, Eltoft had appeared and asked,

'Why are you looking so white?'

Ball said he had then related the entire incident to his workmate and showed him the bloodstains on his trousers.

'Where I had had her head on my knee'.

Eltoft had then remarked,

'It looks black for you George'.

'Yes', I said. 'If anybody comes in now I'll get blamed for it'.

Ball then told the court of how he and Eltoft had put the body in a sack and taken it to the canal on a handcart.

Under cross-examination, Ball's story soon began to look very improbable to say the least. The fact that the victim's handbag was never found was also seen as being significant. On the morning of the murder, Ball had borrowed 3d from his landlady for his tram fare and cigarettes, yet, while in hiding at the lodging house, he had spent very freely, according to some of the other lodgers.

Eltoft, who was tried at the same time, stuck to his story of having helped to push the handcart from the warehouse, without realising what it contained. While neither story seemed particularly convincing, of the two, that of Eltoft appeared the more believable, and the jury decided to give him the benefit of the doubt. In finding him guilty of being an accessory after the fact, they added a recommendation for mercy on account of his youth and because he had clearly been influenced by Ball. The judge, Mr Justice Atkin, handed down a sentence of four year's penal servitude, which resulted in a pitiful scene in court, when the Defendant's mother collapsed weeping and wailing into the arms of relatives.

It was no surprise when Ball was found guilty of wilful murder and sentenced to be hanged. The judge told him,

'It was a cruel and heartless murder of a woman who had been kind to you. Yet you killed her and did away with her body in a most revolting way'.

Ball seemed unmoved as he stood in the dock, and showed no emotion whatsoever as he was escorted from the courtroom to the cells below. There was never any question of a reprieve in his case, and the date of execution was fixed for Thursday, 26th February, 1914.

When Ellis arrived at Walton Gaol on the 25th he went immediately to inspect the scaffold. Later, one of the warders described to him George Ball's behaviour while in custody.

At first he had slept a lot. Sometimes he would rouse himself and sit on the edge of the bed, staring ahead as if in a stupor. Then after a while he would suddenly leap to his feet and start to pace around the cell. He would start to talk to the warders, speaking rapidly and animatedly and wanting to discuss all manner of subjects. He seemed to have a very good knowledge of sport, particularly soccer, and would go on and on for hours at a time.

Then, all of a sudden, he would throw himself down on the bed again and lapse into silence. He would try to sleep, but would toss and turn restlessly. The mental anguish he was suffering was all too evident, and because he spent so much time lying down during the day he slept very badly at night, making life very uncomfortable for his gaolers.

As the fatal day drew nearer he became quieter and began to exhibit signs of real fear. All the bravado now disappeared and the terror-stricken prisoner asked for a priest.

The Bishop of Liverpool, Dr Chavasse, was sent for, and to him the prisoner confessed his guilt. He also asked for Confirmation, and this was carried out.

On the afternoon of Ellis's arrival at the prison Ball's father, sister, brother and brother-in-law visited the prisoner for the last time. Ball, who had protested his innocence from the outset, now told his family what he had confessed to the Bishop. They were shocked, as they had believed implicitly his story of how the crime had occurred.

'I hope you'll forgive me father'. said Ball.

The father, who was extremely upset, just hung his head and tried to hold back the tears.

When Ellis peered through the grille that night Ball was writing a letter. The strain showed clearly on his face. The hangman, noting that the prisoner appeared to be strongly built, went away to make his calculations.

Ellis sat up very late that night, talking to a couple of warders. In the morning his watch suddenly fell from its chain and crashed down on the stone floor. Bending down, he found that the face had smashed. Frowning, he slowly picked up the bits of broken glass. Though Ellis always claimed not to be superstitious, he couldn't help wondering, at that moment, if this was some sort of omen that did not bode well for that morning's execution. He was always tense before a hanging, and somehow the incident with the watch unsettled him just a little.

He knew, however, that he had to put all negative thoughts out of his head, or something surely would go wrong. Ellis went downstairs to the scaffold to measure the drop. Taking into account that Ball weighed 10st. 9lbs. and stood 5ft. 5ins. he had decided on a drop of 7ft. 6ins.

Just before he was due to carry out the execution, Ellis was told that the prisoner was now much more composed than he had been. Apparently, the confession of his crime and the ministrations of the Bishop had worked wonders.

The hangman was also informed that the pinioning would not take place in the cell, but in a storeroom which was much closer to the scaffold. On arriving there, Ellis was astonished to find that the room had been transformed into a miniature chapel almost, with an altar, on which was a crucifix and an array of flowers. Ball was on his knees, praying, with the Prison Chaplain close by.

The hangman and his assistant stood watching the scene for a moment or two, then Ellis stepped forward and touched the prisoner gently on the shoulder. Ball got to his feet and meekly submitted to the pinioning. Ellis then went on ahead and stood waiting on the scaffold as the hanging party approached.

Ball kept his nerve as the rope and the white cap were put in place. As Ellis tightened the noose his assistant completed the strapping together of the condemned man's legs. The hangman then pulled the lever, to complete the job satisfactorily. He thought of the broken watch again, and breathed a sigh of relief.

On the very day that George Ball paid the extreme penalty another horrific crime was committed less than two miles from Walton Gaol.

The wife of a man named Joseph Spooner, who had been having trouble with her husband, went to court to apply for a separation order. While she was there Spooner called at the house and asked whoever was minding her if he could take his three-year-old daughter, Elizabeth, to the local sweetshop. Then, after buying the child a bag of sweets, Spooner callously cut her throat with a penknife. She died in hospital later that day.

When Spooner insisted on pleading guilty, the judge at his trial at first refused to accept the plea. But Spooner earnestly desired death, and the court was ultimately obliged to accept his plea and pass sentence without actually trying him.

A foreigner named Alberto Oliverio Coelho was also condemned to death at the same Assizes, and John Ellis was engaged to carry out a double execution on 14th May. So, some three months after the execution of Ball, he was back at Walton Prison.

As it turned out, only one of the two was hanged, Coelho being reprieved at the eleventh hour. Spooner went to his death without giving any trouble at all, and Ellis remarked later that he had never seen a man who wanted to die as much as Spooner.

In June 1914, Ellis travelled to Winchester, in Wiltshire, to hang Walter White, who had murdered his sweetheart, Frances Priscilla Hunter, at Swindon, in a fit of jealousy, on discovering that she had lived for three months with a married man. Though this had occurred some months before White had even met Miss Hunter, he could not stand the thought of her in another man's arms, especially a married man. So he shot her, before giving himself up to the police.

On checking his victim's build Ellis found White to be small and slight, weighing no more than 9 stone. He gave him a drop of 7ft. 6ins., and the execution was carried out smoothly and without incident.

The following month, on 28th July, Austria declared war on Serbia, initiating a chain of events that would escalate into a bloody conflict involving many nations and which would become known as the Great War.

For the next four years the newspapers would be filled with the progress of the fighting in Europe. Little space was given over to murders, or anything else, though the hangman was kept as busy as ever.

In November of 1914 Ellis hanged two elderly men within six days of each other. Their crimes were somewhat similar and both were getting on in years, one in fact, Charles Frembd, being the oldest man Ellis ever hanged.

Frembd was a seventy-one-year-old German, who had lived in England since the age of seventeen. He had also spent some time in America, but had eventually settled in Leytonstone, London, where he ran a grocer's shop.

Following the death of his first wife Frembd met a widow in Yarmouth and married her early in 1913. After the first few weeks Frembd's new wife began to get on his nerves. She constantly nagged at him and soon he could stand it no longer. When he asked her to stop she would fly into a temper and nag him even more.

One night, at the end of his tether, Frembd attacked his wife with a razor as she lay in bed. He made a good job of it, slicing her throat open and killing her stone dead.

The old man then turned the razor on himself, and was later found lying beside his victim in a pool of blood. He recovered, however, and later faced a judge and jury. He was found guilty of wilful murder and sentenced to be hanged.

When Ellis saw Frembd on the day prior to the execution the old man appeared far from well. Next morning, when the executioners went into his cell, he looked even worse. Apart from that, his throat was still heavily bandaged from the bungled suicide attempt. All this made Ellis quite nervous. He did not want anything to go wrong on the scaffold, and with the old man in such a shaky condition, this was always a possibility. But the main thing to worry about was the fact that Frembd's throat had been cut, and the wrong length of drop might very well result in decapitation. Having decided on a drop of 6ft. 6ins., Ellis was fairly confident that all would go according to plan, but was still nervous.

The first stage of the operation went well enough, Frembd being transferred from his cell to the scaffold without any problem or incident. Ellis felt very sorry for the old man and could feel the tension within himself as he adjusted the rope around his victim's neck. He stepped to one side and reached for the lever. But before he could complete the job he saw the old man sag at the knees. At the very last moment his self-control had given way and he fell into a dead faint. A fraction of a second later the lever was pulled and the trapdoors opened beneath his feet. As he had started to keel over before Ellis had had time to pull the lever he had not dropped into the pit at quite the usual angle, and the hangman held his breath until it had been ascertained that all was well. As it happened, it was, for the doctors were able to testify that Frembd had died instantaneously.

Six days later Ellis was at Northampton Gaol to hang one John Francis Eayres, a Peterborough tinsmith, aged 59, whose wife had been found with her throat cut in the back yard of their house. Close by lay Eayres, also with throat wounds, which were far less serious than the victim's. The murderer had used a penknife on himself and had made a very poor job of it.

Like Frembd, Eayres claimed that his wife had nagged him beyond endurance, and his Defence Counsel fought strongly on his behalf, pointing out that while there had certainly been plenty of provocation, there was no evidence of any malice aforethought, therefore, a verdict of manslaughter might be more appropriate than one of murder.

But Mr Justice Avory would have none of this, pointing out that if a person immediately retaliated against someone who had assaulted him and caused his death, that might be manslaughter, but this was by no means the case here. The jury had but one course open to them, to find a verdict of 'Guilty', which they did.

The day Ellis arrived at Northampton, Eayres received a visit from his only son, a soldier, who was about to go to the Front. It was a meeting both sad and pathetic.

As it had been ten years since the last execution at Northampton the whole thing had to be organised from scratch. The scaffold itself was built in the old coachhouse in which the prison van, a Black Maria, was normally kept. The big problem was that the condemned cell was situated a good distance from the main building, and the hanging party would have to pass by the windows of the cells of the other convicts. So to prevent them looking out on the doomed man as he proceeded to the scaffold a number of large tarpaulins were hung up over the cell windows.

One of the warders told Ellis that the prisoner appeared very shaky, and when the hangman peered through the grille that night Eayres indeed looked upset and depressed.

'I wouldn't be at all surprised if we had trouble with him in the morning', said Ellis. 'You'll have to be ready in case you should need to assist him on the walk from the cell to the drop'.

As it turned out, Ellis's fears were well founded. When the hangmen entered his cell on the following morning, Eayres, a huge man weighing well over two hundred pounds, was sitting on the edge of the bed, his head in his hands.

After being told gently to stand up, he rose and offered no resistance as his hands were pinioned behind his back. When Ellis opened his shirt collar he could see that the big man's eyes were brimming with tears. The hangman turned away quickly and left the cell to make his way to the scaffold. Then, just as the procession began to form up in the corridor, the condemned man finally broke down completely, sobbing pitifully as he set off on what would be his last walk. The officials were clearly affected as they made their way out into the yard and down the path. Even the Chaplain's voice broke from time to time as he prayed aloud.

At the end of the path the procession made a left turn, which brought it to the open doors of the coachhouse. On entering the gloomy interior, the condemned man came face to face with the scaffold. The sight of it, with the noose hanging there, seemed to come as a shock to him. He stopped, his mouth gaping open, then was moved gently on to mount the scaffold and was guided by Ellis onto the drop. He spoke just a few words. The last he would ever utter. 'I'm going to die for a bad woman'.

The big man stood there on the trapdoors trembling with fear. He was so heavy that Ellis had given him a drop of only 5ft. With everything in place the hangman pulled the lever and Eayres disappeared into the pit.

That year, 1914, Ellis hanged Josiah Davis at Stafford. Davis, a 53-year-old ironworker, had strangled his landlady, Martha Hodgkins, with a length of bandage tied around a bedpost. Two weeks later, at Durham Gaol, he hanged Robert Upton, a Jarrow man, for the murder of Charles Gribben, his rival for the love of a local woman, and, also that month, James Honeyands at Exeter. Honeyands, a 21-year-old sailor, had shot dead Amelia Jones, a Plymouth woman with whom he had been having an affair. At Cardiff, Ellis executed Edgar Lewis Bindon for the killing of Maud Mulholland, in yet another case of jealousy and passion.

When boarding the train for the journey back to Rochdale, Ellis, a keen follower of sport, was introduced to the famous boxer, Jim Driscoll, and on settling down in his compartment, found himself in the company of a number of other renowned Welsh fighters, including the legendary Jimmy Wilde, Llew Edwards and Percy Jones, who was due to box the Frenchman, Eugene Criqui, the following day.

Ellis was thrilled to be in such illustrious company and could hardly wait to get back home to tell his tap-room mates all about it. Though the hangman frequented a number of local pubs he was most often to be seen in the Jolly Gardener*, one of a number of beerhouses on a section of Platting Lane known as 'th'alley', which was in the vicinity of the present Roller City. His closest friends were Dr Ward, a local physician, Bert Mills and Simon Bibbington, both bookies, and Dick Wallwork, the landlord. It was at the Jolly Gardener that the Buersil Lodge of the Buffaloes held their meetings, Jack Ellis being one of the most prominent members.

The meetings were very formal and began and ended with prayers. Ellis must have been a fair drinker. When he first entered the pub he would order two pints straight off. The first he would down pretty quickly, then take his time with the second. The "Buffs" held an annual Harvest Festival in an upstairs room of the pub, when hymns were sung, prayers said and a collection taken.

Another of Ellis's 'locals' was the Bull's Head at 591, Oldham Road, now a block of flats. Next door was a chip shop kept by Emily Sutcliffe, who remembered the hangman calling in regularly. When he had had a drink he could be quite jovial, making such remarks as,

'Hey, I'll tell thee what lass, thes getten a lovely neck'.

Customers who called at Ellis's shop for a shave often remarked that they got the "shivers" when the hangman gently fingered their throats as he tied the sheet around their necks.

In August 1915, Ellis travelled to Durham Gaol to hang one Frank Steele, a Gateshead man who had murdered a woman named Nana Barnett, with whom he had been keeping company. Steele was a drunkard, who boasted of having cut his lady-friend's throat, to a number of people in various pubs. His story was so wild and he was in such an intoxicated state most of the time, that he could not get anyone to take him seriously, not even his mother.

* There was also a Jolly Gardener at what is now 362 Oldham Road.

In order to get him out of her house the mother called a policeman, and was amazed to see her son produce a key and tell the constable,

'Here you are. Go to Great Nelson Street and you'll find her dead there'.

When the police went to investigate they found the dead woman, just as Steele had claimed. He was arrested and charged with murder. Found guilty and sentenced to hang, he was scheduled to face the hangman on 27th July 1915, but gave notice of appeal, with the result that, following the dismissal of the appeal, the execution was re-arranged for 11th August.

On arrival at the gaol, Ellis checked the scaffold, then went along to view the prisoner. Steele was 31 years old and quite a big man for those days, standing 5ft. $9^{1}/_{2}$ins. and weighing just under twelve stone. Ellis gave him a drop of 6ft. 6ins. and claimed that Steele died instantaneously.

1. Samuel Dougal – the Moat Farm murderer. *(Courtesy of Topham Picturepoint)*

2. Camille Holland, who mysteriously disappeared – never to be seen alive again. *(Courtesy of Topham Picturepoint)*

3. The exhumed remains of Camille Holland lying in the greenhouse at Moat Farm awaiting forensic examination. *(Courtesy of Topham Picturepoint)*

4. Hawley Harvey Crippen, whose capture by the use of the new wireless telegraphy so captured the public's imagination. *(Mirror)*

5. Ethel le Neve, Crippen's lover, seen here in her disguise as a boy. *(Mirror Syndication International.)*

6. A well-disguised Crippen is escorted down the gangway of the *S.S. Megantic* by Inspector Walter Dew of Scotland Yard, after a dramatic dash across the Atlantic. *(Topham Picturepoint)*

7. The gruesome remains of Cora Crippen in the cellar of 39, Hilldrop Crescent.
(Courtesy of Metropolitan Police)

8. Cora Crippen, alias Belle Elmore, Music Hall artiste.
(Courtesy of Mirror Syndication International)

9. The Martinettis, theatrical friends of Cora Crippen, seen leaving the court during Crippen's trial. *(Courtesy of Hulton-Getty)*

10. Frederick Seddon, whose murderous greed led him to the gallows.
(Courtesy of Hulton-Getty)

11. Mrs. Margaret Seddon, whose misplaced loyalty to her evil husband resulted in a murder charge being brought against her.
(Mail Newspapers-Solo)

12. Frederick and Margaret Seddon in the dock at The Old Bailey, London, in March, 1912.
(Courtesy of Mirror Syndication International)

13. Tragic victim Eliza Barrow was murdered after being systematically robbed by the avaricious Frederick Seddon. *(Photograph attributed to Metropolitan Police)*

14. The unfortunate Ernest Grant, outside the Court during Seddon's trial. *(Courtesy of Hulton-Getty)*

15. George Joseph Smith, the 'Brides in the Bath' killer. *(Mirror Syndication International)*

16. Smith with Bessie Mundy, one of his victims. *(Courtesy of Hulton-Getty)*

17. Edith Pegler, the wife to whom Smith always returned.
(Courtesy of Mirror Syndication International)

18. Alice Burnham, whose father was unable to save her from Smith's evil clutches.
(Courtesy of Mirror Synd. Intl.)

19. Roger Casement, whose humanitarian work earned him a knighthood.
(Courtesy of Mirror Syndication International)

20. A manacled Casement leaves the Old Bailey, London.
(Courtesy of Mirror Syndication International)

21. A German propoganda photograph of Roger Casement (circled) on the conning tower of the U-Boat before sailing on his ill-fated mission to Ireland.

22. Frederick Rothwell Holt, a ruthless killer, for whom Ellis felt no sympathy. *(Courtesy of Blackpool Gazette)*

23. Kitty Breaks who escaped an unhappy marriage only to fall, tragically, into the arms of Frederick Holt. *(Blackpool Gazette)*

24. *(Left)* Ivy Wolfenden, aged seven, stands next to her sister Doris, nine, *(seated)*, both dressed in their 'Sunday best'. *(Courtesy of Oldham Chronicle)*

25. William Waddington cruelly murdered little Ivy Wolfenden after his perverted attack on her. *(Courtesy of Oldham Chronicle)*

26. The shop of Mr. Davies, chemist, who first suspected that his son-in-law, Oswald Martin, had been poisoned. *(Courtesy of Topham Picturepoint)*

27. The dapper solicitor, Herbert Rowse Armstrong, who turned to murder to further his selfish ambitions. *(Mirror Synd. Intl.)*

28. A touching portrait of Katharine Armstrong and her two children. *(Courtesy of Topham Picturepoint)*

29. Major Herbert Armstrong was commissioned in the Territorials before serving his country during the Great War. *(Courtesy of Topham Picturepoint)*

30. A contemporary photograph of Broad Street, Hay-on-Wye, where Major Herbert Armstrong had his solicitor's practice. *(Courtesy of Topham Picturepoint)*

31. The car, with its windows covered, carries Major Armstrong away from the Police Court at Hay-on-Wye, after his indictment for murder. *(Courtesy of Hulton-Getty)*

32. Young Henry Jacoby, guilty of a senseless killing, enjoyed playing cricket with the prison warders. *(Courtesy of Mirror Synd. Interntl.)*

33. Ronald True – flamboyant man-about-town, con. man and bogus war hero. *(Topham Picturepoint)*

34. A hand-cuffed Ronald True being led by Detective Inspector Burton into the West London Police Court. *(Courtesy of Topham Picturepoint).*

35. Edith Thompson, who lived in a dream world of romantic fiction.
(Courtesy of Mirror Syndication International)

36. Freddie Bywaters whose clandestine love affair with Edith led him to the gallows.
(Courtesy of Mirror Syndication International)

37. The fateful, eternal triangle of Freddie Bywaters, Edith and Percy Thompson, apparently relaxing in the garden on a sunny afternoon – but Edith has a pensive, far-away look... .
(Courtesy of Paul Popper Limited)

38. The expectant, ghoulish crowd outside Holloway Prison waiting, on an aptly atmospheric, wet morning, for news of the hanging of Edith Thompson. *(Courtesy of Topham Picturepoint)*

39. John and Annie Ellis with their children *(left to right)* Sarah, Austin, Ivy and young Annie Beaton in the backyard of their home. The eldest son, Joseph, was absent. *(Courtesy of The Courier, Dundee)*

40. John and Annie Ellis at their garden gate. (Inset John as a child).
(Courtesy of The Courier, Dundee)

41. Jack Ellis was fond of keeping poultry and breeding dogs.
(Courtesy of The Courier, Dundee)

42. Ellis was known for his bulldogs and won many prizes. *(The Courier, Dundee)*

43. Ellis with his beloved whippet 'Bob Seivier'. *(Courtesy of The Courier, Dundee)*

44. The Rochdale hangman, John Ellis, relaxing on the moors near his home and enjoying a welcome break from the tedium of hairdressing and the strains and pressures of his official duties as the country's Chief Executioner.
(Courtesy of The Courier, Dundee)

CHAPTER 20

BRIDES IN THE BATH

In 1915, with the fighting raging in Europe, the newspapers were, naturally, full of war stories and related tragedies, such as the sinking of the Cunard liner, *Lusitania*, by a German submarine in May, with the loss of more than eleven hundred lives. Crimes were still committed and reported on, but took second place to the horrors of the war and the stories of heroism and fierce fighting at the Front.

A case of murder and bigamy on a grand scale was, however, about to break, with the leading player as callous and as vicious a monster as any who ever stood in the Old Bailey dock.

George Joseph Smith was a cockney, born at 92, Roman Road, Bethnal Green, in London's East End, on 11th January, 1872. He came from a respectable family, his father being an insurance agent. But from an early age he was wayward and impossible to control. Obstinate and wilful, he was a constant worry to his parents and his teachers, who could do nothing with him.

At the age of nine, he was sent to reform school for stealing. His sentence, eight years, seems a terribly cruel one, but in those days courts did not dole out soft sentences, even to youngsters. They made every effort to impress on a budding criminal that crime did not pay. But neither the harsh sentence, nor the serving of it, had any noticeable effect on Smith. This was a great pity, for several of the staff took a genuine interest in him and encouraged him to try to make something of his life. He responded by taking an interest in poetry, and also learned to play the piano, but that was as far as it went. His basic character remained the same. He would never change.

While Smith was at the reformatory, his father died. On his release the youth went to live with his mother, who had remarried, and her new husband. Perhaps he was unhappy. Whatever the reason, he was soon in trouble again. In 1890, when he was eighteen, he was convicted of stealing a bicycle at Lambeth. This time, he got six months' hard labour. His long-suffering mother remarked sadly, 'George will die with his boots on'. As it later turned out, she was quite correct in her prophecy.

After his release, Smith served three years in the army, joining the Northamptonshire Regiment and eventually becoming a physical training instructor. Not many months after leaving the forces, however, he was back in gaol, again for thieving. During his time in prison, while mixing with other criminals and swapping ideas, he must have realised that petty crime was leading him nowhere, and resolved to make a fresh start. Not that he had any intention of going straight and earning an honest living. It was simply a matter of developing a little cunning and setting his sights higher.

Smith had already discovered that he could exert an extraordinary influence over women, particularly the lonely and the gullible kind. He could win a girl's confidence, make love to her, and then talk her into stealing for him. Of course, she would at first recoil from such a suggestion, but Smith could be extremely persuasive and always got his way in the end. Now he would play for bigger stakes. From now on he would be on the lookout for women of more substantial means. When he found them he would show no mercy, but would be prepared to divest them of all they owned, before callously abandoning them.

Between 1893, when he left the army, and 1896, he was in and out of gaol. For receiving stolen goods from a woman he had been keeping company with, he got twelve months. On his release, he moved to Leicester, where he met a young lady named Caroline Thornhill, to whom he proposed marriage. The young lady's parents did not approve of Smith, but the wedding took place anyway, at a church in Leicester on 17th January 1898.

At this time, Smith was using the name, George Oliver Love, and it was that name which went on the marriage certificate. Miss Thornhill was only eighteen at the time and the bridegroom twenty-six. He did not have a job, but lived by his wits, and before long his young wife was very much involved in his larcenous schemes. These often took the form of stealing from families with whom she had obtained employment as a domestic servant. Coached by her villainous husband, Caroline worked for and robbed a whole string of employers in London and on the South Coast.

Arrested in 1899 with stolen property in her possession, the young Mrs Love was given a twelve-month prison sentence, for which she blamed her husband. On her release, the pair got back together again, but before long were quarrelling, and it appears a distinct possibility that when Smith was arrested at Hastings, in 1901, while attempting to dispose of a quantity of silver cutlery, the police had been tipped off by Caroline Love. He was gaoled for two years and came out of prison in 1903, by which time his estranged wife, having decided to get away from him for good, had emigrated to Canada.

Over the next four or five years he ingratiated himself with, and no doubt used and robbed, any woman with whom he came into contact, though his activities during this period did not bring him to the notice of the police.

In the summer of 1908 Smith met Florence Wilson, a widow from Worthing, with whom he soon struck up an amorous relationship. Within a couple of weeks he had persuaded her to withdraw her savings from the bank. It was by no means a large sum, but Smith very kindly offered to look after it for her. Since he had already proposed marriage, Mrs Wilson trusted him completely. They were staying together in London, and Smith decided to give the widow a treat, taking her to see the White City Exhibition. Leaving her 'for just a few moments' while he went to buy a newspaper, he never came back. Instead he had returned immediately to their lodgings, removed all their belongings and disappeared.

Smith, obviously feeling it prudent to get well away from London for a while, next made his way to the West Country, where he used his ill-gotten gains to set up a second-hand shop in Gloucester Road, Bristol. One of the applicants for the position of housekeeper, for which he had advertised, was a young woman named Edith Mabel Pegler. Twenty-eight years old and no more than moderately attractive, Miss Pegler got the job, and was destined to play a very important role in Smith's life.

Within a month he had married her, and though he would leave her many times, she would always be there when he returned, and later would unknowingly benefit from the property and money of other women, whom he had bigamously married, robbed and murdered.

Smith's marriage to Edith Pegler was, of course, his first excursion into bigamy. Miss Pegler was a very religious person, who had always dreamed of a church wedding, but the groom simply would not agree to it. Whatever his excuse, Smith's will, as always, prevailed, and the couple were married at Bristol Registry Office on 30th August 1908. On this occasion, he used his correct name, George Joseph Smith.

It was not long before the restless Smith became bored with Bristol and sold the shop. Taking his new wife with him, he moved around a lot over the next twelve months or so, living at Bedford, Luton and Croydon for short periods, but never settling. He again tried his hand as a second-hand dealer, and while travelling around the country sometimes referred to himself as an 'antiques expert'. In certain London circles, which he often frequented, mainly for pleasure, he sometimes attempted to pass himself off as a composer of Music Hall songs. In these circles he became acquainted with many young women, quite a number of whom fell under his spell.

This was amazing, as he was not particularly attractive, physically. A little above average height, he was upright in his bearing and walked with what has been described as a military step. Of fair complexion, with brown hair, a bushy, gingerish moustache and a boney face that could hardly be described as handsome, Smith's countenance did, in fact, possess at least one unique feature — the eyes. Many women who had known him, later commented on Smith's piercing, almost hypnotic, staring eyes. Those eyes were not large and expressive. They were not particularly pleasing in shape or colour. They were not warm or welcoming. In fact, they were small and cold. But they became positively mesmeric when fixed upon a woman. It was as though he could look into a person's mind, almost, and instruct that person to do his bidding. Though this may sound fanciful, there can be no getting away from the fact that Smith did persuade many women to do things that were totally out of character, and certainly not in their own best interests.

In the autumn of 1909 Smith met a young lady from Southampton named Miss Faulkner and soon swept her off her feet, after first ascertaining that she was worth several hundred pounds. He introduced himself as 'George Rose', and within three weeks had bigamously married her at the Registry Office, in Southampton.

From there the couple went to London and found lodgings. Smith then persuaded his new bride to withdraw her savings from the post office. Once the money was in his possession he had no further use for Miss Faulkner and got rid of her by employing one of his old dodges. He took her to the National Gallery, left her 'for a few minutes', and never returned. When the distraught young bride made her way back to their lodgings sometime later, she discovered that Mr Rose had already been there and cleared out everything, including her clothes and jewellery. In total, her estimated loss was somewhere in the region of six to seven hundred pounds, leaving her virtually penniless.

Smith promptly returned to Edith Pegler, to whom he confided that he had had the good fortune to find a genuine Turner painting, which he had bought and re-sold at a healthy profit. Soon after this, he took Edith to Southend, where the couple set up house, but only a few months later the Smiths were once again on the move, this time returning to Bristol, where Smith opened another second-hand shop.

Leaving Edith to run the business, Smith again set off on his travels. In the summer of 1910, at Clifton, he met his next victim, Beatrice Mundy, known to her friends as Bessie. Smith introduced himself as 'Henry Williams', and made it his business to discover all he could about Miss Mundy. When she told him that she was the daughter of a bank manager, now deceased, she immediately had his undivided attention, and on learning that her father had left her the sum of £2,500, Smith decided there and then, that one way or another, he was going to get his hands on it.

As always, he set out to woo his victim by flattery and by lavishing attention on her. Within three weeks of their first meeting Bessie Mundy and Henry Williams were married at the Registry Office in Weymouth. The date was 26th August, 1910.

Then came the bad news as far as Smith was concerned. The money was invested in a trust fund, administered by her uncle and brother. She was well provided for and received £8 per month to live on. Apart from that she had around £140 in the bank. This, of course, was soon withdrawn and in Smith's possession, but he was very unhappy about the situation, and annoyed that she had not acquainted him with the full details of her financial affairs before they were married.

He was now irritated by his new bride, and while he still intended to devise a plan to get his hands on Bessie's inheritance, Smith was not prepared to waste much time on her in the interim. After a fortnight's honeymoon he disappeared, taking with him his wife's £140.

The heartbroken Bessie returned to Clifton and shortly afterwards received a letter from her missing 'husband', in which he expressed sorrow at having been forced to leave her, explaining that he had caught a disease from her and had returned to London to be cured. This would be expensive, which is why he had needed the money. He assured her that once he was well again he would return to her, and that in the meantime, he was missing her very much. The letter only made Bessie feel worse. As for Smith, he simply returned to Edith Pegler yet again. As usual, he had money in his pockets and informed her that he had had a reasonably successful trip.

Bessie went to lodge with a friend in Weston-super-Mare, a Mrs Sarah Tuckett, and one day, around eighteen months after her marriage and desertion, she got the shock of her life while walking along the sea front. There, strolling towards her, dressed in fashionable morning attire, was none other than Mr Henry Williams, who professed himself to be amazed that they should suddenly bump into each other after so long.

Bessie's long-lost husband explained that he was now cured and that he had just returned from abroad, where he had been on business. There can be little doubt that the 'chance meeting' had been stage-managed by Smith, for after realising that getting his hands on Bessie Mundy's money was not going to be easy, he had given himself time to think things over. He had finally decided on a plan, the first stage of which was to win back Bessie's confidence.

If she had had any sense, she would have called a policeman and had him arrested, but his glib tongue and hypnotic eyes soon eliminated any hope of that. Within a short time he had talked her into going away with him for a short holiday, and they returned to her lodgings to collect Bessie's belongings. There he met Mrs Tuckett, who took an instant dislike to the man. A very forthright type of woman, she asked him point-blank,

'Why did you leave her like that?'

Mr Williams explained that there were certain personal reasons, which he could not discuss, and added that all problems had now been resolved and that he had been searching for his wife for over twelve months. Though this, of course, contradicted his earlier statement about having been abroad, the gullible Bessie did not query it. Bessie told Mrs Tuckett that she had forgiven her husband and had agreed to return to him. The couple then left, and Mrs Tuckett took it upon herself to write to Bessie's relatives, to inform them of the situation.

Smith took Bessie to Herne Bay, in Kent. One of the first things they did on arriving there was to consult a solicitor named Annesley. Bessie had agreed that her husband should have control of her capital, and now wished to arrange this. The local solicitor did not feel competent to deal with it himself and consulted a more senior colleague, who looked into the matter very carefully before advising that such a move would not be in the best interests of Mrs Williams. The trustees could have found a way to block this move, in any case, but if Bessie made a will in her husband's favour, leaving him everything, and she should happen to die soon afterwards, he would, of course, get her money. Realising this, Smith got Bessie to agree to their making mutual wills, leaving everything to each other.

In Herne Bay the couple rented a house at 80 High Street. It was on the small side and did not afford the luxury of a bathroom, so soon after moving in, Mr Williams bought a tin bathtub, paying £1.17s.6d for it, and taking Bessie along to the ironmonger's to help choose it. The following day he took her to see a physician, Dr French, as she had been feeling unwell. Williams informed the doctor that his wife was subject to fits, which was quite untrue. Bessie had been bothered by headaches, but nothing more serious than that. Yet she did not argue, and Dr French prescribed accordingly.

Once the wills had been witnessed and signed, all was set for Smith to take the next fateful step. Greed had finally ruled over caution and common sense. To get his hands on the money he was about to commit murder.

He did not waste any time. Early on the morning of 13th July Smith went out to buy some fish to cook for breakfast. Half-an-hour later he was banging on the door of the doctor's surgery, shouting,

'Come quickly doctor, something's happened to my wife'.

On arriving at the house, the doctor found Bessie in the bath, her head submerged. In one hand she clutched a bar of soap. She had obviously drowned. Dr French concluded that she must have been seized with a fit while in the bath. Smith's scheme had worked perfectly. There was an inquest, of course, at which the local Coroner came to the same conclusion, and though Bessie's brother later wrote a letter to the Coroner's office asking for a thorough investigation, the verdict, 'death by misadventure', was allowed to stand.

One of Smith's first acts, once the inquest was over, was to return the bath to the ironmonger's, as he had no further use for it, and get his money back. He had already written to Bessie's uncle, informing him of her sad demise, and now began legal proceedings to take possession of Bessie's estate, valued in excess of £2,500. In the meantime, he returned to the ever-faithful Edith Pegler. He told her that he had made a couple of very profitable deals, and when the money from the will eventually came through he invested most of it in property and an annuity. He had always fancied himself as a businessman, but, in fact, was less than successful, for his investments, more often than not, lost money. He would then go on the road again looking for vulnerable females.

On one occasion, he became very angry when Edith told him that during one of his absences she had tried to locate him in one of the South Coast towns. He told her very bluntly that she should never try to get in touch with him in this way again, as he considered it to be interfering with his business. Following a spell in Margate, the couple returned to Bristol, and after a few weeks Smith left Edith there and disappeared once again.

In September, he was on the prowl at Southsea and attended a church service, where he spotted a buxom twenty-five-year-old named Alice Burnham. Outside the chapel he introduced himself, on this occasion for some reason or other, giving his correct name. Later, when Miss Burnham wrote to her sister, she described Smith as a gentleman of independent means and a devoted Wesleyan.

Smith quickly uncovered the details of Miss Burnham's financial and social standing. The daughter of a Buckinghamshire fruit farmer, she held a qualification as a private nurse, and was, at that time, looking after an elderly invalid man.

Smith soon proposed marriage and was accepted, but the love-struck Alice insisted that he should meet her father before they were married. Charles Burnham was less than happy with his daughter's choice. In fact, he disliked the prospective son-in-law on sight. To him, it was not a match. He felt that Smith was totally unsuitable for his daughter and pleaded with her not to rush into something she might regret.

It made no difference. The wedding took place at Portsmouth Registry Office on 4th November, 1913, and Smith lost no time in writing to her father, requesting that Mr Burnham forward to him the sum of £104, which he was keeping for his daughter. Burnham replied, stating that before he did, he would like to know something of Smith's family background.

Outraged, Smith sent back this insolent and nonsensical reply:

> *Sir, In answer to your inquiry regarding my family — My mother was a bus-horse, my father a cab-driver and my sister a rough-rider over the Arctic regions. My brothers were all gallant sailors on a steamroller. This is the only information I can give to those who are not entitled to ask such questions.*

Through a solicitor, Smith eventually extracted the £104 from his father-in-law. Then, having cleared Alice's bank account of the twenty-odd pounds balance, he insured her life for £500 and induced her to make a will, bequeathing everything to him.

Smith was now supremely confident that he had found a winning formula. He had also added a new feature — insuring his victim. This time, possibly as a precaution, he decided to give the South Coast a miss and took his new wife to Blackpool 'for a short holiday'. The first boarding house they called at seemed ideal, but when Smith found that there was no bath, they moved on, eventually boarding with a Mrs Crossley of 16, Regent Road.

Alice was tired after the long journey, and Smith asked her if she had a headache, to which she obligingly replied in the affirmative. Next morning she accompanied him to the surgery of a Dr Billing, where Smith suggested that his wife might be an epileptic. Alice made no serious attempt to contradict him, so in all probability he had been able to convince her, just as he had his previous victim, that she was unwell and that there could possibly be something more seriously wrong. Perhaps he even suggested certain significant symptoms. In any event, neither woman protested when he spoke to the doctor and mentioned the word 'fits'.

After visiting the doctor, Alice said she felt much better, and the couple went to see the sights. Smith was very attentive, and the young bride again wrote to her sister, saying that she had 'the best husband in the world'.

About eight o'clock on Friday night 12th December, Mrs Smith took a bath. At around 8-15 Smith stopped by the kitchen, where the Crossley family were having supper. He was carrying a bag, and mentioned that he had been out for some eggs for breakfast. He went upstairs. It was at this point that one of the Crossleys noticed a stain on the ceiling. As it was just below the bathroom, they realised that the bath had probably overflowed. Just then a shout came from the landing.

'Fetch the doctor — please hurry! It's my wife. I can't get her to speak to me!'

Dr Billing was soon on the scene, and pronounced Mrs Smith dead. She had obviously had a fit and drowned in the bath.

The Crossleys were natually shocked that such a tragedy should occur in their house, and even more shocked at Smith's reaction to it. For though he seemed devastated at first, he soon appeared to get over it, after which he began to display a callous indifference to what had happened. He was intending to sleep that night in the bedroom where Alice's dead body lay, but Mrs Crossley refused to allow it. Next day, he ordered a cheap coffin and arranged a pauper's funeral. When Mrs Crossley protested, he brushed her aside, saying,

'When they're dead, they're done with'.

When writing to Alice's mother, however, he told her that he had suffered a terrible and cruel loss. That same day he sat in Mrs Crossley's front room, playing the piano and drinking whisky, until it was time to go to the Coroner's Court. By then Smith had consumed a large amount of alcohol and was becoming very emotional. Mrs Crossley, however, was not taken in by Smith's histrionic performance as the grieving husband. Though she could not quite put her finger on anything specific, she felt very strongly that something was wrong — Smith's actions and general attitude following his wife's sudden death, made her feel uneasy. At the inquest he appeared very upset, but when the Coroner's verdict, that Alice Burnham's death had been accidental, was announced, he quickly regained control of his emotions, and left the court with a self-satisfied look on his face.

After selling off his wife's belongings, Smith returned once more to Bristol, where he spent a pleasant Christmas with Edith and her mother. His story was that he had just returned from a profitable trip to Spain. As usual, he was not short of funds. There was plenty of food and drink, and Smith entertained family and friends around the piano. Though he did not read music too well, he could play almost any tune by ear, and not surprisingly, was the centre of attention.

By February, Smith was richer by £500, having collected on Alice Burnham's insurance policy. Very prudently he decided to place the money with his insurance company, increasing his annuity by around £30 a year. Then he set off once again on his travels, taking Edith with him this time. They stayed in Torquay and various other South Coast towns, and when the War broke out, in August, the Smiths were living in Ashley Road, Bournemouth. They were reasonably happy, though he did occasionally beat her, and went out most nights, leaving her alone.

The truth was that Smith was on the prowl again, looking for yet another victim. He found her listening to a band on the seafront. Stylishly turned out in boater, blazer and white flannels, Smith must have cut quite a dash as he introduced himself to Alice Reavil as 'Charles Oliver James'. He had obviously taken the smartly-dressed Miss Reavil for a young lady of some means. In fact, she was a servant girl with only a few pounds to her name, which she had painstakingly accumulated by putting away a small sum each week in the Post Office Savings Bank.

Smith swept Miss Reavil off her feet, and within a matter of days they were living together in lodgings at Battersea Rise, Woolwich. Soon after settling in, Smith took Alice to the local Registry Office, where they were married by special licence on 17th September.

On the drive back to their lodgings, Smith flashed around a bundle of banknotes, and told his new bride that it was his intention to open an antique shop in the town. Alice was naturally eager to help her husband all she could in his new venture, and immediately handed over to him all the cash she had, a total of £14. In addition, she told him, she had her Post Office Savings, which amounted to £72. She would be glad to withdraw this and put it into the business. Smith was, no doubt, disappointed to learn that his latest bride was by no means well off after all. Still, he would have to make the best of it. The following day, after she had withdrawn the money and he had relieved her of it, the callous Smith disappeared, taking with him all their luggage, even Miss Reavil's clothes, leaving her stranded without a penny.

Shocking as this was, there can be no denying the fact that Alice Reavil was very lucky indeed. Fortunately for her, Smith had not considered her worth killing, otherwise she might well have died in her bath at the lodging house in Battersea Rise.

Edith Pegler was now back in Bristol, and on his return, Smith made her a present of some of Alice Reavil's clothes. He had bought them at a sale, he told her, and thought they would 'just suit her'.

In early November, Smith bumped into Margaret Lofty, a lady whom he had first met earlier that year in Bath. On that occasion he had introduced himself as 'John Lloyd', estate agent, and on running into her again, Smith immediately sized her up and realised that he might well be looking at his next prospect.

Miss Lofty, the daughter of a deceased clergyman, lived with her sister and mother, and at thirty-eight was considered an old maid, who had been left on the shelf. It was the perfect situation for a predator such as George Smith, and hardly surprising that Miss Lofty should soon fall under his spell. During the next few weeks the couple met frequently, and as the relationship developed, Smith learned all he could about Miss Lofty's family background and financial standing.

Though the liaison had certainly progressed to a point where the lady's thoughts were occupied almost exclusively by her suave and attentive suitor, Miss Lofty was not one to be rushed. Smith must have realised this and was therefore a little more cautious than usual. He knew that to appear too anxious might well have the effect of causing her to question his true motives. Still, a month was a lengthy courtship for an experienced Lothario such as Smith, and by that time he was becoming just a little impatient. By early December, he had decided that he must get things moving, and finally proposed. He somehow managed to persuade Miss Lofty to elope, which was rather surprising, taking into account her maturity, close family ties and the fact that her mother was getting on in years and might not be able to stand the shock of it. On the other hand, she had suffered a big disappointment some years previously, when a young man whom she had hoped to marry had broken off their engagement, leaving her devastated. She was not going to miss out again if she could possibly help it.

On the afternoon of 15th December, 1914, Margaret Lofty went out for tea and did not return. Two days later the couple were married and living in lodgings at 14, Bismarck Road, Highgate, London. On the day of her wedding Margaret wrote to her family.

> *No doubt you will be surprised to learn that I was married today to a gentleman named John Lloyd. He is a thorough Christian man whom I first met in Bath last June. Our tastes and temperaments are exactly in harmony. It is only natural that I should do anything to secure the one I love, and I have every proof of his love for me. He has been honourable and kept his word to me in everything.*

The usual pattern was now repeated: the precautionary visit to a local doctor, followed by an appointment with a solicitor to have mutual wills drawn up. As he had already insured Margaret's life for a sum of £700, Smith was anxious to collect the proceeds.

On Friday evening, 18th December, the landlady, Mrs Blatch, was ironing in her kitchen when she heard the sound of water splashing in the bathroom above, followed by what she later described as 'a sort of big sigh'. Not long afterwards, she heard Mr Lloyd playing the organ in the front room. The tune was 'Nearer My God To Thee' — a not inappropriate choice in the circumstances. Soon afterwards, the music stopped and Mrs Blatch heard the front door slam shut. About ten or fifteen minutes later the doorbell rang, and the landlady answered it to find Mr Lloyd standing on the step holding a paper bag. He explained that he had just been out to buy some tomatoes, and asked if his wife had come downstairs for supper yet. Mrs Blatch said, 'No', and asked him why he hadn't used his key.

'Oh yes, my key', he replied. 'Do you know, I'd forgotten you gave me one'.

He went upstairs, and minutes later Mrs Blatch heard a shout as Smith came rushing down in a panic, shouting that his wife had drowned in the bath.

Dr Bates was quickly on the scene, but could do nothing beyond pronouncing Margaret Lloyd dead. At the inquest, the bereaved husband appeared very upset indeed, and sobbed as he gave his evidence, repeating several times,

'We were only married on Thursday'.

The Coroner's jury had no hesitation in exonerating the husband from any blame for his wife's death. At this stage, his efforts had produced only the sum of £19, all that Margaret Lofty had at her disposal, in spite of her family connections. But Smith's plans were centred on the insurance money, which he knew from experience would take a few weeks to come through.

The amazing thing about George Joseph Smith's career as a bigamist and murderer, was that he was never recognised in the street by those who had known him while he was masquerading under a different identity. Of course, as a precaution against this he had moved around a lot, never staying in the same town for very long and making few friends. In fact, apart from London and Bristol, he was not well known anywhere. He simply turned up, struck up a relationship, then usually persuaded his victim to leave her own familar surroundings and go off with him. He would then talk her into marriage, relieve her of property and money, before either abandoning or murdering her. In Bristol, which he considered his home base, he had committed no crimes and was considered a respectable businessman. Though he had always been extremely circumspect for a man with so many identities, he had also been incredibly fortunate that no one had ever recognised him, or connected him with someone they had previously known. This run of luck, however, was about to come to an end. Smith's greed and his inability to know when to stop was to prove his downfall. He had gone to the well just once too often.

Quite possibly, Smith's apparently anguished outburst at the inquest was what eventually led to his apprehension. The words 'and we were only married on Thursday', and the pathetic way in which they were uttered by the bereaved husband, must have caught the attention of some keen young reporter, who developed what, on the surface, was simply a case of a woman unfortunately drowning in her bath after a seizure, into a romantic tale of elopement, marriage, then tragedy.

The death of Margaret Lloyd made headlines, not just in the local paper, but also in that Sunday's *News of the World*, under the title *'Bride's Tragic Fate On Day After Wedding'*. If Smith read it he must have received something of a shock, though by this time he was back in Bristol and probably feeling quite safe.

Unfortunately for him, several other people whose paths he had crossed, also read it. One was Mrs Heiss of 16, Orchard Road, Highgate, who recalled that a man named Lloyd had applied to her for lodgings, and had made a point of enquiring about having the use of a bathroom. Mrs Heiss had shown him the bathroom and he had remarked that the bath looked rather small, then added,

'Still, I suppose it's large enough for a person to lie in'.

He had said that he would take the rooms, but as he was unable to furnish references, Mrs Heiss had refused to let him move in. He had then become very angry and so offensive that she had been obliged to call a police officer, who soon got him off the premises.

More ominous, as far as Smith was concerned, was the fact that both Mrs Crossley, the Blackpool landlady, and Mr Charles Burnham, also read the article. Both were shocked at the similarity between the deaths of Mrs Lloyd and Alice Burnham. Mrs Crossley at once contacted the police, and after giving the matter some thought, Mr Burnham did the same.

With a full description of the suspect, the police were on the lookout for their man in several towns, and particularly in London. On 1st February, 1915, Smith was on his way to see a solicitor in connection with the latest insurance claim, when he was stopped by a man introducing himself as Detective-Inspector Neil of Scotland Yard.

'Are you John Lloyd?' he was asked.

'That's correct', replied Smith.

'I believe you married Margaret Elizabeth Lofty on 17th December last, and that she was found dead by you in her bath at 14, Bismarck Road, Highgate, the following evening'.

'Yes', replied Smith. 'That's true'.

'You are also believed to be identical', said the Detective-Inspector, 'with George Joseph Smith, whose wife died in similar circumstances in December 1913 at Blackpool'.

'I know nothing about that', came the reply, 'and my name's not Smith, it's Lloyd, John Lloyd. I have no idea what you're talking about'.

'Well, you will have to accompany me to the police station, and if you are found to be George Smith, you'll be charged with causing false entries to be made on your marriage certificate'.

On hearing this Smith became less worried and agreed to go with the policeman. He had expected to be charged with murder, instead, the detective was talking of charging him with making false entries on a marriage certificate.

Once they had him safely in custody, however, and had made further enquiries, the evidence began to pile up. The man arrested as John Lloyd soon turned out to be not only George Joseph Smith, but also George Oliver Love, Charles Oliver James, George Rose and Henry Williams.

The charge of false entries was dropped and one of bigamy substituted. This would later be replaced by an indictment for murder.

Glancing through the morning paper between customers, John Ellis sat in his shop and read of Smith's arrest. What an interesting case, he mused, with just the hint of a smile as he absorbed the intriguing details. What kind of man could commit such horrific crimes? He knew that in all probability he would soon find out, for he would very likely be coming face to face with the monster in question early one morning in the near future.

Once Smith was under lock and key, the Home Office ordered the body of Margaret Lofty to be exhumed. Supervising the exhumation was Dr Bernard Spilsbury, who went from Finchley Cemetery, first to Herne Bay, then to Blackpool, to oversee the disinterments of Bessie Mundy and Alice Burnham, respectively.

On 23rd March, Smith was charged with the murders. Remanded at Bow Street, he was eventually brought to trial at the Old Bailey on Tuesday, 22nd June 1915, when he was indicted for the murder of Bessie Mundy only.

By this time, Smith's crimes were front page news, and people queued for hours to secure a place in the Public Gallery. The prisoner was defended by Edward Marshall Hall, assisted by Montague Shearman and Grattan Bushe, while Sir Archibald Bodkin, Travers Humphreys and Cecil Whiteley appeared for the Crown.

Over the course of the next week or so, a long parade of witnesses was called to the stand and over two hundred exhibits produced in court, including the actual baths in which the three victims had met their deaths. At one point in the trial, a young nurse, dressed in a bathing-suit, was used to demonstrate how the brides had been drowned. This little exhibition almost ended in further tragedy, when the nurse lost consciousness and had to be revived by artificial respiration.

The relatives of the three murdered women who were called to give evidence, did so with great difficulty, being under such emotional stress. Smith listened intently, making copious notes, which he passed to his

Counsel, particularly during the questioning of Edith Pegler, who told the court that he had once warned her of the danger of taking baths.

'I would advise you to be careful', he had said. 'For it's a known fact that many women have lost their lives through fainting and weak hearts while in the bath'.

In the Magistrates' Court, Smith had been loud and disruptive, but at the trial he remained reasonably calm, until Detective-Inspector Neil stepped up to give evidence. He then shouted,

'That man is a scoundrel. He ought to be up here in the dock, not me'. And when another policeman was called, Smith yelled out,

'He's another scoundrel. He's been up to nothing but bribery for years'. He was told by the judge, Mr Justice Scrutton, to sit down.

'You're doing yourself no good', he was advised.

'I don't care tuppence what your witnesses have to say', said Smith. 'You'll have me hung the way you're going on. You might as well sentence me now and have done with it. It's a disgrace to a Christian country. I'm no murderer. I might be a bit peculiar, but I'm not a murderer'.

Marshall Hall cross-examined each witness with his usual thoroughness, and when the turn of the Defence came he announced that he would not be calling any witnesses. This gave him the last word, for where no evidence is called by the Defence, the Prosecution is obliged to sum up first. After Archibald Bodkin had spoken, Marshall Hall delivered a fine speech in defence of his client, the main thrust of which centred on the absence of any marks of violence on the bodies of the alleged victims.

'If you drowned a kitten', he said, "it would scratch you. Do you not think a woman would scratch?'

When the judge had finished his summing-up, the jury retired and took just over twenty minutes to find Smith guilty. As Mr Justice Scrutton donned the black cap the prisoner smiled scornfully, prompting the judge to remark,

'I think an exhortation to repentance would be wasted on you'.

After his appeal had been duly dealt with and dismissed, Smith was transferred from Pentonville to Maidstone Gaol, where he was to be hanged. At Pentonville, he had complained that one of the warders detailed to guard him would not talk.

'He just sits there all the time saying nothing', said Smith. 'Anybody would think it was him that was going to be hanged'.

On 12th August, 1915, John Ellis travelled down to Maidstone and was met at the railway station by the Sheriff and the Under-Sheriff. At the prison, he was told that the Governor was on a visit to France, where his son was lying wounded in a military hospital. In his place was Deputy-Governor

Wintle, who had come down from Liverpool Gaol. Ellis had met Wintle previously, when he had executed George Ball.

'How is Smith holding up?' Ellis asked.

'A bit depressed', was the reply. 'I'm afraid he'll require some assistance in the morning'.

But when Ellis suggested the usual dose of brandy, the Deputy-Governor replied that he was not inclined to order this on his own responsibility.

'I'll leave it to the doctor', he told Ellis.

Before going to examine the drop, Ellis was given the condemned man's measurements: height 5ft. 7½ins., weight 11st. 7lbs. His assistant for this execution was a man named Edward Taylor, from Brighton. It was Taylor's first assignment, and he reminded Ellis that he had written to the Rochdale hangman some time before, asking how he might become a public executioner. Ellis had given him the address to write to and he had eventually taken the examinations and passed. Ellis had also bought his first bulldog from Taylor, four years previously, and afterwards became quite renowned in the dog-breeding world for the bulldogs he bred.

The two men examined the scaffold together, then Ellis arranged with the Chief Warder to view the prisoner. The Chief Warder asked the Prison Chaplain to walk in the yard with the condemned man, while the hangmen got a good look at him, and they observed Smith from a window in the prison hospital. It was a mild summer evening, and as the prisoner came into view, Ellis got something of a shock at the first sight of him. Having seen photographs of Smith in the newspapers, in which he appeared smartly turned out, with dark hair neatly brushed, Ellis was amazed at the dramatic change in his appearance in the space of a few weeks. His brown hair had turned almost white, and was long and unkempt, while his face was drawn and haggard and his back bent like that of an old man. He was 43, but looked more like 63. Ellis decided on a drop of 6ft. 8ins.

Later, the Doctor told Ellis that the prisoner had a bad heart and might well collapse under the strain before they could get him to the scaffold. The Doctor agreed to give him brandy, but the prisoner refused to take it.

'I don't need that!' he said, but it was quite obvious that this was merely bravado.

A few days previously, Smith had been confirmed by the Bishop of Croydon, who asked him if he wished to make a confession.

'I have no confession to make', replied Smith, 'I'm innocent'.

He told a warder that when his estate was settled, there would be about £150 left, which would go to Edith Pegler. Yet he refused to allow her to visit him. He said she had asked to come, but he wanted no visitors.

The last night passed very slowly, but without incident, and the morning dawned fine and sunny. The nerves of the prisoner were now failing him, yet he still would not take the brandy. A breakfast of boiled eggs, bread and butter and tea was left untouched.

At five minutes to eight the hangmen made their way along the hushed prison corridor to the condemned cell. Hearing the shuffling of footsteps, the Chaplain, who was alone with the prisoner in his cell, mistakenly believing that the time had come to take the condemned man to the scaffold, opened the cell door and stepped out into the passage, followed by Smith, who was immediately pushed back inside by a warder. The Acting-Governor then consulted his watch. There was a short wait until one minute before eight o'clock, when the hangman entered the cell to pinion the prisoner, who offered no resistance. Having loosened Smith's shirt collar, Ellis left the cell and headed for the scaffold, leaving his assistant with the condemned man. When the procession reached the scaffold Ellis was waiting. The condemned man stopped just short of the trapdoors and exclaimed,

'I'm innocent of this crime'.

Ellis pulled him to the chalk mark on the trapdoors and slipped the white cap over his head. While he was adjusting the rope, Smith spoke again. From beneath the cap came the muffled words,

'I am innocent!'

Ellis pulled the lever and George Joseph Smith plunged into the pit. One of the most callous murderers the Rochdale hangman would ever put to death dangled at the end of the rope. He would never again prey upon another innocent female.

CHAPTER 21

TERROR ON THE GALLOWS

In the latter part of 1915, the prison authorities introduced a new rule. It was decreed that in future, unless there was very good reason to believe that some sort of trouble was likely to occur, no assistant was to be engaged to work with the Senior Executioner.

While the Senior Executioner himself was normally engaged by the Sheriff of the County, it was the responsibility of the Governor of the prison at which the hanging was to take place, to engage the assistant. Ellis knew nothing of the new rule until he arrived at Bedford Gaol on 15th November 1915, to hang one William Benjamin Reeve for the murder of his wife at Leighton Buzzard.

It was the first time he had been asked to carry out an execution at Bedford, and he was less than impressed by the facilities. On arriving at the prison gates, Ellis made his way through the small crowd gathered there. Among them he noticed a soldier in uniform, and on gaining entry was told that the young man, a corporal, was the son of the condemned prisoner. He had been wounded in France and was home on leave. Ellis felt sorry for him, but of course, it would have been very much out of place for the hangman to speak to the young man.

William Reeve received a large number of visitors during his incarceration, and always seemed in good spirits while they were there. But after they had left he would sink into a deep depression, and very often would weep bitterly. Not many hours later he would have miraculously recovered from his depression and would be again cheerful and talkative. He had been a poacher, and was quite frank about admitting it. It was during an argument with his wife that he had shot her with the double-barrelled gun he used for killing rabbits. He had then tried to cut his own throat, but as with the majority of such suicide attempts, was unsuccessful.

The murderer had been drinking at the time of the killing, and although this had probably led to the argument with his wife, there was also some evidence of intent, as earlier in the day he had indicated to a friend that he had left his gun in the kitchen, and that it was loaded for a purpose.

When Mrs Reeve arrived home from her work she sent the children to the cinema. She knew her husband was out drinking and was obviously anticipating trouble. Soon after Reeve arrived home, the worse for drink, the neighbours heard shots being fired and rushed to investigate. They found Mrs Reeve sitting in a chair with part of her face blown away. She was beyond help and died soon afterwards.

No one ever found out what the Reeves had argued about, and as there was no apparent motive, the Defence entered a plea of insanity, despite the fact that Reeve himself insisted that the shooting had been accidental. He was found guilty, and following the failure of his appeal, the date of execution was set for 16th November.

Soon after his arrival at Bedford, Ellis sat opposite the Governor in his office and heard for the first time of the new rule regarding assistants.

'Well, to my way of thinking, Governor', said Ellis, 'this is a very bad move indeed. As a Senior Executioner this is not going to affect me personally. I've done the job for quite a number of years now, and I've never once been in a position where I couldn't carry out my duties, either through illness, or for any other reason. But nothing is a certainty in this world, and if something *did* go wrong, the assistant, who is after all trained to do the job, could step into the breach'.

'I'm sure you'll manage very well on your own Mr Ellis', said the Governor unsympathetically.

'Very well', replied Ellis, 'but I shall not be strapping the prisoner's legs together when he reaches the trapdoors, otherwise he'll have too long a wait on the scaffold'.

In the condemned cell Reeve was several times given rabbit for his dinner, as he had requested, and appeared to enjoy it. Nevertheless, when they came to weigh him on the day prior to his execution, they got quite a shock, for he had lost 20lbs. in weight.

When Ellis observed the prisoner through the peephole he saw a tall, thin man with a sandy moustache. In fact, Reeve was 5ft. 10ins., but now weighed only 9st. 12lbs. He was 42 years of age, but looked much older. At that particular moment he was sitting at a table with the prison schoolmaster, who was writing letters for him, for Reeve was illiterate and could just about write his own name.

Ellis was disappointed when he saw the scaffold for the first time. First, it was a long way from the condemned cell, and was built in such a way that the condemned man would not be able simply to walk onto the trapdoors as was the usual procedure. Secondly, he would have to make a half-turn after stepping onto the drop. He would therefore need to be guided first of all, then placed in position. As there would be no assistant to the hangman, Ellis asked for two planks, which he placed one on either side of the drop, so that a warder might stand on each in case the prisoner should need supporting. The problem was that Reeve would now also have to negotiate the planks, and if he became uncertain he might very well stumble as he stepped onto the scaffold. All this worried Ellis, for he knew that if anything should go wrong the blame would be placed firmly on his shoulders.

On the penultimate evening the condemned man smoked cigarettes continuously, and next morning had only eight remaining. He was allowed to exercise very early in the mornings and intended to smoke his remaining cigarettes then. Unfortunately, the officer detailed to take him into the yard arrived late and was roundly admonished by the prisoner.

'Hurry up', he was told, 'or I'll have no time to smoke my cigarettes'.

At the end of the day, he was left with only two cigarettes, which he planned to smoke soon after rising on his last day. Reeve was, however, able to indulge in a final orgy of smoking on his last night, as the Prison Doctor visited him and very kindly handed him a box of 25.

Still concerned about the distance between the condemned cell and the scaffold, Ellis decided to have a 'dry run'. Down the long passage, into the open air, then two left turns before the scaffold, which was close to the outer prison wall, was reached. After that lengthy walk the prisoner would be standing in the wrong position on the trapdoors, with only the hangman, without an assistant, to place him correctly, cover his head, then slip the noose around his neck and position the knot.

There was snow overnight and it was still falling next morning, accompanied by a bitterly cold wind. At a few minutes before eight o'clock, Ellis joined the officials waiting outside the door of the condemned man's cell. Usually at this point the Chaplain would be inside the cell with the prisoner, but on this occasion he was standing with the Governor in the passage. Having prayed with Reeve, he had left him inside the cell with two warders. He was now standing there reading from his prayer book. As Ellis watched, he noticed the Chaplain lean close to the Governor and whisper something to him. The Governor approached Ellis and said,

'The Chaplain has asked if you will wait until he gets to a certain passage in the service before you pull the lever'.

'No, I shall not', replied Ellis. 'I think the condemned man has enough to go through without having to wait for a particular moment'.

The executioner's answer was conveyed to the Chaplain, who had no time to react to it, as Ellis then entered the cell. Reeve's eyes betrayed no fear, but just after Ellis had pinioned his hands behind his back and was loosening his collar, he said,

'My neck's still sore, so be careful will you? Don't hurt me'.

He was obviously referring to the injury caused in his abortive suicide attempt. Ellis thought it very odd that a man about to be hanged should be worrying about a minor injury. Nevertheless, he replied,

'I won't hurt you. You have nothing to be afraid of'. Then, remembering that he would not be strapping the prisoner's legs together, he added, 'Place your feet together as soon as we get there, and it will be all over in an instant'. Reeve just nodded.

Ellis left the cell and hurried on ahead to the scaffold. He seemed to reach it a long time before the drone of the Chaplain's voice could be heard, to signal the fact that the procession was on its way. When it finally came into view Ellis could see that Reeve was walking without assistance, his head held high. When the dangling noose came into view he did not flinch, but walked calmly onto the trapdoors, stepping over the planks without stumbling. Ellis slipped on the white cap, then attempted to turn him into the correct position. But as Ellis stepped towards the lever the condemned man suddenly remembered about his feet, and still had the self-possession to shuffle them together, with the result that his position again altered slightly, so that he was no longer in the centre of the trapdoors. Ellis knew that if the victim did not plunge straight down into the pit the job could easily go wrong. However, he felt he could delay no longer and drew the lever. Later, on being informed that Reeve had died instantaneously, Ellis was a very relieved man, and now believed more than ever that it was absolutely essential to employ an assistant.

It was only two weeks later, at Walton Gaol, Liverpool, that Ellis carried out the double hanging of John Thornley, a railwayman from Macclesfield, in Cheshire, and a negro named Young Hill. On this occasion there was no question of doing the job single-handedly, for apart from the fact that there would be two victims to deal with simultaneously on the scaffold, there was also the strong possibility that one of them was likely to give trouble.

After agreeing to do the job, Ellis was asked by the Under-Sheriffs of Lancashire what size of fee he was expecting to receive. He pointed out that in his opinion this was no ordinary double execution, for which he would normally receive £15 plus expenses, and that he would expect to be paid the full double payment of £20 plus expenses. This was turned down and he received only £15 plus expenses, although the assistant received a full double fee of 4 guineas plus expenses, which Ellis considered totally unfair.

Thornley's crime, the murder of a young mill girl named Frances Johnson, was the result of a case of unrequited love. Thornley, a lampman at the

Central Railway Station in Macclesfield, had taken a fancy to Miss Johnson, who was 24 and very pretty. She, on the other hand, did not encourage his attentions, yet he persisted, following her about continuously and hanging around her parents' home. Though feeling rather sorry for him, Frances's father asked him to leave her alone. Thornley, however, ignored Mr Johnson's request, and the father was finally forced to warn him that unless he stayed away from his daughter he would be forced to call in the police. Yet Thornley still refused to comply. He stayed away from the house for a while, but still followed the girl around.

In September, 1915, Mr and Mrs Johnson left for Cleethorpes to take their annual holiday of one week. Frances still had to go to her work while her parents were away, and asked May Warren, a friend who lived next door, if she would like to stay with her.

For a few nights the girls slept together, but on the night of 17th September they occupied separate rooms at Frances's suggestion. Both girls worked at a local mill, and while sleeping together they had chatted into the small hours. As they had to get up early each morning they decided that the time had come to get to sleep a little earlier.

That evening, a Friday, they went to a local theatre, and on the way encountered John Thornley, who spoke to them, but received no reply. He followed the girls into the theatre, taking a seat several rows away from theirs. After leaving the theatre they reached Miss Johnson's house unmolested, had some supper, prepared the fire for lighting in the morning, and went to bed around one o'clock. Frances made a point of checking all the windows and doors, and on going to her room, set the alarm clock for 4·30a.m. She slept in the back bedroom and May Warren in the front.

At around 2·50 in the morning Miss Warren was awakened by what sounded like a bang in the back yard. Next she heard the rattle of a window, and soon after, footsteps on the stairs. Getting out of bed, May quietly opened the bedroom door and peered out at the landing, but could see nothing. However, when she stepped onto the landing she saw what appeared to be the dark outline of a man on the stairs. Terrified, she dashed back into the bedroom, closed the door and leapt back into bed, pulling the covers tightly over her head. May's heart was pounding. She could not move. She was shaking, and paralysed with fear.

Some time passed, she could not be sure how long it was. Then she heard Frances's voice, faintly calling,

'May, oh May', then 'Help! Help!... Oh father!'

But still May dared not move or call out, she was so terrified. The next thing May heard was the sound of heavy footsteps descending the staircase. For a long while she could not move, then eventually, she got up and went onto the landing. From there she could make out a glow downstairs, which told her that someone had lit the gaslight in the kitchen. She felt relieved. Perhaps Frances was all right after all. May was still too frightened to investigate and returned to her bed, where she lay awake a long time. She had left the door ajar and could just make out the glow of the gaslight from the kitchen, though all remained quiet.

Then she received a shock, for suddenly the alarm clock in the other bedroom started to go off. It rang and rang as May listened, until at last the spring ran down and it stopped. She knew then that something had happened to Frances. Still she could not move. At last, with a great effort of will, May leapt out of bed, threw open the front bedroom window and screamed out for help.

As it happened, three young men, one of them May's brother-in-law, were on their way to work at the time and rushed to her aid. On being told what had happened, her brother-in-law ran upstairs, calling 'Frances!' There was no reply. He stuck his head inside the bedroom, then withdrew it hurriedly, gasping out the words,

'I think Frances is dead!'

A policeman, accompanied by a doctor, soon arrived at the scene. May went into the bedroom after them and saw her friend lying on the bed covered in blood, an ugly wound across her throat and several slashes on her arms.

A note, written by Thornley, was found in the kitchen, but there was no sign of the killer, for he had gone on the run, making tracks for the foothills of the Pennines.

A manhunt was undertaken by the police, and though a number of clues were discovered, Thornley himself could not be located. For two days and nights he lived rough, but on the third day he appeared at a farmhouse begging for food, and when given some, wolfed it down ravenously. Suspicious that this was the man the police were hunting for the Macclesfield murder, the farmer got in touch with the local police station and the fugitive was soon under arrest. He was by then in a sorry state and offered no resistance.

Thornley's trial took place at Chester, and his plea was one of insanity. The fact that he had written a note admitting the crime hardly supported such a plea, and it was no surprise when he was found guilty and sentenced to be hanged.

The crime of Young Hill, the negro, was an amazing one. He had sailed from New Orleans as a deckhand on the liner *Antillian* . Before leaving the United States the crew were told that they must give up any knives and razors, or any other dangerous instrument that might be used as a weapon.

The reason for this was that the crew comprised a variety of nationalities, and the Captain felt this could well lead to trouble when they got to drinking during their time off duty. Once the ship reached England the knives, razors and so on, were returned to them. The ship was then lying off the Canada Dock wall in Liverpool.

One of the men was lying sick in his bunk and asked for water. Hill took it to him in a bucket. Another negro deckhand, James Crawford, noticed that the bucket was not very clean and remarked on it, before going to fetch some cleaner water for the sick man.

Hill was so angry and resentful at this that he grabbed Crawford from behind, and pulling his head back, slashed him across the throat with his razor. The jugular vein was severed, but Crawford somehow managed to stagger from the forecastle to the deck. Hill followed and again attacked him, wounding him in the back. The stricken sailor died almost immediately.

A scene of wild excitement then followed, for Hill appeared to have gone completely berserk and was brandishing the razor in a menacing fashion. It was feared that he might run amok and kill or injure others. No one could get near him, and he was subdued and disarmed only when revolvers were produced by the Captain and two other officers. To a policeman who arrived on the scene, Hill said,

'I've cut a man, and they say he's dead'.

Hill was tried at Liverpool and found guilty of murder. On being sentenced to death, he yelled out from the dock,

'I don't believe in putting people to a violent death. Only sick people should be put to death'.

There was only one condemned cell at Walton and Hill was placed in it, while Thornley was accommodated in the prison hospital, the patients being removed to another part of the gaol. Ellis and his assistant were found a room adjoining, but did not sleep much, as they stayed up half the night playing cards with the warders.

Before this, of course, Ellis had to make sure that all was properly prepared for the following morning. First he went to look at the prisoners and to obtain the relevant details. Thornley, who was 11 stone and 5ft. 6ins., was given a drop of 7ft., while for the negro, who was a stone heavier and half-an-inch shorter, a drop of 6ft. 6ins. was decided on. Ellis was informed that Hill had fallen into a deep depression since his trial, and was expected to cause problems before they got him to the gallows.

At seven-thirty next morning, Thornley was removed from the hospital and placed in a cell close to the scaffold. The Church of England clergyman attending him had brought in a portable altar, on which were placed two vases of flowers. As Ellis watched, the minister was administering the Sacrament. Hill, a Roman Catholic, had received the last rites, but this did not appear to have calmed him. A report now reached Ellis that the negro was close to collapse and might be incapable of walking to the scaffold. The Governor wished to know if Ellis would like a chair to be at hand on in case they had to carry him onto the drop, but Ellis knew that this would not be a good idea. For one thing, with two men on the trapdoors, there simply would not be room for a chair as well.

'No', he replied. 'If that turns out to be the case he'll have to be carried bodily. Give him a stiff dose of brandy'.

On going into the cell to pinion Thornley, Ellis saw that the prisoner was heavily tattooed. On his right arm were two hands, inter-twined, while on the left arm was a heart and the name 'Frances'. When Ellis opened his shirt collar he noticed the design of a cross, a dove and the words 'At rest'.

Next he went to Hill's cell and found him sitting there with a priest beside him. Ellis tapped him on the shoulder and he rose to his feet mechanically, as though in a daze. The hangman made his way to the gallows, leaving his assistant in charge of the prisoners. On the way he was stopped by a warder, who told him that Thornley had managed to work the straps on his wrists loose. He had not intended to try anything foolish, but was pleading to be allowed to shake hands for the last time with each of the warders who had attended him.

'No, no', said the Chaplain, who had overheard, 'that will only be prolonging the agony'.

Ellis, of course, agreed, and returned to Thornley's cell to check the pinioning straps. The prisoner was still asking to be allowed this final request, and though Ellis would not relent, as a compromise, each warder went over and gripped him by the hand, after which Ellis tightened the straps and continued on his way to the gallows, quickly followed by the usual procession.

Thornley was the first of the prisoners to step onto the scaffold, and Ellis immediately capped him, then slipped the noose around his neck. One look at Hill's face told the hangman that he had made a bad mistake in allowing Thornley to go first, for on witnessing the capping of Thornley and seeing the rope placed around his neck, Hill began to exhibit signs of terror, and was shaking like a leaf when his turn came.

Once the white cap was over his head Ellis felt sure that the negro would quieten down, but as he stood there on the trapdoors he began to faint slowly away. The assistant was still in the process of strapping his legs together when he fell backwards, into Ellis's arms. The hangman called out to one of the warders to support him while the noose was adjusted, but the moment the officer laid hands on him Hill let out the most blood-curdling sound that the Rochdale hangman had ever heard come from the mouth of a human being.

In the midst of all this, Thornley remained as solid and immovable as a statue, which was absolutely astonishing, for Hill's behaviour was having a very disturbing effect on all those present, including Ellis, despite his vast experience of hangings.

The hangman steeled himself and proceeded to position the noose, but the moment Hill felt the rope around his neck he seemed to lose consciousness completely. As he sagged, Ellis's hand darted to the lever, and the next moment the two murderers were dangling side by side in the pit.

It was one of the most difficult jobs Ellis ever undertook, and afterwards he realised that, by a curious coincidence, at another double execution he had carried out, in 1911, one of the men hanged was also named Hill, and he too, had fainted on the scaffold.

Owing to the fact that this was a double execution, an assistant, George Brown, from Ashton-under-Lyne, was used, but in any case, within a matter of months the authorities decided that they had been wrong and assistants were again appointed.

CHAPTER 22

UNPREMEDITATED

Early in 1916, Ellis received a request to proceed to Holloway Prison in London, on 7th February. His assignment was to carry out the execution of Eva de Bournonville, an espionage agent. Spy or no spy, the idea of hanging a woman was always something Ellis dreaded, and when Eva's case went to appeal, thereby necessitating the execution being called off, he was very relieved, and hopeful that the verdict might be reversed. Unfortunately, this did not turn out to be the case, and a letter was soon received in Rochdale informing the barber that he must carry out the sentence on 23rd February.

But then to Ellis's great relief the Home Secretary intervened, Miss de Bournonville being reprieved at the eleventh hour. She was held in Walton Gaol for six years, then deported to her native Sweden.

The following month Ellis got a job close to home; the double execution of Frederick Holmes and Reginald Haslam, sentenced on the same day at Manchester Assizes for two quite unrelated, but very similar, murders.

Holmes was amazingly frank in confessing his crime. He had known his victim for over six years. When they first met, Sarah Woodhall was married, but after separating from her husband she set up house with Holmes in Clifford Street, Chorlton-on-Medlock, Manchester. One day in December, 1915, the landlady called at the house to collect her rent, but found the door locked and the blinds drawn. On returning the following day, she was faced with the same situation and decided that she must now somehow gain entry. A locksmith was called and soon had the door open. Then a terrible discovery was made. The woman whom the landlady had known as 'Mrs Holmes' lay there on the bed with her throat cut. It was later ascertained that she had been dead between 24 and 36 hours.

An immediate hunt was begun for the missing Frederick Holmes, and within a matter of hours he was in custody. He admitted his guilt at once, but at his trial told a lengthy and dramatic story of how he had come to kill the woman he loved.

'We had a quarrel', he told the court, 'and she attacked me. Then I was bending down to pick my hat up from the floor when I felt several blows on my head and shoulders. At first I tried to cover my head with my arms. Then I just grabbed at whatever it was she was attacking me with and struck out at her with my fists. She slumped back against the wall and made a hoarse noise'.

Holmes had tears in his eyes as he continued,

'I could see her white jumper going discoloured. All dark and with blood coming through it. I said, "Oh Neta, what's happened?" I then realised how serious it was and took hold of her arm, and said, "Neta darling, You're going to heaven, pray..." She kept repeating "Doris, Doris", the name of her daughter, and I said, "Yes darling, I'll look after her". Then she collapsed and I took hold of her and laid her on the bed, and soon after that she died. I stayed with her all that night. I slept with her in my arms'.

The accused man was very much affected as he gave his evidence and almost broke down a number of times. He was asked by Counsel about the razor, and replied that on the following morning he found it on the bed.

'Is that the razor?' he was asked.

'Yes, that's the razor, curse it!'

He was asked by the Prosecuting Counsel, Mr Lindon Riley,

'When you knew she was dead, why didn't you call someone into the room and tell them what had happened?'

'I wanted to keep her with me on this earth for as long as I could'.

'But you must have known that sooner or later the police would be informed'.

'Yes, but I was going to be with her for as long as I could'.

'Why didn't you tell the police this story?'

'I was never asked. I thought this was the proper place to tell it in any case'.

Holmes' own Counsel submitted an eloquent appeal, pointing out that his client had acted under severe provocation. He was being attacked by the woman and merely retaliated. He had snatched whatever she was attacking him with, as it turned out, a razor, and struck out with it. At the worst, he contended, the charge should be one of manslaughter, not murder.

There is no record of Holmes having sustained any cuts, which seems odd, as he claimed that Sarah Woodhall had initially attacked *him* with the razor.

The judge, in summing-up, said that the Defendant's explanation of what had happened was not beyond the bounds of possibility, but highly unlikely. The jury were clearly of the same opinion and found him guilty.

Also brought up that day was Reginald Haslam, who had walked into the Central Police Station at Burnley on the evening before Christmas Eve, 1915, and informed the sergeant on duty that if he would send an officer along to a house in Ellis Street he would find the body of a woman there.

The sergeant wondered at first if the man were drunk, but decided that his claim must be investigated. Ellis Street is a short side street a mile or so out of Burnley town centre, and sure enough, on going to the house Haslam had mentioned, the police discovered the body of Isabella Conway, a thirty-five-year-old winder, whose husband, from whom she was separated, was fighting in France.

Haslam, who claimed to have caused Mrs Conway's death, was also married and separated, and he and Mrs Conway had been seeing each other over the previous few months. Haslam told the police that he had gone to her house and had seen through the letter box that another man was there. When Mrs Conway had refused to let him in he had forced the door. After the other man had left there was a heated argument. Haslam told the police,

'I grabbed her by the throat, and being hot-tempered, my strength overcame me. I had my hands around her throat for about two minutes. When I let go she slumped into an armchair and I knew she was dead. I felt her heart. It wasn't beating, so I placed her on the sofa and tied a piece of silk round her neck. Then I placed a shawl over her and put a pillow under her head'.

Before going to the police station Haslam had visited several pubs. In one he met a soldier friend and told him,

'Listen, I've murdered Belle'.

'You haven't!' said the amazed soldier. 'You couldn't have. You think too much of her for that'.

'Yes I have', said Haslam. 'I did it in a fit of temper. Now I'm going to give myself up'.

The jury at Haslam's trial did not take very long to decide that he was guilty, and after the judge had passed the death sentence the prisoner made a quite remarkable speech from the dock.

'I want to thank you all', he said. 'I think you have gone into my case very well and given me a patient hearing. I believe I've had a very fair trial. Thank you for the recommendation for mercy, but quite honestly I do not wish for a reprieve'.

Later, Haslam changed his mind, or at least he agreed to file an appeal. This had the effect of causing the original date of execution to be postponed and complicated matters as far as John Ellis was concerned. Initially, Ellis had received a letter asking him to carry out the double execution of Holmes and Haslam at Strangeways on 8th March 1916. He replied that he would be available on that date. However, because of Haslam's appeal, Holmes went to his death alone. After the appeal was dismissed, a new date, 29th March, was set for the execution of Haslam.

When Ellis arrived at Strangeways on 7th March for the purpose of dispatching Frederick Holmes on the following morning, he was taken to an upstairs room, the window of which overlooked a part of the prison yard. As the hangman watched, two men were led out by the warders and began to stroll around the yard together. Haslam walked just in front, smoking a cigarette, while Holmes, who was due to die early next morning, plodded along just behind, his head bent and his hands clasped behind his back.

Holmes was by far the older of the two, being 44, while Haslam was just 25. He was also much bigger at 5ft. 7ins. and 11st. 3lbs. to Haslam's 5ft. 2ins. and 10st. 5lbs. Ellis weighed up his victim's build from the window, making sure that he was not observed, and though he could not see his face clearly he noted that the man's hair was grey and his moustache was turning the same colour.

Ellis spent part of that evening playing billiards with the warders in their recreation room, and during the course of the evening learned that Fred Holmes was by no means a stranger to them, having been imprisoned in Strangeways a few times before, but of course, for less serious offences.

That evening the prisoner was removed from the hospital section to a cell closer to the scaffold. Ellis decided to take a look at him in his cell, not realising that Holmes had not yet been transferred. As he walked along a corridor he saw a prisoner, flanked by two burly warders, coming towards him, and realised in time that it was Holmes, on his way to the condemned cell. Quick as a flash Ellis changed direction, turning off down an adjoining passage, just in time to avoid coming face to face with the man he had come to Strangeways to hang. He was fully aware that to confront a condemned man with his executioner any sooner than was absolutely necessary might be very unsettling for him, and was therefore glad that he had been able to avoid doing so. Ellis observed the prisoner through the peephole, later that night, and decided on a drop of 7ft. 1in.

Just before he went into the cell next morning the Chaplain whispered to him,

'He's very strong. He's been given no brandy or any other stimulant, but he's holding up well. He's very brave'.

While Ellis was pinioning the prisoner the Governor came into the cell and Holmes greeted him with a bright 'Good morning, sir'. The Governor was rather taken aback and mumbled an embarrassed reply.

The execution went swiftly and smoothly. Ellis slipped on the white cap the instant that Holmes stepped onto the scaffold, then quickly completed the rest of the operation and engaged the lever. He always believed that the quicker it was over the more merciful it was for the prisoner. This particular execution went so well that it was over almost before those in attendance realised it. The Chief Warder, in fact, was at the rear of the procession, and never even saw the condemned man go into the pit.

Edward Taylor, who had recently been added to the list, was the assistant appointed for the execution of Haslam and, surprisingly enough, he had to come all the way from Brighton, which seemed totally unnecessary as far as Ellis was concerned, for there were several other men living much closer. Normally perhaps, it would not have mattered, but that week a tremendous gale broke out over Central and Southern England. By the morning of 28th March it had not abated, and all forms of transport, including rail, were badly disrupted.

Ellis travelled the short distance from Rochdale to Manchester without any trouble, but as the hours went by the man from Brighton still did not put in an appearance. Ellis went to the condemned cell to take a look at the prisoner. He had already been informed that Haslam, having complained that the cell was very cold, had been moved. The new cell did not have the usual inspection grille in its door. Instead, Ellis had to slide back a small wooden wicket to enable him to look inside. In doing so he disturbed the condemned man, who looked up sharply at the noise. Fortunately, he did not realise that he was being sized up by the man who was about to hang him, and he soon turned his attention once again to the conversation he had been having with the warders. As Ellis had not been able to observe him properly the Chief Warder was asked if he could get Haslam to go outside for some exercise, but when he attempted to do this the prisoner replied that he did not want to go. The Chief Warder then snapped,

'You'll go whether you want to or not'.

Haslam got to his feet and reluctantly made his way out of the cell and down the passage on his way to the exercise yard, accompanied by two warders. Unfortunately, the fact that several labourers, who were not convicts, were at that time working in the prison, had been overlooked. It was a strict rule that a condemned man must not come into contact with anyone other than an authorised person, but the workmen not only saw the prisoner, but actually spoke to him and he to them, one or two grim jokes being exchanged before the warders could get Haslam out of the way and into the yard.

After observing the condemned man and checking the scaffold, Ellis went along to see the Governor, as he had a request to make, although he was somewhat apprehensive about making it.

Ellis, always a keen dog fancier, particularly in regard to bulldogs, was aware that there was a show on in Manchester that very afternoon, run by the Manchester and Counties Bulldog Society, and he was desperate to go, even though he knew full well that once inside the prison the executioner was not allowed to leave until his work was completed. Despite this, and also the fact that his assistant had still not arrived, Ellis put his request to the Governor, hoping he might be inclined, taking Ellis's past record into account, to allow him leave of an hour or two.

The Governor listened courteously to that Ellis had to say, then shook his head.

'No, I'm very sorry Mr Ellis, but the rules state that you must remain within the prison until the execution has been carried out, and I have no intention of breaking them'.

Ellis could only accept this and resign himself to staying in, so once again, he spent the evening playing billiards in the warders' mess. At around 10-30 that night the new assistant finally arrived.

That afternoon Haslam's family had been to see him for the last time. One of his sisters remarked,

'Well Reggie, you're going on a long journey tomorrow'.

'Nay', he replied with a grin, 'it'll only be a short 'un'.

After being a little depressed, Haslam was feeling somewhat brighter, mainly due to the ministrations of the Chaplain. He had never been baptised, so the Chaplain carried out this ceremony in the cell.

When they came to weigh him and measure his height, Haslam said,

'What's this for? Is it something to do with the length of the drop?'

The warders did not admit it, of course, but he had guessed correctly. Haslam had actually gained more than half-a-stone while in prison. He had an excellent appetite and enjoyed a large slice of fish with a couple of slices of bread each morning, with beef, potatoes and rice pudding for his dinner. Three rounds of bread and a Spanish onion was his favourite tea, with a cup of Bovril at supper time. He also smoked between 20 and 30 cigarettes a day.

He got to know the warders very well, and always asked about their families. On the night before his execution, Haslam shook the hand of one of the warders, who was just going off duty.

'Give my love to your wife', he said, 'and tell her I hope she'll soon be better'.

One of the warders came from Haslam's home town of Burnley, and the condemned man asked the Governor if this particular man might be allowed to accompany him to the scaffold. It was another request that the Governor quite rightly refused to grant.

The morning of the execution dawned bright and sunny. To know one will never see another day is terrible enough on a cold, drizzly morning, but to go to one's death on a beautiful spring day must have been positively heart-breaking.

When Ellis went to pinion him the prisoner pulled his hands away, saying,

'It's all right, you don't have to worry. I'll give you no trouble'.

'That's fair enough lad', replied the hangman, 'but I still have to do this'. With that Ellis strapped the prisoner's hands behind his back.

The hangman waited on the scaffold, and soon the grim procession came into view, the Chaplain intoning the prayers in the forefront, with the condemned man immediately behind him. When almost at the gallows, Haslam suddenly went down on his knees and started to pray.

'You mustn't do that lad', said one of the warders. 'Get up on your feet'.

'Almighty God', wailed the prisoner, dramatically, 'I wish to state that I am innocent of the charge of malicious murder, and hope that if I'm guilty you will strike me dead while I'm kneeling here before thee!'

Perhaps he was hoping for exactly that, so that he would not have to face the hangman's rope. However, he did not get his wish and was quickly yanked to his feet by the warders and led onto the trapdoors.

'Gentlemen', he persisted, 'I am innocent of the crime of murder'.

Even with the white cap covering his head and the noose around his neck he continued to speak. His very last words were,

'Lord Jesus, have mercy on my soul'. Seconds later he was dead.

CHAPTER 23

THE TRAGEDY OF ROGER CASEMENT

One sultry afternoon in 1916, with the war in Europe still raging, a tall, handsome, bearded Irishman sat in the condemned cell at Pentonville Prison, flanked by armed guards. Also at the table were the prisoner's legal representatives, while a pair of hefty warders guarded the door.

The prisoner's lawyers were there to explain to their client that nothing further could be done to save him from the gallows. It was quite obvious from the expression on his face that he had not expected to hear anything different and that he was resigned to his fate. In rich, clear, mellifluous Irish tones he thanked them for all they had done on his behalf and smiled bravely. As there was clearly no more to be said, they rose from the table and each in turn shook hands with the prisoner and murmured a sad final farewell before leaving the cell. Standing there in his convict's garb with its broad arrows, Sir Roger Casement, very tall and erect, dwarfed most of those present, even the warders. Yet, despite his towering presence, there was no aura of menace about the man. He was, in fact, the epitome of the proverbial gentle giant.

Casement had devoted much of his life, not only to the Irish cause, but also to that of oppressed peoples as far away as Africa and South America. That such a man should end up in the death cell at Pentonville was as much a tragedy for Ireland as it was for Casement himself, for he had seemed destined to emerge as a leader of his people, perhaps one of the greatest. Instead, Ireland was about to gain yet another martyr.

Whenever this great tragedy is discussed or written about, it is nearly always the British authorities who emerge as the villains of the piece, which is hardly surprising, taking into account that they were the rulers of Ireland and the hated subjugators of its people. Casement was a noble, sincere but very foolish man; a man whose high ideals and naive schemes were far removed from reality. Not only by plotting against Great Britain, but also by consorting with and aiding her deadly enemies, with whom she was engaged in a bloody war, he, a British subject and the holder of a knighthood, gave the authorities little choice. Whatever his achievements in the service of humanity, Casement was, on his own admission, guilty of treason. However, in such a many-sided and complex case as this it is extremely difficult, even for those who would wish to be fair and unbiased, to get a clear picture of the truth. Best, therefore, simply to look at the facts and let them speak for themselves.

Roger David Casement was born on 1st September 1864, at Sandycove, in County Dublin. His father, also named Roger, was a Captain in the 3rd Dragoon Guards, a British Army regiment stationed in Ireland, who is said to have resigned his commission rather than disobey his orders to evict poor farmers and peasant families in the West of Ireland and burn down their humble hovels. Later, while in what was possibly self-imposed exile, he fought in the war for Hungarian independence. He also mixed with revolutionaries from various other countries in the city to which so many of these people gravitated, Paris.

With a Wexford girl named Anne Jephson, whom he had married, the former Captain returned to Ireland and set up home in Dublin, where the younger Roger Casement was born. Tragically, his father died while Roger was still a small boy, and when he was only eight his mother also passed away, leaving him an orphan. Luckily for the boy, however, an uncle living at Ballycastle, County Antrim, offered him a home. After a period of adjustment, Roger settled in very well and spent a year with his uncle before being sent to the Ballymena Academy. He was to remain there until the age of seventeen, spending his holidays with his uncle at Ballycastle.

Roger's father, a Protestant, had always had very strong patriotic feelings, and his uncle was no different, the result being that as he grew up the boy learned all about Ireland's years of oppression under the British, and of the great patriots of the past — men like Wolfe Tone, Robert Emmet, the Fenians John Devoy, O'Donovan Rossa, O'Mahoney, Stephens, O'Leary, and John Mitchel, who had been a close friend of his father before being transported for life to Van Diemen's Land. This knowledge, passed down from generation to generation, left a lasting impression on young Casement, and planted within him deep-rooted Republican feelings which would come to the surface later in his life.

When he was nineteen, Roger, with a little help from his uncle, who was well-connected, secured a clerical position with the Elder Dempster Shipping Company, and was sent to work in Liverpool. In 1883, his uncle's influence no doubt still standing him in good stead, Roger was posted to the West Coast of Africa, where he remained for over three years. When an American explorer, Henry Sandford, organised an expedition to the Congo's interior in 1887, Casement, because of the knowledge he had gained during his time in Africa, was invited to join the party. Once the expedition ended, the principals returned to the United States, while Casement, by this time regarded as an expert on Central Africa, secured a Foreign Office appointment in Nigeria.

During the eighteen-nineties his career blossomed. At various times he held consular positions in Portuguese West Africa, the French Congo Colony and the Independent Congo State. At the outbreak of the Boer War he was sent on a special mission to Cape Town. Casement made it clear, at a much later date, that he sympathized greatly with the Boer's cause, and when an Irish Brigade of several hundred men was formed to fight on their side he must have been secretly delighted.

The year 1903 found Casement in Leopoldville, named after the Belgian King, in the Congo Free State. Leopold's motive in annexing the Congo, was primarily to gain control of the region's rich rubber resources, for with the coming of the automobile the manufacture of tyres was now a booming world-wide industry. To obtain the rubber in the required quantities, Belgian companies were allowed to use native forced labour and encouraged to employ cruel, bullying methods in order to boost output.

Casement wrote down, in great detail, all he witnessed during his time in the Congo. His report, published as a Parlimentary White Paper, made the most appalling reading. It shocked the world and greatly embarrassed King Leopold.

The report made it abundantly clear that the natives, apart from being used as slave labour, were also being murdered, raped and mutilated by their callous, malevolent masters. These poor people were subjected to the most horrifying treatment imaginable. Men, women and even little children were chained together and whipped, while those who failed to bring in their alloted quota of rubber were brutally beaten, and any who resisted paid for their folly by having their hands chopped off.

In a three month's trek through the interior Casement saw all of this and much more. The trip, through hundreds of miles of fever-ridden jungle and swamp at the height of a scorching hot summer, severely undermined his health, yet he forced himself on. In the midst of so much human suffering his own ills seemed of little consequence.

During his time in the Congo, and later in South America, the plight of his own country was ever more on his mind, and he always believed that had he not been an Irishman, though he would still have felt very strongly indeed for the poor suffering natives, he would perhaps not have committed himself to the extent that he did on their behalf.

Following his investigations, he returned to London and immediately set about compiling a full report of all he had seen and discovered. Always most thorough in everything he did, Casement had reams of hand-written manuscript to assist him, along with numerous maps and copious notes scribbled at odd times during his travels.

On completion, the report was passed on to the Foreign Secretary, Lord Lansdowne. Casement did not bother to wait for a reaction, he went ahead with his own plans to form what he called The Congo Reform Association, his initial aim being to gain the backing of as many prominent people as possible. Perhaps he doubted that the Foreign Office would take any action on his report. Whether they did or not he was not prepared to allow them to sit on it or delay things in any way. As each day passed he knew that more Congo natives were being tortured and murdered. It had to be stopped, and quickly.

The report was published early in 1905 and copies sent to most European goverments. The reaction was not long in coming. A tremendous storm of anger and protest was heard around the world as the story of Casement's journey through the Congo and the harrowing details of the atrocities he had witnessed were reported in the newspapapers.

Suddenly Roger Casement was a household name. In the summer of 1905 he was awarded the C.M.G.* in recognition of his outstanding work in the cause of humanity. It was an honour which, in one sense, was a great embarrassment to him, for it was awarded by the British Government, and he as an Irishman was becoming increasingly more aware of his own deep-rooted and extremely strong nationalist feelings. Yet he did not refuse the award, and claimed later that he had been in no position to do so. Instead, from that time on, Casement criticised the Government at every opportunity, publically castigating Britain for her dedication to imperialism and her treatment of those in her power. No doubt because of the fact that Casement was now such a high-profile figure, no action was taken against him, though his scathing comments were noted, and filed away for future reference.

In 1906, despite all the disparaging remarks he had directed at the Government, Casement accepted another Foreign Office appointment, this time as His Majesty's Consul-General in Rio de Janiero. Once there, his official duties took a back seat while he proceeded to organise an expedition to the upper reaches of the Amazon, his prime aim being to investigate the rumours he had heard regarding the exploitation of native workers by the Peruvian Amazon Rubber Company. The activities of this company, which was registered in Britain, with offices in London, were concentrated on an area of the upper Amazon known as the Putumayo. Casement spent several weeks in the region, and found ample evidence that the stories of lashings, torture and even murder were by no means exaggerated. Returning to Rio, he took the first available ship to England, and on arrival, lost no

* Commander of the Order of St. Michael and St.George.

time in passing on to the Foreign Office a full report of his findings. In June of that year, 1911, Casement was again honoured, this time with a knighthood. It was an honour he did not desire and could well have done without, but as his work on behalf of the oppressed natives of the Putumayo was not yet completed, he felt he had no option but to accept, though it went very much against the grain.

Two months later he sailed again for South America, reaching Iquitos in the Putumayo, in October, to find things just as bad as they had been when he left. Through his exposure of the Congo horrors, reforms had certainly been made there over the previous five years, and Casement was determined that the people of the Putumayo should similarly benefit from his exposure of their plight.

From South America he now proceeded to the United States, where he met the British Ambassador and also President Taft, who gave his wholehearted support to Casement's campaign, with the result that the press very soon made the entire world aware of the terrible atrocities being perpetrated in the Putumayo. Still more weight was added when Casement returned to London, where his latest report was published.

There can be no doubt that his magnificent work did eventually result, if not in the total abolition of cruelty and slavery in West Africa and South America, at least in a significant improvement in the lot of the natives of these and other countries living under the rule of a foreign power.

There was, however, a personal price to be paid for all of Casement's wonderful achievements. The strain of the years spent in such hostile and unhealthy regions of the world had taken a heavy toll on his health. In 1913 he was forced to give up work, and retired to Antrim on a pension of £420 a year. A part of his income he pledged towards the establishment and maintenance of two Irish schools, in Dublin and Galway, and a training college in Donegal, each dedicated to the teaching of Ireland's history and her language. Though £420 a year was a comfortable enough sum to live on in 1913, it was certainly a most generous act on Casement's part to pledge a part of his income in this way.

It was at this point in his life, perhaps, that Casement took a wrong turn, choosing to take the road that would eventually lead to the gallows. With his health permanently impaired, the possibility of a career in politics was no longer a realistic option. However, as a well-read, much travelled and highly-respected figure, he was still capable of exerting his influence on the political scene in Ireland. In doing so, he had no qualms about alienating the British Government and openly supporting her enemies. With the probability of war between Great Britain and Germany becoming ever greater, Casement wrote,

'I pray for the Germans and their coming'.

He firmly believed that in any conflict Britain was always the aggressor or provocateur, conveniently disregarding the fact that a number of other European nations, including Germany, also held extensive territories in Africa and in other parts of the world.

At that time, a Protestant Ulster Volunteer force was raised by Orangemen, aimed at preventing the implementation of Home Rule, which would clearly have been a major step on the road to Irish independence. Ulster Protestants were very much against this, as they still are to this day, and were quite prepared to fight the Government forces if necessary, to retain their own independence from the rest of Ireland. The Orangemen's defiance of the British Government both saddened and angered Casement. The realisation that some Irishmen did not wish to see their country freed from British rule came as a bitter blow to him. He also recognized that such a situation could well result in civil war. He therefore threw his weight behind a move to raise an opposition force, to be known as the Irish Volunteers. Quite apart from his concern about all that was happening in Ireland, however, Casement had an ulterior motive. By the summer of 1914, it was clear that the uneasy peace in Europe was about to be shattered, and Casement welcomed this, for he saw obvious possibilities in an alliance between his own country and Germany. If Ireland were to be taken seriously by the Germans, however, she would have to be capable of raising a strong armed force, and with this in mind, Casement left for New York on a fund-raising mission. He was well aware that it had all been tried nearly fifty years before by James Stephens and his Fenian followers, and had produced only moderate results.

This time, however, there was much more reason to feel optimistic, for the Irish population in America had by now increased significantly, and many Irishmen had prospered in the New World — even the poorest among them were far more affluent than their brethren back home in Ireland.

It was while Casement was in New York conferring with Irish-American leaders, that war was declared. He issued a statement to the effect that in his opinion no Irishman should join the British Armed Forces. They should, instead, immediately enlist in the Irish Volunteers, for not only was a strong Volunteer presence necessary, in view of the threat of the Orangemen, who were armed to the teeth, but a well-drilled citizens' army could be a real thorn in the side of the British authorities in Ireland, who would be faced with war on two fronts. When Casement's statements were made public he was branded a traitor by newspapers, not only in Britain, but in America also.

Soon after this, Casement left New York on a Norwegian ship, the *Oskar II*. Not wishing to have his movements made public, he travelled under the name of 'Mr J. Landy' and was accompanied by a Norwegian sailor named

Adler Christensen, with whom he had become friendly while in New York. It was not clear whether Christensen was a friend or a servant, for he usually carried Casement's luggage, but rather ominously, in view of what would come out at a later date, it was rumoured that he used face make-up and behaved as a rather 'unmanly' way.

In Christiania*, he Norwegian capital, Casement booked into the Grand Hotel. Fearful of spies, he had shaved off his beard, which gave him a completely different appearance. Nevertheless, it was clear that he had been recognised, for while walking in the street he got the feeling that he was being followed. This was confirmed by Christensen, who told Casement that earlier he had been approached by a stranger, who had asked questions about the 'tall dark gentleman' who was staying at the Grand.

Very much on his guard now, Casement's next stop was the German Embassy, where he was met by the German Minister to Norway, Count Von Oberndorff, whom he asked to supply him with the necessary entry papers to Germany. Oberndorff assured him that this would be done as quickly as possible. Later, back at the hotel, when Christensen claimed that the British Ambassador himself, Mr Findlay, had actually attempted to bribe him to assassinate his friend, Casement decided that he must leave Norway immediately and try to get into Germany without papers. Travelling via Copenhagen, they entered Germany by train and eventually arrived in Berlin at the end of October.

At the German Foreign Office he was received by Count Von Wedel, to whom he imparted his plan to form an Irish Brigade made up of Irishmen from among the ranks of British prisoners of war held in German prison camps. He was later granted an interview with the German Chancellor, Bethmann Hollweg, who thought Casement's plan an excellent one, and also indicated that Germany would look favourably on any scheme to help Ireland in her fight for independence. Casement replied that rifles and ammunition were urgently needed, along with trained officers, and Von Wedel promised to set the wheels in motion.

The attempt to persuade Irish prisoners of war to fight against Britain was, however, largely unsuccessful, despite a tour of the camps by Casement, who spoke with great fervour, pleading with them to join up.

'It is idle to talk of Irish liberty if we are not men enough to fight for it ourselves', he told them. It made no difference. Few Irish prisoners were prepared to take the risks involved. In the end Casement was forced to give up the idea.

In January 1916, Casement's health took a turn for the worse and he was forced to enter a Munich sanatorium. Whilst laid up there, he received

* In 1925, Christiania reverted to its original name of Oslo.

a communication from New York, stating that a rising was planned for Easter Sunday in Ireland, and that the promised arms and ammunition were now urgently needed.

Leaving his sickbed, Casement made the journey to Berlin to plead with the German authorities to act without further delay. His hosts did not appear to be impressed, no doubt sensing that the planning of the rebels left much to be desired. They reluctantly agreed to send 20,000 captured Russian rifles, plus 1,000,000 rounds of ammunition. It was agreed that the shipment would be landed at Fenit Pier in Tralee Bay on the Kerry coast, sometime between Holy Thursday, 20th April and Easter Sunday, 23rd April. The arms were to be sent by steamer, while a submarine was to be placed at Casement's disposal to transport him to Ireland, though the truth was that he was in no condition to embark on such an arduous mission.

Captain Robert Monteith, an American sent to Germany to train the proposed Irish Brigade, urged Casement to call off the whole thing, as it was obviously ill-conceived, insufficiently well organised and therefore bound to fail. Casement told him that there was no alternative but to proceed with the plan, as he felt certain that the revolt would go ahead with or without him, and whether the arms were delivered or not, which would result in an even worse situation. His idea was to get the arms and ammunition landed, then attempt to persuade the rebels to postpone the insurrection until they were better drilled and organised, but if his pleas fell on deaf ears and they insisted on carrying out their plan of action, he was quite prepared to join in and fight alongside them. Although not persuaded that this plan would be viable, Monteith would not hear of Casement going alone, and insisted on joining him.

On 9th April the steamship *Aud* sailed from Lubeck carrying the arms shipment, and three days later the submarine *U20* left Wilhelmshaven with Casement on board, also Captain Monteith and Daniel Bailey, one of the few Irish prisoners of war to volunteer for the Irish Brigade. After experiencing engine trouble the *U20* was forced to put in at Heligoland*, where Casement and his men were transferred to another sub., the *U19*.

The *Aud* and the submarine were to rendezvous at Inishtooskert, a small island off the coast of Kerry, where a pilot boat would make contact by flashing two green lights. Once contact had been made, the pilot was to bring her into Tralee Bay, to Fenit Pier. These arrangements had been cabled to the old Fenian, John Devoy, in New York, whose reply, confirming agreement to them, was dated 14th March. It was subsequently decided that Easter Saturday would be the safest time to land the arms and ammunition, for if they were in the country several days prior to the Easter Sunday rising they

* Now known as 'German Bight', Heligoland is a North Sea Island 36 miles off the coast of Germany.

would have to be hidden, and might well be discovered should the British authorities get wind of what was planned and decide to carry out searches.

By the time all this had been agreed the *Aud* had already sailed. As she was not fitted with a wireless there was no way to contact her. Unfortunately, word had already been sent to Ireland that the rebels should not expect the *Aud*, which carried a Norwegian flag, to arrive until Easter Saturday, the 22nd. Consequently, when she arrived at the rendezvous point at 4·15p.m. on Holy Thursday, 20th April, there was no sign of any pilot boat to meet her, and the Captain, Karl Spindler, after waiting for over an hour, tentatively headed at half speed into the bay, until they were quite close to Fenit Pier. For over two hours the German ship cruised around the bay, and though Spindler signalled a number of times, no acknowledgement came back from the shore to indicate that they had been spotted. Several times the *Aud* showed her lights. Still no signal from the shore. At last the Captain decided that to remain in the bay was too risky, and he steamed back to the open sea to wait for daybreak.

At around 3a.m. that morning, Friday 21st April, the *U19* approached the coast of Kerry. Casement and his men, believing they were now too late to rendezvous with the *Aud*, were put ashore at Banna Strand, a bleak and lonely spot, just north of Tralee Bay, where they were unlikely to be spotted. The first thing they did was to bury their pistols and a quantity of ammunition, before setting off on foot in the direction of Tralee town.

Unfortunately for Casement and his men, Michael Hussey, a farm labourer, who was walking home in the early hours, had noticed a light not far out to sea, and decided that he would go back at daybreak to investigate, in case there had been a shipwreck. Several hours later a farmer named John McCarthy, who was up and about very early, spotted a dinghy on the beach. McCarthy contacted a neighbour, Pat Driscoll, who went to fetch a policeman while McCarthy waited by the boat.

On being aroused by Driscoll, Police Constable Thomas Riley alerted several other officers and headed for the beach. At about 4·30 that morning, a servant girl, Mary Gorman, saw three men hurrying along a country road close to the house where she was employed. They were, of course, the would-be insurgents, Casement, Monteith and Bailey, and on reaching a ruin known as McKenna's Fort, they stopped to rest. It was obvious that Casement, soaked to the skin and utterly exhausted, could not go on, and he quickly persuaded his companions to continue their journey, while he rested and tried to regain his strength. Monteith and Bailey made him as comfortable as they could and told him to wait until they could return with some sort of vehicle. Then they pressed on to Tralee, arriving there at around 7a.m. The people they made contact with were extremely suspicious of them, but they were eventually put in touch with a local group of the Volunteers. Shortly afterwards they were told that Casement had been captured.

By this time, the British authorities had been made aware of the *Aud*'s presence in the area, and at approximately 6p.m. that evening she was challenged by *H.M.S. Bluebell* , which fired a volley across her bows. Before a boarding party could be put on the *Aud*, however, Captain Spindler lowered his lifeboats and abandoned ship, having already set explosive charges in the hold, which detonated only minutes after the lifeboats had got clear. The *Aud* sank very rapidly, weighted down as she was by such a hugh quantity of arms and ammunition. With those badly-needed munitions of war at the bottom of the sea, the Irish Volunteers would be even more at a disadvantage now, but the planned insurrection would go ahead, for the rebels were still capable of putting over twelve hundred armed men out on the streets of Dublin. They captured the Post Office, made it their headquarters and declared themselves a provisional government. The rebellion, however, was soon crushed. When it was over, several of the ringleaders were tried and executed, but the insurrection of Easter week 1916 would lead directly to the birth of an Independent Republic of Ireland within three short years.

Sitting shivering in the ruins of McKenna's Fort, Casement heard the sound of voices, and knew that the law was close at hand. Constable Riley was talking to a little girl, who had unearthed the rebels' cache of guns on the beach. Noting that the weapons were Mauser pistols, and having seen the dinghy and interviewed the servant girl, he came to the conclusion that German spies had landed on the Kerry coast.

Realising he was about to be discovered, Casement attempted to burn a number of coded documents he was carrying, but the matches were damp and refused to ignite. He was in the process of tearing the papers to shreds when he felt the barrel of Constable Riley's carbine on the back of his neck.

Casement, blue with cold and in a weakened state, was escorted to nearby Ardfert Barracks. On the following morning, he was removed to the barracks at Tralee and later transported by train to Dublin. From there he was taken to London, the first stop being Scotland Yard, where he was interviewed and later lodged in Brixton Prison. It was Easter Sunday. Finally, on the following day, he was locked up in the Tower of London. In addition to a sentry, placed outside the door, two soldiers were stationed inside the cell. These were relieved every couple of hours by a new pair. The electric light burned day and night, making it very difficult for the prisoner to get any sleep.

At the outset it became clear that no solicitor in London wished to be involved in Casement's defence. Then one came forward of his own volition. He was Gavin Duffy, an Irishman. Subsequently, in order to comply with the law, two barristers were appointed to defend the prisoner. They were Mr Serjeant Sullivan, K.C. and a Junior Counsel, Mr T.A. Jones. The result of the trial was a foregone conclusion. Nevertheless, the authorities, not content simply to rely on the evidence to be produced in court, embarked on a smear campaign aimed at turning public opinion totally against Casement, which was really an unnecessary exercise, for the British public were hardly likely to feel sympathetic towards a traitor in time of war.

When Casement's lodgings were searched certain documents had been found. These became known as the 'Black Diaries', and would soon be leaked to the press. They apparently originated from an agent of the Peruvian Amazon Rubber Company, by the name of Armando Normand, working in Putumayo. Over a period of six years or so, hundreds of Indians were tortured and murdered on his orders. Many of the atrocities he carried out personally. In addition, he corrupted innumerable boys and young men with his bestial and perverted practices.

Normand, learning that Casement's Commission was about to pay a visit, had fled his station at Matanzas and had become a fugitive from justice. On arriving at Matanzas, Casement had occupied the agent's rooms for several days, and came across the diaries, which described in great detail the perversions Normand had indulged in while in the Putumayo.

Casement later claimed to have copied the diaries, before forwarding them, along with the rest of his report, to the Foreign Office in London, but owing to their disgusting content they were omitted from the official published report. The papers, which ran to more than 200 pages, were discovered in Casement's lodgings, and were stated to be written in his own hand, thereby suggesting, by innuendo, that Casement was their author. He had not kept the diaries secret, having spoken to a number of his friends about them and mentioning that the originals were in the hands of the Foreign Office.

At the time of Roger Casement's arrest and trial, the War had been going on for two years, with no end in sight. The Great War, as it came to be known, was one of the bloodiest in history. To die for King and Country was considered brave and honourable, but the obituary columns of every newspaper in every town and city in the country told another story. Each week, long lists of the names and very often the pictures of young men reported missing, killed or wounded, were carried. Some families lost more than one son. To the relatives of those killed in action no medals could make up for their tragic loss. It made pitiful reading. So much heartache and so many lives lost or ruined.

A typical case, from the pages of the *Rochdale Observer*, highlights the horrors of the war. It is that of a young man, an outstanding sportsman with so much to look forward to, until that fateful day in August 1914 when war was declared. Walter Roman, an international Rugby Union star, signed professional for Rochdale Hornets Rugby League Club in January 1910. Later, he became Captain and developed into one of the finest forwards in what was then known as the Northern Union. Rough, tough and very powerful, but always fair, he soon came to the notice of the international selectors. In the summer of 1914, just before the outbreak of the war, he was picked to tour Australia and New Zealand, but instead of realising a lifetime's ambition, he found himself in the trenches in France. Walter fought heroically at Ypres and Armentières before receiving serious wounds and being invalided home to England. He had been shot in both arms and one leg, and as he lay in hospital at Cheltenham his wife was sent for, and travelled down from Rochdale. Unfortunately, Roman died before she reached his bedside.

Heart-rending reports such as this, surprisingly enough, did little to dampen the intense patriotic fervour of the British public. Our own Government's actions and motives were never for a moment questioned. The Germans were the villains and that was the end of it. If fathers and sons were being killed and maimed on the battlefields of France, then all the suffering and sadness must be borne bravely, and the glorious fight continued until the hated enemy was crushed. It was in this highly-charged atmosphere that Roger Casement, the reviled traitor, stood his trial. There was absolutely no chance whatsoever of an acquittal, and he knew it.

Two cousins of the prisoner, named Bannister, contacted the prison authorities requesting permission to visit him and also to provide him with certain items of underwear and other clothing. These requests were ignored, and it was only after Gavin Duffy had badgered the authorities and practically forced them to let him talk to Casement and find out what he required, that permission was given for the clothes to be delivered to the prison. Several days later Casement's relatives were granted their visit. They were dismayed to find that the clothes they had sent in had not been handed over to the prisoner, and that he still had on the same garments, socks and boots he had worn when apprehended at McKenna's Fort, soaked to the skin, some three weeks before. After they had complained, the clothes were hurriedly produced and Casement was able to change at last. It would appear that at this point, he had not been issued with the usual prison garb.

On the fourth day of his trial, Casement addressed the court. His speech from the dock was one of the finest ever delivered on the subject of Ireland and her struggle for freedom. In his cell, after sentence of death had been passed on him, he was told of the campaign to blacken his name. He was extremely angry and instructed his solicitor, Gavin Duffy, to demand that these so-called 'Black Diaries' be produced in open court and the authorities either prove that Casement was their author or withdraw them and make a public statement, clearing his name of these libellous accusations. Duffy did exactly that, but his letters to the Home Office went unanswered, and repeated requests for an interview with the Home Secretary were ignored.

Casement heard the death sentence passed on him by Judge Rufus Isaacs on 29th June, 1916. The following day, it was announced that His Majesty had seen fit to strip Casement of his knighthood. On that day, he was visited in his cell by James McCarroll, a Catholic priest and Chaplain at Pentonville. From then until his execution the two prayed together daily, and it would appear that the priest was a great comfort to the condemned man during those last painful days, when he was received into the Catholic Church.

Two hundred miles away in Rochdale the Roger Casement trial was avidly discussed by the locals, particularly in view of the fact that their own Jack Ellis would soon be playing a major role in the drama still to unfold.

One man later told a newspaper reporter,

'Jack wer' very patriotic tha' knows. He said he'd willingly give £10 to charity for the chance to hang Casement. He wer' as pleased as Punch when he got t'job. He went off to London as happy as a schoolboy'.

During this period, Ellis had temporarily given up hairdressing and was keeping the Bridge Inn at 320, Oldham Road, where the Roger Casement scandal was naturally the main topic of conversation among the regulars. When he received the letter asking if he would be available to carry out the execution on 3rd August, Ellis was indeed pleased with himself, and over the following weeks felt very important, which was hardly surprising, for he could not walk down the street without someone stopping him and asking what he thought of the Casement business.

It was at these times that he became officious and tight-lipped.

'Sorry', he would say, 'but I'm not allowed to discuss it'.

On arrival at Pentonville, on the day prior to the execution, Ellis had a meeting with the Governor and was taken to view the prisoner through the cell door grille. Casement was pacing up and down his cell, apparently deep in thought. Ellis saw at once that he was a big man; tall, slim, but well made. He wore a short beard and moustache, and reminded Ellis of the former American President, Abraham Lincoln.

275

It has been stated, elsewhere that Casement stood 6ft. 4ins., but although he certainly was a big man for those days, his actual measurements, as recorded at Pentonville Prison, were 6ft. 1^1/$_2$ins. and 168lbs., or 12 stone. After noting that his neck did not appear particularly muscular, Ellis decided on a drop of 6ft. 5ins., making a slight adjustment to this after inspecting the scaffold and determining that the pit was not quite as deep as he had thought.

Great efforts were being made to save Casement from the gallows, with many prominent people drawing up petitions on his behalf. It was felt in some quarters that the Black Diaries had seen used in an effort to discourage the Irish from making a martyr of him. If so, the campaign was doomed to failure, for Casement was to become one of Ireland's most renowned and revered sons. At the time, though, as he languished in his prison cell, despite knowing that there were many who sympathized with his plight, he felt alone and helpless. It is recorded that one of Casement's last statements in Pentonville was,

'Don't let my bones lie in this dreadful place. I wish to be buried in my own country'.

He was not to get his wish, for the request was ignored. He was to be buried within the walls of Pentonville, along with Crippen and all the other murderers.

Father McCarroll remained in the death cell for the whole of the condemned man's last evening. Casement did not sleep well and was up very early. He took no breakfast, and by 7-50 was in the prison chapel, where he received his first Holy Communion. Between then and nine o'clock, when he was due to die, he continued to pray with Father McCarroll.

At a few minutes before nine, Ellis and his assistant, Robert Baxter, entered the cell. The prisoner did not acknowledge them, but stood there detached and aloof as he was pinioned, Ellis having to reach up to loosen his collar. As he walked to the scaffold he continued to pray, Father McCarroll reciting the litany for the dying and the condemned man responding.

Ellis let it be known later that although he considered Casement a traitor, he had to admit that he went to his death bravely and was certainly no coward. His last words are believed to have been, 'God save Ireland', and 'Jesus receive my soul'.

While the execution was taking place a number of Irish men and women, among whom was an Irish M.P., began a hostile and noisy demonstration outside the goal. They were quickly removed by the police.

Shortly after nine o'clock the prison bell tolled, announcing the death of Roger Casement. Many of those amongst the large crowd assembled outside the prison gates actually cheered, while groups of Irish men and women knelt in silent prayer.

Soon afterwards three notices were posted up outside the prison, the first a declaration that judgment had been carried out in the presence of the Under-Sheriff of London, the Governor of Pentonville, a Roman Catholic priest and others.

The second notice stated:

> *I, P.R. Mander, surgeon of His Majesty's Prison of Pentonville, hereby certify that I this day examined the body of Roger David Casement, on whom judgment of death was this day executed at the said prison, and that on that examination I found that the said Roger David Casement was dead. Dated this third day of August 1916.*

Another notice bore the signature of A.R. Preston, Under-Sheriff of Middlesex, and stated that the verdict at the inquest was that the sentence had been carried out in a humane manner. This was quite correct. Casement had died instantaneously. In fact, everything had gone smoothly enough, the worst aspect of the whole affair being the unsavoury behaviour of the ghouls who came to jeer and cheer. Father McCarroll, who was the only mourner at the graveside when the body was buried within the precincts of the prison, said that Roger Casement went to his death 'proud and erect, like the man he was.'

If Jack Ellis returned to Rochdale feeling like a hero he was in for a nasty shock, for the word was out that Irishmen from Manchester had been seen in the town who were said to be 'looking for' the hangman. If this story is correct they apparently never found him, but as a precaution he was issued with a gun by the Home Office, which was a great pity, for though he was never called upon to defend himself, it was still in his possession when he later began to entertain thoughts of suicide.

Repeated requests from the Irish Government for Casement's body to be disinterred and transported to Ireland were totally ignored for almost fifty years. Until, at the beginning of 1965, the English at last relented and the remains were flown to Dublin, where they lay in state at the Church of the Sacred Heart. Many thousands filed past the coffin before it was escorted to St Mary's Pro-Cathedral for a state funeral, then on to Glasnevin Cemetery for reburial. Another Irish martyr was home at last.

The Rochdale hangman was again in action only two weeks later, when he made the journey to Birmingham to execute William Allan Butler, who had stabbed to death a married woman with whom he had been having an affair.

The execution was carried out without any problems arising, and when it was over, the Chaplain approached Ellis and asked him,

'Don't you remember me, Mr Ellis?'

'Well, I seem to know your face sir, but I can't quite place you', replied the hangman.

'Do you remember Samuel Dougal? The Moat Farm Murder?'

'Yes, of course I do. How could I forget it?'

'I was the Chaplain at Chelmsford'.

'Of course, you're the Reverend Blakemore', said Ellis, beginning to recall how the Reverend had interfered with the carrying out of the execution by attempting to elicit a confession from the condemned man as he stood on the trapdoors.

The Reverend Blakemore began to explain to Ellis some of the background to the dramatic events on the scaffold and his reasons for his actions. Apparently, Dougal had been on the point of making a full confession a number of times during his last few days of life, but always drew back at the last moment.

In his capacity as Chaplain, the minister felt that here was a man whose soul was crying out to be saved, but who could not, or would not, allow himself to weaken and confess. It was as if Dougal's two inner selves, the good and the evil, were fighting a battle within him. The Reverend Blakemore knew that he must do all in his power to tip the scales.

He assured Ellis that when he had led the procession from the condemned cell to the scaffold he had not already made up his mind to do what he did.

'It was not until he stood on the trapdoors that it flashed into my mind that I must make one last effort to save his soul, for he was standing there on the brink of eternity, ready to go to his Maker with a lie on his lips'.

Without even considering the shock he would cause, the minister had then yelled, 'Stop! Dougal, are you guilty or not guilty?'

'It was a risky thing to do I know', Blakemore admitted, 'but it worked. Dougal confessed'.

The incident had caused Blakemore many subsequent problems, for his interference had been widely resented, and resulted in his being transferred to Winson Green Prison.

'That was thirteen years ago and I've been here ever since. I was heavily criticised at the time I know, but if you remember, Dougal always claimed that his wife's death was the result of an accident when the gun went off. By getting him to confess to the crime I've always felt that I helped remove any lingering doubts regarding Dougal's guilt or innocence'.

CHAPTER 24

WHIMPERING BULLIES

Jack Ellis's career as a pub landlord was not a success, and was short lived, as was a further venture into the licensed trade, when he took over the Jolly Butcher at Middleton. So it was back to barbering, while at the same time remaining steadily employed in his capacity as Senior Executioner.

During the latter part of 1916 Ellis was called upon to hang two murderers whom he regarded as big men, at least physically. The first was Dan Sullivan, perpetrator of one of the most horrendous domestic crimes imaginable, and the other James Howarth Hargreaves, who murdered a fellow lodger, a woman, in the house of his sister, at Ashton-under-Lyne, Lancashire.

These two murderers had one other thing in common. When the time came to face the gallows they showed their true colours, going to pieces and behaving in the most cowardly way.

In the case of Hargreaves, he was also the only man Ellis ever hanged with whom he was personally acquainted, although he did not realise it until it was too late to do anything about it, otherwise he would certainly not have been allowed to accept the appointment, and probably would not have wished to.

Dan Sullivan was an Irishman from County Cork, who had settled in Dowlais, Glamorgan, where he worked as a coker in the steelworks. He had married a widow with two children, and later two others were added to the family.

Dan could not be described as a good father, for though he was a hard worker, his free time was spent mostly in the beerhouses, and when he came home drunk he was often in a savage temper. His wife and children would then suffer.

It was during one of his drunken rages that the tragedy occurred, and a terrible tragedy it was. On arriving home one night he asked one of his daughters.

'Where's your mother?'

'In bed', was the reply.

'I want my bloody supper', roared the drunken Irishman, and with that he rushed up the stairs, shouting at his wife to get up. When she did not move quickly enough he dragged her out of bed and proceeded to punch her. Mrs Sullivan, a small lady, was naturally unable to stand up to him and begged him to stop. This only made him worse and he began to kick her.

Even when the children came into the room and begged him to stop, the Irishman's frenzy continued unabated.

One of his little boys pleaded with him to, 'Stop kicking Mama, she's had enough!' but still he carried on assaulting his wife until her pitiful cries of agony ceased and she lay there unconscious. She died the following morning.

When the police arrived there was no sign of the husband anywhere in the house. He was eventually found hiding in the back yard, in a shed with the hens, and for a while resisted all attempts to remove him. Eventually he was dragged away kicking and struggling to the police station, where he was charged with murder.

Sullivan naturally came up with the usual excuse — that because he had been drinking he did not know what he was doing. But in passing sentence of death on this loathsome, cowardly bully, the judge described the crime as, 'a killing as brutal as could possibly be conceived'.

The Under-Sheriff of Glamorgan engaged Ellis to carry out the execution on 6th September, and on the day before, a Tuesday, he left Rochdale for Manchester, from where he would travel to Swansea Prison. When he booked his ticket he imagined he was going via Cardiff. He would then have reached Swansea before 4p.m., but found, too late, that the ticket clerk had booked him to Swansea via Shrewsbury, where he would have to change trains. As there was a wait of an hour and three-quarters for his connection at Shrewsbury, he wired ahead to the prison to say that he would be late, and eventually arrived at 5·30p.m.

Ellis was apologetic and very annoyed about it, as he prided himself on punctuality and was well aware that the rules required him to be at the prison by 4p.m. at the latest, on the day prior to an execution.

At the gaol, he was taken to the Governor's office, where he was interviewed by Chief Warder White, who was Acting-Governor, as the Governor himself was away on leave. White readily accepted Ellis's explanation and took him along to see the prisoner.

Sullivan, known as 'Big Dan', was lounging in his cell, contentedly puffing at his pipe. He was 36 years old and 5ft. 11ins. in height, but would have been well over six feet had he not had such a pronounced stoop. At 12 stone he was considered a very big man, and it had taken half-a-dozen policemen to drag him out of the hen-house and take him to the police station.

Ellis went to inspect the scaffold and was not very happy with it. There was no special execution chamber at Swansea. Instead, a large weaving shed, where the prisoners manufactured rugs, was used, the trapdoors having been cut out of the floor, with a temporary beam, to take the rope, built above it.

Ellis, who considered himself a thorough professional, did not relish having to work with such a make-shift arrangement, yet there was nothing he could do but make the best of it. Also, as the distance between Sullivan's cell and the weaving shed was over a hundred yards, it was decided to have the prisoner moved closer in advance of the execution.

On going into the warders' mess, he was rather taken aback to find several females there. Because of the war many male prison warders were in the forces, and rather than train temporary male staff, the authorities had taken the decision to bring in qualified female warders from the women's prisons. As well as the normal warders' duties, the women waited on the male warders at mealtimes.

Two of these wardresses asked Ellis if they might be allowed to see the apparatus to be used at the execution, and were very interested when Ellis led them to the scaffold to take a look. Not content with that, one of them asked if she could be allowed to witness the execution itself.

'I'm having nothing to do with that', Ellis told her. 'You must ask the Acting-Governor'.

Undeterred, the woman actually went to the Governor's office and formally made her request.

'Oh yes?' said the Acting-Governor. 'Well, you would first have to go before the doctor'. 'The doctor, sir? Why is that?'

'To see if your heart can stand it'.

The woman then began to have second thoughts and decided to withdraw her request.

While passing the time that evening Ellis strolled down to the main gate to have a chat with the man on duty. There was another warder present, and from him Ellis learned that as Big Dan was completely illiterate, the warders had written his last letters for him. He had put on weight while awaiting execution, which was hardly surprising, as he was no longer working at the steelworks and was sitting around all day smoking and eating regular, wholesome meals. Apart from the food, he was smoking half-an-ounce of plug tobacco a day, plus cigarettes, and was also allowed one pint of beer.

'How's he holding up?' asked Ellis.

'Fairly well, I think. When I left him earlier today he said he would not give any trouble'.

Early the next morning the condemned man was removed from his cell and placed in a small office close to the weaving shed. When Ellis entered the room to pinion the prisoner he could see at once that Sullivan was trying hard to keep his composure, but as Ellis took hold of his left hand to strap it to the right he found clasped in it a coloured handkerchief, and on prising it free, he saw that it was soaking wet. One look at the big man's reddened eyes told him the reason. The hulking bully had been weeping. Ellis opened up Sullivan's collar, then turned away and headed for the scaffold.

It was fortunate that the journey to the scaffold was now a very short one, for the condemned man was a pitiful wreck and stumbled along with head down and almost on the point of complete collapse. He could just about stand up on the trapdoors and no more than that. As the cap went over his head he muttered something that the hangman did not catch. A drop of just 6ft. had been allowed, and this resulted in instantaneous death.

Dan Sullivan's four children were now homeless orphans and were sent to the local workhouse, but on hearing of their plight, Sullivan's mother wrote to the authorities from her home in Glengarriff, County Cork. Though she was living in very poor circumstances herself, she was quite prepared to find a home for the two younger children. But the local Guardians of the Poor, at one of their weekly board meetings, then surprised everyone with their meanness, for having readily agreed to Mrs Sullivan's suggestion, they refused to furnish the cost of the journey.

On hearing of this, one of the Guardians, an Irishman, let it be known that the Irish people of Dowlais would collect enough money to cover the passages. In the end the cost of the journey was met by the authorities after all and the innocent victims sent over to Ireland. What became of the other children is not known.

James Howarth Hargreaves was 54, and lived in the house of his sister at Ashton-under-Lyne, Lancashire. He was none too keen on work but very fond of the drink, and when under the influence had an appalling temper.

Also living in the house was Caroline McGee, a thirty-year-old woman who was separated from her husband, a school teacher. One evening, when Hargreaves returned from the pub, he and the lady, who had also been drinking, began to quarrel. Hargreaves' temper was quickly out of control. He grabbed a poker and began to beat her over the head with it, and did not stop until she was lying dead on the floor.

The surprising thing was that Hargreaves' sister, who had gone to bed, heard nothing of this, and went off to her work next morning completely unaware that murder had been committed in her house. Hargreaves, however, could not live with his secret and gave himself up. He was duly found guilty of murder and sentenced to be executed at Strangeways, only a few miles away.

When Ellis arrived at the prison on the afternoon of the 18th December, he was informed by the Governor that Hargreaves was about to be taken to the prison hospital, where he would be weighed.

'You could see him then', said the Governor.

Ellis agreed, but suggested that it might be a good idea to get there in advance of the prisoner's arrival, so that a spot could be found from where Ellis could observe Hargreaves without being seen by the prisoner. The Governor agreed, but on being shown the room to which Hargreaves would be brought, the hangman saw at once that there was no spot from which he could observe without being seen. It was therefore decided that it would be best to find a spot somewhere in one of the passages along which the prisoner would pass on his way to the hospital. As an extra precaution, Ellis borrowed a warder's jacket and cap, and when the prisoner approached with his escort, the hangman stood there in the dimly-lit corridor with a real warder and waited to get a good look at the condemned man.

As Hargreaves came closer the hangman received something of a shock, for he recognised the prisoner as a man he had met at various dog racing handicaps around the county. He had not been a friend, just an acquaintance, but he was a man with whom Ellis had spoken on several occasions, and it was an odd and very unpleasant feeling to think that he was about to hang the man. Hargreaves, of course, did not take the slightest notice of Ellis as he passed him, though he was so close that he could have reached out and touched him.

On weighing him, they were surprised to discover that he had gained fifteen pounds, and tipped the scales at 14 st. 7lbs., although he was only 5ft. 5ins. tall. Ellis regarded the prisoner as a very bulky man indeed and gave him a drop of only 5ft. 4ins.

Hargreaves was now beginning to display the same sort of symptoms that Ellis had seen in the other big man, Dan Sullivan. First the deep depression, followed by abject terror. He was so frightened in fact, that when Ellis went into the cell to pinion him and loosen his collar there was no longer any need to worry about the prisoner recognising him, for Hargreaves just stared into space, his mouth open and his whole body shaking.

Ellis left the cell and made his way to the scaffold, then waited for what seemed like an age for the procession to come into view. The hangman was worried. He could not understand it, for the scaffold at Strangeways was only yards away from the condemned cell.

The problem was that Hargreaves was in such a pitiful state that the warders were having trouble getting him to leave the cell and proceed along the passage. They had no wish to drag him, except as a last resort, but he was so disorientated that he could scarcely put one foot in front of the other.

At last the little group appeared. Ellis could see the terror in the condemned man's eyes as he approached the gallows, and made up his mind that the job must be carried out as quickly as possible, for there was no doubt at all in his mind that Hargreaves was on the point of collapse. The cap was immediately slipped on and the rope adjusted while the assistant strapped the prisoner's legs together. Then, while the Chaplain intoned the prayer, Ellis pulled the lever. The execution was a successful one, for Hargreaves died instantly, but it had taken all of 50 seconds from the hangman entering the cell to the condemned man plummetting down into the pit. By Ellis's standards this was an unusually long time, which did not please him at all, though the authorities had no complaints and he was once again congratulated on the very professional way in which he had carried out his duties.

John Ellis's schedule for that week was a pretty hectic one. Within half-an-hour of hanging James Hargreaves he was on his way to the station to catch a train for the North-East, where he was due to execute a man named Joseph Deans at Durham Gaol on the following morning.

Deans, a former gold miner in South Africa, had returned to this country only a few months before, having worked abroad for over 17 years. As well as having saved some money, he was in receipt of two pensions; one of £2 a week from the South African Government, and another of 10 shillings a week from the South African War Department, for a period of service in the Imperial Light Horse.

Not long after returning to England he had become very attached to a widow named Catherine Convery, who lived at Monkwearmouth, near Sunderland. Very foolishly, Deans began spending his hard-earned money on her. When it had more or less run out she began to go about with other men and thought nothing of it. Deans, who had become far more serious about their relationship than she apparently had, took it very hard.

One evening he arrived at her house and accused her of being unfaithful, then struck her in the presence of her daughter, who later told the police that he had picked up a knife and threatened to kill her mother.

On another occasion Catherine Convery was seen running, pursued by Deans, and screaming,

'Somebody stop him. He's going to choke me'.

Deans attempted to purchase a gun at a shop in Sunderland, but the gunsmith, Mr Garrick, believing him to be drunk, would not let him have it. Instead, Garrick gave him a form, which he told him to take to the Chief Constable. Deans did not go to the police station, nor did he return to the gun shop.

He was still determined to kill Catherine Convery, however, and spoke of his intentions to a number of people. To one acquaintance he showed the inside of his hat. Pasted in the band was a photograph of the widow.

'I love every hair on her head', he told the man, 'but I'm going to finish her off tonight'.

'Don't be silly', was the reply.

But Deans then took a ring from his finger and handed it over, saying, 'Here, I want you to have this as a keepsake. I won't be needing it now, I can't stand it any longer. I'll have to do away with her tonight'.

Once again his friend tried to make him see some sense, and advised him to go to the Houghton Feast*, 'to take his mind off it'.

That afternoon Deans bought an axe at an ironmonger's shop. Later he repaid a debt to a man named Donkin, and told him,

'It's no use. I can't stand it any longer. I must do the lady, then myself'. He showed Donkin the axe and also a razor. 'The axe is for her and the razor for me', he said.

That night the customers in a local pub received a terrible shock when Catherine Convery rushed in, her head covered in blood, shouting,

'He's murdered me this time, he has!'

Apart from her obvious hysteria, she appeared to be under the influence of drink, and though badly hurt, she made her way on foot to the hospital, where she was found to have terrible head injuries. Apart from wounds on her neck and shoulder, she had a long, deep gash running across the top of her head, and the blow she had received had also split the skull, opening up the bone to a width of half-an-inch. After lingering for nearly a week, Catherine Convery died in the hospital, death being due to the exposure of the brain.

Deans' attempt to end it all by cutting his own throat was not successful, and he was arrested and charged with murder. The Defence pleaded temporary insanity on Deans' behalf, but Deans had made so many threats before killing his victim that such a plea was quite unrealistic, and the jury returned the only verdict possible — guilty. Deans was therefore sentenced to be hanged.

Asked if he had anything to say, the prisoner replied,

'Yes, I killed her, and I'm glad I did'.

Originally fixed for 5th December, Deans' execution had to be postponed pending the hearing of his appeal. Once this was out of the way a new date of 20th December was arranged, to which Ellis agreed, despite the fact that he was on a very tight schedule that month.

When his appeal was dismissed Deans seemed disappointed, but after his outbursts at the trial he had no grounds to expect any other result. It was yet another example of a person charged with a crime, opening his

---

* A fair, held at Houghton-le-Spring, a few miles North-East of Durham, where an ox was roasted in the market place for the poor of the parish.

mouth where a professional criminal would not have done so. In other words, a still tongue makes a wise head.

As the appeal was heard in London the prisoner was transported there by rail, handcuffed to a policeman, and accommodated overnight in Pentonville. On returning to Durham Gaol he began to complain about the food, saying,

'If they can do it at Pentonville they can do it up here'.

There was some argument at this point, but Deans eventually got his own way, the Governor reasoning that perhaps a condemned man should be given certain concessions. From then until he was hanged Deans received the best of everything, plus plenty of tobacco.

In Durham Gaol at that time were a number of men who had simply dug in their heels and refused to fight in the war. These conscientious objectors were serving sentences ranging from six months to two years, and though despised by many people, particularly those with relatives at the Front, they were resolute in their beliefs and were not cowards by any means.

On examining the scaffold, Ellis ran into something of a problem. In order to guard against the possibility of the lever being tampered with, a cotter pin had been inserted in the mechanism. This was pointed out to Ellis by the engineer, and the hangman thought it an excellent idea.

'All you have to do is remove it once the condemned man is in place on the trapdoors'.

'I see', replied Ellis. 'Yes, a very good idea'.

Fortunately, he decided to test it there and then, and discovered that it was so tight that he could not move it. To have this happen in the middle of an execution would be disastrous, so Ellis asked the engineer to stand by in the morning and to be ready at a signal to knock the pin out.

'Not me', was the reply. 'I want nothing to do with a hanging'.

In the circumstances Ellis thought it prudent to have the pin removed, and replaced it with a slimmer piece of metal which he could slip in and out quite easily.

Deans was forty-four years old, and taking his measurements, 5ft. 9ins. and nearly 11 stone, into account, Ellis worked out a drop of 6ft. 4ins. The wound on his throat caused by the razor was now no more than a scar, and the execution went smoothly enough, Ellis remembering to remove the substitute cotter pin just before pulling back the lever.

It was the last hanging he would perform that year, and within a couple of hours he was on a south-bound train to spend Christmas with his family at home in Rochdale.

CHAPTER 25

THE HANGING OF THREE SOLDIERS

In 1917 Ellis was called upon to execute three young soldiers, all in the space of a month, and in three totally unrelated cases.

Private Thomas Clinton of the Royal Welch Fusiliers was in training at Barrow when he got into the bad books of a superior, Company Sergeant-Major Lynch. One day Clinton walked into the Sergeant-Major's office carrying a loaded rifle. A minute or two later, a shot was fired and Lynch staggered from his office before collapsing on the steps. He was dead before they could get him to the hospital.

Clinton admitted that there had been an argument, but insisted that the rifle had gone off by accident. His defence therefore, was based on 'accidental death', but the fact that when taken to the police station Clinton had asked,

'Did the bullet hit him? Well it's a wonder he hasn't been shot before. He deserves all he got', did not help his cause at all. He was duly found guilty and sentenced to be hanged. His appeal was dismissed and Ellis instructed to carry out the execution on 21st March at Strangeways.

On arrival at the gaol on the previous afternoon, Ellis noticed two women at the gate waiting to be admitted. Inside he was told that Clinton had received the staggering total of 21 visitors that day and that the two women at the gate were also waiting to see him.

'It's very unusual for a condemned man to have as many visitors as that', said the Chief Warder. 'I had to send them through half-a-dozen at a time'.

The Governor was concerned that so many people had turned up that day, and felt that it put a greater strain on the prisoner than was necessary. He felt so strongly about it that he refused to allow the two late-comers to see Clinton, and they were turned away, very disappointed.

In his last letter home the condemned man wrote 'I shall die like a man and a soldier'. He seem quite resigned to his fate, and on the last morning started to sing hymns from the moment he awoke.

When Ellis entered the death cell at a few minutes to nine o'clock Clinton stood up at once and offered no resistance as he was pinioned. Unlike most condemned men Clinton still wore his prison clothes, for it would have been considered an insult to the King to have hanged him in his army uniform. Allowing a drop of 7ft. 3ins., Ellis completed the job in 45 seconds.

Before leaving the gaol Ellis was told by one of the warders that Clinton had as good as admitted his guilt when he said, 'Lynch was a proper bully. We drilled in a place where a lot of women used to come and watch us, and it was his hobby to make me look silly in front of them. I could never forgive him for it and for all the other things he did to me, so I meant to do him in some day'.

It was only a week later that Ellis travelled to Winchester to execute Leo George O'Donnell, a sergeant in the Royal Army Medical Corps.

The case of Leo O'Donnell was one of the oddest that Ellis was ever involved in, for before the trial was over the accused had not only denied killing the victim, he had also tried to blame someone else for the murder, and when that failed he attempted to bribe two of his friends to give him an alibi for the night the murder was committed. In the end he even claimed that he was not Leo O'Donnell at all, but had assumed this identity on joining the army.

O'Donnell, who was stationed at Aldershot Barracks, had been courting the daughter of a Quartermaster-Lieutenant Watterson, who had charge of the Isolation Hospital, and on the evening of 1st January 1917, he went to see Watterson with the intention of seeking his consent to marry his daughter. Miss Watterson herself went out for the evening, leaving her father and the young man alone together. At around 8-15 the two men were seen to leave the house. Sergeant O'Donnell returned to the barracks at 10-30, but Lieutenant Watterson did not come back at all. The following day he was found at the bottom of a practice trench, battered to death. The instruments of death, a stone and a worn-down lavatory brush, which had obviously been used as a club, were both found lying nearby, heavily stained with blood. Sergeant O'Donnell was soon under arrest, charged with the crime.

In the dock at Winchester Assizes, O'Donnell told an amazing story. Three months before the murder, he said, he had been approached at the barracks by two young men, one of whom asked him if he was Lieutenant Watterson's son. He replied that he was not, and the stranger then handed him a note and asked if he would mind going into the house and passing it on to Watterson. Rather dubiously, he agreed to do this, and after reading it, Watterson said, 'Don't let them in Leo'.

He did, however, eventually agree to see them, and was alone with them for over half-an-hour. When they had gone Watterson confided in O'Donnell that he was in serious trouble.

'If I tell you about it Leo', Watterson is supposed to have said, 'you must never reveal it to anyone. Not even my daughter'.

O'Donnell went on to relate to the court all that Watterson had told him. While stationed in Gibraltar he had often made trips to the mainland, and had met a young lady who came from a well-to-do Spanish family. They had planned to marry, but the family objected and the girl had been forced to abide by their wishes. The problem was, that she was pregnant, and when the child, a boy, was born, it was arranged that he would be brought up by a woman who lived on one of the islands, and who would regularly receive money from the mother for his upkeep. This arrangement had worked quite well for many years, but when the woman died, the son, now grown up, made it his business to find out the identity of his father.

'He's now demanding a large sum of money from me', Watterson, was alleged to have said, 'and in return he will not cause trouble for me here by declaring himself to be my son'.

O'Donnell stated that he advised the Lieutenant to resolve the problem by simply offering to continue paying the allowance the woman had previously received for his upkeep, but Watterson replied that this would not satisfy the blackmailer and he could not afford to have the truth revealed, as the scandal would very much endanger his position as Quartermaster.

'I'm at my wits end', he is supposed to have told O'Donnell, a couple of weeks later. 'This business is affecting my health. I think I'm going to have a breakdown'.

'He was in a very bad state', O'Donnell told the court.

'He told me that he felt certain his son was out to kill him'.

This yarn was a little too far-fetched to be swallowed by the jury, and the Defendant continued with his romanticising when it was established that the bloodstained lavatory brush belonged to him.

'Yes', he said. 'The bristles are worn down because it's very old. It's a souvenir from the Irish Rebellion'.

Asked to account for his movements after he was seen leaving Watterson's house in the company of the murdered man, O'Donnell said he had had so much to drink at Watterson's that he lay down on the rifle range and fell fast asleep. When he woke up it was nearly half-past-ten and there was no sign of the Lieutenant. This story sounded just as false as the one about the long-lost son. To make matters worse the Prosecution next produced copies of two letters alleged to have been written by the Defendant to acquaintances whom he expected to furnish him with an alibi. To one he wrote:

> *'For God's sake clear up those two hours for me. Say you saw me at a social or somewhere'.*

In a letter to another person he wrote:

> *'Help me clear up those two hours. Say you spoke to me at about a-quarter-to-nine in D block. I'll give you £100 when I come out'.*

He also offered the sum of £250 to two other men if they would be prepared to testify that he was drunk and had had to be put to bed that night.

He had insisted that the men who received the letters should destroy them and each had complied, but before they had left the prison they had been opened by the Governor, according to prison rules, then read and copied before being re-sealed and posted. When O'Donnell was confronted by all this he was not a bit put out, and even had the effrontery to tell the judge that he would have been only too pleased to have provided an alibi for any friend of his who needed it if the positions had been reversed.

Now that all else had failed, the accused had only one final card to play. 'My name is not O'Donnell', he told the court. 'I substituted myself for a man of that name'.

At this point he refused to say who he really was. Not that it made any difference, for it was obvious to all those in court that the man in the dock was guilty of the murder of Lieutenant Watterson. He had already admitted that the blood-stained brush was his. Also, banknotes found in his possession, which bore traces of blood, were proved to have belonged to the murdered man.

With regard to motive, it was stated by the Prosecution that O'Donnell had received his orders to go overseas, but did not want to go. He had intended to desert and needed money. He was aware that a large sum was held in a safe at the barracks and that Watterson kept a key in his pocket.

Though this might not appear very convincing, particularly as O'Donnell had apparently made no attempt to get the key and open the safe, there was still more than enough evidence to link him to the killing.

'You stand convicted of a cruel and heartless murder', Mr Justice Darling told him. 'I should be wanting in my duty if I were to hold out to you any hope in this world. You had better make your peace with God'.

As sentence was pronounced, the murdered man's daughter, who was seated close by, fainted, and was attended to by friends. The prisoner, however, showed no emotion whatsoever, but just strode from the dock to the cells below without even glancing in Miss Watterson's direction.

The appeal having failed, Ellis was engaged to execute the prisoner on 29th March. When he arrived at Winchester on the 28th he was told that the condemned man had now given what he insisted was his correct name — Sutcliffe.

On going to the cell to take a look at his victim, Ellis found him lounging on his bunk, talking to a Catholic priest. He was lying in such a position that it was impossible to get a good look at the prisoner's build, and in particular, the thickness of his neck. He did, however, manage to get a clear view of his face, which was large and square. His hair was very dark, almost black, and the prominent nose and thick lips suggested, at least some Jewish blood. When at last O'Donnell stood up, Ellis could see that he had a thick, strong-looking neck and was well-built. On learning that his measurements were 5ft. 7ins. and $11^{1}/_{2}$ st. Ellis decided that, although the Home Office table recommended a drop of 6ft. 2ins. for a man of O'Donnell's height and weight, he would give a drop of 6ft. 9ins.

O'Donnell's behaviour while in prison was very odd indeed. At one moment he would be smiling and apparently quite happy, the next silent and morose. Once he attacked a 50-year-old warder for no apparent reason. Suddenly seizing a heavy water jug, he swung it with great force at the man's head. Fortunately, the warder saw it coming and raised his arm to protect himself, just in time. With the help of a colleague he wrestled O'Donnell to the floor and pinioned him there. His hands were lashed to his sides and he was forced to remain that way for the next few hours, until they could be fairly certain that he had calmed down. O'Donnell showed no further aggression, nor did he explain why he had attacked the warder, nor apologise to the man.

Not one single person from the outside would come to visit the prisoner. Not that he had many friends, but even the few he had now turned their backs on him. To an army friend, O'Donnell sent a telegram requesting him to come to see him, but no reply was received. The only person he had to turn to was the Roman Catholic priest. On the night before he was due to die Ellis peered into the cell and saw that O'Donnell was being given Holy Communion. Ellis found this very significant, for he knew that the priest would have received the prisoner's confession and he would undoubtedly have confessed his guilt of the murder of Lieutenant Watterson, which the priest could not, of course, reveal.

O'Donnell took his last meal that evening, telling the warders that he did not want any breakfast. Just before eight o'clock in the morning, Ellis and an assistant approached the death cell, passing the Chaplain in the doorway. On seeing the prisoner Ellis got something of a shock, for O'Donnell was as white as a sheet and very upset. All the cockiness had now disappeared and he looked as though he might burst into tears at any moment.

Like the soldier Ellis had executed just a few days before, O'Donnell was not allowed to wear his uniform, but was dressed in prison garb and wore a pair of old leather slippers. After the pinioning, Ellis left the cell and made his way to the scaffold. The prisoner had only about 40 or 50 yards to walk to get there, but the hangman seemed to be kept waiting a terribly long time before the procession finally came into view. Ellis then saw the reason why, for the Chaplain, who led the procession, was an old man who walked very slowly indeed as he intoned the prayers. Ellis realised at once that this put an even greater strain on the nerves of the condemned man, and as O'Donnell was already in a very shaky state, the hangman began to worry.

As the procession drew closer, he could see that the prisoner's face was a mask of terror. Ellis at once motioned him to step forward and toe the chalk mark he had made on the trapdoors. Mechanically, O'Donnell complied. Ellis could see that he was very close to collapsing and realised that he must move quickly. As the assistant dealt with the strapping of the legs Ellis slipped on the white cap and fixed the noose. Then just as he released his grip on the rope O'Donnell began to sag at the knees and would have slumped to one side had Ellis not acted swiftly.

'Get out of the way!' he shouted at his assistant, who stepped clear of the trapdoors almost at the moment that Ellis pulled the lever. As they shot open and O'Donnell disappeared into the pit the rope did not appear to jerk unduly, and Ellis insisted afterwards that the victim never felt the slightest thing from the moment he began to swoon.

The third soldier to be executed by Ellis at this period was, to be absolutely accurate, an ex-soldier, as William James Robinson had recently been invalided out of the forces after being wounded in action.

Shortly after his discharge he was in a public house with another man when he noticed a Canadian soldier at the bar who appeared to be carrying a large sum of money. It was later alleged that the two had followed the Canadian out of the pub and attempted to rob him. In the struggle the victim was stabbed in the neck and died on the way to hospital. The two were tried for the murder before Mr Justice Coleridge at the Central Criminal Court. After a trial lasting three days, Robinson was found guilty of murder and received the death penalty, while his companion got three years' penal servitude after being found guilty of manslaughter.

Both men appealed and the latter sentence was quashed, leaving Robinson with every hope of a reduction of sentence. Had he not written a certain letter to a lady friend this might well have happened. In it he revealed that he was guilty, and was quite satisfied with the sentence.

'But it was not done for robbery', he wrote. 'I took him for somebody else whom I'd had a row with on the previous day. I had no intention of killing him, but I do not look for sympathy. I don't deserve it'.

At the appeal, Robinson's Counsel had intended to plead that the evidence at his trial had been insufficient and controversial, but when the letter was read out it did not help his case at all and the sentence was upheld. The date for Robinson's execution was set for 17th April at Pentonville.

Ellis arrived on the afternoon of the 16th and was taken to inspect the scaffold. Waiting there was a group of officials, including the Governor of the prison. After Ellis had tested the structure he was asked by the Governor what length of drop he proposed to give. As he had only just been given the condemned man's basic measurements of 5ft. 3ins. and 9 st., plus his age, 26, he naturally replied,

> 'Well sir, not yet having seen the prisoner, I can't really say for sure, but from these particulars I should think it would be about 8ft. 2 or 3'.

Nothing more was said about the matter and Ellis proceeded to Robinson's cell to take a look at him through the grille, but on arriving there, was told that he was in one of the interview rooms talking to a visitor. Shortly afterwards, Ellis, making sure that he was not observed, watched as the prisoner left the interview room to be escorted back to his cell, and noted that he limped very badly. This was owing to wounds received in the war, which had left one of his legs almost four inches shorter than the other. After seeing him, Ellis was now quite convinced that, to avoid any suffering, a drop of at least 8ft. 3ins. would be necessary, and he let the Governor know his decision at once. The Governor, after discussing it with the Under-Sheriff and the Doctor, pointed out to Ellis that, as the Home Office table recommended a drop of only 7ft. 11ins. for a man of Robinson's height and weight, they were very dubious about his decision to give him 8ft. 3ins. On the understanding that they would bear the responsibility if anything went wrong, Ellis compromised at 8ft.

Next morning at 6-30 a warder brought him a cup of tea and some toast. The execution was set for 9 o'clock. Just before the hangman put in an appearance, the Doctor entered the cell and asked if there was anything Robinson required.

'Yes', he replied. 'I could do with a cigarette'.

The Doctor, not sure what to do, stepped out into the passage and informed the Governor of the prisoner's request.

'No', said the Governor. 'Not now, it's too late'.

He nodded to Ellis who had now arrived on the scene, to go into the cell and pinion the prisoner. When they entered Robinson was sitting in a chair waiting for his cigarette, and made no attempt to rise as the hangmen approached him. Ellis took hold of his left hand. He then got to his feet. But before Ellis could place his right hand behind his back he reached out and gripped the hand of one of the warders. After he had said his final farewells to the rest of the warders, Ellis completed the pinioning and the prisoner was soon on his way to the scaffold. It took him some time to get there and he made a sad and pathetic figure as he limped slowly down the passage in the wake of the Chaplain.

Before Ellis could place the white cap over his head, Robinson looked him bravely in the eye, and smiling, said,

'Goodbye'.

'Goodbye', replied Ellis, taken aback by the man's calmness and fortitude.

'Lord have mercy on my soul', Ellis heard him murmur, after the white cap had been put in place.

Everything seemed to be going perfectly, but the moment Ellis let go of the rope the condemned man suddenly seemed to sway to one side. Fortunately, one of the warders, standing nearby, acted very quickly. Stepping close to the trapdoors, he grabbed the prisoner's arm and steadied him. In that split second Ellis reached for the lever and pulled. The victim shot down into the pit, dropping plumb through the trapdoors, and after a few seconds hung quite still.

Ellis breathed a sigh of relief, but the Governor was not at all happy and motioned Ellis to step over to where he stood with the other officials.

'You did it far too quickly', he snapped. 'Why rush things? You should take your time over it'.

'Well sir', replied the hangman. 'I believe that it's my duty to get the job done as quickly as possible'.

Ellis knew full well that, although the execution had been carried out successfully, it had not looked good as far as the officials were concerned. The truth was that while the assistant had been strapping Robinson's legs together Ellis had been supporting him. Once that support had been removed, the victim, owing to his disability, had lost his balance and would have slumped right over had it not been for the warder's timely intervention.

As far as Ellis was concerned, he was very relieved that it was all over. To be called upon to execute three soldiers while the war was still going on, one of whom had been badly wounded while fighting for his country, was an experience he could well have done without and was glad to put behind him.

CHAPTER 26

THE WALLASEY DOUBLE MURDER

Though John Ellis had travelled the length and breadth of Britain in his capacity as Public Executioner, he found it rather surprising that his visits to Scotland were so infrequent. The reason for this is not altogether clear. Either unlawful killings were less common North of the Border than elsewhere in the British Isles, or Scottish courts were loath to impose the sentence of death.

Whatever the reason, when the Rochdale hangman was engaged to carry out the execution of one Thomas McGuiness on 16th May 1917, it would be the first execution to take place in Glasgow for over eleven years.

McGuiness had murdered Alick Imlach, a little boy of five. Alick was the son of a domestic servant whom McGuiness had met in Aberdeen, and the woman had become so attached to him that she went to live with him as his common-law wife. Though, apparently, he was genuinely attracted to her, McGuiness did not like the idea of having the boy around and was often cruel to him. So much so that it was noticed by several people that Alick sometimes had ugly bruises on his face. There were also marks on the backs of his hands and on his arms which appeared to indicate that cigarettes had been stubbed out on him.

When the boy's mother took McGuiness to task he shouted at her,

'Shut your mouth or I'll do for you!'

She was so terrified of him that she was afraid to communicate her suspicions to anyone, which was a great pity, for the time came when McGuiness's temper went completely out of control. He flung the little boy down a flight of stairs, on account of some trifling incident. Only a few hours later he gave the child such a beating that his face became badly swollen and his eyes discoloured. Still the mother failed to act.

Next morning, she left McGuiness and the child alone while she went out shopping, and returned to find Alick gasping for breath. His eyes were closed, blood was coming from his mouth and ears and his lips were badly swollen.

'He's had a fit', was the only explanation McGuiness could offer.

Half-an-hour later the boy was dead, and at the instigation of a neighbour, the police were called.

The mother's failure to intervene was almost as criminal as the monstrous, inhuman behaviour of McGuiness, who was duly found guilty of murder and sentenced to die on the scaffold.

Almost a week after his trial had ended John Ellis received a letter from Mr Samuel, secretary to the Lord Provost of Glasgow, requesting him to report to Duke Street Prison on 15th May, to carry out the execution of Thomas McGuiness on the following day.

Knowing that Duke Street Prison did not possess a scaffold or the necessary apparatus, and also that it was not the normal thing for Scottish prison authorities to provide an assistant to the hangman, Ellis replied:

> *Dear Sir, Re Thomas McGuiness. Please accept my thanks for your letter of the 1st. Inst. My fee for the execution will be ten guineas, with a third class train and cab fares. In the event of a reprieve my retaining fee will be two guineas. I believe it is usual to apply to the Prison Commissioners in London for the necessary articles to be used for the execution. I presume you will be engaging an assistant executioner. It is always advisable to do so.*
>
> *Your humble servant,*
>
> *John Ellis*

Ellis's terms and suggestions were all quite acceptable, and he travelled north on the night of 14th May. The old steam trains were much slower than today's modern electric ones, and it was almost 8a.m. on the following morning when Ellis arrived in Glasgow.

On reaching the prison, he was taken to see Mr A.D. Drysdale, the Governor, who told him that a box containing ropes and other apparatus had arrived from London, and that a scaffold had been erected. It was a structure owned by the city of Glasgow, from whom it had been borrowed for the occasion. Ellis recognised it at once as one he had used before, in executions carried out at Perth in 1908 and 1909. Compared to scaffolds then in use in England it was very antiquated indeed.

This worried Ellis somewhat. To the majority of people a scaffold was just a scaffold. But to an experienced executioner, who constantly strove to carry out his assignments as smoothly and as clinically as was humanly possible, the difference could be absolutely crucial. As far as Ellis was concerned the structure with which he was now confronted was nowhere near the required standard. For one thing the trapdoors were not flush with the floor surrounding them, but were over four inches higher. Bearing in mind that the average condemned person was likely to be in a dazed or panic-stricken state when he approached the drop, he might quite easily fail to negotiate the step up and fall headlong. More important still, the overhead beam did not have the usual length of adjustable chain fixed to it. Consequently, the rope would have to be tied directly around the beam itself, making it very difficult indeed to measure the length of drop correctly.

Ellis pointed out these things to the Governor, who immediately arranged for the faults to be rectified. Two joiners soon fashioned a sort of ramp, which would enable the condemned man to walk straight onto the trapdoors, while in the blacksmith's shop a length of chain was forged and fixed to the beam.

After dealing with these problems Ellis thought it might be a good idea to check the ropes, and was glad that he had, for they were very poor specimens indeed. The problem actually lay in the gutta-percha* covering the metal eyelets through which the rope ran, ensuring that the noose closed tightly around the victim's neck. Without the gutta-percha covering it was possible for the metal eyelet to cut quite easily into the neck of the victim once the full weight of the body was transferred to the rope. As the gutta-percha on the rope he now examined was well worn, Ellis felt he had every reason to be worried, and carried out a test in the presence of one of the prison officials, dropping a sandbag, to which the rope was attached, into the pit. On examining it he discovered that the gutta-percha had rubbed clean through, leaving the bare metal exposed. There was one other rope to try, and on testing, this seemed to stand up well enough, so Ellis left it dangling in the pit with a sandbag attached to it.

Having done this, Ellis asked to see the prisoner, and was taken to a window overlooking the exercise yard, from where he was able to observe McGuiness strolling around, accompanied by a couple of burly warders. He turned out to be a very small man, being under five feet in height and weighing just nine stone.

After lunch, Ellis and his assistant went for a walk around the city, returning at teatime to find quite a large crowd standing by the gates. The pair managed to get inside without being recognised, and on passing through the waiting-room noticed a young woman sitting there, obviously in some distress. They were told that she was the condemned man's sister, and was waiting for her mother, who was at that moment in McGuiness's cell, seeing her son for the last time. A few minutes later Ellis watched as the two tearful women left the prison, and felt very sorry for them.

Later that evening the hangman and his assistant were entertained to an excellent supper by the Governor, and Ellis later remembered it as one of the most pleasant days he had ever spent in the course of his duties.

Perhaps he paid too little attention to those duties that night, for having left the second rope dangling in the pit, with the sandbag attached, he

* A grey rubber-like susbatnce obtained from the juice of a Malayan gum tree.

examined it early on the following morning and was dismayed to discover that the gutta-percha on this one had also rubbed away, leaving the metal on the ring exposed. To have used this rope would have been very risky indeed, and could quite easily have led to unnecessary suffering and possibly serious mutilation. Ellis, therefore, felt that he had no alternative but to substitute one of his own ropes, which he always carried in case of emergencies. The problem was that it had not been hung overnight with the sandbag to take the stretch out of it. Nevertheless, Ellis felt obliged to take a chance and use it. Because of the condemned man's slight build the hangman decided on a drop of 8ft. 6ins., and measured out his new rope accordingly.

With the execution still an hour or so away, Ellis was informed that he might well experience a few problems with the condemned man, as McGuiness had been getting very jumpy, and it appeared that his nerve might be about to crack. Ellis at once suggested his usual remedy — brandy. The Governor, however, was not prepared to prescribe alcohol on the word of the hangman, and told him,

'No, this is a matter for the Doctor to decide upon'.

'Well, it's quite usual in such cases Governor', said Ellis.

Dr Borland, the Prison Doctor, was consulted, and agreed that the condemned man should be given the brandy. The Governor, accompanied by the Doctor, entered McGuiness's cell to find him sitting on his bed with two Roman Catholic priests in attendance. If he had begun to lose his nerve there was now very little sign of it, possibly because the priests had managed to calm him down somewhat. On being offered the brandy, he declined.

'No thank you, Governor. I've been a tee-totaller all my life. I've no intention of starting now', he said, firmly.

As it was now almost eight-o'clock the procession began to form up, and Ellis went on ahead to the scaffold. As he waited he began to worry about the stretch in the new rope and hoped that it would not let him down. As the procession came into view he saw at once that the prisoner appeared composed, but knew that his nerve might give way at any moment.

No sooner had the little man stepped onto the drop than Ellis had the rope around his neck and the white cap over his head. It was at this point that the hangman almost made what could well have turned out to be a fatal blunder. So anxious was he to get the execution over with, that Ellis failed to notice that his assistant was still in the process of strapping the condemned man's legs together. Moving quickly towards the lever, he was almost in the act of pulling it back when he suddenly realised that his assistant was still kneeling partly on the trapdoors as he put the finishing touches to his part of the job. Even so, Ellis checked himself for no more than a split second, at the same time yelling out to his man to stand clear.

The assistant hastily stepped off the drop, and at almost the same instant Ellis pulled the lever and the murderer disappeared from view.

There was a slight pause, then Ellis peered down into the pit. The body of Thomas McGuiness swung gently to and fro. There had been no undue suffering. He had died instantaneously.

Governor Drysdale then stepped forward and congratulated Ellis on the efficiency of his work. The Rochdale hangman breathed a sigh of relief, as he always did after a hanging had been successfully carried out.

During this period Ellis was spending far more time in his barber's shop than he had for quite a while, the reason being that with the nation still very much occupied with the war and thousands of young men at the Front, serious crime had significantly decreased, which was good news, unless you happened to follow the profession of Public Executioner.

Over the years, the hangman had barbers' shops at three different locations, all on the Oldham Road, near to his birthplace in Broad Lane. The first shop he occupied was at 451, which is now part of a poultry shop close to the bottom of Charter Street. The second was at number 413, close to the busy junction where Kingsway cuts across the main thoroughfare to become Queensway. The hangman's old shop still stands, and is now a florist's. Even in the early part of the century this was a bustling area, and Jack Ellis was not slow to realise that a man in his position was bound to attract a number of curiosity seekers. As he could do only so many haircuts and shaves in a day — a job on which he was not particularly keen anyway, he might as well expand his business in other directions. Soon he was doing quite a brisk trade in newspapers, stationery and the repair of umbrellas.

With a wide range of newspapers on sale in his shop, Ellis would spend time reading each day between customers. Though he was very keen on sport, particularly Rugby League and to a lesser degree, boxing, crime was what interested him most of all. Many of his customers, who were also his cronies, liked to kid him by remarking that the only reason he devoured the daily papers as he did, was because he was looking for any 'business' that was likely to be coming his way following a murder case. Though there could well have been some truth in this, he was just as morbidly interested in murders as most people, and would have followed them in the newspapers even if he had not had a vested interest.

Jack sold number 413 to a Robert Ashworth, before moving on to his third and final shop at 513, which was part of what became the local Co-op, at the corner of Fraser Street.

Ellis was very much one of the 'locals', despite his unusual calling, and liked to spend an hour on most evenings in one of the nearby pubs, where he enjoyed a game of cards or dominoes, and in the war years, with hanging jobs coming up much less frequently, he tended to get bored at home and to stay out longer in the evenings. He would often call in after closing up the shop, and would occasionally stay out rather late, arriving home to face a tongue-lashing from the stockily-built and very formidable Annie, before sitting down to a dried-up meal.

Ellis found the year 1917 particularly slow as far as his 'professional' work went, with very few cases of any great interest coming up. One which did, however, caused quite a stir in the North of England at least. It was a case which became known as the Wallasey Double Murder, and a more horrendous crime would be very difficult to imagine.

It occurred a week after Easter, and the victims were a Mrs Hodgson and her four-year-old daughter, Margaret, who were found by a neighbour on the floor of their kitchen in a pool of blood. It was immediately obvious that they had been hacked to death, for a blood-stained hatchet lay against the woman's body, while a second hatchet had been deposited in the sink. Upstairs, a young baby was crying.

It did not take the police long to arrive at the conclusion that although the crime was not discovered until around five-thirty in the evening, it had been committed early that morning. On the kitchen table stood a loaf of bread with the top slice half cut through. The walls were thin and the Hodgsons usually talked quite loudly, but after hearing voices at some time between 7-30 and 8a.m. that morning, the next door neighbour, Mrs Law, had not heard another sound from the house all day, which was unusual, she told the police. Normally, she would hear and see her friend Mrs Hodgson and the children a number of times in the course of a day. By late afternoon she began to feel uneasy. There was no sign of any movement next door and she could hear the baby crying in an upstairs room. Knowing that it was very unlike Mrs Hodgson to leave her child unattended for so long, she eventually decided to find out if anything was wrong, and knocked on the front door. Getting no response, she pushed it open and entered. Upstairs the baby was still wailing. Mrs Law made her way down the hall, calling out as she went. At the door of the kitchen she stopped dead in her tracks and almost fainted at the sight she was met with. There lay her neighbour, quite still and covered with blood, her little girl's dead body beside her.

The police arrived soon after 6p.m. and began their investigations. There was no sign of the husband, but around six-thirty William Thomas Hodgson arrived home from work, and though his face registered surprise on finding an ambulance outside his door and the house full of policemen, he did not act in quite the way that would have been expected in the circumstances. On entering the house, he did not ask where his wife and children were, but merely enquired,

'What's going on here? What's up?'

He was told that he would have to speak to the Chief Constable. Hodgson made no reply to this, but looking around the kitchen, suddenly pointed to a large portmanteau and exclaimed,

'Look at that! What's that doing there?'

On being opened, the portmanteau was found to contain a sugar bowl, a biscuit barrel, a toast rack and an assortment of cutlery. On the mantelpiece lay a diamond ring, two gold bracelets and several other pieces of jewellery.

It certainly appeared very odd that a thief should pack into a suitcase items of such low value as sugar bowls and toast racks when there was expensive jewellery lying about. Hodgson soon came under suspicion. Mrs Law had heard voices in the Hodgson's kitchen not long before eight o'clock that morning, and knew that Hodgson usually had his breakfast at around eight. Soon afterwards the house had fallen silent and the evidence of the half-cut slice of bread strongly suggested that Mrs Hodgson had been in the process of preparing breakfast when she was attacked. Mrs Law also mentioned that the voices she had heard appeared to be raised, as if in argument. Hodgson admitted that he had left the house that morning at his usual time, eight-thirty, but emphatically denied that there had been any arguing or raised voices. It appeared clear from the evidence that the wife and child had been dead before Hodgson left the house, and he was placed under arrest and charged with murder. It was later established, through the medical evidence, that the killer had not only used a hatchet to strike down his defenceless victims, but had then struck them both a number of times as they lay helpless on the floor.

At the trial, it was mentioned that no person other than the accused had been seen to enter or leave the house on the day the crime was committed, and Mr Justice Avory, presiding, remarked that the murders must have occurred before Hodgson left the house.

The Defence could offer very little explanation, apart from the suggestion that an attempt had been made to rob the house by person or persons unknown. The Defence also put the question to the jury:

'Is it likely that the Defendant could murder his wife and child, then simply go off to his work as usual, carry out his business as if it were just a normal day, then calmly return to his home in the evening ?'

The jury decided that he could and did. They clearly found the idea of an attempted burglary quite unconvincing, and must have concluded that

Hodgson was responsible for the packing of the portmanteau. They were out only fourteen minutes before returning a verdict of 'Guilty'. Hodgson registered no emotion as the judge pronounced the sentence of death on him.

The one thing which the Prosecution had failed to prove conclusively, was motive, although an attempt was made to show that he had committed the crime to gain his freedom, as he had been having an affair with a young girl, who had become pregnant.

Hodgson was a Yorkshireman, who in 1915 had left his native Huddersfield to take up a position with a firm of drapers at Birkenhead, moving his wife and children to nearby Wallasey. At that time, Hodgson had seemed quite happy and contented with his marriage, but after a year or so he became friendly with a young waitress named Lena, who worked in the cafe where he often went for lunch. Before long an intimate relationship had developed between them, and Hodgson began to lead what can only be described as a double life. For despite being obsessed with the young waitress, his attitude towards his wife did not change in the least. At home, he was still the loving husband and father he had always been. Meanwhile, he was seeing the waitress more and more. They took long walks together and held hands in the darkness of the local picture house. He even met her mother, which would appear to indicate that he was posing as a single man.

On discovering that her daughter was pregnant, the mother bluntly asked Hodgson what he intended to do about it.

'I'll stand by her', he replied. 'Only I can't do anything till after Easter'.

He would not explain why, and the mother and daughter had to be satisfied that he had admitted to being the father and had not attempted to wriggle out of it. He also stated, in a letter to the girl, that he would look after her and that they would be together before long.

All this was brought out at Hodgson's trial, but in the witness-box he insisted that he had never had any intention of leaving his family for Lena, and had not really been serious about the affair.

'Were you in love with her?' he was asked.

'No, I was never in love with her'.

'Were you fond of her?'

'Not particularly', he replied, rather callously, 'and I am not the father of her child and never admitted that I was'.

If Hodgson was telling the truth there could have been no motive for the crime. But the jury were in no doubt that he had lied from beginning to end.

John Ellis followed the progress of the case in the newspapers and was confident that he would soon have another customer. Sure enough, within a week of the trial's ending he received a letter from the Under-Sheriff of Cheshire, asking him if he would be available on 1st August. He accepted at once, but after Hodgson's appeal was dealt with, and dismissed, his execution was re-scheduled for 16th August at Walton Gaol, Liverpool. Ellis had, in the meantime, accepted a job in Northern Ireland on the 14th, and knew that he would be working to a tight schedule, as he would have to travel direct from Londonderry in order to be at Walton on the day prior to the execution. However, the condemned man in Londonderry was reprieved, and Ellis received a letter informing him that his services would not be required after all. Of course, there was little or no chance of Hodgson being reprieved, and when Ellis arrived at Walton on 15th August he was asked by the Governor if there was anything he needed.

'No, just to be allowed to see the prisoner', he replied.

He was taken to a shed known as The Ropery, where the convicts were engaged in the making of ropes. At that time, the prisoners were actually working overtime as their contribution to the war effort. When Ellis entered the shed the convicts had just gone to the dining hall for tea, so he was quite alone except for a warder. Taking up his position at a window overlooking the exercise yard, he waited for Hodgson to appear. A few minutes later the prisoner came into view, flanked by two warders. Ellis was surprised at his appearance, and later described the murderer as, 'A big, fine fellow of well over six foot, and very well made'.

In fact, Hodgson's official measurements were 6ft. $1^{1}/_{2}$ ins. and his weight twelve stone. He appeared quite cheerful as he smoked a cigarette and chatted with the warders. At one point the little group stopped, and stood around for a few minutes. The hangman now got a chance to view the prisoner from behind, paying particular attention to the thickness of his neck. Hodgson's build reminded Ellis of that of Sir Roger Casement. In fact, on consulting his notes later, he discovered that the two men were almost exactly the same height and weight, except that Casement's neck was somewhat slimmer, as he recalled. After giving it some thought Ellis decided on a drop of 6ft. 4ins., and later recorded in his notes that he had given Hodgson a slightly longer drop than the Irish martyr because he appeared to be that bit more powerful in the area of the neck.

Ellis sat for an hour or two having a quiet smoke with his assistant. It was going up to eight o'clock in the evening when they brought Hodgson in from the yard, having allowed him an extra-long exercise period. At some point between Ellis observing him in the prison yard and his being returned to his cell, the prisoner had been informed that there was no question whatsoever, of a last-minute reprieve. Ellis watched as he was escorted along the long stone passage, and the change in him was quite striking. In contrast to his demeanour in the prison yard, he now appeared to be languishing in the depths of despair. Despite the hopelessness of his position, he had obviously still clung to that last forlorn hope. Now that it had gone and he knew that he was doomed, Hodgson appeared absolutely stunned. He could not bring himself to eat that night, nor to talk to anyone. He sat there on his bunk, staring into space and from time to time shaking his head in utter despair.

Ellis had never been inside the condemned cell at Walton, for the simple reason that the prisoners were never pinioned there, but brought to a small cell quite close to the scaffold. It was here that he first came face to face with his victim. Hodgson looked pale and shaky. Beside him stood a clergyman reading from a prayer book.

Ellis stepped forward, and drawing Hodgson's arms behind his back, pinioned him within seconds. He could tell that the condemned man, although close to breaking point, was striving desperately to keep his nerve, but Ellis gained the impression that he was likely to crack at any moment.

Immediately the pinioning was completed, Ellis left the cell and made his way to the scaffold. The hangman had drawn a chalk-mark on the trapdoors. It was the letter 'T'. When the procession arrived at the scaffold the prisoner's eyes took in the scene, and it was clear that he immediately understood the chalk-mark's meaning. Ellis took him gently by the arm and placed him on the trapdoors, with one foot on either side of the downward stroke of the T and both toes just touching the horizontal line at the top. Ellis was well aware that Hodgson was still fighting to hold on to his nerve. Even as he struggled to do so the lever was pulled and his body plunged down into the pit.

When the Doctor descended the ladder he found that although Hodgson's heart had stopped there was evidently still some life remaining in him, for his chest heaved up and down, although every other part of his body remained immobile. When told of this Ellis became somewhat apprehensive, but on taking his leave of the Governor, he was told,

'I'm pleased to tell you that my report will say that your work has again been more than satisfactory'.

Ellis was relieved to hear this, in view of all the circumstances, but one thing which gave him great satisfaction was the knowledge that the entire operation had been accomplished in the space of thirty seconds.

In February of 1918 Ellis was called upon to execute two murderers who had committed particularly vicious crimes. The first, Victor De Stamir, had been convicted of the slaying of a 55-year old ex-army Captain, Edward

Kenrick Tighe, while the second, Joseph Jones, a hardened criminal who had been to prison a number of times for robbery with violence, was found guilty of the murder of a Canadian soldier. Both were hanged at Wandsworth within a few days of each other.

De Stamir, aged 27, was born in London of French parents, and had been difficult to control from an early age. For a burglary at Croydon when he was 15, De Stamir was sent to Reform School for a period of three years. While in custody, an attempt was made to teach him a trade, but on release he made no effort to find a job and simply ignored his parents' pleadings to settle down and go straight.

Not long afterwards he left home without telling anyone where he was going, and it was some months later that his parents received word that he was in prison in Australia. After doing his time, he returned to England soon after the outbreak of war and immediately enlisted in the London Yeomanry, but it was not long before he was occupying a cell in a military prison after threatening an officer.

One night he broke out of the prison and returned to London. Moving from one place to another, he defied all efforts to track him down, and lived by his wits, getting himself involved in all kinds of shady deals and also committing a series of robberies. The police were well aware of De Stamir's activities, but were finding it difficult to pin anything on him, until one day in November 1917, when they received a call from a jeweller in London's West End, who reported that a man had come into his shop only a few minutes before and tried to sell him jewellery which he suspected had been stolen.

The man, who turned out to be De Stamir, was soon under arrest, and was found to have in his possession jewellery which the police believed to have been the proceeds of a burglary from a house in Streatham. On searching the arrested man's lodgings, they made a very important discovery in the shape of two silver watches and a Mackintosh, known to have been taken from Winkfield Lodge, Wimbledon, the home of Captain Tighe, on the night of 12th November, 1917, when the Captain was murdered.

Captain Tighe had only recently retired from the Rifle Brigade when he moved into Winkfield Lodge with his wife, three children and several servants. He had only been in occupation for about a week, in fact, before being done to death in his own bedroom by a person, or persons, unknown.

The Tighes were a well-bred, well-connected family, the Captain himself being a cousin of the Earl of Bessborough, while his wife was a cousin of Sir Francis Younghusband.

As the Captain was subject to periodic attacks of asthma, he preferred to have his own bedroom. On the morning of 13th November the maid found him lying unconscious between his bed and the wall, and assumed that he had fallen out of bed and banged his head. A doctor was quickly summoned, and after lifting the Captain back into bed and examining him, quickly came to the conclusion that his injuries suggested something more serious than a fall from his bed.

The doctor left the house and soon returned with dressings for the patient's wounds. He was also accompanied by a second doctor. Following further examination, the medical men agreed that Captain Tighe had been struck a number of times on the head with a heavy, blunt object.

The police were sent for and a search of the house and grounds soon produced the weapon. It was a poker, which had been removed from the dining room, and was heavily blood-stained and bent from the force of the blows rained on the victim. It was ascertained that he had been struck at least eight times about the head. Four days later Captain Tighe died without regaining consciousness.

As two silver watches and a raincoat were found to be missing from the house, it was assumed that the murder had been committed during the course of a burglary, although the haul had been a meagre one to have cost a man his life. The police came to the conclusion that the Mackintosh had been taken to cover the murderer's blood-stained clothing.

It was established that the intruder had gained entry via a ground floor window and picked up a poker from the dining room before proceeding upstairs. As there was no soft ground beneath the window where the burglar had entered, there were no footprints, and the police had really very little to go on until they were fortunate enough to lay hands on De Stamir. They now had good reason to believe that he could help them with their enquiries into a series of burglaries, and, more important still, the murder at Winkfield Lodge. But when charged, De Stamir simply refused to co-operate, insisting that he knew nothing about any Winkfield Lodge and had been at home on the night of the murder. When asked to account for the incriminating articles in his possession, he refused to answer. Later on, he changed his mind and told the police a lengthy and complicated story about meeting an Australian soldier in a pub and agreeing to accompany him on a burglary.

At Winkfield Lodge, they had discovered an open window and had entered. After searching through the lower rooms, De Stamir's companion, who called himself Reginald Fisher, picked up a poker from the dining room, saying it was for breaking open drawers. The two of them then went up the main staircase and opened a bedroom door. Fisher switched on the light. On the bed lay a man in pyjamas. It was Captain Tighe, who woke up and was about to rise when Fisher struck him a heavy blow to the head with the poker.

'As soon as I saw what he had done', said De Stamir, 'I flew out of that room and rushed downstairs. Fisher did not come down right away. When he did, he followed me out of the side door and said he'd searched but only found a couple of watches. He had this Mackintosh on. Said he'd taken it to cover up the spots of blood on his army tunic. He gave me the watches and we split up. Two days after that we met up by arrangement in Balham. Fisher had the Mackintosh with him and I gave him ten bob for it. He said it would be too dangerous for us to stay together, and left, but a few days later I tried to find him at an address he'd given me in Kennington — Brook Street, Kennington it was. But I couldn't find him. Nobody at the address knew of any Reg. Fisher'.

This rambling tale was, not surprisingly, viewed rather dubiously by all in court, certainly by the jury members, who did not take very long to arrive at a verdict of 'Guilty'. They were in no doubt that the recovered articles clearly tied De Stamir to the murder scene, and therefore the killing. In any case, as Mr Justice Darling pointed out, even if De Stamir's story were true, he would still be guilty of murder, as he had been involved in the commission of a crime which had resulted in the death of the victim.

After sentencing, the prisoner was removed to Wandsworth Prison to await his execution at the hands of John Ellis, who duly received a communication from the office of the Under-Sheriff, appointing him to carry out the job on 12th February. It was mentioned in the letter that the Under-Sheriff himself would be present when Ellis tested the drop, and the hangman was requested to report to the prison on the day prior to the hanging at 3p.m., an hour earlier than the usual time.

This necessitated his leaving home before six in the morning. Even so, he did not arrive at Wandsworth until after one-thirty in the afternoon. The testing of the scaffold went smoothly enough, and the following morning, as Ellis was measuring off the rope, the Prison Doctor arrived and enquired what length of drop he intended to give.

'Seven feet', replied the hangman.

'Do you think that's sufficient?' asked the doctor.

'Quite sufficient', said Ellis, who was in no doubt that it would be. For, as he knew full well, this was five inches longer than was recommended by the Home Office table.

The condemned man had no trouble eating his breakfast — two new-laid eggs, with tea, bread and butter — but even though he appeared reasonably in control of his emotions, Ellis still recommended to the Doctor that a glass of brandy would not go amiss.

Ellis's two conversations with the Doctor turned out to be very significant, in view of what happened on the scaffold. All went as planned up to the point when the Doctor went down into the pit to make sure that De Stamir was dead. He was down there just a little longer than usual, which caused Ellis to feel somewhat uneasy. When he came back up the ladder it was obvious that he was in an agitated state.

The Doctor went straight to Ellis and snapped,

'Ellis, you got it wrong. You did not give him enough rope!'

'What?' said Ellis. 'What do you mean? Is he dead or not?'

'He's dead, yes. But he did not die instantaneously. As I said, you did not allow a long enough drop!'

'I told you the length of drop I intended to give him. You didn't argue with me then Doctor'.

Ellis was very upset at the Doctor's accusation, made in front of a number of people, including the Governor of the prison. The medical man must have realised that his outburst questioned Ellis's professional judgement and he later apologised. He explained that he had since been told by one of the senior warders that he had seen De Stamir fall forward, as if in a faint, and that this could quite easily have affected the length of drop, as he would not go straight down into the pit.

Ellis could not be sure whether this was true or not. He realised that as he had stepped away from the trapdoors and moved to the lever his attention would have left the condemned man for a split second; so it was possible that the Doctor could well have been correct in his assumption.

'So you think he fainted?' asked Ellis.

'Yes, I think that's probably what happened'.

'It would have been better, Doctor, if you had given him the brandy, as I suggested'.

'But I did', replied the Doctor.

It was discovered later that what had actually happened was that the warder who was sent to De Stamir's cell with the brandy, had arrived to find the prisoner deep in prayer with a Catholic priest. The warder, not wishing to disturb them, had gone away again, intending to go back later. There had not been enough time, however, before De Stamir had been taken from his cell, and so he had never been given the brandy. It is possible therefore that his courage failed him at the very last moment.

In Wandsworth Gaol, while De Stamir was there, was one Joseph Jones, who was also waiting to pay the extreme penalty. Along with two Australian soldiers, he had conspired to rob Oliver Gilbert Imley and John McKinley, two soldiers in the Canadian army, who also happened to be in London at that time.

The attempted robbery had occurred in an alley known as Valentine Place, off Waterloo Road, and in the subsequent fight, Imley was struck on the head with a stick and later died. The perpetrators of the crime were soon under arrest. Jones, who had already served time and had a number of convictions for robbery with violence, was sentenced to death, while one of his accomplices received ten years. So, a little over a week after he had executed De Stamir, Ellis was back at Wandsworth to hang Jones. On arrival, he was taken aside by Mr Metcalfe, the acting Under-Sheriff, who gave him the prisoner's measurements, then asked what length of drop he intended to give.

'According to the Home Office scale, this man should get 7ft. 3ins., but after what happened the last time I was here I'd prefer to get the Doctor's opinion before deciding. He believes in long drops the same as I do'.

'Yes', replied the acting Under-Sheriff, 'but I don't want us to get away from the Home Office scale if we can help it. However, if the doctor suggests a longer drop than the scale provides for, then he takes the responsibility off our shoulders'.

The Doctor, however, appeared to be absent from the prison, as no one could find him. When Ellis viewed the prisoner through the grille in his cell he found him to be a small man of 26. According to the warders he had been very awkward while in prison, and though everyone had gone out of their way to treat him kindly he had responded by being sulky and argumentative.

Ellis did not encounter the Doctor until early the next morning. The hangman had already decided to give a longish drop, and had a little trick up his sleeve which he intended to use to get the Doctor to agree. When asked what drop he intended to give, he replied,

'I thought perhaps eight feet doctor'.

'Eight feet? Oh no, I could never sanction that'.

'What about seven-foot-ten then?'

'Well... it's still well over the recommended figure, but yes, I'll agree to that'.

This suited Ellis fine, since it was longer than he had expected the Doctor to agree to.

On entering the prisoner's cell, he found Jones smoking a cigarette. He rose and offered the hangman his hand, but instead of shaking it as Jones had intended, Ellis twisted it behind his back and proceeded to pinion him. When this was done the prisoner asked if Ellis would release him, so that he might shake hands with the warders who had attended him during his time in prison. Ellis refused, telling him, 'No, I'm sorry, but you've had plenty of time to do that. We must get on with it'.

The prisoner would not be put off and continued to insist. It seemed obvious to Ellis that he was very frightened and was simply trying to prolong his life, even if it were only for a few minutes. But the hangman refused to give way, and in the end the warders pacified Jones by filing behind him, each one in turn gripping him by the hand. Then, after being given a stiff glass of brandy, Jones went to his doom. This time the Doctor congratulated Ellis on his work, expressing his satisfaction with the way the condemned man had met his end, and the hangman returned North feeling considerably happier than he had following his previous visit to Wandsworth.

CHAPTER 27

THE GRUESOME REMAINS IN REGENT SQUARE

On the morning of 2nd November 1917, a male nurse from a nearby hospital was walking through Regent Square, Bloomsbury, when his attention was drawn to what looked like a soldier's kit-bag tied up with slim rope in the bushes of the public gardens. He stopped and peered at it through the railings, then reached through and touched it. It felt heavy, yet soft. Determined to investigate further, as his curiosity was now aroused, he climbed over the railings to get a closer look.

The package, done up in sacking, was tightly bound, and on finding that he could not unfasten the knots with his fingers, he took a knife from his pocket and cut the ropes. As the sack fell open to reveal a headless torso, he recoiled in horror.

The torso was wrapped in a white sheet and clothed in a white lace undergarment trimmed with blue ribbon. The resourceful and apparently well-equipped male nurse, produced a tin whistle from his coat pocket and blew on it, then, while awaiting the arrival of the police, he took a further look around and soon discovered a second, smaller parcel. It contained a leg and a foot. By this time, as a crowd had begun to gather, the male nurse did his best to keep people back until the police arrived on the scene, followed by Dr Gabe, the Police Surgeon. After examining the body, Dr Gabe expressed the opinion that the woman had been dead for at least twenty-four hours. As there had been heavy rain from just after midnight until the early hours, and the sacking was only a little damp from the morning dew, it was obvious that the gruesome parcels had lain in the park no more than an hour or so before their discovery.

One thing which struck the doctor, was the clean and expert way in which the limbs had been severed, as if by a butcher, or even a surgeon. Of the other limbs and the head there was no sign. Apart from the white sheets, in which the body parts were wrapped, the only other item to be found was a piece of torn brown paper on which the words 'Blodie Belgian' were scrawled in pencil. On three pieces of the white fabric was a circular stamp bearing the words *'Argentina La Plata Cold Storage'*, which could perhaps indicate that a butcher might be involved. More important though, was the laundry mark *'II II'*, found on the white sheet in which the torso was wrapped. This was photographed and circulated to the newspapers and very quickly produced results, for it was identified by the laundry proprietor, who lost no time in contacting the police.

The victim's identity was soon established. She was Emilienne Gerard, wife of a soldier in the French Army, who was serving on the Western Front. Madame Gerard had been living in rooms at Munster Square, St. Pancras, no more than a mile or so from where her body was found.

After Scotland Yard had communicated with the French military authorities, the husband, Paul Gerard, was brought to London and had the heartbreaking task of identifying his wife's dismembered body. In life she had been a very pretty woman of thirty, with fair wavy hair.

The identification could not have been easy, in view of the fact that the victim's head had not been found. She was also known to have had a prominent scar on the back of one of her hands, but as the hands had been cut off, this piece of information was of little use to the police in establishing that the body was that of Mme. Gerard. Paul Gerard, however, was in no doubt, and was led away from St Pancras Mortuary weeping bitterly.

On questioning the victim's landlady at her lodgings, the police elicited the information that Mme. Gerard had received frequent visits from a stockily-built, middle-aged man, who always arrived at Munster Square in a pony and trap, which was of rather odd design, being driven from the back like a governess cart. Instead of a horse or pony, it was pulled by a mule. The day after Mme. Gerard's disappearance the man drove up in a modern-looking trap, and informed the landlady that her tenant had gone to stay in the country for a couple of weeks.

The police soon tracked down the man in question. He was a fifty-seven-year-old Frenchman named Louis Voisin, who lived in Charlotte Street, Soho. The strange-looking trap which he usually drove, he had designed and built himself, and it was well-known to everyone in the district, being completely enclosed at the top, side and front, except for a hole through which the reins passed, but was open at the rear.

After receiving this information Scotland Yard detectives called on Voisin and asked him when he had last seen Mme. Gerard. In very poor English, he told them,

'Last Wednesday, at Munster Square. She told me that she was going to Southampton to see a friend off, a woman named Marguerite, who was going abroad. I saw them leave for Southampton on Wednesday morning. Madame Gerard said she might stay down there for a few days and asked me to pay her lodgings'.

Though not satisfied with what Voisin had to tell them, the police left, but returned the following day and asked him to accompany them to Bow Street Police Station. With him was a woman named Berthe Roche, who asked if she could accompany him. The detective in charge agreed at once, and on arriving at Bow Street, Voisin was again questioned, this time with the help of an interpreter. He was asked if he had any objection to writing the words 'Blodie Belgian'. He replied that he had no objection at all, and complied, writing the words several times on a sheet of paper. It was at once apparent that the writing was the same as that on the sheet of brown paper found with the torso. Voisin was immediately placed under arrest. Also taken into custody was Roche, who was believed to be implicated in the crime.

It was soon established that Madame Gerard had worked for Voisin as a sort of cleaner-housekeeper for over a year. Some months before the murder he met Berthe Roche, and had then removed Mme. Gerard from her position and installed Roche in her place.

Once the pair were safely under lock and key, Voisin's rooms were thoroughly searched. In a concealed drawer several items of jewellery were discovered, which were known to have belonged to Mme. Gerard. In a tub of brine in the kitchen, the gruesome discovery of the victim's head, along with both her hands, was made.

At the trial it was established that Mme. Gerard had been murdered during an air raid on London, which commenced around 11-30 on the night of Wednesday, 31st October, 1917. Not long after the air raid warning was given she was heard moving around her room at Munster Square. She was probably very frightened. At any rate, it was ascertained that she went to Louis Voisin's house at Charlotte Street, possibly to seek shelter, as the house had a cellar. What happened there that night was never fully brought out during the trial. According to Berthe Roche, she herself left Voisin's room on hearing the air raid warning and went down into the cellar to shelter with the other occupants of the house. After the raid was over she had returned to Voisin's room to find him asleep. Not one witness, however, could be produced by the Defence to corroborate this statement.

Sir Bernard Spilsbury stated in evidence that the murdered woman had been struck many times on the head, yet the blows had not been powerful enough to fracture the skull, although the scalp was pierced in a number of places. The jury members were transported to Charlotte Street and taken down into the cellar to view for themselves the scene of the crime. There were bloodstains all over the stone floor.

A most remarkable feature of the case was that Mme. Gerard's room at Munster Square revealed bloodstains, the police coming to the conclusion that blood had, in some way, been taken to Munster Square and splashed around the room to mislead the police into believing that the murder had been committed there.

Though Voisin was careful not to run the risk of facing cross-examination by electing to go into the witness box, he told the police a rambling tale of how he had gone to Mme. Gerard's room on the night of the air raid, to find blood everywhere. Mme Gerard was nowhere to be seen. But on entering the kitchen, he said, he had found a flannel jacket in which were wrapped the head and hands of Mme. Gerard.

Fearing that he would be blamed, he had done his best to clean the place up, and had even removed the body parts to his own house.

'Why should I kill her?' he pleaded. 'She had no money. I know she was mixed up with bad company though. I know she took men to Munster Square, and I think she had had someone there that night'.

Voisin was not believed by the jury, and his allegations regarding the character of Mme. Gerard were proved to be quite unfounded. The Defendant was at pains during the trial to stress that Berthe Roche was in no way implicated, and though it could not be proved that she was, the judge, Mr Justice Darling, expressed the opinion that there was 'Very strong suspicion against her'. The jury, therefore, was instructed to acquit her of the murder charge, although she was held in custody, to go on trial at a later date on a charge of being an accessory after the fact. The jury took no more than fifteen minutes to find Voisin guilty of murder. The verdict was delivered first in English, then in French by the Clerk of the Court, to be certain that the Defendant clearly understood.

When the judge pronounced the sentence of death, this was also delivered in French as well as in English.

The only reply Voisin made was,

'I am innocent'.

He was removed to the cells beneath the court. His execution was eventually fixed to take place on Tuesday, 26th February, with Jack Ellis engaged to carry it out. It was realised belatedly, however, that if he were to die before the trial of Berthe Roche, the Defence might claim that a possible key witness was no longer available, if required to testify, so although it was not intended at this point to call Voisin as a witness, the date of his execution was put back to 2nd March, just as a precaution.

Though Roche strongly proclaimed her innocence of any involvement in the murder of Mme. Gerard, it was proved beyond doubt, that she had, at the very least, attempted to cover Voisin's tracks, for she had washed his shirt, which was covered with blood, knowing full well that Mme. Gerard had been cruelly murdered. In fact, it was widely suspected that she herself had actually done the killing, though it could not be proved.

On being found guilty, Roche screamed out from the dock that she was innocent, then burst into tears and sank to the floor. She was lifted to her feet by two female warders and placed on a seat by the side of the dock, where she wept and wailed uncontrollably. When she had calmed down somewhat the judge told her,

'Madame Roche, the sentence upon you is that you will be kept in penal servitude for a period of seven years'.

At this the Defendant then broke down completely and had to be carried to the cells. As there was no apparent motive for the murder of Mme. Gerard it can be safely assumed that the killing was not premeditated, and was no doubt the result of a violent argument, either between Voisin and the victim, or between the two women.

As the war was still in full swing, with food shortages and ration cards now an accepted part of life, it came as no surprise to Ellis, when he received a letter from the Governor of Pentonville Prison, reminding him either to bring his food ration card with him, or his own meat, bacon, sugar, butter or margarine.

On the afternoon prior to the execution, Ellis and his assistant were having their tea when a warder arrived to say that Voisin was about to be weighed. The weighing machine was set up in a passage on the ground floor of the prison. So that the hangman could get a close look at the prisoner, without his being aware of it, he and his assistant were placed in an adjacent room behind a glass door.

Voisin was brought to the scales wearing carpet slippers, and as he stepped onto them Ellis was able to get a good look at him from behind. Though only 5ft. $3^1/_2$, he weighed close to 13 stone and had a remarkably thick neck. Dark-complexioned, and with a heavy moustache, he could not be described as good-looking, and Ellis, in fact, remarked to his assistant that he thought the fellow rather ugly.

The two hangmen went to inspect the scaffold, where they met the Governor of the Prison, Mr O.E. Davies, Mr Metcalfe, the Under-Sheriff, and the Prison Medical Officer, Dr Mander. Ellis was asked the usual question,

'How long a drop are you thinking of giving, Mr Ellis?'

Ellis had an idea that the three of them had already been discussing the subject and soon discovered that his assumption was correct, for when he replied,

'Oh, perhaps about six feet', the Doctor remarked,

'Ah, yes, I said you would say that'.

'Well', said Ellis, 'if it were up to me entirely, I would probably give a bit more than six feet, but as that's already a few inches over the Home Office scale I felt that you would not be happy with more than six feet'.

The matter was discussed at some length, before it was finally agreed to stick to the drop which Ellis had worked out. In testing the rope, he made sure that the sandbag hanging from it was approximately as heavy as Voisin, and discovered that the weight was too much for the gutta-percha to withstand, for on inspection, it was found to have cracked very badly. A second rope was tried, with the same result. Both ropes had been used a number of times previously, so a brand new one was brought in. This stood up to the test very well and was left hanging in the pit with the sandbag attached to it.

Ellis arose early next morning and by seven-thirty was checking the scaffold to make sure that everything was in order. As the execution was set for nine o'clock, he and his assistant then ate a leisurely breakfast and were outside the condemned man's cell by ten minutes to nine. They could hear Voisin screaming and shouting as they arrived. He had refused to eat his breakfast and out of sheer terror was behaving like a demented coward.

As they waited outside the cell, a warder appeared with a bottle of brandy and a glass. The Doctor was with the prisoner in his cell and was heard to say, 'Go on, drink it all up'.

After that, the prisoner seemed to quieten down, and the hangmen entered the cell. Voisin was seated on his bunk between two chaplains, who were praying. The prisoner was clutching a handkerchief and sobbing quietly. The assistant hangman removed the handkerchief from Voisin's hand so that Ellis could pinion him. It was wet through from his tears. He was then asked to stand up while Ellis went about his work. As the two clergymen rose to their feet they continued to pray, while Voisin made his responses in French.

The condemned man was soon on his way to the scaffold, where Ellis waited for him. The moment he was on the trapdoors the hangman had the white cap over his head and the rope around his neck. Voisin's courage had deserted him completely and he fell into a faint. As he sagged at the knees Ellis, a man of slight build, struggled to hold him up and immediately called for assistance. This quickly arrived in the shape of a couple of hefty warders, who grabbed hold of the prisoner, one on either side, and supported him while Ellis attempted to adjust the noose. This proved no easy task. Voisin's neck was so fat that it was very difficult to get the rope firmly under his chin. The only sure way was to tighten the noose, and Ellis was afraid that the victim would cry out that he was being throttled. However, Voisin was now too far gone to make any sort of protest. All he could do was mumble and moan, and the hangmen could not be sure whether he was praying or just rambling on dementedly.

The prisoner's head now hung, almost limply, to one side. Ellis knew he would have to get things over with as quickly as possible, and though he was still not altogether sure that the noose was quite correctly in place, he signalled to the two warders to stand clear. As they did, Ellis pulled the lever and the murderer dropped into the hole.

After the Doctor had descended into the pit to examine the body, the hangman was anxious to hear his report. He was assured later, by the Governor, that he had done an excellent job and that all those in attendance had been amazed at how quickly the execution had been carried out.

Only three days after the execution of Louis Voisin, Ellis was at Shepton Mallet Military Prison in Somerset to hang one Verney Asser, an Australian soldier found guilty of murdering a comrade in a military camp at Sutton Veny in Wiltshire on the night of 27th November, 1917.

The victim was Joseph Harold Durkin, and the two men, both of whom had served in France, were very good friends and worked together at Sutton Veny as Lewis Gun instructors. They also slept in the same hut.

On the night in question, Asser reported to the Sergeant of the Guard that Durkin had shot himself. The sergeant, along with the Duty Officer and a doctor, were at the hut within minutes and found Durkin lying on his bunk, with a rifle close to his right hand. The bullet that killed him had entered his left cheek and came out by his right ear, before passing through a blanket and a kitbag, which he was using as a pillow, and embedding itself in the wall of the hut.

Following an investigation by the military authorities, Asser was arrested and charged with the murder. It came out at the trial that both men had been interested in the same girl, and that Asser, realising that Durkin was beginning to emerge as favourite for her affections, had become insanely jealous. The two men had quarrelled, but continued to sleep in the same hut and to work together.

It was proven in court by the Prosecution that Durkin could not possibly have shot himself while lying on his bed. The weapon had been discharged several inches away from his face and the bullet could not have taken the direction it travelled had it been fired by the dead man. In addition, the body was covered with a blanket drawn neatly over the chest.

A soldier named Milner, who was based in the next hut, stated that ammunition was kept there and Asser had taken some, between 9-30 and 11p.m. on the night Durkin was killed. A verdict of 'Guilty' was brought in by the jury and Asser was sentenced to death.

On arriving at Shepton Mallet, Ellis was not able to look at his victim, for by the time he asked to see him, around 6p.m., he was informed that

Asser had already gone to bed. He learned from the warders that the prisoner was a very queer fellow indeed. Two of them had been detailed to sit with him in the condemned cell and sometimes did not manage to get a word out of him for hours on end. At times, he would go as long as two days without uttering a single word. When he did speak his conversation was very odd, to say the least.

He told the warders that he believed people had a number of lives to live and visited and re-visited the earth in various forms. He actually claimed that he could clearly remember the last time he was on earth, as a dog, adding that he had been wondering just what he would be 'after tomorrow,' which was, of course, the day he was due to be hanged.

Asser did not get on very well with the Prison Chaplain, who visited him on a number of occasions and never felt completely safe with him. Normally, a Chaplain would prefer to be left alone with a prisoner in his cell, but after a couple of visits, when Asser had become quite aggressive, the Chaplain, fearing he might be attacked, requested that the warders remain while he attempted to establish some sort of rapport with the condemned man.

From the Chaplain, Ellis learned that Asser was not an Australian, but a Lancashire man, born at Bootle, whose parents had emigrated to Australia when he was only two years old. When he was fourteen the family had returned to Liverpool, but Asser went back to Australia a few years later. When war broke out, he joined the army and eventually fought in France, before being transferred to Sutton Veny camp.

When Ellis learned a little more about the condemned soldier he began to feel sorry for him. Asser appeared to be an outcast and had not had a letter, or a single visitor, while awaiting execution.

Ellis's first glimpse of the prisoner came at around 6a.m. on the morning he was to die. Peering through the inspection grille, he saw that Asser was already up, and smoking a cigarette. He was around thirty, of average height and weighed eleven stone.

From the condemned cell Ellis went to the scaffold and measured off a drop of 7ft. 3ins. At five minutes to eight, he entered Asser's cell with his assistant to find the prisoner smoking what was to be his last cigarette. Ellis pinioned his arms, then turned him around and loosened his shirt collar. On his face there was no sign of fear. Still Ellis assured him, 'Don't worry, I'll have it over quickly'.

Asser nodded, and Ellis, leaving his assistant in charge of the prisoner, made his way to the scaffold. The prisoner maintained his composure to the end, and on entering the execution shed, stepped firmly onto the trap doors. It was all over within seconds. Then the Chaplain stepped forward and shook Ellis by the hand, as did the Chief Warder, who remarked that the execution had been carried out in exactly 33 seconds,

'The quickest job I've ever witnessed'.

As for Ellis, he could not help thinking what a contrast the unflinching courage of Asser had been to the whining, cowardly behaviour of Voisin, the man he had hanged only three days before.

In April 1918, Ellis and his assistant, George Brown, hanged Louis Van der Kerk-Hove at Birmingham. Van der Kerk-Hove had stabbed to death his lady-friend, Clementine Verelist, in an hotel room. Following this execution, Ellis did not get another job until December, when he executed William Rooney, a Liverpool man, at Strangeways.

After his brother had been killed in France, Rooney had made repeated advances to the brother's widow, who refused to have anything to do with him. Convinced that she was interested in another man, he flew into a jealous rage and stabbed her to death. His plea of insanity was not accepted by the jury.

Ellis's first assignment of the following year took him to Oxford, with Edward Taylor as assistant. The condemned man was a gypsy, twenty-five-year-old Joseph Rose, found guilty of murdering his cousin Sarah, who was nineteen. The two had gone through a form of marriage peculiar to their race and had a six-month-old child. One day in the autumn of 1919, the family, who were living on a camp site at Enborne, near Newbury, Berkshire, set off for Newbury Market, stopping along the way to eat lunch. They were seen in a field by a passer-by, who noted that the man and woman appeared to be engaged in a struggle, but concluded that they were just 'acting the goat'.

Not long afterwards, another man came by and was accosted by Joseph Rose, who was holding a wad of cloth to his neck. He appeared to be injured and could not speak. Seizing the witness by the arm, he pulled him into the field, where the man was horrified to find the bodies of a young woman and a child. They were covered in blood.

The police were quickly on the scene, while Rose was conveyed to the nearest hospital. When questioned, he claimed that the family had been attacked by a man with a knife, but though Rose himself had sustained a superficial neck wound, there was really no evidence to indicate that he had done anything to fend off the alleged assailant. Nor did an exhaustive search of the field and surrounding terrain produce footprints, or any other evidence to show that another person had recently been in the vicinity.

Rose was charged with murder, found guilty at Oxford Assizes in January 1919, and executed the following month at Oxford Gaol.

At the Old Bailey in May 1919, Henry Perry, a former soldier, was found guilty of murdering an entire family at Forest Gate, London. Perry had previously lodged with a Mr and Mrs Cornish, but had been ordered to leave following a dispute. Still angry over the incident, he returned to the house. In the course of further discussions, which blew up into a violent row, he seized the nearest weapon, an axe, and crashed it down on the woman's head, killing her. Perry was cold-blooded enough to lie in wait for the husband and two children, aged five and fourteen. He killed them all, and ransacked the house, taking money and anything of value he could lay his hands on. The murderer, who had a long string of convictions for various crimes, was soon apprehended. He was hanged at Pentonville in July 1919, by John Ellis, with William Willis assisting.

Less than two weeks after this, Ellis made the short journey from Rochdale to Liverpool to hang John Crossland for the murder of his wife, Ellen, at Blackburn. After a series of rows Crossland left the family home in Prince Albert Street and went to live in lodgings. When visiting his wife one day, he completely lost control of his emotions and attacked her, savagely beating her about the head until she lapsed into unconsciousness. At that point, two of the children entered the room and were horrified to see their mother lying on the floor, obviously in a very serious condition. Crossland, realising what he had done, immediately panicked and fled from the scene. He was soon picked up and pleaded his innocence, claiming that his wife had fallen and injured herself. This did not, of course, tally with the medical evidence, and the jury had no hesitation in finding Crossland guilty.

After he was sentenced to death, a petition for reprieve was launched, which gained several thousand signatures, but to no avail, the sentence being carried out on 22nd July by John Ellis and Robert Baxter, from St. Albans. Baxter had carried out his first job as assistant to Tom Pierrepoint in the summer of 1915, when Robert Rosenthal, a German spy, was hanged at Wandsworth.

Ellis's quiet spell the previous year was more than made up for in 1919. Following the Crossland execution the work came in thick and fast. Just over a week later he was at Pentonville, with Edward Taylor, to carry out the sentence on Thomas Foster, a Bethnal Green man, who had cut the throat of his wife Minnie as she lay in bed.

Only a week after this, he hanged Henry Gaskin at Winson Green Prison, Birmingham. Again it was a wife murder, that of Elizabeth Gaskin at Cannock, Staffordshire. The husband had attempted to dismember the body and get rid of the pieces to avoid detection, but was quickly arrested, tried and condemned to death. Ellis's assistant this time was William Willis.

In October, Ellis, assisted by George Brown, executed Frank Warren at Pentonville for the murder of Lucy Nightingale by strangulation, and the following month he disposed of one James Adams in Glasgow for the murder of a soldier's wife, Mary Doyle, with whom he was having a relationship. The crime was committed at the home of the victim in Cameron Street. Mrs Doyle had informed Adams that she was going back to her husband, whereupon he became very angry. He admitted that he had taken a razor from his pocket, but claimed that he had intended to use it on himself. However, a struggle had ensued during which Mary Doyle had sustained a serious throat wound, from which she had quickly expired. Adams had given himself up to the police. His story was not believed by the jury and he was sentenced to die on the scaffold.

Next on the agenda came Ernest Scott, who had murdered his girl friend, Rebecca Quinn, after she had decided to end their relationship. Scott cut her throat and was hanged at Newcastle at the end of November. Edward Taylor and Robert Baxter assisted in a double execution, the second victim being Ambrose Quinn, who had also been found guilty of murdering his wife by cutting her throat. Scott was executed at eight o'clock and Quinn at 9-15a.m.

A week after this Ellis and Edward Taylor hanged a Chinaman at Worcester. Djang Djing Sung had used a hammer to bludgeon to death another Chinaman, Zee Ming Wu, in a wood at Warley, near Birmingham. The crime was committed for the sake of a savings' book, from which the killer attempted to draw money at a local post office. He was convicted of the brutal and senseless murder of his fellow countryman at Worcester Assizes and was duly dealt with, this being Ellis's last job of 1919.

On 2nd December, 1919, the trial had taken place at Manchester Assizes of David Caplan for the murder of his wife and their two children at their home in Derby Road, Kirkdale, Liverpool. Caplan, a very violent man, had beaten his wife many times, yet had always been full of remorse afterwards and had been forgiven. However, he had lost control of himself just once too often, and in a frenzy, had battered his family to death with a flat-iron. Caplan deserved no mercy and received none, despite a plea of insanity, which was all the Defence could offer.

Just three days later, Hyman Purdovitch, a Russian Jew, was also sentenced to death at Manchester for the murder, by stabbing, of Solomon Franks, a foreman at the factory where Purdovitch was employed.

The two Jews were hanged together at Strangeways by John Ellis, assisted by Edward Taylor and Robert Baxter, on 6th January 1920.

CHAPTER 28

THE BODY IN THE SANDHILLS

The signing of the Armistice on 11th November, 1918, finally brought to an end four years of horror and bloodshed in Europe. Thousands of lives had been lost and many more ruined. Quite apart from the dead, the maimed, and the families at home who had suffered greatly, there were also those who returned from the trenches carrying scars that were less obvious. Many men, who had cracked under the stress and strain of battle, finished up in mental hospitals, in some cases, never to emerge. Others came home and resumed their lives, but were never the same again. Such men might suffer from periods of depression and feel suicidal. In others, the mental torment, while not so apparent, nevertheless remained below the surface; like a time-bomb ready to explode at any moment.

Frederick Rothwell Holt, known as 'Eric', was an officer in the Territorial Army prior to the outbreak of war, and one of the first to be called up at the commencement of hostilities. He was sent to France and came under rifle fire and heavy shelling in the trenches, being in the thick of things from the outset. Though Holt was one of the lucky ones, who came through it, the experience left its mark. He was invalided out of the army suffering from acute neurasthenia and what was termed 'shell-shock', which is perhaps best described as a kind of nervous breakdown brought on by exposure to gunfire, including exploding shells and grenades.

Following a period of employment in the Far East, Holt returned to England, where he set himself up as an insurance agent at Lytham St. Annes, Lancashire. On the surface at least, he appeared by this time to have shaken off the effects of his war-time experiences, and soon became prominent in local middle-class society. His personality was bright and outgoing, making him popular with friends and acquaintances.

It was in 1919 that Holt first met Kathleen Elsie Breaks. Miss Breaks, who was known as Kitty to her friends, was an exceptionally pretty twenty-five-year old from Bradford, Yorkshire. It is not clear how or where the two first met, but it was not long before they were meeting on a regular basis. Though a deep romantic attachment was clearly developing between them, Kitty did not appear to be particularly happy.

She was troubled by the fact that she had not been entirely frank regarding her past life. Realising that she was very much in love with Holt, she knew that, if there were to be any hope at all of a future together, she would have to be honest with him. She summoned up all her courage and wrote a letter, in which she confessed to being a married woman. The marriage, she said, had gone wrong from the very beginning, and she had lived apart from her husband since shortly after the wedding. She had been very lonely since then, and meeting Holt had changed her life completely. She did not want to give him up, but would understand if he wished to end the relationship.

Holt was soon in touch, assuring her that he loved her very much and that her past made no difference. They would get her a divorce as soon as it was possible to do so. In the meantime, he told her, their love would grow stronger. He was very glad she had unburdened herself, as he could not stand the thought of her being so worried and unhappy.

Kitty felt as though a great weight had been lifted from her shoulders. She should have known, she told herself, that Eric would not shy away. His reaction had shown her that he not only loved her, but also that he was a sincere, genuine person. Nothing, however, could have been further from the truth, for Holt had plans of his own, which did not include a long-term relationship with Miss Kitty Breaks.

It would appear that, almost from the beginning, he had been turning over in his mind a scheme to insure her, get rid of her and collect the money. Her confession, which would seem to have drawn them even closer together, now proved fortuitous as far as Holt was concerned, for it placed the gullible, love-stricken Kitty firmly under his influence, and therefore in a far more vulnerable position. He had already been turned down by one insurance company when he had attempted to take out a policy on her life, in the sum of £10,000. As an accredited agent he must have known that as he was not related in any way to Miss Breaks, he had no insurable interest in her, and could not, therefore, take out a policy on her. He had attempted to do so nevertheless, and had been unsuccessful. Now that he had so completely won her confidence, all Holt had to do was to continue to be loving and solicitous and he could get her to go along unquestioningly, with almost anything he proposed.

His next move was to persuade her to take out a policy on her own life, for £5,000. He even paid the premium, then got her to make a will, naming himself the sole beneficiary. Had Kitty possessed anything else, he would no doubt have had that also, but as she was not wealthy, the insurance money was all he could expect to gain — though £5,000 was a fortune in 1919. The scheming Holt must have been in a great hurry to get his hands on the money, for it was only a few days later that the body of Kitty Breaks was discovered in a shallow grave in the sandhills at St. Annes.

On the previous day, 23rd December, Holt had travelled by train to Bradford and returned later, accompanied by Miss Breaks. People who saw them on the train, later mentioned how much in love the pair appeared to be, holding hands and never taking their eyes off each other. Holt left the train at Ansdell Station, near his home, while Kitty carried on to Blackpool, where he had booked her into an hotel. They met again later that evening, but Kitty was never seen alive again. At some time between 9 and 10p.m., Holt was seen boarding a tram near the sandhills. He was alone, and on reaching home, he had his supper and went to bed.

On the following day, Christmas Eve, two schoolboys, playing on the sandhills, found what they thought was a toy gun, half buried in the sand. On realising that the gun was no toy, they decided to take it to the police station. A couple of police officers then accompanied them to the spot, and further probing around in the sand resulted in the grim discovery of the body, in which were three bullet holes. Close by, a pair of men's gloves were found, and several clear footprints were visible in the damp sand, made by a man's shoe of a large size.

Detectives were immediately called in, and with so many clues to work with, rapid progress was made. The gun was quickly identified as belonging to one Frederick Rothwell Holt, as were the gloves. On visiting his home, the police removed several pairs of shoes, one of which exactly corresponded with the footprints in the sand. Holt, who was not at home when the police called, was eventually traced to the hotel in Blackpool where Kitty had been staying. He told them that he had been out shopping, had bought his fiancée a Christmas present, and was waiting for her to come down from her room. He was arrested and charged with murder.

Of all the people who read of the murder in that evening's newspaper, one of the most interested was John Ellis. From then until he received a letter from the Under-Sheriff's office asking if he would be available to hang Holt at Strangeways on 16th March, 1920, Ellis followed the case in the newspapers with rising anger at the attitude of some members of the public.

At his trial in Manchester, Holt had been found guilty and sentenced to be hanged, despite the tremendous fight put up by his Counsel, headed by Marshall Hall, who tried hard to convince the jury that his client was insane, and therefore unfit to plead. Though this claim was supported by the opinions of several doctors, brought into court by the Defence, it was not accepted.

The prisoner had been found fit to plead, but Marshall Hall had no intention of dropping the insanity angle. He was able to show that Holt's mother had died in an asylum. The prisoner's war record was, of course, brought up, also the horrors he had experienced on the battlefield, which, it was argued, could well have pushed him 'over the edge'. In addition to this line of defence, an alibi was furnished for Holt by several members of his family, each one of whom insisted that he had never left the house on the evening of the murder. But the Prosecution's case was far too powerful, and Holt was duly found guilty and sentenced to death.

Holt had been acting very oddly, almost from the time of his arrest, this being construed as an attempt to lay the foundations for an insanity plea. In court, he sat almost throughout the entire proceedings with his arms folded, looking thoroughly bored and totally uninterested in all that was going on around him. On being brought back up from the cells to hear the jury's verdict, he was seen to be carrying a rolled-up evening paper, which he casually shoved into his jacket pocket as he stepped into the dock. After hearing the dreaded word 'Guilty', he was asked by the clerk if he had anything to say, and just shrugged his shoulders in an unconcerned manner. The judge then pronounced sentence of death, whereupon the prisoner remarked,

'Well, that's over with. Now I'm ready for my tea'.

Marshall Hall immediately filed notice of appeal and requested that he be allowed to introduce new evidence, which had come into his possession too late to be used at the trial. After deliberating, the Appeal Judges decided that the circumstances were exceptional enough to warrant the new evidence — which proved to be quite sensational — being introduced.

An English doctor working in Malaya had been reading about the trial in a newspaper, when he suddenly realised that the Defendant was the same Frederick Holt whom he had treated for syphilis a couple of years previously. He had contacted the Defence Counsel and was brought over from the Far East to testify that while treating the patient he had noted that Holt was obviously also suffering from shell-shock. Another doctor who had given evidence at the trial, unaware at the time that Holt had been treated for syphilis, said he now believed that Holt had been suffering from general paralysis of the insane at the time of the murder.

Marshall Hall attempted to show that Holt had been unable to resist the impulse to murder the woman he loved. He argued that it had already been shown that there was insanity in the family, that Holt had been treated for syphilis and that his mind had been badly affected by his frightening experiences in the trenches. The appeal failed, which was hardly surprising, considering the fact that the insurance policy and the will in his favour showed obvious premeditation. Yet it was clear that the condemned man had been through more than his share of suffering in one way and another. It was this, more than anything else, which prompted many people to feel pity for him and to urge the Home Secretary to show compassion in the form of a reprieve and commutation of the sentence to life imprisonment, or more appropriately, that Holt be placed in an asylum for the criminally insane.

This attitude angered Ellis, who felt very strongly that the sympathizers seemed more concerned with the welfare of the murderer, than with the fact that he had cold-bloodedly extinguished the life of a beautiful young girl for greed of gain.

When Ellis, received the Under-Sheriff's letter he had just returned from a trip to Ireland, where he had been engaged to hang three men in Londonderry, who were under sentence of death for their involvement in a politically-motivated killing. Two detectives escorted Ellis from Rochdale to Manchester, where they were met by two assistant hangmen. These two men, along with Ellis, were locked in a railway carriage and remained there until the train arrived in Liverpool. They were then taken under escort to the docks and put on a boat bound for Belfast. It turned out to be a wasted journey, however, for one of the first things Ellis spotted on stepping off the ship was a newspaper placard announcing, in bold letters, the reprieve of the condemned men. At the prison, they were told by the Governor that the reprieves had come through too late for him to get word to the authorities in Liverpool before their boat sailed. He apologised for the inconvenience and agreed to pay their full fees.

Following the failure of Holt's appeal, a new execution date was set — 13th April. While his family organised a petition for a reprieve and got hundreds of people to sign it, the condemned man showed not the slightest sign of gratitude for all that people were doing on his behalf. Even his relatives were more or less ignored when they came to visit him.

To the Governor and the warders, Holt was a constant problem, going out of his way to be as unpleasant and as awkward as possible, though as a condemned man he was given every consideration. He kicked up a fuss when told to remove his civilian clothes and put on the broad-arrow prison uniform, then caused a further commotion because he did not care for the fit.

It was particularly trying for the warders, who were detailed to sit with him day and night leading up to the execution, for they were supposed to talk to him and try to keep his spirits up. With Holt, this was almost impossible.

When Ellis first laid eyes on him, the prisoner was at exercise. Over six feet in height and quite well-built, he was striding along at such a brisk pace that the two warders who flanked him were having a difficult time keeping up.

Soon after seven on the following morning, Ellis was in the execution shed, making sure that all was in order. With the help of his assistant, he drew up the rope from the pit, removed the sandbag from the end of it, and after satisfying himself that the rope was fully stretched, left it hanging over the drop. The trap-doors were then pulled up and everything was ready.

At a few minutes to eight o'clock Ellis and his assistant met the prison officials in the corridor outside the condemned cell. The Governor told Ellis that he was very worried about the prisoner's mental state and anticipated trouble. Holt had eaten very little breakfast and seemed tense and agitated.

'Did you give him brandy?' asked Ellis.

'We tried to', replied the Governor, 'but he refused it'.

Ellis pushed open the cell door and stepped inside. Holt was standing there, a cigarette dangling from his mouth, with the Chaplain, prayer book in hand, trying unsuccessfully to gain his attention. On seeing the two hangmen enter, Holt glared at them, then as the Chaplain began to pray more earnestly, Holt waved him aside and turned away. Ellis immediately stepped up behind him and gently took hold of his left arm. But before the pinioning straps could be applied the prisoner jerked his arm free.

'Is this really necessary?' he asked angrily.

'Yes it is', replied Ellis, trying to remain as calm as possible.

Holt was not satisfied. He now turned to the Chief Warder and asked aggressively,

'Is it necessary?'

'Yes', he was told again. 'It's very necessary'.

Holt's face was now twisted in anger, his fists clenched tightly, and it certainly appeared at that moment that he was about to put up a fight. But he could see from the determined looks on the faces of the warders that they were ready for him, and thought better of it.

Ellis met with no further resistance as he proceeded to pinion the prisoner. While he loosened Holt's collar he tried not to look into his eyes, but could feel the loathing and anger as Holt looked down at him. Without glancing up, Ellis left the cell and proceeded to the execution shed, the rest of the party close behind him.

As Ellis reached the scaffold, he turned to see Holt striding quickly towards him, still ignoring the Chaplain, who was praying furiously while trying to keep up. The prisoner stopped short of the trapdoors. As Ellis met his gaze he saw no fear there, only hatred. A gentle touch from the assistant hangman and Holt stepped onto the trapdoors. Ellis immediately produced the white cap.

'You're not putting that on me', snapped Holt.

'I must', Ellis told him.

He reached up and with great difficulty managed to get the hood over the prisoner's head. Around his neck went the noose, the knot was quickly adjusted, then Ellis stepped smartly to one side and pulled the lever. There were sighs of relief all round as the murderer disappeared into the pit.

Outside the prison, hundreds of people stood in the rain to await the announcement that the execution had been carried out, among them many who sympathized with Holt and had signed the petition. Most of those inside the prison felt very differently, one of the warders remarking,

'Well that's the last of him, and I'm certainly not sorry'.

On leaving Strangeways that morning, Ellis took the train to Cardiff, where he was due to hang Tom Caler, a negro, who had cut the throats of a woman friend and her baby at a house in Christina Street, Cardiff.

Ellis was at once struck by the difference in Caler and the man he had hanged that morning in Manchester, for the negro was praying earnestly in his cell with the Chaplain when the hangman looked in on him. The execution went very smoothly and Ellis marked it down in his diary as an interesting and quite profitable week.

CHAPTER 29

THE CHILD IN THE CELLAR

In 1920, William Waddington was thirty-five years old. He was unmarried and lived with his father, mother, two brothers and a sister in Edge Lane Road, in the Higginshaw district of Oldham. Higginshaw, bordering on the out-district of Royton, was a typical working-class part of the town, with the old boilerworks at the top of the hill and the local gasworks near the bottom of the road. Directly opposite the Waddington house the steep slopes of Oldham Edge rose up to the town centre and beyond. Early records show that coal mining had taken place on Oldham Edge as far back as the early seventeenth century. It continued, intermittently, until the coal strike of 1912, when local stocks ran out. Small bands of desperate men re-opened old seams on the slopes of the Edge and poverty-stricken women and children queued with sacks, buckets and various other receptacles for the precious fuel. When the strike was over this once pleasant, green landscape was left rough and badly scarred.

The Waddingtons lived at number 192, in the last row of twenty or so houses at the bottom end of the road. Though all were occupied by working-class families, the dwellings were quite large, each consisting of three storeys and an attic at the back, and two storeys and an attic at the front, the lower rooms at the back being used by most of the tenants, as cellars, the back doors of which opened into a yard.

The three Waddington brothers, William, the eldest, George aged thirty-two and Thomas, who was twenty, were all single and liked a drink. In fact, they tended to drink too much, and on several occasions had been in trouble with the law for disorderly conduct.

William had served in the forces during the Great War, first joining the Manchester Regiment and later being transferred to the King's (Liverpool) Regiment. He was wounded, and following the Armistice was discharged, but could find no employment and re-enlisted. Evidently, peace-time soldiering was not to his liking, for after a short time he deserted and returned home. For some unknown reason the authorities made no effort to track him down. Perhaps his records were lost or misplaced. In any event, he was left alone, but remained constantly on his guard and was always afraid that he might be arrested at any time.

In the early part of 1920, Waddington was working as a piecer at the Monarch Mill, Royton. On Saturday, 14th February, he started work at 7-30 in the morning and finished at 11-30, then went into the Royal Hotel close by and had a couple of pints. Around one o'clock he went up into Oldham town centre, where he met a married sister, Mrs Emma Roberts, who accompanied him to the Boilermakers' Arms in Henshaw Street. They drank together until around a-quarter-to-two, when Emma left him to go shopping.

Meanwhile, brother George, after finishing work at the Glebe Mill, Hollinwood, at 12 noon, also headed for Oldham town centre and had seven pints of beer in the Cheshire Cheese in Henshaw Street, then decided he was hungry and went home. When he got there, at around 2-15, his father and mother were in the house, along with his sister, Mary, and a few five minutes later his brother William arrived. Soon afterwards mother and daughter left the house to go shopping, the father, Tom Waddington senior, also going out at around the same time.

George, who was feeling somewhat the worse for drink, ate his dinner, then told his brother that he was going to bed, and asked William if he would wake him up at 5 o'clock. Before George could get off to sleep he heard the front door open and shut. Thomas, his younger brother, had arrived with his pal, Ernest Lupton. Thomas went upstairs and handed over a new hat that George had asked him to get for him. Thomas and his friend then left the house and George soon drifted off into a deep, drunken sleep.

Outside in the street three little girls were playing. They were Doris Wolfenden, aged nine, her younger sister Ivy, and Elizabeth Roberts. Elizabeth, who was ten years old, was the daughter of Emma Roberts, William Waddington's sister.

While they were playing on the pavement near the Wolfenden home, number 170, William Waddington appeared at the doorway of 192 and called out to his niece, who went to see what her uncle wanted.

'What?' she asked.
'Go and tell that little girl of Wolfenden's I want her,' said Waddington.

Elizabeth ran back to her friends and spoke to Ivy Wolfenden, who shook her head. Waddington then called out to her, and the little girl, who was seven years old, reluctantly went to find out what he wanted her for.

Waddington said he only wanted her to go an errand for him, to Whittingham's shop on the main road. He just wanted change for sixpence and told her that if she would go, she could keep a penny for herself. Ivy went off to the shop and was seen a few minutes later going up the street in the direction of Waddington's house, clutching the coins.

A short while after this William Waddington emerged from his house. His niece Elizabeth and Doris Wolfenden were still playing in the street. They had apparently forgotten all about Ivy, or perhaps assumed that after completing her errand she had passed by without their noticing and gone home.

On seeing her uncle at the door, Elizabeth asked him,

'Can me and Doris go and play in Grandma's?'

'No', he replied. 'I'm going out and your Uncle George is in bed'.

Elizabeth then suddenly remembered Ivy, and asked Waddington if he knew where she was. He replied that he didn't know, and shut the door, leaving the key in the lock, for when his mother and sister returned. 'Look after the house will you', he said, 'while your Grandma comes back'. He then crossed the street and went off towards Oldham Edge, by way of a 'broo', or steep hill, known locally as 'The Nip'. As he went up the street he passed a neighbour, Mrs Clara Newsome, but did not speak, which she thought strange, as he usually did.

Emma Roberts was returning home that afternoon from her trip to Oldham town centre, accompanied by another woman, Mrs Hester Davies. It was late in the afternoon, and they were crossing Oldham Edge when they saw Waddington coming towards them. He appeared somewhat agitated, and when asked where he was going, replied, rather abruptly,

'For a walk'.

He hurried past them, and though it seemed odd, the women thought no more about it and carried on towards home. On reaching Edge Lane Road, Emma Roberts saw her daughter playing in the street outside the Waddingtons' house. Elizabeth locked the door, removed the key and handed it over to her mother. Then the two of them went home to number one Higginshaw Road. It was not long after this that Mrs Eliza Waddington and her daughter Mary came back from their own shopping. They stopped by Emma's house, and were handed their key, staying only a few minutes before leaving for home. No more than five minutes later both women returned, screaming.

'What is it?' asked Emma. 'Calm down, just calm down and tell me...

'The cellar. I opened the door and heard something in the cellar', Mary told her.

'Oh my God', wailed her mother. 'What's happened...?' 'Oh please, what's happened?'

Unable to make any sense of what they were telling her, Emma ran to her mother's house and looked around frantically, afraid of what she might find. Nothing appeared to be amiss, but as she checked each room she suddenly heard a faint noise coming from the cellar. It sounded like someone groaning. Emma crept slowly down the steep steps. It was very dim and she could see nothing. Now very frightened, she ran back up the steps and out into the street. As it happened, a postman named John

McHugh was delivering letters. As Emma came out of the house her sister Mary was just coming up the street, having left her mother at Emma's house. Both women, who were almost hysterical, ran up to him and pleaded with him to help them.

'Please come with us will you. Somebody's been murdered in our house.'

McHugh did not hesitate. He followed the women into the house, and when told about the noise in the cellar, asked for a candle. As he reached the foot of the steps the moaning had ceased, then was heard again. Mrs Waddington, who had now come back to the house, also heard it, and cried out in anguish,

'Our Willie's done it!'

McHugh peered into the darkness, the candle giving off a very poor light. In one corner he could make out a pile of coal. Then, in a recess, he spotted what appeared to be a pool of blood. The next thing he saw looked like a small foot. On moving closer with the candle he peered into the gloom and saw that it was a little girl. She was lying on her left side and he noticed at once that her clothing was disarranged. Horrified, McHugh picked the child up and carried her upstairs. She was still alive and continued to moan as he took her into the kitchen and laid her down on a couch. He asked who the child was, but no one seemed to know. This was no doubt due to the fact that she was covered in blood and coal-dust, particularly around the head. McHugh went to the front door and called out to two young lads who were returning home after playing football, asking for their assistance. Leaving them in charge of the situation, he then went to several houses, enquiring if anyone had a telephone, but failed to locate one. At around 5p.m., a policeman on the beat, PC William Bradbury, was stopped in Shaw Road by a boy named Travis Marsh, who told him that he was wanted at number 192, Edge Lane Road. Setting off in that direction, he ran into John McHugh. After hearing what he had to say Bradbury ordered an ambulance, then returned with the postman to the Waddington's. One of the lads was bathing the little girl's face with lukewarm water. She was still breathing, but appeared extremely weak. A few minutes later the ambulance arrived and PC Bradbury picked up the child and carried her out of the house. Just as he was about to get into the ambulance she sobbed, then went limp. The constable travelled in the back of the ambulance to the Oldham Royal Infirmary, but he knew it was too late. From the Infirmary he took the body to the mortuary, then returned to 192 Edge Lane Road.

After the ambulance had left for the Infirmary, young Elizabeth Roberts tugged at her mother's sleeve,

'Mam'..., Mam'.

'What is it?'

'Uncle George is upstairs'.

George Waddington, who had slept through all the commotion, was awakened by his two sisters, Emma and Mary, shaking him. He heard one of them say,

'George ..., George ..., Get up! You might get blamed for it!'

'What's wrong?' asked George sleepily.

'George, for God's sake get up before you're blamed for something'.

Unable to get a clear picture of what was going on from his sisters, but realising that something was badly amiss, George got up quickly and ran down the stairs. Finding no one in the house, he hurried to his sister Emma's house, to find his mother in a state of shock. She had fainted and was being looked after by the neighbours.

The police had now arrived at the house, headed by the Chief Constable, Mr A.K. Mayall, Superintendent Pigott and Inspector Hobson. They found blood in the front room, which was used as a bedroom, and also in the cellar. Members of the family, including the children, were questioned. It was soon quite clear that William Waddington would have to be tracked down as quickly as possible, and his description was circulated, along with the information that he had been seen crossing Oldham Edge in the direction of Royton. Chief Constable Mayall called out every available policeman to scour the town and outskirts. In addition, several taxis were requisitioned to convey police officers, including plain clothes men, to neigbouring towns, with orders to make enquiries in pubs and to search all lodging houses for the wanted man. Among the towns visited were Rochdale and Ashton-under-Lyne, and parts of Manchester.

While the search was going on in these areas, Waddington was heading over the moors. Later that evening, having walked some twelve miles or so, he reached the little country town of Todmorden, just over the border in Yorkshire. It was a town with which he was quite familiar, having tramped to various parts of that area looking for work, a common thing in those days. At around 9p.m. he walked into the Woodpecker Inn, on the Rochdale Road.

'How do Bill?' said John Newall, the landlord, who knew him quite well. 'Well..., tha' looks to be in a bit of a state lad'.

'Aye, I'm done up. I've just walked from Leeds', replied Waddington.

In the taproom at the Woodpecker were two brothers, James and Thomas Murray, who came from the nearby village of Walsden. They also knew Waddington and paid for a pint for him. From the Woodpecker, the three of them went to the Spinner's Arms. At the Spinner's, Waddington was treated to another pint of beer, and after hearing that he was out of employment and down on his luck, the brothers gave him the money for a night's lodgings. The Murrays left the pub and Waddington went off to look for somewhere to put up.

In the meantime, the Oldham police had been told that Waddington had a friend at Todmorden named 'Jack', and decided to travel there, in case he had gone in that direction. After receiving this information, Inspector Musgrave and Detective Wrigley set off in a taxicab. With them was the fugitive's father, Thomas Waddington. When they arrived there, they immediately made inquiries in the town, which convinced them that Waddington was not very far away.

There are three roads leading in and out of Todmorden: to Rochdale, Burnley and Halifax, and after combing the town centre, the police travelled a short distance along each one of these roads out of the town. As it was mid-winter, and getting quite late, the streets were all but deserted, so it was not difficult to spot any stray pedestrian wandering abroad at that time of night. It was after 10-30 when Detective Wrigley came face to face with a man in Rochdale Road. The officer did not know Waddington, but he appeared to answer the fugitive's description. Taking a shot in the dark, Wrigley called out,

'Hello Bill'.

Waddington replied 'Hello'.

The Detective then approached the man and asked him,

'What's your name?'

'William Waddington', came the reply.

He was then cautioned and told that he was under arrest on suspicion of murder. All Waddington could say was, 'Oh'.

As he travelled back to Oldham in the taxi, Waddington asked where he was being taken and why. On being told, he said,

'I know nowt about it'.

'What are you doing over here then?' he was asked.

'I came to see a friend of mine. I was at work till dinner time. I went into the Royal pub and stayed there till turning-out time. Then I went home, had my dinner and after that I came over here to see my pal, Jack Shaw'.

The prisoner was delivered to the cells at Oldham police station in the early hours of Sunday morning and brought up before the Magistrates on the following morning, charged with murder. Waddington presented a sorry sight as he stood in the dock. He looked very unkempt after his tramp over the moors and his night in custody. His trousers, which were dirty and rumpled, were supported by a thick leather belt. He wore no coat, just a waistcoat, which was open, and under it an army shirt. The prisoner was remanded for a week.

At the inquest, it was stated that the murdered child had attended Higginshaw Council School, and had been in Standard One. She also went to the Wesleyan Sunday School in Edge Lane Road, close to her home, and was described as a bright, intelligent little girl. She was the youngest of eleven children, four of whom were married. Her mother, fifty-two-year old Eliza Wolfenden, was a widow, her husband, Ben, having died the previous year. Ironically, Ben Wolfenden and the accused prisoner had soldiered together during the war.

Dr MacKinnon, Honorary Pathologist at the Oldham Royal Infirmary, gave the report of a post mortem examination of the body of the deceased, made on 15th February, the day after she was murdered, stating that Dr Fort, Surgeon to the Oldham Police, was present at the time.

There were a number of wounds on the face and head, several of which were so severe that parts of the skull and brain were exposed. The skull, in fact, was extensively fractured.

Asked by the Coroner,
'What was the cause of death?' the pathologist replied,
'Fracture of the skull, causing perforation of the brain'.
'What is likely to have caused the injuries?'
'Some of the facial injuries could have been caused by a brick, like the one produced. Other wounds, those on the head for example, could have been caused by a blunt instrument'.
A hammer was then produced, and the Coroner asked,
'Would you call a coal hammer that kind of instrument?'
'Yes, they might be caused by a hammer'.

The child had been interfered with sexually, and when a piece of rag, found near the body in the cellar was produced, the Coroner enquired if there was any evidence to show that this had been used to gag the victim.

'It's possible', said Dr Fort. 'but there are no marks to show that this happened'.

Dr Fort told the court that he had been present when Waddington was brought in on the Sunday morning, and had examined him. He found scratches on his left hand and left elbow. There were also scratches on the inside of his left thigh. All the scratches were new, and could have been caused by a girl's finger nails.

Examining Waddington's clothing, he found bloodstains on his waistcoat and trousers. There were also buttons missing from both articles of clothing. He later went to the Waddington home with the Chief Constable and other policemen. In the cellar he found two pools of blood, and brain matter on the coal cellar floor. There was also blood on the brick wall to a height of over three feet, and bloodstains on the handrail leading up to the kitchen and on the steps. He saw a hammer and a piece of rag among the coal near the blood, and a penny, [produced in court], which was found on the cellar floor. In the front room on the ground floor was a bed with a pink coverlet, underneath this were a quilt, an army blanket and a white sheet, all bearing bloodstains.

Nine-year-old Doris Wolfenden, sister of the murdered child, gave evidence standing on a chair. She was dressed in a black coat and wore a white hat trimmed with black ribbon. She told of the children playing together in the street and of Ivy being sent to a shop by William Waddington. Her story was corroborated by Elizabeth Roberts, who told the court that Waddington was her uncle and that he had asked Ivy to go to Whittingham's shop for a packet of 'tabs'[cigarettes].

When William Whittingham, shopkeeper, of 6 Higginshaw Road, gave his evidence, he denied that he had served the child with cigarettes. She had come into his shop on the afternoon of Saturday, 14th February and asked if he could give her change for sixpence. He gave her six pennies, and she remarked,

'A penny of this is mine'.

In summing-up, the Coroner said that this was a case of murder as foul and revolting as the mind of man could conceive. The little girl was lured to the house, and after being inhumanly assaulted, was dragged down into the coal-cellar and battered to death with fiendish cruelty.

'In all the annals of crime', he said, 'I should think it would be impossible to find a more unnatural beast than the murderer of this little girl, whoever he might be'.

A verdict of 'Wilful Murder' was returned against the prisoner.

When the prisoner was next brought up before the magistrates he was again remanded, and later the same day his two brothers were also before the court, charged with being drunk and disorderly, the younger one, Thomas, also being charged with assaulting the police, and George with obstructing the police.

PC Connard told the court that on the previous Sunday at 9-25p.m. he was on duty in Market Place when he saw the two prisoners, drunk and behaving in a disorderly manner. Several times he requested them to go away, and one of them, George, did so. As Thomas refused to move, the Constable took him into custody.

On the way to the police station he became very violent, striking the officer and tearing his tunic. George Waddington then came back and attempted to rescue his brother, but another officer, PC Hartley, arrived on the scene, and Thomas was placed on a tramcar and taken to the Town Hall.

PC Hartley stated in evidence that Thomas Waddington was behaving like a madman.

'He had gone wild. Kicking and striking, and George was trying all he could to get his brother away'.

Superintendent Pigott said that Thomas had been before the court five times for being an army absentee, and George had been there for larceny and sleeping out. Both prisoners expressed sorrow for their behaviour. George was fined ten shillings in each case and Thomas twenty shillings in each case.

On being brought up again at the Magistrates' Court, when he was represented by Mr J. Nicholson, William Waddington was allowed to sit at the solicitor's table, owing to the fact that he was deaf and found it difficult to hear the evidence against him. The magistrates concurred with the findings of the Coroner. Waddington was found guilty of murder. Mr F. Houghton, Chairman of the Magistrates, asked the prisoner if he wished to say anything, to which he replied,

'No sir'.

The Magistrates' Clerk, Mr H. Booth, then read over the committal and cautioned the prisoner, who again responded with the words, 'I have nothing to say'.

'You have not attempted in any shape or form, to ask any questions', said the Chairman. 'Have you fully understood what has been going on?'

'I've heard the witnesses', was all that Waddington would reply.

He was committed for trial at Liverpool Assizes and removed from the court. All of the witnesses, thirty-four in number, were bound over to appear at the Assizes.

The funeral of little Ivy Wolfenden had taken place nearly two weeks previously, when a remarkable demonstration of sympathy was shown by the people of Higginshaw and surrounding areas. At least an hour before the mourners were due to leave the deceased's house for the interment at Greenacres Cemetery, a large crowd had gathered in the street. They were so densely packed outside the Wolfenden house that the police had to move them back off the pavement. Most then took up a position on raised ground opposite.

Eight girls from Ivy's class at Higginshaw Junior School attended the service, which was held at the house. They were in the charge of Mr Fish, one of the teachers. The service was conducted by the Reverend W. Hindes, a Wesleyan minister, and four boys from the Wesleyan Sunday School were also present, while four others stood by to act as bearers.

By the time the funeral party left the house, there were upwards of a thousand people in the street, including a number of girls and women who had left their work at nearby cotton mills to see the funeral procession leave for the cemetery. Along the whole length of Edge Lane Road the householders paid silent tribute by drawing their blinds, and at around 11·30a.m. the door of number 170 opened and the coffin, covered with floral tributes, was carried from the house. A hush fell over the crowd and both men and women wiped the tears from their eyes as the little box was placed in the hearse.

Thirty-four witnesses, police, legal people and others, travelled from Oldham to the Liverpool Assize Court on Monday, 19th April, 1920. Unfortunately for them, it was to prove a wasted journey, as the trial of a man charged with fraud and false pretences, begun two days before on the Saturday, had not been completed. Yet, no one had thought to inform the Oldham contingent.

The fraud case took up a further two days, and the trial of William Waddington commenced on Wednesday the 21st, before Mr Justice McCardie, the prisoner being represented by Mr J.G. Helm, instructed by Mr J. Nicholson, while Mr A.J. Ashton, K.C. and the Hon O.S.G. Stanley prosecuted on behalf of the Crown. The Defendant pleaded 'Not Guilty'.

There was very little that the Defence Counsel could say in the face of such overwhelming evidence of Waddington's guilt. Faced with witness after witness called by the Prosecution, Mr Helm could put up what amounted to little more than a token defence on behalf of his client.

Emma Roberts told the court that her brother William was always hasty-tempered, and when he was worried his eyes stared in a strange way and he looked as he did when she passed him on Oldham Edge on the day of the murder.

Thomas Waddington senior, father of the prisoner, in reply to Mr Helm, stated that he was a blacksmith's striker. His son, he said, had fought in the war, being wounded three times, once very seriously.

In summing-up, Mr Helm contended that a great part of the evidence proved nothing against the prisoner, and argued that an innocent interpretation could be placed on some of his acts that day, as well as the explanation the Prosecution sought to place upon them.

It was hardly a convincing argument, and the jury, after being out only a short time, not surprisingly returned a verdict of 'Guilty'. The square of black velvet was placed on the judge's head and he gravely uttered the dreaded words. Waddington stood quite still as he listened to the sentence, and remained so even after the judge had finished speaking. Then a tap on the shoulder from a warder caused him to turn quickly and descend the steps leading from the dock.

Mr Helm then informed the judge that there were certain facts relating to the mental history of the condemned man's family which it would seem desirable to place before those in authority. His Lordship remarked that the instructing solicitor should communicate these facts to the Home Secretary, who would no doubt pay due regard to them.

There is not the slightest doubt that Jack Ellis followed the Oldham murder case from the day it first appeared in the local newspapers until sentence of death was pronounced on William Waddington in Liverpool. This time, should he receive the appointment to hang the murderer, it would hardly be likely to make him unpopular or despised by a section of the Oldham public, as the Kelly/Hilton case of seven years before had done. The violation and murder of little Ivy Wolfenden had been so horrifying that any number of people would have been only too willing to have pulled the lever, given the chance.

The case was, of course, much discussed in the Oldham Road barber's shop, with the hangman remaining very discreet as he shaved his customers and snipped away with the scissors. At the same time, he was unable to refrain from voicing an opinion here and there.

Just a few days after Waddington was condemned to death, it arrived…a letter asking Ellis if he would be available to carry out the sentence of death on the Oldham murderer. He wrote back at once, accepting the job. As it turned out it would be a double event. The second condemned man's name was Herbert Edward Rawson Salisbury. He was a former soldier, who was invalided out of the forces in 1918. He began an affair with Mrs Alice Pearson, whose husband then filed for divorce, naming Salisbury as co-respondent.

One evening Salisbury and Mrs Pearson went out drinking in the town of Formby, north of Liverpool. They were discussing the forthcoming divorce case, and Salisbury got very drunk. Later that evening he was in such a state that he was arrested, and informed the police that he had shot his girl friend. He told them where he had left the body. It was located exactly where he had said it would be, near the river. Salisbury pleaded guilty at Liverpool Assizes and was sentenced to death.

Ellis duly arrived at Walton Gaol, Liverpool, on the afternoon of Monday, 10th May. There he met the man assigned to assist him, Robert Baxter, the two of them then going to inspect the scaffold. Ellis had been a regular visitor to Walton over the years and it was not the first time that he had carried out a double execution there, having dispatched Hill and Thornley in December 1915. The Walton scaffold was built in such a way that two men could be hanged simultaneously, which, in Ellis's opinion, made the job more difficult. This had proved to be so in the case of Hill and Thornley. Hill, the young negro, had simply gone to pieces on seeing the noose and the white cap being placed over the head of his fellow victim. He had screamed out in sheer terror, then collapsed, and had to be supported on the trapdoors by the warders, while Ellis sprang to the lever. Ellis knew full well that in such situations there was the possibility that a condemned man might not die quickly, as was always the intention. The hangman might then be criticized, whether it was his fault or not. He was, therefore, hoping and praying that neither prisoner would cause him problems.

Up to that point, both Waddington and Salisbury had retained control of their emotions. As suggested in court following the trial, Waddington's solicitor had forwarded a statement to the Home Secretary, detailing the mental history of members of his client's family, and had received a reply to the effect that the matter was being given careful consideration. Time, however, was rapidly running out, and Waddington seemed quite resigned to his fate. He was enjoying his meals and was never short of a cigarette. That night Ellis went to take a look at him through the grille. He was sitting there chatting with the warders, the habitual 'tab' dangling from his mouth, as if he had not a care in the world.

No one from the Waddington family visited him on the Monday, the day prior to the execution, but two days before, on the Saturday, his brother Thomas had turned up at the prison. William told his brother,

'I'm ready. It'll be like going home'.

He also said that he would have liked to have seen all the family, but apart from a letter sent to his mother by the Onward Mission, which she forwarded to him, Waddington had no further contact with them.

'If they're worried', he told Thomas, 'tell them to think no more about it. I'm quite happy, so tell 'em to buck up'.

Only a small number of people, mostly workers on their way to their occupations, bothered to congregate outside the prison that morning. Standing there on the scaffold, the wretched pair looked around at the world for the last time. Like Waddington, Salisbury had fought in the war and been wounded at the Front.

It was all so tragic. Yet no pity could not be felt for them when one considered their poor innocent victims. As the *Oldham Chronicle* commented:

Even in these times of hysteria and revolting crime, Waddington's offence stands out as matching almost the worst, and few people will regret the last act of a tragedy which revealed such brutality and cruelty on the part of the principal actor.

The double hanging was carried out smoothly and without incident, both men accepting the inevitable and going to their deaths as bravely as could be expected. With all those years of experience behind him, Ellis was the perfect man for such an assignment. From the moment he entered their cells to pinion the condemned men, until he drew the lever to send his victims plummetting into eternity, the entire procedure was conducted in a thoroughly professional manner, duly commented on by the Governor of the Prison.

John Ellis was extremely busy throughout 1920 and 1921. Only two weeks after the executions of Waddington and Salisbury at Liverpool, came yet another double hanging, this time in Glasgow, for a vicious murder committed in the city's Queen's Park.

The victim was Henry Senior, lured into the park by a girl, who was in league with a couple of villains named Rollins and Fraser. The two men had hidden among the bushes, and when the couple strolled by they leapt out. Pinning their victim to the ground, they beat him viciously about the head, robbed him, then left him there to die. They were tracked down a few days later and arrested. The girl escaped the death penalty, but Rollins and Fraser were sentenced to die on the gallows, Ellis and William Willis carrying out the assignment on 26th May.

On 16th June Ellis executed Frederick Storey, a forty-two-year-old tram driver, at Ipswich, for the murder of Jane Howard, a domestic servant, whose body was discovered lying close to the lines by a railway worker. She had been badly battered around the head. The post mortem revealed that the dead girl had been pregnant, a fact which soon led the police to Storey, who claimed he had not seen Miss Howard for several days. A search of the suspect's house, however, produced numerous items of her clothing, which showed traces of blood. Storey was charged with the crime and duly paid the penalty.

Six days later Ellis hanged William Aldred at Strangeways. The condemned man, a cotton mill worker from Pendlebury, had murdered Ida Prescott, a forty-odd-year-old widow, who worked at the same mill. Angry and frustrated when she repelled his advances, Aldred had lost his head and cut her throat with a razor.

The following month, July, Ellis and Edward Taylor executed the bigamist and murderer, Arthur Goslett, at Pentonville, the dead body of Goslett's last bride having been pulled out of the river at Golders Green.

In August, the same pair of executioners ended the life of one James Ellor, who had been found guilty of the murder of his wife Ada, at Hyde, in Cheshire. At his trial it came to light that the accused had been wounded during the war and badly gassed. It would appear also that Ellor was one of those who came out of the war with mental as well as physical scars, and there can be no doubt that he had found it extremely difficult to settle again into a normal peacetime existence. His wife found him virtually impossible to live with, and finally, after much upheaval and many bitter arguments, she had left him and found lodgings with a woman friend. Of course, Ellor soon turned up and begged her to return to him, insisting that there would be no more rows. But Ada had had enough. She told him that everything was over between them and she would never go back. On hearing this, Ellor seized a hammer and beat his wife to death with it. At Chester Assizes his plea of insanity was rejected and he was sentenced to death.

CHAPTER 30

KEVIN BARRY
'FOR THE CAUSE OF LIBERTY'

In Mountjoy Jail, one Monday morning
High upon the gallows tree
Kevin Barry gave his young life
For the cause of liberty
Just a lad of eighteen summers
Yet there's no one can deny
As he walked to death that morning
He proudly held his head up high...

So begins the ballad of Kevin Barry, an Irish Martyr, whose arrest and trial for his part in the murder of three British soldiers made headlines in September 1920.

Barry was a Dublin medical student who joined the ranks of Sinn Fein, the political wing of the I.R.A., because, like many another young idealist, he was determined to do all in his power to further the cause of Irish Independence. Unfortunately perhaps, he had made up his mind that he would stop at nothing, and would even give his life for the cause if necessary. As it turned out, he did just that.

Kevin had been brought up to despise his country's oppressors, the British. To see the occupying forces patrol the streets of Dublin, where he was a student, was anathema to Barry, who was weaned on the exploits of the great Irish patriots — Wolfe Tone, Smith O'Brien, Robert Emmet and the Fenians, James Stephens, John O'Mahoney, John Devoy, and O'Donovan Rossa.

Sinn Fein is a simple motto. It means 'We ourselves', which is plain enough. In other words, the people themselves must act to rid Ireland of the invaders, who had established themselves in the country some 120 years before and still remained. The Irish people had suffered greatly in consequence of British soldiers being in occupation of Ireland and of the British laws imposed on them.

Like many of his fellow students, Kevin Barry felt very deeply about his country, and it took little persuasion to get him to enlist in the ranks of

Sinn Fein. From that moment his studies became secondary to his political activities. He was now on the road to the gallows.

On Monday, 20th September, 1920, a lorry carrying military personnel was attacked in North King Street, Dublin. There were six armed and four unarmed British soldiers in the vehicle, which was collecting bread from a bakery when it was fired upon by a number of men with revolvers. One soldier was killed outright and two others badly wounded. Two of the attackers were shot while attempting to get away. One of these, who was killed, was in possession of a home-made bomb. Several others were arrested, including nineteen-year-old Kevin Barry, who was discovered lying injured under the lorry.

The two wounded soldiers died soon afterwards, making a total of three British casualties, these being Privates Henry Washington, Thomas Humphreys and Matthew Whitehead. When dragged from beneath the lorry, Barry was clutching a German automatic pistol. A bullet in the body of Private Whitehead was of the same calibre and character as one found in Barry's weapon.

The British Government had already acted unconstitutionally by setting up military courts to try such offenders as Barry, so when placed in the dock, the young Irishman at once made it clear that he did not recognise the court, whereupon his solicitor withdrew. Sixteen witnesses were lined up by the Prosecution, Barry being found guilty and sentenced to death.

The turmoil in Ireland at that time was at its worst. On Saturday, 25th September 1920, less than a week after the attack on the lorry in Dublin, two Sinn Feiners, John Gaynor and John McFadden, were murdered by a gang of armed men at their homes in Springfield Road, Belfast. Gaynor's mother was present, and Edward Trodden, a local barber, was dragged into a yard, placed in a chair and shot.

Soon after this the police barracks at Trim, in County Meath, was doused in petrol and burnt to the ground. Then followed a terrible catalogue of wanton destruction carried out in revenge by the occupying forces.

A company of over 200 Black and Tans* raided the historic town of Trim, population around 1,500, and set fire to some of the principal buildings, starting with the large premises of J and E Smyth, and the wholesale store, bakery and mineral water manufacturers' owned by Mr J.J. Reilly, Chairman of Trim Town Commissioners. These premises were completely burnt out.

Another party went to the house of a Mrs Mooney in Watergate Street and forced the occupants outside. They were made to stand in the street and watch their home set on fire. The soldiers then knocked at the door of an adjoining house and gave the people there five minutes to get out,

---
* A para-military police force. Named for their uniforms – a mixture of khaki battledress and police blue – and after a famous Limerick pack of hounds, The Black & Tans.

as Mrs Mooney's house was being fired. The occupant turned out to be ex-Sergeant Tobin, a Royal Irish Constabulary pensioner, and after some discussion the raiders changed their intentions and ransacked a nearby shop instead.

In High Street, the large drapery store of Allen Brothers was burnt and damage done running into thousands of pounds. In Castle Street, just outside the walls of the old castle, the Town Hall was gutted and all the town's records destroyed. After burning down other properties, the Black and Tans marched triumphantly out of town, singing 'Rule Britannia' and 'Boys of the Bulldog Breed'.

Little or nothing is known of Ellis's movements beyond the fact that he was given the job of hanging the young student and that he travelled to Ireland by train to Liverpool, then by boat to Dublin. Lord French, the Lord Lieutenant of Ireland, who had been in England, had made a special journey to Dublin the week previously to investigate the case personally, and had decided that there were no grounds to consider exercising the royal prerogative.

Even as Ellis made his preparations for the execution, desperate, last-minute appeals were still being made to save the condemned prisoner on the grounds of his youth, but the fact that the three dead soldiers were also young lads, two being twenty and the other nineteen, certainly did not help Barry's case.

It would appear, though, that he had already accepted his fate, for he remained composed from the time of his arrest until the final morning, when he told the Catholic priest attending him that he was proud to die for Ireland 'like Roger Casement', and that he forgave his enemies. If, as the Irish claim, he was tortured while in Mountjoy Gaol, this could not have been an easy thing to do, but in any case, while no doubt sincere, such a sentiment would have been dictated by his religion.

Long before 8a.m. a large crowd had gathered outside the prison gates. In unison, hundreds of people recited the rosary, while military vehicles patrolled the area. Many remained in the streets long after the notice proclaiming the death of yet another martyr had been posted up.

Kevin Barry would never be forgotten. For like many other Irish martyrs, his name would live on in the folklore of his native country, thanks to the ballad, by an unknown lyricist, which is sung to the air of 'Rolling Home To Dear Old Ireland', and which contains a reference to the alleged torturing:

Just before he faced the hangman,
In his dreary prison cell
British soldiers tortured Barry,
Just because he would not tell,
The names of his brave comrades,
And other things they wished to know.
'Turn informer, or we'll kill you'.
Kevin Barry answered 'No!'

Having completed the job in his usual efficient way, Ellis quietly left Dublin and returned home. On trips such as this he was usually shadowed by detectives for his own safety, and his movements kept as secret as possible. Yet getting safely out of Ireland was no guarantee that he would not become a target for Republican sympathizers in England, where large numbers of Irish immigrants had now settled, in order to escape poverty and oppression in their own country.

Ellis was always uneasy about going to Ireland to carry out executions, but within a matter of months he would be called upon again to make the journey, this time to carry out a multiple execution. In the meantime, there was work to be done closer to home.

At the end of November Ellis travelled to Exeter Gaol to hang Cyril Saunders, who had stabbed to death his cousin, Dorothy Saunders, with whom he had been emotionally involved.

At the end of that year, three executions were scheduled to take place, all on the same date, 30th December, with the result that a new man, Robert Wilson, yet another Lancastrian, was 'blooded'. William Willis, who had been an assistant since 1906, at last got his first appointment as the man in charge.

In what must surely have been one of the busiest hanging days of modern times, John Ellis and his new assistant, Robert Wilson from Manchester, hanged Samuel Westwood at Birmingham, for the murder of his wife at Willenhall in yet another stabbing case. Thomas Pierrepoint and Edward Taylor executed Edwin Sowerby at Leeds for the murder of Jane Darwell at Croston, near Wakefield. While at the same time, William Willis, assisted by Robert Baxter, was hanging Marks Goodmarcher, a fifty-eight-year old Jewish tailor, at Pentonville, for the murder of his own daughter.

Only one day later, on New Year's Eve, Ellis was back in Manchester to execute Charles Colclough, from Hanley. Colclough, who ran a fish shop in the town, became romantically involved with a customer, Anne Shenton. The affair developed to the point where the woman left her family and moved in with the fishmonger. When things did not work out she decided to end the affair and return home.

Colclough, however, was not prepared to accept this and followed her. On being confronted by her husband, he produced a knife. A fiece struggle then ensued which ended with George Shenton lying dead on the pavement. Realising that the situation was now hopeless, Colclough turned the knife on himself, but as was usual in such cases he did not cut his own throat with anything like the same ferocity and force that he had attacked his victim. The result, of course, was that he survived to face the hangman.

At the time, the story was put about that a postman, walking up the street near the prison gates just as the clock struck eight o'clock, enquired as to whom they were tolling the bell for. A man in the crowd replied that it was for the murderer, Colclough. The postman is then supposed to have told some of those standing around that he was just about to deliver a letter to the prison, which was, in fact, a last-minute reprieve. The postman remarked that it had obviously arrived too late to save the condemned man. A most unlikely story to say the least.

The year 1921 was to prove a milestone in the career of the mild-mannered Lancashire barber. If the hanging of Kevin Barry had not already made Ellis, in the eyes of the Irish, one of the most hated of all living Englishmen, his activities in this particular year most certainly would.

It came about partly as the result of a horrifying series of incidents that occurred on Sunday, 21st November, 1920, when large numbers of rural Irishmen turned up in Dublin, ostensibly to attend a Gaelic football match between Dublin and Tipperary at Croke Park. The authorities, however, had been warned to expect trouble and were ready. It was decided to take no chances, and a mixed party of military, Royal Irish Constabulary and auxiliary police was placed on duty.

As they approached the ground from different directions they were spotted by pickets posted at various entrances, who not only raised the alarm, but also opened fire on the forces of the Crown. The gunfire was returned, with the result that a number of innocent people watching the match were injured. Many more were badly crushed in the stampede that ensued. As many people as possible were searched. Some men dropped their firearms and ran off, and more than 30 revolvers were eventually recovered from the field.

It was a terrible day for the city. With armed police and troops plus a crowd of around fifteen thousand, it was inevitable that there would be a number of fatalities, and so it proved. There were at least twelve deaths at the football ground, mostly from rifle and machine-gun fire, while one man was bayoneted, another died from heart failure and a woman was trampled to death. A great mass of people at the end of the ground near the canal bridge, swept like an avalanche onto the pitch. As the firing increased, apple-sellers were pushed over and their baskets of fruit trodden underfoot. Women and children were knocked over and trampled on in the rush to reach the exits, which were blocked with people, some praying aloud, while others fainted. One of the dead was Michael Hogan, a well-known Tipperary footballer.

There was fighting in other parts of the city that day. The whole thing was believed to have been planned and carried out by revolutionaries from various parts of the country. Though a number of the invaders were killed and several more taken into custody, the death toll among the occupying forces was truly horrendous, a Major, six Captains, three Lieutenants and two Cadets being among the dead, while four other officers, including Colonels Woodcock and Montgomery, were wounded. Later that day, three Sinn Fein prisoners were reported to have been shot dead while attempting to escape.

Following this, and other incidents, a series of trials took place which resulted in death sentences being passed on six men. Two of these, Patrick Moran and Thomas Whelan, were convicted of the murders of British officers Captain Baggally and Lieutenant Aimes on 'Bloody Sunday', 21st November, 1920. Four others, Patrick Doyle, Francis Flood, Bernard Ryan and Thomas Bryan were found guilty of High Treason, by taking part in an ambush of British soldiers at Drumcondra.

It was with some trepidation that Jack Ellis once again travelled to Dublin, and as he made his way, as inconspicuously as possible, to Mountjoy, he was aware of the atmosphere of smouldering unrest in the city. He was not mistaken, for on the following morning a massive crowd converged on the prison. Eventually, the number of people packing the streets around Mountjoy was believed to have been in excess of 20,000. It was an amazing spectacle, with some weeping and others offering up prayers for the condemned men. There was an entire withdrawal of labour, which resulted in the closure of all post offices and the stoppage of public transport, while shops remained shuttered and hotel staff failed to report for work, leaving guests to wait for their breakfasts.

Jack Ellis was certainly faced with a daunting task that morning. The identity of his assistant or assistants is not known, but Ellis certainly hanged all six men. The first two to go, at 6a.m., were Moran and Whelan, followed by Ryan and Doyle at seven and Bryan and Flood at eight. No details are known of the lead up to these executions or of how the six went to their deaths, but in all probability it was with the cry 'God save Ireland' on their lips. For Ellis, even taking into account his vast experience and undoubted professionalism, it must have been a harrowing time.

Not long after returning to Rochdale, Ellis was again on duty at Strangeways. The victim was Frederick Quarmby, who had murdered his wife at their home in Blackpool by cutting her throat. Quarmby had been so insane with jealousy that he had almost decapitated the woman, and paid the extreme penalty on 5th April, 1921.

Later that month, Ellis was back in Dublin to hang Thomas Traynor for the murder of a young serviceman in the course of an ambush. The father of ten children, Traynor was dispatched by Ellis and William Willis.

Following another job at Strangeways, where he executed Thomas Wilson for the murder of Olive Jackson, in yet another eternal triangle slaying, Ellis again set sail for Dublin, where he was required to hang three more Irishmen — Edmund Foley, Patrick Maher and William Mitchell.

Foley and Maher had been found guilty of the murder of a British Army sergeant, while Mitchell had been sentenced to death for his part in the robbery and murder of a Justice of the Peace named Robert Dixon.

The first two were executed at 7a.m. and Mitchell an hour later.

When Ellis hanged Lester Hamilton, a negro convicted of the murder of a teenage girl in South Wales, he broke in a new assistant, Seth Mills, a Welshman, who remained on the list for a relatively short time before giving up the job. At the end of that year, Ellis executed Edward O'Connor at Birmingham. It was the culmination of a particularly horrific case of murder, in which the father of five children had attacked four of them with a razor. Following a series of rows, for which he blamed his mother-in-law, he had become temporarily deranged and had evidently decided to do away with his entire family. The wife and youngest child were not in the house at the time. O'Connor began wielding the razor, and after slashing the other four children he gave himself up to the police. Though all four were badly injured, only one child died, the other three eventually recovering.

O'Connor was executed on 22nd December, 1921.

Ellis's first assignment of 1922 was the result of an horrific murder in the Whiteinch district of Glasgow.

A young Jewish girl, Elizabeth Benjamin, aged fourteen, selling door to door in the area, was invited to enter the house of a man named William Harkness. Harkness and his wife were heavy drinkers and deep in debt. After ascertaining that the girl was carrying money, they bludgeoned her to death with a hammer and robbed her of the modest sum she had on her.

The Harknesses then dumped the body, which was quickly discovered. It was not long before the killers were under arrest. Both were charged with murder and found guilty. William Harkness was hanged by Ellis on 21st February, 1922, his wife having been reprieved only a few days previously.

The following month, Ellis was engaged to carry out hangings on consecutive days, 23rd and 24th March. The first was at Usk, in Wales, where he executed William Sullivan for the murder of Margaret Thomas. A new assistant, Thomas Phillips from Little Lever, near Bolton, made his debut. Phillips would remain an assistant for the next seven years, retiring from the job in 1929 without ever achieving senior status.

From Wales, Ellis travelled to Exeter to hang Edward Ernest Black, an insurance agent who had poisoned his wife Ann at Tregonissey, near St Austell in Cornwall.

Mrs Black, who was a great deal older then her husband, ran a small confectioner's shop which turned over a steady trade. She had no money problems, although Ernest Black had. Either his business was not going well or he was not as efficient at running it as he might have been. Whatever the reason, he was in serious financial trouble and began using clients' money to cover his own bills, making the situation even worse.

In November 1921, Mrs Black became very ill with what was diagnosed as gastro-enteritis. Within a matter of days she was dead. Black himself had gone missing, presumably as a result of the financial mess he had got himself into. Meanwhile, a post mortem was carried out on his wife and certain organs removed from the body. On analysis they were found to contain traces of arsenic. Following information received by the police, Black was arrested at Liverpool and charged with murder. An ugly wound on his neck revealed that he had tried unsuccessfully to take his own life.

Black was tried at Bodmin Assizes in February 1922. Defending him was John Pratt, a young barrister whose brother William found fame and fortune in Hollywood as 'Boris Karloff'. Pratt did his best, but could not save his client from the gallows. Black was executed by Jack Ellis, assisted by Seth Mills, on 24th March.

Two weeks later the Rochdale hangman was at Nottingham, where he hanged Percy Atkins for the murder of his wife Maud, whose body was found in a shallow grave after she had been missing for several weeks.

When arrested, Atkins admitted that there had been a domestic quarrel, in the course of which she had flung her wedding ring at him and run off. After searching for the ring, he claimed that he had gone to look for his wife and found her lying dead on the ground. In a panic, he dug a hole and buried her.

When the body was eventually discovered several weeks later, it was in such an advanced state of decomposition that the pathologist was unable to ascertain the exact cause of death. In spite of this, the husband was found guilty of murder and hanged by Ellis at Bagthorp Gaol, Nottingham, on 7th April, 1922.

Because we live in such violent times, we tend to forget that in bygone days the newspapers were never short of stories when it came to crime, much of it involving cases of murder. The appalling details of many of these slayings make the most horrifying reading. The courts were kept busy, the prisons remained pretty full and a certain barber from Rochdale was seldom short of work in his other profession. Another boom year was 1922. After the hanging of Percy Atkins there were two further jobs before the month of April was out. Frederick Keeling, the landlord of a Tottenham boarding house, was hanged at Pentonville on 11th April for the murder of Mary Dewbery, a woman with whom he had once lived.

On the 18th, Ellis returned to Pentonville to execute Edmund Hugh Tonbridge, for the murder of Margaret Evans, his lady-friend, who was pregnant. Tonbridge, a married man of thirty-eight, was many years older than his victim, who was putting pressure on him to divorce his wife and marry her. She was found drowned in highly suspicious circumstances, Tonbridge ultimately being tried for murder and convicted.

Ellis's next assignment would be the hanging of Hiram Thompson, the Bamber Bridge murderer, at Strangeways, which will be dealt with in the next chapter. After that he would travel to Gloucester to hang Major Herbert Rowse Armstrong, the central figure in what would become one of the most famous murder cases in the annals of British crime.

CHAPTER 31

ARSENIC AND MAJOR ARMSTRONG

For an ex-army officer, Major Herbert Rowse Armstrong cut a somewhat less than imposing figure. Under five-foot-seven inches in height, he was very slimly built and weighed no more than seven stone. Yet the Major walked proud and erect and was always smartly turned out, his neat military-style moustache waxed at the ends and a fresh flower in his button-hole each morning.

Born at Plymouth in 1869, the son of a colonial merchant, Armstrong more than made up for his physical shortcomings by a tenacious approach to his studies and meticulous attention to detail. He graduated from Cambridge University in 1891, and within four years had qualified as a solicitor and was working as an articled clerk for a firm at Liverpool, where his family had settled after leaving Devon some years earlier.

Apart from his law work Armstrong was an ardent churchgoer. He was also keenly interested in anything connected with the armed forces, and joined the local Volunteers at some time in the 1890s. In 1900, at the time of the Boer War, he was commissioned as Second Lieutenant in the Lancashire Fusiliers, but did not go abroad. From Liverpool, Armstrong returned to Devon, where he worked for a law firm at Newton Abbot, and it was there that he met Katharine Friend, the daughter of a Teignmouth printer. In 1906, they were married. At that time, Armstrong was thirty-seven and his bride thirty-four.

Once she had the ring on her finger Katharine's true nature began to emerge. A humourless, austere woman, she ran the house and the servants with an iron hand. The Major also, surprisingly enough, was very much under her domination — a highly unusual situation for those days, when it was accepted that the man was the undisputed head of the family, with the woman being cast in the role of dutiful wife and mother, who never argued with her husband and carried out his wishes unquestioningly. In the Armstrong household, Katharine made the rules. No alcohol was allowed, except for a little wine on the odd occasion when guests came to dinner. Smoking was another thing of which she disapproved, and the Major was allowed to smoke in only one room of the house.

As well as continuing with his church work, Armstrong joined the Devon Volunteers, and it was not long before he was made full Lieutenant. As for his daytime occupation, he now had plenty of experience behind him, and decided that the time had come to strike out on his own. He found the perfect opening in the tiny Welsh market town of Hay-on-Wye, on the Herefordshire border.

For many years there had been two solicitors in the town, Edmond Cheese and Robert Griffiths. Their offices stood on opposite sides of the main thoroughfare, Broad Street. Keen, though friendly rivals, both men were getting on in years, and wanted to cut down on their work to some extent. It was in 1906 that Armstrong took up the position of Managing Clerk for Edmond Cheese. He was later taken on as a full partner, the firm then becoming known as Cheese and Armstrong.

At that time the Armstrongs had no children, and occupied a small house just outside the town, but after a few years they moved into a large detached property known as Mayfield, an impressive country house in the village of Cusop, which nestles in the valley, just a mile or so out of Hay. The dapper little solicitor, still very active with his weekend soldiering, had now reached the rank of Captain, and was put in charge of the local Territorials.

In April 1914, old Edmond Cheese died of cancer, and Armstrong took over the business completely. The sign on his door now read: *Herbert Rowse Armstrong, Solicitor and Notary Public, Clerk to the Justices.* Meanwhile, his rival across the street, Robert Griffiths, was still plodding on, and sensing an opportunity, Armstrong suggested a merger of the two companies. As well as eliminating a rival, he probably had the idea that he might eventually take over Griffiths's business in the same way as he had that of Edmond Cheese. But old Griffiths was not keen on the idea of working alongside the little Territorial officer and turned him down flat. Instead, at a later date, he took on a young man named Oswald Norman Martin, who had fought in France and been wounded. After a few months, Griffiths made the young man a full partner and never regretted it, for Martin proved to be an excellent choice. He worked extremely hard and took much of the weight off the older man's shoulders.

In August 1914, the Great War broke out and Armstrong was immediately called up. He must have had ambivalent feelings, for he loved soldiering and was glad to have the opportunity of a stab at the real thing. Yet, at the same time, he was worried about his practice. He was fortunate however. No doubt because of his background, he was not sent to the Front, but given administrative duties in the South of England.

Armstrong discovered that the life of a full-time army officer suited him very well. He was a good organiser and extremely punctilious in every task he undertook, which greatly impressed his superiors, while at times irritating those under him. He also enjoyed the social side, particularly those 'singalong nights' in the Officers' Mess, where he could drink and smoke to his heart's content, without having to answer to Katharine.

Meanwhile, his law practice had to tick over without him, although he was close enough to keep an eye on things. The last few months of his army career were spent in France, though well away from the action, and he came home with the rank of Major, a title he was allowed to keep and use in civilian life if he so wished, which he most certainly did.

It was with mixed feelings that Armstrong left the army in 1919. By this time he had three young children, a boy and two girls, and though he must have been pleased to be home again with his family, he did not relish the idea of having to knuckle down to Katharine's rigid regime. Her attitude seemed to have hardened even more while he had been away. She was always grumbling and would criticise him severely over the most trifling misdemeanour, quite often in front of the servants. Armstrong never argued with her, but it was noticeable that he tried to stay out of her way as much as possible, spending a lot of his free time pottering about in the garden, even though he employed a part-time gardener. He was still with the Territorials, involved in the church and also a Freemason. In addition, he had to work hard to try and resurrect a business which had become somewhat run down, due to his absence.

The opposition across the street, on the other hand, was doing very well indeed. As the longer-established local solicitor, Robert Griffiths had the advantage, but quite apart from this, the introduction of Oswald Martin had given the business a shot in the arm. The young solicitor had turned out to be very capable, had won the confidence of Griffiths's clientele, and was well-liked in the town.

All this was bad news for Armstrong, who was respected, but still looked upon as an outsider. It was not long before he began to harbour strong feelings of jealousy, though of course, he kept these feelings to himself. He was always courteous when he and Martin bumped into each other, and on the surface quite friendly, but even then was probably racking his brains to think of a way to get rid of his rival. Late in 1919, Robert Griffiths died. However, this made very little difference as far as Armstrong was concerned, for Martin was by this time well-established in his own right as head of the firm, in which Robert Griffiths's son, Trevor, though yet to qualify as a solicitor, was also a partner.

In the meantime, Katharine's health began to deteriorate. She had always been something of an hypochondriac, her bedroom being littered with all sorts of medicines and homoeopathic remedies. Now, she seemed to sink into a deep depression. Her appetite was poor and she was losing weight. Dr Hincks, the local physician, began to call regularly, but did not seem able to halt his patient's downhill slide. She constantly complained of rheumatic pains in her shoulder joints and arms, and had great difficulty in sleeping. For many years she had played the piano to a very high standard.

It had always been very important to her. Now she lost interest completely and could not be persuaded to go near the instrument.

Early in August 1920, Armstrong called at the chemist's in Hay and bought three tins of weed-killer in powder form. As the Major was a regular customer, Mr Davies, the chemist, did not think the purchase at all unusual, apart from the size of the order, which, Armstrong explained, was necessary because the weeds on his garden paths had been particularly persistent that summer. In fact, he was having such a struggle with them, he told Davies, that he might very well be back for further supplies.

It was around this time that the Major called at the office of Dr Hincks and told him that he was very worried about his wife, and feared that she was having a mental breakdown. She was in an almost constant state of melancholia and suffered from delusions. She fancied she could hear voices and strange people moving about the house.

The doctor seemed baffled by Mrs Armstrong's symptoms, and in particular by the fact that they were so varied. Hincks decided to call in a friend, Dr Jayne, for a second opinion. After Jayne had given the patient a thorough examination he consulted with Dr Hincks. He had come to the conclusion that Mrs Armstrong was indeed suffering from some form of mental illness, possibly brought on by the change of life, and was in need of urgent treatment. The two doctors then informed Armstrong that the only course was to get her into a mental institution, where she would receive the best attention. Armstrong replied that if that was their advice he would go along with it. The necessary papers were obtained and signed by Armstrong and the two doctors, and Mrs Armstrong was duly committed to Barnwood House Mental Institution, a private hospital at Gloucester.

With his wife safely out of the way, Armstrong lost no time in indulging in an orgy of drinking and smoking. It felt good to be able to do as he pleased in his own home. He also took the opportunity to visit London at the weekends, and later in the year was horrified to discover that he had contracted a sexual disease, which took several months to cure.

On arrival at Barnwood, Mrs Armstrong was found to be in a very low state physically as well as mentally. She was sedated, and over the next couple of months was calmed down. Gradually she began to eat solid food again and gain a little weight. By the end of the year she was feeling much better and looking forward to going home. While still at Barnwood she talked of making a new will. There was one in existence, made in 1917, in which she had left her husband only £50 per annum, apart from which there were various bequests, mainly to the children. This will was in the possession of her sister Bessie, who lived at Teignmouth. Katharine now apparently felt that she had been rather ungenerous in her bequest to

Herbert and wished to rectify this, she told her sister in a letter. When Bessie mentioned this some time later to the Major, he informed her that a second will had indeed been made. He did not add that he was now the sole beneficiary.

Armstrong had been visiting his wife in the asylum every couple of weeks, and had now reached the point where he was finding it very difficult to resist her pleas to be allowed to come home. He discussed the situation with Dr Townsend of Barnwood Mental Hospital, whose opinion was that Mrs Armstrong was far from well and not fit to be released, but the Major insisted, settled his bill and took his wife home.

When Mrs Armstrong returned to Mayfield in January 1921 she was hardly any better than when she had left five months before. As she was too weak to attend to herself, a nurse, Muriel Kinsey, was hired to take care of her. Nurse Kinsey would wash and dress the patient, sit with her and try to get her to eat her meals, but the nurse soon realised that she was dealing with a serious mental case, and when Mrs Armstrong began to talk about killing herself she informed the Major that she could no longer cope.

A full-time nurse named Eva Allen was then engaged, but very little change was seen in the patient, who now took to spending long hours sitting out on the porch wrapped in a heavy blanket, with her feet on a hot-water bottle and another on her lap. In the middle of February, she was again experiencing muscular pain and could not keep her food down. She was put to bed and Dr Hincks sent for. He found her to be in a very bad way, her cheeks sunken and her skin a dreadful colour. After injecting the patient with morphia to relax her and ease the pain, the Doctor took Armstrong to one side and told him that the possibility of his wife's recovering was very remote. The Major seemed to accept the news stoically and just nodded.

Dr Hincks arrived at Mayfield on the following morning, 22nd February, to find that his patient had lost consciousness. He informed the Major that there was nothing more he could do for her and doubted that she would last out that day. As the Doctor was about to leave, Armstrong asked him for a lift into town, saying that although he hated to leave his wife, he was snowed under with work and needed to go to his office. Dr Hincks dropped him off in Broad Street and went on to his surgery.

Armstrong had barely had time to remove his hat and coat and settle down at his desk when the telephone rang. It was Nurse Allen, informing him that his wife had passed away. Armstrong at once informed the Doctor, sent off a telegram to his wife's sister, then made this simple entry in his diary: *Jan 22nd — K died*. On returning to Mayfield, Armstrong found the curtains drawn as a mark of respect. He immediately opened them.

Dr Hincks, who had been puzzled by the patient's symptoms during the whole time he had attended her, recorded on the death certificate that Mrs Armstrong had died from gastritis, but mentioned the presence of heart disease and nephritis, or inflammation of the kidneys. On the night before the funeral the Major told the young maid, Inez Rosser, to bring a lighted candle and follow him into the main bedroom, where her former mistress was laid out in her coffin. She was told to bring the candle close, which she did, holding it with shaking hands as Armstrong soaped his dead wife's fingers prior to removing several rings.

The funeral took place three days later in Cusop Cemetery, with just the family and a few friends in attendance. One of these was Arthur Chevalier, also a solicitor, whom Armstrong had known since his younger days in Liverpool. Chevalier had drawn up Katharine Armstrong's will of 1917, and was also one of the executors. He was rather surprised, therefore, to be told by the Major that Katharine had made a new will, leaving everything to Armstrong and appointing him sole executor. The estate amounted to over two thousand pounds.

The grieving husband now treated himself to an extended holiday on the Continent. He was away for a month, and on his return, when he ought to have been getting back to his business, he decided to travel to Bournemouth to visit a middle-aged widow named Marion Gale. Armstrong had first become acquainted with Mrs Gale when he was in the army, stationed at Christchurch. She lived with her mother at Bournemouth and was not without money. After the war, although his wife was not aware of it, he occasionally met the widow in London while there on business. They would have dinner, sometimes followed by a visit to the theatre.

The Major made it quite clear to Mrs Gale that he would like to see more of her, and that as he was now a free man, he would not be averse, perhaps, to taking their relationship more seriously. The widow, however, did not encourage him. She was devoted to her ageing mother and did not wish to complicate her life in any way.

Armstrong was now forced to turn his attention to business, and it soon became obvious that his own practice had lost ground, while the firm across the street was forging ahead, mainly, Armstrong felt, at his expense. He refused to accept that Oswald Martin's success was well-deserved, the result of hard, painstaking work.

In the summer of 1921, Martin married Constance Davies, daughter of the local chemist. The young couple, who had bought a house at Cusop, received quite an array of wedding presents, including some silverware from Major Armstrong. The Martins had been married nearly three months when a package arrived at the house, which they took to be a belated wedding gift. There was no card attached, and on opening it, the newly-weds were surprised to find a 1lb box of Fuller's chocolates. Though they had no idea who had sent the chocolates, Martin and his wife sampled a couple, then put the box away and forgot about it.

Around this period, Martin and the Major became involved in the conveyancing of a substantial estate in Brecon. There were two separate purchasers, both of whom were represented by a local solicitor, Mr Lewis Jones, who had paid over to Major Armstrong, acting for the vendor, deposits received from clients. When Lewis Jones died suddenly and Oswald Martin was approached by the purchasers to act on their behalf, he was informed that the sale, which appeared to be straight-forward enough, had been dragging on for months. At first, he put this down to the fact that Armstrong had suffered a bereavement, following which he had taken an extended holiday. It was clear, however, that more than enough time had now elapsed for Armstrong to have completed his part of the sale, but when asked to explain what was holding things up, the Major made a vague excuse and said that completion could be expected within a few days.

Early in October, Oswald Martin's two brothers and their wives arrived at Cusop to spend the weekend. After dinner on the Saturday evening the mysterious chocolates were brought out and offered around the table. Only one person ate any, Mr Gilbert Martin's wife, Dorothy. Later in the evening she complained of feeling sick, and in the middle of the night was violently ill and was rather alarmed to find that her heart was beating at a rapid rate. She was not much better next morning, and it was another couple of days before she was well enough to be taken home. It was not realised then, that she had been the only person to have eaten any of the chocolates.

In the meantime, the property deal had still not been resolved. Oswald Martin was becoming exasperated, and again spoke to the Major, who told him that the main reason for the hold-up was the fact that more than one purchaser was involved. Martin was not satisfied with this explanation. When another week had passed without the relevant papers having been received from Armstrong's office, Martin informed the Major that he had been advised by his clients that unless the deal was completed by the end of that week the purchasers would withdraw their offer and claim repayment of their deposits, a matter of around £500. Armstrong now paid a personal visit to Martin's office and practically pleaded with him for a little more time, though he could not furnish a satisfactory explanation as to why it was necessary. Martin told him point blank that he could allow no more time, and on the following morning Armstrong received a letter from Martin cancelling the deal and requesting the return of his clients' deposit money.

Armstrong made no further attempt to argue about the matter, but instead, surprised Martin by inviting him to take tea at Mayfield that day. Martin replied that he was sorry, but he would not be able to come. Armstrong then suggested the following day, and though Martin again turned him down, he felt guilty. Perhaps the little man was feeling embarrassed about his failure to complete the property deal and was eager to remain on friendly terms. After all, he was now a widower and had few close friends in the town. Maybe he was lonely. When several other dates were suggested, Martin finally gave in and agreed to go to tea on the following Wednesday.

'What time would you like me to be there?' he asked.

'Oh, around five, if that's all right'.

'Yes, I'll drive up straight from the office'.

Knowing that the Major always walked the short distance to and from Hay, Martin offered him a lift, but Armstrong declined, saying that he would be going home early as he had one or two things to do at the house before tea.

When Martin arrived, Armstrong was in the garden. After a brief stroll around the paths the Major led the way into the house and through to the drawing room, where a small table by the window was laid for tea. On a tiered cake stand were slices of currant bread and several buttered scones. The maid brought in the tea. After she had left the room Armstrong poured out two cups and passed one to Martin. He took a scone from the cake-stand and handed it over to his surprised guest, saying 'excuse fingers'. Though it did not worry him at the time, Martin thought it odd that a man who had always been so fastidious should pick up the scone with his fingers, instead of either offering his guest the cake-stand or inviting him to help himself.

Apart from the buttered scone, Martin also ate some currant bread. The meeting proved to be no more than a friendly chat, and Martin left after about an hour, wondering why he had been invited, as nothing of any importance had been discussed. Perhaps he had been correct to assume that Armstrong was just lonely and craved company.

That evening, as Martin did some work in his study, he began to feel a little queasy, and when his wife came in to say that supper was ready he told her that he was not feeling hungry. However, as she had gone to a lot of trouble to produce a meal of jugged hare, to be followed by coffee cream, he decided not to disappoint her. After supper Martin began to feel sick. He was experiencing violent stomach pains and started to vomit. During the night he became ill with diarrhoea and more frequent vomiting.

Next morning, Dr Hincks was called in and noted that the vomit was dark brown in colour and that the patient's pulse rate was unusually high. The Doctor asked Martin what he had eaten the previous evening and was told that he had taken tea with Major Armstrong before having supper later on with his wife. Dr Hincks assured the Martins that it was nothing more serious than a bilious attack, probably brought on by something he had eaten. He made out a prescription and told Mrs Martin not to give her husband any food for a day or so, and only cold drinks.

During the day, Major Armstrong called in at Martin's office on business and was told by a clerk that his employer was ill and would not be coming in that day. In fact, it was several days before Martin could return to work, and he was still very pale and by no means back to normal.

While he was laid up, his father-in-law, John Davies, called round to visit, and was shocked at his appearance. When told that the illness had been diagnosed as a bilious attack he was very surprised indeed. As a chemist he was familiar with all kinds of illnesses. To him the symptoms pointed to something more serious. When he learned that his son-in-law had taken tea with Major Armstrong the first thing that sprang to his mind was the large amounts of poison purchased by the Major in recent weeks.

The chemist made it his business to call at the office of Dr Hincks to inform him of his suspicions. The Doctor naturally dismissed the idea that his patient had been given poison by his business rival as utterly ridiculous. Davies knew that he was only guessing, but realised that if he was correct, then Oswald Martin could be in mortal danger, as the Major might well try again. So he persisted, eventually persuading the Doctor, at least to take a sample of the patient's urine and have it analysed.

While this was being done, Davies remembered that Dorothy Martin had also been taken ill some weeks before, and questioned his daughter about her symptoms. While discussing what she had eaten that evening, mention was made of the chocolates sent by the anonymous well-wisher, and it came out that Dorothy had been the only person to eat any. Davies's suspicions now hardened. He asked his daughter if she still had any of the chocolates.

'Yes, I think so', was the reply.

Davies took the remaining chocolates over to a table by the window and examined them very closely. After a few minutes he looked up.

'Did either Oswald or yourself eat any of these when you first received them?'

'Yes, just one or two, that's all. Why?'

'You were very fortunate', said Davies. 'Some of these have been tampered with'.

'Are you sure Dad?'

'Quite sure. Look at this... see that one? It's got a puncture mark in it. And see, there are traces of a white powder'.

'What do you think it is?'

'It could be arsenic'.

'Oh Dad!'

'Well, it seems highly suspicious to me that Armstrong should be buying such quantities of weed-killer, that you should receive those chocolates, sent anonymously, and that Dorothy Martin should be taken ill after eating them. Then Oswald goes to tea at Major Armstrong's, and he's also taken ill, with the same symptoms'.

'But I told you, I ate some of those chocolates too. I didn't feel sick or anything'.

'Perhaps not all of them had been tampered with'.

'What are you going to do?'

'Have these analysed too'.

Davies arranged this also through Dr Hincks, who sent the chocolates, along with a sample of Oswald Martin's urine, to the Clinical Research Association in London, though the Doctor was still convinced that John Davies's suspicions were unfounded and that his imagination was running riot.

The Research Association did not appear to be in any great hurry to complete their findings and report back. They received the samples in early November and by the end of the month had still not contacted Dr Hincks.

Meanwhile, Oswald Martin had been bombarded with further invitations to take tea with the Major, and was forced to make one lame excuse after another. When he failed to persuade his business rival to visit him at Mayfield, Armstrong began to suggest that he stop by his office for a cup of tea and a chat. Still Martin resisted, feeling embarrassed and even a little guilty, despite the fact that the invitations were now viewed with suspicion.

Christmas came with still no word from the Clinical Research Association, but among the Christmas cards was an invitation to Mr and Mrs Martin to visit Mayfield over the holiday period. Martin sat on it for a few days, then made an excuse for not going. Finally, on 31st December, the Martin's were at last put out of their misery. It was a bitterly cold morning, with snow threatening, as the diminutive figure of the Major came into view, striding along briskly, dressed in riding breeches and neatly-tailored officer's greatcoat. Armstrong nodded courteously to a couple of passers-by before entering his Broad Street office, a converted shop. As he removed his coat and prepared to settle down to his work, he had no idea that within the next half-hour he was to receive a nasty shock.

At around 10 o'clock that morning the Deputy Chief Constable of Hereford, Superintendent Weaver, entered the premises, accompanied by two plain clothes detectives, and asked if Major Armstrong was in his office. The Head Clerk, Arthur Phillips, replied that he was. Without waiting to be announced, the Superintendent, followed by the two detectives, went upstairs and knocked on the Major's door. If Armstrong was shocked to see them he did not show it, but when the Superintendent introduced his companions as Inspector Crutchett and Sergeant Sharp from Scotland Yard, his heart must have missed a few beats.

The Inspector informed him that he was conducting an investigation into a mysterious illness suffered by Mr Oswald Martin, the symptoms of which suggested that he might have been poisoned, as arsenic had been found in his urine. The chocolates, some of which also contained traces of arsenic, were mentioned, and also the fact that Martin had taken tea at Mayfield only a few hours before becoming ill. The Major was asked if he wished to make a statement, and replied that this was indeed a very serious matter, and he would help the police all he could. Having made a statement, Armstrong was told that he was being placed under arrest on the charge of having administered arsenic to Oswald Martin on 26th September 1921 at Mayfield. The Major's only comment was:

'I'm innocent'.

He was escorted downstairs, past his bemused staff and lodged in a cell in the Hay Police Station.

News of the arrest of Major Armstrong went round the tiny town of Hay like wildfire. Very few people could believe what they were hearing. It was inconceivable that one of the town's two solicitors, a highly respected man, would go so far as to poison the other. Or if so, what was the motive? Surely not to remove a business rival.

With their man safely in custody, the police made a thorough search of his office premises. Nothing of any significance was unearthed, but a quantity of arsenic was discovered in a cupboard in the library at Mayfield. In the light of recent happenings the police now harboured suspicions about the death of Katharine Armstrong, and an application was made to obtain an exhumation order.

On Monday morning, 2nd January 1922, Major Armstrong was brought up before the magistrates and remanded for a week pending further police inquiries. That same day, Home Office pathologist, Dr Bernard Spilsbury, travelled from London by train to Hereford, then on to Hay by car. He was driven to Cusop churchyard, which was covered by snow, accompanied by Superintendent Weaver. A heavy canvas screen was set up around the grave of Mrs Armstrong and two gravediggers went to work with their picks and shovels. It was tough going, as the ground was frozen hard, and as it was also beginning to get dark, oil lamps were lit to aid the diggers. Eventually the coffin was raised and carried to a small building close by, where Spilsbury carried out a preliminary examination, at the same time removing several organs and other specimens which were placed in jars and sealed. The remains were then returned to the coffin and re-interred. Two days later, the inquest on the exhumed body of Katharine Armstrong was opened, and adjourned for three weeks.

On 9th January, Major Armstrong again faced the Magistrates. The little market town was over-run with reporters from every leading newspaper in the country, and there was very little space left in the tiny courtroom to accommodate all those who wished to be present as spectators.

The Major was transported from Worcester Gaol, where he was now held, and escorted into court still dressed in the same military outfit he had worn at his previous appearance. It must have seemed very odd indeed, to see the man who normally acted as Clerk to the Magistrates, up there in the dock. The accused was also one of the town's most prominent citizens, being a leading light in church activities and Worshipful Master in the local Freemasons' lodge.

Armstrong was represented by Mr Thomas Matthews of Hereford, while his position of Clerk was taken by eighty-two-year old Mr Cambridge Phillips. As it was by now common knowledge that the body of Katharine Armstrong had been exhumed, there was a strong feeling that the case before the court was merely Act One of a far more sensational drama yet to unfold.

The case against Major Armstrong for attempted murder was resumed that morning and continued until 12th January. At the end of that day's proceedings, Mr St John Micklethwait, for the Prosecution, requested a further adjournment of one week, as he had certain scientific evidence to put before the court, which would take several more days to complete and prepare. Despite strong objections from the Defence, his request was granted.

On 19th January, Armstrong was again brought to Hay and placed in a cell prior to going into court. There he was visited by two policemen, one being Superintendent Weaver, who now formally charged the little man with the murder of his wife. On being cautioned, Armstrong again stated that he was completely innocent.

You could have heard a pin drop as St John Micklethwait rose to address the court. He began by stating that it was now his duty to bring a far more serious charge against the prisoner, Major Herbert Rowse Armstrong — that of the wilful murder of his wife, Katharine Armstrong, by arsenic poisoning. Though the announcement was not unexpected, it hit the court like a bombshell, and at once there was uproar, with everyone talking at once and reporters attempting to push their way through the packed courtroom to get to the telephones. It was some minutes before order could be restored and the proceedings resumed. During the following weeks Armstrong would be transported daily to and from Hay Magistrates' Court.

From the very first day in court, the Major had maintained his composure. He seemed quietly confident and even cheerful, in spite of the grave position he was in. But as the case dragged on and the evidence against him piled up, the strain began to show on his features and also in his general appearance, for he was nowhere near as smart and well turned out as he had been at the outset. This was hardly surprising, in view of the fact that some of the evidence against him seemed pretty damning. Micklethwait was attempting to prove that the Major had removed his wife from the asylum, knowing she was not cured, so that he might set about poisoning her systematically. After her death, Armstrong had produced a will, by which he inherited everything. Her original will, made three years earlier, in 1917, was in her own handwriting, whereas the new will, dated July 1920, was written out by Armstrong. It had been signed by two of the servants, as witnesses, but they had witnessed nothing, for Mrs Armstrong was not even present when the will was signed. In fact, it was doubtful whether they knew it was a will that they were signing.

Those in court were shocked to hear that the Major had been receiving treatment for a venereal disease, contracted while his wife was in the asylum. This revelation had come from Dr Hincks, who had been reluctant to speak of it, but knew that it was his duty to do so. On the witness stand he was asked if Armstrong was suffering from syphilis, and replied that this was so.

Mr Micklethwait sought the Magistrates' permission to introduce a witness who did not wish to be named. This was granted, and the witness, a woman, who appeared to be of middle age, took the witness stand. Her face was covered by a veil, and she was introduced as 'Madame X'. She was, in fact, Mrs Marion Gale, the widow from Bournemouth. Mrs Gale told the court that she had known Major Armstrong since 1915. She had met him by arrangement in London, in July 1920, and had seen him on more than one occasion during the following year. In October 1921, some eight months after the death of his wife, she had stayed at Mayfield for one night. This was after he had returned from his continental holiday. Entries in the Major's diaries indicated that he had consorted with quite a number of women, both in London and abroad.

At the end of what had been a lengthy ordeal, during which the Majors' reputation had been dragged through the mud, the Magistrates concluded that there was sufficient evidence to warrant the prisoner being sent for trial to the Assizes at Hereford. He was now transferred from Worcester to Gloucester Gaol, and on 3rd April 1922, brought up for trial before Mr Justice Darling for the murder of Katharine Armstrong. Though it was now early spring, it was extremely cold, with the country still in the grip of winter, as the court convened at the Shire Hall in Hereford. Sir Ernest Pollock, the Attorney-General, assisted by Mr Charles Vachell and St John Micklethwait, led for the Prosecution, while the accused was represented by one of the country's most distinguished lawyers, Sir Henry Curtis-Bennett, K.C.

Bernard Spilsbury proved to be a most convincing witness for the Prosecution. He told the court that several of the organs he had taken from the body of the dead woman were remarkably well-preserved considering the length of time she had been in her coffin, and that this could only have been explained by the amount of arsenic found in her body. It was suggested by Curtis-Bennett that Mrs Armstrong might well have committed suicide by poisoning herself. This was easily refuted by the Prosecution, when it was pointed out that a person attempting suicide would be most unlikely to take poison over a period, but would surely take sufficient to kill in one dose.

Curtis-Bennett was of the opinion that the Prosecution had failed to show a strong enough motive if, in fact, a crime had been committed. He maintained that to suggest that Armstrong had poisoned his wife in order to get his hands on her property and money, when under the terms of a new will he was the sole beneficiary, was ridiculous, as was the suggestion that the will was not genuine. For it had been clearly established that Katharine Armstrong had previously told her sister that she intended to make a new will. This would effectively cancel out the one made in 1917, in which she felt that she had been less than generous to her husband.

When the Defence called Major Armstrong to the witness stand a buzz of excitement went round the court, and every eye in the room followed the little man as he made his way from the dock. He was examined by one of the Defence team's leading figures, Mr Ronald Bosanquet K.C., and did not seem in the least bit nervous, answering each question in a clear, well-modulated voice. But when cross-examined by the Attorney-General, Armstrong began to lose his composure just a little. A small packet of arsenic was produced, and he was asked:

'Didn't you say in your statement to the police that this was the only arsenic in your possession?'

'Yes'.

'That wasn't true, was it?'

'No, but before I could correct that statement I was arrested, and I decided to say nothing more until I'd seen my lawyer'.

The Major, who was on the stand for almost six hours, did not make a particularly good witness under cross-examination, and must have been very relieved when he was finally allowed to step down. He had been given a hard time of it, not only by the Prosecution, but also by Mr Justice Darling, who asked him a number of awkward questions, which he did not answer in a very convincing manner.

As the Oswald Martin case clearly had a bearing on the poisoning of Katharine Armstrong, a close examination of the facts surrounding the visit of Martin to Mayfield, to take tea, was inevitable. It was pointed out by the

Prosecution that, according to the servants, the scones were unbuttered when they left the kitchen, yet when Oswald Martin sat down to his tea there was butter on them. Therefore, it was obvious that the butter had been applied sometime between their leaving the kitchen and Martin being shown into the drawing room.

It was also probable that something else had been added, and it had already been shown that Armstrong had a quantity of arsenic in his library cupboard. The servants had not touched the scones again after placing them on the drawing room table, and as Major Armstrong was the only other person in the house, the only possible conclusion to be drawn was that he was the person who had tampered with them.

The jury did not find it easy to arrive at a verdict. They were out for a total of forty-eight hours before finally sending word that they were ready to return. There was a hushed silence as the foreman of the jury was asked to deliver the verdict. After a slight pause, the foreman uttered the fateful single word, 'Guilty'.

When asked if he had anything to say before sentence was passed, Armstrong, showing little or no emotion, replied,

'No, nothing'.

The little man stood stiffly to attention in the dock as the judge donned the black cap and sentenced him to death. He then did a smart about-turn and marched from the dock and down to the cells flanked by the two warders. Many of those in court waited outside the Shire Hall to witness the prisoner's departure. Armstrong looked pale and shaken as he left the court building and got into the vehicle that was waiting to return him to Gloucester Gaol.

Following the inevitable appeal, which was unsuccessful, John Ellis, who, as usual, had been following the case with great interest, received a letter from the Herefordshire Sheriff's office, informing him that the date set for Armstrong's execution was 31st May, 1922, and enquiring as to his availability. The first thing that came into his mind was that the 31st was Derby Day; the second was that he was engaged to hang one Hiram Thompson at Strangeways on the 30th. Easily solved, thought Ellis. The Governor of Strangeways would certainly let him get away as quickly as possible after the execution, to catch a train for Gloucester, and one of the warders, with whom he was friendly, would place a bet for him on the Derby.

Ellis always said that Hiram Thompson was one of the most callous and unfeeling men he was ever called upon to hang. Thompson had murdered his wife at Bamber Bridge, near Preston. When arrested he readily admitted his guilt, showing not the slightest sign of remorse. At his trial he conducted himself as though he was not in the least concerned, and when found guilty he stood in the dock with his arms folded, the expression on his face never changing, as sentence of death was pronounced upon him.

When Ellis arrived at Strangeways on the day prior to the execution, he got into conversation with a warder named Sharrocks, who told him that he and the condemned man had been at school together and that he knew him and the murdered woman very well.

'It's affected me very much, seeing him here in these circumstances', said the warder, 'but he doesn't seem the least bit bothered. When the Governor asked him why he hadn't lodged an appeal, he just said, "Oh, it's no use appealing. It's not worth it".'

It was not the first time that Ellis had encountered this sort of resignation, and he felt pretty certain that when the time came for Thompson to face the final moments he would probably change his tune. However, when the hangman entered his cell on the following morning he was rather surprised to find the condemned man sitting there quite contentedly puffing at his pipe. After being pinioned he was led out into the passage and greeted the prison officers who were waiting to escort him to the gallows with a cheery 'Good morning'.

The execution was carried out with Ellis's usual efficiency. Afterwards, the hangman was told by one of the warders that Thompson had slept so soundly on his last night that he had had to be shaken several times before he finally woke up. He then began to complain that they ought to have woken him earlier, and remarked that he had slept better in prison than he ever did at home.

On leaving Strangeways, Ellis made his way to London Road Station and took the 10a.m. train, changing at Birmingham and finally arriving at Gloucester about 3-30. Around teatime, a warder came in with an evening paper. Ellis asked him if he might have a glance at the racing results and was delighted to find that a horse he had backed named Trumpeteer had dead-heated at odds of 100-8. As the Derby was due to be run the following day, he would no doubt have found a way to put a bet on, though there is no record of whether or not he backed the winner, Captain Cuttle, ridden by the great Steve Donoghue.

Soon afterwards, the assistant hangman, Edward Taylor, arrived, and Ellis was told that he could go and take a look at the prisoner. He was led down into a cellar with an office at the far end, through the window of which he could look out onto a small yard.

'He'll come out through that door', he was told.

The condemned man did not emerge immediately, and while he waited Ellis produced his notebook and asked the warder to give him Armstrong's height and weight. He was astonished to learn that the prisoner had not been weighed during the previous three weeks.

'That's not good enough', Ellis told him. 'You must weigh him without any further delay, or I won't be able to calculate the length of drop'. Just then the prisoner stepped out into the yard, two warders close behind him. Ellis was shocked. 'That's never him!' he exclaimed. 'Surely that can't be Armstrong'.

He was assured that the little man in the yard most certainly was the notorious Major Armstrong. Ellis had seen pictures of the condemned murderer in the newspapers, showing him in his army officer's uniform, smartly turned out and looking every inch a soldier and a gentleman. Now here he was, with face unshaven and shoulders hunched. He struck Ellis as just about the most pathetic-looking specimen he had ever laid eyes on.

After taking note of Armstrong's build, Ellis went to check the scaffold, then talked to the Head Warder. Apparently, the prisoner had given no trouble, and spent most of his time reading. He did not talk much, but when he did his conversation centred mainly on his children. He was very worried, he said, about them and what would happen to them. He also expressed great admiration for Sir Henry Curtis-Bennett, and felt confident that with such a man in his corner he had an excellent chance of winning his appeal.

On the day the appeal was heard Armstrong had spent most of the time pacing his cell. When word came through that the appeal had failed he became very downhearted. He appeared almost on the point of collapse and felt even worse when he was ordered to strip off his civilian clothes and put on the broad-arrowed prison garb. This seemed finally to bring home to him the hopelessness of his position. It could be said that the Major all but went to pieces at that point, but by the time Ellis saw him on the day before his execution he had recovered his composure, though he looked far from well.

That day the prisoner received his last visitors — his solicitor, Thomas Matthews, the Vicar of Hay, the Rector of Cusop and a fourth man described as a family friend, probably Arthur Chevalier. To them he again proclaimed his innocence. There were rumours that Armstrong also received a visit from 'Madame X', but this report was unconfirmed, and it is highly unlikely that Marion Gale ever visited Gloucester Gaol.

When the prisoner was weighed it was found that he tipped the scales at 8st. 3lbs. At the age of fifty-two he had put on a little weight since his younger days, but was still quite light for a man of 5ft. $6^1/_2$ ins., as measured by the prison authorities, and the hangman, after considering very carefully, decided to allow a drop of 8ft. 8ins., one of the longest ever given by Ellis, or any other hangman for that matter. It was a known fact that executioners fought shy of long drops for obvious reasons, and there can be no doubt that Ellis was taking something of a gamble in Armstrong's case, for though the lightness of his body clearly indicated that a long drop would be necessary to hang him, there was always the chance that, because of the slimness of his neck, the head could be torn from the body, a possibility that every executioner dreaded.

Armstrong was told that he could have anything he wished to eat or drink, and before retiring for the night he consumed a couple of glasses of whisky. This did not, however, induce sleep, and perhaps not surprisingly, he tossed and turned in his bed almost the entire night. A couple of times he got up, put on his slippers and walked aimlessly around the cell. When told of this later, Ellis made a remarkable statement, saying that he felt at least a measure of pity for Armstrong because in his opinion an educated man would suffer more mental anguish than 'the more stolid type with underdeveloped brains!'

Eventually, the prisoner lay down again, and after a while, dropped off to sleep. After twenty minutes or so, he awoke with a start and asked what time it was. On being told that it was not long after midnight, he groaned and said,

'Waiting to die is very, very hard'.

Of course, he got through the long tortuous night, but on rising, he appeared very shaky indeed. Slowly and mechanically, he dressed himself in the clothes he had worn on his arrival at the prison, for that was the usual procedure when a person was about to be executed. After putting on his shirt Armstrong asked for his collar, then immediately realised that this would not be returned to him, as his shirt would have to be open at the neck when he reached the scaffold.

Ellis, who had already checked the equipment and tested the drop, was sent for by Mr James, the Under-Sheriff, at around seven-thirty, and assured him that all was in order. James told him,

'I won't be present at the execution. You see I've known Armstrong well for a number of years, and I don't want him to know I'm here'.

At five minutes before eight o'clock Ellis was outside the condemned cell with the Governor, the Chaplain and several prison warders. They all appeared tense, and one or two said they would be glad when it was all over.

At two minutes to eight the cell door was opened and the Chaplain, the Reverend Macklin, entered, followed by the Governor, who shook hands with the prisoner, then came out into the passage again and signalled to

Ellis to go in. Armstrong was standing by his bed with two warders close by. The hangman took hold of his left arm, drew it behind his back and proceeded to pinion him. When Ellis turned him around to make sure that his shirt was unbuttoned at the neck the little man looked him in the eye and said,

'Goodbye'.

'When we get up there', said Ellis. 'Look straight at me and it will be all over very quickly'.

Armstrong nodded, then Ellis left him with the assistant hangman and went on ahead to the scaffold. The hanging party's progress over the short distance from the cell to the scaffold seemed to take an age, owing to the slow pace set by the Reverend Macklin, who led the way as he intoned the prayers for the dying. This seemed to make the doomed man, who followed immediately behind the Chaplain, very edgy. He appeared to be looking anxiously over the clergyman's shoulder, as though he wanted to hurry past him and get it over with.

At last, the party reached the scaffold. Now that the final moment had arrived, Armstrong's military training stood him in good stead, and at the very last minute he managed to pull himself together. The little Major was determined to die like a soldier. Stepping onto the drop, he stood very erect and remained so while the white cap and the rope were placed in position. Then, as Ellis stepped back and pulled the lever, he heard a stifled cry from the condemned man,

'I'm coming Katie!'

They were the last words Major Armstrong ever uttered. There were no problems regarding the length of drop. Armstrong died instantaneously and Ellis was congratulated by the Governor on an excellent job.

There was quite a crowd outside the prison when Ellis and his assistant left an hour or so later, but they managed to slip away without being accosted. At the railway station the hangman got a nice surprise when he bumped into Jack Robinson, a well-known former Rochdale Hornets' player who was then living in Gloucester. Robinson had been a great favourite between the years 1908 and 1914, when the war broke out. A strong-running centre or wing, he set a club record of 28 tries in the 1910-11 season, which stood until 1934-5.

As a keen Rugby League fan, Ellis was delighted to meet one of his favourite players, and spent a pleasant half-hour with him over a drink while reminiscing. Then, catching the 10-15 train for Birmingham, he arrived back in Rochdale at four that afternoon, tired out. The hanging of Major Armstrong had been quite a strain for him, possibly owing to the worry of having gambled with such an unusually long drop. He was certainly relieved that it was all over, and flopped down in his favourite armchair by the fire feeling completely drained.

Sixty-five-year-old Emily Pearce, who had served the Armstrongs as housekeeper for a number of years, stayed on at Mayfield for a while to look after the children, until arrangements could be made for their welfare. The estate was bankrupt and a sale of the furniture and effects was held and drew a large crowd, which included a number of dealers as well as curiosity seekers. The sale appeared to be very successful and it is to be hoped that the Armstrong children received some benefit from it, as well as the creditors.

The children were taken in by Arthur Chevalier and his wife, who looked after them for a number of years. Chevalier apparently did everything he could to keep their true identities secret, even going so far as to have their names changed. The Armstrong children were fortunate to have the Chevaliers to care for them and protect them from the press and the morbidly curious. After a few years people seemed to forget about them, though it was rumoured that on reaching maturity the family went to live abroad. But, young as they were when disaster struck, they would never be able to forget Mayfield and the horrors associated with it.

CHAPTER 32

RONALD TRUE AND HENRY JACOBY

The year 1922 produced a number of sensational murder cases, among them the slaying of a prostitute, Olive Young, in south-west London, and the murder of Lady White, widow of Sir Edward White, a former Chairman of the London County Council, at a private hotel in Portman Street — crimes which made national newspaper headlines.

John Ellis was given the job of hanging the killers of both women. One murderer was ultimately reprieved. No such mercy, however, was shown to the slayer of Lady White, a young boy of eighteen named Henry Jacoby. The ordeal of hanging Jacoby caused Ellis much anguish and soul-searching, and probably had a lasting effect on him.

The murder of Olive Young, however, is without any doubt the more interesting of the two cases, simply because the chief protagonist was Ronald True, whose amazing career and twisted mind have fascinated criminologists over the years.

True was born illegitimately in Manchester, in 1891. His mother, only sixteen years of age at the time, later met and married a decent man, who was also quite wealthy. True's stepfather was prepared to do all he could for the boy. He was given a good education, although he was far from being a diligent pupil. Rather than buckle down to his school work he preferred to indulge in flights of fancy, which were not viewed seriously by his parents. Eventually though, as True grew up, it became increasingly obvious that he was lazy, unreliable and not above telling the odd lie if he thought he could benefit from it.

Realising that something positive would have to be done about young Ronald, his stepfather arranged for him to be sent off to New Zealand, to learn farming, hoping that this would bring some sort of stability into his life. Faced with the tough, back-breaking work and long hours, True soon walked away from it, and over the next few years drifted around the world, visiting Canada, South America, Mexico and the Far East, sometimes scratching a bare living, but more often sending letters home asking for money. Whatever form of employment he undertook, it always ended the same way. He was either fired or just walked out.

At the outbreak of the war in 1914 he was back in Britain, and managed to use his persuasiveness to get himself accepted as a trainee pilot in the Royal Flying Corps at Gosport in Hampshire. True proved to be a very poor pupil when it came to grasping the theoretical side of the training, which was not surprising, as he had never been able to apply his mind to anything. As for the flying itself, he was very erratic, but could just about get by. His fellow students therefore, were absolutely amazed when he managed to scrape through his exams and gain his wings. Once these had been sewn on his uniform he strutted around as though he had just been made Squadron Leader.

Over the following months, True proved to be an absolute disaster and wrecked several aircraft, almost killing himself on one occasion, before ending up in a military hospital with severe concussion.

He was also found to have contracted a venereal disease. A report, dated 22 March 1916, stated that the patient was suffering from 'Gonorrhea with Arthritis' and added that he would be unlikely to be fit for duty within a period of three months.

A further report, dated 5 July 1916, stated that True was suffering from,

> *'Obstinate Gonorrheal rheumatism, complicated with old syphilitic infection. He is now emaciated and anaemic'.*

Soon after this True was transferred to a convalescent home at Southsea. A doctor who examined him in February of 1916 and again in December of the same year, concluded that he was, 'Suffering from after effects of concussion due to crash'. The report also mentions injuries to spine and hip joint.

By this time he had been invalided out of the forces, and though now a civilian again, he was passing himself off as Major Ronald True of the Royal Flying Corps. He often carried in his pocket a loaded revolver, and informed friends and acquaintances that if they wished to have anyone removed he would be only too willing to do the job — for a price. No one took him seriously. In fact, his friends must have found him quite amusing, this dare-devil ex-pilot, who was prepared to have a crack at just about anything.

True, however, was by this time beginning to exhibit clear signs of mental instability. He began to believe that there was a second Ronald True, a man who was going around impersonating him and getting him into trouble. Once, when presented with a bill he owed, he flew into a rage, insisting that it was 'the other man' who had run up the debt, and not he.

After leaving the RFC he managed to get himself taken on as a test pilot, but proved less than satisfactory and was soon dismissed. True next turned up in New York, where no one knew him, and created quite an impression with his tales of air battles in which he was always depicted as the hero. It was there that he met Frances Roberts, an aspiring young actress, who obviously found him attractive. Foolishly, she agreed to his sudden proposal of marriage, and from then on accompanied him on his travels. For a brief spell he held down a position with a gold mining company in South Africa, but his unreliability and cavalier attitude soon lost him that job. True now returned to England, his young wife in tow. His step-father, by this time, had had enough of him, and although still willing to continue giving him a small allowance, informed True that he wanted no more to do with him.

True had been taking morphia for some time, possibly since being hospitalised following his near-fatal plane crash, and had become badly addicted. In 1921, he was arrested and fined for tendering a false prescription at a chemist's shop in Portsmouth.

His fantasies now began to get much worse. When he was caught out in a forgery, or one of his cheques bounced, he would immediately put the blame on the other Ronald True. By this time, the young couple had a two-year-old son, and her husband's irrational behaviour caused Frances to fear for the boy's safety. She had come to realise that True was mentally ill and needed help. Before she could do anything about it her erratic husband disappeared. He simply left the house one day and did not return. Frances knew that it was her duty to try to trace him, but had no idea of his whereabouts.

He was, in fact, staying at various West End hotels. Every night he would be out dancing, in bars or hotel lounges, making friends quickly and easily, regaling them with tales of his exploits during the war and describing how he had sent many an enemy plane plummetting down to earth after an epic air-battle.

With the sort of life-style he had adopted, True's allowance went nowhere, and he simply lived off his wits; walking out of hotels without settling his bills, borrowing money and 'bouncing' cheques all over London.

One night in February 1922, True met Olive Young, a high-class prostitute who worked the West End. Her clients were mainly well-to-do, and several visited her on a regular basis. Olive looked after her earnings, had money in the bank and a nice basement flat in Finborough Road, Fulham. She was quite taken by the dashing Flying Corps officer, who was well-spoken and could be very charming. Once in her flat, however, she became alarmed by his behaviour, especially when he produced the revolver and began to wave it around. She became frightened and tried to persuade him to leave. At first he refused, then suddenly changed his mind and left rather abruptly. Miss Young was relieved to see the back of him, but on checking her handbag later, she discovered that a five-pound-note had been removed from it.

After that, whenever she saw True in the West End, she made a point of giving him a wide berth. But he refused to be put off. Sometimes he telephoned, and when told that she was too busy to see him he would still turn up at the flat in a hired car driven by a man whom he referred to as his chauffeur. When Olive was aware that he was at the door, she would pretend to be out.

On the night of Sunday, 5th March, the hired car drew up outside her flat in Finborough Road. For once, Olive was caught off guard. On hearing a knock on the door, she did not call out to inquire who was there. Perhaps she believed it to be one of her regulars, who had arrived without making a prior appointment. Whatever the reason for her lack of vigilance, she opened the door, and was dismayed to find the imposing figure of 'Major' Ronald True standing there, smiling that sickly, yet somehow menacing, smile of his. Before she could speak he had stepped inside. She knew that there was nothing she could do short of creating a scene, and considering the nature of her profession, this was the last thing she wanted to do. The hired car drove off and Miss Young was left alone with her unwelcome caller.

Around 9-15 on the following morning, Emily Steel, a cleaning woman, let herself into the flat. There was no sound of any movement and the bedroom door was shut, which was not unusual, as Olive Young often slept late. On a table in the sitting room the cleaner noticed a man's overcoat, a pair of gloves and a scarf. Obviously, someone had spent the night with Miss Young, which again was not unusual.

Emily Steel was pottering about in the kitchen when she heard a door open and shut again, and looking into the sitting room saw a man, whom she knew as 'Major True', having seen him at the house two or three times previously.

'Good morning', he said, with a smile 'I shouldn't wake Miss Young just yet. We had a very late night. I'll send the car round for her at twelve o'clock'.

'Oh, right you are sir', replied Emily, helping him on with his coat.

True slipped a half-crown into her hand. The surprised cleaner thanked him, closed the door behind him and returned to her chores in the kitchen. About half-an-hour after True had left she looked at the clock. It was ten minutes to ten. Time to wake up Miss Young she decided. Emily tapped on the bedroom door, then entered. There were bloodstains on the carpet and also on the bed. Though badly shaken, she forced herself to draw back the bedclothes. Beneath them she found two pillows heavily stained with blood, and a rolling-pin. The pillows had been placed length-ways down the bed, obviously to create the impression that Miss Young was still asleep. The room had been ransacked, with drawers pulled out and various items scattered about the floor. There was no sign of Olive Young. Fearfully, Emily crossed to the bathroom and pushed open the door. There on the floor lay the almost naked body of Miss Young, her head covered in blood and the cord of a dressing gown knotted tightly around her neck. As well as being brutally bludgeoned, she had been choked and a towel rammed down her throat.

Emily, screaming hysterically, ran to get help. It was not long before the police arrived. In charge of the investigation was Chief-Inspector Bill Brown of Scotland Yard. Brown knew at once, of course, who the killer was, for not only was Emily Steel able to provide him with a full description and a name, but True had also left his calling card on a sideboard in the sitting room, stating his address as being 23, Audley Street, W.1, which turned out to be false. His correct name, though, was on the card.

After leaving Finborough Road in a taxi, True was dropped off at Piccadilly Circus and went straight to a men's outfitters' shop in nearby Coventry Street, where he bought a ready-made brown suit for five guineas, a bowler hat, and a shirt, collar and tie. True told the salesman that he would keep the new clothes on, and asked him to make a parcel of the ones he had just taken off, which were blood-stained. True casually mentioned that he was a pilot. He had flown over from France that morning, he said, and been forced to make a crash landing, injuring himself in the groin. As he emptied the pockets of his old suit the salesman noticed several items of jewellery, including a woman's wrist watch, a couple of rings and a necklace. These had belonged, of course, to Olive Young, as had the cash with which he paid for his new clothes, for his funds had been very low the previous day.

Next, True visited a barber's shop, where he had a shave and a haircut. At a pawnshop in Wardour Street he got a loan of £25 on the jewellery. Then, having already telephoned the car hire company, he was picked-up at the Prince of Wales Theatre, in Coventry Street, by his usual driver, Luigi Mazzola. He mentioned to Mazzola that after being dropped off at the flat in Finborough Road the previous night he had stayed only twenty minutes, then left.

It does not appear to have occurred to True that unless he intended to give himself up, the time had come either to go into hiding, or on the run. Instead, he picked up a friend named James Armstrong and told him to jump into the car, as they were going to have 'a good day out'. The first stop was Hounslow, then Feltham, before stopping at Croydon for tea. Then it was off to the Hammersmith Palace of Varieties, where True paid off the driver and dismissed him.

When the hire car arrived back at its base, Mazzola found four police officers waiting to question him. It was almost ten o'clock when they reached Hammersmith. Having located their quarry, the officers quietly stepped into the box where he was sitting with his friend and led him out into the foyer, where they searched him and found a loaded revolver. Asked if he wished to make a statement, he denied any knowledge of the murder, and said that he had stayed at the Finborough Road flat only a short while on the previous evening, as there had been another man with Miss Young, a tall man. There had been an argument, and he had left them there, still quarrelling. In a further statement he said he had seen a tall man running along the Fulham Road from the direction of Finborough Road. Curiously, he told the police that the man was about thirty-one, his own age. In fact, the general description of the man, or men, he said he had seen could have fitted True himself. Perhaps he was once again attempting to put the blame for what he had done on the other Ronald True. Oddly enough, there really was another Ronald Trew, a club singer, whom True could have heard about. If so, this could have put the idea into his mind to invent a double. As he persisted with this claim at his trial, a Mr Victor Trew was produced by the Prosecution. He was there because his brother Ronald was in hospital. The two were identical twins and it was obvious from one glance that there was no similarity, whatsoever, between them and the accused.

The Defence claimed that True was mentally unbalanced, which was undoubtedly the case. The jury, however, decided that he was guilty of murder as charged and he was sentenced to death.

In the weeks leading up to his trial True was held at Brixton Prison, where he spent some time in the hospital, under close observation. At Brixton, True met and talked to a young boy named Henry Jacoby, who was also awaiting trial for murder.

On the face of it, the slaying of Lady White in her bedroom at the Spencer Hotel, Portman Street, London, had all the ingredients of a first-class murder mystery, one that would have taxed the ingenuity of a Sherlock Holmes. There was no apparent motive for the crime. She had no known enemies and had not been robbed, though there were many items of value in the room, including various pieces of expensive jewellery lying around on the dressing table. Lady White had been found by her maid, lying on the bed with severe head injuries. Scotland Yard detectives were told that the doors were kept locked at all times, and no one could get in unless they either had a key or were let in. There were no signs of any forced entry on either doors or windows, nor was there a single fingerprint to be found anywhere. The police, in fact, were completely baffled and had no idea where to begin.

It was at this point that Henry Jacoby, a pantry boy at the hotel, calmly announced that he had committed the crime. Without any prompting he told the police the whole story.

He was sitting on his bed in the early hours of the morning when he decided to go upstairs to the visitors' bedrooms to try to steal some money.

Dressed in jacket, trousers and socks, he left his room around 2a.m. carrying only a torch, and went to a room in the basement, where he knew the maintenance men employed by the hotel, left their tools. He handled various tools before finally deciding to take a hammer, admitting that the idea was to use it if he got caught. Upstairs he tried the first door he came to, No. 9. It was locked. Further along the corridor he tried another door. This was also locked. Moving stealthily to the next door, No. 14, Jacoby turned the knob and the door opened. He stepped quietly inside, leaving the door ajar. He saw that there were two beds, one of which was occupied. It was the one nearest to the window.

Jacoby told the police,

'The person in the bed woke up and I saw it was a woman. She screamed out and I got the wind up and hit her on the head with the hammer. She partly raised herself up on the bed when she screamed, and I struck her the blow. I struck her at least twice, because after I struck her the first time, she was moaning, and I struck her again. I first of all went back to my bedroom and wondered what I was going to do with the hammer. Then I went and washed it under a tap in the basement. It was covered in blood and I washed all the blood off and wiped it with my handkerchief'.

Jacoby was placed in a cell and later asked to make another statement. After going over the story of the murder once again, he added,

'I didn't go for jewellery, I went for money. I tried a box on the table, but it was locked. They found some blood on my clothes and thought it was Lady White's blood, but it isn't. It's my own blood. You see the porter hit me on the nose and made it bleed. Yes, I killed her all right, but what's done can't be undone. What's the difference between manslaughter and murder?'

After this had been explained to him, he added,

'I feel a lot better now that I've spoken. I knew it was Lady White's room— If I get out of this I'll take good care not to get mixed up in anything else'.

Of course there was no possibility of Jacoby 'getting out of it', and he was duly found guilty of murder and sentenced to be hanged. At the Court of Criminal Appeal the point was made by his Counsel that the boy had not gone to his victim's room with the intention of killing anyone, and had taken the hammer for his own protection in the event of discovery. He had struck out in blind terror when the woman screamed. But the Lord Chief Justice said that the jury had come to the conclusion that 'the fatal act was not only done in the course of, and for the furtherance of the perpetration of a felony, but was done with the intention of inflicting grievous bodily harm'. Therefore, Jacoby was guilty of the capital offence.

Though a number of petitions pleading for the commutation of the death sentence had been sent to the Home Office, no communication had come through to the Governor at Pentonville Prison indicating that the sentence would not be carried out. On Sunday, 4th June, 1922, John Ellis received a letter informing him that there was no hope of a last-minute reprieve, and requesting him to report to Pentonville Prison on the following Tuesday at 4pm. Only a few days before he had been engaged to carry out the sentence of death on Ronald True, who was also in Pentonville, and efforts were being made to save his life also, on the grounds of insanity.

It was with a feeling of dread that Ellis travelled to London on that Monday morning. There had been much in the newspapers about the case, and a great deal of criticism directed at Edward Shortt, the Home Secretary, who insisted that although he had gone over the details in great depth, he could find no grounds for granting a reprieve. Most people who were aware of the facts, felt that Jacoby had struck out at the woman in the bed in panic, being as frightened as his victim, when she discovered him and screamed. In addition, it hardly seemed right to hang such a young boy, who was also obviously simple-minded. Surely, the correct and more humane course would be to detain him at His Majesty's pleasure?

When Ellis arrived at the prison he was taken to a window overlooking the exercise yard and was astonished to find the young boy who was to die early the following morning, enjoying a game of cricket with the prison warders. He was holding the bat while one of the warders bowled to him, and seemed to be engrossed in the game. Perhaps he was so simple-minded that his impending demise had been momentarily forgotten.

In an article in the *Empire News*, many years later, Ellis stated,

> 'I saw the poor lad playing cricket the day before his death, and he were nobbut a child. It wer't most harrowing sight I ever saw in my life. And I had to kill him t'next day'.

After his game of cricket young Jacoby sat down in his cell to write some last letters, which were very brief. To his solictors he wrote:

> 'The only way I can show my gratitude is by keeping a stiff upper lip and going through it bravely'.

Another letter, to Major Blake, the Governor of Pentonville, read as follows:

Dear Sir,

I am just writing these few lines to thank you and all the officers who have looked after me since I've been here. If you would not be put to an inconvenience I would like you to thank these men for me. Once again thanking you for all the kindness.

Yours obediently, Henry Jacoby.

The previous week, Jacoby had been confirmed by the Bishop of Stepney, and afterwards told the warders that when the Bishop had laid his hand on his head he got the feeling that 'he was now ready to go through with it'.

Ellis tested the drop in the presence of the Under-Sheriff, the Governor, his deputy and the Prison Doctor, and when he arrived at the door of the condemned cell at a few minutes to eight he found the usual group of officials gathered there, the Governor standing with his watch in his hand.

'All right Ellis', said the Governor, 'let's get it over with'.

The hangman entered the cell, his right hand, which held the pinioning straps, behind his back. Jacoby, who had been sitting on the edge of his bed, got to his feet and shook hands with the Chaplain, who was standing nearby. The prisoner had been given a glass of brandy at his own request, and seemed reasonably steady.

'Look straight at me when you get there, laddie', muttered Ellis, 'and it'll all be over quickly'.

Jacoby did not answer, but Ellis was sure he understood. As Ellis left the cell to make his way to the scaffold he heard Jacoby say to the Governor,

'I want to thank you sir, and all the officers for the kindness you've shown me'.

Some of those present afterwards admitted that they had almost been moved to tears. Jacoby followed the Chaplain out of the cell and walked firmly to the scaffold. It was soon over. Within a matter of seconds Henry Jacoby was dead.

In general conversation with some of the warders afterwards, Ellis stated bluntly, that in his opinion, it was wrong to hang such a young boy. He was told that there had been so many crimes, including murder, by youngsters recently, that something had to be done to stop it.

John Ellis could not wait to get home that day. He felt sick at heart and profoundly unhappy about the part he had just played in the death of one who to him, was really a child.

Two days later Ellis received a letter from the Home Office, informing him that he would no longer be required to execute Ronald True. On the intervention of the Home Secretary, the murderer had been reprieved and committed to the Criminal Lunatic Asylum at Broadmoor, where he was to spend the rest of his life. True proved to be very popular, both with the staff and his fellow inmates, and seemed quite happy there, still playing the part of the gallant flying officer. He died in Broadmoor in 1951, in his sixtieth year.

The commutation of Ronald True's death sentence caused a public outcry, more especially in view of the fact that young Jacoby had just been hanged. The letter informing him of True's reprieve had caused Ellis to feel even worse. During all the years he had served as Public Executioner he had been well aware that many people despised him on account of the job he did. Now he had come to despise himself. Perhaps it was at this point that the long, downward spiral, that was to end in tragedy, began.

Before the year 1922 came to a close Ellis had executed a further six men, two of them members of the IRA, living in London. They were Reginald Dunn and Joseph Sullivan, both in their mid-twenties. They had lain in wait for Sir Henry Wilson, a retired army officer, intending to assassinate him in the street in broad daylight. Sir Henry was returning from an official function and was in full dress, including sword. As he approached his house they opened fire, and though he was hit twice he showed great courage in withdrawing the sword from its scabbard and charging at the two Irishmen, who fired further shots at the plucky ex-soldier, bringing him to the ground. He died shortly after the perpetrators of this cowardly attack had run off, with police and several members of the public hot on their heels. When cornered, the fugitives again opened fire, hitting a policeman and also a civilian, before they were finally overpowered and taken into custody. They were lodged in Wandsworth Prison, before being tried and sentenced to death.

Rumours of attempts to storm the prison, to free them, soon began to circulate, but no rescue attempt ever materialized, though there were noisy demonstrations outside the walls on the day the two were hanged by Jack Ellis, assisted by Edward Taylor and Seth Mills.

CHAPTER 33

MRS THOMPSON AND BYWATERS

The hanging of young Henry Jacoby had a profound effect on the mind of John Ellis, for soon after, he began to talk about 'packing it in'. Had he done so he would have been spared involvement in a case that probably created more public controversy than any before or since. Moreover, Ellis, as executioner, was right at the centre of it, and forever afterwards regretted the part he played, though he always told himself that he had only done his duty.

The brutal killing of Percy Thompson and the subsequent arrest of his wife Edith, a handsome woman of twenty-eight, and her lover, Freddie Bywaters, who was almost nine years her junior, first hit the newspaper headlines on 4th October 1922. As the facts began to emerge over the next few days, public interest grew to such an extent, that by the time the trial opened at the Old Bailey three months later, it was becoming increasingly clear that here was another classic to rival the great murder cases of the past.

Ellis, as always, followed the story day-by-day in the newspapers, and no doubt discussed it with his customers as he cut their hair, for though he made a point of remaining tight-lipped when asked to recount specific details of executions in which he was involved, he had no such reservations when it came to discussing the facts of a case as reported in the papers. Though he must have been aware that as Chief Public Executioner he would very likely be called upon should there be a conviction and sentence of death, he was not to know that this particular case, and the part he was destined to play in it, would affect him in a way that no other ever had. To say that the Thompson-Bywaters case left its mark on him would be an understatement. The truth is, that when it was all over, he was never the same man again. The spectre of Edith Thompson on the gallows would haunt him until the end of his life.

When nineteen-year-old Frederick Bywaters came into their lives, Percy Thompson and his wife Edith had been married for five years and appeared happy enough, though there were no children. Thirty-two-year old Percy, who had been invalided out of the army with heart trouble in 1916, worked as a shipping clerk in the City, while his wife held the responsible position of book-keeper and manageress at a wholesale milliners, Carlton and Prior, of 168, Aldersgate Street, London.

Edith had known the Bywaters family for a number of years. Freddie, in fact, had been a school friend and playmate of her three younger brothers, Newenham, William and Harold Graydon, at Kensington Avenue School in Manor Park, East Ham, but of course, would hardly have been noticed by Edith then as he was so much younger.

Freddie Bywaters grew up to be a well-proportioned, handsome young man. He had only one ambition, to go to sea, and after trying unsuccessfully a number of times to get into the Merchant Navy, was eventually taken on by the P & O Line in February 1918. Had his parents known, they would probably have made every effort to stop him, for with the war still on there was obviously great danger to shipping, and Freddie was not quite sixteen. He left the country without bothering to let them know until after he had sailed and there was nothing they could do about it. His duties on board ship were those of laundry steward and ship's writer, or clerk. He loved the life and over the next four years would travel the world, visiting such faraway places as China, India and Australia; trips which in those days took weeks and even months. It was while away in the Far East in 1919 that Freddie received the sad news that his father, who had been gassed while serving in France, had died. On returning home, he spent some time with his mother at the family home in Upper Norwood, South London, and early the following year, while again on shore leave, he decided to visit his old school friends, the Graydons, in Manor Park. Apart from the three brothers and older sister Edith, there was also another girl in the family, Avis, then aged twenty-four.

Though he was several years her junior, Avis found Freddie Bywaters extremely attractive. He was not yet eighteen, but being already well-travelled and well-read, he possessed a maturity far beyond his years. Of medium height, he was now broad-shouldered and muscular, with a clear complexion and a good head of thick, curly, light brown hair.

By this time, Edith and her husband had bought a house at Kensington Gardens in the more up-market suburb of Ilford. Though the marriage was quite stable, the Thompsons were not particularly well-matched. Edith was something of a dreamer, who could easily lose herself in romantic novels and accept the characters in them as living people, identifying with them and all their joys and heartaches. Percy, on the other hand, was staid and unimaginative. He would often take his wife to the theatre and quite enjoy it simply as entertainment, though he never took it seriously, while Edith liked to discuss the plots and the characters in great depth.

The Thompsons were now comfortably off. With Edith bringing home an excellent wage and Percy's respectable salary of five pounds a week, they were able to afford good clothes, holidays and regular evenings out.

Some months after his initial visit, Freddie Bywaters again turned up at the Graydons. They were delighted to see him and made him very welcome. He was still there in the evening when Edith Thompson stopped by to see the family on her way home from work, and it is possible that a spark was ignited between them the moment they were re-introduced. Percy Thompson also met the young seaman around this time at the Graydon's, and must have liked him, for in the summer of 1921 Bywaters was invited to accompany the Thompsons on holiday to the Isle of Wight. This was probably Avis Graydon's idea, as she was also going. No doubt Freddie was expected to spend most of his time with Avis. Whether he did or not, it can be safely assumed that Mrs Thompson would have been the main focus of his attention, and it is quite possible that the two took the opportunity to snatch brief moments alone together during the holiday. Whatever took place on the Isle of Wight, their relationship certainly blossomed, for when the holiday was over Freddie was invited to stay with the Thompsons for the remainder of his leave, as a paying guest at 41, Kensington Gardens. It would seem more than likely that the invitation was engineered by Edith.

The arrangement appeared to work quite well at first, with Thompson completely oblivious to what was developing right under his nose. Edith seemed so happy all the time, in fact, she was positively blooming — the reason being that she had fallen in love. Bywaters was showing very little interest in going back to sea. He had some money saved and seemed content to remain ashore indefinitely. He would occasionally go over to Manor Park and take Avis out, but to her great disappointment Freddie exhibited no more than a platonic interest in her.

When the Thompsons called at the Graydon's, Bywaters was usually in tow. If any of the family thought this odd, nothing was said. What neither they nor Percy Thompson knew was that the lovers were now meeting regularly for lunch and snatching what precious time they could together whenever Thompson was out of the house.

As the weeks turned into months Percy began to wonder if young Bywaters would ever go back to sea. Whenever he came home Freddie would be there with Edith. When they went out, Freddie would go with them. If they decided to stay in, he would stay in too. In the end, Thompson decided that he had had enough, and began to grumble. This led to quarrels between the couple. They were both now thoroughly unhappy, for different reasons. Percy, clearly irritated by Freddie's constant presence, tended to sit around and sulk, while Edith had reached the point where she wanted desperately to be with Freddie all the time, and though trying hard not to make it too obvious, was paying far more attention to him than she was to her husband. It was an awkward situation, especially for Percy Thompson, who, rather than tell Bywaters point blank that he had outstayed his welcome, continued to sulk and to snap at his wife over the most trifling things. Instead of holding her tongue, as wives invariably did in those days, Edith would argue, which maddened Thompson. There were rows, sometimes in front of the lodger. Bywaters, feeling embarrassed, angry and frustrated because he was in no position to intervene, would leave them quarrelling and go up to his room. He knew that it was a bad situation to be in, but he was now completely besotted with Edith Thompson. She had become everything to him, and he could not even consider giving her up. However, things were about to come to a head.

August Bank Holiday 1921 turned out to be fine and warm, and the afternoon found the Thompsons sitting in the garden enjoying the sunshine. As usual, Bywaters was there also. Both men were reading, while Edith was sewing, and no doubt casting her eyes from time to time in Freddie's direction. After a while, she announced that she needed a pin. Bywaters immediately offered to go inside and get one for her. After Freddie had left the garden Thompson turned to his wife and told her that she should have gone for it herself. When Bywaters returned he found them arguing again, and was glad when Edith put down her sewing and went into the house, saying that she had to lay the table for tea. But Percy followed her and the argument continued, Bywaters remaining in the garden with his book, very unhappy and wishing that Thompson would let the matter drop.

Eventually things quietened down, which was just as well, as Avis was expected for tea. Unfortunately, she was late, which resulted in Thompson starting to grumble again and demanding that the meal be served, as he was hungry. When Edith insisted on waiting for her sister he flew into a temper, and according to Mrs Thompson's later statement, made uncomplimentary remarks about her family, which resulted in her becoming very angry. She claimed that her husband struck her several times and flung her across the room.

On hearing the commotion, Bywaters ran in from the garden. Edith was crying hysterically, while Thompson was still yelling at her. Freddie was now incensed, and shouted at Thompson,

'Stop this! Just stop it!'

Thompson turned on him angrily,

'You keep out of this. In fact you can get out!'

At this point, Edith ran upstairs, crying, and Freddie, realising that the time had come to speak out, told Thompson that he was disgusted with his behaviour and that he was making Edith's life a living hell.

'What business is it of yours?' Thompson demanded.

'Why don't you divorce her? Neither of you are happy'.

'Whether we are or not, is of no concern to you'.

'Edith has had enough!' snapped Freddie.

'Oh has she? Well she's my wife and that's the way it's going to stay. Now you can leave us alone and get out!'

If Thompson had any idea of attempting to remove the young sailor by force he thought better of it. Later that evening Edith went to Bywater's room. Freddie comforted her and told her not to worry, everything would turn out right in the end.

Edith Thompson claimed that, following the Bank Holiday incident, her husband agreed to a separation, but had later gone back on his word. Freddie left the house a few days later, but only after he had got Thompson to promise that he would not beat Edith again. He stayed at his mother's house in Westow Street, Upper Norwood, but continued to see Edith Thompson almost every day. The lovers would meet for lunch, stroll hand-in-hand through St Paul's Churchyard, then meet again after she finished work in the evening and steal another hour together.

Meanwhile, things had gone from bad to worse in the Thompsons' home, with the arguments increasing and becoming more bitter. Edith and Freddie must have regretted the Bank Holiday quarrel, for it was now much harder to see each other, but both were determined that nothing ultimately would keep them apart.

About a month after leaving the Thompson house, Freddie managed to get a ship, the *Morea*, a cruise liner, bound for the Mediterranean. While he was away they exchanged letters, Bywaters collecting his at the ship's various ports of call, while Edith's were addressed to her at Carlton and Prior's. There was no problem with that, for her boss, Mr Herbert Carlton, valued her highly, and if he was aware that she was receiving personal correspondence, made no objection to it.

Over the next twelve months or so, Bywaters made a number of voyages on the *Morea*, some lasting several months. During the times he was away Freddie wrote many letters, while Edith wrote to him almost every day. Most of her letters were long and rambling, and often involved lengthy analyses of plays she had seen, or books she had read. There were, of course, long loving passages in them. Usually, they began with her addressing him as 'Darlingest', sometimes abbreviated to 'Darlint'. In these letters she mentioned that she could not bear her husband to touch her, and there were certainly periods when their sex life was practically non-existent. At such times, the frustrated Percy would naturally become angry and Freddie's name would crop up. Thompson would ask if Edith was receiving letters from Bywaters and she would deny this. Percy would accuse her of lying, and threaten to go down to Carlton and Prior's and have a word with her employer.

In subsequent letters, Edith began to enclose newspaper cuttings detailing various murder cases. One, headed *'Mystery of Curate's Death'*, involved alleged poisoning by hyoscine, another poisoned chocolates and a third ground-up glass. In one letter she wrote:

> *Darlingest boy, this thing I am going to do is for both of us. Will it ever make any difference between us? Do you understand what I mean? Will you ever think less of me, because of this thing that I shall do? Darlint, if I thought you would, then I could not do it'.*

In another letter she asked:

> *Darlint, will you do all the thinking and planning for me — for this thing? Be ready with every little detail when I see you. I'm relying on you for all your plans and instructions — not for the act. What about the Wallis case? You said it was interesting, but you did not discuss it with me.*

Parts of other letters mentioned that her husband complained that his tea tasted bitter, and added:

> *Now I think that whatever else I try, it again will still taste bitter, and he'll recognise it and be more suspicious still... I'm going to try the glass again occasionally — when it's safe. I've got an electric light globe this time.*

In a letter sent during September, 1922, when Bywaters' ship was returning from a trip to Australia, Edith attached a cutting which mentioned rat poison. These references to murder cases, poison and various plots to get rid of her husband could well have been flights of fancy, for it is a fact that Edith Thompson was very much inclined that way. But whether she was serious or not, Bywaters made the fatal mistake of keeping all her letters.

Freddie celebrated his twentieth birthday while at sea, and arrived home on 23rd September after a trip lasting over three and a half months. The lovers were soon meeting again almost every day for lunch. Freddie would be there again when Edith left work and they would travel on the train together, and perhaps spend half an hour in the park. Then she would go home and he would return to his mother's house in Upper Norwood, sometimes stopping at Manor Park to visit the Graydons.

They must have felt, at this point, that their situation was hopeless. Freddie was home again, but they were no nearer a solution to their problems. Percy Thompson had no intention of giving his wife a separation. The law was on his side, and if things came out into the open he would not only have the full support of the courts and the Graydon family, but — this being the 1920s — Edith would be shunned and regarded as a woman of loose morals.

Because of the letters and the tragedy that followed, a jury would later come to the conclusion that on Freddie's return from Australia, when the lovers met, their plans to get rid of Percy Thompson were discussed further and a course of action eventually agreed upon. Mrs Thompson and Bywaters would strenuously deny this.

Tuesday, 3rd October, 1922, was a typical autumn day, damp and chilly. At lunchtime, Freddie was waiting outside Carlton and Prior's to take Edith to the Queen Anne's Restaurant. Both were probably feeling a bit low, as he was due to sail two days later. That evening she had promised to go to the theatre with Percy, which could not have made Freddie feel any better. The lovers met again briefly, after she had finished work, Edith no doubt apologising for not being able to spend more time with him that evening, and arranging to meet him the following day.

After leaving Freddie, Edith met her husband. The Thompsons travelled by tube to Piccadilly Circus and walked to the Criterion Theatre, where they met another couple by arrangement, the Laxtons, Edith's uncle and aunt. The play they saw that night was *The Dippers*, a Ben Travers' farce, starring Cyril Maude and Binnie Hale.

When Edith left him outside Aldersgate Station Freddie must have been feeling very low indeed. The woman he loved so desperately, but could not have, was going off to enjoy herself at the theatre with the man he had come to despise. Despite her declarations of love and her constant talk of leaving Percy, so that they could be together, Freddie must have felt that she was having the best of both worlds. When she had gone he felt really miserable. He had nowhere in particular to go that evening and found himself heading east towards Manor Park. He would spend an hour or two with the Graydons. They were always glad to see him. He stayed all evening, not leaving until nearly eleven. Before he went he told Avis that he would come by the following evening and take her to the cinema, to which she agreed. Freddie went down the road towards East Ham Station, a forlorn, lonely figure. He was not quite sure where he was going. All he knew was that he did not feel like going home.

Around this time the Thompsons were leaving the theatre. They said goodnight to the Laxtons and took the underground to Liverpool Street, then the 11-30 train to Ilford, arriving just before midnight. They were now faced with a mile-long walk from the station to 41 Kensington Gardens.

The route took them along Belgrave Road, a lengthy, not very well lit thoroughfare, intersected by a series of avenues. They were walking on the right-hand pavement, past Empress, Mayfair and Courtland Avenues and De Vere Gardens. They had just crossed the next intersection, Endsleigh Gardens, the last one before Kensington, when it happened. A man in an overcoat and trilby hat, who had obviously been hiding in the bushes in one of the gardens, rushed up from behind and shoved Edith violently to one side. She fell, banging her head either on the pavement or on a garden wall. Badly dazed, she was vaguely aware that the man was attacking her husband. Thompson was being driven back many yards up Belgrave Road. The men seemed to be arguing and at the same time struggling and fighting. The assailant was wielding a knife, stabbing Thompson a number of times in the neck, the arm and the side. Mrs Thompson cried out,

'Oh don't, please don't!'

As she stumbled towards the scuffling men the fight ended almost as suddenly as it had begun, Thompson falling against a wall and slithering down into a sitting position. As Edith screamed and rushed to his aid the attacker ran off up Belgrave Road towards Seymour Gardens. As he passed under the lamp at the corner of Kensington Gardens, Mrs Thompson, though by now hysterical, got a good look at what he was wearing and recognised the hat and the overcoat.

On reaching her husband Edith saw at once that he was in a serious condition. He was groaning and blood was pouring from his mouth. In a blind panic, she ran down Belgrave Road and saw two people — Percy Clevely and Dora Pittard — walking home from the direction of the station. Edith rushed up to them and cried

'Oh please…will you help me? My husband's ill. He's bleeding. I must get a doctor'.

'There's a doctor's surgery just up the road', Mrs Pittard told her.

'Where, where…? Please take me', cried Mrs Thompson.

Dora Pittard and her companion led the way to the surgery and home of Dr Maudsley. Mrs Thompson rang the bell over and over again, until the doctor was finally roused from his sleep. By that time she had returned to her husband's side and was joined by a man named John Webber, who lived in De Vere Gardens and had heard Edith's cries. Dr Maudsley, having dressed hurriedly, was quickly directed to the scene by Percy Clevely and Dora Pittard. Matches were struck in order that the doctor might get a better look at the stricken man, as it was quite dark at the spot where Percy Thompson had fallen. The doctor saw at once that the man was dead, and said so. To which Mrs Thompson replied,

'Why didn't you come sooner and save him?'

Dr Maudsley ignored this remark, as he could see that the woman was extremely upset. At around 1a.m., the police arrived in the shape of Sergeant Walter Mew and two constables, who had been on patrol in the area. The ambulance was already there, and Edith Thompson, naturally distraught, was being comforted and physically supported by some of the bystanders who had now gathered at the scene. The body was removed to the mortuary, while Mrs Thompson was escorted by Police Sergeant Mew and a constable to her home nearby. As the body was being taken away Mrs Thompson, despite the fact that she had already been told that her husband was dead, asked,

'Will he come back?'

Mew simply answered, 'Yes'.

'They'll blame me for this!' said Mrs Thompson.

Sergeant Mew, believing the woman to be suffering from shock, did not ask her to elaborate. On arriving at 41 Kensington Gardens it was seen that Edith's clothes were covered in blood.

Daybreak found the scene of the crime swarming with police officers. There were numerous bloodstains covering the pavement at a spot midway between Endsleigh Gardens and Kensington Gardens. At the mortuary Percy Thompson's body was found to have a number of stab wounds. Only then did the police realise that they were dealing with a case of murder.

While Percy Thompson lay dying on the pavement in Belgrave Road, Freddie Bywaters was running through Seymour Gardens, the murder weapon clasped in his hand. He was heading towards Wanstead Park when he suddenly realised that he still had the knife, and dropped it down the first grid he came to. From Wanstead, Freddie carried on to Leytonstone and then Stratford. Panting and gasping for breath, he hailed a taxi, which took him part of the way home. By the time he reached Westow Street it was almost 3a.m. He let himself quietly into the house, hoping not to disturb anyone, but his mother was lying awake, and called out,

'Is that you Mick?' [Her pet name for him].

'Yes, Mum'. replied Freddie. He then slipped into his room and went to bed. It is unlikely that he slept that night. Of course, he did not know at this stage whether Percy Thompson were dead or alive. If Thompson were alive he could readily identify his attacker. If he were dead, he would be a murderer. In that event, would Edith identify him? He knew that she had seen him.

In Belgrave Road and the surrounding avenues, the hunt was on for the murder weapon. All the newspapers, sensing a big story, were represented, even the major ones, such as the *Daily Express* and the *Daily Mail*, their reporters knocking on doors, stopping people in the street and interviewing almost anyone prepared to talk to them. Did they know the Thompsons? Were they friends of the Thompsons? Did they have any photographs of the Thompsons?

Edith's family, of course, had rallied round her. All that morning Mrs Graydon remained at 41 Kensington Gardens. It was well after 9-30a.m. before Edith managed to drag herself downstairs, still distraught. Later in the morning she received a visit from a Police Inspector Hall, who asked her to recount to him everything that had happened in Belgrave Road earlier that morning, which she did, omitting to mention the fact that her husband had been attacked. According to Edith, he had simply groaned and fallen against her, as though he had suffered some sort of seizure. She had tried to save him from falling and found that her hands were covered with blood, which seemed to be coming from his mouth. He had staggered up the street for several yards before slumping down against a garden wall.

'And you saw no one else about at that time?' the Inspector asked her.

'No', was the reply. 'We were just walking home side by side, talking. I saw no one else until I ran down the road and met the man and woman coming up'.

The Inspector was far from satisfied with this story, and informed her that they were now dealing with a case of murder. Within a matter of hours Edith Thompson was at Ilford Police Station, being questioned by a senior detective from Scotland Yard named Wensley. One of the first questions he asked her was,

'Do you know of anyone who might have wanted your husband dead?'

'No', was the reply. 'I can't think of anyone'.

That day Detective-Inspector Wensley talked with various members of the Graydon family. There was very little they could tell him. He also questioned Percy Thompson's relatives and had a lengthy interview with Richard Thompson, the victim's brother, who did not appear to have much time for his sister-in-law, the bereaved widow. It is possible that the name of Freddie Bywaters was first mentioned at this point, for Richard Thompson was well aware of the wedge that had been driven between his brother and Edith by their lodger, and would not have hesitated to tell the police about it.

Edith was now asked about Bywaters, and members of her family, who were at the Ilford Police Station with her, were able to tell the police that Freddie had spent the previous evening with them at 231 Shakespeare Crescent, Manor Park, leaving around 11p.m.

In view of all he had been told, Wensley concluded that Freddie Bywaters must be found and questioned. However, all efforts to track him down that day proved fruitless. He had not gone into hiding, but was simply roaming around London, doing odd bits of shopping in readiness for his departure on the following day. He must have been worried sick and hoping against hope that his name would be kept out of it until after his ship had sailed. When the evening papers appeared on the street he bought one. His mouth felt dry as he scanned the headlines. *'SHIPPING CLERK MURDERED'*. Freddie's heart sank. As he read on he was only slightly relieved to note that the murdered man's wife claimed that she had not seen an attacker.

What should he do? Stay under cover, then try to board his ship at the last minute? Of course, the police might be keeping a watch on the docks at Tilbury. But then he had no way of knowing at that moment if he was yet a suspect.

Bywaters now made what would appear to have been a surprising decision: he took the tube to East Ham and made his way to 231 Shakespeare Crescent. On arriving at the house, Freddie learned from Mr Graydon that Edith had been taken to the police station and that Avis and her mother were there with her. What he did not realise was that the police were watching the Graydon house at that moment. Once he was inside there was a sharp knocking on the door and a Police Sergeant entered, accompanied by a plain clothes detective. Freddie was asked to identify himself and was then taken to Ilford Police Station for questioning.

Though reluctant to say much, he did make a statement, or rather he answered questions put to him by Detective-Inspector Wensley. Freddie admitted that he had quarrelled with the murdered man some months previously, and that the quarrel had resulted in his leaving his lodgings at 41 Kensington Gardens. He also admitted that he had remained on friendly terms with Mrs Thompson, that they had exchanged letters when he had been abroad, and that when he was at home they had occasionally met for lunch. When asked if Percy Thompson had been aware of these meetings, Bywaters stated that he had known about some of them, but not all.

When asked to account for his movements on the previous day and evening, through to the early hours of that morning, he was obliged to begin by admitting that he had lunched with Mrs Thompson, without Percy Thompson's knowledge. He appeared rather vague about what he had done during the afternoon. Most of the evening he had spent at the Graydons' in Manor Park, leaving some time between 10 and 11p.m. He had gone to East Ham Station and booked to Victoria. Then, after missing his connection, he had crossed the river at Vauxhall Bridge and walked all the way home to Norwood, a distance of several miles. He did not mention that he had taken a taxi part of the way home, but stated, quite correctly, that it had been around 3a.m. when he arrived at his mother's house. He had then gone straight to bed.

Asked if anyone had seen him after he left the Graydon's, he replied that he had not met anyone he knew. He had not known anything about the murder until he bought a newspaper around teatime that evening. Yes, he had written letters to Edith Thompson and she to him, mostly while he was at sea. He had destroyed her letters after reading them, he told the Inspector. On being asked if he ever carried a knife, Bywaters replied that he did not. Finally, he was asked what clothes he had been wearing on the previous evening, and replied,

'The same clothes I'm wearing now'.

The Inspector pointed out some dark spots on the sleeves of Freddie's overcoat, and asked him what they were. As Freddie could not give a satisfactory explanation, the overcoat was removed and the spots analysed. It was quickly established that they were, in fact, bloodstains. Freddie was informed that he would be held in custody.

While Bywaters was undergoing interrogation at Ilford Police Station, his room at his mother's house in Upper Norwood was being searched. The only items of any significance were a couple of letters from Edith Thompson, which would later prove very damaging.

At Ilford Police Station, Mrs Thompson, though still in a highly emotional state, had made a lengthy statement, in which she described all that had happened after she and her husband had left home to go to the theatre on the previous evening, right up until the time his body had been removed from Belgrave Road in the ambulance.

Asked about Freddie Bywaters, she described him as a long-standing friend of the family. Under questioning, she admitted that he had intervened on her behalf during a quarrel she had had with her husband, and that he had been asked to leave the house. She insisted, however, that before Bywaters moved out he and Percy Thompson were back on friendly terms. Mrs Thompson admitted that she and Freddie had written to each other while he was at sea, and said that she had destroyed all his letters, as she did with all correspondence she received.

Bywaters knew that Edith Thompson was also in custody, or at least had been taken in for questioning. She may or may not have known that he was being held. It would appear, however, that at some point the police deliberately allowed her to catch a glimpse of Freddie through an open door while she was being escorted along a passage and he was being interrogated for the second time. If this little manoeuvre was intended to shock Mrs Thompson and loosen her tongue it certainly worked, for her immediate reaction was to exclaim,

'Oh God, what can I do? Why did he do it? I never wanted him to do it'.

She was cautioned, then made a further statement, in which she described being pushed out of the way by a man, who then attacked her husband. They struggled, then Percy Thompson slumped to the pavement. Though dazed and shaken, she had seen the man running away, and had recognised him by the clothes he was wearing. It was Freddie Bywaters. Mrs Thompson maintained, however, that she had no idea of Bywaters' movements on the previous evening, nor any reason to believe that he was planning to attack her husband.

Faced with Edith Thompson's confession, Freddie appeared non-plussed, and at first refused to say anything more. He was informed that the police intended to charge him and Mrs Thompson with wilful murder.

'Why her?' he asked. 'Mrs Thompson is not involved. She knows nothing about it'.

Freddie then made a further statement, in which he described how he had waited for Mrs Thompson and her husband near Endsleigh Gardens, and had approached them, pushing her to one side,

'I said to him, "You've got to separate from your wife". He said "No, I will not".'

'We struggled. I took my knife out of my pocket and we fought. He got the worst of it. The reason I fought with him was because he never acted like a man to his wife. He always seemed several degrees lower than a snake. I loved her and I couldn't go on seeing her lead that life. I didn't intend to kill him though. I only meant to injure him. I gave him the opportunity to stand up to me like a man, but he wouldn't'.

Freddie told the police how he had disposed of the knife, which had still not been found. Soon after this he and Edith Thompson were jointly charged. Following the Magisterial hearing, Bywaters was lodged in Brixton Gaol, while Edith Thompson was taken to Holloway.

It was several days before the murder weapon — an ugly-looking dagger — was finally discovered. It had been purchased from a shop in Aldersgate Street, not far from Carlton and Prior's. The police now had all they needed to convict Freddie, but no evidence, whatsoever, to implicate Edith Thompson in the murder of her husband. This situation, however, was about to change. On 11th October, over a week after the killing of Percy Thompson, the two accused made their second appearance at Stratford Magistrates' Court. On the following day, detectives visited the *SS Morea*, berthed at Tilbury, where they took charge of a box, or sea chest, belonging to Freddie Bywaters. The ship was then given permission to sail.

Once the box had been unlocked and its contents scrutinised, the police knew that they had all they needed to link Mrs Thompson to the murder of her husband, for while she had destroyed the letters she had received from Bywaters, he had kept every one of hers. Their contents could not have been more incriminating.

At the inquest on Percy Thompson, held in the Town Hall at Ilford, a verdict of wilful murder by Frederick Bywaters was returned. A few days later both he and Edith Thompson again appeared at Stratford Magistrates' Court, which was packed to capacity. Despite strenuous efforts by Mr Stern, Mrs Thompson's solicitor, to prevent her letters being produced as evidence, the presiding magistrate, after considering the matter, decided that they should be submitted. For the first time, but by no means the last, Edith Thompson was forced to listen as her most secret thoughts were read out and her soul laid bare to the public.

After a harrowing day for the prisoners, there was still no end in sight, the Prosecution requesting a further week's remand, which was granted. On their next appearance in court the Crown asked for yet another extension of the remand, which was again granted. Further extensions were to follow as the Prosecution built up its case, and it was almost the end of November before the Magisterial hearings were finally concluded and the prisoners knew the worst — committal to stand trial for murder at the Old Bailey.

When the trial opened on 6th December, 1922, Sir Henry Curtis-Bennett, who had been briefed to represent Mrs Thompson, made an early objection to the letters being produced, arguing that they could only become evidence if it could be shown that she took an active part in the killing of her husband, for even though she might have desired Percy Thompson's death, she had no involvement in it, and was as shocked as any innocent person would be when it happened. For the Crown, the Solicitor-General, Sir Thomas Inskip, disagreed, maintaining that the letters were evidence of intent. Mr Justice Shearman, presiding, eventually ruled in the Prosecution's favour. After the judge had rejected an application for the accused to be tried separately, both prisoners pleaded 'Not guilty' to the charges.

The Prosecution had successfully applied for an exhumation of the body of Percy Thompson. In view of the references in the letters to poison and also powdered glass, a post mortem was expected to reveal either one substance or the other, perhaps both. In this the Prosecuting Counsel was to be disappointed, however, for Bernard Spilsbury could find no evidence of poison, no signs that it had been present in the body, nor any indication of glass, either in pieces or in powdered form. Sir Thomas Inskip did get Spilsbury to admit that if poison or powdered glass had been present in the body, and several months had passed since, it might very well leave no trace.

Over sixty of Mrs Thompson's letters to Bywaters had been seized. During the course of the trial, passages from around thirty of them would be introduced as evidence. Copies of these were now passed out to the jury.

Mr Travers Humphreys, who was assisting the Solicitor-General, rose and began to read from one, whereupon Mrs Thompson hung her head and wept. There was a mention of quinine, with the implication that Mrs Thompson had used this sustance on more than one occasion to terminate a pregnancy.

The reading of the letters went on for the best part of an hour, before the reader was cut short by the judge, who remarked that they were mostly 'gush'. Apart from the gush though, there were some passages which would prove to be very damaging indeed.

Bywaters, who was granted legal aid, was called upon to testify by his Counsel, Mr Cecil Whiteley, who took him painstakingly through his evidence, in which he explained his relationship with the Graydons and subsequent friendship with Mr and Mrs Thompson. Whiteley went over several passages from the letters and asked Bywaters to comment on them. There was little he could say, except that Edith had a very vivid imagination. Regarding such passages as,

> *'I used the light bulbs three times, but the third time he found a piece — so I've given it up — until you come home', and, 'You said it was enough for an elephant' —*

Bywaters could only shake his head.

Mr Whiteley pressed on,

'As far as you could tell, reading these letters, did you ever believe in your own mind that she herself had ever given any poison to her husband?'
'No', was the reply. 'It never entered my mind at all. She'd been reading books'.

The likelihood of his being correct in this opinion, was surely borne out by another passage from one of Edith's letters, which ran,

> *'It must be remembered that digitalin is a cumulative poison, and that the same dose, harmless if taken once, yet frequently used becomes deadly. Darlingest boy, the above passage I've just come across is in a book I'm reading, Bella Donna, by Robert Hitchens. Is it any use?'*

Edith had sent this book, in which a wife poisons her husband, to Freddie, and later asked him in a letter what he thought of it. This was by no means unusual, as she had sent him a number of books during his trips abroad, and was always keen to initiate discussions on them via their letters to each other.

It seems more than probable that Edith was simply letting her imagination run riot. Or, it might have been that all the talk of poison and references to getting rid of her husband, by one means or another, were intended to prove to Freddie that she was prepared to do anything to bring the two of them together. In truth, she had made not the slightest attempt to harm her husband and had no intention of doing so.

One passage though, which could not be explained away quite so easily, read:

> *Yes darlint, you are jealous of him — but I want you to be. He has the right by law to all that you have by nature and by love. Yes darlint, be jealous, so that you will do something desperate.*

This would prove to be extremely damaging, for Bywaters had indeed done something desperate. Therefore, it was only natural that the jury should conclude that Edith Thompson had set the whole thing up and was as guilty as her lover. Cecil Whiteley would, without doubt, have attempted to portray his client as a gullible young man besotted by an older woman, who had persuaded him to get rid of her husband, but Freddie would not hear of this, and did all he could from the time he was arrested to protect Edith Thompson. In the end Whiteley could do little, apart from admitting that the boy had been very foolish and pleading with the jury to take his youth into account before arriving at a verdict.

Very much against the advice of her Counsel, Edith Thompson insisted on giving evidence. Curtis-Bennett always maintained that she went a long way towards ruining her own case. She had the idea that she could somehow sway the jury, but proved to be a very bad witness.

Questioned by her Counsel regarding the letters and cuttings, Mrs Thompson explained that she had deliberately deceived Freddie into believing that she wished to poison her husband, but had no intention of doing so. She had written those things only because she was anxious to retain Freddie's love.

Cross-examined by Sir Thomas Inskip, she was soon in difficulties. He began by reading from one of her letters:

> 'Why aren't you sending me something? I wanted you to. If I don't mind the risk why should you?'

'What was it he was supposed to be sending you?'
'I've no idea'.
'Have you no idea?'
'Except what he told me'.
'What did he lead you to think it was?'
'That it was something for me to give to my husband'.
'With a view to poisoning him?'
There was a lengthy pause, then she replied,
'That was not the idea. That was not what I expected'.
'Something to give to your husband that would hurt him?'

'To make him ill. I did that to make Freddie think I was willing to do anything he might suggest, so that I would keep his affections'.

'Mrs Thompson, is that really a frank explanation. Of this urging him to send rather than bring?'

'It is absolutely. I wanted him to think I was eager to help him'.

'That does not answer the question you know', said Mr Justice Shearman.

Curtis-Bennett's heart must have sunk as he listened to her muddled and unconvincing replies to the Prosecution's questions. He knew that much damage had already been done by allowing Edith Thompson to testify in the first place. With a deep sigh he rose from his seat and attempted to put things right.

'As far as you recall, from the moment you got to your feet following the attack on your husband, did you do everything you could for him?'

'Everything I possibly could', was the reply.

In his closing speech Curtis-Bennett pointed out that no evidence had been produced to show that his client had any prior knowledge of what was going to happen on the night that Percy Thompson was murdered. He submitted that the accused woman lived in a fantasy world a good deal of the time, which explained why she had come to write some of the things contained in her letters.

'She reads a book and then imagines herself as one of the characters in it', he told the jury.

As far as her relations with Bywaters were concerned, Curtis-Bennett said he did not care whether they were described as 'an amazing passion' or 'an adulterous intercourse'.

'Thank God', he said, 'this is not a court of morals. Because if everyone immoral was brought here I should never be out of the place, nor would you. Whatever name you wish to give it, it was certainly a great love that existed between these two people'.

He was interrupted by Mr Justice Shearman, who took it upon himself to warn the jury that they should not listen to advocacy which might distract their minds from the one thing that mattered — that they were trying a vulgar and common crime, and added that he did not like invocations to the Deity and that the jury must not be frightened by them.

In his summing-up the judge left no one in any doubt as to which way he was leaning.

'This charge really is', he began, — 'I am not saying whether it is proved — a common or ordinary charge of a wife and an adulterer murdering the husband. We are told this is a case of great love. Take one of the letters as a test — *"He has the right by law to all that you have a right to by nature and by love".*' 'If that means anything it means that the love of a husband for his wife is something improper, because marriage is acknowledged by law, and that the love of a woman for her lover, illicit and clandestine, is something great and noble. I am certain that you, like any other right-minded persons, will be filled with disgust at such a notion'.

The judge also cast doubt on the testimony of a witness who claimed to have heard a woman cry out on the night of the tragedy... 'Oh don't, Oh don't!' He remarked, 'You know he was some way off. I'm not saying it's true'.

He made no mention of Bernard Spilsbury's evidence, which could have made the summing-up a little more balanced. The jury, comprising eleven men and one woman, were out for just over two hours. There was a hushed silence as the packed courtroom waited to hear their verdict. Despite all that had gone before, it still seemed to come as a shock to most of those present when the Foreman of the Jury made his announcement...

'Guilty in the case of both prisoners'. There was not even a recommendation from the jury for mercy.

When asked if he had anything to say, Bywaters' first inclination, even now, was to protect Mrs Thompson.

'She is not guilty', he replied. 'and I'm no murderer. I'm not guilty of intentional murder'.

As for Edith Thompson, she appeared to be in a state of shock, and could only keep on repeating;

'I'm not guilty. Oh God, I'm not guilty'.

Before leaving the court Freddie shook hands with Mr Cecil Whiteley, and thanked him for all his efforts. In the cells below, the Graydons, obviously shaken, but trying hard not to break down, took their leave of Edith, who was weeping uncontrollably. Everyone was telling her not to worry, that the verdict was clearly unjust and would surely be quashed on appeal. No doubt they also had plenty to say about the performance of Mr Justice Shearman, who had certainly not done the Defence any favours.

At Holloway, Edith was lodged in the prison hospital and sedated, while half-a-mile away, at Pentonville, Freddie Bywaters was placed in the cell previously occupied by, amongst a number of other notorious murderers, Dr Hawley Harvey Crippen. One of his first acts was to write a letter to Mrs Thompson, in which he exhorted her to keep up her spirits; that all would turn out right in the end, but the Prison Commissioners refused to allow her to receive it.

The day after the trial ended, Freddie was visited by his mother and his sister Florence. He appeared to be in reasonably good spirits, but became upset when they were discussing Edith Thompson's evidence in the witness box.

'I never thought she would turn against me like that', he said.

Yet when discussing the coming appeal with his Counsel a few days later, he still insisted that nothing must be said in his defence that might possibly harm Mrs Thompson.

During her visits to Holloway Mrs Graydon constantly assured her daughter that her father was doing everything possible on her behalf, and was confident that she would soon be released. Edith told her mother that she was being treated very well in the prison hospital, getting breakfast in bed and being allowed to read and write and also to take exercise if she chose to. There was a meal at mid-day and another at around four in the afternoon, though she was not allowed a knife and fork, and had to manage with a spoon. As the days went by, she became downhearted and listless, and would not exercise at all, but just lay on her bed for hours.

On Thursday 21st December the Court of Criminal Appeal convened to consider the cases of Thompson and Bywaters. They were to be heard separately. Freddie attended, accompanied by three warders. Edith, however, decided that she could not face the ordeal and remained at Holloway to await the outcome.

Cecil Whiteley again spoke on behalf of Freddie Bywaters, submitting that the court's decision not to allow the prisoners to be tried separately had been wrong, as it had resulted in the letters being admitted in evidence, which had proved prejudicial to the Defence, as had the fact that the Prosecution had been allowed the last word before the summing-up, and that Mr Justice Shearman had mis-directed the jury.

The three judges were unimpressed, taking only a few minutes to dismiss the appeal. Mr Cecil Whiteley was followed by Sir Henry Curtis-Bennett, who had prepared his case well and took his time as he painstakingly presented it to the court, using all the guile and eloquence at his command in a last-ditch attempt to save his client, though he must have realised from the outset that there was really very little hope.

Again the admissibility of Mrs Thompson's letters was re-examined, and Sir Henry's submission that they confused fact with fiction certainly appeared valid. It surely had not been proved that a plot had been hatched to poison Thompson, and there was not a shred of evidence to show that Edith Thompson had played a part in, or was even aware of, any plan to murder her husband on the night of 3rd October, though the Lord Chief Justice pointed out that Edith Thompson had shielded her husband's killer. The judges did not take long to decide that, as in the case of Bywaters, the verdict should stand.

That night Mrs Thompson received a visit from the Governor, who regretfully informed her of the Appeal Court's decision, adding that the execution was scheduled to take place on 9th January.

John Ellis, who had followed so many murder cases through the newspapers in his time, realised at an early stage that here was one that was clearly destined to capture the imagination of the public in a big way. Every conceivable element was there... The eternal triangle... the wronged husband, jealousy... passion... the younger man enticed by an older woman... clandestine love... the horrific slaying of the husband in the unlikely setting of a leafy suburban street... the hunt for the killer... his arrest and also that of the wife... the discovery of the letters with their sensational and damning revelations... the alleged murder plot... talk of poison and powered glass... the lovers in court... the young man nobly attempting to shield the woman who had helped to bring about his downfall.

Of one thing Ellis was certain. A man had been murdered and someone would have to pay. Obviously, it would be the young sailor, Freddie Bywaters. He would surely be hanged, but there was every possibility that the woman would also be found guilty. If that happened, Ellis was fairly certain that she would never face death on the scaffold. It had been fifteen years since the last woman was executed in Britain*,

Ellis himself had never hanged a woman, although he had assisted William Billington in the execution, in 1903, of Emily Swann at Armley Gaol, Leeds. He did not wish to see another woman hanged.

On learning that Mrs Thompson's appeal had been turned down, Ellis told his cronies who gathered in the shop and down at the pub, that this had not surprised him in view of all the evidence. He was, however, still adamant that he would not be called upon to hang her, as he firmly believed that the Home Secretary would now intervene and that the sentence would be commuted to life imprisonment. Not even the receipt of a letter from the office of the Under-Sheriffs for the County of Essex, asking if he would be available on the 2nd and on the 3rd of January, was enough to convince Ellis that the execution of Thompson would be carried out.

Initially, he was asked to hang Bywaters on the 2nd and Mrs Thompson on the following day, and replied that he would, in fact, be available, still confident that there would be only one execution, that of Bywaters. Following the failure of the appeals, the date was put back to January 9th, for both prisoners. It was then decided that two hangmen would be used. At Pentonville, Tom Pierrepoint would execute Freddie Bywaters, while Ellis would hang Mrs Thompson at Holloway, the two executions to take place simultaneously, at 9a.m. As it turned out, Pierrepoint was not involved at all.

* This being Rhoda Willis, executed at Cardiff by Henry and Thomas Pierrepoint for the murder of a child.

Christmas 1922 was a bleak one indeed for the families of the condemned prisoners. In Holloway Gaol, Edith Thompson was in a very low state. She could not sleep and ate very little. In Pentonville, Freddie spent his time playing cards and draughts with the warders, or strolling in the exercise yard, though as a condemned man he was not allowed to have any contact with the other prisoners. It was a very bad time for both of them, and most probably the joys and pleasures of past Christmases constantly invaded their thoughts.

In going over, in their minds, the events of the previous few weeks… that tragic night in Belgrave Road… arrest and interrogation, when neither knew what was happening to the other… the court proceedings, when everything seemed to go against them, followed by incarceration… the horror, the shame and the suffering they had brought down on their families… the failure of the appeals… it was fully brought home to Freddie now that by keeping Edith's letters he had effectively placed a rope around her neck, while Edith must surely have realised that her own fertile imagination had put the final nail in her coffin. The lovers were now at their lowest ebb, as were their respective families.

It was at this point that a remarkable thing happened. The British public — which had been so appalled at the killing of Percy Thompson, and had indignantly condemned both the killer and, more particularly, the wicked, wanton woman who had led astray an innocent young man several years her junior — now did a complete about-face. Suddenly, those who had been so revolted by the crime, felt such loathing for its perpetrators, and exhibited such smug satisfaction when they were found guilty and sentenced to death, now began to realise that the authorities were actually intending to carry out the sentences. There began to develop among the public, strong feelings of compassion for the young lovers. Freddie Bywaters was a mere youth with his whole life before him. He had lost his head over an older woman, but he had never actually intended to commit murder. In the case of Mrs Thompson, it was generally acknowledged that she had been very foolish, and could, perhaps, be considered as guilty of the crime as her lover, but to hang the woman was unthinkable. The very thought of it filled most people with revulsion.

Petitions were organised all over the country. *The Daily Sketch* launched one, making petition forms available in most cities and in a number of towns, also in theatres, cinemas and outside tube stations. There were huge placards displayed with the words THOMPSON and BYWATERS REPRIEVE … SIGN HERE!

The movement gathered such momentum that within a matter of days many thousands had signed and van loads of parcels containing the petition forms were being delivered to the Home Office in London.

Buoyed up by this flood of sympathy and emotion, the families, the Graydons in particular, began to feel that there was now real hope of a reprieve. But on 5th January, four days before the scheduled execution date, those hopes were cruelly dashed. At noon on that day the Home Secretary made his final decision. After giving very careful consideration to all the circumstances in the case, he had failed to discover any grounds which would justify him in advising His Majesty to interfere with the due course of the law. Dr Morton, who acted as Prison Doctor and was also the Governor, delivered the sad news to Edith Thompson that afternoon.

Freddie Bywaters had already been told, as had his mother, who was absolutely devastated. But, determined to fight on to the very end, Mrs Bywaters went so far as to write directly to the King, enclosing a letter signed by His Majesty, which her late husband, Frederick Samuel Bywaters, had received from the Palace in recognition of his war service. The anguished mother pointed out that her husband had made the supreme sacrifice for King and Country. She was now begging for mercy for his son.

Ellis must have gone cold when he opened his evening paper and read of the Home Secretary's decision. He now knew that he would almost certainly be forced to hang a woman for the first time in his career, and he was dreading it almost as much as the victim herself. But like her, Ellis still clung to the faint hope that the Home Secretary would yet relent. After all, there had been last-minute reprieves in the past.

Edith Thompson was visited in Holloway by a Church of England chaplain, who constantly exhorted her to confess to the crime, and appeared totally oblivious to her protestations of innocence. Soon she began to discourage his visits, making it very clear that she did not wish to talk to him. As the day of reckoning drew ever closer, Edith became more and more frightened and was frequently on the brink of hysteria. She was constantly receiving medical attention, with the result that she was drugged most of the time. She could sleep only for short periods, complained of bad headaches, and would often weep and wail

'I never did... I never did anything', and 'Why did he do it? Oh, why'?

When it became clear that the authorities fully intended to carry out the sentence of death on Edith Thompson, the wrath of the public knew no bounds. As the man who would actually put the condemned woman to death, John Ellis was obviously a prime target, and received shoals of angry letters. A typical one read:

> *Be a man and not a machine—refuse to hang her—revenge is mine—I will repay—law is not always justice—Think!*
>
> *(From, an ex-soldier)'*

On the reverse side of the note was written:

> *'Bywaters is a victim of sympathy—drawn into it through that agent, in the first instance.*
> *Mrs Thompson's fall is through vanity, which is no credit, and next to greed the worst sin in the world—But as she did not actually do the crime, and being a woman, should, like Bywaters, be reprieved.*

Another letter, enclosing a picture of Mrs Thompson cut from a newspaper, ran:

> *Dear Sir, Be a man and don't hang a woman. You know you have to die yourself in a few years. Just think.*

Another read:

> *If you go and pull that lever and take a woman's life Government ain't to answer for it. God will send the bill to you.*
>
> *Nemesis.*

Of course, Ellis had received correspondence such as this before, as did every other executioner. The letters themselves did not worry him in the least. What did, was the growing realisation that time was running out fast, and it appeared that the Home Secretary would not be influenced by public opinion, which had taken such a dramatic swing since the trial, when Mrs Thompson was perceived as an evil, scheming murderess. Many of the same people who had been so vindictive at the time, were now clamouring for her reprieve and demanding that the authorities show compassion. Ellis agreed. After all, commutation to life imprisonment would still be a terrible punishment. He knew though, that this was now extremely unlikely.

His fears were confirmed when, a couple of days before he was due to leave for London, a letter arrived from Gepp & Sons, acting on behalf of the Under-Sheriffs of Essex, informing him that there would be no reprieve. Mrs Thompson, though, never completely lost hope, in spite of the terrible state she was now in. When her family visited Holloway they continued to express their belief that she would be spared. She was now being visited by a Roman Catholic priest, Canon Palmer of Ilford. Although she was not of that faith, she apparently felt more comfortable with him than she did with the regular Prison Chaplain.

John Ellis had never been in an aeroplane. In fact, in 1923 very few people had, or would have wished to. But for some reason or other Ellis decided that he would make enquiries about the possibility of flying to London rather than going by train as he normally did. Quite possibly the reason behind this was that, in this particular instance, he was worried about being recognised. There would be far less risk of this in travelling by air, for the planes were small and carried only a few passengers at a time. In fact, on arriving at the airport in Manchester, on Monday morning 8th January, Ellis found that he was the only passenger.

The clerk in the booking office mumbled something about the weather not being ideal for flying, but Ellis went ahead and bought his ticket. It cost two pounds five shillings, one way, which was around the same as it cost to travel to London by train, except that the train fare also covered the return journey. The flight was uneventful and the hangman claimed afterwards that he did not feel in any way nervous. On landing at Croydon Aerodrome he was directed to an hotel close by and told to wait there, as he would be picked up and taken to London by car. After a rather long wait Ellis began to get edgy and went over to the booking office to enquire about his transport. It appeared that as he was the only passenger there was some reluctance to send out a car for just one person. Ellis was somewhat put out on hearing this, but before an argument could ensue a car arrived with a passenger who was taking the plane back to Manchester, so the hangman got his ride into the city. On arriving in London he met one of his assistants by arrangement, Tom Phillips from Bolton, who had come down by train. There was also a second assistant, Robert Baxter from Hereford, who was already at the prison when they got there.

Outside Holloway Gaol a large crowd had gathered. A handful of policemen were trying to keep some sort of order, while several newspaper photographers took pictures of the scene. Ellis and his colleagues were at pains to appear as inconspicuous as possible, and managed to give their names at the gate and gain admittance without being recognised by people in the crowd.

Soon afterwards the hangman and his two assistants went to examine the scaffold. They were met there by the Governor and learned that the Under-Sheriff had arranged for two prison officers to be sent over from Pentonville in case Ellis needed any additional assistance. He was assured that the officers were unlikely to crack under the strain, as both had previously attended a number of executions. Though Ellis felt that an extra two men at the scaffold was totally unnecessary and that they might even get in the way, he made no comment. As things turned out it was just as well, for those two officers would indeed be needed.

When Ellis was told about the condition Mrs Thompson was in he immediately recommended a stiff dose of brandy, to be given to her about five minutes before he arrived at the cell to pinion her, and though the Governor agreed at once to this, he confided to Ellis that he feared they would have serious trouble with the prisoner in the morning.

'She's a very puzzling woman', he told Ellis. 'At times she can be quite cheerful. She can be this way for hours, then she'll fall into a sham faint. She's done this several times, but she fainted today and really was quite unconscious. If this should happen in the morning we might have to use the chair, which I've ordered to be put in readiness'.

'Well, I hope not sir', replied Ellis, 'and if you do as I suggest regarding the brandy I think you'll find she will walk to the scaffold under her own steam'.

'Yes, of course', said the Governor, though he still appeared to be worried.

Ellis found Dr Morton to be a very courteous gentleman, who, unlike the majority of prison Governors, was always ready to listen to suggestions with an open mind. The Doctor now went over a detailed plan, showing the position of the condemned cell and the approach from it to the scaffold. He explained that he would like the Under-Sheriff, himself and two junior doctors to leave the cell along with Ellis after he had completed his pinioning of the prisoner. But when the hangman respectfully pointed out that this was not the usual procedure as far as he was concerned, Dr Morton listened carefully to what Ellis had to say, then told him to carry on and do it his way.

'Just one question though, what will you do if she faints?'

'If that should happen we would have to complete the pinioning in the cell. I mean strap her legs as well. My two assistants would then carry her to the scaffold, and support her while I do the rest'.

That evening Ellis had a long conversation with Miss Elizabeth Cronin, the Prison Superintendent, whom he had met previously at Lancaster and Maidstone Gaols. She admitted to him that the strain of looking after Mrs Thompson had proved very great. The condemned woman, she said, had been very considerate to the wardresses, who were spending many long hours with her, but from time to time she would experience very bad emotional breakdowns. Ellis told Miss Cronin that he would need to have a good look at the prisoner, so as to get a general idea of her physique. He was told that the best time to do so would be when she was moved from her present quarters to the condemned cell.

Earlier in the day Mrs Thompson's family had paid her a final visit. When they arrived she was lying on her bed and had to be helped up by the wardresses. She was deathly pale and appeared to be on the brink of total collapse. The sight of her made them feel even worse. Still they refused to give up hope altogether, and as each hugged her in turn, her father, mother, brothers and sister, they tried desperately to lift her spirits, as well as their own, with such pathetic words as,

'Don't worry Edie, there's still time for word to come through. You must not give up hope. You'll be back home with us by tomorrow'.

Of course, all went away in tears. They would never see Edie again. Their lives were ruined. They would never be able to forget.

Much the same scene was being played out at Pentonville. Freddie's mother, his two sisters and several other relations were there. He told his mother that she should not worry. That she had done everything possible for him and must now look after herself. He told them how sorry he was for Edith Thompson and hoped that she would not suffer too much. The family remained for most of the afternoon, and though all were in tears on leaving, they must have felt very proud at the great courage Freddie was showing.

Bywaters had proved popular with everyone who came into contact with him at Pentonville. As well as playing card games and draughts with the warders he was forever discussing football with them and was also interested in boxing. The Governor, Major Blake, struck up a great friendship with the young sailor, and was impressed by his quiet, respectful manner and his appreciation of all that had been done to make his last few weeks as comfortable as possible.

While Freddie was holding up so well, his mistress was rapidly going to pieces. It was soon after her family left the prison on that last afternoon that the Governor entered her cell to inform her gently, as was his duty, that he had received a final communication from the Home Office to the effect that, having given full consideration to all of the representations made to him, the Home Secretary regretted that he could find no grounds to alter his decision. On hearing this Mrs Thompson started to moan, then worked herself up into such a state that she was practically screaming, and had to be given another morphine injection. This did not put her to sleep immediately, but calmed her down a little.

At about 8-30p.m. a wardress came to fetch Ellis, who accompanied her to where a glass door gave access to a long passage,

'She'll come down that corridor', she told him.

'If you look through the glass you'll be able to get a good look at her'.

A few minutes later Ellis saw three figures come into view.

'She's here', whispered the wardress. 'They're having to hold her up'.

There she was. The woman that all England had been talking about... Edith Thompson. Ellis noted that she was tall for a female, 5ft. $7^{3}/_{4}$ ins. in fact, and though she had obviously once been a handsome woman, she now presented a pathetic picture indeed, accentuated by the ill-fitting, arrow-marked prison dress she was wearing.

It was at this point that an unfortunate incident occurred. Perhaps Ellis was not as careful as usual, or else he was fascinated by his first glimpse of the now notorious Mrs Thompson. Whatever the reason, he suddenly realised that the prisoner had caught sight of him through the glass and was staring back at him. Ellis turned away and quickly withdrew. The incident upset him very much, for he felt that she had recognised him, or at least realised who he was.

When asked by the Governor that evening what length of drop he had decided on, Ellis told him 6ft. 10ins. Dr Morton was very surprised, as this was 10 inches less than the Home Office regulations suggested for a woman of Mrs Thompson's height and weight, which was 9st. 4lbs.

'I understand that you normally give more than the regulations state. Why are you doing otherwise in this case?' asked the Doctor.

'Because we're dealing with a woman', was Ellis's reply. 'A matter of physical difference, which the Home Office scale does not take account of'.

Edith Thompson slept very little on her last night, despite having been drugged. When she did drop off it would only be for an hour or so at a time. For most of the night she seemed to drift between fitful sleep and half-awake stupor. At times she called out for her mother and father, and at others murmured 'Freddie... Freddie'. She was offered food, but refused it, then a cigarette, which she accepted, dragging slowly on it, her eyes almost closed.

The wardresses on the day shift arrived well before 7a.m. Those going off duty sadly said goodbye to the prisoner. After a while the day wardresses told Edith to get dressed, this time in her own clothes. As they helped her to do so she was trembling, and wept continuously. Some toast was brought in, but she could not eat it. As they were brushing her hair, the Chaplain, the Reverend Murray, arrived, and tried to persuade her to pray with him, but failed to get her attention.

At Pentonville, Freddie was spending his last night in the cell once occupied by Sir Roger Casement. Like Edith, he had not been able to sleep much. After retiring for the night he had tossed and turned until he finally realised that sleep was not going to come. He then got up and sat talking with the warders, chain-smoking. Eventually he lay down again, but still could not rest, and was up very early and getting dressed in the navy blue suit he had been wearing when arrested. When he was ready he was escorted to the prison chapel, and afterwards had a good breakfast of fish, bread and butter and a pot of tea.

It has been claimed that Thomas Pierrepoint was the man given the job of hanging Bywaters, assisted by William Willis and Seth Mills, and though Pierrepoint was appointed initially, there was obviously some alteration in the arrangements, for Willis ultimately carried out the execution, with Mills as his assistant.

Bywaters was given a drop of 7ft. 4ins. When they came for him just before nine o'clock Freddie was as calm as any man in his position could be expected to be, though it was obvious to those present that he was under an enormous strain and making a great effort not to crack. As far as is known he succeeded in this, and went to his death with great courage.

In the early morning mist a crowd had gathered outside the prison, despite the weather, which was cold and wet. Over at Holloway an even greater mass of people packed the pavements around the prison gates in the drizzling rain, a few parading up and down with placards and sandwich boards, proclaiming that the killing of Edith Thompson was a travesty of justice, and that as she had taken no part in the murder, she should not be hanged. Some claimed that the woman was really being executed for adultery, and this was not too far from the truth. Several mounted policemen were present to keep the crowd in order and make sure that there were no unruly scenes.

At 8a.m. the two officers, Wood and Young, who had been detailed to assist Ellis, arrived from Pentonville. By this time Mrs Thompson was in such a terrible state that she could barely stand. All the time she was wailing and moaning, and pleading with those around her not to let the hangmen kill her. It was a pitiful scene, and the wardresses, who were very tough women, not readily given to expressions of emotion, were in this case very much affected.

The three hangmen rose at 6-30a.m. and each had a mug of hot tea, then made their way to the execution shed to check that all was in order. Leaving his two assistants in the shed, Ellis went to the condemned cell to take a look at Mrs Thompson through the inspection hole. It was now around 8a.m., and Mrs Thompson was fully dressed. As the hangman peered through the hole one of the wardresses was fastening the prisoner's suspenders. As far as he could tell, Mrs Thompson did not appear distressed. He returned to the shed feeling quite relieved and confident that all would go smoothly.

The sandbag was drawn up from the pit and removed from the end of the rope. Everything was now ready, including the provision of a chair, which was placed close to the drop. This had been requested by the Reverend Murray, who had informed Ellis that he was subject to fits of dizziness and might need to sit down at some point in the proceedings.

At five minutes before nine o'clock Ellis and his two assistants were outside Mrs Thompson's cell, along with the Governor, two junior doctors, the Chaplain and various other officials and wardresses. The Governor was holding his watch in his hand. As they stood waiting, a low moan was heard from within the cell. Ellis was startled by it, but the Governor and his staff did not react. They knew, of course, that the condemned woman's nerves had already given way. In fact, after being given a sip of brandy early that morning and a little more at around 8 o'clock, she appeared to be much steadier. It was at that point that Ellis had looked in on her. Half-an-hour or so later, she had gone to pieces completely. What happened next was by far the most harrowing scene Ellis had ever witnessed, or ever would witness. It was a scene that would come back to haunt him again and again for the rest of his days.

At one minute to nine o'clock Ellis entered the cell. Mrs Thompson was sitting on the bed, weeping. Beside her the Chaplain was trying hard to get her to pray with him, but without success. Two wardresses were whispering encouraging words to her, but she just shook her head over and over again and continued to cry. Ellis nodded to the Chaplain, who understood, and moved out of the way. As the prisoner, who was now wailing and moaning pitifully, was unable to stand unaided, she was lifted gently to her feet by the two wardresses, who held her while Ellis quickly pinioned her hands behind her back. The hangman himself, very much affected, had to make a big effort to pull himself together.

Once the pinioning was completed Mrs Thompson was allowed to sink down into a chair. Ellis knew that there was not the slightest chance of getting her to walk to the scaffold, even supported, and realised that the emergency measures, discussed with the Governor, would have to be put into operation. First he instructed his assistants, Phillips and Baxter, to strap her skirt around her ankles, and told them that they would have to carry the condemned woman, who was now no more than semi-conscious, to the scaffold, with the help of the two Pentonville officers. He then went on ahead of them.

As the procession set off for the execution shed, those carrying Mrs Thompson were forced to negotiate a narrow doorway and struggled to get through it with their trussed-up burden. She was placed on the trapdoors and held upright by the four men. Before Ellis placed the white cap over Mrs Thompson's head he noticed that her eyes were closed and that she was no longer moaning. She was unconscious. Swiftly, he slipped the noose over her head and adjusted the knot. Her head had now fallen forward onto her breast. Quickly, Ellis gave the signal, and as the four men stepped back and he went for the lever, the body momentarily sagged at the knees, held up only by the rope. Then the trapdoors banged open and Mrs Thompson disappeared into the pit. The rope went taut, quivered, then swung slowly from side to side.

All those present, including the experienced Ellis, were badly shaken by what they had just witnessed. The hangman spoke soon afterwards to the Governor. He was very surprised that the brandy had, for the first time in his experience, failed to work. He then learned that the prisoner had been given several small quantities over a period of a couple of hours. He always maintained that if the Governor had followed his suggestion that she be given a good dose about five minutes before nine o'clock, it might have been a very different story. The victim was in such a state by then though, that this seems highly unlikely.

After hanging for an hour the body was taken down and washed in the prison mortuary. It was said to have been in a bad state, and persistent rumour had it that Mrs Thompson's 'insides had dropped out of her'. This was never verified, but if there is any truth in it, it could either have been that she was pregnant and had miscarried, or more likely it was just the fluids and waste matter being released from her body after death.

To have hanged a person, and a woman at that, who had been in a state of total collapse, was something that Ellis had never imagined he would have to experience. It had really shaken him. He always felt a great sense of relief once a hanging was over, but in this case, as he travelled back to Rochdale by train, he felt not just relieved, but positively shattered. He fervently hoped that he would never again be called upon to hang a woman. Had he known at that moment, that within a few short months he would have to do it all over again, he would probably have tendered his resignation immediately.

On arriving home he picked up a newspaper and got a further shock. The aircraft on which he had travelled to London had crashed on the return journey to Manchester, killing its two passengers and the pilot.

CHAPTER 34

STEADY DECLINE

Though John Ellis could not deny that the execution of Edith Thompson had been a harrowing experience for all those involved, he would never admit that it had left its mark on him. He certainly did not like the idea of hanging a woman, but was only too well aware that if a woman was found guilty of the crime of murder the law decreed that she must pay the penalty in the same way as a man. Yet, after witnessing the disintegration of Mrs Thompson and then being forced to hang what had become a pitiful wreck of a woman, who was barely conscious, there is no doubt that he was a changed man, badly shaken by the experience and thinking very seriously about his future.

There were clear indications that Ellis was losing his grip, at least to some extent, for he was drinking a lot more, and it was noticeable that often when he drank he became morose and withdrawn. Some evenings, on returning from the pub, he could be quite jovial, but usually he would have his supper then sit in his chair, smoking and staring into space, not uttering a word for hours on end.

Had it not been for a murder that occurred in Scotland, in June 1923, it is just possible, though unlikely, that Ellis might have pulled himself together and carried on as Public Executioner for several more years. As it was only a few months after the Thompson and Bywaters case, however, it must have come as something of a blow to be handed the assignment of executing another female so soon after his ordeal at Holloway.

Susan Newall was on very bad terms with her husband. On a number of occasions he had deserted her and their eight-year-old daughter, Janet, leaving them to fend for themselves in the one-room apartment where they lodged, at the house of a Mrs Young at Coatbridge, near Glasgow.

One morning Mrs Newall was seen pushing a pram through the streets. In the pram was a bundle, on top of which was perched the little girl. They were on the main road, heading in the direction of Glasgow, when a hawker's dray pulled up and the driver offered them a lift. With his help, Mrs Newall lifted the pram and its contents onto the back of the lorry, then she and the child climbed aboard. On reaching the city, Newall asked to be put off. As the pram was being lowered from the back of the lorry, it slipped, and a foot protruded from the bundle. Whether the driver noticed it or not, he made no comment, but left them there and drove on.

The incident had, however, been witnessed by a woman from an upstairs window. She contacted the police and Newall was arrested within an hour or so in a back court where she had just left the gruesome bundle, which contained the trussed-up body of a young male. The victim, who had been strangled, was a thirteen-year-old newpaper boy, who had been seen by Mrs Young, the landlady, going into Susan Newall's room earlier that morning. A search was now made for John Newall, the husband of the arrested woman, but he could not be located. On hearing that the police were enquiring as to his whereabouts, however, Newall reported voluntarily to the police station at Haddington.

The Newalls were brought up in court on 18th September 1923, one of the witnesses being Mrs Young, who told the court that after seeing the boy enter the Newall's room on the morning of 20th June she had not seen or heard him come out again. She had, however, heard several loud bumps, and soon after this Mrs Newall asked her if she had a cardboard box.

Mrs Young replied that she did not have one. Mrs Newall then returned to her room and no more was heard of her until the following day, when she was seen wheeling the pram through the streets.

It was soon established that John Newall had taken no part in the crime and knew nothing about it. There appeared to be no motive for the murder and Mrs Newall's Defence team attempted to show that the woman was insane, but after a psychiatrist, brought to court by the Prosecution, stated that she was perfectly normal mentally, she was found guilty and sentenced to death.

When John Ellis received a letter bearing a Scottish postmark soon after the trial, he knew it was the one he had been dreading. Would he be available to travel to Glasgow on 9th October to execute one Susan Newall on the following day? There was no possibility of getting out of doing the job. He was the Chief Public Executioner and it was his duty to carry out the sentence of the law on whomsoever was found guilty of murder, man or woman.

When he entered Duke Street prison that day, perhaps he had already decided that the time for retirement was looming ever nearer. Not a great deal is known about the execution itself, except that Ellis was so nervous when he entered the death cell that morning to pinion the prisoner that he made a very poor job of it. Unlike Mrs Thompson, Susan Newall did not go to pieces, but steeled herself and walked to the scaffold as bravely as any man that Ellis had ever hanged. On the trapdoors she objected to the white bag being placed over her head, and while arguing with the hangman managed to get her hands free because of the insecure way in which they were fastened. Ellis now began to show signs of panicking, but, helped by his assistant, William Willis, he quickly got the situation under control and successfully completed the job.

Afterwards, Ellis was asked to give an explanation, and told the Governor that, as he believed that Mrs Newall was going to be difficult, he had simply wound the strap around her wrists without fastening it fully, in order to get the execution over with as quickly as possible. As the victim had died instantaneously the Governor was satisfied to let the incident pass without taking further action, but he must have been less than impressed by Ellis's performance. The execution of Susan Newall was only one of fourteen carried out by Ellis in 1923, the last of these being that of John Eastwood for the murder of John Clarke at Sheffield. The hanging took place at Armley Gaol, Leeds, where he was assisted by Seth Mills. Possibly neither realised it, but it would be the last time that either would officiate at an execution.

While the Susan Newall hanging had certainly not disturbed Ellis in the same way as the execution of Mrs Thompson, there could be no denying the fact that he had come very close to bungling the job. He now began to give some serious thought to retirement. His health generally was not good. He was suffering more and more with his nerves and found it difficult to sleep. Because of this, perhaps, his drinking had increased to the point where it was becoming a big worry to Annie, who made every effort to persuade him to give it up, but to no avail.

At last, in the early part of 1924, he finally made the decision. He had held the office of Public Executioner for twenty-three years, during which time he had taken part in over two hundred executions, numbering among his victims some of the most notorious murderers in the annals of crime. As far as Ellis himself was concerned it had been a long and honourable career. He had no regrets. He had always carried out his duties to the best of his ability and had many letters from Governors and Under-Sheriffs from all over the country bearing testament to his skill and efficiency. Ellis's letter of resignation was tendered and accepted in March 1924, leaving Thomas Pierrepoint as Senior Executioner. Tom's brother, Henry, after retiring from the job in 1910, had died in 1922, at the age of 48. Ellis could now look forward to a much quieter life. No more long, tiring train journeys, arriving home late at night and having to be up early next morning to open the shop. No more worry and tension over the executions themselves, knowing that one little slip could spell disaster, with the blame inevitably falling on the executioner. All these were things he most certainly would not miss. In fact, he wondered sometimes how he had managed to carry such a burden for all that time... twenty-three years. Looking back he could hardly believe it. Well, it was over, and he felt a great sense of relief. He would give more time to his business, his family and his hobbies, and in particular to his chickens and his beloved whippets, which he now favoured in preference to bulldogs.

And so Jack Ellis settled down to a comfortable life in Kitchen Lane,* Balderstone Fold, to where the family had moved from 400, Oldham Road. Next door but one lived his eldest daughter, Sarah, who by this time had become Mrs Robinson. The Ellis's eldest son, Joe, was also married and living in the Fold. In fact, all the Ellis clan, including Jack's sisters and brothers, had remained more or less in and around Balderstone, which was by no means unusual, for in those days very few people ever moved any great distance away from their roots. Annie Ellis had every reason to hope that the change in her husband's life and the lifting of the tensions and pressures which came with the executioner's job would help to stabilize him and make him less reliant on the drink.

One thing that did not change much was the public's morbid curiosity. People still came into his shop just to meet the Rochdale hangman, or peered in at him through the window as he served at the counter, or cut hair. He received 'fan' letters from all over the country, as well as some from abroad, many from men interested in becoming public executioners themselves, and asking how they should go about applying for the job. There were offers of lecture tours, both in this country and in America, while several national newspapers expressed an interest in publishing his memoirs. Eventually, he accepted an offer from *Thomson's Weekly News*, and collaborated with their staff writers to produce a series of articles based on his experiences. Around this time he was also approached by certain theatrical impresarios, who had the idea of presenting the former hangman on stage in music halls around the country. Ellis showed some interest, but nothing was to come of it until a later date.

In the meantime, on the domestic front, things had not worked out quite so well as Annie had hoped. Jack Ellis's health was not good. His drink problem, far from improving, had become worse, and with it his mental state. When he had been drinking he could be very trying and sometimes treated the family badly. Even the strong-minded Annie Ellis had a breaking point. At one stage she became so angry and frustrated that she walked out of the house and got herself a job as a reeler at Balderstone Mill. It is not known where Annie went to live during this period, probably with a

*Roughly the site of the present Wasp Avenue

relative. In the meantime, the erring husband was looked after by Sarah, who also worked at the Balderstone Mill, as a beamer. Sarah stuck with her father through this difficult time. It has even been suggested that she went to the pub with him, but this is doubtful. It is more likely that her reason for going to the pub was to get him out and bring him home.

Eventually, Annie softened and came back to Kitchen Lane. Jack promised to keep his drinking to a minimum, but the new resolution did not last long. As Public Executioner he had once possessed nerves of steel. Now they had gone to pieces. For over two years he had suffered from neuritis, heart trouble and nervous trouble, and was getting steadily worse.

On the night of Sunday 24th August, 1924, Mrs Ellis went up to bed, leaving her husband alone in the front room, sitting in an armchair, smoking his pipe. It was well after midnight when Annie was woken from a sound sleep by a loud bang. Along with other members of the family she rushed downstairs to find her husband lying on the floor, bleeding from the neck. Beside him lay a revolver.

A doctor was sent for at once and arrived within a short time, followed soon afterwards by a policeman, PC Parker, who later stated in court that when he arrived at about 1-15a.m. Ellis was sitting in a chair, a bandage around his face and the front of his shirt covered in blood. The local bobby saw at once that the injured man was under the influence of drink. When asked what had happened, Ellis replied,

'I shot myself. I'm sorry. I shall say no more'.

PC Parker took charge of the gun, along with eight rounds of ammunition, while a careful search of the floor produced a spent bullet and an empty cartridge. The constable accompanied Ellis to the Rochdale Infirmary, and on the way asked him why he had shot himself.

'I've had a drink', was the reply, 'and it's caused some trouble at home'. Ellis refused to say any more, but the obvious inference was that he and his wife had had a row about his drinking. She had then gone up to bed, leaving him downstairs, probably angry and brooding.

At the Infirmary Ellis was cleaned up and given a thorough examination, which revealed a fractured jaw. He was in no danger of expiring, however, but was kept in, and on the following morning was stated to be 'comfortable.'

Two days later Ellis appeared at the Rochdale Magistrates' Court, charged with attempting to commit suicide. The case aroused a great deal of interest in the town and long before the magistrates took their places on the Bench the public section was packed to capacity. Hundreds of people, mostly working men in cloth caps, had been crowding the pavement outside the court since early morning. Some had literally fought to gain their places, and several hundred people were turned away. An outside door leading to the police office had to be barred against a crowd of people who attempted to force their way in. There was much banter. One man was heard to say to his mates,

'Ellis wer' used tut rope and t'razor, and he goes and tries to do away with his self with a revolver'.

When John Ellis appeared it was seen at once that the right side of his jaw was bandaged and a coloured scarf tied loosely around his neck. He was unshaven, and presented an altogether forlorn and dejected figure.

Before proceeding with the case, the Chairman, Alderman J. Blomley, addressed the court:

'It is the desire of the Bench that no sketches or photographs be taken. In fact, they will not be allowed. So I should be glad if any lady or gentleman present for this purpose would bear that in mind'.

In answering the charge against him, Ellis said,

'I don't intend to commit this act again'.

Asked if he wished to question PC Parker, who brought the charge, he shook his head and replied,

'No, everything is true'.

The Chairman asked him,

'Have you anything to say why you committed this act?'

'No', was the reply.

'You have no reason to give?'

'No reason at all'.

'I take it you're prepared to give an undertaking to the bench that you will not attempt this thing again?'

'I will give that promise, yes'.

'I'm very sorry to see you here Ellis', said the Chairman, gravely shaking his head. 'If your aim had been as straight as the drops you've given, it would have been a bad job for you. Your life has been lengthened, and I hope you will make the best use of it... the spared life which has been granted to you.'

Mrs Ellis gave evidence, and assured the Bench that she would fully support her husband and do all she could to help him keep his promise.

'My colleagues want me to say', said the Chairman, 'that in your own interests, as well as those of your wife, it would be advisable for you to give up the drink. I hope you will be able to give that promise, for the drink has obviously led you to this'.

After promising, Ellis was bound over for twelve months and discharged. Perhaps drink *had* led him to this, but what had led him to the drink?

When his fellow executioner, Tom Pierrepoint, read about the shocking incident in a newspaper, he remarked,

'Bloody 'ell! Ellis has tried to commit suicide! He should have done it years ago. He wer' bloody impossible to work with'.

Over the next three years Ellis's life continued as before. He still followed Rochdale Hornets, remained a member of the 'Buff's' and tended his chickens and other animals. He always treated them kindly, and it was often said that although he had had few qualms about hanging a human being, he could not bring himself to wring the neck of one of his hens.

Despite now being relieved of the weight of responsibility associated with his former profession, Ellis was finding it hard to settle down. Something was still playing on his mind, and though he would never have admitted it, he was also missing the feeling of importance and possibly even the notoriety he had previously enjoyed.

Eventually, in the latter part of 1927, he finally succumbed to one of the many offers that continued to come in. The idea was to feature the former hangman in a play, *The Life and Adventures Of Charles Peace*. Though the part Ellis would play was to be quite small, he would be the star attraction, for it was expected that the crowds would flock to see a real live executioner carrying out the hanging, on stage, every night, of the notorious Peace, who had paid the extreme penalty at Armley Gaol in 1879.

Charlie Peace was without doubt one of the most fascinating criminals this country has ever known. Born at Angel Court in The Wicker, one of the poorer districts of Sheffield, in 1832, Charlie had to fend for himself from a very early age, and grew up to be extremely cunning and resourceful. He was small and wiry, and walked with a slight limp, the result of an horrific accident sustained while working in a steel mill at the age of fourteen. Yet, despite his handicap, he was very strong and agile, and later, when he graduated from picking pockets to burglary, he was able to climb drainpipes and clamber over rooftops with the ease of a monkey. Peace was also a master of disguise, and had such rubbery facial features that he could distort them so completely as to be virtually unrecognisable. A man whose talents seemed limitless, he played jigs on the violin and had a wonderful way with animals. Peace also had an insatiable appetite for women, a great many of whom found him very attractive in an odd sort of way, despite the fact that he was small, ugly and lame.

It was this lust for certain members of the opposite sex that led him to the gallows, for he was convicted of the murder, at Banner Cross, Sheffield, of one Arthur Dyson, the husband of a woman on whom he had a strong designs. She had allowed herself to become involved, later regretting it and attempting to end the association. But having used all his wiles to charm

Catherine Dyson in the first place, Peace had no intention of simply stepping out of the picture and letting the Dysons get on with their lives. He continued to hang about outside their house at Banner Cross, taunting Arthur Dyson and pestering his wife. In the end, Dyson confronted his tormentor and was shot dead. Peace went on the run, moving with his family to various towns, while continuing to live by his wits. It was while living in Peckham as Mr John Thompson, that he was apprehended when leaving a house he had just burgled, and was later identified as the notorious Charlie Peace.

Though no one knew it at the time, Peace, in the course of committing a burglary at Whalley Range, Manchester, had also shot and killed Police Constable Nicholas Cock, in 1876. A young Irish labourer named William Habron was arrested and charged with the murder. Peace had the audacity to attend his trial at Manchester Assizes, and was a very interested observer from his seat in the public gallery, greatly impressing his fellow spectators with his knowledge of the law and court procedures. Habron was found guilty and sentenced to death, later commuted to life imprisonment.

Two-and-a-half-years later, while awaiting execution in Armley Gaol for the Dyson murder, Peace decided to clear his conscience by confessing to the Manchester killing. Charlie co-operated fully with the police and was able to furnish them with proof of his guilt. He drew a detailed plan of the area where the murder was committed, showing the house he had targeted to burgle. He also suggested that if they were to compare the bullet taken from the breast of PC Cock with one from Peace's own gun, they would find that the two were of the same calibre, and had, in fact, been fired from the same weapon.

The result was that William Habron was released from a life of hard labour at Portland Prison, where he had spent the previous two years breaking rocks. Charles Peace was hanged on 25th February 1879, by William Marwood, who served as executioner from 1872 until 1883.

The Life and Adventures of Charles Peace opened at the Grand Theatre, Gravesend, on Monday evening, 12th December, 1927, and though the actor, Thomas Morris, was cast in the starring role of the notorious thief and murderer, it was on John Ellis's dressing room that a posse of reporters converged prior to the curtain's going up. They were not disappointed, for Ellis obliged by providing them with several quotable comments.

> 'I'm more nervous now', he told them, 'than I was before a real execution. But I can tell you that if Mr Morris complains afterwards, he'll be the only one I've handled who ever did'.

After answering a number of questions, Ellis told the reporters:
'During my service as executioner I carried out a total of 203* hangings at £10 a time, plus travelling and other expenses. The pay for executions is the only thing that hasn't gone up. Now that I'm no longer employed by the Government I have to earn a living in the best way I can. I retired in 1924, and it's often been said that I gave up the job through the Edith Thompson case. But that had nothing whatever to do with it, although it was a terrible task to have to carry out. You know, I once hanged six men before breakfast. They were Sinn Feiners. I hanged two at six o'clock, two at seven, and two at eight. That was a very bad day, dreadful. The strain was something terrible'.

Returning to the question of the hangman's remuneration, he told them,

'There's no pension at the end of it and the pay is the same today as it was twenty years ago, apart from the assistant's money, which has gone up from two to three guineas. The executioner should really get a regular salary. You can be away from your normal work or business for several days at a time. I had to carry on working as a barber because there wasn't a living in it. People don't have any idea of the jeers and insults a hangman has to put up with. In company, some people won't even sit in the same room with you. They get up and walk out. I was once proposed as a Mason, but because of my position as executioner they wouldn't accept me. I had to withdraw'.

The melodrama turned out to be a series of episodes suggested by the extraordinary life of the subject, Charlie Peace, which included a scene depicting the trial of William Habron at Manchester Assizes.

When the point came where Peace was about to be executed, an expectant hush fell upon the audience, for they knew that the man they had all come to see was about to step onto the stage. When he did they were somewhat taken aback, for before them stood a man who did not conform in any way to the popular image of a public executioner. The man on stage, dressed in a black suit with white shirt and stiff collar, a silk handkerchief protruding from his breast pocket, looked as innocuous as a kindly middle-aged uncle. Of medium height and slightly built, with thinning hair, heavy auburn moustache and pale blue eyes, John Ellis was the last man in the world you would have taken for a hangman.

His first action was to pinion the condemned man's hands behind his back, as he had done so many times in real executions. Spontaneous applause broke out from the audience as he completed this task. The condemned man, contrary to actual practice, was dressed in conventional broad-arrow

* He was exaggerating; a figure of 203 included those executions at which he acted as assistant, earning just two guineas each time.

convict garb, instead of his own clothes, which were always worn on the day of an execution.

The tension of the audience was palpable as Peace was led away by the executioner, with the clergyman in close attendance. Once on the scaffold, Ellis placed the noose around the neck of the murderer, covered his head with the white cap, then deftly stepped to one side and drew the lever. Down into the pit plunged the actor Thomas Morris, as the audience gasped in unison.

The whole thing was cleverly contrived to appear absolutely authentic, and Ellis afterwards remarked that,

'It went beautifully'.

'I must say', declared Thomas Morris. 'that it was rather uncanny to feel a rope placed around one's neck by a man who has hanged so many people'.

Ellis went on to perform the execution of Charlie Peace twice nightly for the rest of the week at Gravesend. In the meantime, the play was attracting a storm of protest all over the country, and before the week's run had been completed, the manager of the company had had talks with the Lord Chamberlain, but declined to disclose the details of the meeting to the pack of reporters who lay in wait for him as he left the Lord Chamberlain's office.

Many prominent people, including a number of MPs, were loud in their condemnation of what was happening at Gravesend.

'It's a scandal', said one, 'and should not be allowed'.

Another described it as,

'An absolute degradation of the stage, to use it for such an exhibition. It is simply trading on the love of horror, which, unfortunately, is inherent in human nature'.

Mr Monty Bayly, Secretary of the Variety Artists' Federation, described it as, 'Pandering to the morbid interests of the public', pointing out that the presence of a number of children in the audience made it even worse.

Mr Philip Snowden MP, expressing his indignation to a group of reporters, told them,

'This is an outrage on public decency. I really cannot imagine how any man not lost to all sense of human feeling could use his past gruesome experiences for such an exhibition'.

As things turned out, there was very little that the outraged objectors could do about it, for the fact was that the play had been licensed in the ordinary way by the Lord Chamberlain's office, and though there was no indication, at that time, that Ellis was scheduled to appear in the role of executioner, the Lord Chamberlain did not, in any case, have the power to prohibit the engagement of any particular individual in a play, either on the grounds of his personal character, or his former occupation.

Following the press agitation and public outcry, an official from the office of the Lord Chamberlain attended a performance of the play, and following his report, it was decided that there were no grounds for banning the hanging scene.

Despite this victory, however, the play was not destined to run for very long. The novelty quickly wore off and the audiences were soon down to a trickle. This, along with continued public feeling against the morality of the play, eventually led to a management decision to cut its losses and bring down the final curtain. It would appear that Ellis had put money into the venture, for when the scenery and props were sold off it was reported in the newspapers that he had donated his share of the proceeds to a fund for poor children in Manchester. He retained ownership of the scaffold, which he arranged to have transported to Rochdale and stored in a garage close to his home.

That the theatrical venture was aborted did not mean the end of Jack Ellis as a thespian, for not long afterwards he undertook a tour of the nation's fairgrounds and seaside resorts, giving lectures on the executioner's craft and demonstrations of the skills required in hanging, using the scaffold which had done duty at Gravesend. At sixpence a time the entertainment proved quite successful, and Ellis accepted an offer of £20 a week to take the show to Southall in London. Unfortunately, after a couple of days, he became ill with chest trouble and was forced to spend several days in bed. On recovering, he took a week's engagement at Redcar, in Yorkshire. At the end of the tour Ellis brought the scaffold back home to Rochdale, where it was again placed in storage, this time for good. One newspaper report claimed that he had erected it in his back yard, but this seems highly unlikely. What actually happened to it is not known.

Life now became much harder for the former Public Executioner. The great depression of the 'thirties had already taken a firm hold. In towns such as Rochdale thousands of men were on the dole and hard-pressed even to put food on the table, let alone afford a haircut. In consequence, Jack Ellis's business was struggling, along with the rest. For a time he took on an extra job to help bolster finances. This involved making the rounds of public houses in the area for the purpose of selling towels and counter cloths. It was not profitable and soon fizzled out.

Ellis was nearly fifty-eight, but appeared older. He was drinking heavily and his health had deteriorated alarmingly. He could not get a sound night's sleep and had become so depressed that his mental condition was causing the family grave concern. He would come home in the evenings to the cottage in Kitchen Lane, usually the worse for drink, have his tea, though his appetite was poor, then settle down in his chair in the front room and smoke his pipe.

Annie knew that he was brooding over his problems, which, given his mental state, were greatly magnified in his own mind. She was finding it difficult to come to terms with the change that had taken place in this man who had always been so inoffensive and mild-mannered. In the past he would never have argued with her, even about important matters. Now he could fly into a temper over the most trifling incident or minor difference of opinion. Most evenings though, he would sit there, his favourite dog, a fawn-coloured whippet, on the rug beside him, and stare into space. The dog was about the only living thing he had any time for. He called it Bob Seivier, after R.S. Seivier, the well-known racehorse owner and tipster. When he spoke to the dog it would look up into his eyes, and like all dog owners, Ellis was sure that Bob understood every word he was saying. Perhaps he did, for the pair had been together for many years and he seldom left his master's side.

On the evening of Tuesday, 20th September, 1932, Ellis returned home earlier than usual. It was obvious that he had been drinking. He told Annie that he did not want any tea and went into the front room, where he fell asleep in his chair. A couple of hours later, at about 7-15, he woke up and went into the kitchen, telling her he would now like his tea. When it was ready he sat down at the kitchen table, and according to Mrs Ellis's later statement he seemed to enjoy it. Afterwards, he went into the front room again and lit his pipe, leaving Annie in the kitchen, sewing. The only other person in the house at that time was their daughter, Ivy, then aged twenty-one, who was upstairs.

A short while after this, Ellis came back into the kitchen, removed his collar and tie and took his razor down from a shelf. Suddenly he made a rush at his wife, and brandishing the razor, shouted,

'I'll cut your head off first!'

Terrified, Annie Ellis dropped her sewing basket and dashed out of the house. She ran straight to the home of her son, Joe, close by. Ivy, on hearing the commotion, came downstairs to find her father holding the razor, a strange expression on his face. She realised at once that he had been drinking, but was shocked when he came towards her and shoved the razor close to her face, then told her,

'If I can't cut your mother's head off, I'll cut yours off'.

Ivy screamed and pushed him away. He stared menacingly at her for a moment, then turned and went into the front room. Terrified, Ivy cowered in the kitchen, not knowing what to do next.

It is not known whether Joe was at home when his mother rushed into the house, but his brother Austin, who still lived with his parents in Kitchen Lane, was there visiting. On seeing the state his mother was in and hearing what had happened, he immediately left for home, with Annie close behind. As they neared the house Austin saw his father standing at the front door, the razor still clutched in his hand. His neck was bleeding and there was a wild look in his eyes. It was obvious he was not normal. It was as if they were looking at a stranger. As they approached they saw him go back into the house. Austin followed, but it was too late. Entering the front room, he saw his father draw the blade of the razor across his throat, then stagger and fall to the floor. There was blood everywhere and Austin did not want his mother to see it. Though realising at once that the situation was extremely serious, he refused to panic, but managed to persuade his mother to return to his brother's house while he went off to telephone for a doctor, leaving his sister with her stricken father.

Doctor Harris was soon on the scene, but there was nothing he could do beyond examining the body and pronouncing life to be extinct. Jack Ellis had managed to do away with himself at the second attempt. A local bobby, PC Clarke, arrived soon afterwards, at around 8-20p.m., to find the dead man lying face downwards in a pool of blood. There were two deep cuts, both at least five inches in length, one on each side of the throat. There was a bruise on the deceased's forehead, just above the left eye, obviously caused by the fall. The razor lay at his feet.

In spite of the fact that he had attempted suicide some years previously, Ellis's sudden, violent end still shocked his friends and neighbours. He had never been ostracised locally, because of his profession. In fact, he had always been considered something of a minor celebrity, and because of his sporting interests, his connection with the Buff's and strong family ties in the district, he had been well liked, generally speaking.

The death of the hangman was naturally almost the sole topic of conversation in Rochdale over the following days and weeks. Almost everyone had an opinion or a story to tell. One neighbour, a woman who lived close by, described him as 'a bad un', no doubt referring to the way he had treated his family during the last few years of his life.

A friend and fellow Buffalo member, who was one of the coffin bearers at the funeral, described Ellis as an alcoholic, who could drink a full bottle of whisky, neat, between 8 and 10p.m. He also claimed that the hangman had a foul mouth in drink, but when sober was the perfect gentleman.

Another added,

'Jack had a keen eye for business tha knows. When he came back from hanging Crippen he said that if only he'd been allowed to keep the rope he could have sold it for £5 an inch!'

Others talked of his generosity, claiming that he gave annual treats to ex-soldiers and gifts to charity. Father Thomas of the Church of St Mary, Balderstone, spoke kindly of Ellis, describing him as a well-intentioned man, who sometimes drank to excess. He had regularly gone to the vicarage to cut Father Thomas's hair, and the vicar mentioned that Ellis had reduced his prices to customers who were out of work.

Austin Ellis told a reporter that his father's death had seemed almost inevitable.

'Dad hadn't had a proper night's sleep for many years', he said. 'We all knew what the trouble was. He was haunted. I don't think it was the memory of the two hundred and odd executions he had taken part in, but the recollection of the hanging of two women that drove him to suicide. He was a quiet man, who would sit in a corner and listen to the conversation of other people. But he became a nervous wreck. It was definitely his old job that drove him to his death'.

No one would ever have described Ellis as a 'nervous wreck' just a few years earlier. When he died, one newspaper report stated that the Prison Commissioners regarded him as one of the coolest, most self-possessed executioners ever known. On entering the cell to pinion a condemned man he never betrayed the slightest sign of emotion. Nothing in his face or manner ever indicated that he was affected by the terrible task he was employed to carry out.

At the inquest, Annie Ellis stated that, apart from ill-health, her husband had had no real worries. She was asked by the Deputy County Coroner, Mr J.M. Chadwick, if she had ever before seen him in the condition he was in when he rushed at her with the razor.

'No', was the reply. 'It struck me that he had suddenly gone mad'.

Mr Chadwick recorded a verdict of suicide while of unsound mind.

On the day of the funeral, neighbours stood at their front doors and watched as the cortège left the house in Kitchen Lane. Apart from the hearse, there were seven cars carrying the mourners, the last one with members of the Buersil Lodge of the Royal Antediluvian Order of Buffaloes, who acted as coffin bearers.

Notwithstanding the prevailing view of suicide, or the fact that the deceased had not attended church for many years, Father Thomas insisted that the body be brought to St Mary's and a service be held there before burial. The church was packed, and later the cortège arrived at Rochdale Cemetery to find around three hundred people crowded around the gates. Those assembled followed the funeral procession into the cemetery.

The Reverend Thomas officiated at the burial, following which, in accordance with their custom, the Buffaloes formed a chain around the grave, leaving one significant space.

There was one other sad footnote to this tragic affair. It concerned the old dog, Bob Seivier. He had been with his master for twelve years, and at the time of Ellis's death was lacking several teeth and had become very slow of foot. During the few days before the body was interred, he would not eat, sitting outside the door of the room where his master lay in his coffin, whining and looking with pleading eyes at the other members of the family.

Jack Ellis, who had lived the last few years of his life in steadily declining health, both physically and mentally, his mind tortured and tormented by past horrors he could never forget, was finally at peace.

A RECORD OF THE EXECUTIONS IN WHICH JOHN ELLIS WAS INVOLVED

John Miller and John Robert Miller	Newcastle "	December 7th 1901	as Assistant
Richard Wigley	Shrewsbury	March 18th 1902	as Assistant
George Woolfe	Newgate	May 6th 1902	as Assistant
William Brown	Wandsworth	December 16th 1902	as Assistant
George Place	Warwick	December 30th 1902	as Assistant
Charles Howell	Chelmsford	July 7th 1903	as Assistant
Samuel Dougal	Chelmsford	July 14th 1903	as Assistant
William Joseph Tuffin	Wandsworth	August 11th 1903	as Assistant
Charles Wood Whittaker	Manchester	December 2nd 1903	as Assistant
William Haywood	Hereford	December 15th 1903	as Assistant
John Gallagher and Emily Swann	Leeds "	December 29th 1903	as Assistant
Henry Jones	Stafford	March 29th 1904	as Assistant
George Breeze	Durham	August 2nd 1904	as Assistant
Samuel Holden	Birmingham	August 16th 1904	as Assistant
Eric Lange	Cardiff	December 21st 1904	as Assistant
John Foster	Cork	April 25th 1905	as Assistant
Albert Stratton and Alfred Stratton	Wandsworth "	May 23rd 1905	as Assistant
Ferat Mohamed Benali	Maidstone	August 1st 1905	as Assistant
Arthur Deveraux	Pentonville	August 15th 1905	as Assistant
William George Butler	Pentonville	November 7th 1905	as Assistant
William Yarnold	Worcester	December 5th 1905	as Assistant
Henry Parkins	Newcastle	December 6th 1905	as Assistant
Frederick William Edge	Stafford	December 27th 1905	as Assistant
George Smith	Leeds	December 28th 1905	as Assistant
John Silk	Derby	December 29th 1905	as Assistant
John Griffiths	Manchester	February 27th 1906	as Assistant
Frederick Reynolds	Wandsworth	November 13th 1906	as Assistant

Walter Marsh	Derby	December 27th 1906	as Assistant
John Davies	Warwick	January 1st 1907	as Executioner
Edwin James Moore	Warwick	April 2nd 1907	as Executioner
William Edward Slack	Derby	July 16th 1907	as Assistant
Richard Brinkley	Wandsworth	August 13th 1907	as Assistant
John Ramsbottom	Manchester	May 12th 1908	as Assistant
Thomas Siddle	Hull	August 4th 1908	as Assistant
Edward Johnstone	Perth	August 19th 1908	as Executioner
Henry Taylor Parker	Warwick	December 15th 1908	as Assistant
Noah Percy Collins	Cardiff	December 30th 1908	as Assistant
Thomas Meade	Leeds	March 12th 1909	as Assistant
Edmund Walter Elliot	Exeter	March 30th 1909	as Executioner
William Joseph Foy	Swansea	May 8th 1909	as Assistant
John Edmunds	Usk	July 3rd 1909	as Assistant
Alexander Edmunstone	Perth	July 6th 1909	as Executioner
Madar Dal Dhingra	Pentonville	August 17th 1909	as Assistant
John Freeman	Hull	December 7th 1909	as Assistant
Joseph Wren	Manchester	February 23rd 1910	as Assistant
George Henry Perry	Pentonville	March 1st 1910	as Assistant
William Butler	Usk	March 24th 1910	as Assistant
John Alexander Dickman	Newcastle	August 9th 1910	as Executioner
Thomas Rawcliffe	Lancaster	November 15th 1910	as Executioner
Henry Thompson	Liverpool	November 22nd 1910	as Executioner
Hawley Harvey Crippen	Pentonville	November 23rd 1910	as Executioner
William Broome	Reading	November 24th 1910	as Executioner
Noah Woolf	Pentonville	December 21st 1910	as Executioner
William Scanlan	Cork	January 4th 1911	as Executioner
George Newton	Chelmsford	January 31st 1911	as Executioner
Thomas Seymour	Liverpool	May 9th 1911	as Executioner
Michael Collins	Pentonville	May 24th 1911	as Executioner
Arthur Garrod	Ipswich	June 20th 1911	as Executioner
William Henry Palmer	Leicester	July 19th 1911	as Executioner
Francisco Carlos Godinho and Edward Hill	Pentonville "	October 17th 1911	as Executioner

Frederick Henry Thomas	Wandsworth	November 15th 1911	as Executioner
Michael Fagan	Liverpool	December 6th 1911	as Executioner
Walter Martyn and John Edward Tarkenter	Manchester "	December 12th 1911	as Executioner
Henry Phillips	Swansea	December 14th 1911	as Executioner
Joseph Fletcher	Liverpool	December 15th 1911	as Executioner
George William Parker	Maidstone	December 19th 1911	as Executioner
Charles Coleman	St Albans	December 21st 1911	as Executioner
Myer Abramovitch	Pentonville	March 6th 1912	as Executioner
John Williams	Knutsford	March 9th 1912	as Executioner
Frederick Henry Seddon	Pentonville	April 18th 1912	as Executioner
Arthur Birkett	Manchester	July 23rd 1912	as Executioner
Sargent Philp	Wandsworth	October 1st 1912	as Executioner
William Henry Beal	Chelmsford	December 10th 1912	as Executioner
Alfred John Lawrence	Maidstone	December 18th 1912	as Executioner
Albert Rumens	Lewes	January 13th 1913	as Executioner
John Williams	Lewes	January 29th 1913	as Executioner
Eric James Sedgewick	Reading	February 4th 1913	as Executioner
George Cunliffe	Exeter	February 25th 1913	as Executioner
Henry Longden	Pentonville	July 8th 1913	as Executioner
Thomas Fletcher	Worcester	July 9th 1913	as Executioner
James Ryder	Manchester	August 13th 1913	as Executioner
Hugh McClaren	Cardiff	August 14th 1913	as Executioner
Patrick Higgins	Edinburgh	October 2nd 1913	as Executioner
Augustus John Penny	Winchester	November 26th 1913	as Executioner
Frederick Robertson	Pentonville	November 27th 1913	as Executioner
Ernest Edwin Kelly	Manchester	December 17th 1913	as Executioner
George Ball	Liverpool	February 26th 1914	as Executioner
Josiah Davis	Stafford	March 10th 1914	as Executioner
James Honeyands	Exeter	March 12th 1914	as Executioner
Robert Upton	Durham	March 24th 1914	as Executioner
Edgar Lewis Bindon	Cardiff	March 25th 1914	as Executioner
Joseph Spooner	Liverpool	May 14th 1914	as Executioner
Walter White	Winchester	June 16th 1914	as Executioner

Herbert Brooker	Lewes	July 28th 1914	as Executioner
Percy Evelyn Clifford	Lewes	August 11th 1914	as Executioner
Charles Frembd	Chelmsford	November 4th 1914	as Executioner
John Francis Eayres	Northampton	November 10th 1914	as Executioner
Arnold Warren	Leicester	November 12th 1914	as Executioner
George Anderson	St Albans	December 23rd 1914	as Executioner
Frank Steele	Durham	August 11th 1915	as Executioner
George Joseph Smith	Maidstone	August 13th 1915	as Executioner
George Marshall	Wandsworth	August 17th 1915	as Executioner
William Reeve	Bedford	November 16th 1915	as Executioner
Young Hill and John James Thornley	Liverpool "	December 1st 1915	as Executioner
Lee Kun	Pentonville	January 1st 1916	as Executioner
Frederick Holmes	Manchester	March 8th 1916	as Executioner
Reginald Haslam	Manchester	March 29th 1916	as Executioner
Roger David Casement	Pentonville	August 3rd 1916	as Executioner
William Allan Butler	Birmingham	August 16th 1916	as Executioner
Daniel Sullivan	Swansea	September 6th 1916	as Executioner
Fred Brookes	Exeter	December 12th 1916	as Executioner
James Howarth Hargreaves	Manchester	December 19th 1916	as Executioner
Joseph Deans	Durham	December 20th 1916	as Executioner
Thomas Clinton	Manchester	March 21st 1917	as Executioner
Leo George O'Donnell	Winchester	March 29th 1917	as Executioner
Alexanda Bakerlis	Cardiff	April 10th 1917	as Executioner
William James Robinson	Pentonville	April 17th 1917	as Executioner
Thomas McGuiness	Glasgow	May 16th 1917	as Executioner
William Thomas Hodgson	Liverpool	August 16th 1917	as Executioner
Thomas Cox	Shrewsbury	December 19th 1917	as Executioner
Victor De Stamir	Wandsworth	February 12th 1918	as Executioner
Joseph Jones	Wandsworth	February 21st 1918	as Executioner
Louis Voisin	Pentonville	March 2nd 1918	as Executioner
Verney Asser	Shepton Mallet	March 5th 1918	as Executioner
Louis Van der Kerk-Hove	Birmingham	April 9th 1918	as Executioner
William Rooney	Manchester	December 17th 1918	as Executioner

Joseph Rose	Oxford	February 19th 1919	as Executioner
Henry Perry	Pentonville	July 10th 1919	as Executioner
John Crossland	Liverpool	July 22nd 1919	as Executioner
Thomas Foster	Pentonville	July 31st 1919	as Executioner
Henry Thomas Gaskin	Birmingham	August 8th 1919	as Executioner
Frank George Warren	Pentonville	October 7th 1919	as Executioner
James Adams	Glasgow	November 11th 1919	as Executioner
Ernest Scott and Ambrose Quinn	Newcastle "	November 26th 1919	as Executioner
Djang Djing Sung	Worcester	December 3rd 1919	as Executioner
David Caplan and Hyman Purdovitch	Manchester "	January 6th 1920	as Executioner
William Hall	Durham	March 23rd 1920	as Executioner
Frederick Rothwell Holt	Manchester	April 13th 1920	as Executioner
Thomas Caler	Cardiff	April 14th 1920	as Executioner
Herbert Edward Salisbury and William Waddington	Liverpool "	May 11th 1920	as Executioner
Albert James Fraser and James Rollins	Glasgow "	May 26th 1920	as Executioner
Frederick Storey	Ipswich	June 16th 1920	as Executioner
William Thomas Aldred	Manchester	June 22nd 1920	as Executioner
Arthur Goslett	Pentonville	July 27th 1920	as Executioner
James Ellor	Liverpool	August 11th 1920	as Executioner
Kevin Barry	Dublin	November 1st 1920	as Executioner
Cyril Saunders	Exeter	November 30th 1920	as Executioner
Samuel Westwood	Birmingham	December 30th 1920	as Executioner
Charles Colclough	Manchester	December 31st 1920	as Executioner
George Bailey	Oxford	March 2nd 1921	as Executioner
Patrick Moran Thomas Whelan Bernard Ryan Patrick Doyle Thomas Bryan Francis Flood	Dublin " " " " "	March 14th 1921	as Executioner
Frederick Quarmby	Manchester	April 5th 1921	as Executioner
Thomas Traynor	Dublin	April 25th 1921	as Executioner
Thomas Wilson	Manchester	May 24th 1921	as Executioner

Edmund Foley	Dublin	June 7th 1921	as Executioner
Patrick Maher	"		
William Mitchell	"		
Lester Hamilton	Cardiff	August 16th 1921	as Executioner
Edward O'Connor	Birmingham	December 22nd 1921	as Executioner
William Harkness	Glasgow	February 21st 1922	as Executioner
William Sullivan	Usk	March 23rd 1922	as Executioner
Edward Ernest Black	Exeter	March 24th 1922	as Executioner
Percy James Atkins	Nottingham	April 7th 1922	as Executioner
Frederick Keeling	Pentonville	April 11th 1922	as Executioner
Edmund Hugh Tonbridge	Pentonville	April 18th 1922	as Executioner
Hiram Thompson	Manchester	May 30th 1922	as Executioner
Herbert Rowse Armstrong	Gloucester	May 31st 1922	as Executioner
Henry Jacoby	Pentonville	June 7th 1922	as Executioner
Reginald Dunn and	Wandsworth	August 10th 1922	as Executioner
Joseph O'Sullivan	"		
Elijah Poutney	Birmingham	August 11th 1922	as Executioner
Thomas Allaway	Winchester	August 19th 1922	as Executioner
William Yeldham	Pentonville	September 5th 1922	as Executioner
William Rider	Birmingham	December 19th 1922	as Executioner
George Frederick Edisbury	Manchester	January 3rd 1923	as Executioner
Edith Thompson	Holloway	January 9th 1923	as Executioner
George Perry	Manchester	March 28th 1923	as Executioner
Bernard Pomroy	Pentonville	April 5th 1923	as Executioner
Frederick George Wood	Liverpool	April 10th 1923	as Executioner
John Henry Savage	Edinburgh	June 11th 1923	as Executioner
Rowland Duck	Pentonville	July 4th 1923	as Executioner
William Griffiths	Shrewsbury	July 24th 1923	as Executioner
Albert Burrows	Nottingham	August 8th 1923	as Executioner
Susan Newall	Glasgow	October 10th 1923	as Executioner
Phillip Murray	Edinburgh	October 30th 1923	as Executioner
Frederick Maximillian Jesse	Wandsworth	November 1st 1923	as Executioner
William Downes	Dublin	November 29th 1923	as Executioner
John Eastwood	Leeds	December 28th 1923	as Executioner

Total Hanged 203.

SELECTED BIBLIOGRAPHY

Catholic Bulletin, various dates.

Daily Mail, various dates. London, UK. Northcliffe Newspapers Ltd.

De Balderston II by Hannah Haynes and David Tipper. Published 1994 by H.M. Haynes, Rochdale.

Empire News, various dates. London, UK.

Mormon Records. Church of the Latter Day Saints, Rochdale.

New York Times Magazine, 13 August, 1916. New York, USA. New York Times.

Oldham Chronicle, various dates. Oldham, Lancashire, UK. Hirst, Kidd & Rennie Ltd.

Registry of Births, Deaths & Marriages, London.

Rochdale Observer, various dates. Rochdale, Lancashire, UK. Manchester Evening News Group.

Sunday Chronicle, various dates. UK.

The Hangman's Record by Steve Fielding. Published 1995 by Chancery House Press, Beckenham, Kent.

Thomson's Weekly News, various dates. Dundee, Scotland, UK. D.C. Thomson.

INDEX

A

Abbey Lane, West Ham 171
Aberdeen 297
Abertridwr 84
Abramovitch, Myer 145 – 147, 149
Accrington xi
Adams, James 323
Africa 263 – 265, 267 – 268
Aimes, Lieutenant 352
Alderley 186
Aldersgate Street, London 387, 393, 399
Aldershot Barracks 290
Aldred, William 345 – 346
Allen Brothers, Trim 349
Allen, Eva 361
Allen, Harry xi
Allen, Mary 45
Alnmouth 87 – 88
Alverston, Lord 117
Angel Court, Sheffield 423
Annesley, solicitor 232
Ansdell Station 327
Antediluvian Order of Buffaloes 158, 160, 173, 225, 423, 429 – 430
Antillian 250
Antrim 264, 267
Antwerp 114 – 116
Appeal, Court of 16, 119, 132 – 133, 147, 158, 166, 328, 383, 405
Ardfert Barracks 272
Argentina La Plata Cold Storage 313
Armley Gaol, Leeds 45 – 47, 84, 91, 95, 350, 406, 419, 423 – 424
Armstrong, James 381
Armstrong, Major Herbert Rowse 355, 357 – 371, 373 – 375
Armstrong, Mrs Katharine 357, 360 – 362, 367 – 370
Ashford, Kent 54
Ashley Road, Bournemouth 235
Ashton, Mr. A. J., KC 342
Ashton-under-Lyne xi, 253, 281, 284, 337
Ashworth, Alderman 208
Ashworth, Robert 301
Askern, Thomas xi

Asser, Verney 319 – 321
Assize Court, (Assizes) 26, 41, 49, 53, 55, 59, 77, 125, 137, 198, 221, 255, 323, 341 – 342, 344, 346, 354, 369, 424 – 425
Aston, Birmingham 68
Ather, John 88, 90
Atkin, Mr. Justice 219
Atkins, Maud 354
Atkins, Percy 354 – 355
Attorney General 149, 156 – 157, 369 – 370
Aud 270 – 272
Audley Street, London, W1 381
Australia 274, 307, 320, 388, 392 – 393
Avondale Road, Chesterfield 72
Avory, Mr. Justice 130, 132, 146, 223, 303

B

Bacup, Lancashire 3
Baddesley Ensor, Warwickshire 17
Baggally, Captain 352
Bagthorp Gaol, Nottingham 355
Bailey, Daniel 270
Balderstone ix, 1, 4, 134, 420 – 421, 430
Balham, London 309
Ball, George 218 – 221, 242
Ballycastle, Co. Antrim 264
Ballymena Academy 264
Bamber Bridge, Lancashire 355, 372
Bank Hall Pit, Burnley 86
Banna Strand 271
Banner Cross, Sheffield 423 – 424
Bardsley, Daniel Wright 185 – 197, 199 – 202, 204, 209, 214
Bardsley, John 56
Bardsley, John Andrew 185, 189
Barnett, Nana 225
Barnwood House Mental Institution, Gloucester 360 – 361
Barrow, Eliza 150 – 157
Barrow-in-Furness 150, 289
Barry, Kevin 347 – 351
Bassely, Newport 86
Bates, Dr. 238

441

Bath   236 – 237
Bath Road, Slough   100
Battersea Rise, Woolwich   236
Baxter, Mr. Wynn, Coroner   146
Baxter, Robert   276, 322 – 323, 344, 350, 410, 415
Bayly, Mr. Monty   426
Beal, William Henry   171 – 172
Beck, Richard and Elizabeth   77
Bedford Gaol   245 – 246
Belfast   329, 348
Belgrave Road,   394 – 396, 398, 407
Bell, Charlotte   103
Benali, Ferat Mohamed   45
Benjamin, Elizabeth   354
Berlin   269 – 270
Berry, James   xi, 7
Bessborough, Earl of   307
Bethnal Green   227, 322
Bibbington, Simon   225
Billing, Dr.   234 – 235
Billington, James   xi, 6,
Billington, John   xi, 38 – 39, 41, 44 – 45
Billington, Thomas   xi
Billington, William   xi – xiv, 11 – 14, 16 – 17, 27 – 29, 33 – 34, 38, 41 – 44, 406
Bindon, Edgar Lewis   225
Binns, Bartholomew   xi
Birkbeck Bank   23 – 24
Birkenhead   140, 217, 304
Birmingham   42, 68, 278, 321, 350, 353, 372, 375, 436
Bishop of
   Croydon   242
   Liverpool   220
   Manchester   62
   Stepney   385
Bismarck Road, Highgate, London   237, 239
Bitteswell, Leicester   124
Black and Tans   348 – 349
Black Diaries   273, 275 – 276
Black, Ann   354
Black, Edward Ernest   354
Blackburn, Lancashire   xi, 322
Blackpool, Lancashire   234, 239 – 240, 327, 353
Blackwell, Mr., solicitor   209
Blake, Major, Governor of Pentonville   384, 412

Blakemore, Reverend   27 – 29, 278
Blatch, Mrs.   237 – 238
Blomley, Alderman J.   422
Blue Bell Inn, Shaw   49, 62
Bluebell, H.M.S.   272
Bodkin, Sir Archibald   240 – 241
Bodmin Assizes   354
Boer War   167, 265, 357
Boilermakers Arms, Oldham   334
Bolton   xi, 28, 95, 354, 410
Booth, Hesketh   189, 341
Bootle, Lancashire   320
Borland, Dr.   300
Bosanquet, Ronald, K.C.   370
Bournemouth, Hants.   235, 362, 369
Bow Street Police Station, London   117, 132, 314 – 315
Bow, London   19
Bowen, Mary   17
Bower, Detective Inspector   25 – 26, 100, 164
Bradbury, PC William   336
Bradfield, Christina   217 – 218
Bradford, Rev. W. J.   6
Bradford, Yorkshire   xi, 31 – 32, 325 – 326
Bramwell, Mr. Justice   198, 200
Breaks, Kathleen Elsie (Kitty)   325 – 327
Breeze, George   41 – 42
Brewster, Alice Emily   131
Bridge Inn, Balderstone, Rochdale   134, 275
Bridge Inn, Castleton, Rochdale   38
Brierley, William   49, 63
Brighton, Sussex   43, 168, 242, 259
Brinkley, Richard   76 – 77
Bristol   229 – 230, 233, 235 – 236, 238 – 239
Brixton   128, 272, 382, 399
Broad Lane, Balderstone   1, 4 – 5, 301
Broad Street, Hay-on-Wye   358, 361, 366
Broadmoor   386
Brook Street, Kennington   309
Brooklyn, New York, USA   103
Broome, William   100 – 102, 119
Broughton, Salford, Lancashire   173
Brown, Chief Inspector Bill   381
Brown, George   xi, 253, 321, 323
Brown, Michael   85
Brown, Mr. T.E., solicitor   179

Brown, William   17
Broxburn, Scotland   174
Bryan, Thomas   352
Buckingham Palace   209, 408
Buckley, Mr.   185
Bucknill, Mr. Justice   157 – 158
Bucks Head, Camden Town, London   151, 156
Buersil Fold, Rochdale   1
Burnham, Alice   233, 235, 239 – 240
Burnham, Charles   233 – 234, 239
Burnley, Lancashire   3, 85, 256 – 257, 260, 338
Bury, Lancashire   4
Bushe, Grattan   240
Butler, William   86
Butler, William Allan   29, 278
Butler, William George   45
Butterworth, J. H., solicitor   53, 55, 61
Bywaters, Freddie   xii, 387 – 393, 395 – 409, 412, 414
Bywaters, Frederick Samuel   408
Bywaters, Mrs.   395, 408

C

Calcraft   7
Caler, Thomas   331
Calton Gaol, Edinburgh   173, 176
Cambridge University   357
Camden Town, London   100, 105, 108, 151
Cameron Street, Glasgow   323
Canada   20, 115, 175, 186, 228, 377
Canadian Scouts   167
Cannock, Staffordshire   322
Cape Horn   149
Cape Town   167, 265
Caplan, David   323
Cardiff   42, 84, 224, 282, 331
Carlton & Prior   387, 391 – 393, 399
Carter, Clara   171 – 172
Casement, Anne (née Jephson)   264
Casement, Roger David   19, 263 – 277, 305, 349, 413
Castle Street, Trim, Co. Meath   349
Castleton, Rochdale   4, 38
Central Criminal Court, London   132, 146, 294
Chadderton, Oldham   57
Chadwick, Mr. J. M. Deputy Coroner   430

Chamberlain, Lord   426 – 427
Channell, Mr. Justice   146 – 147
Charlotte Street, Soho   314
Charlton, William   87
Chatham, Kent   19
Chaucer Street, Oldham   186
Chavasse, Dr., Bishop of Liverpool   220
Cheapside, Oldham   197
Cheese, Edmond   358
Cheeseman, Charlotte   14 – 15
Cheetham Hill Road, Manchester   213
Chelmsford Gaol   27, 29, 128, 171 – 172, 278
Cheltenham, Gloucestershire   274
Cheshire Cheese, Oldham   334
Chester   250, 346
Chesterfield, Derbyshire   48, 71 – 72
Chetwynd, Eliza   17
Chevalier, Arthur   362, 373, 376
China, S.S.   131
Chisholm, Margaret Jane   41
Christchurch, Hants.   362
Christensen, Adler   269
Christiania, Norway   269
Christie, Mrs.   80
Church Lane, Oldham   187
Clarke, John   419
Clarke, PC.   429
Clavering, Essex   27
Claybrooke Magna, Leicestershire   125
Clayton, Bradford, Yorkshire   xi
Cleethorpes, Lincolnshire   249
Clegg, Mr. W. E.   185
Clements, Capt., Governor of Winchester Gaol   179 – 180
Clevely, Percy   394
Clifford Street, Chorlton on Medlock   255
Clifton   230 – 231
Clinical Research Association   366
Clinton, Thomas   289 – 290
Clover, Alice   45
Coatbridge, Scotland   417
Cock, P.C. Nicholas   424
Coelho, Alberto Oliverio   221
Cohen, Herman   92 – 93
Colchester, Essex   27
Colclough, Charles   350 – 351
Coldham Farm   21
Coldwater, Michigan   103
Coleridge, Justice Lord   71, 74, 91, 294

443

Collins, John 86
Collins, Noah 84
Collyhurst, Manchester 38
Colne, Lancashire 3
Colombo, Ceylon 131
Commercial Road, London 145
Conduit, William xi, 129
Congo Free State 264 – 267
Congo, French Colony 265
Connard, PC. 340
Convery, Catherine 286 – 287
Conway, Isabella (Belle) 257
Copenhagen, Denmark 269
Copythorne 178
Corbyn Street, London 155
Cork, Eire 42 – 43, 281, 284
Cornish, Mr. & Mrs. 322
Correll, Anne 86
Coulson, John Roper 95
Courtland Avenue, Ilford 394
Coventry 84
Coventry Street, London 381
Cowlishaw Lane, Shaw 49
Crawford, James 251
Criminal Lunatic Asylum, Broadmoor 386
Crippen, Andresse 103
Crippen, Cora 103 – 112, 114 – 116, 118, 120, 155
Crippen, Dr. Hawley Harvey 19, 35 – 36, 87, 99 – 101, 103 – 122, 173, 183, 276, 404, 429
Crippen, Myron 103
Croke Park, Dublin 351
Crompton, Lancashire 61
Cronin, Miss Elizabeth 411
Crossland, Ellen 322
Crossland, John 322
Crossley, Mrs. 234 – 235, 239
Croston, near Wakefield 350
Croydon Aerodrome 410
Croydon, Surrey 77, 229, 307, 381, 410
Cruikshank, Major R. D., Governor of Strangeways 6
Crutchett, Inspector 367
Cuddy, William 135 – 136
Cullercoats, Whitley Bay 9
Curtis Bennett, Sir Henry, K.C. 369 – 370, 373, 400, 402 – 403, 405
Curtis, Samuel 45 – 46
Cusop 358, 362 – 363, 367, 373

D

Daily Express 395
Daily Mail 115 – 116, 395
Daily Sketch 407
Darling, Mr. Justice 292, 309, 316, 369 – 370
Darwell, Jane 350
Davenport, PC Harry 50, 53, 56
Davies, John 68 – 70
Davies, John (Chemist) 360, 365 – 366
Davies, Mrs. Hester 335
Davis, Josiah 224
Dawn Mill, Shaw 50, 52 – 53, 56, 58
de Bournonville, Eva 255
De Stamir, Victor 306 – 311
De Vere Gardens, Ilford 394
Deans, Joseph 286 – 288
Deptford, London 44
Derby 71
Derby Gaol 46, 48, 65, 72, 75
Derby Road, Kirkdale, Liverpool 323
Deveraux, Arthur 45
Devon 357
Devon Volunteers 357
Devoy, John 264, 270, 347
Dew, Chief Inspector Walter 111 – 113, 115 – 117
Dewbery, Mary 355
Dewsbury, Yorkshire xi
Dhingra, Madar Dal 85
Dickman, Annie 92
Dickman, John Alexander 87 – 94
Dieppe, France 111
Dixon, Robert, J.P. 353
Donegal, Eire 267
Donkin, (Mr.) 287
Dornan, Agnes 209
Dougal, Samuel 19 – 29, 164, 278 – 279
Dovecot Colliery 89 – 90
Dowlais, Glamorgan 281, 284
Downing Street, London 209
Doyle, Mary 323
Doyle, Patrick 352
Driscoll, Mr. Pat 271
Drumcondra 352
Drysdale, Mr. A. D., Governor of Glasgow Prison 298, 301
Dublin, Eire 20, 44, 264, 267, 272, 277, 347 – 353
Duffy, Gavin 273 – 275

Dugdale, Richard   135
Duke of York, Shaw   51, 53, 57
Duke Street Prison, Glasgow   298, 418
Dumbarton, Scotland   4
Dumfermline, Scotland   80
Dunn, Reginald   386
Durham Gaol   42, 224 – 225, 286, 288
Durkin, Joseph Harold   319
Durkin, Patrick   45
Dyer, Dr.   128
Dyson, Arthur   423 – 424
Dyson, Catherine   424

E

Ealing, Middlesex   86
East Ham, London   388, 393, 397
Eastbourne, Sussex   163 – 164, 168, 171
Eastwood, John   419
Eaves, Rev.   203
Eayres, John Francis   223 – 224
Edge, Frederick William   46
Edge Lane Road, Oldham   333, 336
Edinburgh   57, 166, 173 – 174, 176 – 177
Edmunds, John   85
Edmunstone, Alexander   81, 85
Edward, Dr.   139
Edward Street, Oldham   212
Egerton Street, Oldham   185 – 186, 190
Elder Dempster Shipping Company   264
Elgin Crescent, London   21
Elkin, Mr.   146 – 147
Elliot, Edmond   84
Ellis Street, Burnley   256 – 257
Ellis, Ann (sister)   1
Ellis, Annie (née Whitworth) (wife)   4, 6 – 8, 55, 69 – 70, 302, 419 – 422, 428 – 430
Ellis, Annie Beaton (daughter)   76
Ellis, Austin (son)   76, 429 – 430
Ellis, Ellen (sister)   1, 4
Ellis, Emily (sister)   1
Ellis, Isabella (sister)   1
Ellis, Ivy (daughter)   134, 428
Ellis, James Preston (brother)   1
Ellis, John   xi – xiv, 1 – 9, 16 – 17, 19, 27 – 29, 33 – 39, 41 – 49, 54 –55, 63 – 65, 67 – 71, 75 – 77, 79 – 87, 91 – 95, 97, 99 – 102, 107, 118 – 121, 123, 125 – 135, 137 – 141, 147 – 149, 158 – 161, 164 – 166, 169 – 173, 176 – 180, 183 – 184, 204, 208, 210, 213 – 215, 219 – 226, 240 – 243, 245 – 248, 251 – 253, 255, 257 – 261, 275 – 278, 281 – 290, 292 – 302, 304 – 306, 309 – 312, 316 – 323, 327, 329 – 331, 343 – 346, 349 – 355, 371 – 375, 377, 384 – 387, 406, 408 – 431
Ellis, Joseph James (father)   1, 7, 134
Ellis, Joseph James (son)   7, 420, 428 – 429
Ellis, Sarah (daughter)   7, 420, 421
Ellis, Sarah Ann (née Dawson) (mother)   1, 134
Ellor, Ada   346
Ellor, James   346
Elmore, Belle (Crippen, Cora)   105, 112, 115
Eltoft, Samuel   217 – 219
Emmet, Robert   264, 347
Empire News   384
Empress Avenue, Ilford   394
Enborne, Newbury, Berks.   321
Endsleigh Gardens, Ilford   394 – 395, 399
Euston Station, London   117, 208
Evans, Margaret   355
Evans, Mrs.   46
Evershot Road, London   150, 155
Exeter, Devon   84, 224, 350, 354

F

Failsworth, Manchester   212
Falkland Islands   149
Farnworth, Bolton   xi
Farrow, Thomas   44
Faulkener, Miss   230
Featherstall Road, Oldham   212
Feltham, Middlesex   381
Fenit Pier   270 – 271
Ferguson, Joseph   9
Fife, Scotland   80, 85, 175
Finborough Road, Fulham   379 – 382
Finchley Cemetery   240
Findlay, Mr., British Ambassador   269
Fish, Mr.   342
Fisher, Reginald   308 – 309
Flood, Francis   352
Foley, Edmond   353
Folkestone, Kent   124 – 125, 168
Forbes Kinnear, Dr., Police Surgeon   50, 56 – 57

445

Forest Gate, London   322
Formby, Lancashire   343
Fort, Dr. , Police Surgeon   188, 339
Foster, John   42 – 44
Foster, Minnie   322
Foster, Thomas   322
Fox, Inspector   28
Foy, Mary *See Sloppy Mary*   84
Foy, William Joseph   84 – 85
Frankhill Street, Oldham   187
Franks, Solomon   323
Fraser, Albert James   345
Fraser Street, Rochdale   301
Frederick's Place, London   25
Freeman, John   85
Frembd, Charles   222 – 223
French, Dr.   232
Fry, William   46
Fulham Road, London   382

G

Gabe, Dr., Police Surgeon   313
Gale, Mrs. Marion   362, 369, 373
Gallagher, John   31 – 34
Galway, Eire   267
Garrick, Mr., Gunsmith   286
Garrow, Chief Constable   81
Garside, Joe   51
Garston, Liverpool   68
Gaskin, Elizabeth   322
Gaskin, Henry   322
Gaynor, John   348
General Prison, Perth   84
Gepp & Sons   409
Geraghty, John   49, 62
Geraghty, Katherine   49 – 51, 54 – 55, 60 – 62
Gerard, Emilienne   314 – 317
Gerard, Paul   314
Gibson, Mrs. Elizabeth   124
Gilbert, Dr.   41
Gilbert, Mary   39
Glasgow   82, 297 – 298, 323, 345, 353, 417 – 418
Glasnevin Cemetery   277
Glebe Mill, Hollinwood, Oldham   334
Gloucester Gaol   355, 369, 371 – 373
Glynn, Edward   65
Godinho, Francisco Carlos   131 – 133
Golders Green, London   346

Goodmarcher, Marks   350
Gorman, Mary   271
Gorton, Manchester   79
Gosforth   89
Goslett, Arthur   346
Gosport, Hants.   377
Grant, Ernest   150, 152 – 156
Grantham, Mr. Justice   55 – 56, 58 – 59 128
Gravesend, Kent   424, 427
Gray, Mr., Under-Sheriff of Yorkshire   91
Graydon, Avis   388 – 390, 393, 397
Graydon, Harold   388
Graydon, Mr.   397
Graydon, Mrs.   396, 405
Graydon, Newenham   388
Graydon, William   388
Great Nelson Street, Gateshead   226
Greaves, James   187
Greenacres Cemetery   190, 341
Greenfield Lane, Shaw   49, 51 – 52, 55 – 57, 63
Greenfield Mill, Shaw   50, 52
Gribben, Charles   224
Griffiths, Charlie   51, 59
Griffiths, Edith   135
Griffiths, John   49 – 65, 204
Griffiths, Robert (junior)   63 – 64
Griffiths, Robert (senior)   49 – 50, 63 – 64
Griffiths, Robert, solicitor   358 – 359
Griffiths, Trevor   359
Grosvenor Street, Oldham   197
Guildford   77
Guildford Street, London   106
Gwilliam, John   17

H

Habron, William   424 – 425
Hackney, London   144, 180
Haddington, Scotland   418
Hahnemann, Dr.   103
Haigh, Detective Inspector   181
Halifax, Nova Scotia   20
Halifax, Yorkshire   338
Hall, Clara   186, 188
Hall, Inspector   396
Hall, Percy   87 – 88, 90
Hall, Sir Edward Marshall   117, 149, 156 – 158, 240 – 241, 327 – 328
Hamilton, Lester   353

Hamilton, Mr. Justice   146
Hamilton, Sydney   168
Hammersmith, London, 381
Hanbury Street, Spitalfields, London   143
Hanley, Staffs.   350
Hannaford, Clara   84
Hannan, Rev. J. H.   139
Hargreaves, James Howarth   281, 284 – 286
Harkness, William   354
Harris, Ann   123 – 126
Harris, Cecilia   85
Harris, Dr.   429
Harrison, Jane   68 – 69
Hartley, PC.   341
Harvey, Mr. E. G., Under-Sheriff of Northumberland   91
Haslam, Reginald   255 – 261
Hastings, Sussex   228
Haynes, Captain 139
Haynes, Hannah 17
Hay-on-Wye   358, 360, 364, 367 – 368, 373
Haywood, William   39
Heard   77
Heaton, Northumberland   87 – 88
Heiss, Mrs.   239
Heligoland   270
Helm, Mr. J. G.   342 – 343
Henshaw Street, Oldham   334
Hepple, Wilson   88 – 89
Hereford   39, 366 – 369, 410
Herne Bay, Kent   232, 240
Hewart, Mr. Gordon, KC, MP.   198 – 199
Heyside, Oldham   56, 135
Heywood, Lancashire   135
Hibbert, Mr. and Mrs. George,   202
Higgins, Patrick   173 – 178
Higginshaw Road, Oldham   335, 340
Higginshaw, Oldham   335, 339, 341 – 342
Highfield Road, Chesterfield   72
Hill, Edward   131 – 133
Hill, Young   248, 250 – 253, 344
Hilldrop Crescent, Camden Town, London   107, 110 – 112, 118
Hilton, Edward Wild   186, 188 – 192, 194 – 210, 212 – 215
Hilton, Mr. and Mrs. 190
Hincks, Dr.   359 – 362, 364 – 366, 369

Hindes, Rev. W.   342
Hinds, Inspector   51, 53
Hirst's Jewellers 188
Hobson, Inspector   337
Hodgkins, Martha   224
Hodgson, Mrs and Margaret   302 – 303
Hodgson, William Thomas   302 – 306
Hogan, Michael 352
Hogg, Mr. W.   89 – 90
Holden, Samuel (hanged by Ellis)   42
Holden, Samuel (of Shaw) 49
Holland, Camille Cecille   21 – 24, 26 – 27
Hollinwood, Oldham   191, 194, 196, 334
Holloway Prison, London   37, 255, 399, 404 – 410, 414, 417
Hollweg, Bethmann, German Chancellor   269
Holmes, Frederick   255 – 258
Holt, Frederick Rothwell   325 – 331
Honeyands, James   224
Hook, Mr. and Mrs.   150 – 151
Horton Street, Shaw   53
Houghton, Mr. F.   341
Houghton-le-Spring, Durham   287
Hounslow, Middlesex   381
Howard, Jane   345
Howarth, Kay   135
Howell, Charles   27
Howerton Workhouse   181
Hoxton, London   15
Huddersfield, Yorkshire   xi, 37, 304
Hull   80, 85
Humphreys, Mr. Travers   156, 240, 401
Humphreys, Private Thomas   348
Humphries, Susan   42
Hunter, Frances Priscilla   221 – 222
Hussey, Michael   271
Hyde, Cheshire   346

I

Ilford, Essex   388, 393, 396, 398, 400, 409
Ilkley, Yorkshire   46 – 47
Imlach, Alick   297
Imley, Oliver Gilbert   310 – 311
Imperial Institute, London   85
Imperial Light Horse   286
India   70 – 71, 100, 175, 388
Inishtooskert isle, Eire   270

Inskip, Sir Thomas, Solicitor-General 400 – 402
Ipswich 345
Isaac, Rabbi 147 – 148
Isaacs, George 85
Isaacs, Mr. Justice Rufus 149, 156, 275
Isabella Pit 89
Isle of Wight 389
Islington, London 150, 155, 182

J

Jackson, Dr. 154
Jackson, Olive 353
Jacoby, Henry 377, 382 – 387
James, Charles Oliver
   See Smith, George Joseph 236, 240
James, Mr., Under-Sherrif 374
Jayne, Dr. 360
Jelf, Mr. Justice 47
Jersey City, USA 104
Jesmond, Northumberland 88
Johannesburg, South Africa 168
Johnson, Frances 248 – 250
Johnson, Inspector 187 – 188
Johnson, Mr. and Mrs. 249
Johnston, Lord 176
Johnstone, Edward 80 – 84
Jolly Gardener, Rochdale 225
Jones, Amelia 224
Jones Brothers Ltd., Holloway 113
Jones, Detective 188 – 190
Jones, Henry 39
Jones, John 42
Jones, Joseph 307, 310 – 312
Jones, Norah M. 104
Jubilee Colliery, Shaw 59

K

Keeling, Frederick 355
Kelly, Ernest Edwin 188 – 196, 198 – 210, 212 – 215
Kendall, Captain Henry 114 – 116
Kennington, London 309
Kensal Green Cemetery 156
Kensington Avenue School, London 388
Kensington Gardens, Ilford 388 – 389, 393 – 397
Kenyon, Mr., Barrister 130
Kerk Hove, Louis Van der 321
Kerry, Eire 270 – 272

Kerslake, PC 136
Kimberley, South Africa 167
King's Liverpool Regiment 333
Kinsey, Muriel, Nurse 361
Kirkdale, Liverpool 323
Kitchen Lane, Balderstone 420 – 421, 428 – 430
Knutsford Gaol 140 – 141

L

Lancashire 1, 5 – 6, xi, 27, 35, 139, 173, 320, 351
Lancashire Fusiliers 357
Lancaster Castle 97, 411
Langdon, Mr., KC 55, 58
Lange, Eric 42
Lansdowne, Lord, Foreign Secretary 266
Laurentic, S.S. 115 – 117
Law, Mrs. 302 – 303
Laxton, Mr. and Mrs. 393
Le Neve, Ethel 107, 115 – 116, 118
Leach, Annie 186, 188
Leach, Clementina 52
Leach Street, Shaw 52
Lee, Rev. Walter E. 83
Lee, River 43
Leeds, Yorkshire 45 – 47, 84, 91, 95, 337, 350
Leek, Staffordshire 125
Lees, Alderman Mrs. 205 – 211
Lees, Mr. W. 190 – 191, 195 – 196, 198
Leicester Gaol 123, 125
Leighton Buzzard 245
Leman Street, London 145
Leopoldville, Congo Free State 265
Lewes Gaol 165 – 166, 169 – 170
Leytonstone, London 222, 395
Liddon, Mr. 180
Lightbody Street Lock, Liverpool 217
Lincoln, Abraham 275
Linlithgow, Scotland 173
Liverpool 99, 115, 117, 119, 129, 149 – 150, 217 – 218, 251, 264, 320 – 321, 329, 341 – 344, 349, 354, 357, 362
Lloyd, John
   See Smith, George Joseph 236 – 237, 239 – 240
Lofty, Margaret Elizabeth 236 – 240
London 7, 14, 16, 20 – 22, 24, 26 – 27, 38, 63, 85, 99 – 100, 103,

105, 108, 116, 122, 124, 131, 149 – 150, 163 – 164, 168 – 171, 177, 206, 208 – 210, 214, 218, 228 – 231, 237 – 239, 265 – 267, 272 – 273, 275, 277, 288, 298, 307, 311, 314 – 315, 322, 360, 362, 366 – 367, 369, 377, 379, 382, 384, 386 – 388, 396, 408 – 410, 416
London Yeomanry   307
Londonderry, N. Ireland   80, 305, 329
Longley, Mrs. Emily   154
Lord, John   49
Love, George Oliver
  See Smith, George Joseph   228, 240
Lubeck, Germany   270
Luff, Dr.   113
Lumb, Albert   xi
Lupton, Ernest   334
Lusitania, S.S.   227
Luton, Bedfordshire   229
Lutterworth, Leicestershire   124
Lydenburg, battle of, South Africa   167
Lynch, Company Sergeant Major   289 – 290
Lyon Mill, Shaw   49 – 50
Lytham St. Annes   325 – 326

M

Macclesfield, Cheshire   248 – 250
MacKinnon, Dr., Hon. Pathologist   339
Macklin, Rev.   374 – 375
Macnaughten, Sir Melville, Asst. Commissioner   113, 115
Madame X
  See Gale, Mrs. Marion   369, 373
Maher, Patrick   353
Maidstone Gaol   45, 169, 241, 411
Malaya   328
Maltby, Yorkshire   xi
Manchester   xi, 2, 38, 49, 53, 55, 61, 65, 79, 81, 123, 125 – 126, 129, 135, 137, 139, 198 – 199, 208, 211 – 213, 255, 259 – 260, 277, 282, 323, 327, 329, 337, 350, 377, 410, 416, 424 – 425, 427
Manchester Regiment   333
Manchester Street, Oldham   188, 212
Mander, P. R., Surgeon   277, 317
Mann, Lionel   xi
Manor Park, London   388 – 389, 392 – 393, 396 – 397
Market Place, Oldham   185, 204, 340

Market Street, Shaw   50 – 51, 58
Marsh, Travis   336
Marsh, Walter   65
Martin, Oswald Norman   358 – 359, 362 – 367, 370 – 371
Martinetti, Clara   108, 110 – 111
Martinetti, Paul   108, 110
Martyn, Walter   135, 138 – 139
Marwood, William   xi, 7, 424
Matanzas, Peru   273
Matthews, Mr. T.   368, 373
Maudsley, Dr.   394 – 395
Mayall, Chief Constable A. K.   337
Mayfair Avenue, Ilford   394
Mazzola, Luigi   381
McCardie, Mr. Justice   342
McCarroll, Father James   275 – 277
McCarthy, John   271
McCleary, Mr. R.   191, 195, 198 – 200
McConnell, Sarah Ann   65
McFadden, John   348
McGee, Mrs. Caroline   284
Mc'Graw, James   79
Mc'Graw, Mrs.   79
McGuiness, Thomas   297 – 301
McHugh, Mr. John   336
McKay, George
  See Williams, John   166 – 168
McKenna's Fort, Kerry, Eire   271 – 272, 274
McKenna, Mr. Reginald, Home Secretary   135, 209, 214
McKinley, John   310
McQueen, Superintendent   53 – 54
Meade, Clara   84
Meade, Thomas   84
Megantic, S.S.   116 – 117
Megson, Mr. F.,   189
Mersey, River   217
Metcalfe, Mr., Under-Sherrif   118 – 119, 183 – 184, 311, 317
Mew, Sergeant Walter   395
Mexico   377
Micklethwait, Mr. St. John   368 – 369
Middle Street, Shaw   49
Middlesbrough   32
Middleton Road, Oldham   197
Middleton, Lancashire   4, 281
Miller, Bruce   109, 111
Miller, John   9, 12 – 14
Miller, John Robert   9, 12 – 13

449

Millfields Road, London   181
Mills, Bert   225
Mills, Jesse   203
Mills, Seth   353 – 354, 386, 414, 419
Millstein,   143 – 146
Millstein, Mrs   143 – 145
Millward, Mr. Police Court Missioner   186
Milman, Colonel, Governor of Newgate   8
Mitchel, John   264
Mitchell, Detective Sergeant   111 – 112, 115 – 116
Mitchell, William   353
Moat Farm   21 – 23, 25 – 27, 164, 278
Moffat, PC David   50
Monarch Mill, Royton   333
Monkwearmouth, Sunderland   286
Monteith, Captain Robert   270 – 271
Montgomery, Colonel   352
Montreal Star, S.S.   116
Montrose, S.S.   114 – 116
Mooney, Mrs   348 – 349
Moore, Edwin   70 – 71
Moorgate Railway Station, London   164
Moran, Patrick   352
Morea, S.S.   391, 399
Morpeth, Northumberland   88 – 90
Morrell, Chief Warder   74
Morris, Maria   52
Morris, Mr. John   61
Morris, Thomas, actor   424, 426
Mortlake, Surrey   17
Morton, Dr., Prison Doctor   408, 411, 413
Moss Hey Street, Shaw   49, 52, 56, 63
Mountjoy Jail   347, 349, 352
Muir, Mr. Richard   117, 156
Mulholland, Maud   225
Mundy, Beatrice (Bessie)   230 – 233, 240
Munster Square, St. Pancras, London   314 – 316
Munyon, Professor   104, 106 – 107
Murray, James   337 – 338
Murray, Reverend   413 – 414
Murray, Thomas   337 – 338
Musgrave, Inspector   338

N

Nash, John and Lil   111
Needham, Miles   55
Neil, Detective Inspector   239, 241

Neilson Street, Newcastle-under-Lyme   46
Nelson, Lancashire   3
Nelson, Major, Prison Governor   141, 202, 213
New Radcliffe Street, Oldham   197
New York, USA   103 – 104, 268 – 270, 378
New Zealand   274, 377
Newall, John   418
Newall, John, collier   55
Newall, John, publican   337
Newall, Susan   417 – 419
Newcastle   4, 11, 87 – 91
Newcastle Gaol   8, 11, 45, 92, 323
Newgate   7 – 8, 16 – 17
Newhey, Lancashire   55
Newsome, Mrs. Clara   335
Newton Abbot, Devon   357
Newton, Arthur   117
Newton, George   128 – 129
Nicholson, Mr. J.   189, 191, 341 – 342
Nightingale, Lucy   323
Nisbet, John Innes   87 – 91, 93
Noble, Irene   17
Normand, Armando   273
North King Street, Dublin   348
Northampton Gaol   223
Northamptonshire Regiment   227
Norway   269
Nottingham   65, 354 – 355

O

O'Brien, Smith   347
O'Connor, Edward   353
O'Connor, John   51
O'Donnell, Leo George   290 – 294
O'Leary (Fenian)   264
O'Mahoney, John   264, 347
Oberndorff, Count von, German Minister to Norway   269
Old Jewry, London   24
Oldham Chronicle   54, 208, 345
Oldham Edge   333, 335, 337, 342
Oldham Road, Balderstone   1, 4, 6, 134, 225, 275, 301, 343, 420
Oldham Royal Infirmary   188, 336, 339
Oldham, Lancashire   1, 49, 51, 135, 150, 185, 187, 190, 198, 202 – 206, 208 – 213, 215, 333 – 335, 338 – 339, 342 – 343
Oldham Lyceum   185, 194

450

Oldham Motor Company 212
Old Market Chambers, Rochdale 61
Orchard Road, Highgate 239
Oskar II, S.S. 268
Oxford Gaol 321 – 322

P

Painter Street, Oldham 190
Palmer, Canon 409
Palmer, William Henry 123 – 128
Parker 77
Parker, Henry 84
Parker, PC 421 – 422
Parkins, Henry 45
Peace, Charles 423 – 426
Pearce, Emily 376
Pearce, Mr. 190, 194, 198
Pearson, Mrs Alice 343
Pegler, Edith Mabel 229 – 231, 233, 235 – 236, 241 – 242
Pendlebury, Lancashire 345
Pendlebury, Mr. J. H. 125
Penny, Augustus John 173, 178 – 180, 183
Pentonville 45, 86, 99 – 100, 118 – 119, 131, 133, 147, 159, 173, 177, 183, 241, 263, 275 – 277, 288, 295, 317, 322 – 323, 346, 350, 355, 384, 404, 406 – 407, 410, 412 – 415
Pepper, Dr. George, Home Office Pathologist 26, 113
Perry, George Henry 86
Perry, Henry 322
Perth 81 – 82, 85, 298
Peruvian Amazon Rubber Company 266, 273
Phillips, Tom xi, 354, 410, 415
Piccadilly Circus, London 381, 393
Pickford, Mr. Justice 125
Pierrepoint, Albert xi
Pierrepoint, Henry xi, 17, 37 – 39, 41, 44 – 48, 63 – 65, 67, 71, 75 – 77, 79 – 80, 84 – 86, 94, 140, 160
Pierrepoint, Thomas xi, 38, 91, 94 – 95, 160 – 161, 322, 350, 406, 414, 419, 423
Pigott, Detective Inspector 188, 190, 337, 341
Pilkington, Sir George, High Sheriff of Lancashire 139
Pinniger, Rev. James W. 61
Pittard, Dora 394

Place, George 17
Platt Bros. Company, Werneth, Oldham 185, 195, 203 – 204
Plumpton Wood, near Heywood 135
Pollard, Henry xi
Pollock, Sir Ernest, Attorney General 369
Poor Defendants Act 53, 198
Portland Prison 424
Portman Street, London 382
Portsmouth, Hants. 233, 379
Potter, Mr. David 163 – 165
Pratt, Mr. John, Barrister 354
Prescott, Ida 345
Preston, Lancashire 6, 68, 372
Price, G. Meyrick, Commissioner for Oaths 104
Prince Albert Street, Blackburn 322
Pryke, Superintendent John 23 – 25
Purdovitch, Hyman 323
Putumayo, South America 266 – 267, 273

Q

Quarmby, Frederick 353
Quebec, Canada 114 – 116
Queen Street, Oldham 185
Queen Victoria Street, Balderstone 4
Queen's Park, Glasgow 345
Quinn, Ambrose 323
Quinn, Rebecca 323

R

Ramsbottom, John 79 – 80
Range, Ellen 38
Rawcliffe, Thomas 97
Reading Gaol 100, 119
Reavil, Alice 236
Redcar, Yorkshire 427
Reeve, William Benjamin 245 – 248
Regan, William 42 – 43
Regent Road, Blackpool 234
Regent Square, Bloomsbury 313
Registry Office 229 – 231, 233, 236
Reilly, Mr. J.J., 348
Reynolds, Frederick 65
Rhodes, Mr. 55, 57
Ridley, Mr. Justice 69, 146
Rifle Brigade 307
Riley, Mr. Lindon 256

Riley, PC Thomas   271 – 272
Roberts, Elizabeth   334 – 336, 340
Roberts, Mrs. Emma   334 – 336, 342
Roberts, Frances   378 – 379
Robertson, Beatrice   180
Robertson, Frederick (junior)   180
Robertson, Frederick (senior)   173, 180 – 184
Robertson, Nelly   180
Robinson, Jack   375
Robinson, Mrs. Sarah   134
Robinson, William James   294 – 296
Rochdale   xi, 1, 3 – 4, 8, 17, 19, 28, 38, 49, 54, 61, 70, 81 – 83, 87, 102, 118, 123, 127 – 129, 135, 139, 158, 160, 169, 172 – 173, 177, 183, 204, 208, 214, 225, 242 – 243, 253, 255, 259, 274 – 275, 277 – 278, 282, 288, 297, 301, 322, 329, 337 – 338, 353 – 355, 375, 416, 420 – 421, 423, 427, 429
Rochdale Cemetery   430
Rochdale Infirmary   421
Roche, Berthe   314 – 317
Rock Street, Oldham   193, 197, 204
Roe-Rycroft, Mr.   198, 200
Roker, Ada   128
Rollins, James   345
Roman, Walter   274
Rooney, William   321
Rose, Joseph   321 – 322
Rose, Sarah   321
Rosenthal, Robert   322
Rossa, O'Donovan   264, 347
Rosser, Miss Inez   362
Rowlett, Mr. Sidney   156
Royal Army Medical Corps   290
Royal Engineers   19
Royal Flying Corps   377 – 378
Royal Hotel, Royton   334
Royal Irish Constabulary   349, 351
Royal Military Hospital, Dublin   20
Royal Navy   178
Royal Scots Regiment   167
Royal Warwickshire Regiment   70
Royal Welch Fusiliers   141, 289
Roylatt, Mr. George, Under-Sherrif   125
Royton, Lancashire   1, 49 – 50, 137, 333, 337
Rumens, Albert   165 – 166
Rushden, Northamptonshire   125

Ryan, Bernard   352
Rylance, Dr. Gilbert   107

S

Saffron Walden, Essex   21
St. Albans   322
St. Andrew's Church, Oldham   203
St. Austell, Cornwall   354
St. Mary's Hospital, London   113
Salem Moravian Church, Oldham   185
Saline, Fifeshire   80
Salisbury, Herbert Edward Rawson   343 – 345
Salvation Army   181 – 182, 204, 208
Samuel, Mr.   298
Sandalbridge Institution, Alderley   186
Sanderson, Mark   52
Sandford, Henry   264
Sandycove, Dublin   264
Saratoga Road, London   180 – 181
Saunders, Cyril   350
Saunders, Dorothy   350
Scotland   4, 80, 83, 176 – 177, 297, 417
Scotland Yard, London   25, 100, 115 – 116, 145, 163 – 164, 239, 272, 314, 367, 381 – 382, 396
Scott (Chief Warder)   7
Scott, Ernest   323
Scott, Thomas   xi
Scottish Rifles   175
Scrutton, Mr. Justice   241
Seaham Harbour   41
Seddon, Frederick Henry   19, 149 – 161, 173
Seddon, Mrs. Margaret   149, 153 – 155, 157 – 158, 160
Seivier, R.S., (Bob)   428, 431
Senior, Henry   345
Seven Sisters Road, Islington   150
Seymour, Florence   165 – 166, 168 – 170
Seymour, Thomas   129 – 131
Shaftesbury Avenue, London   105
Shakespeare Crescent, London   396 – 397
Sharp, Sergeant   367
Shaw Road, Oldham   336
Shaw, Jack   338
Shaw, Oldham   1, 49, 52, 54, 60 – 63, 65, 136, 202, 204
Shaw Temperance Society   61
Shawcross, Mr.   55 – 58

Shearman, Mr. Justice   240, 400, 403 – 405
Sheffield, Yorkshire   65, 419, 423
Shenton, Anne   351
Shenton, George   351
Shepherd (Assistant Warder)   8
Shepherd, Father   172
Shepherdess Walk, City Road, London   181
Shepton Mallet Military Prison   319
Shortt, Edward, Home Secretary   384
Shrewsbury   17, 282
Siddle, Thomas   80
Silk, John   48
Simpson, Thomas   91
Sinn Fein   179, 347 – 348, 425
Slack, William Edward   71 – 76
Slater   15
Sloane-Stanley, Mr. R.C.H.,   179
Sloppy Mary   84
Slough, Berkshire   100
Smith, Bridget (Delia)   56
Smith, George   46 – 47
Smith, George Joseph   19, 169, 227 – 243
Smith, James   80
Smith, Martha   46 – 47
Snowden, Mr. Philip, MP   426
Somerset   168, 319
South Africa   100, 126, 167, 286, 376
South America   263, 265, 267, 377
South Cliff Avenue, Eastbourne   163
Southall Street, Manchester   212
Southall, Middlesex   427
Southampton   230, 314
Southend, Essex   155 – 156, 230
Southsea   233, 378
Sowerby, Edwin   350
Spa Lane, Chesterfield   48
Spilsbury, Dr. Bernard   113, 117, 156, 240, 315, 367, 370, 400, 404
Spindler, Captain Karl   271 – 272
Spinners' Arms, Todmorden   337
Spink, John   87 – 88
Spooner, Elizabeth   221
Spooner, Joseph   221
Springfield Road, Belfast   348
Stafford Gaol   39, 46, 224
Stanley, the Hon. O. S. G.   342
Stannington, Northumberland   88 – 89
Stanstead, Essex   23

Steel, Emily   380 – 381
Steele, Frank   225 – 226
Stephens, James   264, 268, 347
Stern, Mr., solicitor   400
Stobswood Colliery   87
Stone, Mary   35 – 37
Storey, Frederick   345
Stott's Yard, Shaw   53, 56, 58
Stott, Thomas Kay   52
Strangeways Prison, Manchester   6, 38, 59, 61, 67, 79, 86, 135, 137, 190, 199, 202 – 203, 207 – 208, 210 – 211, 257 – 258, 284 – 285, 289, 321, 323, 327, 331, 345, 350, 353, 355, 371 – 372
Stratford, London   128, 395, 399 – 400
Stratton, Albert   44
Stratton, Alfred   44
Sullivan, Daniel   281 – 285
Sullivan, Joseph   386
Sullivan, Mr. Serjeant, KC   273
Sullivan, William   354
Sumner, George   217 – 218
Sunderland   4, 41, 92, 286
Sung, Djang Djing   323
Surrey   35, 158
Surrey Militia   15
Sutcliffe, Arthur   51
Sutcliffe, Emily   225
Sutcliffe, Fred   52
Sutton Veny, Wiltshire   319 – 320
Swann, Emily   19, 31 – 35, 406
Swann, William   31 – 32
Swansea   84, 282
Swanston, Rev.   160
Swindells, Henry Hammond   135
Swindon, Wiltshire   221
Sydney, Australia   131
Sztaray, Countess   163 – 165

T

Tait, Detective Inspector   88 – 89
Tarkenter, John Edward   135 – 139
Tarkenter, Rosetta   135 – 136
Tattersall, Rebecca   45
Tattersall, Thomas   45
Taylor, Detective Inspector   125
Taylor, Edward   242, 259, 321 – 323, 346, 350, 372, 386
Taylor, James   52
Teignmouth, Devon   357, 360

453

Temperance Hall, Shaw 51 – 52, 57 – 58, 62
Thames Ditton, Surrey 35
The Red School, Balderstone 1
Thomas, Charles 86
Thomas, Margaret 354
Thomas, Mary 86
Thomas Street, Shaw 52
Thompson, Edith Jessie xii, 19, 387 – 409, 411 – 419, 425
Thompson, Henry 97 – 99, 119
Thompson, Hiram 355, 371 – 372
Thompson, Percy 387, 389 – 400, 403, 405, 407
Thornham, Lancashire 1, 4
Thornhill, Caroline 228
Thornley, John 248 – 253, 344
Tighe, Captain Edward Kenrick 307 – 308
Tilbury, London 397, 399
Tipper, David 134
Tipperary, Eire 351 – 352
Tobin, ex-Sergeant 349
Tobin, Mr. Alfred 117 – 118
Todmorden, Yorkshire 337 – 338
Tollington Park, Islington 150, 155
Tomkins, Thomas 84
Tonbridge, Edmund Hugh 355
Tone, Wolfe 264, 347
Torquay, Devon 235
Tottenham, London 14, 355
Tower of London 272
Townsend, Dr. 361
Tralee, Kerry, Eire 270 – 272
Traynor, Thomas 353
Tregonissey, Cornwall 354
Trent, River 71
Trew, Ronald 382
Trew, Victor 382
Trim, County Meath 348
Trodden, Edward 348
Troup, Sir Edward, Permanent Secretary 209
True, Ronald 377 – 382, 384 – 386
Tuckett, Mrs. Sarah 231 – 232
Tuffin, Caroline 35 – 36
Tuffin, William Joseph 35 – 38
Turner, Mr. D. H., Chief Constable 189
Turner, Will 51
Tweedale & Smalley's, Castleton 4, 6

U

U-19 270 – 271
U-20 270
United States 113, 250, 264, 267
Upper Norwood, London 388, 391 – 392, 398
Upton, Robert 224
Usk 85 – 86, 354

V

Vachell, Mr. Charles 369
Valentine Place, London 311
Vaughan, Deputy Chief Constable 213
Vauxhall Bridge, London 397
Verbloot, Marks 143 – 145
Verelist, Clementine 321
Victoria Station, Manchester 208
Voisin, Louis 314 – 319, 321
Vonderahe, Frank 150, 155 – 156

W

Waddington, George 333 – 335, 337, 340 – 341
Waddington, Mrs Eliza 335 – 337
Waddington, Thomas, junior 333 – 334, 340 – 341
Waddington, Thomas, senior 334, 338, 342
Waddington, William 333 – 345
Wade, Robert xi
Wadhurst, East Sussex 165
Wagstaff, Mr. Ernest Arthur, analyst 199
Wakefield 47, 65, 135
Walcote, Leicestershire 123 – 124, 126
Wallasey, Cheshire 302, 304
Walls, Parade Inspector 163 – 164
Wallwork, Dick 225
Walsden, Yorkshire 337
Walters, Harry 65
Walton Gaol, Liverpool 97 – 98, 119, 130, 219, 221, 242, 248, 251, 255, 305 – 306, 322, 344 – 345
Wandsworth Gaol 17, 37 – 38, 44, 65, 76, 307, 309 – 312, 322, 386
Wanstead, Essex 395
Warbrick, William xi, 95
Ward Street, Oldham 188, 210
Ward, Dr. 225
Ward, Rev. C. E. 124
Ward, William 52
Wardour Street, London 381

Warley, Birmingham   323
Warren, Frank   323
Warren, May   249 – 250
Warwick Gaol   17, 68 – 70, 84, 91
Washington, Private Henry   348
Watergate Street, Trim, Co. Meath   348
Waterloo Road, London   311
Watson, Hugh   80
Watterson, Quartermaster-Lieutenant   290 – 293
Weaver, Superintendent   366 – 368
Webber, John   394
Weddell, Superintendent   89
Wedel, Count von   269
Wells, Somerset   168
Wensley, Inspector   145, 396 – 397
Werneth, Oldham   203, 205, 210 – 212
West Ham, London   171
Westbury, Shropshire   17
Weston-super-Mare, Somerset   231
Westow Street, London   391, 395
Wexford, Eire   264
Westwood, Samuel   350
Weymouth, Dorset   46, 231
Whalley Range, Manchester   424
Whelan, Thomas   352
White, Lady   377, 382 – 383
White, Sarah   20 – 21, 23
White, Thomas   51
White, Walter   221 – 222
Whitehead, Private Matthew   348
Whiteinch, Glasgow   353
Whiteley, Mr. Cecil   240, 401 – 402, 404 – 405
Whittaker, Charles Wood   38
Whittingham, William   334, 340
Whitworth, Samuel   4
Widdrington, Northumberland   87
Wigley, Richard   17
Wild, James   135
Wilde, Alderman Herbert, Mayor of Oldham   203 – 204
Wilhelmshaven, Germany   270
Willcox, Dr. William H.   100 – 101, 113, 156, 182
Willenhall, Staffordshire   350
William Henry Street, Rochdale   134
Williams, John (1)   140 – 141
Williams, John (2)   163, 165
Williams, Mrs. Hilda   140 – 141

Willis, William   xi, 65, 70, 84, 92 – 93, 322 – 323, 345, 350, 353, 414, 419
Wilson, Florence   229
Wilson, Isabella   100
Wilson, Lucy   71 – 72, 74 – 75
Wilson, Robert   xi, 350
Wilson, Sir Henry   386
Wilson, Thomas   353
Wimbledon, London   307
Winchburgh, Scotland   173 – 176, 178
Winchester Gaol   173, 179, 183, 221, 290, 292
Winkfield Lodge, Wimbledon   307 – 308
Winson Green, Birmingham   29, 278, 322
Winterburn, Mrs.   51, 60
Wintle, Deputy Governor   242
Withers, Jane Wallace   80
Wolfenden, Ben   339
Wolfenden, Doris   334 – 335, 340
Wolfenden, Ivy   334 – 335, 341 – 343
Wolfenden, Mrs. Eliza   339
Wombwell, Barnsley   31 – 32
Woodcock, Colonel   352
Woodhall, Sarah   255 – 256
Woodpecker Inn, Todmorden   337
Woolf, Noah   120
Woolfe, George   14 – 17
Woolwich, London   236
Worcester Gaol   45, 323, 368 – 369
Worthing, Sussex   229
Wren, Joseph   85 – 86
Wright, John   59 – 60
Wrigley, Detective   338
Wu, Zee Ming   323
Wyllie, Sir William Curzon   85

Y

Yarmouth, Norfolk   222
Yarnold, William   45
York   80
York Street, Liverpool   97
Yorkshire   xi, 3, 32, 91, 337, 427
Yorkshire Street, Oldham   185, 187, 189
Young, Olive   377, 379 – 382
Younghusband, Sir Francis   307